# GENESIS 🍎 *The Beginning of Desire*

# GENESIS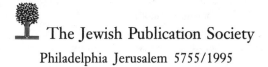

## The Beginning of Desire

AVIVAH GOTTLIEB ZORNBERG

The Jewish Publication Society
Philadelphia Jerusalem 5755/1995

The Jewish Publication Society,
1930 Chestnut Street,
Philadelphia, PA 19103.
Manufactured in the United States of America

Library of Congress Cataloging-in-Publication Data

Zornberg, Avivah Gottlieb.
Genesis : the beginning of desire / Avivah Gottlieb Zornberg. —
1st ed.
p.    cm.
Includes bibliographical references and index.
ISBN 0–8276–0521–8
1. Bible.  O.T.  Genesis—Commentaries.  I. Title.
BS1235.3.Z67   1995
222'.1107—dc20                                        94–40776
CIP

"...*not to have is the beginning of desire.*"

WALLACE STEVENS
from "Notes toward a Supreme Fiction"

# Contents

# Acknowledgments

The genesis of this book was in the loving teaching of my parents, Rabbi Dr. and Mrs. Wolf Gottlieb, whose Torah of life animates me to this day. Many teachers have opened up for me the depths of Torah, among them, Rabbi Shmuel Sperber *z'l*, Rabbi Chaim Brovender, and Rabbi Daniel Epstein, whose scholarship and imagination inspired me to explore my own resources in learning Torah.

Friends and students have been a source of insight and of warm support. I especially thank David Shulman, who responded to the manuscript with extraordinary understanding, grace, and enthusiasm. Susan Handelman, Baruch Hochman, Micha Odenheimer, Susan Shapiro, Debbie Weissman, and Linda Zisquit read some chapters and made illuminating comments. Other peopole helped in other ways, among them Julie Greenblatt, Diane Levenberg, Paul Mandel, Tessa Manoim, and Eva Weiss. I am grateful to Tamar Ross for many stimulating conversations, not directly on Genesis, and for encouraging me to begin a career in Torah teaching; to my late uncle, Rabbi Moshe Rosen *z'l*, for his constant interest and wisdom; to Freema Gottlieb, my sister and friend; to Judy Goldstein, for her cheerful readiness to help in computer crises; to Fern Seckbach for indexing; to the staff of JPS, especially Diane W. Zuckerman. Ellen Frankel has been an ideal editor, scholarly and sympathetic and unfailingly enthusiastic.

"I have learned from all my teachers, and from my students most of all" (Ethics of the Fathers). I am deeply grateful to the many students who have responded with passion and insight, in class and after class, to my teaching.

I wish to thank the Littauer Foundation for its financial support.

My book is dedicated to my husband, Eric, whose love and encouragement created space for thinking and writing. It is also dedicated to our children, Bracha, Moshe, and Avraham; their life and growth have brought us much joy.

Translations from the *Tanakh* are reprinted by permission of The Jewish Publication Society. All other translations from Hebrew texts are my own work.

Excerpts from *Mr. Palomar* by Italo Calvino, copyright © 1983 by Giulio Einaudi editore s.p.a., Torino; English translation copyright © 1985 by Harcourt Brace & Company. Reprinted by permission of Harcourt Brace & Company. Copyright © by Palomar S.r.l., reprinted with the permission of Wylie, Aitken & Stone, Inc.

Excerpts from *Collected Poems* by Wallace Stevens, copyright © 1954 by Wallace Stevens. Reprinted by permission of Alfred A. Knopf Inc. and Faber and Faber Ltd.

Lines from "Sailing to Byzantium" are from *The Poems of W.B. Yeats: A New Edition*, edited by Richard J. Finneran. Copyright © 1928 by Macmillan Publishing Company, renewed 1956 by Georgie Yeats. Reprinted with permission of Macmillan Publishing Company.

Lines from *The Sonnets to Orpheus* by Rainer Maria Rilke, copyright © 1985, translated by Stephen Mitchell. Reprinted by permission of the translator.

# Introduction

❦ These essays on the weekly Parsha emerged from ten years of teaching the biblical readings to classes here in Jerusalem. I was fortunate to have eager and intelligent audiences, whose spoken—and even unspoken—responses made it possible for me to discover, year after year, what further might be said on the matter-of-the-week.

These audiences were composed of a wide range of people, of all ages, professional and intellectual backgrounds, and levels of Jewish learning. The gamut ran from young American women and men studying in Israeli *yeshivot* (colleges of advanced learning) for a year or more before proceeding to college study in the United States, to professionals, housewives, artists, poets, and professors; from those who had had little previous contact with biblical and midrashic literature to those who had spent many years delving into the layers of meaning within these texts. The meeting places were some of the many colleges for adult Jewish education that have burgeoned in Jerusalem over the last twenty years.

What I did over the years was to share my own personal struggles for meaning, to discover the ways in which life and text inform each other. My audiences were in the position of "eavesdropping" on my meditations, on the literary and philosophical resonances emerging from these texts. These personal meditations were a weaving of biblical, midrashic, and literary sources; my students would receive a list of the sources and use them as a basis for further study.

My mode of inquiry was closer to the "rhetorical" than to the "methodical," in terms of Gerald Bruns's distinction—the "rhetorical" having "no greater ambition than to discover what can be said, in any given case." The rhetorical mode, which Bruns sees as characteristic of most literary criticism, is "more concerned with finding than with proving, is more speculative than analytical, more heuristic than polemical." It explores problems, relationships, patterns, without arriving at single-minded or schematic theories. The rhetorician is a "public meditator."[1]

My teaching mode, exploratory, ironic, open to turbulence, suspicious of fixities, had to be translated into an equivalent written text. There is no one specific audience I have in mind for these essays. I expect that readers from different backgrounds, "eavesdropping" on these meditations, in their written form, will find different parts of the book either strange or familiar. In introducing it, I am, however, reluctant to engage in *post facto* methodological framings of my approach to biblical and midrashic sources. For essentially my way of reading these sources is highly un-theoretical: the work of interpretation is done "in the field," in close attention to themes and motifs I sense within the words on the page. It is a kind of *listening* for the meta-messages of the text. My assumption is that the narrative block that constitutes a Parsha has thematic integrity, that the midrash is concerned to draw out the implicit dynamics of the biblical narrative, and to limn the internal tensions that continue, to our own day, to trouble and animate human beings. The field of energy that is thus set up I have tried to register in these essays.

I make use of an extensive range of sources to release the expressive internal logic of each Parsha. Some of these sources are exegetical, others are drawn from my reading in such areas as literature, literary criticism, psychology, philosophy, and anthropology. The exegetical sources range from the Talmud and Midrash to medieval and modern commentaries on the Bible, to hasidic meditations and homilies. The other sources consti-tute my mental "in-scape," the landscape of my mind, and, as such, must inform my responses to the implicit dynamics of the biblical text.

Here, I would like to spell out certain assumptions that may help the reader in engaging with a perhaps unfamiliar approach to the biblical narrative. One of my assumptions is that the sources I refer to set up a field of tension and mutual illumination with the biblical text. I am not looking simply to elucidate either what the Bible "really means" or what moral or homiletical uses can be made of the biblical narrative. I am looking to loosen the fixities, the ossifications of preconceived readings. To do this, a dialectical hermeneutics is essential: an opening of the ear, eye, and heart to a text that reflects back the dilemmas and paradoxes of the world of the reader.

Two examples may clarify my point. When Rashi comments on the birth of Joseph's sons in Egypt, "before the years of famine came"

(Genesis 41:50), he observes that we learn from that nuance of timing that it is forbidden to have sexual relations in time of famine. This comment, drawn from the Babylonian Talmud (Ta'anit 11a), is a legal principle gleaned from a close reading of the narrative. Normally, readers will assume that we are learning about life, about how to behave in time of famine, from the biblical text. Life is strange territory; it requires the compass, the orientation of biblical guidance. The Bible is familiar, life is strange. We bring the two together, to shed light on life. What is produced in the end becomes a commonplace of proper behavior, derived from, or—in a more sophisticated approach—drawing authority from the Bible.

My assumption is that a much more complex, dialectical dynamic is possible. If Rashi introduces into his commentary an observation about sexuality and famine, this can be read back into the original text. We are now encouraged to reflect on Joseph's larger situation, in terms of the dynamics of fertility, sexuality, famine, and corruption: Joseph's sense of normalcy in a strange land is reflected in his oblivious fertility. We use Rashi's legal observation as a way to probe beneath the surface of Joseph's inner conflicts. An apparently homiletical or legal comment is also an exegetical one.

Another example would be Rashi's comment on the beautiful ending to Isaac's "courtship" of Rebecca. Isaac meets his bride, after an extremely long account of the matchmaking adventures of his father's servant. "Isaac then brought her into the tent of his mother Sarah, and he took Rebecca as his wife. Isaac loved her, and thus found comfort after his mother's death" (Genesis 24:67). Rashi comments: "It is the way of the world (*derekh eretz*) that as long as a man's mother is alive, he is attached to her [lit., bound up, involved]; when she dies, he comforts himself in his wife."

Here, again, a realistic observation about life is gleaned from the text; one might even describe Rashi's comment as Freudian, opening his readers' eyes to the dynamics of intimate family relationships. But, again, I would suggest that Rashi's apparent generalization provides us with a key to the narrative itself.

Rashi seems to be describing a tension between two loves—for mother and for wife—experienced at the same time; only after the mother dies does the man turn "for comfort" to his wife—implicitly, the marriage relation then assumes fuller proportions. In Isaac's story, of course, there is a gap, probably of several years, between his mother's death and his marriage to Rebecca. Indeed, the discrepancy between the situation in the Bible narrative and that described by Rashi should deter the reader from making too-facile extrapolations from the text to life.

Precisely because the two cases are not symmetrical, Rashi's observation leads us to reflect again upon Isaac's relation with his mother, his involvement (*karukh etzla*) with her life and her death, and the nature of the comfort he later finds in Rebecca. This more complex vision of Isaac's situation would then reinform the reader's sense of what Rashi calls *derekh eretz* — the way of the world — which means, basically, the uncommon commonness of things, the ways human beings struggle with the nature of the world.

It seems to me that Rashi usually writes in such a multivalent way, transforming the reader's comprehension of the biblical text, even in his most — apparently — fantastic citations from the midrash. His commentary works as a dreamtext, suggesting many alternative — but not exclusive — facets of reality. In both the cases I have discussed, the feedback loop radiates a field of energy that includes both the reader, with his/her life situation, and the text. For to understand Isaac, Sarah, and Rebecca through a Freudian reading of Rashi is, of course, to reunderstand ourselves.

This field, or circle of understanding, yields endless illumination. If at first the text seems familiar, while life is strange, needy of privileged guidance, at a later stage of reading the situation may be reversed: life acquires a new familiarity, a new intelligibility, in the light of Rashi's deployment of midrashic sources, while the original text suddenly seems alien, uncanny, needy of reinterpretation.

This dialectic of strangeness and familiarity is the gift of art; in this sense, I would regard Rashi and his midrashic precursors as poets. George Steiner alerts us to this paradoxical effect of art: on the one hand, "all representations, even the most abstract, infer a rendezvous with intelligibility or, at the least, with a strangeness attenuated"; on the other, "much of poetry, music and the arts aims to . . . make strangeness in certain respects stranger."[2] It is the tension between these two statements that underlies my readings of Genesis.

This cycle of desire is present in all dimensions of life, intellectual, interpretive, as well as overtly emotional. The reader needs most of all the animation of desire, which is generated, paradoxically, by the experience of "not to have:"

> *the priest desires. The philosopher desires*
>
> *And not to have is the beginning of desire.*
> *To have what is not is its ancient cycle.*
> *It is desire at the end of winter, when*
>
> *It observes the effortless weather turning blue*
>
> . . . .
>
> *It knows that what it has is what is not*
> *And throws it away like a thing of another time*
> *As morning throws off stale moonlight and shabby sleep.*
>
> — *Wallace Stevens,*
> *"Notes toward a Supreme Fiction"*

"What it has is what is not": the economics of desire apply to priests and philosophers and readers of ancient and modern texts. The aim of interpretation is, I suggest, not merely to domesticate, to familiarize an ancient book: it is also, and perhaps more importantly, to "make strangeness in certain respects stranger," to make the reader aware, in the current that runs between his/her lived situation and the text, of the ways in which we are "at key instants, strangers to ourselves, errant at the gates of our own psyche."[3]

My approach, therefore, has been concerned to detect the intimations of disorder within order, instability within stability, the tensions evoked by questions about human life and the search for God that the midrash expresses to such ambiguous effect. On the one hand, we are reassured to find ourselves, with our most radical dilemmas, reflected in these ancient texts. On the other hand, the midrashic strategy will not allow us to rest in a formalized, serenely fixed image of human life, with merely homiletical messages to brace us in desirable postures. In its variety and restlessness of versions of the narrative, the midrash invites us to read the text with the truest — that is, with the least conventional, platitudinous, or even pious — understandings available to us.

This is so because the Torah text that seems so plainly "there" can be approached only by the strenuous and imaginative "making" of the reader. This "making" has much to do with the intimate experience of the human being in the world; more than that, according to Jewish mystical and exegetical sources, it is God's will of the readers of His book. Whenever, for instance, the Torah speaks of the imperative *la'asot*, usually translated "to fulfill, to obey," the words of the Torah, the Netziv of Volozhin, author of *Ha'amek Davar*, consistently translates "to *construct the meaning* of the words of the Torah." *La'asot* indicates the "making," the creation of Torah in the mind of the reader. This is not passive receptivity, but expresses a post-Kantian understanding of the active processes of perception.

If this reading of personal history in the Torah is not to degenerate into a "reading *into* the Torah," there should, of course, be rules, decorums, a sense of traditional understandings. But ultimately, what I have attempted in these essays is to articulate a personal meditation on themes evoked by the biblical text. This may perhaps be termed an eisegetical, rather than an exegetical, approach. It takes its cue from the kind of reading of Torah that one poignant midrash sets in sharp focus. Rarely, indeed, is the act of reading the subject of midrashic narration. Here, however, the midrash powerfully reflects on its own enterprise.

In this passage (*Yalkut Shimoni* 1, 764), God asks Moses to help Him with the difficult task of telling Aaron that he is to die:

> God said to Moses, "Do Me a favor and tell Aaron about his death, for I am ashamed to tell him." Said R. Huna in the name of R. Tanhum bar Hiyya: What did Moses do? He rose early in the morning and went over to Aaron's place. He began calling out [*korei*], "Aaron, my brother!" Aaron came down to him and asked, "How is that you have come here so early today?" Moses answered, "There is a *davar*, a thing/word, a problem from the Torah that I was mulling over [*meharher*] during the night, and it gave me great difficulty. That is why I have come over to visit you so early in the morning." Aaron asked, "What is the problem?" Moses answered, "I don't know what it was — but I do know that it is in the book of Genesis. Bring it, and let us read [*nikra*] in it." They took the book of Genesis and read in it, story by story, and at each one, Aaron said, "God did well, He created well." But when they came to the creation of Adam, Moses said, "What shall I say about Adam who brought death to the world?" Aaron replied, "My brother Moses, you surely would not say that in this we do not accept the decree of God? We have read how Adam and Eve were created and how they merited thirteen wedding canopies, as it said, 'You were in Eden, the garden of God' (Ezekiel 28:13), and how Adam ate of the Tree, and was told, 'For dust you are, and to dust you shall return' (Genesis 3:19) —

and after all this glory, that they should come to this . . ." Then Moses said, "What about me—who had control over the ministering angels? and what about you—who halted the spread of death? Is our end not the same? We have another few years to live—perhaps twenty years?" Aaron said, "That is only a few years." Then Moses brought the number down more and more, until he spoke of the very day of death. Immediately, Aaron's bones felt as if they were quaking. He said, "Perhaps the *davar*, the word, the thing, was for me?" Moses answered, "Yes." Immediately, the Israelites saw that his stature had shrunk, as it is said, "The whole community saw that Aaron was about to die" [lit., had died] (Numbers 20:29). Then Aaron said, "My heart is dead within me, and the terror of death has fallen upon me." Moses asked him, "Do you accept death?" And he answered, "Yes . . ."

Moses is faced with the task that God Himself finds shameful. How to tell Aaron of his imminent death? He approaches the subject by indirection, through a reading experience in the book of Genesis. In doing so, he models for us a way of reading. He introduces his project by "calling out" (*korei*) to his brother: the word is identical with the word for reading—"Let us read in the book of Genesis." This gives us a sense that to read—especially to read the *mikra*, the Bible—is to call out for response to a text that itself calls out, summons, and addresses the reader. Essentially, to read is to invite the text to yield up its meanings.

In this case, Moses and Aaron will read in order to find the lost *devar torah*—the word, the idea that troubled Moses during the night. *Meharher*, the word I translate here as "mulling over," has connotations of agitation; Moses recalls being uneasy over a thought, an image, a problem from the Torah, which he now can no longer remember. He proposes to search for it in the book of Genesis, the book of beginnings, where the origins of all things are to be found. We have a sense that the *davar* is of utter—and threatening—importance. Perhaps we should understand that Moses has, in fact, repressed his memory of God's mission. It is no fiction that he is presenting to Aaron, not a strategy to communicate his brother's impending death but a real experience in which God's word has disappeared from his memory, leaving only an intuition that the book of Genesis will yield it back again.

There follows a poignant scene, in which Aaron enthusiastically endorses the narratives of creation. Clearly, he reads with his whole being, almost comically applauding God for the beauty (*yafeh assa*) of His making of the world. It is Moses who asks the dark question of death.

Aaron at first gives the theologically correct, Job-like answer (reminiscent of Job's retort to his wife, "Should we accept only good from God and not accept evil?" [Job 2:10]). In the context of the whole narrative of creation, human sin and punishment, death has its organic place. Moses then reads himself and Aaron into the text, making death a matter of personal, looming, and tragic import, until Aaron reluctantly (*shema* evokes an unwilling thought) realizes, "Perhaps the word, the mystery, the terror is *for me?*"

Moses has interrogated the text of the book of Genesis by bringing it into the closest confrontation with the lives of Aaron and himself. He challenges Aaron to a sense of pain and outrage at the very idea of death — and then mobilizes his brother's acquiescence to the tragic narrative in a personal acceptance of death. The result of this reading of biblical narrative is much more than the conveying of information: Aaron not only learns of his death, but experiences its imminence, in a dialectical mode of fear ("his bones quaked") and acquiescence. He can contain this tension, only because it is generated by a way of reading the Bible. Strangely, with all the terror of such an intimate reading comes a sense of destiny, of existing in the mind of God, of being oneself the subject of God's word.

Such a reading — initiated and guided by Moses (our Teacher, as he is commonly named) — is not a matter of reading personal concerns into the text. Rather, it is a responsive summons to the meanings inherent within the text, that await the "hearing" reader. Moses, more questioning, more restless, is also a better reader than his brother. He is not entranced by the words of the text, but senses what is hidden in the spaces between the letters, in the silences between the words.

What is hidden is, essentially, the reader's most intimate life, the things and words of the night, fears and longings and questionings. It is these that I have tried to "hear" from within the text of the Torah.

In terms of these underlying — and often subversive — concerns, the essay on Parshat Bereshit can be read as a kind of "preamble" to this book and to Genesis as a whole. The belfry daydream, which represents the vertical, distant, theoretical perspective, is opposed to the swarming, earthbound dimension of mass human and animal life. The tension between the two, the paradox of the human situation, cross-chained, in Kafka's image, to both axes, throttled by one or the other chain, yields no resolution. Kafka points up the beauty and absurdity of the human response:

"And yet all the possibilities are his, and he feels it; more, he actually refuses to account for the deadlock by an error in the original fettering."[4]

The experience of highest tension, between immanence and transcendence, between the limits of human experience and the "signals of transcendence" that are secreted within these limits, is what draws me in the biblical texts and in the midrashic and later versions of those texts. There is a sense of the turning point, the fulcrum of transformation that affects the characters in their relations to God, to each other, and to themselves.

Ultimately, the interpretive act becomes similar to the creative act. One reads, and one begins to hear a certain hum in one's ears. I think of Nadezhda Mandelstam's account of how her husband would begin to write a new poem: "a poem begins with a musical phrase ringing insistently in the ears; at first inchoate, it later takes on a precise form . . . I have a feeling that verse exists before it is composed . . . The whole process of composition is one of straining to catch and record something compounded of harmony and sense as it is relayed from an unknown source and gradually forms itself into words. The last stage of the work consists in ridding the poem of all the words foreign to the harmonious whole which existed before the poem arose."[5]

The hum in the ears of the reader generates a personal response to the text. There are, of course, decorums and limits to be observed; but the intimate encounter between self and text must create something new, something neither "stale" nor "shabby," in Wallace Stevens's words, but with that essential "this-ness," which is the classic midrashic description of what it is to "receive" the Torah:

> "*On this very day*, they entered the wilderness of Sinai": the words of Torah should be new to you as though they were given this very day. (Rashi, Exodus 19:1)

# A *note to the reader*

There is no doctrinaire intent in my usage in this book of the traditional forms of reference to God as "He" nor to the use of "man" for humanity. I am aware that these are sensitive issues, but in order to avoid stylistic awkwardness, I have followed the JPS translation, particularly in the "Creation" and "Flood" narratives.

# GENESIS 🍃 *The Beginning of Desire*

# BERESHIT 🍎
## *The Pivoting Point*

### The mystery of creation

"We live," writes Lev Shestov, "surrounded by an endless multitude of mysteries. But no matter how enigmatic may be the mysteries which surround being, what is most enigmatic and disturbing is that mystery in general exists and that we are somehow definitely and forever cut off from the sources and beginnings of life."[1]

*Bereshit bara Elokim*: "In the beginning, God created heaven and earth" (King James translation). Boldly and lucidly, the originating words and acts of God are described. The narrative tells of an ordering and a goodness that shapes all the categories of creation. Smoothly, powerfully, and seamlessly, the text (Genesis 1:1–2, 4), through formal devices of sequence, repetitions of key words, and the leitmotif of "Let there be . . . and there was . . . ," produces "several theological meanings: that Elohim, alone, 'at the beginning,' created a good ordered world; that He 'separated' and hierarchically ordered the primordial mass into a 'good' pattern; that the created world of nature is, as a result, a harmony; and that Elohim is Omnipotent and without rival."[2]

The clarity of this account of "the sources and beginnings of life" seems to leave no room for the existential sense of "mystery in general" that Shestov describes. And yet Rashi, the foremost of the traditional commentators on the Torah text, begins his great work with these words: "This text is nothing if not mysterious" (lit., this text says nothing but "Explain me!"). What Rashi claims, in effect, is that the opening sentence tells us nothing about beginnings, nothing about sequence, that it means little more than "When God created heaven and earth. . . ."

The mystery of the beginning is based, for Rashi, on syntax: How does the opening sentence hold together? What is the grammatical form of the very first word? "Bereshit" is the construct form, meaning "In the

3

*beginning of* God's creation of heaven and earth." Heaven and earth, he argues, were not created first. "You should be ashamed of yourself" if you try to argue that this is a chronological description of the order of creation, for, strangely, the water appears in the second verse with no account of its creation. So the water, it seems, is already there when the account of beginnings begins.

What emerges from Rashi's provocative statement ("The text does not reveal anything regarding the sequential order of creation") is a sense of the gaps, the unexplained, the need to examine and reexamine the apparently lucid text, with its account of a harmonious, coherent cosmology. There is a tension between the benevolent clarity and power of the narrative and the acknowledgment of mystery that inheres in the very first word and that develops as the implications of the beginning are realized.

## Primal disintegrations

For six days, the process of creation continues, seen from the viewpoint of God, who speaks, sees, and names His work in its increasing complexity. Essentially, the original binary reality of "heaven and earth" is split into smaller binary, contrasting units: darkness and light, the lower waters and the upper waters, seas and dry land, sun and moon. The act of *havdalah*, "separation," is central. Unlike the other days of creation, which are summed up by reference to their place in sequence — "a second day," "a third day" — the first day is simply "one day": "And there was evening and there was morning, one day." Rashi takes this as a reference to primordial unity. God was alone, *yahid ba'olamo*. The concept of "first-ness" would have no relevance to that day; the main business of that day was the radical transformation of reality from the encompassing oneness of God to the possibility of more-than-one.

Even the angels, in Rashi's narrative, are not created until the second day. The angels play a complex and often adversarial role in the midrashic versions of the creation narrative; this culminates in Rashi's classic understanding of God's decision, "Let us make man" (1:26). "We learn of the humility of God from here. Since Man was to be in the likeness of the angels and they would be jealous of him, He consulted them (*nim-lakh*). . . . He asked permission of His court."

The role of the angels is to suggest a "many-ness" of viewpoints, a spectrum of opinions, that God has to convince, placate, ultimately to "receive permission." And what is God's main argument in favor of creating humankind, in Rashi's version? "He said to the angels, 'You exist in the upper worlds after My likeness. If there is to be no one in the lower worlds after My likeness, then there will be jealousy among the works of the beginning.'" In other words, God desires a proliferation of His image in lower as well as upper worlds, a mitigation of His oneness, even, in a sense, of His greatness. God, as it were, submits (*nimlakh* is the passive form of the verb "to be king," "to rule") His greatness and seeks permission from those smaller than He.

This imagery of consultation and proliferation is employed, as Rashi notes, even though its associations are obviously disconcerting to a monotheistic theology. Despite the unwelcome resonances from the discussions and disputations that accompany creation in pagan mythologies, the Torah uses a plural verb to communicate a moral teaching: "In spite of the license given to heretics by this formulation, the text does not restrain itself from teaching the virtue of humility: the *great* one should consult with, request permission from the *small* one. For if the text had said, 'Let *Me* make man,' we should not have learned that He spoke with His angelic court, but merely with Himself."

The text, then, according to Rashi, risks heretical interpretation, in order to make a point of vital importance for human life. The point has to do with the One, the Great One, who begins on Day One alone in the Upper Worlds and then engages in an activity that apparently compromises His Oneness and His Greatness.

From a midrashic perspective it seems that *havdalah*—separation, specialization, the formation of difference and opposition—is generally achieved at some sacrifice. When, for instance, the lower waters are separated from the higher waters on the second day of creation, the lower waters are described in midrashic sources[3] as weeping: "We want to be in the presence of the King." The essential act of this second day is this act of division: "He divided His works into different groups and reigned over them."[4] From now on, the notion of the sovereignty of God will depend on the differences and many-ness of His subjects. But the idea of separation and difference has a tragic resonance: gone is the primal unity of "God alone in His world." New possibilities, new hazards, open up. The primary image of such separation, the division of the waters and their weeping expresses the yearning of the split-off parts of the cosmos for a primordial condition of unitary being.

With division begins alienation, conflict, and yet, paradoxically, a new notion of divine sovereignty. In this new perspective, God is recognized as King only by that being who is most radically separated from Him. Man, created on the sixth day, is foreshadowed by the splittings and differentiations of matter that begin on the second day; his freedom to perceive and to act is founded on those primal disintegrations.

## Nature comes into being

God's will to divide the waters is expressed in the fiat of *yehi*: "God said, *Let there be* an expanse in the midst of the water, that it may separate water from water. . . . And it was so" (1:6–7). The word of God effectively achieves His will: "Let there be" division, definition. Rashi quotes the Jerusalem Talmud[5] on the force of this willing word of God—*yehi*—"Let there be. . . ."

> *"Let there be"*: Let the separation be *strengthened*. Even though the heavens had already been created on the first day, they were still *liquid*. They crystallized on the second day, in response to God's rebuke: "*Let there be* a separation." This is what is written, "The pillars of heaven tremble, are astounded at His rebuke" [Job, 26:11 — my translation]. All that first day, the pillars of heaven [*amudei shamayim*—lit., "that which the heavens *stand* on"] were trembling, but on the second day, they were astounded at His rebuke, like a man who is stunned and frozen in place [*omed*—"stands still"] under the rebuke of one who intimidates him. (Rashi, 1:6)

The Jerusalem Talmud, Rashi's source, extends the kinetic, tactile basis of the imagery. "Rav said, 'Let there be a separation'—let the separation strengthen, let it crystallize, let it freeze, let it consolidate." "To be" is represented as a sort of jelling process, as the formless liquid primary substance finds its limits in space, solidifies, assumes its proper form. Previously, the waters are described in Rashi's prooftext from Job as "trembling" (*y'rofefu*). Ibn Ezra traces the root to two sources, one denoting weakness, the other movement. In the primary state of unachieved being, there is a slackness, an uncontrolled motion. (See Ralbag's comment, too: "They move and they shudder" [Job 26:11]. In midrashic language, the root, *rofef*, is used to describe the failure of milk to curdle—it quivers;[6] the form, *rifref*, indicates a fluttering, vacillating mode.[7] To come into real being is to be strengthened, hardened into specific form: "They stood in dryness and strength—like a man who is astounded and stands [*omed*] in one place" (Rashi, Job 26:11).

Finding one place to stand: this is Rashi's definition of being. As we have seen, the midrash insists that this is not achieved without tears. Being is achieved in the cosmos by the power and terror of God's word; "Let there be. . . ." A kind of fascination takes hold of the waters: necessity constrains them. They must *be*.

What I have called the jelling process in the creation of the heavens continues in the rest of Rashi's account. The waters are "suspended in the air" above the expanse—they "depend on the word of the King" (Rashi, Genesis 1:7). This is the consummation of God's making (*asiyah*); Rashi defines *asiyah* here as *tikno al omdo*—He fixed, completed it in its position (*al omdo*—lit., on its stand). This stage of creation is definitively completed only on the third day, with the movement and containment of the lower waters and the exposure of dry land. Only then, Rashi remarks, can God see "goodness": the unfinished, that which has not achieved full being, cannot be called "good."

The model of coming-to-be that is suggested by Rashi's commentary here pictures a primary fluid stage, followed by the transformative thrill of God's word. There is a firming, a finding of proper place, a new density and rigor. The effect of God's word is constraint. We are close to the notion of Necessity, as Aristotle understood it. "Cry halt before Necessity"—*Ananke stenai*. Nature cannot argue with the word of God. "Necessity does not allow itself to be persuaded."[8] Natural phenomena can only freeze into place, assume their necessary posture in space.

## The belfry daydream

Kenneth Burke suggests that the six days of creation may be considered as six major classifications of reality.[9] The narrative translates these classifications into terms of temporal sequence. Man comes last, not merely in temporal terms: he culminates, he dominates. These are the terms in which he is conceived by God: "Let us make man, in our image, after our likeness. They shall rule the fish of the sea, the birds of the sky, the cattle, the whole earth, and all the creeping things that creep on the earth" (1:26). God's first words, when He blesses man, are: "Be fertile and increase, fill the earth and master it; and rule the fish of the sea, the birds of the sky, and all the living things that creep on the earth" (1:28). Man is to rule, to dominate all categories of created reality, even those that he cannot physically control — that is, creatures of the sea and the air, who do not share his habitat. He is to evolve strategies to overcome physical barriers and make himself master of nature.[10]

What does share his natural habitat — all animal life on earth — is described as crawling (*romesset*). This is rather an unexpected use of the term, which had answered previously to one specific form of animal life — small, swarming creatures of water, air, and land (1:21, 24, 25). The related term *sheretz* is defined by Rashi as "any living being that is *not higher than the ground* — like flies, ants, beetles, worms, rats, mice and all fish" (1:20). Rashi's definition seems to consist of the height criterion only. Yet a few lines later, he adds another factor, to define *remess*: "insects that are low, crawling on the ground, and look as though they are being dragged, because their movement is not clearly perceived" (1:24). There is a quality of *movement* that characterizes the *remess — sheretz*, as well as a quality of *height* — "not higher than the earth." This is an unwilled, unindividuated movement — these creatures move in crowds, driven by instinct. They wheel and swerve in a way that is perceived by man as irrational. The word *remess* is strangely used, then, to describe *all* animal life on earth. It is as though Man is conceived of as towering physically over all animal life.

This conception, which is inherent in the blessing of domination, is figured by an image of *verticality*. In *The Poetics of Space*, Gaston Bachelard, the French philosopher of art, writes of what he calls "belfry daydreams," in which one watches others "running about . . . irrationally, like ants . . . the size of flies." This is a "dream of high solitude"; the dreamer enjoys "an impression of domination at little cost. . . . From the top of his tower, a philosopher of domination sees the universe in miniature. Everything is small because he is so high. And since he is high, he is great, the height of his station is proof of his own greatness."[11]

The insistence of the Creation narrative on man as vertical (high, therefore great) comes always in a context of horizontal spread: "Be fertile and increase, fill the earth and master it; and rule" (1:28).[12] The blessing of fertility, the instinct of what Elias Canetti calls the "increase pack" ("to be more"), is first given to fish, fowl, and animal life (1:22;

8:17). To proliferate is, in a sense, the *sheretz* modality, as Ramban, following on the Targum, translates the term (1:20).

Here is Canetti's account of the phenomenology of the increase pack:

> Characteristic of the pack is the fact that it cannot grow. It is surrounded by emptiness and there are literally no additional people who could join it. It consists of a group of men in a state of excitement whose fiercest wish is *to be more*. . . . Density within the pack is always something of an illusion. Men may press closely together and enact a multitude in traditional rhythmic movements, but they are not a multitude; they are a few, and have to make up in intensity what they lack in actual numbers.[13]

Canetti's reading of the pack phenomenon is informed by the despair and vulnerability of the few fevered by the desire to be more. When God blesses Adam and Eve, or commands Noah and his few survivors after the Flood, the imperative of density—"to be more"—is poignantly recognized: "Fill the earth. . . . abound on the earth [lit., swarm] and increase on it" (9:7). Surrounded by emptiness, man seeks the animal faculty of increase. What man is blessed-commanded to do is not simply to propagate; the process is one, in Canetti's terms, of transformation:

> Early man, roaming about in small bands through large and often empty spaces, was confronted by a preponderance of animals . . . Many of them existed in enormous numbers. Whether it was herds of buffaloes or springboks, shoals of fish, or swarms of locusts, bees or ants, their numbers rendered those of man insignificant.
>
> For the progeny of man is sparse, coming singly and taking a long time to arrive. The desire to be *more*, for the number of people to whom one belongs to be larger, must always have been profound and urgent, and must, moreover, have been growing stronger all the time. . . . Man's weakness lay in the smallness of his numbers. . . . In the enormously long period of the time during which he lived in small groups, he, as it were, incorporated into himself, *by transformations*, all the animals he knew. It was through the development of transformation that he really became man; it was his specific gift and pleasure.[14]

Canetti goes on to discuss the rites of the Australian aborigines, whose ancestors are treated as having a dual nature, both animal and human at once. Each ancestor embodies a particular animal as part of his being. These Canetti sees as products of transformation. A successful and established transformation became a kind of endowment: it signified a connection with the *numbers* of the animals incorporated into the human identity. Man desired the increase of the animals, since they were connected with man: "When they increased, he also increased; the increase of the totem animal was identical with his own." Plants, as well as animals, even insects, scorpions, lice, flies or mosquitoes can be designated as a totem: "it can only be their immense number which attracts them; in establishing a relationship with them he means to ensure their numbers for himself."[15]

Canetti's model of the increase pack and the process of "transformation" that achieves the desired animal numerousness provides us with a way of reading the connection in the Creation narrative between increase and domination. For man is told in the same breath that he is to proliferate and to rule. His motion is to be swarmlike, horizontal, attached to the earth, and to necessity, blindly following the instinct to be more, to fill the emptiness; and, equally, it is to be Godlike, concentrated, vertical, affirming an all encompassing vision of the world. As in the belfry daydream described by Bachelard, part of the human experience is the "dream of high solitude. . . . From the top of his tower, a philosopher of domination sees the universe in miniature."[16]

## The vertical and the horizontal

Here is an essential paradox of the human, as God conceives, blesses, and commands His culminating creation: he is to live on the horizontal and vertical plane at once. He is to transform himself into a creature preoccupied with swarming, proliferation, incorporating the strength of the animal world. He is at the same time to rule, to conquer. Rashi's comment here is evocative: the word for "rule," *ve-yirdu*, can be read as a play on the alternative meanings of "rule" and "descent." "If he merits, he will *dominate* [*rodeh*] the animal world, if he does not merit, he will *become low* [*yarood*] before them and they will dominate him" (1:26). The necessity for a kind of philosophical detachment, the solitude of higher and larger perspectives, creates an implicit tension with the imperative blessing of increase. To spread over the earth, to fill the earth, to know the urgent rhythmic passion of increase is to be invested in the immediate, the experienced, the contingent.

It is in these terms that we can read God's final statement of disappointment at the outcome of the human creature:

When men began to increase on earth and daughters were born to them, the divine beings saw how beautiful the daughters of men were and took wives among those that pleased them. The Lord said, "My breath shall not abide in man forever, since he too is flesh; let the days allowed him be one hundred and twenty years." It was then, and later, too, that the Nephilim appeared on earth—when the divine beings cohabited with the daughters of men, who bore them offspring. They were the heroes of old, the men of renown. (6:1–4)

Here are the themes of giant size and increase over the face of the earth. But some essential misarticulation affects these two modalities. In the midrashic accounts, the Nephilim are giants who wear the sun around their necks,[17] their heads disappear into the heavens, they command the rainfall—and, in accordance with their name, they "fall and bring the world down with them" (Rashi, 6:4). The monstrous excess of the vertical leads to a shattering destruction.

Many centuries later, as the Israelites roam the wilderness, they send spies to the Holy Land. The spies return with eyewitness reports of giants: "All the people that we saw in it are men of great size; we saw the Nephilim there—the Anakites are part of the Nephilim—and we looked like grasshoppers to ourselves, and so we must have looked to them" (Numbers 13:32–33). There, too, the two modalities are disastrously polarized. The spies are filled with awe before the invulnerable, the vertical; they sense themselves as humiliated at their own grasshopper dimensions, their *sheretz* reality.[18] This splitting-off, the incapacity to bear the tension of their own equivocal existence, leads to a real despair, an acceptance of the lowest human profile—"And so we were in their eyes" (Numbers 13:33). The spies see themselves reflected in the eyes of the fantasy giants: an intimate vision of self is corroborated at every turn.

The catastrophe of the narrative of the spies is conveyed through the imagery of "falling." They complain of a destiny, in which any claim to vertical stature will be doomed ("Why is the Lord taking us to that land to fall by the sword?" [Numbers 14:3]). Moses "falls on his face" (Numbers 14:5) in despair. And God decrees, "In this very wilderness shall your carcasses drop. . . . But your carcasses shall drop in the wilderness . . . until the last of your carcasses is down in the wilderness" (14:29, 32, 33). In the words of Midrash Y'lamdenu: "The spies fell to the ground [in hysterical fits]—they would stand on their feet and make themselves collapse in front of their families" (14:3).

The narrative of the spies is one of failure to contain a radical tension. The vertical being is assailed by the vertigo of his dual nature. His origin and ultimate destiny are in the earth, the issues of fertility, increase, and survival dominate his experience. And yet he knows himself invested with a singular Godlike power. From his vantage point, he can see immense perspectives, come to conclusions far beyond the contingencies of the moment; yet he is a participant in the driven, spawning multitudes he can observe so splendidly from his metaphysical solitude.

This is the essential dilemma of man, as God conceives of him, blesses him, and charges him with imperative of his duality. How to deal with the unthinking conformity of the increase pack, the vision of men as "bugs, spawn, as a mob"? These are Emerson's terms, in "Self-Reliance," which Stanley Cavell calls a "study of shame": "How do we, as Emerson puts it, 'come out' of that? How do we become self-reliant? The worst thing we could do is rely on ourselves as we stand — this is simply to be slaves of our slavishness: it is what makes us spawn. We must . . . transform our conformity."[19]

The problem is implicit in the blessing: we are to spawn, and we are to rise upwards. Hamlet has his tortured view of the dilemma: "Get thee to a nunnery! Why wouldst thou be a breeder of sinners? I am myself indifferent honest, but yet I could accuse me of such things that it were better my mother had not borne me. . . . What should such fellows as I do, crawling between earth and heaven?"[20]

To breed, to crawl, these are the acts of the *sheretz*. At one pole of failure, the midrash imagines men as grasshoppers, who compulsively "climb up and fall back down" into their jar, are incapable of learning from experience.[21] To be trapped in the reality of "crawling between earth and heaven" is to be doomed to repeat irrational patterns of the pack, the rhythmic movements generated by the blind urge simply "to be more." And, on the other hand, there is the "terror of standing upright," which Kafka describes in one of his letters to Felice, responding to a dream of hers: "Had you not been lying on the ground among the animals, you would have been unable to see the sky and the stars and wouldn't have been set free. Perhaps you wouldn't have survived the terror of standing upright. I feel much the same; it is a mutual dream you have dreamed for us both."[22] There is a violence, even a guilt, inherent in the posture of greatness, of power. Kafka expresses the dream conviction that to lower one's profile is to preserve innocence and, perhaps, even to see more of the sky.

# Greatness and procreativeness

The paradox of the vertical and the horizontal is fleshed out in the midrashic narratives of Creation. Two things are called "great" in the Biblical text: the lights ("God made the two great lights, the greater light to dominate the day and the lesser light to dominate the night, and the stars" [1:16]) and the great sea monsters (1:21). The lights are great, and they dominate: the two concepts clearly cohere. But in both cases, the lights and the sea monsters, the midrash opens up tantalizing perspectives on the problematics of greatness.

Responding to the apparent textual contradiction—both lights are great? Only one is great?—and the defective spelling of *me'orot* (lights), the midrash deciphers a hidden narrative: "They were created equal, but the moon was diminished, because she complained, 'It is impossible for two kings to wear one crown'" (Rashi, 1:16). The moon knows that inherent in the idea of greatness is singularity. Two cannot be called great, since to be great is by definition to dominate, to loom over, to see a world from a unique perspective. In Rashi's source, therefore, God tells the moon, "Diminish yourself."[23] Here is a voluntary act of self-diminishing, an acceptance of the small rather than the great role, which is compensated for by the many hosts of stars that will now accompany the moon.

Maharal, in fact, offers an arresting reading of "diminishment": the moon becomes, not smaller, but a being capable of waning—to the point where the sun remains truly alone—that is, truly great—in the sky.[24] The moon yields up her eternal and transcendent being and accepts a role of contingency, mutability, and proliferation. There is a powerful suggestion of a relation between greatness and solitude, on the one hand, and smallness and increase, on the other. The moon experiences both loss and gain.

The sea monsters, too, are great; they, too, are spelled defectively (the plural indication lacks a *yod*). This is Rashi's version of the midrashic tradition: "This is the Leviathan and its mate. God created them male and female, and killed the female and salted it away for the righteous in the world to come. For if they had been fertile and increased, the world could not have survived in their presence" (1:21). (In the midrashic source, the male Leviathan is castrated to ensure that its destructive powers of procreation — or even of sexual relations — are totally neutralized).[25]

In this extraordinary midrash, what commands our attention once again is the theme of greatness and solitude. To have a partner, while remaining in the mode of greatness, is an existential impossibility. The world as we know it would cease to exist. Only in the world-to-come, in a different (and presumably richer) version of reality can the righteous flourish on the free play of greatness and procreativeness.

## The problem of man

All this is a preamble to the problem of man. Although he is to dominate creation, Man is not called "great," because he is, from the very outset, to be many. ("Be fertile and increase . . ." [1:28].) Yet there is ambiguity in the account of his origins. He was formed from the clay of dust and water, of earth and heaven, in one whole "image of God"; yet immediately, he is described as a plural being: "And God created man in His image, in the image of God He created him; male and female He created *them*" (1:27).[26] The narrative later describes the removal of one of his ribs to make woman. And the midrash, in Rashi's version, resolves the question of unity and duality in one striking image: "God created him first with two faces, and separated them" (1:27).

One of Rashi's sources narrates a previous stage of the process, which Rashi does not quote: "At first, God intended to create two separate beings, but in the end man was created as one being."[27] God's first thought represents an ideal reality. The decision to create man as one androgynous being ("in the image of God He created *him*") then seems inscrutable, especially since there is an almost immediate return to the original plan: man is split into the two entities of God's first intention ("male and female He created *them*"). The splitting-off is prefaced by a thought of God: a soliloquy — perhaps the first "God said" that has no direct effect on reality. God thinks: "It is not good for man to be alone; I will make a fitting helper for him" (2:18). Rashi comments: "So that people should not say, 'There are two powers; God is alone in the upper worlds, and has no partner, and this one is in the lower worlds, without a partner.'"

The association of aloneness with power, greatness, is clear here. To have a *ben zug*, an equivalent Other, with whom one must reckon, who limits the grandeur of one's solitude, with whom one speaks and struggles and brings offspring into the world—all this is the very definition of the not Godly, the not great. One who has a *ben zug* is yoked to contingency, lives on the horizontal plane, whose blessing and imperative is increase.

God is without a *ben zug*; angels are not fertile and do not increase—unlike men, animals, and demons (who share also the facts that they eat, drink, defecate, and die!);[28] the Leviathan is deprived, for the duration of present time, of his partner; the Sabbath has no *ben zug*, and complains as the other days of the week pair themselves off—in the end, God matches her, matchless as she is, with Israel; the tribe of Dan is described as a lonely, independent warrior—"as *one* of the tribes of Israel" (49:16): "like the solitary One of Israel who needs no help in war," and his emblem is the snake, who goes alone: "All the beasts walk in pairs, while the snake travels alone."[29] "God said to Israel, All that I have created, I created in pairs: heaven and earth, the sun and the moon, Adam and Eve, this world and the next. But My glory is One and unmatched in the world."[30]

In view of all this, man's aloneness is "not good": it lends itself to a misconception about the nature of man. What he requires is a "fitting helper." This arresting description (lit., a help against him) draws an equally arresting comment from Ramban: it was important to realize man as two matched creatures, rather than as one androgynous being (even if he were capable of procreation), because "God saw that it was good that his helpmate should stand in front of him [*kenegdo*, translated here as "fitting," has confrontational implications], so that he may see her, and separate from her, and unite with her, according to his will" (Ramban, 2:18). For Ramban, man as alone and autonomous is "not good," because he would live a static, unchanging, and unwilled life. Man needs to live face-to-face with the Other, dancing to the choreography of his own freedom.

The splitting-off of man is, however, achieved not by the pure word of God. This remains "private," a reminder to the reader that God's original idea of the human good has not yet been implemented. It is achieved only when man himself comes to recognize the pains of solitude. Only after he has named the animals does the text insert into Adam's consciousness the search for the Other: "And the man gave names to all the cattle and to the birds of the sky and to all the wild beasts; but for

Adam no fitting helper was found" (2:20). Who was it who sought and could not find? The midrash fills the gap. Rashi says, "When God brought the animals to Adam, He brought each species in pairs, male and female. Adam said, They all have a *ben zug*, a partner. Only I have no partner. Immediately, he fell asleep."

The powerful implication here is that God's original intention can be consummated only by Adam's free perception and desire. Only when Adam comes to feel the solitude of the angelic, unitary existence is he split into two separate beings. He must, in a sense, diminish himself, come to know the rightness of a more complex form of unity. That is, God sets aside His original vision, creates man alone and great, complete in himself—a plausible version of the human reality, but one that will be undermined by the restless experience of *"he could not find* a fitting help" (literal translation of *lo matza*). "Not to find" is the purpose of man's lone creation. He knows in his pain and searching both that "For my sake the whole world was created"[31]—he dreams of belfries, and of "monuments of unaging intellect"—and that his humanity requires the "sensual music"[32] of horizontal relationship, the fusing and parting, the changing reflections of face meeting face.

Man's greatness, therefore, his creation in the image of God, his dominating the sensual swarming landscape, locks in an inescapable tension with his participation in that world of proliferation and change, of waxing and waning. He is attached to two mutually exclusive ways of being, called in the shorthand of the midrash "the upper worlds" and "the lower worlds."

In his creation, for the first time, the word *vayyitzer* is used—"He *formed* man from the dust of the earth" (2:7). The doubling of the *yod* in *vayyitzer* suggests the surplus of possible meanings and identifications that man is endowed with. Unlike the cattle, which "do not stand to be judged" (Rashi, 2:7)—that is, which are not accountable for the choices and conflicts inherent in a paradoxical existence—man is formed both of the dust of the whole earth (the four corners of the earth), so that he will be accepted for burial in whatever part of the globe he dies, and of the dust of the sacred center, Jerusalem: "God took his dust from the place of which it is said, 'You shall make an altar of earth for Me—I wish that he may gain atonement, and that *he may be able to stand*'" (Rashi, 2:7).

There is a striking pathos in God's wish for man: "*Halevai!*—Would that it might be so!" The difficulty of man's situation is focused here: the material of his body (only at the next stage, God animates him with His spirit-breath) comes both from the four corners of the earth, from all the instincts and processes of the horizontal, from the dust into which he will disappear, and from the place of unity, the sacred spot of original creation, the *axis mundi*, where this world intersects with the higher worlds. There is an "opposition between space that is sacred—the only *real* and *real-ly* existing space—and all other space, the formless expanse surrounding it."[33] And man, in the midrashic view, is the meeting point of the two kinds of dust, of the one and the many.

The Jerusalem Talmud puns on the agony of the dilemma: "Woe to me, because of the One who formed me [*yotzri*]! Woe to me, because of my unruly desires [*yitzri*]!"[34] In the very fibers of his being, he belongs to both dimensions at once.

Kafka expresses a similar torment of irresolubility:

> He is a free and secure citizen of the world, for he is fettered to a chain which is long enough to give him the freedom of all earthly space, and only so long that nothing can drag him past the frontiers of the world. But simultaneously he is a free and secure citizen of Heaven as well, for he is also fettered by a similarly designed heavenly chain. So that if he heads, say, for the earth, his heavenly collar throttles him, and if he heads for Heaven, his earthly one does the same. And yet all the possibilities are his, and he feels it; more, he actually refuses to account for the deadlock by an error in the original fettering.[35]

Man is chained to incompatible universes of being; and yet within his chains he feels unaccountably that all the possibilities are his. There is no error; yet he cannot live comfortably in either heaven or earth, while he is a "free and secure citizen" of both.

## The hands of God

The two sources for human dust are given, in Rashi's version, as alternatives. But, in a source midrash, the two are aligned into one narrative: in the first hour of the sixth day of creation, God gathered dust for man; in the second hour, He molded him in a pure place, at the very umbilicus of the world, the Holy Temple in Jerusalem.[36] That is, man has his origins in both kinds of space, in the dust of the Many and the One.

But here it is the image of *molding* man that is arresting. Man alone in creation is described as formed out of a clammy combination of earth and water. "A flow would well up from the ground and water the whole surface of the earth" (2:6). Rashi comments: "For the purpose of creating man, the depths released a vapor that seeded the clouds and moistened the dust, so that man was created — *like this baker*, who adds water to his dough and then kneads it! So here, first there was a moistening and then, 'God formed man.'"

The audacity of the image is reinforced by another comment of Rashi: "'And God created man in His image': Everything else was created by an *act of speech*; only man was created *with the hands of God*, as it is said, 'You placed Your hands upon me'" (Psalms 139:5) (1:27).

There is an imagining here that cannot be glibly dismissed under the rubric of anthropomorphism. What does it mean, to be created by the hands of God, rather than by His word — ("'Let there be an expanse in the midst of the water'")? Man comes to *be* differently, it seems. Even before God breathes the breath of life into him, the circumstances of his physical making are radically different. It is no longer a matter of the water's swarming spontaneously with new life (1:20), or of the earth's "bringing forth" animal life (1:24), in response to God's word, "'Let it be. . . .'"[37] As we noticed before, the creative fiat induces a spasm of realization of new forms in the rest of nature. There, God's word is all-powerful: it constrains chaotic possibilities into the desired shape and posture. In such a hegemony of the word, it would be absurd to conceive of rebellion, or even of dialogue: "Necessity does not allow itself to be persuaded."[38]

Quite different is the imagery of the potter and his clay (or the baker and his dough). For here, the midrash dares to make a statement about the Frankensteinian nature of all creation. True, the potter has total control of his material. As in the famous image in Jeremiah 18, "if the vessel he was making with clay in the potter's hands was spoiled, he would make it into another vessel, such as the potter saw fit to make" (18:4). Like God, the potter "sees" and "makes." But there is another truth in the relationship of potter and clay:

> Then the word of the Lord came to me: O House of Israel, can I not deal with you like this potter? says the Lord. Just like clay in the hands of the potter, so are you in My hands, O House of Israel! At one moment I may decree that a nation or a kingdom shall be uprooted and pulled down and destroyed; but if that nation against which I made the decree turns back from its wickedness, I change My mind [*veniḥamti*]

concerning the punishment I planned to bring on it. At another moment I may decree that a nation or a kingdom shall be built and planted; but if it does what is displeasing to Me and does not obey Me, then I change My mind [*venihamti*] concerning the good I planned to bestow upon it. (Jeremiah 18:5–10)

Here is surprise, rather than the inevitability of God's power. In all creative work (the word *la'asot*, "to make," is central in this passage), there is play between the artist and his material. The characters of the novel begin to talk back, to declare their own reality and destiny. Thomas Mann intended his Joseph cycle to be a short story: it grew into a long novel that took ten years to complete. Edward Hopper says that for him painting is about a vision, yet when he makes a painting he reluctantly surrenders the vision to what he has made.[39] Erich Neumann writes of the "autonomy of the unconscious": the artist lives within the tension created by his consciousness and the unconscious that "often breaks through with a 'will of its own,' which by no means coincides with the will of the artist."[40] This tension in the experience of the creative person is precisely evoked by the passage in Jeremiah, and by the midrashic image of the baker kneading his dough. For God indeed "diminishes" His solitude and His power in order to create man. He responds to man's autonomous motions, to his "turning back," with a "change of mind":

the spirit of re-creation which masters this earthly form
loves most the pivoting point where you are no longer yourself.[41]

## Ambiguities of independence

In the Creation narrative, God "changes His mind" about the work of His hands—and destroys the world. Just before the Flood, "the Lord regretted [*va-yenahem*] that He had made man on earth, and His heart was saddened" (6:6). The anthropomorphism here is most poignant: but it is an organic outgrowth of the imagery of the artist, who projects but cannot control this one part of his work that is made *ba-yadayim*—"with His hands." Rashi's comment makes the connection clear. What is the meaning of *va-yitatzev* (translated here as "He was saddened")? "He mourned the loss of the work of His hands." There is a relation of the hands to the work, which is the contrary of everything abstract and detached. It is the relation of loving involvement, the mutual vulnerability to surprise and failure, the power and the risk of making.

When Adam sins, God's response, according to the midrash, is not verbal; rather "He laid His hand upon him and diminished him."[42] God "mourns for the loss of the work of His hands." Rashi's translation of *va-yitatzev* (6:6) is precisely related to the meanings that Rashi attributes to the word *etzev* (translated here as "sadness") where it first appears, in God's response to Eve's sin: "I will make most severe your pangs in childbearing [*itzvonekh*]" (3:16). Rashi veers away from this obvious meaning of *itzavon* ("pain of childbearing") and quotes the Talmud: "This refers to the pain of bringing up children."[43]

One might say that the difficulty in rearing children has to do with the ambiguities of independence. The child must separate from the parent; the parent must allow the child to discover his or her own reality. Where there was one, there must be two. But this separation, though necessary, is a complex and often tormented experience. The relationship between separation and loving attachment has to be negotiated each time afresh. There is no theory that can totally guide the parent or the artist. No belfry can house this kind of experience. In the act of creation, there is perhaps inevitable sadness, as the work works itself loose from the vision.[44]

The original verb, *vayyitzer*—"And He formed [man]" (2:7) — expresses this mystery of formation, of transformation. Wherever hands are involved, wherever there are "les traces des mains," even in the kneading of dough, there is the surprise of becoming: the viscous mixture of flour and water becomes the fragrant loaf of bread, the clay of dust and water becomes man. And it is this mystery, of how man becomes real, that is central to the midrashic vision of the narrative.

## Standing upright

At this point, I would like to quote a passage from *Nine Talmudic Readings*, by Emmanuel Levinas. He describes his approach to those rabbinical sources in which the psychology and intentionality of God are central.

> My effort always consists in extricating from this theological language meanings addressing themselves to reason. . . . [This] consists, first of all, in a mistrust of everything in the texts studied that could pass for a piece of information about God's life, for a theosophy; it consists in being preoccupied, in the face of each of these apparent news items about the beyond, with what this information can mean in and for man's life.[45]

If we are to speak of God's sadness, of His restraint in listening to and observing the freedom of man, of His frustration and sense of mourning, and, above all, if we are to unpack the imagery of God's hands, making and unmaking, molding and reducing man, then our effort will be toward an understanding of what this "can mean in and for man's life." Man knows himself created and freed from constraint. He feels himself as full of possibilities, and yet mysteriously cross-chained. He has had God's hands upon him; they created him whole, and he struggles to free himself from their total hold.

Like the child, like the vessel, he must find a space of separateness, in order to be; but to separate from God is to cut the ground of being from under his feet. For however one understands the nature of the sin that turns Adam and Eve out of Eden, its effect is to undermine their standing in the world. The tension between the vertical and the horizontal was once successfully accommodated by Adam and Eve. They could hold their ground in the presence of God. This, essentially, is the meaning of being — *kiyyum*: to rise up (*la-koom*), to be tall (*koma zekufa*) in the presence of God. To be banished from the Garden is to lose a particular standing ground.

To be banished, as Cain is later much more totally banished, is to have the earth cursed under one's feet: "You have banished me this day from the soil, and I must avoid Your presence and become a restless wanderer on earth" (4:14). Cain's connection with the earth is disrupted. Ramban emphasizes that restlessness is an inner quality of Cain's being, an essential character of his "curse": "His heart will not rest nor be quiet enough *to stand in one place*." Cain's protest focuses on this subjective torment: "Since I am to be a restless wanderer, I can not *stand in one place* — that is what banishment from the soil means — I have no place of rest. 'And I must avoid Your presence' — for I cannot stand before You to pray." In Ramban's reading, prayer, or sacrifice, is a profound expression of the existential stance of man-in-the-presence-of-God, able to hold ground and rise vertically, between earth and heaven.

In this context, the motif of Adam's "standing" acquires great resonance in midrashic sources. One of the essential stages of his creation, which is charted over the course of the hours of the sixth day, is when God "stood him on his legs."[46] This is Adam's first experience, after God has filled him with the breath of life — an experience of "standing on his legs":

He looked upwards and downwards, and his stature [*komato*] extended
from one end of the world to the other . . . and he saw all God's
creatures. He began to glorify his Creator's name, saying, "How many
are Your works, O God!" He stood on his legs and looked like one made
in the image of God. The creatures saw him and were afraid, thinking
that he had created them. So they all came to worship him. He said to
them: "You have come to worship me. Come, you and I, let us go and
put on clothing of majesty and strength and make Him King over us,
who created us all." So then Adam went by himself and was the first to
make God King. And all the creatures followed him, while he said,
"God reigns: He is clothed in majesty." (Psalms 93:1)

The imagery in this passage is potent with paradox. Adam stands on
his legs; and his stature (*komato* — as in English, the words "stature" and
"stand," are related) extends from one end of the world to the other.
Because of his height, he can see both vertically and horizontally, to the
full extent of empirical reality. There is, in fact, an ambiguity about the
"end-to-end" image: whether it indicates a horizontal grasp of the world
or an earth-heaven range.[47] But clearly, Adam is depicted as possessing
both powers, and the meaning of his stature is that he can see to the full
extent of both planes, the vertical and the horizontal. That is, unlike
Kafka's dreamer, lying on the ground in a refusal of the erect position (the
"terror of standing upright"), Adam occupies a vantage point from which
he sees not only the stars, but all created beings on earth. He can see
downwards as well as upwards, he is rooted in a reality which he can
perceive and map.

Nothing is said to indicate that he sees the animals as minuscule, but
clearly they see him as awesome in his verticality. They assume, indeed,
that he is their creator. That is, man knows himself as conspicuous, self-
conscious, not an indigenous part of the world of nature. There is danger
and fear in the loneliness of this position, the hazard of hubris. For what
the animals perceive is something truly Godlike. In standing, he is the
equivalent, in the lower world, of the angels. Sardonically, Canetti writes:
"We always overrate the man who stands upright. . . . Because standing
is . . . the antecedent of all motion, a standing man creates an impression
of energy which is as yet unused."[48] The reserves of possibility signified
by the standing position may be something of an illusion, Canetti suggests. We see Adam's godlikeness, here, from the viewpoint of the
adoring animals.

But the authentic greatness of Adam emerges in his response. He abandons his belfry grandeur and proclaims a common identity with the animals as created beings who owe adoration to an invisible Creator. And he does this in no obsequious humility but in a paradoxical perception that "to stand in the presence of God" is precisely to achieve full "majesty and strength." In voluntary acknowledgment, firstly of the vast gamut of created life ("How many are Your works, O God!") and then of the ultimate coherence under God of this "pied beauty," Adam becomes most Godlike. He makes common cause with the animals (lit., I and you, let us go put on majesty), but he, in fact, goes first and alone.

The paradox consists of Adam's diminishing himself—surrendering a speciously Godlike role and assuming an authentic one. The paradigm for this is the enigmatic rabbinic statement: "Wherever you find the greatness of God, there you find His humility."[49] Power and humility are both implicit in this vision of Adam standing in the presence of God: "man in his wholeness wholly attending."

This is a posture that he does not hold for long, however. It is striking that midrashic accounts of the sin that deforms his posture are so often cast in the imagery of the "incapacity to stand." We have already noticed the wistful tone of God's wish: *Halevai*—"Would that he might be created from the place of the altar and *have standing*."[50] Before the sin, Adam could "hear God speaking and stand on his legs . . . he could withstand it."[51] After the sin, he hides; the midrash imagines Adam and Eve as shrinking, essentially pretending *not to be*.[52] In another midrash, God says, "Woe Adam! Could you not stand in your commandment for even one hour? Look at your children who can wait three years for the fruit tree to pass its forbidden stage [*orlah*]."[53] This is a strange analogy: the capacity to *wait* seems to be the issue here, to hold ground, in spite of tensions of various kinds.

Another version of the same image is found in *Shemot Rabbah*. God reproaches the Israelites after the sin of the Golden Calf: like Adam, the people were destined to live for ever, but "when they said, 'These are your gods, O Israel!,' death came upon them. God said, 'You have followed the system of Adam, who *did not stand* the pressure of his testing for three hours. . . .' 'I said, "You are gods. . . ."' But you went in the ways of Adam,' so 'indeed like Adam you shall die. And like one of the princes you shall fall' (Psalms 82:6–7)—you have brought yourselves low."[54]

The midrash uses the imagery of the Fall, with a perfect consistency. The sin, as such, is not mentioned. Instead, what Adam, and again the Israelites, represents is a kind of spinelessness, a vapidity. A splendid being decomposes before our eyes. The word that is used in Sanhedrin 38b to describe the sin is *sarah*, which implies exactly this aesthetic offensiveness: it holds nuances of evaporation, loss of substance, and the offensive odor of mortification. "O my offense is rank, it smells to heaven."[55] It signifies a failure to stand in the presence of God, to maintain the posture of eternal life. "You have brought yourselves low": man, the midrash boldly implies, does not really want full and eternal being. He chooses death, lessened being. What looks like defiance is an abandonment of a difficult posture.

In connection with this notion of flight from the demands of reality, there is an evocative sentence in the Vilna Gaon's reading of the story of Jonah. The central enigma of that story is the act that initiates the plot: Jonah flees from the presence of God. Much ink has been spilled on the theological absurdity of such a flight. The Gaon says simply: "Everyone flees from the presence of God; no one wants to stand in His presence."[56] In this allegorical reading, Jonah is Everyman, protesting at the paradoxical demands of his condition. "To stand in the presence of God" is to resist the temptations of flight, to bear the tensions of freedom and obedience, of a position where vertical and horizontal axes meet. No one, says the Gaon, chooses to be; it is normal to decompose, to evade the demands of a whole consciousness. Unlike the phenomena of nature, man cannot be shocked into being, by fear, by Necessity, by the fiat of God. His is a more complicated story. It is the story of the quest for *amidah*, for a solid reality on which to base his life. Adam could not hold his position long: "things fall apart; the center cannot hold."[57] And in his failure to be, the whole world loses solid specification.

## The suspension of being

Here we approach the heart of the matter, an important, much-quoted midrash in which the narrative of Creation is undone, as it were, by the failure of Adam to stand. At the very end of the saga of Creation, just before the Sabbath (and therefore after Adam has begun to "evaporate"), the Torah says, "And God saw all that He had made and found it very good. And there was evening and there was morning, the sixth day"

(1:31). God reviews a work of art that now includes failure and death, and calls it—as never before—*very* good.[58] But the midrash that Rashi quotes, in his commentary on the verse, gives us a sense of a world not really created at all:

> "*The* sixth day": the definite article [*heh*] is added here [compare the conclusion of each of the previous days of creation—*a* second day, *a* third day] to teach that God had made a condition with all the works of the beginning, depending on Israel's acceptance of the Five [the numerical value of *heh*] Books of the Torah. Another reading: All the works of the beginning are suspended [lit., hanging and standing] until *the* sixth day of Sivan, which is destined for the Giving of the Torah.

Before we confront this midrash, however, the Torah text itself should provoke us to uneasiness. Why is the totality of things very good, since it now implicitly includes exile and shame, the flattening and dulling of the human body and face. " 'And God banished him from the Garden of Eden': his stature was diminished, his light was dimmed, his food changed, he became a restless wanderer on the earth, and death was inflicted on him and on all generations to the end of time."[59] Some essential light has faded from man's face; his range of vision is stunted. Job cries to God about the hopelessness of man's fate: "You overpower him for ever and he perishes; You alter his visage and dispatch him" (Job 14:20). "You dispatch him"—*va-tishalḥehu*—the same word used for Adam's banishment from Eden—holds a terror of summary execution. The banishment of man is interwoven with his mortality; it is to be read in his face, in his body. He knows himself unable to stand where he stood before. Is this change irreversible, as Job asserts? And in what sense is this "very good"?

One suggestion is that banishment is a merciful alternative to the finality of immediate death, which was, indeed, the apparent punishment that God had decreed originally: "on the day that you eat of it, you shall die" (2:17). Instead of dying on the very day of his fall, he is punished with exile; he lives on for nine hundred and thirty years. "If it were not for Your mercy, Adam would have had *no standing (amidah)*."[60] The simplest reading of "standing" would be "survival." But, implicitly, both Adam and the world are in need of some Archimedean point of stability, in a situation in which disintegration threatens. Here, the Archimedean point is defined as the "mercy of exile"; in another midrashic text, it is called the "strength of the Sabbath, without which the world could not have stood."[61] The main question facing man from now on will be precisely this quest for a foundation of being, for "one thing only which is certain and indubitable."[62]

Man sets off on a journey in which no form of solid assurance of reality and sanity accompanies him. In Descartes's vision of this radical anxiety, the ultimate dread is of madness, the fear of waking from a self-deceptive dream world, of having "all of a sudden fallen into very deep waters," where "I can neither make certain of setting my feet on the bottom, nor can I swim and so support myself on the surface."

The instability, the tendency of the world to change, to wear out, to fall apart, will lead the descendants of Adam to beliefs and rituals whose common aim is to make the world strong and solid again. Mircea Eliade narrates many such rituals of renewal, which reenact the creation, the original encounter of God and the world, and thus "repair" or "fix" the world:

> In Kimberley, the rock paintings, which are believed to have been painted by the Ancestors, are repainted in order to reactivate their creative force, as it was first manifested in mythical times, that is, at the beginning of the World. . . . Among some Yurok tribes the strengthening of the World is accomplished by ritually rebuilding the steam cabin. . . . [The priest] climbs a mountain. There he finds a branch, which he makes into a walking stick, saying: "This world is cracked, but when I pick up and drag the stick, all the cracks will fill up and the earth will become solid again." Going down to the river, he finds a stone, which he sets solidly in place, saying: "The earth, which has been tipped, will be straight again. People will live to be stronger." He sits down on the stone. "When I sit on the stone . . . the earth will never get up and tip again." The stone has been there since the time of the Immortals, that is since the beginning of the World.[63]

Eliade's notion of the continual or recurrent need to participate in the original "right" creation of the world is one response to a common existential anguish. The response described in classic talmudic literature is radically different. For the beginnings, the sources of man's being are clear and solid (the heavens become strong, congealed, come to *be*) only until the point where he begins to be conscious, to name the world, himself and God.[64] From this point, it is a matter of hours till he has named his reality[65] in such a way that what remains is a world that *is not really there*, in which the whole creation story is subtly undermined.[66]

# The world decomposed and recomposed

In such a situation, no return to the firm splendors of origins is possible. Another, more difficult act of regeneration is required. Here, again, is Rashi's comment on God's final assessment of the already disintegrated world:

> "*The* sixth day": the definite article [*heh*] is added here to teach that God had made a condition with all the works of the beginning, depending on Israel's acceptance of the Five [the numerical value of *heh*] Books of the Torah. Another reading: All the works of the beginning are suspended (lit., hanging and standing) until *the* sixth day of Sivan, which is destined for the Giving of the Torah. (1:31)[67]

Rashi's source[68] reads like this: "The definite article is not necessary. Resh Lakish taught: God made a condition with the works of the Beginning — If Israel accepts the Torah, you will continue to exist; if not, I will bring you back to chaos."

The radical effect of this talmudic passage is to undermine all the clarities, the achieved articulations, the crystalline firmness of Creation. For the question of meaning remains unresolved: "to be or not to be" is a question that is "suspended and standing" till Mount Sinai. There is a provisional quality to the reality of the world, a *rofef* ambivalence about meaning, which no fearful utterance of God can shock man into crystallizing. The world, till Sinai, awaits its true creation; man feels the question hanging over him, nothing is solid in his consciousness until some essential point of equilibrium is discovered.

This is not simply a matter of a shotgun commitment being demanded of the people at Mount Sinai. Their standing at the mountain is an experience *in extremis* of the instability, the terror, and madness of the world. Here is the version of the narrative found in *Pesikta Rabbati*:

> "Earth and all its inhabitants dissolve: it is I who keeps its pillars [*amudeha*, standing supports] firm" (Psalms 75:4). The world was in the process of dissolving. Had Israel not *stood* before Mount Sinai and said, "All that God has spoken, we will faithfully do [lit., we will do and we will listen (Exodus 20:7)] the world would already have returned to chaos. And who made a foundation for the world? "It is I — *anokhi* — who keeps its pillars firm" — in the merit of "I — *anokhi* — am the Lord your God who brought you out of the Land of Egypt."[69]

On a first reading, it seems that what saves the world from decomposing is God and His Law, which the people obediently accept. ("It is I who gives solidity to the world, through My commandments, encoded in the opening word of the Ten Commandments, *anokhi*—I. . . .") But there is another possible—and compelling—reading. Here, the *anokhi*, which gives substance and coherence to reality, is the "I" of human beings. Rashi reads the prooftext, the verse from Psalms (75:4), in just this unexpected way: " 'It is I who keeps its pillars firm'—when I said, 'We shall do and we shall listen.' " The people are responsible for the "I" that "fixes," that congeals a dissolving reality. The world is saved by a human affirmation, a human "standing at Sinai," which halts the process of disintegration.

In an even more paradoxical version of this idea, the midrash quotes provocatively: " 'But now thus said the Lord—Who created you, O Jacob, Who formed you, O Israel': (Isaiah 43:1) God said to His world, 'My world, My world, I shall tell you who created you, who formed you. Jacob created you, Jacob formed you—as it is said, "Who created you: Jacob. Who formed you: Israel." ' " [70]

God speaks lovingly to *His* world—and assigns it another creator. It is apparently human consciousness, in all its contingency, that "creates the world." In this sense, God "becomes" the Creator of the world, only when the question of meaning has been decided by man.

The notion of "world making," which, according to Rashi, is the chief enticement of the serpent in the Garden (" 'You shall be like God'— Creators of worlds" [3:5]) is one that has become very familiar since the advent of cognitive psychology. Nelson Goodman's central thesis, for example, is that "what we call the world is a product of some mind whose symbolic procedures construct the world."[71]

Jerome Bruner offers a succinct account of Goodman's notion of the creation of realities, and the complex—and changing—symbol systems that allow for constant "transformation of worlds":

> These constructions have in common that they take certain premises for granted, as stipulations. What is "given" or assumed at the outset of our construction is neither bedrock reality out there, nor an *a priori*: it is always another constructed version of a world that we have taken as given for certain purposes. . . . So, in effect, world making involves the transformation of worlds and world versions already made.[72]

This transformation is achieved when we

> compose and decompose worlds, impelled by different aims in doing
> so. . . . We weight and emphasize features of previous worlds in creat-
> ing new ones. . . . We impose order, and since all is in motion, the
> order or reordering we impose is a way too of imposing alternate
> stabilities. . . . We deform the given that we took and create carica-
> ture, the caricature itself being principled rather than entirely fanci-
> ful. . . . [73]

Transformation as distortion of the given, as principled caricature: this
is the core of Goodman's concept of world making. We recall the famous
midrash that describes God Himself as "creating worlds and destroying
them," before He achieved an opus that gave Him satisfaction.[74] The
model for creativity sketched here is not remote from Goodman's model;
constructions follow each other, each a "world," with its own givens, its
"stipulations," decomposing world versions already made.

If we try to make use of this model, we can ask: what, in all seriousness,
is the transformative moment of Sinai? In what sense is it true to say that
Jacob creates the world, as he stands before the mountain, as he says, "We
shall do and we shall listen"? Clearly, in making this resonant declaration
(which is rather tidied away in the JPS translation: "We will faithfully
do"), they are distorting the normal processes of cognition and action. It
is common sense that first one hears, understands, and then one acts.

The Talmud, continuing from the passage we read previously about
the conditional nature of God's creation, has a heavenly voice cry out,
"Who has revealed to My children this secret the angels make use of, for
it is written (Psalms 103:20): 'Bless the Lord, O His angels, mighty
creatures who do His bidding, hearkening to the sound of His word' —
They do before hearing."[75]

To distort the order of doing and hearing is a secret of the angels. As
Emmanuel Levinas points out, we are not dealing with "the consciousness of children," with an infantile concept of blind faith.[76] A rational
world is decomposed here; what is composed, set in its place, is a possible
world that only angels (who "stand upright") have represented until now.
Levinas calls this the world of "any inspired act, even artistic, for the act
only brings out the form in which it only now recognizes its model, never
glimpsed before. . . . [It indicates] a going beyond knowledge . . . [that]

could not be the deed of an underdeveloped human nature. It is a perfectly adult effort."[77]

We might, in fact, call the mode of action before knowledge a kind of spiritual virtuosity. Angels do what is complex and difficult with organic ease. In order to achieve the same effect of simultaneity, in which commands are transmitted from the brain to the nervous system to the muscles so fluidly that performance seems to precede input, human beings normally have to work very hard. But there is a triumphant moment when the normal laborious procedures of will and execution are short-circuited. In that virtuoso moment, a new world is created.

This is the experience of Jacob-Israel, as he discovers in himself the *anokhi*, the "I" of the world maker. He meets the *anokhi* of the World Maker and responds with the spontaneous energy of the unitary self. In that moment, a new map of reality is drawn—strange, imposing new stabilities. The "deep structure of subjectivity," as Levinas calls it, is acknowledged by human beings, when they encounter that same subjectivity expressed by God.

It is the *anokhi*, the "I," that creates a foundation for the world. In the original Creation, there is no *anokhi*: there is Necessity, there is the fiat that freezes the world into its forms. When God says *anokhi* at Sinai, however, something very different happens; a process that had begun in the enigmatic "very good," of failure, exile, and death, reaches its culmination.

This culmination is described in *Shemot Rabbah*, 29:9:

> When God gave the Torah, no bird sang, no fowl flew, no ox bellowed, the Ophanim spread no wings, the Seraphim did not declare, "Holy, Holy, Holy. . . ." The sea did not rage, people did not speak, but the world was in utter silence. And there came forth the Voice, "I am the Lord your God. . . ." It is written, "The Lord spoke these words— these and no more—to your whole congregation with a mighty voice. . . ." What is the meaning of "these and no more"? When one calls out to one's friend, one's voice echoes; but the Voice that came out of the mouth of God had no echo. And if this surprises you, think of Elijah, who came to Mount Carmel, gathered all the priests of Baal, and told them, "Shout louder! After all, he is a god!" [1 Kings 18:27]. What did God do? He silenced the whole world, muted upper and lower worlds, till the world was again unformed and void, as though there were no created being in the world, as it is said, "There was no sound, and none who responded or listened" [18:26]. For if anyone had

spoken, they would have said, "Baal answered us." How much greater was the silence of the world when God spoke at Sinai! Only so could God's creatures know that there is nothing aside from Him. And then He said, "*anokhi*—I am the Lord your God."

The extraordinary claim of this midrash is that the Torah is given when the process of decreation, the decomposition of the world, has reached its completion. In the silence of a time before Creation, before individuation and separation, none of the "stipulations," the found constructions of previous worlds exists. The question of meaning erodes all the facades of reality.

Mircea Eliade writes of an "archaic ontology," a "belief in an absolute reality opposed to the profane world of 'unrealities'; in the last analysis, the latter does not constitute a 'world,' properly speaking; it is the 'unreal' *par excellence*, the uncreated, the nonexistent: the void."[78] In "primitive societies," there is a profound sense that "everything that lacks an exemplary model is 'meaningless,' i.e., it lacks reality. . . . [Man] sees himself as real, i.e., as 'truly himself,' only, and precisely, insofar as he ceases to be so."[79]

"In the last analysis, [the world] does not constitute a 'world' ": the midrash, too, is concerned with "the last analysis"; but it offers a different response to the despair of a world returned to ultimate unreality. The question inherent in Creation emerges with full force. This is the question that the angels are recorded as asking in so many midrashic narratives: "Why? . . . Why create man? And with him, for him, the whole complex environment that is the universe?" What the Israelites experience at Sinai is the devastation, the return to "unreality," of the world. Out of this emerges, not the primal *Yehi*, the first fiat, "Let there *be*," but instead, this time, simply the voice of God saying, "*Anokhi*—I am."

The terror of such an experience is palpable. "It has been clearly demonstrated to you that the Lord alone is God; there is none beside Him" (Deuteronomy 4:35). Rashi's comment emphasizes the visual-mystical experience of de-realization: "When God gave the Torah, he opened the seven firmaments, upper and lower worlds were torn apart, and they saw that He is alone; that is why it says, '[lit.] you were *shown*.'" In other words, what the people overwhelmingly see is that there is nothing, nothing to stand on. "If you do not accept the Torah, I shall return the world to chaos and emptiness."

What saves the world, indeed what in a real sense *creates* the world, is the capacity of the people to encounter the terror of the *anokhi*. "It is *anokhi*, it is I who keeps the pillars — *amudeha* [lit., standing supports] — firm" (Psalms 75:4). What is the infrastructure that gives substance to reality? One perspective emphasizes the *anokhi* of God — the transcendent and only reality. But another — audacious and difficult — emphasizes the *anokhi* of human beings. It is man's ability to meet the voice of God out of the void, and to respond with his own *anokhi*: "We will do, we will *make* the world."

In this perspective, Israel creates the world, simply by finding a place to *stand* at Sinai. The giving of the Torah is, of course, idiomatically and commonly referred to as *ma'amad har sinai* — the standing at Sinai. To be able to stand "face to face" (Deuteronomy 5:4) with the God who alone exists and whose *anokhi* emerges from a vast silence is to take that immensity of the *anokhi* immediately within oneself. Analogously, perhaps, with the effect of great poetry, "an intimate call of immensity may be heard, even more than the echo of the outside world."[80]

To "make" the world is the charge that God left man with at the end of the original creation process, when "God ceased from all the work of Creation that He had done." *La'asot*, translated here as "that He had done," is actually the infinitive form, "to do"; the world is created open-ended, open to the doing, the making of man. And the word that recurs in God's reproaches to Eve and the Serpent is precisely this verb, *la'asot*: "What is this you have done? . . . . Because you have done this . . ." (3:13, 14). What a disappointing act this is! Immediately, the possibility of standing in the world is reduced.

At Sinai, a covenant is made both with a people "who are *standing* here with us this day before the Lord our God and with those who are not with us here this day" (Deuteronomy 29:19). This last group, says the midrash,[81] refers to future prophets, yet unborn. Of them, the word *omed*, "standing," cannot be used, as it is used to describe those physically present at Sinai. For *ein ba-hem mamash* — the unborn "have no reality." Only those who are substantial, live within time and space and the contingencies of the earth, can be depicted as *omed*, as standing.[82]

The people of Sinai affirm their ability to stand face to face with God. But what seems a static position is exposed, in a midrash quoted by Rashi, as a fulcrum of desire and fear, a point of equilibrium in the eye of the storm: "'And all the people saw the voices . . . and they moved backwards and they stood at a distance' (Exodus 20:15): they were repelled to the rear a distance of twelve miles—that is, the whole length of the camp. Then the angels came and helped them forward again." If this happened at each of the Ten Commandments, the people are imagined as travelling 240 miles in order to stand in place! The ebb and flow, the awe and the passion, are contained within a human "stance," that allows them to hold ground as *anokhi* encountering *anokhi*.

There may be something angelic about the capacity to say, "We shall do and then hear." But the people stand as human beings do, aware of tensions and countertensions. And, of course, they "fall" very soon after; "like princes you fall" (Psalms 82:6–7).

The Talmud makes an extraordinary observation about the paradoxes of "standing": "No man stands on [i.e., can rightly under-stand] the words of Torah, unless he has stumbled over them."[83] To discover firm standing ground, it is necessary to explore, to stumble, even to fall, certainly to survive the chaotic vibrations of a world that refuses to *be*. The gelid certainties of the fully created world are immediately undermined; only because of death and failure is man impelled to create the world anew. "Tremble in His presence, all the earth! The world stands firm; it cannot be shaken" (1 Chronicles 16:30). One might read this by tuning the strings of paradox tighter: "Tremble in His presence—*so that* the world may stand firm and not collapse." For how can one stand at all, if one does not know the tremor?[84]

## The experiment in form

To stand in the presence of God is not, then, to be static: it is a kind of dance, invisible to the naked eye. Neither rigidity nor chaos is God's desire of man. What He desires is the human response of transformation. Erich Neumann writes: "For Satan as antithesis to the primordial living world of transformation is rigidity . . . but at the same time he appears as its opposite, as chaos. . . . The smooth, undifferentiated fixity of the one is inseparable from the molluscous, undifferentiated chaos of the other. . . . In the creative sphere, they give rise to a third term, which embraces and transcends them both, and this is form. . . . [that] is menaced from both sides, by sclerosis and by chaotic disintegration."[85]

When the first experiment in human form seems to have failed, and God contemplates the "loss of the work of His hands," He mourns as a human artist or father would mourn. "And His heart was saddened" (Genesis 6:6). Rashi here quotes a provocative midrash, which purports to deal with the theological absurdity of the anthropomorphism:

> A certain skeptic asked R. Yehoshua ben Korḥa, "Do you not believe that God foresees the future?" He answered, "Yes." "But it says, 'His heart was saddened'?" "Did you ever have a son born to you?" "Yes." "And what did you do?" "I rejoiced and made everyone else happy." "But didn't you know that your son would eventually die?" "In time of joy, there is joy; and in time of mourning, there is mourning." R. Yehoshua said, "That is the way of God. Even though it was revealed to Him that His children would eventually sin and be destroyed, He *was not prevented from creating them* — for the sake of the righteous who were destined to descend [lit., to stand up] from them."

The skeptic asks about God's "disappointment," in view of the doctrine of God's omniscience. He uses the idiomatic expression for "foreknowledge": "Does God see the *nolad*, that which is already, barely born?" Within the frame of God overseeing the vistas of space and time—a transcendent God, who, in His "high solitude," knows what must be, as though it already were—within the frame of Necessity, what room is there for tears or for laughter, for hope or disappointment?[86]

"Yes, of course," answers R. Yehoshua: that is an obvious frame within which to view God. But the question R. Yehoshua asks, instead of answering explicitly, has to do with human experience, with the irrational freedom to rejoice, to mourn, not as one at the top of a belfry, not metaphysically, or theoretically. *Theoria*, in Greek, suggests taking a view of a large stretch of territory from a great distance, and favors the idea of a vertical view downward. It rises above "the plurality of appearances in the hope that, seen from the heights, an unexpected unity will become evident—a unity which is a sign that something *real* has been glimpsed."[87] In place of the *nolad* metaphor, the foreknowledge of a necessary future, that is not yet, but that can be seen from the top of the belfry as "already born," there is the contingency of the live child, who will die.[88] It is this frame, of contingency and passion, that God chooses to inhabit. Just as a human father does, God assumes the risks of the live process of creation.

However, the analogy with human fatherhood breaks down on one essential point. Unlike the father, God did not *have* to create the problematic, volatile being who will sadden Him. It is not by free choice that the father brings his son into the world. Why does God, in His freedom and power, choose to create this admittedly doomed creature? To respond to this implicit question, Rashi adds his last sentence, which does not occur in his source midrash:[89] "He was not prevented from creating them — for the sake of the righteous who were destined to 'stand up' from them."

Here, Rashi answers the question implicit in the father-son analogy. The question, again, is "Why?. . . . Why create man at all, why create a problem?" He was not prevented by His foreknowledge from engaging in the whole frustrating project — "because of the righteous" — *bishvil ha-tzaddikim*. The price to be paid for a *tzaddik* — a righteous man — is creation. The hazards and contingencies of the creative act are the loam out of which true form emerges. There is no way of achieving true form without opening possibilities of all manner of travesties. For to create is precisely not entirely to control. "If I create man," says God, in Rashi's second source midrash,[90] "wicked people will emerge from him. But if I don't create him, how will righteous people 'stand up' from him?"

To consummate creation with a free-standing *tzaddik* — that always was the point of the enterprise. We return here to the beginning, to that so-clear and structured and "real" description of unities breaking down into smaller and increasingly specific parts. "In the beginning, God created heaven and earth." Rashi says: "This verse is nothing if not mysterious [lit., This verse says nothing but "Explain me!"] — as the Sages said, 'God created the world for the sake of the Torah, which is called "*reshit* — the *beginning* of His way" (Proverbs 8:22) and for the sake of the righteous, who are called "*reshit* — the *beginning* of His produce" ' " (Jeremiah 2:3).

On no account, Rashi declares, can the opening verse be a description of the origins of the universe.

> The text does not intend to teach the order of creation. . . . And if you say that this verse teaches that heaven and earth were created first . . . be ashamed of yourself! [lit., be surprised at yourself]. For the waters were already in existence, as it is written, "And the spirit of God hovered over the face of the waters." Since there has not yet been any reference to the creation of the waters, they must already have been in existence before the earth and heaven were created. Clearly, then, the text does not propose to give a chronological account of creation.

Significantly, Rashi opens his great commentary on the Torah with a
response to the mystery of the words. He does offer a *peshat* reading—a
straightforward contextual reading[91]—but only in second place. He
draws his primary energy from the enigmatic midrashic decoding of the
mystery. *Bereshit*, "In the beginning," describes not the clarities of origin
and cause, but the potentialities of purpose. "For the sake of the righteous" means that all is open. There is no foundation; the beginning of a
pathway glimmers. (*Bishvil*—"for the sake of"—but lit., on the path
towards). In the future, at some time, in some place, a human being may
create the world. God now authors the work that will go in search of
authors. What is given at the beginning challenges man to the self-
transformations that will allow him, in spite of everything, to stand in the
presence of God.

> *Will* transformation. Oh be inspired for the flame
> in which a Thing disappears and bursts into something else;
> the spirit of re-creation which masters this earthly form
> loves most the pivoting point where you are no longer
>        yourself.
>    . . .
>
> He who pours himself out like a stream is acknowledged at
>        last by Knowledge;
> and she leads him enchanted through the harmonious country
> that finishes often with starting, and with ending begins.[92]

# NOAH ❦
## *Kindness and Ecstasy*

T*he collapse of God's project*

When men began to increase on earth and daughters were born to
them, the divine beings saw how beautiful the daughters of men were
and took wives from among those that pleased them. The Lord said,
"My breath shall not abide in man forever, since he too is flesh; let the
days allowed him be one hundred and twenty years." — It was then, and
later too, that the Nephilim appeared on earth — when the divine
beings cohabited with the daughters of men, who bore them offspring.
They were the heroes of old, the men of renown. The Lord saw how
great was man's wickedness on earth, and how every plan devised by his
mind was nothing but evil all the time. And the Lord regretted that He
had made man on earth, and His heart was saddened. The Lord said, "I
will blot out from the earth the men whom I created — men together
with beasts, creeping things, and birds of the sky; for I regret that I
made them." But Noah found favor with the Lord. (6:1–8)

God's decision to "blot out" the whole of creation follows on an
account of births and deaths over ten generations, culminating in the
birth and naming of Noah. The central event of each generation is the
birth of the significant heir; the father's years are numbered before and
after this pivotal act of propagation. Intense expectation builds up, therefore, in this objective account of numbers and names, an expectation that
becomes explicit when the reason for Noah's name is given by Lamekh,
his father: "This one will provide us relief [*y'nahamenu*] from our work
and from the toil of our hands, out of the very soil which the Lord placed
under a curse" (5:29). That Noah's name is derived from the word *neh
ama*, "comfort," is in itself strange: etymologically, the word *noah*, meaning "rest," would seem more appropriate; and, in fact, Rashi insists on
treating *y'nahamenu* as a pun on *yaniah mimenu* — "God will give us rest —

37

relief—from the labor of our hands." (Otherwise, as he points out, Noah should have been named Menaḥem!)

There begins to be woven, therefore, a tissue of verbal plays on the words *noaḥ*, *naḥem*: the comfort Noah will bring to mankind is the relief from a relation with nature that is misarticulated and, in some real sense, perverse. (Rashi: "Noah invented the plough—before his time, people would plant wheat and the earth would produce thorns and thistles.") Noah is therefore seen, at least by his father, as representing a readjustment of man's relation with the world; in effect, he will neutralize the primal curse on Adam.[1] This is the human expectation; it is followed by Lamekh's and Noah's significant age-data, until the birth of Noah's three sons.

Chapter 6 begins with the cryptic description of the sexual relations of the "divine beings" with the "daughters of men"—including reference to the Nephilim, giants, heroes, men of renown. Only at this point does God, it seems, reenter a drama of sexuality, procreation, and death in which human beings have been evolving their own destiny without comment from or dialogue with their creator. Even the function of creating man in His image has been taken over, apparently, by man himself: "When God created man, He made him in the likeness of God. . . . When Adam had lived 130 years, he begot a son in his likeness after his image." (5: 1, 3)

Man replicates himself; in so doing, indirectly, he will replicate the divine image. That is the model suggested by Adam's first act of procreation after the sin. But the image of man is distorted. God "sees" that evil has swollen to enormous proportions (6: 5, 12). An act of divine perception occurs: no human being is capable of such an act, it seems. Man had desired the "knowledge of good and evil"; by now, he seems unaware of the evil that, ambiguously, he has both generated and suffers. Evil overshadows his life; he no longer knows, or can discriminate between, those radical opposites that Buber describes: "the fortune and the misfortune or the order and the disorder that are experienced by a person, as well as that which he causes."[2]

A kind of sensitivity is lost to man. At this point, God, with a terrible humor, quotes the word-play on Noah's name, subtly transforming the meanings and indulging in a positive flurry of puns. The root *naḥem*, "comfort," which held out hope of comfort or relief, now denotes "regret," a radical revision of the entire Adam project (6:6). The curse, in which the relation of Adam to *adama*, "ground," had been skewed ten generations previously, was, in the human perspective, to have been lifted by Noah. When God acts on His vision of things, however, it seems that the curse is, instead, to be intensified to the point of utter destruction.

There is a clear sense that something problematic, even bizarre, is at work in the very use of language itself: the explosion of puns raises questions about limits and liberties, about structure and play. As we shall eventually see, this is a powerful issue: what does it mean to use language truly or wrongly? The shadow of catastrophe looms, even as language begins to display its resources.

The word God uses for destruction is *emḥeh* — "I will blot out" (6:7). Rashi translates to different effect: "He is dust, so I shall bring water upon him and *dissolve* him." This is to be a watery destruction, not a dry one. The original dust-earth of man — his relation to the *adama* — is to be radically annulled by an overapplication, as it were, of water. It then transpires that man's destruction is also to be the destruction of all life — animal, reptile, and bird — again under the rubric of *neḥama* — the cosmic "regret" of the creative God. The root words, *naḥem, noaḥ*, are joined in an associative cluster with the root *maḥah*, "dissolution."

The last verse of Parshat Bereshit returns explicitly to Noah and evokes a fundamental unease about the relation of this one individual, who was to have given relief to a strained world, and the total destruction that God has just declared, in His own voice. The narrative voice takes over for a short, final half-verse: "And Noah found favor with the Lord" (6:8). *Noaḥ matza ḥen* — the words *noaḥ* and *ḥen* form a palindrome, suggesting a subversive relation between the man and the "favor" he finds, the grace with which God sees him. So many expectations are being undermined; there is a kind of mirror-reflection of Noah that God sees and saves from the debacle. It is as though only by an imaginative act of vision can God decide to exempt Noah from the clearly stated general fate of the whole Adam project.

# The choice of Noah

There is a profound tension in this passage: in a sense, God declares an intention, based on a vision, and immediately revokes it, because of another vision of things. The tension is subtly reinforced by the fact that it is the narrative voice that seemingly undercuts the decisiveness of God's declaration — as though shrewdly making a comment on the emotional reservation of which God Himself is, as yet, unaware. A few verses later, this tension has surfaced in God's speech. He communicates it to Noah, in His first words to him: "I have decided to put an end to all flesh. . . . Make yourself an ark of gopher wood" (6:13–14).

"An end to all flesh" could not be more unequivocal: it is qualified only by an augmentation — "I am about to destroy them *with the earth.*" And yet there is the exception. Noah is at first not told the reason for his survival. Rather, God speaks of the technical details of the Ark, of a covenant that will cover his family and two of every living species, of food arrangements. It is only when God again speaks to Noah, telling him to board the ark he has already constructed, that an explanatory clause is added: "for you alone have I found [lit., seen] righteous before Me in this generation" (7:1).

The rationale is apparently simple and ethically reassuring. Noah is *different* from his generation. They are full of evil, of violence; he is righteous. Buber, indeed, comments that he is the first human being to be described by any epithet. He is certainly the only human being in the entire biblical narrative to be described as "righteous"[3] both in direct encounter with God and in the authoritative narrative voice that begins the Parsha: "Noah was a righteous man; he was blameless in his age" (6:9). The great emphasis on Noah's difference from his contemporaries serves an obvious moral purpose. It justifies his exemption from the universal disaster, and the choice of him to found a new race of Adam.[4] In a creative project that has proved a total failure (the text harps constantly on totality, through the repetition of the word *kol*, "all"[5]), there is yet one detail that can be salvaged and can provide a basis for a reworking of the idea. God's act in destroying and saving is seen to be ethically coherent: there is an unarguable logic to the ruthlessness of the artist who shreds all unsuccessful drafts and retains only the one that approximates his original intent.

But, close beneath the surface of the text, and glaringly exposed in many midrashic versions of the narrative, there is another reading. On this reading, Noah is chosen not because he is absolutely different, but because he "finds favor in the eyes of God." In what merit, asks the midrash, was he saved? The very question, with its multiple answers, is damning. In a famous comment, Rashi questions the qualifying phrase, "righteous *in his generations*." Does this damn him with faint praise (only in his corrupt time did he look like a hero)? Or does it praise him for transcending the sociomoral pressures of his period? In either case, the full-blown epithet, "perfectly righteous," is subjected to a refracting process that troubles its immaculate surface.

Ultimately, the suggestion that Noah is saved more because of the grace of God than because of any intrinsic grace of his own being is unavoidable. Midrash Tanḥuma elaborates on this possibility:

> This is like one [*eḥad*] who was traveling along and saw another traveler [*eḥad*] and sought his company. To what extent? Till he formed bonds of love with him. That is why it says here, "Noah found favor." Compare this with "Joseph found favor in [Potiphar's] eyes" [39:4]. It is like one who was traveling along and saw another traveler and sought his company. To what extent? Till he gave him power. . . . To what extent? Till he gave him his daughter. . . . To what extent? Till he could tell which animal is to be fed at the second hour of the day, and which at the third hour of the night.[6]

The traveler's choice of companion as narrated here is almost arbitrary. It is because He is One-alone-matchless that He seeks another one — any one — so that He may love, empower, and educate him. The anonymous hero, undeserving, finds himself married to the King's daughter. In many midrashic parables, the King's daughter is identified as wisdom. So, here, God chooses Noah, not because he has achieved significant wisdom or virtue, but because He seeks to convey to *some one* the knowledge of Himself. The commoner marries the King's daughter. But what is the intention of the end of the midrash? The acme of wisdom that Noah attains is a knowledge of the feeding schedules of the animals in the ark! Is this bathos, a satiric comment on Noah's limitations, or a serious insight into the nature of the wisdom that God has to teach Noah?

At any rate, Noah's heroic status, his difference from his generation, is undermined. The ethical underpinning to God's choice becomes less clear. The most explicit shattering of ethical clarities, however, is to be found in Sanhedrin 108a: "Noah had a death sentence sealed against him. But he found favor in the eyes of God."[7] In this reading, Noah is of a piece with his generation. He is essentially included in God's "regret," *neḥama*. Only love can invert *Noaḥ* into *ḥen* — an object of beauty: "you I *have seen* as righteous before Me" (7:1).

Disturbing questions about God's dealings with human beings arise inevitably from such a reading. If Noah is not such an unequivocal tzaddik, if his election is not entirely on merit, then what is the ethical statement of the Flood narrative? Perhaps there were others like Noah who were destroyed in the cataclysm? The midrash does not evade such a possibility. Indeed, Midrash Tanhuma goes so far as to construct an evolving model of individual justice; the rules of the game change when the Torah is given: "From the time that Israel stood before Mount Sinai and God gave them the Torah, any individual who sinned would be punished by God. Previously, one man might sin and the whole generation be punished. Of the generation of the Flood, our sages said that there were many decent people like Noah who were obliterated with the generation."[8]

On this view, the giving of the Torah marks a turning point in God's relation with human beings. Now, every man is treated after his deserts; previously, God's dealings with mankind were summary and rough-hewn. On such a view, however, there would be no motivation for a post-Sinai generation to read the Flood narrative at all. Beyond the purely historical interest, what is to be gained from such a reading? We read, says Paul Valéry, to "acquire some power." If radical questions of evil and punishment are confronted in the narrative in ways that are no longer relevant, then our knowledge and power as readers are not significantly increased.

## The theological question

Moreover, in Rashi's reading, based on a plethora of midrashic sources, the Torah itself instructs the reader to read with a different assumption. In several passages, the Flood narrative becomes the epicenter of questioning about God's ways with mankind. The Flood remains a live issue; no statute of limitations has withered its relevance. Moses tells the people at the end of his life, in his final song: "Remember the days of old, consider the years of generations past" (Deuteronomy 32:7). Rashi comments: " 'Remember': What He did to those first people who angered Him. 'Consider': This refers to the generation of Enosh, when the ocean flooded them, and to the generation of the Flood, which *washed them away* [shotfam]."

A people that does not read history and that therefore has no sense of the vast spectrum of possibilities within God's range is called a "dull and witless people" (Deuteronomy 32:6). Rashi unpacks the description: "They have forgotten what happened in the past, and therefore cannot understand the future: that He has the power to do good and to do evil."

The idea that history is to be read for the sake of the present and the future focuses on the Flood and its earlier warning version in the time of Enosh.[9] And the main affirmation Rashi has to make about the Flood relates precisely to our question of individual justice (Deuteronomy 32:4):

> *"The Rock! His deeds are perfect"*: Even though He is strong, when He brings retribution on those who transgress His will, He brings it, not in a *flood* [*shetef*], but with justice, for "His deeds are perfect."

> *"A faithful God"*: to recompense the righteous for their righteousness in the world to come. And although He may delay their reward, in the end
> He will fulfill His words.

> *"And without iniquity"*: Even to the wicked, He pays the reward of their righteousness in this world.

One of the basic theological questions is addressed here, the enigma of God's relations with mankind. Essentially, Rashi reads the verse as saying that *despite appearances*, ultimately (that is, from the perspective of the world to come), God is just to each individual. What may look like the neglect of the righteous, or the pampering of the wicked in this world, is "in the end" deciphered as coherent and morally just.

For our purposes, however, what is interesting here is the imagery implicit in the word *shetef*, "flood." God brings retribution not in one indiscriminate cataclysm, but with justice — that is, commensurate with the individual and his merits. The word *shetef* implicitly evokes the Flood. It is the word that Rashi himself uses a few verses later, as we have seen, to describe the fate of the Flood generation: "He washed them away." On one occasion, at least, God did, quite literally, "wash away" an entire generation, a mass of people and animals and insects, and the very earth itself, to a depth of three handbreadths below the surface — as far as the plough of human (agri)culture could fathom.[10] And Rashi, it seems, is inviting us to consider the questions raised by the apparently undiscriminating destruction exemplified by the Flood. Indeed, he insists that without such a searching reading, there is no way for the people to face essential problems of the present and future.

Rashi essentially affirms his faith in an ultimate justice, in spite of a world where His power is more apparent than His discrimination. What may look like *shetef*—the overpowering surge of mighty waters[11] that washes away guilty and innocent alike—is to be seen in the total context of the world-to-come. But the problem of *shetef* is not so easily dismissed by Rashi himself, nor indeed by his sources in the midrash. When God consigns the whole world to destruction, with the words "I have decided to put an end to all flesh" (6:13), Rashi comments: "Wherever you find sexual sin and idolatry, *andralamousia* comes to the world and kills good and bad (indiscriminately)."

*Andralamousia* is the term, borrowed from the Greek, for summary mass execution, the same notion as was indicated by the word *shetef*, "flood." Rashi here draws on the acknowledgment in many sources[12] that there may indeed be a disaster in which individual merits are entirely ignored. In one midrash, Noah is the king's friend and therefore is sealed away in a prison, to exempt him from the general fate (*andralamousia*).[13] On the other hand, there are many midrashic sources that stoutly deny any such possibility. Their message is clear: unlike a human king, who cannot discriminate between friend and foe, God saves the sterling individual, even as He punishes the corrupt masses. And the case of Noah is brought in evidence for this affirmation.[14]

The anxiety generated by the question of God's discrimination and providence is expressed in Rashi's reading of the two most poignant complaints on this subject in the Torah. First, there is Abraham's passionate defence of Sodom: "Far be it from You, to do such a thing, to bring death upon the innocent as well as the guilty, so that innocent and guilty fare alike. Far be it from You! Shall not the Judge of all the earth deal justly?" (18:25). Rashi comments: " 'Far be it from You!' It is a travesty of You! People will say, That is His usual work—He washes away everyone, righteous and wicked alike! That is what You did to the generation of the Flood and to the generation of the Tower of Babel."[15]

Abraham here imagines what people will say. He projects a possible reading of the Flood narrative, in which God's character, what He habitually does, His "speciality" (lit., craftsmanship) is subject to fits of irrational and petulant anger. "Far be it from You!" Clearly, Abraham is as concerned for God's reputation as he is for the threatened city of

Sodom. In one of Rashi's sources, Abraham says: "This is a profanation of God—people will be held back by this from returning to You."[16]

The interesting assumption here is that the Flood narrative has become a paradigm of interpretation in Abraham's time. People obviously are saying the kinds of things that Abraham projects here. In another midrashic version, Abraham does not, in fact, project the nihilistic view onto "people," but simply—though rhetorically—asks, "Is this not a travesty of You? Is this what You did to the generation of the Flood and to the generation of the Tower of Babel? This is not Your way."[17] Here, Abraham is confronting an obvious reading of the Flood paradigm. On this reading, there is a grotesque consistency to God's arbitrariness: He acts true to character. "Master of the universe, far be it from You! . . . Let people not say, 'That is his usual work: He destroys the generations *in the mode of cruelty*. He destroyed the generation of Enosh and the generation of the Flood and of the Tower of Babel. He does not change from His usual work!' "[18]

Twice, Abraham protests, "Far be it from You!" The second time, Rashi comments, "in the world to come." Such a view of God's relationship with human beings cries to high heaven: it affects not only what his contemporaries may say in their particular historical situation, but all future generations. Gur Arye translates "the world to come" here, as "in future generations." The Flood will never lose its potency to generate questions about *shetef*—about mass destruction and the relation of God to the individual. Wherever a similar situation recurs, the Flood paradigm will be cited, and people's darkest fears about their existential situation will be confirmed.

For the *shetef* model, with its image of a cruel, undiscriminating God, will always have enough apparent evidence to support it. Gur Arye emphasizes that no proof of God's response to the individual can ever be convincing. Noah's survival, for instance, will be attributed to the need for the species to survive, and not to his personal affirmation of values different from those of his time. The Flood model of *shetef* will be confirmed particularly by its triple occurrence as the basic mechanism of God's dealings with mankind. But perhaps, Gur Arye suggests, there are *specific* reasons, in each of these generations, for the general destruction that is called *shetef*? In the case of the Flood, he refers to Rashi's cryptic assertion, quoted previously, that sexual sin results in indiscriminate disaster. We shall return to this notion later.

The second example of the Flood as a paradigm for mass, irrational destruction in the thinking of later generations is the midrashic reading of the episode involving Avimelekh and Sarah. Avimelekh has kidnapped Sarah, and God has spoken to him in a dream, threatening death for adultery. Avimelech pleads ignorance: he was told Sarah is Abraham's sister, not wife; and, in any case, he has not touched her. According to the midrash, he cries to God: "Will You kill a righteous nation as well?" The unexpected word, "nation," in Avimelekh's protest of innocence suggests that his own case leads him to ask universal philosophical questions: "Even if he is innocent, will You kill him? Is that Your way—to destroy nations for no good reason? That is what You did to the generation of the Flood, and to the generation of the Tower of Babel. *I too say* that You killed them for no good reason, as You intend to kill me" (Rashi, 20:4).

Rashi's source[19] depicts Avimelekh as motivated by a deep sense of his own innocence. If he is to be condemned nevertheless, then he is forced to assume that, in the paradigm Flood situation, the victims must also have been innocent. He affirms absurdity in God's relations with mankind; his speech is a combined text, woven of his personal situation and his understanding of large historical and philosophical questions. In his thinking, there is little dialectical tension: "I too say" commits him squarely to an imagery of absurdity and cruelty.

The Flood, then, in its most radical imagery, becomes for all time a paradigm of the problem of God's dealings with man. Before we look more closely at Rashi's cryptic acknowledgment that where there is sexual sin or idolatry, mass indiscriminate destruction really does occur, it will be fruitful to consider again the *shetef* image. *Shetef* expresses the rash haste with which tyrants punish their populations. "When a king condemns his people, no one praises him, because they know that there is *shetef*—an angry surge of passion—in his judgment. *But God is not so.*"[20] Human beings, in a condition of *shetef*, become blind to individual differences and circumstances. There is a lack of *curiosity* about this condition that is the very definition of cruelty. God is not like this, asserts the midrash: He can always maintain high moral ground in any questioning of His judgments.

It is undeniable, however, that the savage imagery of the *shetef* is to be found in descriptions of God's dealings with the world. In Isaiah 28:18, for instance: "When the *sweeping flood* passes through, you shall be its victims." And in Nahum 1:8: "With a sweeping flood, He makes an end of His place." And it is one of the most common ways in which the effects of the Flood are described in talmudic metaphor: all life is swept away, washed away (*nishtafin*). It is the violent surge that uproots trees and mountains, in Ramban's translation of "The waters swelled" (*va-yigberu*, Genesis 7:18).

*Shetef* denotes a quantity of water — *mayim rabbim* — and a force that leaves nothing intact. The word used in the Torah narrative to describe the effect of the waters — *mahah*, "dissolve" — indicates a return to the "watery" condition of the universe before Creation. Man, as we noticed in our previous chapter, was originally formed out of the judicious mixture of dust and water; he was kneaded like dough, by the divine Baker (Rashi, 2:6). All that is necessary to ruin the structure of his being is to infiltrate him with an excess of water: in this destruction, the apparent solidity of the flesh is melted, thawed, and dissolved. All identities disintegrate; "they were obliterated from the earth" indicates, according to Ramban, that there is even no memory of their ever having existed (7:23).

## The drama of language

In a powerful midrash,[21] the primordial water acquires a symbolic force that will inform our understanding of the *shetef* modality:

> *"Let the waters be gathered into one area"* [1:9] — Let there be a *limit* (*kav*) to the waters, as it is said, "The measuring line is being applied to Jerusalem" [Zekhariah 1:16]. "Let the waters *hope* [*y'kavvu*] for Me, for what I am about to do with them." This like a king who built a palace and settled dumb people in it. They would rise up early in the morning and greet the king in sign language. The king said, "If these dumb people rise early to greet me in sign language, how much better it would be if they could speak!" So the king settled speaking people in his palace. They rose up and took over the palace. They said, "This palace does not belong to the king, it belongs to us." So the king said, "Let the palace return to its previous state." So, in the beginning, God's praise rose up only from the water, as it is written, "From the voices of many waters." And what did they say? "God is majestic on high" [Psalms 93:4]. God said, "If these waters, which have no speech, praise Me, when man is created, how much more will he praise Me!" The generation of Enosh arose and rebelled against Him; the genera-

tion of the Flood rebelled; the generation of the Tower of Babel rebelled. God said, "Let these be removed, and let those who were here before come in their place."

The return to "wateriness" is a return to speechlessness. The drama of the generations leading up to the Flood and following it becomes a drama about language, about the paradoxes inherent in the human capacity to create symbol-systems; it is a drama about civilization and its discontents. Apparently, the two modalities described here are those of language and silence: the waters are the dumb servants, while human beings are the articulate servants. And yet, a kind of inversion of values happens in the midrash. "From the voices of many waters" — dumb waters speak magnificently, giving ecstatic, unequivocal expression to the glory of God. Their very bodies speak. And the articulate — called *pikḥim*, the intelligent (lit., with open mouths) — so misuse their power of speech that they can be considered as not having said anything. It is a natural consequence of what they do with language that the dumb waters replace them.

The paradoxes are acute: the waters express a total oceanic acquiescence to God's power, while the poignancy of man's power of language is that it represents a narrowed, filtered inspiration. (There is a "line" drawn to limit the power of the waters and to make human speech possible. But that very limit holds out "hope" to the waters that their retrenchment is only temporary.) To speak as human beings speak is to make choices at every level of articulation. Which particular version of reality is to be created through this selection of words? What is *not* to be said? Many things, many more than are to be said. How can any model of reality, expressed in any form of language, vie with the devastating power of the "voices of many waters"? And yet, it seems, God has expectations of human beings, in their verbal expressiveness and their intelligence. Theirs is the power that He wants, apparently. Their structures, their freedoms, whatever is separate, distinct, and limited in them, can express a consciousness of God more valuable to Him than the involuntary ecstasy of the waters.

The "rebellion" of the generation around the Flood can be understood as a failure to speak, to communicate with God — or, indeed, with each other. There is a pathology in the very "openness" (*pikḥim*) of the Flood generation, which converts openness to a dumbness, a dumbness of babble rather than of silence.

# The exile of speech

One of the central midrashic motifs on the Flood is a quotation from Psalms 142:8: "Free me from prison [lit., from closedness] that I may praise Your name." Here is one version:

[God said to Noah:] *"Come out of the ark."* David said, "Free my soul from prison." When Noah was in the ark, he prayed constantly, "Free my soul from prison," as it is said, "Therefore let every faithful man pray to You, in a time when You may be found, that the *rushing mighty waters* [*shetef mayim rabbim*] not overtake him" [Psalms 32:6]. God said to Noah, "It is decreed before Me that you shall not leave this prison [closed condition] till twelve months are up." So we find in Isaiah 49:8, "In an hour of favor I answer you . . . saying to the prisoners, 'Go free.'" For they [the people in the ark] were forbidden [lit., imprisoned] to have sexual relations. Why? Because when the world is in trouble and destruction, human beings are forbidden to procreate; so that there should not be a situation in which man is building while God is destroying.[22]

In this complex and poignant midrash, Noah prays constantly in the ark. He prays to be saved from the prison of his ark. That, at least, is our opening understanding of Noah's prayer. But the quotation from Psalms 32:6 forces us to realign our perspective on Noah's dilemma. Noah, like "every faithful man," prays to be saved from the "rushing mighty waters"—the expression combines *shetef* with *mayim rabbim* to communicate the undifferentiated dumb violence of the world just outside the prison of the ark. The prison is both the closed space of the ark and the too-great openness of the wild raging silence beyond. In his enclosure within the ark, he is, of course, saved from the waters, but the midrash emphasizes that, thus imprisoned, he shares the general "decree" against mankind. He is not exempted from the general malaise; he too must endure twelve months, immobilized by fear of both openness and closedness. In a final move, the prison is associated with sexual death, which expresses most intimately the breakdown of speech in the rushing mighty waters surrounding him.

That is, Noah shares with his generation a pathology that is called in kabbalistic sources "the exile of speech."[23] And since "In every generation, there is something of the people of the Flood generation,"[24] this pathology is not unknown in the world since the Flood. A fundamental disaster has befallen the language powers of human beings. They have become so open that they are closed to one another. Communication between subjects has degenerated into a babble of indiscriminate voices. The silent compression of the ark (the *teiva*, meaning both "box" and "word") is the mirror image, the alter ego of the cacophony outside. Noah, man of his generation, endures the Flood, the misarticulation of openness and closedness, in an inversion of a deluge all his own.

For what, after all, according to classic midrashic sources, was the pathology of the Flood generation? The almost formulaic expression for their sin is that they were *shetufim be-zima* — "awash with sexual sin." The sense of *shetef*, of undiscriminating passion that sweeps away all boundaries, is central to the life of the time. The "corruption of all flesh," of which God speaks to Noah (6:12), is a profound disintegration of identity that is simply mirrored in God's declared intent to "disintegrate . . . all flesh" (6:13). The structures are already lost. According to Sanhedrin 108a, "cattle had perverse relations with wild beasts, wild beasts with cattle, everything with man, and man with everything." If sexuality is a mode of communication, then a sexual pandemonium has taken over. Something in the delicate balance of likeness and unlikeness that makes communication possible has been violently dislocated. In sending the Flood, the *shetef* that deconstructs all differences, God is, in a sense, merely registering what human beings have made of themselves. Or, to put the point differently, the Flood is an objective correlative, in T. S. Eliot's sense, for processes that psychologically and spiritually have long been under way.

Relevant here is the tradition, which Rashi refers to, that the Flood was not a single cataclysmic event, but a process. When Enosh was born, "it was then that men began to invoke the Lord by name" (4:26). This is interpreted by Rashi to mean that people began to call human beings and natural phenomena by God's name. At that time, in other words, people lost the capacity to discriminate between God, man, and nature. A linguistic rigor was lost. And at that time, by no coincidence, "a third of the world was flooded by the overflowing ocean" (Rashi, 6:4). This can, of course, be read as sin and punishment; it can also be read as an objective correlative for the blunted distinctions and misarticulations, by which people then defined themselves and their place in the world.

There are several indications in midrashic sources that the Flood was a process that men and women knew to be under way. In a fascinating midrash, quoted by Rashi, for example, Lamekh's wives refuse to have sexual relations with him (to "speak" to him), under the plea that "Tomorrow the Flood will come and wash away everything" (Rashi, 4:24). The Flood is intimated in the lives of men and women and animals, before Noah's time. Lamekh's wives speak out of a sense of impending doom — quite literally, *après moi, le déluge!* They react to the catastrophic openness of their time by refusing speech, sexuality, entirely. What they affirm in doing this is that the apparent openness smothers life as fatally as any prison.

# Rapacious sexuality

At this point, it will be important to look more closely at the sin that precipitates the Flood, that *is* the Flood. There is a strange ambiguity in the midrashic account: on the one hand, Rashi defines the sin as sexual sin and idolatry ("And the earth was corrupted before God"); on the other, he defines it as robbery ("And the earth was filled with violence" [6:11]). The same ambiguity recurs when God speaks to Noah, but this time Rashi schematizes the situation that precipitates the Flood:

> *"An end of all flesh"*: Wherever you find immorality and idolatry, in-discriminate punishment — *andralamousia* — comes to the world and kills innocent and guilty alike.
>
> *"For the earth is filled with violence"*: The divine decree was sealed against them only because of robbery (6:13).

The total indiscriminate destruction comes as a response to sexual sin and idolatry. But it is only because of robbery, disrespect for private property, that the edict is finally signed and sealed. What does Rashi intend here, when he aligns sexual immorality with idolatry as the essential factor, and robbery separately, as the final determinant? We might suggest that a comment is being made on the nature of the open sexuality and idolatry of the time, and on the mass destruction that is commensurate with it. For both sexual sins and idolatry often seem to be "generous" sins. In them, human beings often experience and express a yearning to transcend self, to relate to the other. It is no etymological coincidence that incest and other sexual taboos are called *ḥesed*.[25] This is the modality of expansiveness, impatient of limits and laws, eager to speak many languages, and know many other selves.

But the midrashic comment on the sexuality of the Flood generations reveals a grim counterreality. This is a sexuality of rapacious egotism: "The divine beings saw how beautiful the daughters of men were and took wives from among those that pleased them" (6:2). Rashi draws on the midrash:[26]

> *"The divine beings"*: These are princes who go about the business of God [*Elohim* in the Torah has the root meaning of mastery, leadership].
>
> *"How beautiful"*: The word used is *tovot* — "goodly," written defectively [without a *vav*]. When a girl was being prepared and adorned to enter the *ḥupa* [the marriage canopy], the ruler would enter and have intercourse with her first.
>
> *"From among those that pleased them"*: Even married women, even males, even animals.

The sexual temperament of the time is focused vividly in this image. The bride adorned on her wedding day, about to "enter" her new condition, to cross a threshold—"A threshold is a sacred thing," wrote Porphyrus in the third century[27]—is snatched away to the bed of the "great one." This custom—known in later times as *ius primae noctis*, the right to the first night—exemplifies the institutionalization of barbarity. If we are to speak of passion here, it is the arrogant passion of the self, for whom no Other exists, in her own subjectivity, her own readiness to open doors or leave them closed. The ruler simply *enters* the intimate domains of others and expresses his mastery. He ignores the sacredness of thresholds, the dangers, the hesitations, the temptations, the respect, due to doors.[28] His act of entry is a way of saying, in the words of the midrash: "Either me or you. . . ."[29] It is not an act of love, but an act of robbery.

Richard Rorty discusses the passion of the torturer in similar terms. Referring to Elaine Scarry's book, *The Body in Pain*, he speaks of "the tearing down of the particular structures of language and belief in which [the victims] were socialized. . . . The worst thing you can do to somebody is not to make her scream in agony but to use that agony in such a way that even when the agony is over, she cannot reconstitute herself. . . . You can thereby, as Scarry puts it, 'unmake her world' by making it impossible for her to use language to describe what she has been."[30]

The essential paradigmatic act of sexual sin is thus an act of rapacious self-assertion, which sweeps away all other "worlds," all other selves.

When Rashi says that the verdict against the Flood generation was sealed only because of the sin of *robbery*, we can understand him to be describing the *nature* of the prevailing sexual fantasy (and idolatrous fantasy) of the period. This is a fantasy in which self swells to fill all worlds, a colonial expansionism that radically denies the existence of other worlds of self and culture. "Either me or you. . . ." Essentially, this is a sexuality of cruelty, not of erotic relationship. It is a "pursuit of ecstasy which necessarily excludes attention to other people."[31] At base, it is, to use Rorty's term, a "lack of curiosity."[32]

The context in which these terms occur is a discussion of the work of Nabokov, and the theme of cruelty as related to the ecstasy-seeking of the artist. The central question, as Rorty sees it, is whether the obsessional nature of the artist does not entail a kind of fatal *incuriosity*, as to anything irrelevant to his own obsession. Nabokov claims that art is identified with the compresence of "curiosity, tenderness, kindness, and ecstasy." Curiosity, as Rorty notes, comes first.[33] But Rorty treats Nabokov's manifesto as something of a pious hope, rather than a realized assurance. In reality, Nabokov "fears most . . . that one cannot have it both ways—that there is no synthesis of ecstasy and kindness."[34]

## Ecstasy and kindness

These motifs provide us with a model that will be helpful in discussing the dilemma of the Flood generations. The main problem of the time— called sexual sin—is the very converse of love. Love is to be identified with curiosity, with that *attentiveness* to the self-made worlds of others, which the midrash represents the Flood people as lacking. What we see in them is the excess of openness, manifested in the "desire to conquer all reticent beings."[35] This is the *gezel*, the rapacious mode of sexuality.[36] When this is the prevailing mode, then mass destruction, indiscriminate of selves and worlds, comes like a madness and washes away all selves, innocent and guilty alike.

It is this issue of love-kindness-curiosity, as opposed to obsessive narcissism, that divides the Flood generation from the Tower of Babel generation. Rashi, quoting the midrash, asks why the Flood generation is punished so much more radically, why they are "washed away" (11:9). He answers by contrasting the "robbery" of the Flood generation with the "love and friendship" of the Tower of Babel generation. This, it seems, is the core of the matter.

It is on this score, of the cruelty that is basically incuriosity, that the Flood narrative evokes associations with the sin and fate of Sodom. There are verbal echoes in the two narratives,[37] including the use of the word *ḥamas*, "violent robbery." In a provocative passage, the prophet Ezekiel sketches the Sodom-like character of his own people: "Only this was the sin of your sister Sodom: arrogance! She and her daughters had plenty of bread and untroubled tranquillity; yet she did not support [lit., hold the hand of] the poor and the needy" (16:49). Nahum Sarna writes of the "callous disregard of the existence of poverty amidst an economy of plenty."[38] Callous disregard is the existential meaning of the sexual openness of the Flood period, too.

In many midrashic sources, there is a recurrent comment on the long-term effects of the Flood on the cultural-sexual modalities of future generations. In the story of the rape of Dinah, for example, her brothers' anger is explained: "because Shekhem had committed an outrage in Israel, by lying with Jacob's daughter—a thing not to be done" (34:7). This phrase—"a thing not to be done"—is explained by Rashi: "to rape virgins, because the nations of the world had banned [lit., fenced themselves off from] sexual crimes, *as a result of the Flood*." Such crimes are simply "not done" after the Flood. They are taboos, even where an unmarried woman is concerned, suggests Mizraḥi, in his commentary on Rashi, because of the factor of *gezel*—of robbery, of violence against her autonomy, which is expressed in kidnapping and which is punishable by death.

Rambam, in his legal codex,[39] even justifies the massacre of the whole city of Shekhem, on the basis of the fact that the prince had committed the crime of *gezel*—of robbery—and the whole city was silent accessory to the crime. This is a failure in justice, in the values of privacy and the rule of law, which became the foundation of the post-Flood era.[40] And Shekhem's act of rape is thus seen as an exceptional rather than a typical act—"as a result of the Flood."

A similar point is made by Rashi on Jacob's tears when he meets Rachel for the first time: even a kiss, he fears, will be interpreted as an outrage against the decencies of the post-Flood ethos: "From the time that the world was punished by the Flood, all the nations resolved to ban [fence themselves off from] sexual immorality."[41] In similar vein, when

Avimelekh kidnaps Sarah, he expresses horror at the "great sin" of adultery (20:9), in which Abraham almost involved him, by claiming that Sarah was his sister (and not his wife).

The implication in these and other sources is that a kind of sexual puritanism was, at least for a certain period, the consequence of the Flood. Even the animals in the ark restrict themselves to their own kind. They leave the ark *le-mishpeḥoteihem*—"by families" (8:19): the midrashic comment is that the structures of family life, the taboos of civilization, are inculcated into the animal world, too, during the twelve-month period in the ark, so that when they emerge, it is with a changed nature, as it were—"They left in families—and *not themselves*."[42]

In these two words ("not themselves"—*ve-lo heim*), the midrash, it seems, focuses the essential paradox that Freud describes in *Civilization and Its Discontents*—the costs and gains of repression of sexual energy. By focusing on the animal world, the midrash makes a radical statement about the transformations and sublimations possible in a new cultural-spiritual order. The power of the Flood, its destructive disregard of all privacies, gives rise to an era in which human beings set up voluntary fences and walls.

But the motive for the new puritanism is fear—a fear of the nihilism glimpsed in the unfocused expansionism of the Flood era. And the problem of the Flood generation is, therefore, not resolved; it merely undergoes metastasis, into different, even opposite forms. For the problem of "incuriosity," of "cruelty," in which only self exists, is diagnosed in the midrash as the arrogance of radical insecurity—"Either me or you." The obsessions of the self swell to fill the universe; the more they swell, the more remote they become from any stable ground of being. Human beings are driven to dominate external space, to act out their vertiginous freedoms. But vertigo then drives them inwards again, to construct prison houses of safety from the "mighty waters." These do not cure the vertigo; they merely exclude it.

The post-Flood generation, the builders of the Tower of Babel, have as their motto, "Me and not You." They set up safe houses of human solidarity, which are mere oases in the treacherous and indescribable world. It is, when all is said, a pathetic avoidance. What neither generation can encompass is a world with God at its center, so that one may dare to imagine a multiplicity of selves, of worlds, existing together, even interacting with one another in modes that build and do not destroy.

The radical problem, then, is that of imagining the world. All the pathologies of openness and closedness relate to imaginative obtuseness. According to the midrash in *Bereshit Rabbah* (36:1), the Flood people see God as blind, indifferent, callous to the world. What follows is that human beings feel themselves free to be likewise blind, indifferent, and callous:

> "When He is silent, who will condemn? If He hides His face, who will see Him, be it nation or man?" [Job 34:29]. R. Meir said, "This is what the generation of the Flood said: He is silent toward His world; He hides His face from His world, like a judge who has a curtain drawn over his face, so that he does not know what is happening outside. 'The clouds screen Him so He cannot see'" [Job 22:14].

God's silence, the curtain of cloud that screens man from His view— this is a philosophical understanding that justifies human cruelty. If God either ignores what is happening just beyond His line of sight, as it were, or if He is *shotef hakol*—indiscriminately destroys whole generations— then human society is freed from the yoke of justice and responsibility. Or, at least, until the terrors of such freedom become so palpable that a backlash sets in.

To link God's justice in this way with human justice is not, of course, inevitable. George Eliot's manifesto to a godless world comes to mind: "She, stirred somewhat beyond her wont, and taking as her text the three words which have been used so often as the inspiring trumpet-calls of men—the words, *God, Immortality, Duty*—pronounced, with terrible earnestness, how inconceivable was the *first*, how unbelievable the *second*, and yet how preemptory and absolute the *third*."[43]

Though not inevitable, however, the Flood people's response has a desperate logic to it. Their cruelty is indeed the cruelty of despair. Where such a vision of the world prevails, even "the compassion of the wicked is cruelty" (Proverbs 12:10). In another midrash, God and human beings are set in high relief against one another, precisely in relation to this question of cruelty and kindness:[44]

> "*And God remembered Noah*": It is written, "A righteous man knows the needs of his beast. But the compassion of the wicked is cruelty." The Righteous One of the world knows the needs, even of animals, even in His anger. He is unlike human kings, who send in their legions to quell a rebellion and kill both innocent and guilty alike—because they do not

know rebel from loyal citizen. God, however, even in a generation that angers Him, saves the one righteous person in the generation: "He knows the needs of His beast." "But the compassion of the wicked is cruelty": these are the people of the Flood, who were cruel. The sages said: When God raised the depths over them, and they saw the fountains of the deep threaten to submerge them, what did they do? They had many children . . . and some of them would take their children and place them into the depths, pressing them down mercilessly. That is why it says, "The compassion of the wicked is cruelty." How do we know? Because Job said, "May the womb forget him; may he be sweet to the worms; may he be no longer remembered; may wrongdoers be broken like a tree" [Job 24:20] — his womb [*sic!*] no longer remembers that they were his children.

Rashi adds[45] that the children were placed under their parents, in order to "block the openings of the deeps." The violent imagery of callousness, in which a child — one's own child — becomes a bung against one's own destruction, represents a failure of memory, of imagination. One's child is, after all, that being in the world of others in whom one's own face is reflected. God, by contrast, is exquisitely aware, "knows"; He can focus on the needs of the righteous man (strangely called "His beast") among the mass of the wicked. This is the opposite of cruelty — to know the individual and his needs. It is essentially curiosity, awareness of the otherness of the other. The animal imagery suggests the difference — the lower order — represented by man's reality and God's. Yet He focuses His attention and concern on "His beast."

The analogy is, of course, particularly appropriate in a context where Noah has earned the loving attention of God, precisely by his own loving attention to the animals. Here we can recall the midrash, quoted earlier, in which the traveler meets "one" on his journey, seeks his company to the point of giving him his daughter in marriage, and teaches him wisdom — which animal is to be fed at the second hour of the day, and which at the third hour of the night.[46] We noticed that the King's daughter in midrashic symbolism is often a figure for Wisdom. God gives Noah, in token of His love, wisdom — the wisdom to know the feeding schedules of the animals! The anticlimax is palpable. But what looks like a bathetic ending to a midrash that is clearly designed on a principle of intensification in fact makes, possibly, the most important point of all about Noah and his relation to the world.

# Noah's silence

At this point, and before we discuss Noah's role in the ark, we can return
to the questions we raised earlier about Noah's involvement in the death
sentence imposed on his world. Noah is indeed a man of his world and his
time. He shares in the prevailing pathology; he is saved more for what he
may be than for what he is.

If we are in any doubt about who Noah is, we have only to consider the
central fact of his silence. From beginning to end of the Flood narrative,
Noah says not a word. God talks to him twice before the Flood, telling of
what is to come, telling him how to build the ark, to enter it with his
family and representatives of the animal world. And after each of God's
long speeches (6:13–21; 7:1–4), the text tells us impassively, "And Noah
did just as the Lord commanded him" (6:22; 7:5). Rashi distinguishes
between the two acts of obedience: the first time, he obeyed by building
the ark, the second time by entering it. But the impact of Noah's silent
acquiescence in the destruction of the world is devastating.

His "unqualified apathy," as André Neher calls it,[47] is not largely
mitigated by the midrashic scenario, which has him building the ark over
120 years—a process that begins with planting the cedars that are to
provide wood for the ark, so that they may become a topic of general
conversation and lead to the rebuke and repentance of his contemporaries.[48] Even in this midrash, Noah's imaginative solipsism is clear: he
tells his interlocutors, "God intends to bring a Flood on the world, and
told me to make an ark, so that I and my household may escape." It is not
surprising that he is not effective in swaying his contemporaries. His
silence is the reverse image of their babble.[49]

Noah's silence, I suggest, is essentially a metastasis of the sickness of
his time. He is incurious, he does not know and does not care what
happens to others. He suffers from the incapacity to speak meaningfully
to God or to his fellow human beings. He, too, is imprisoned by the
"mighty waters," even though his prison takes the form of a small,
enclosed, safe space.

Just here, however, is the paradoxical arena of Noah's transformation.
Within the intimate but teeming space of the ark, Noah becomes, in the
midrashic view, a new person—effectively, and retroactively, a person
whom the Torah can describe as a tzaddik, a righteous man: "Said R.
Levi, 'Even the mill stones were obliterated in the water—and yet you say,

"And the sons of Noah who came out of the ark *were*" [9:18]? But Noah saw a new world.' ["Were" is understood as indicating new being.] . . . The Rabbis said, 'Anyone of whom it is said, 'He *was*,' is a feeder, a life sustainer.' "[50]

The midrash treats Noah as one among five cases of people who are described as "seeing a new world," on the one hand, and "feeding and sustaining," on the other. To see a new world, in the case of Joseph, or Moses, or Job, or Mordecai, is to be understood metaphorically; these men underwent radical changes of fortune, so that their entire perspective on the world was transformed. In the case of Noah, of course, quite literally, the world itself was transformed around him. And yet even in his case, the midrash is to be read as a comment on Noah's subjective vision. Even the massive mill stones were turned to water. How could Noah *be*, in such a world of "mighty waters," if it were not that *he* was profoundly changed? When he comes out of the ark, he no longer belongs to the babble of the waters, nor to the silence of the withdrawal. And what has changed him is suggested in the second part of the midrash. "He *was*" means that he became a feeder and a life sustainer.

## Noah as life sustainer

The core of the ark experience is Noah's relation to the animals he brings with him, "to keep alive with you" (6:19). When God speaks to Noah the first time, He tells him to do three things: to build the ark, to enter it with his family, and to bring into it representatives of the animal world. The culmination of God's speech is the last verse (6:21): "For your part [*ve-ata*], take of everything that is eaten and store it away, to serve as food for you and for them." "For your part" — *ve-ata* — parallels the "For My part" — *ve-ani* — of 6:17. God's role is to bring the Flood: Noah's role is complementary, even contrapuntal. He is to prepare food, for human beings and for animals. "Noah did so; just as God commanded him, so he did" (6:22). He takes food for all, but *kaḥ lekha* — literally, "Take for *yourself*" — though an idiom, introduces the suggestion that feeding the animals will be in some sense conducive to his own welfare.

*Bereshit Rabbah* engages in a serious discussion of the type of food Noah brings into the ark.[51] One view is that he brought pressed figs, an acceptable neutral diet for men and animals. ("Food for you and for them" indicates a single diet for both.) But another view is that he brought a different, individual diet for each species. ("For you and for them" indicates specific, individual foods for each species, with the human diet primary.) Ultimately, the midrash concludes, "You shall store it away *for yourself*" (literal translation) indicates that "No one brings something in [lit.], unless he has need of it."

All the feeding that Noah does in the ark, all the varieties of food that he stores there, all have to do with the question of *need*—in the obvious sense, the animals' need, but ultimately, *his* need. To "bring something in" is to satisfy need—the basic model is the human body, with its apertures, through which vital requirements are absorbed. And yet, paradoxically, in this and in many other versions of the midrashic narrative, all attention is focused on the variations and details of the *animals'* needs.

In Tanḥuma 2, for instance, the animals are fed not only the kinds of food they are used to, but at the times they are used to. Here, we recall the midrash about the traveler who teaches his new-found friend the acme of wisdom ("marries him to his daughter")—the timing of animal meals. Here, too, the prooftext is, "A wise man captivates people" (lit., takes souls) (Proverbs 11:30). This refers, claims the midrash, to Noah, who fed and sustained the cattle. Noah's wisdom is demonstrated in his painstaking, detailed knowledge of the feeding schedules of every species within the ark. "For twelve months in the ark, he had not a wink of sleep, neither by day nor by night, for he was occupied in feeding the creatures who were with him—'The wise man takes souls.'"

It is clear that Noah plays a God-like role in "feeding the creatures." Like God, he is the type of the "righteous man, who knows the needs of his beast" (Proverbs 12:10). We have discussed the kind of concern, of curiosity, that according to Tanḥuma 7 God demonstrates, by contrast to the cruelty of the Flood people. The knowledge of the tzaddik is focused on the needs (lit., the soul) of the animal. In another midrash (Tanḥuma 5), Noah as tzaddik is defined specifically by his "feeding the creatures of God." To be a righteous man is to care for and provide the needs of all creatures—like God Himself. But the basis of such concern is spelled out in our midrash: to be able to feed, one must have not simply sterling character, but a kind of curiosity, a kind of wisdom.

The animals are the prototype objects of this kind of nurturing knowledge. Without verbal communication, the righteous man is still expected to intuit the dumb world of the Other. He is defined by his capacity to nurture the needy, with the right food, at the right moment. The knowing of need is the highest measure of that curious, tender concern that characterizes God and God-like man.

In a startling comment on "the needs of his beast," Rashi explains, "What his cattle *and his family* need." He is not inhibited about equating cattle and human beings under the basic rubric of need. "Your justice is like the great deep; man and beast You deliver, O Lord" (Psalms 36:7). Here, again, Rashi emphasizes that there is no shame in the animal needs of the whole human being; indeed, there is an existential realism and humility, in the recognition of these needs.

For the relation of a human being to his needs can be a matter of joy and affirmation of life. Emmanuel Levinas writes:

> Nourishment as a means of invigoration, is the transmutation of the other into the same, which is in the essence of enjoyment: an energy that is other, recognized as other . . . becomes, in enjoyment, my own energy, my strength, me. All enjoyment is in this sense alimentation. . . . The bare fact of life is never bare. Life is not the naked will to be, an ontological *Sorge* for this life. Life's relation with the very conditions of its life becomes the nourishment and content of that life. Life is *love of life*, a relation with contents that are not my being but more dear than my being: thinking, eating, sleeping, reading, working, warming oneself in the sun. Distinct from my substance but constituting it, these contents make up the worth [prix] of my life. . . . The human being thrives on his needs; he is happy for his needs. . . . Happiness is made up not of an absence of needs, whose tyranny and imposed character one denounces, but of the satisfaction of all needs. . . . Happiness is accomplishment: it exists in a soul satisfied and not in a soul that has extirpated its needs, a castrated soul.[52]

Ultimately, the relation of Noah to the animals' needs is symbolic of the relation of the self to its own needs, to its most real and intimate interactions with the other. To be hungry and eat is to experience enjoyment and power—the independence of "a subject capable of ensuring the satisfaction of its needs."[53] The very concrete animal quality of the need for food generates the sense of personal potency.

The traditional midrashic view is that sexuality receives no expression in the ark. Instead, there is feeding, the acute awareness of timing and taste in nurturing the other. I suggest that feeding animals becomes a year-long workshop in the kindness that Rorty defined as "curiosity."

The sexual area is too dangerous, for the time being: too much abuse, too much cruelty has become part of its essential fantasy. Feeding animals, too, however, can be dangerous. The midrash, quoted by Rashi (7:23), depicts Noah as injured by a lion when he is late with its meal. Dealing with the Other is never safe, apparently. His "alterity" (Levinas's term) is essential and irreducible; yet, as Levinas puts it, "it is visible only from an I." All the feeding, the storing of foods, the exquisite concern and attentiveness, are ultimately functions of Noah's relation with his own needs.[54] The "I" of Noah is being trained to an alertness that makes sleep impossible ("He never tasted the taste of sleep!"[55]). He gives food to the animals and gains enjoyment for himself. His work is altruistic and nurtures his own sense of potency.

## Kindness and ecstasy

Over twelve months, the ark becomes a crucible in which a new type of sensibility is nurtured. It is a closed interior, cut off from the raging waters outside. Entering this interior is not simple. Many midrashic sources stress the difficulty of God's command, "You shall enter the ark" (6:18): the smallness of the ark for so many inhabitants,[56] Noah's delay until the water is lapping around his ankles,[57] the attacks by enraged contemporaries, of giant size and force.[58] "You shall enter the ark" can be read as a promise, rather than a command[59] — an assurance that Noah will find the strength needed for this entry. And Rashi reads the second statement of Noah's obedience — "Noah did just as God commanded him" (7:5) — as referring simply to the act of entry, in all its apparent banality.

It seems that Noah senses great danger in this entry, a cutting-off from all previous experience. Gaston Bachelard writes evocatively of the power of doors:

> Is there one of us who hasn't in his memories a Bluebeard chamber that should not have been opened, even half-way? Or — which is the same thing for a philosophy that believes in the primacy of the imagination — that should not even have been imagined open, or capable of opening half-way?. . . . [The poet] knows that there are two "beings" in a door, that a door awakens in us a two-way dream, that it is doubly symbolical.[60]

Indeed, the narrative emphasizes, after the several variations of the clause, "Noah came into the ark," "And God shut him in" (7:16). An ambiguous slam of the door, protecting, imprisoning. Claustrophobia sets in, as we read of all the animal flesh, male and female, enclosed with Noah for twelve months. All this flesh is to be seen by him, in one sense, as his own flesh, its needs are to be his needs: "to keep alive *with you*" (6:19). The ark is to be a laboratory of kindness, of attentiveness to the needs and the enjoyment that are, in Levinas's terms, the "contents of life." But how does Noah deal with the claustrophobia, the sense of being cut off from that other world that Rorty defines as one in which "ecstasy" is pursued? Are the two modalities incompatible — kindness, curiosity, attentiveness to others *as* other, on the one hand, and ecstasy, obsession, at worst, cruelty, on the other?

Midrash Tanḥuma, as we have seen, imagines Noah's constant prayer to have been "Release my soul from enclosure" (Psalms 142:8). This, in fact, becomes a leitmotif in the Tanḥuma narrative: the paradox of Noah's desire to be free of the ark, on the one hand, and his reluctance to leave, on the other. God has closed him in. When He tells Noah, finally, "Come out of the ark" (8:16), He means a most intimate form of release — a release from the sexual abstinence, the nonecstatic modality of the ark.[61] Noah has prayed for this release, yet he refuses it, on the grounds of his apprehension that further floods may sweep away all his efforts to live at the margins of ecstasy. There is an unresolved dilemma in Noah's consciousness: between openness and closedness, between the mighty waters of ecstasy and the alert attentiveness of kindness.

When he prays, "Release my soul from enclosure," he expresses his claustrophobia at being entirely committed to the feeding of others. The *Pirkei d'Rabbi Eliezer* version of the narrative[62] paraphrases the meaning of his prayer: "for my soul is weary of the smell of the lions and the bears." A profound angst cries from these words. It is not simply a physical weariness that afflicts him, the unremitting rigor of a feeding schedule that never allows him a "taste of sleep." The smell of the animals, in the final analysis, unnerves him. The sense of smell evokes intimations, essences of an experience. To be totally present to the needs of the animals — this is the very meaning of the ark experience. Within the density and compression of the ark, multiple relationships and forms of knowledge open up. And yet, through that very saturation in the feeding mode, Noah becomes achingly aware of a "weariness," a fatigue that dreams of another way of being. "O God!" says Hamlet, "I could be bounded in a nutshell and count myself a king of infinite space, were it not that I have bad dreams."[63]

## The *two-way dream*

Noah's dream is a dream of the door, the window, the opening. God closes him in; nothing is left of the world but what is *inside* the Ark: "Only Noah and those with him in the ark" survive (7:23). But, adds *Pirkei d'Rabbi Eliezer*, with magnificent disregard for the apparent clarities of the text, Og, the king of Bashan, also survived. He "sat on a plank of the ladders of the ark, and swore to Noah and his sons that he would be a slave to them for ever. What did Noah do? He pierced a hole in the ark, and handed him his food every day, so that he too survived."[64] Through the giant Og, the race of giants survives the Flood, the race of lordly, rapacious heroes, who recognized no bar to their pursuit of ecstasy.[65] Og, too, must survive, if Noah is to survive in that "half-open" form that Gaston Bachelard describes so evocatively:

> For the door is an entire cosmos of the Half-open. In fact, it is one of its primal images, the very origin of a daydream that accumulates desires and temptations: the temptation to open up the ultimate depths of being, and the desire to conquer all reticent beings. The door schematizes two strong possibilities, which sharply classify two types of daydream. At times, it is closed, bolted, padlocked. At others, it is open, that is to say, wide open.
>
> But then come the hours of greater imagining sensibility. On May nights, when so many doors are closed, there is one that is just barely ajar. We have only to give it a very slight push! The hinges have been well oiled. And our fate becomes visible.[66]

"There are two 'beings' in a door, [it] awakens in us a two-way dream." Noah must enter the ark, cut himself off from the world and discover the closed daydream, with its "temptation to open up the ultimate depths of being." But, "in hours of greater imaginary sensibility," he must pierce a hole in the ark, must feed the giant, who now swears eternal subjugation to the domain of kindness. The opening in the ark acts as a kind of valve, regulating the flow of nourishment from Noah to the giant. Implicitly, however, the flow is not all one way; Noah perforates the shell of his safety to maintain relations with the giant who is outside and inside.

The most significant use of the opening in the ark's surface occurs when, after forty days, Noah "opened the window of the ark that he had made and sent out the raven" (8:6–7). The "window," Rashi identifies with the *tzohar*, the "opening for daylight," which Noah had built into the ark from the first (6:16). This is distinct from "the opening of the ark, which is made for coming in and going out." After the raven fails to return, Noah sends out the dove, "to see whether the waters had decreased from the surface of the ground" (8:8). The verb, "sent out," is explained by Rashi: "This is not the word for 'sending a messenger,' but for 'sending off on its way.' The bird is set free, and thus Noah will see if the waters have decreased—for if she finds a resting place, she will not return."

Rashi makes a subtle point here. The dove is not being sent to fulfill a mission, to "see" the world and report. Noah simply releases her to act as is natural to her. It is Noah who will "see" from her behavior what is the reality outside the ark. In other words, the dove represents a kind of communications system: Noah is mobilizing a symbolic language, by which he may make statements about the world. For this, he needs an "opening" in the ark, an expression of his need to read what he cannot empirically see. When the dove finally returns with the torn olive leaf in her mouth, Noah "knew" that the waters had abated. This is a knowledge with no practical effect. Noah makes no move to leave the ark, until he is told to do so. But he must "see," he must "know."

What the opening in the ark suggests, in fact, is the growth of a new, human, sensibility: Noah "sees a new world." In the narrative of the dove, we find, for the first time, a self-awareness, a consciousness of expectation and disappointment, as Noah trains his eyes on the hole that perforates his box (the literal meaning of *teiva*—usually translated "ark.") The word, *va-yahel*—"he waited another seven days"—is repeated (8:10, 12): for the first time, we are given a sense of human loneliness, as time is endured, as Noah waits for something new to begin. The word contains nuances of "anticipation." But, as Samson Raphael Hirsch suggests (8:12), the second *va-yahel* (because of its passive *niphal* form) actually conveys a contrary mood: he was *disappointed* in his expectations.

The flickering of hope and disillusion through time is conveyed here for the first time in the Torah. Noah, cut off, plumbing the depths of his being, measures time — again, as no one has before — by the years of his life. The Flood is his private history: "In the six hundredth year of Noah's life, in the second month, on the seventeenth day of the month, on that day, all the fountains of the great deep burst apart" (7:11). "In the six hundred and first year, in the first month, on the first of the month, the waters began to dry from the earth" (8:13). The objective date is controversial: is the first month Tishrei or Nisan?[67] The perspective is subjective: Noah suffers the Flood, it is he who needs both to experience the inwardness of the ark and to devise ways of seeing what is unseen beyond its opening.

## Adam and Noah: building and contemplating

Noah's "half-open" condition is a new variation on a theme whose classical form is articulated in an earlier narrative. Eve was created from one of Adam's ribs. There, too, there was a cutting and a closing. It was God who put Adam to sleep. With man unconscious, God removed a part of him, closed the flesh over the incision, and "built" the rib into a woman (2:21–22). Man was separated from himself so that he hardly knew of his loss, until he met it face to face. It was God who did the cutting, the closing, and the building.

The building — va-yiven — is the subject of important punning in the midrash: "This teaches that God gave superior bina — understanding — to woman over man."[68] The root, "to build/understand," evokes a kind of knowledge in which one constructs from what is merely implicit in a given situation. For example, in another midrash, God "contemplates from what organ to create Eve — not from the head, so that she should not be haughty, not from the eye, so that she should not be inquisitive etc."[69] God intuits the implications for the future of the choices of the present. Something not yet present is to be evolved; for this, bina — understanding — is required. (In the terms of this midrash, the characteristic desired by God is modesty.)

All this happens while Adam is unconscious. When he meets woman for the first time, he knows she is bone of his bone, flesh of his flesh, but has no idea of the processes, the choices, the incisions and closures that have gone into her making. With Noah, the theme is replayed with significant variations. Now, it is Noah who has to "enter" the ark and cut himself off from the world — in fact, from a part of himself. It is God who closes him in, seals him from infection and an overpowering sense of loss. But Noah does not sleep—not a wink, insists the midrash—he is conscious during the entire twelve-month operation. And, as we have seen, he is not really sealed. He is ajar, half-open, committed to the ark, and to all "who are with him" — the repeated phrase describes his attentiveness and alert kindness—but also discovering in his vision of his lost world a wonder in alienation that was not his, when he lived a citizen in that world.

For now, the building/contemplating response is his, not God's. The result of the whole ark experience, imprisonment and release, is crystallized in that one word, *va-yiven*—"And Noah *built* an altar to the Lord" (8:20). He meets his world as he emerges from the ark, like Adam meeting Eve with the gratitude and wonder, with the "wild surmise"[70] of encountering a part of himself grown immeasurably more valuable in its new otherness.

But Noah, unlike Adam, is conscious; it is he who "constructs" the experience. "He contemplated—'Why did God command me to bring more pure than impure animals into the ark?—if not to offer sacrifices from them?'"[71] "He searched his heart, and said, 'God has saved me from the waters of the Flood and brought me out of that enclosure—am I not obliged to offer Him sacrifices and burnt offerings?'"[72] In both versions of the midrash, Noah explores the implications of the known, to arrive at what has not, in fact, been told him. He discovers the capacity to read the text of God's words, in the first version. Or—in the second version—he learns to read the text of his own most intimate experience: he "searches his heart" for what he must do, for what is entailed in the story of his double salvation. Neither of those "strong possibilities" that Bachelard schematizes through the imagery of the door—padlocked, or wide open—is the home of his soul, in "hours of greater imaginary sensibility." God has saved him both from the "waters of the Flood" and from "that enclosure." And Noah "builds" his response to the implications of that double escape.

## Noah enlarged

There is a peculiar aptness to Noah's response. One who is saved from prison, one who has been "brought out" into the air and the light, celebrates his redemption by an act of *consciousness*: "I am the man who has known affliction" (Lamentations 3:1). Unlike Adam, who slept

through both opening and closing, Noah builds his world by understanding it. The dynamic is perhaps most clearly presented in the Psalmist's
cry: "O peoples, bless our God, celebrate His praises; who has granted us
life, and has not let our feet slip. . . . You have caught us in a net, caught
us in trammels. . . . We have endured fire and water, and You have
brought us through to prosperity. I enter Your house with burnt offerings, I pay my vows to You, vows that my lips pronounced, that my mouth
uttered in my distress" (Psalms 66:8–14). The Psalmist directly relates
his entrapment, enclosure, and release, his coming in and coming out—
the Hebrew text is subtly transfused with the root words for entry and
exit[73]—with the act of sacrifice—burnt offerings, the voluntary "coming
in" to the House of God.

But why are burnt offerings, specifically, the instinctive response of
both Noah and the Psalmist? Would a thanks-offering (shelamim) not
have been more plausible? One answer is suggested by Radal, quoting the
Zohar.[74] Noah offers burnt offerings (which are considered as atonement
for wayward motions of the heart) because of his apprehension during his
time in the ark, that he would be left in the lurch, that he had, in a sense,
exhausted all his credit with God in being saved from the Flood. Noah
now acknowledges the complex love of God that transcends the simplistic
expectations of human beings. Caught between openness and closedness,
Noah suffered despair: perhaps God can save only in the mode of closure,
of kindness? Perhaps Noah is not sufficiently versatile to be saved from
his own salvation? In the wonder of release, Noah's gratitude is irradiated
with a desire to atone for the meagerness of his faith.

The Psalmist speaks of past speech: "that my lips pronounced, that my
mouth uttered in my distress." "In my distress" (lit., in my narrowness)
suggests the pressure of a condition in which one can imagine no enlargement. What Noah experiences, when he is released, is the subtle gratitude of one who now realizes the implications of where he was and where
he is. The burnt offering articulates the evolution of consciousness that is
now part of the human repertoire.

The history of Noah is, then, the history of man's first exercise in self-
construction. Between the worlds of kindness and ecstasy, between
closedness and openness, Noah reads and interprets the texts of God's
words and of his own heart. "These are the generations of Noah:
Noah. . . ." Noah is his own primary creation. Midrashic commentary
on Noah's narrative is filled with references to the problems and privi-

leges of interpretation, translation, word play, to the whole area of the Oral Law, of what the mouth may say, as it engages in the complex act called "reading." "The unexamined life is not worth living," said Socrates. With Noah and his children, self-criticism, searchings of the heart and of the words of God, become a measure of the life that is worth living.

## Human infancy and "transitional space"

The end of Noah's story is his first speech (9:25–27). Noah's only words come close after he has drunk the wine that celebrates his return to the world of ecstasy. He sleeps—for the first time in twelve months?—and unspeakable things are done to him by Ham, his son. He wakes, he knows, and he curses and blesses his children. Instead of the wicked being destroyed by God, they are from this point on *described* by man. Noah, dumb till now, takes over God's role of blessing and cursing. He declares his commitment to a certain model of reality, in which he recognizes the variables of "less" and "more." (Conceptually, "blessing" is the modality of "more," while "cursing" is the modality of "less.") In other words, he composes a world: it is "as though he made himself."[75]

After the Flood, God looks with new, almost inexplicable tolerance on the very problem of intrinsic evil that had precipitated destruction just a year before: "The Lord smelled the pleasing odor [of the sacrifices], and the Lord said to Himself: Never again will I doom the earth because of man, since *the devisings of man's mind are evil from his youth*" (8:21).[76]

Rabbenu Bahya offers a compelling reading of this diagnosis of the human condition:[77]

> The Sages have said, " 'From his youth' means, 'from the time that he shakes himself free [*nin'ar* puns on *ne'urav*, "youth"] from his mother's womb.' "[78] Evil enters him from that moment on. It is known that a man is not obligated to keep the commandments (which are addressed to the good inclination) until the age of thirteen. That is why the Sages said, "The evil inclination is older than the good intention by thirteen years!"[79] And that is why Solomon said, "Better a poor but wise youth . . . for [he] can emerge from a dungeon to become king" [Ecclesiastes 4:13–14]. From the time he leaves the womb, where he was incarcerated like a man in prison—immediately, he wants to rule. He seeks out the nipple and is drawn after his desires.

In Baḥya's reading, man is seen as an evolving being. God looks at the post-Flood generation as a new and more hopeful infancy. It is true that "evil"—that is, the energy of powerful and uncompromising desires—is at its strongest at this stage. But the prospect of maturity is the reward of an evolutionary view of man. Human history is still in its infancy; the arrogance of the libido is expressed in an oral mode (even the nipple is called the "mouth of the breast"!), as the new-born seeks to attach everything to itself, to "become king." George Eliot uses the same metaphor to describe the process by which human beings grow out of moral "stupidity" to the realization that the world is not "an udder to feed our supreme selves."[80]

In a sense, Noah is reborn Adam. He emerges from the womb-prison and, in one midrashic view, he proceeds to make exactly the same mistakes that the first Adam made. "Noah, the tiller of the soil, was the first to plant a vineyard" (9:20). The Babylonian Talmud, in Sanhedrin 70a, has God reproach Noah: " 'Noah, should you not have learned from the first Adam, whose fate befell him only because of wine?' So we learn that the tree Adam ate of was the vine." Another midrash notes that from being called a "righteous man," he is now called an *am ha-aretz*, an ignoramus (lit., an earthy man—see 9:20): "God said to him, 'What are you doing in a vineyard? Was not Adam punished with mortality, just because of wine?' "[81]

The difference between Adam and Noah is precisely this—that Noah has Adam's narrative as his text to decipher. He has undertaken the task of construction, the work of the Oral Law, which speaks what is not written. It is the task of reading. If he sins, because of his "lateness," his sin has something of the character of a "misreading." "He was the first— *va-yiḥal*—to plant a vineyard." In many midrashic renderings, the expression is understood as something like, "He construed profanely," or, in Rashi's version, "He made himself profane."

Noah comes as the second Adam; he sees a new world, but he remembers the old world, he has a sense of the choices that have gone to the making of his evolving identity. God's new-found tolerance may be a function of just this new self-awareness of man. For if it is emotional stupidity to treat the world as an udder, it is at the same time an essential phase of human growth. D. W. Winnicott writes of the illusion of the infant that he creates and controls the breast. This illusory omnipotence of the small being who has just emerged from a dungeon and imagines himself king is a *sine qua non* of healthy growth. Only if the infant has been given sufficient opportunity for illusion can he be successfully disillusioned. Physically, the child is weaned; emotionally, he comes to recognize objective reality and his own unkingly place in it. Yet in the space between breast and the world, which Winnicott calls "transitional space," the child learns to play, to construct the "transitional phenomena" that link him with both mother and world. This is the area of culture that partakes of imagination and reality, tenderness and ecstasy.[82] And this area is Noah's invention, as he chooses meanings, identities, versions of a world that is new and old at the same time.

# LEKH LEKHA  ❦
## *Travails of Faith*

*That is no country for old men. The young*
*In one another's arms, birds in the trees*
*—Those dying generations—at their song,*
*The salmon-falls, the mackerel-crowded seas,*
*Fish, flesh, or fowl, commend all summer long*
*Whatever is begotten, born and dies.*
*Caught in that sensual music all neglect*
*Monuments of unageing intellect.*

*An aged man is but a paltry thing,*
*A tattered coat upon a stick, unless*
*Soul clap its hands and sing. . . .*

        *—W. B. Yeats, "Sailing to Byzantium"*

## The starting point

The story of Abraham is both beginning and end. Here begins the drama of the central family-nation of the Torah; here ends the prehistory, the rough drafts of God's intent. One such essay in creation had ended in exile (Adam driven from the Garden), the second in destruction (the Flood).

The first important phase of his life is introduced by God's command: "Go forth from your native land, from your birthplace, and from your father's house to the land that I will show you" (Genesis 12:1). There is no indication of circumstance, of previous encounter. Only a short preface, in which family context is sketched out:

When Terah had lived 70 years, he begot Abram, Nahor, and Haran. Now this is the line of Terah: Terah begot Abram, Nahor, and Haran;

72

and Haran begot Lot. Haran died in the lifetime of his father Terah, in his native land, Ur of the Chaldeans. Abram and Nahor took to themselves wives, the name of Avram's wife being Sarai and that of Nahor's wife Milcah, the daughter of Haran, the father of Milcah and Iscah. Now Sarai was barren, she had no child. Terah took his son Abram, his grandson Lot, the son of Haran, and his daughter-in-law Sarai, the wife of his son Abram, and they set out together from Ur of the Chaldeans for the land of Canaan; but when they had come as far as Haran, they settled there. (11:26–31)

Against the flow of generations of chapter 11 — "This is the line of Shem. . . ." (11:10) — is set the central absence of Abraham's life: "Sarai was barren, she had no child" (11:30). *Toledot*, the word translated here as "line" and more commonly as "generations," is rich with a sense of the power of generation, of the multiple birthings, the realized consequences of potentialities inherent in each lifespan. And, ironically, it is the root of this word (*vlad*) that is used to refer to Sarai's childlessness: it is precisely this that she has not: the *vlad* that is the barest notation for some expression of self that lives on beyond self, an essence projected toward eternity.

"She had no child" — *ein la vlad* — the three pungent Hebrew words are freighted with irony. For this significant pair are marked by an emptiness, while all the "dying generations" (Yeats) effortlessly reproduce themselves. This is essentially the business of all other lives, as each generation enacts an identical ritual: the individual, generated by his father, lives a specified number of years; he then generates, projects a version of self beyond self, after which he lives a further tally of years and produces "sons and daughters." In this scheme, a central act of self-propagation is flanked by a period of immaturity and by a historically insignificant period of biological fertility. The expectation built up by the repeated formula is brought to a head in the almost feverish emphasis on Terah's generativeness: clearly, the narrative is closing in on its focus.

But here the rhythm changes: there is death (not the natural kind, but before the shocked face of the father [11:28]), and there is sterility. The resounding negation *ein la vlad* cruelly confirms: what was expected as part of the natural thrust of existence *is not*. Here, the language of the Torah enacts what Bergson calls "the peculiar possibility of the negative." In nature, Bergson argues, there are no negative conditions; only in the realm of consciousness, of desire and expectation, disappointment and frustration, does the knowledge of the negative exist. Memory and imagination attach to a phantom object, in this case the *vlad*, the off-spring, which bestrides positive reality and cries out *ein* — "no!" "Every human action has its starting-point in a dissatisfaction, and thereby in a feeling of absence."[1]

The "human action" of Abram and Sarai begins in this absence. The midrash expresses this paradox of generation as follows: "Wherever it is written '*Ein la* — there is not,' there essentially *is*."[2] A similar comment is made on the poignant leitmotif of absence in Lamentations: *ein la menaḥem* — "there is none to comfort her" (1:2); *ein av* — "we have become orphans, *fatherless*" (5:3). In the latter case, Midrash Rabbah refers to the paradigm of Esther, who is fatherless and motherless, and therefore is nurtured to a singular sensibility of absence and hope (Esther 2:7). What is suggested here in this first human experience of *ein*[3] is a new and difficult mode of being and having: absence leads a man and a woman to travel far in search of a realization of self that comes effortlessly to those who preceded and surrounded them.

## Abram's wanderings

Here begins the journey of *Lekh lekha* (12:1) — with its strange order of abandonments — first land, then community ("moladetkha" — again, the *vlad* root: "Leave that which produced you as one possible realization of its potential"), and, finally, father's house. For the first time, a journey is undertaken not as an act of exile and diminution (Adam, Cain, and the dispersed generation of Babel), but as a response to a divine imperative that articulates and emphasizes displacement as its crucial experience.

For what is most striking here is the *indeterminacy* of the journey. What is left behind, canceled out, is defined, clearly circled on the map of Abram's being; but his destination is merely "the land that I shall show you": from "your land," the landscape of your basic self-awareness, to a place that you will know only when the light falls on it with a difference.

There is some discussion in the commentaries about the extent of Abram's knowledge of his destination. Ramban considers the possibility that Abram knows from the beginning that his destination is Canaan, since his father began a family journey to that destination, which was interrupted and resumed by Abram at this point after his father's death (11:31). However, the other possibility, radical and disturbing in its implications, is that Abram has *no* idea of his destination when the call comes to him.

> *"To the land that I shall show you"*: he wandered aimlessly from nation to nation and kingdom to kingdom, till he reached Canaan, when God told him, "To your seed I shall give this land" (12:7). This was the fulfillment of "to the land that I will show you," and therefore he settled there. . . . Before that, he did not yet know that that land was the subject of the command. . . . That is why he later said to Avi-melekh, "God made me wander from my father's house" (20:13). For indeed, he wandered like a lost lamb.[4]

On this view, Abram wanders from place to place, till God "appears" to him and, in a revelation that includes Godhead and Land, "shows" him the place of destination. ("And he built an altar *there* to the Lord who had appeared to him" [12:7].) This reading is powerfully underwritten by the verse, quoted by Ramban, in which Abraham himself sums up his life on the road, in his apologia to Avimelekh: "So when God *made me wander* from my father's house . . ." (20:13). Ramban hears in the word *hitu* ("made me wander") a resonance of the poignant image in Psalms: "I have strayed like a lost sheep; search for Your servant" (119:176). The Psalmist cries out of his sense of imperiled contingency. His journey is trackless, unmapped; but his cry evokes the ultimate responsibility of the absent Shepherd to choreograph a meeting with His lost sheep. The disoriented consciousness of the Psalmist retains a core sense of relation-in-absence: he concludes his appeal, "for I have not forgotten Your commandments."

What Ramban evokes here is an Abraham who is set on a course of total displacement, a series of encounters with *mekomot*, geocultural environments to be entered, known, and left.[5] This directionless travel-ing is in one sense a *travailing* that is intimately connected with the quest for birth. The Oxford English Dictionary glosses *travel*: "1. torment, distress, suffer afflictions, suffer pains of parturition. 2. make a journey, from one place to another."

Rashi, too, seems to understand the nature of Abraham's journey in this way: "When God took me out of my father's house to be a vagrant, roaming from place (*makom*) to place. . . . Anyone who is exiled from his place (*makom*) and is not settled is called a wanderer" (20:13). Even the plural verb, strangely used for "made me wander" (*hitu*), suggests a plurality of *mekomot*, of existential frames of being, lacking coherent connection in an unmapped universe. Rashi's final prooftext, "They wander about without food" (Job 38:41), suggests the full paradox of a vital (and in that sense tensely focused) quest, enacted in empirical randomness.[6]

Midrash Tanḥuma espouses this view of Abram's first trial: "Is there a man who travels without knowing to what destination [*makom*] he travels?"[7] A journey without apparent destination: absurdity at each step. The midrash gives us mocking voices that weave through Abram's consciousness as he travels: "Look at this old man! Traveling through the country, looking like a madman!"[8]

If the experience of indeterminacy is of the essence of this first trial of Abram (called in the midrash "the test *within* a test"—the heart of darkness within the travail of *lekh lekha*), then it is echoed hauntingly and even more explicitly in the mystery of his last trial, that other *lekh lekha* of the Binding of Isaac (22:2). Abraham is to take his son, Isaac, the long-delayed fruition of his longing, and sacrifice him on one of the mountains, "which I shall tell you." For three days he travels "to the place [*makom*] of which God had told him" (22:3). What is this "place"? Does God *name* the place? Then why the indeterminacy of the original demand? Or does he travel to No Place, to the place that God has told him He has not yet told him?

Abraham's life of vital experience ("God put Abraham to the test" [22:1]—*nissa* is trial, experiment, the knowing of self in muscular action) is thus framed by journeys that are travails of contingency, knowing what it means not (yet) to be shown, to be told.

## Barrenness and alienation

"Sarai was barren"—the barrenness of Sarai evokes the other meaning of the word *akara*: the couple is uprooted, the ground cut from under their feet. Voluntarily, they respond to a call to alienation from all that gives self a placement in the world. By removing themselves from the normal conditions of fruitfulness, they—at least on the face of things—cut off vital sources of nourishment, doom themselves to a sterile nomadic existence, in which no organic fibers of connection and fertility can grow. That is why, according to Rashi (12:1), the blessings that follow immediately on the call of *lekh lekha* are so necessary and so paradoxical. The divine command thrusts Abram and Sarai into the eye of the storm, takes the problem of *akarut* (barrenness) and has them act out all the meanings of deracination, of disconnection from a succession of pasts.

An act of radical discontinuity is, it seems, depicted in the Torah as the essential basis for all continuity: for that act of birth that will engender the body and the soul of a new kind of nation. At the very beginning of human life on earth, after God had created Eve — had made Adam unconscious, removed a rib, and closed the flesh — the narrative voice had proclaimed: "Hence a man leaves his father and mother and clings to his wife, so that they become one flesh" (2:24). The Targum translates, "*Therefore shall a man leave his parents' bedroom*": there is a profound and often wrenching act of relinquishing to be undertaken, before new unions can be established. The sterility of the child's involvement in the "family romance" has to be left behind, in order that the self may find the Other and, according to Rashi, in order that the new being, the *vlad*, may be born. The Oedipal problem indicated by the Targum here is the basis for a cultural and probably counterinstinctual directive by God.[9]

Abram's journey "from your father's house" can perhaps be seen as a realization on a much more complex plane of this original and universal demand. He detaches himself from a spurious or at least outgrown place within an organism. He and Sarai are *akarim*, they recognize the sterility of the place that nurtured them. In the full tension of that paradox, they exile themselves to place after place and encounter new possibilities of being.

Their *akarut*, in its double sense of infertility and rootlessness, is placed in a context of ultimate blessing. ("And I shall make you into a great nation and I shall bless you and make your name great, and you will be a source of blessing" [12:2].) However, the midrash allows us no facile resolution of the tension of their lives: " 'He makes the *akara*, the woman who is the essence of the house [lit., the barren woman] to sit as the happy mother of children' [Psalms 113:9]: this refers to Sarai, as it is said, 'And Sarai was *akara* — barren.' "[10] Sarai is described as both the barren one and the joyous mother; these are not simply successive stages of a life, but both remain necessary functions of her identity. Her later happiness never obviates the twin image of alienation: the pun that the midrash sets in focus insists on alienation-sterility as the very condition of Sarai's significant maternity.

The essential drama of Abram and Sarai is always to be expressed in paradoxical terms: Sarai is *always* both *akara* and "mother of children." Or, as the midrash puts it, " '*I will make of you a great nation*' [12:2]: coinage was issued with his image on it. What image was engraved on the coinage? An old man and woman on one face, a young man and girl on the other."[11]

Abram and Sarai acquire "currency" in the world, their image acquires a mythic potency, just because it is *two-faced*: they are forever old and young, barren and fruitful.[12] Through them, a dialectical vision seizes the imagination of human beings.

## The imperative of transformation

The imperative of transformation is the driving force of Lekh Lekha. To leave one's place is ultimately to seek to become other. *Makom*, the word that becomes a leitmotif in midrashic meditations on Abraham's life, indicates not only physical space, but existential condition. *Makom* is the horizon of one's *kiyyum*, one's existence: the two words are clearly related. When Rashi (15:5) sees in Abraham's change of name yet another facet of his change of "place," he includes both imperatives under the rubric of a desired self-realization: "Abram has no son, but Abraham has a son. Similarly, Sarai shall not give birth, but Sarah shall give birth. I call you by a different name and your destiny shall change." The demand on Abraham and Sarah is to leave one existential environment, one set of paradigms, to emerge ("He took him outside" [15:5]) from their enclosure in the present (deathly sterile when outgrown) into a new condition, in which a fertile self-realization becomes possible.

The promise/demand of God is "I will make of you a great nation," which the Tanhuma translates, "I shall create you anew."[13] In this reading, the call of *lekh lekha* is an urging to self-transformation: at base, that is the meaning of a change of name, or a change of place.

Rambam speaks of teshuva, the penitential process, as involving the same enactment of transformation: "The penitent should . . . change his name, as if to say, I am another, I am not the same person who did those things."[14] To become *other* is to cut oneself off from the existential conditions of previous nurturings.

Saul, for example, is to be transformed in a prophetic trance: "You will become another man" (1 Samuel 10:6–11). The response of his social world ("All who knew him previously") is a blank skepticism: "What's happened to the son of Kish? Is Saul too among the prophets?" The abrupt discontinuity in Saul's identity rings false to those who have known him organically over time, going back to his origin as "son of Kish." Significantly, "another person there," an inhabitant of Saul's new world, responds to the skeptics: "And who are *their* fathers?" (10:12) — "What has the past, its social-psychological structures, to do with the inspiration of prophecy?" "Is Saul too among the prophets?" then becomes an aphorism. Saul's case crystallizes the radical but not uncommon phenomenon of conversion. In this instance, the conversion is charismatic: a turn of Saul's shoulder and God gives him another heart. Perhaps that is why he finds it so difficult to live his new condition authentically. That way madness lies.

The model of transformation presented by Abraham is more complex and ambiguous. The Talmud[15] speaks of a number of possibilities for transforming the perceptions of a life. The givens and predictabilities of a particular destiny may be subverted by acts of passionate will — by, for instance, a change of name — on some views, by a change of place (*makom*). For this strategy in "shredding a predetermined destiny," Abraham's odyssey is the paradigm: "Go forth from your land. . . . I will make of you a great nation." The "shredding of destiny" — there is *kri'ah*, a tearing apart of a *gestalt* apparently cut-and-dried. (*Gezar din* is literally the "cutting edge of judgment," the irrevocable sentence of fate.) It *is* possible, the Sages insist — and Abraham is the first to live this possibility — to move to a new place, to deconstruct all the structures of the old place of being, and in a radical act of *kri'ah*, of *akirah*,[16] to create entirely new paradigms of reality.

"I shall create you anew" — the call of God is the quasi-autonomous urge of man to create himself anew: "God took on the guise of a man who urges [*dohek* — presses, squeezes, creates a sense of pressure or need] his friend, 'Go from your land.' "[17] The midrash, using the figure of God-as-friend, reduces the transcendent force of the command-from-beyond: *lekh lekha* becomes a divine-human drive, mysteriously originating within Abram himself, for the sake of his own enlargement and self-realization.[18] A voice urging discontinuity seduces him: only through a destabilizing process can Abraham move from being Abram (*av ram*), the father of Aram ("which was his place, *mekomo*," says Rashi [17:5] — suggesting the mastery over a known modality of existence, a sterile fatherhood) to being Abraham (*av hamon goyim*), the father of many nations — master of multiple, successive places, who can then engender his true being ("Abraham has a son").

## Rambam's view: Abraham as intellectual innovator

But how is such transformation achieved? In the Torah text, the call and response are instantaneous: culture and sense of self are jettisoned in an act without past or future.[19] It is relevant here to consider William James's discussion of instantaneous conversions, in *Varieties of Religious Experience*. What lies behind such experiences, in James's analysis, is a long incubation period, in which subconscious elements prepare themselves for a flowering, which is as much of a process as an event. "To say that a man is 'converted' means, in these terms, that religious ideas, previously peripheral in his consciousness, now take a central place, and that religious aims form the habitual centre of his energy."[20] The explosive emergence into daylight of hot and live ideas has had to bide its time, while a hidden process of growth takes place.

The complexity of Abraham's incubation emerges from Rambam's classic account of the spiritual and intellectual prehistory of Lekh Lekha:

> When this giant was weaned, he began to *roam around in his mind*, while he was still small, and began to think by day and by night, and he would wonder, "How is it possible that this sphere moves constantly without there being a mover, or one to turn it, for it is impossible that it turns itself?" And he had no teacher or source of knowledge but he was sunk among senseless idol worshippers in Ur of the Chaldeans; his parents and the whole people worshipped idols and he worshipped with them. But *his mind roamed* in search of understanding till he achieved the true way and understood out of his own natural intelligence. He knew that there is one God who moves the spheres, who created everything, and there is none beside Him. He knew that the whole world was in error and that the cause of their error was that they worshipped idols and images, so that they had lost the truth. Abraham was forty years old when he recognized his Creator. As soon as he achieved this knowledge, he entered into dialogue with the people of Ur of the Chaldeans and contended with them about the truth of their beliefs, and he broke the idols, and began to tell the people that it is not right to worship anyone but the God of the world, and it is right to worship Him and bring sacrifices to Him, so that all future generations will recognize

Him; that it is right to smash all the images so as to remove error from the people. . . . When his arguments prevailed over them, the king sought to kill him and a miracle happened for him, and he left Haran. Then he began to stand and to cry out aloud to the whole world and to tell them that the whole world has one God, whom alone it is right to worship. He would cry out while traveling, and gather people around him from city to city and from kingdom to kingdom till he reached the land of Canaan, and there too he cried out, as it is said, "And he cried out in the name of the Lord, God of the world." And when people gathered round him and asked him the meaning of his words, he would tell each one individually according to his capacity, till he brought him back to the true way. Thousands and myriads gathered round him and become part of his household, and he implanted in their hearts this great principle and wrote books and taught it to Isaac, his son.[21]

On this reading, Abraham undergoes an autodidactic process, from the age of three (he begins "small," though he is called a giant from the outset) to the age of forty. It is a process of cognitive questioning that leads him logically to the First Cause ("How is it possible? . . . It is impossible"). This inner process alienates him, teacherless and fatherless, from his entire world. Externally, however, he remains integrated into his society, until the process is completed.

Then begins, literally, his iconoclastic phase, which in Rambam's account is primarily a philosophical contesting of ideas, in which Abraham defeats his opponents. As part of his development, he becomes a peripatetic teacher of monotheism, arriving finally (and without mention of the originating *lekh lekha* moment) at Canaan. In Rambam's account, Abraham's life is essentially the continuous growth of a thinker, teacher, and writer. His early development is characterized by a striking and repeated expression: —"he began to wander in his mind [*le-shotet be-da'ato*]." This suggests a freedom from the cognitive norms of his society, a kind of inner vagabondry, even while he maintains an outward conformism.

Thomas Kuhn, in *The Structure of Scientific Revolutions*, writes of the process by which scientists come to reject old paradigms—the activity of puzzle solving within the parameters of "normal science"—and to see reality in terms of new structures: "discovering a new sort of phenomenon is necessarily a complex event, one which involves recognizing both *that* something is and *what* it is."[22] Characteristics of such discoveries include "the previous awareness of anomaly, the gradual and simultaneous emergence of both observational and conceptual recognition, and the consequent change of paradigm categories and procedures often accompanied by resistance. There is even evidence that these same characteristics are built into the nature of the perceptual process itself."[23]

Kuhn describes a psychological experiment, in which subjects are asked to identify anomalies in playing cards shown in brief exposure. "The anomalous cards were almost always identified, without apparent hesitation or puzzlement, as normal."[24] Only on increase of exposure did hesitation and confusion ensue, and for most subjects — "sometimes quite suddenly" — correct identification of anomalous cards. The experiment provides Kuhn with a "wonderfully simple and cogent schema for the process of scientific discovery. In science, as in the playing card experiment, novelty emerges only with difficulty, manifested by resistance, against a background provided by expectation."[25]

Normal science tends to suppress novelties but paradoxically is also effective in causing them to arise. This is because the scientist's vision becomes immensely restricted by increasing professionalization but at the same time achieves a detail and precision that allows him, knowing with precision what he should expect, to recognize that something has gone wrong. "Anomaly appears only against the background provided by the paradigm."[26]

Seen against these observations, Rambam's account of Abraham's complex and gradual movement toward a revolutionary paradigm (philosophical rather than physical)[27] yields its ambiguous force. On the one hand, "he began to roam in his mind": a perceptual process in which, just because one has mastered the current models of vision and expectation one becomes increasingly aware (an "uncomfortable" experience)[28] of anomalies that are resolved more or less suddenly in the new paradigm. (Perhaps this professionalized mastery is indicated in Rashi's note on Abram's name: "father [*av*] of Aram, *which was his place*" (17:5), where he had expertise and full familiarity.) On the other hand, there is the *gestalt* switch, the change of paradigm that "must occur all at once or not at all"[29] — he "recognized his Creator."

On this view, scientific development is "a succession of tradition-bound periods punctuated by noncumulative breaks." To describe Abraham's intellectual searchings as a process of "roaming in his mind" is to suggest a freedom to perceive anomalies, without recourse to preconceived paradigms. There is an open-ended quality to the expression, a free-wheeling motion set in paradoxical relation with Abraham's conformist behavior as a "normal" scientist ("and he worshiped with them")—until the breakthrough is achieved, until he sees both *that* He is and *what* He is ("He knew that there is one God—and that He moves the spheres").

## M idrash Ha-Gadol: *The passionate search*

If we compare Rambam's account with that in *Midrash Ha-Gadol*, however, we find a significantly different emphasis, indeed a different order of development:

"You love righteousness and hate wickedness; rightly has God, your God, chosen to anoint you with oil of gladness over all your peers" [Psalms 45:8]. This was said with reference to Abraham, who loved God and approached close beneath the wings of His presence, and hated the idolatry of his father's house. For his father's family were idol worshippers, they manufactured images and gave them to Abraham to sell in the market. And when someone would come to buy an image from him, what would he do? He would take a hammer and batter the head of each idol, saying, "Is it this one you want? Or this one?" And when the buyer saw this, he would give up his intention and go away. And Abraham would *roam in his mind*, thinking, "How long shall we bow down to the work of our own hands? It is not right to worship and bow down to anything but the earth, which brings forth fruit and sustains us." But when he saw that the earth needs rain, and that without the sky opening and sending down rain, the earth would grow nothing at all, then he thought again: "It is not right to bow down to anything but the sky." He looked again and saw the sun which gives light to the world, and brings forth the plants, and thought, "It is not right to bow down to anything but the sun." But when he saw the sun setting, he thought, "That is no god." He looked again at the moon and the stars that give light at night, and thought, "To these it is right to bow down." But when the dawn broke, they were all effaced, and he thought, "These are no gods." He was in distress at the thought: "If these phenomena have no mover, why does one set and the other rise?" To what can this be compared? To a traveler who saw a tremendous large castle, and wanted to enter it. He examined it from all sides but could find no entry. He called out a few times but there was no response. Then he lifted up his eyes and saw red woolen cloths spread out on the roof. After that, he saw white flaxen cloths. The traveler thought, "Surely a man lives in that castle—for otherwise how would the cloths appear and disappear?" When the master of the castle saw that he was in distress over this, he asked, "Why are you in distress? I am the master of the castle." Similarly, when Abraham saw the appearance and disappearance of phenomena in nature, he thought, "Unless there were someone in charge, this would not happen. It is not right to bow down to these, but to the One in charge." And he wandered in his mind, trying to find the truth of the matter. When God saw him in distress, He said to him, "You love righteousness" — to justify the world.[30]

Here, the inner process of search ("roaming in his mind"), is accompanied by physical expressions of rejection, anger, a kind of impatience approaching contempt for the unenlightened responses of his world and indeed of himself — "How long shall we bow down . . . ?" The anger of his iconoclasm is literally enacted here in the smashing of idols; while in Rambam's account, Abraham engages in philosophical encounters: "he entered into dialogue with the people of Ur of the Chaldeans and contended with them. . . ." The actual smashing of the idols is there merely a logical outcome of his arguments: "he began to tell them that *it is not right* to serve any but the God of the world."

In *Midrash Ha-Gadol*, Abraham acts with an immediacy and passion that Rambam modulates into a philosophical key. Even the idolatrous belief Rambam explains (in a famous passage just preceding the one we have quoted) as a philosophical error, a result of quite plausible stages of response to the world. In the midrash, the existential confrontation with each stage of hope and faith reduced to absurdity is lived through primarily by Abraham himself; it is a shared human dilemma that he endures. "When he saw . . . he looked again": repeatedly he suffers disillusion as his passion for worship is denied ("It is not right. . . ."). He lives the vicissitudes of his temporality as though he were primal man first set in the world of nature. The setting of the sun is the fading of a world of hopes and beliefs. As the cyclical dimension of time dawns on him, he comes to an utter recognition of "le néant" — "When they were all effaced, he thought, 'These are no gods.'" His reaction is emotional and personal — "he was in distress." His search issues from imperative need, like the need of the traveler to *enter* the castle, to find an opening, ultimately to receive an answering cry to his cry.

Faced with the closed facade of the castle, he observes the changing phenomena on the battlements and concludes that there *must* be a Being who contains and harmonizes contraries within Himself. This faith is characterized by the pain and constriction of not knowing. Only after he has reached the impasse of overwhelming desire confronting total opacity ("When He saw that he was in distress"), does the Master of the Castle speak to him. In the *mashal* (parable), what He says is simply that He *is*; in the *nimshal* (the decoding of the parable), what God says is a return to the opening prooftext, now demonstrably descriptive of Abraham.

The whole thrust of the midrash, indeed, is a phenomenological account of the passion for *tzedek*, for righteousness: for a vision of the natural human world that is spiritually coherent. Abraham here becomes archetypal man in quest of meaning, the *experience* of meaning. What he wants is to *enter into* the castle, not merely to observe its changing colors. The rovings of his mind are passionate and needy; his intent finally ("to find the truth of the matter") is to find a stable core to his own existence (the truth is figured as a *basis*, a *standing* ground), and the pain of his quest is essential to the revelation he is granted. The recognition of God is not a final conclusion reached after a long private philosophical odyssey, but— as the verse about the love of righteousness indicates—an unlocated passion which inspires him with an energy for hope and disillusion that takes him through the phases of his experience.

In the midrash, then, the evocative expression, identical with Rambam's—"the roaming of his mind"—is used to very different effect. Here, Abraham bears the whole world with him in his personal anguished search. *Le-shotet*—To roam, implies full exposure to the hazards of experience. The resonance of *shoteh*—"fool"—lingers on: the radical "folly" of those who abandon safe structures and fare forth on unmapped roads.[31] In terms of the "normal science" of his world, his is a non-paradigm problem and is therefore viewed as a "distraction"[32]—irrelevant, even crazed. He is armed with no alternative paradigm but only with a pressing sense of anomaly that may find no resolution at all. His question can never be solved within the puzzle-framework of "normal science"; the question he asks is a different, a larger one; and in seeking to "enter into" the castle, he intuits an experience that is latent, not manifest in the material world.

Here, we approach the essence of the *lekh lekha* experience. In *Midrash Ha-Gadol*, after the quoted passage, the bold statement ensues: "The first trial was *tiltul*, which is the hardest of all." *Tiltul* is a kind of harassed, distracted, even confused movement. Is Abraham's journey indeed a movement of *distraction*, in the full irony of its two senses: a drawing away, a truancy from the fruitful pursuits of life, and, ultimately, a madness? *Tiltul* is the word that is most vividly descriptive of exile;[33] to be in exile is to be "off the point," it is to be reduced to a handled passivity in which drives and compulsions dominate freely regulated motion. Like a ball, says the midrash, which is caught in the air, and can never touch ground. Or like a dove that never rests; folds one wing at a time and flies on, obedient to some instinct of the species.

*Tiltul* is the hardest experience of all, and it is this that is the measure of Abraham's passion: " 'Your ointments yield a sweet fragrance, Your name is like finest oil' [Song of Songs 1:3]. What did Abraham resemble? A flask of myrrh, surrounded by wadding placed in a corner, so that its fragrance could not escape. But when it was carried from place to place [*tiltul*], its fragrance wafted out."[34] The transformation of Abraham's being, which is signified in the change of his name (the "extension" of his name) can be achieved only through a readiness to submit himself to the "distractions" of placelessness. The perfume is released and diffused in the transforming discontinuities of the *lekh lekha* travail.

## Bereshit Rabbah: The castle afire

Another version of the castle midrash is found in *Bereshit Rabbah*; the differences are significant:

> "The Lord said to Abram, Go forth from your land." "Take heed, lass, and note, incline your ear: forget your people and your father's house" [Psalms 45:11]. This is like a man who was traveling from place to place, when he saw a castle on fire. He thought, "Can you say that this castle is without a master?" Then, the master of the castle looked out at him, and said, "I am master of the castle." In the same way, since Abraham was constantly wondering, "Can you say that this world is without a Master?" God looked out at him and said, "I am Master of the world." "And let the king be aroused by your beauty; since He is your Lord" [Psalms 45:12]: And let the King be aroused by your beauty, that is, to show your beauty to the world. "And you shall bow down to Him."[35]

Here, the traveler moves from "place to place"; he sees a castle on fire, and he articulates in *negative* form a hypothesis about the meaning of the fire: "Would you say that this castle is without a master?" An uncontrolled conflagration suggests that there is no one to care for the castle, to extinguish the flames. In the negative form, the question expresses expectation disappointed. In Bergson's terms, Abraham indulges in the "peculiar possibility" that language affords: the confrontation with the "Idea of Nothing" that does not exist in nature. Only verbally can man formulate absence, and only man can move "from place to place"; can yield his firm footing in one existential frame for vertiginous space between places of *kiyyum* (clearly located being).

It is in response to this form of the question that the Master looks out at him — a revelation that reinforces the enigma. This *hatzatza*, the glance of the Master, is an intimation, a glimmer produced by the courage of the question. Ultimately, this intimation reveals the *traveler to himself*: it is a moment of self-awareness, of the extent of his protest and his terror/wonder at the Masterless world. In this flash of knowledge, the question becomes the answer; through the contingency of frustration, the traveler finds an avenue to consciousness.

## L*ove and madness*

This is, in fact, the reading of the midrash offered by the hasidic writer, Mei Ha-shiloah (the Ishbitzer). The emphasis here is on Abraham's quest for *himself*, for the "root of his own life." This is the literal rendition of *Lekh lekha* — "Go to *yourself*"; only in the movement inwards is the God-joy that is true life to be found. Mei Ha-shiloah also renders literally the phrase in the midrash, "The Master of the castle *looked out at him*" — the preposition *al* suggesting that Abraham is the focus of the Master's gaze. Abraham's attention, in the moment of anger and despair at the absurdity of a Masterless world, is drawn to himself. In a Kantian movement of self-awareness, he turns inward, finds a point of contact with a power not himself in his moral consciousness, in the "search for righteousness rather than . . . for truth"[36] — "You love righteousness. . . ." This is a theology that, in Peter Berger's terms,[37] begins with anthropology; the sense of outraged questioning is itself the first confrontation with God.

*Sefat Emet*, in commentaries on this midrash,[38] speaks of this essential capacity to detach oneself from the psychological conditions of one's being, one's standing place in the world ("Go forth *from your land*"). To move onwards to new "places" is the creative gift of the tzaddik, which is called "greatness." "I shall make you into a great nation" is the promise, then, of the continuing expansion of possibilities and of visions. The great enemy, in this perspective, is torpor, habituation. Abraham becomes emblematic of man discovering his own life's energies, as he confronts the hiddenness of God. "Where you are, there arises a place" (Rilke). Or, in the words of the *Sefat Emet*, "Go to the Land that I shall show you — where I shall *make you visible*, where your potential being will be realized in multiform and unpredictable ways."

From this last version of the midrash, then, there emerges a sense of the journey itself, the travail, as essential to the birth and growth of self. *Tiltul*, the not always graceful lurching of uncertainty, releases the perfume; it also teeters on the verge of madness — "Look at that old man traveling about the country like a madman!" And ultimately, that is the finest compliment that is paid to Abraham. Rambam describes Abraham as the epitome of the "love of God," an ideal but rare condition, testified to by God Himself, who speaks of "Abraham, My lover" (Isaiah 41:8).[39]

> What is this condition of right love? It is, that one should love God with an excessive, powerful love, till one's soul is totally involved in love of God, and one is constantly obsessed [*shogeh*] by it, as though ill with love sickness, when there is no place in one's mind free of the love of that woman with whom one is obsessed — neither when one sits nor stands, eats nor drinks. More than this, should be the love of God in the heart of those who love Him and are obsessed by Him. This is the meaning of the command, "You shall love your God with all your heart and with all your soul. . . ." And also of King Solomon's allegory, "for I am love-sick" [Song of Songs 2:5]: indeed, the whole of Song of Songs is an allegory for this.[40]

To love is total obsession: the word used is *shogeh*, which is clearly related to *shaga*, madness. Rambam describes a kind of pathology of passionate love, human as image for the divine. The characteristic of this "love sickness" is that it *leaves no space* — it is a constant accompaniment to all the normal activities of life. It represents, then, a paradoxical union of fixity and dispersion. It is the capacity to live on two planes at once; to seem to be in possession of oneself, so that one acts within the normal limits of culture and society, and yet to know inwardly that one is utterly lost in a not-here distraction of love.

The most interesting aspect of the word *shogeh* is perhaps the fact that though it is used to express focused fascination,[41] the root meaning is almost the opposite: to be unfocused, to reel away from, to be off target (related to *shogeg*, unwilled action). (Rashi acknowledges the paradox:[42] "Beware the *distracting* effects of passion, even for your own wife!") To be *shogeh*, or *meshugga*, is at root to be absent. In the ideal model of love of God offered by Rambam, a passionate absence from the world is paradoxically set at the heart of behavioral normalcy.

This model of Abraham's achievement represents a fragile equilibrium; on the one side, worldliness, on the other, madness. It is the awareness of this tension that characterizes Abraham's "reeling" motion. Current explanations of the world no longer work for him;[43] the *shogeh*-alienation caused by "love of righteousness" contains within it (in the English word, as well as in the Hebrew—alienation was once one of the clinical terms for madness) both hazard and the birth of a "terrible beauty."[44]

## Love and mystery

Abraham's active spiritual life begins and ends, we noticed, in indeterminacy. The *lekh lekha* of the first trial is echoed by the *lekh lekha* of the last, the Akedah. In both, the nub of his experience (the "trial within the trial") is indeterminacy. ("Go . . . to the land that I shall show you" [12:1]; "Sacrifice him as a burnt offering on one of the mountains that I shall tell you" [22:2].) No destination is specified. In the Akedah narrative, Isaac's name, too, is not at once revealed ("Take your son, your favored one, whom you love, Isaac" [22:2]). Rashi's comment on all three points of mystification is enigmatic: "'*that I shall show you*': He did not reveal to him the land right away, so as to endear it to him, and to give him reward for each word spoken" (12:2).

Rashi affirms a relation between mystery and love. He adds that there is a reward for each word spoken: where there is total revelation, there is no room for language; where meaning is uncertain, words, approximations of interpretation and communication, proliferate.[45] And this state, it seems, offers an opportunity to Abraham—the reward that is called *ḥiba*, love ("so as to endear it to him"). Maharal, in his supercommentary on Rashi, suggests that in the veiling of the truth, there is distress for a human being, who wants to know clearly what is God's will. This distress generates an intense receptivity to every shred of communication that comes from God. When one strains for intimations of relationship, one demonstrates *ḥiba*.

When, however, we compare Rashi's comments on the other two
passages he includes here to illustrate his point, we find that they are not
identical:

> "*your son*": why did He not reveal the son's name initially? So as not to
> confuse him abruptly, with the result of sending him out of his mind
> and driving him mad. Also, so as to endear the command to him and to
> give him reward for each word spoken. (22:2)

> "*on one of the mountains*": God keeps the righteous wondering (*mat-
> heh*), and only afterwards reveals meaning explicitly to them — and all
> this in order to increase their reward. (22:2)

Clearly, Rashi wants us to understand these three phrases as illustra-
tions of a single motif. In the second example, however, he adds as a
reason for delayed clarification the desire to preserve Abraham's sanity,
which might crack under too sudden and too brutal a statement. The
danger of *teruf ha-da'at*, literally, the rending of the mind, an experience
of sharp dislocation and discontinuity, is thus woven into the text about
love and reward. Are they quite separate reasons for delaying clarification, or has this delay, which preserves the integrity of the psyche, got
something to do with love and the rewards of language? In the third
example, Rashi significantly generalizes his point, to make a statement
that transcends the particular narrative; it is characteristic of God's
relation with the righteous that He allows them time for questioning and
wonder, and only reveals the determined reality *aḥar kakh* — afterwards,
ultimately.

The expression Rashi quotes from *Bereshit Rabbah* is highly evocative:
*mat-heh* means to wonder, gaze, be astonished, be plunged into a sense of
the unfathomable (*tehom* is the unfathomable deep, which contains all
and expresses nothing: out of it emerges heaven and earth). It can mean
regret, an openness to conflicting responses. The capacity to move to
new paradigms of perception is the creative possibility in human life and,
to the anthropomorphic imagination, it is the basis of the concept of
divine forgiveness. It is called *tehiya*, the waste space between clarities.[46]

In another version of Rashi's text, the word used is *mash-heh* — delay, a
time that stands still, as it were, when the flow is retarded and a freedom is
granted for contemplation.[47] God gives the righteous time-out-of-time,
like a still in a film, in which a different sense of being-with and being-in
the crisis develops. This is the irreducible word, colorless, transparent,

for being; simple survival, the gift, the interval between the named, the placed — that exile-in-time in which selves are born.[48] In this condition of *akarut*, where nothing is assumed, between worlds of naming, a radical astonishment abides. As with Rashi's alternative term *mat-heh*, God's grace to the righteous is the "wild surmise" of discovery.[49] In this interval, each *dibbur*, each speech act, is crafted by man's articulation of God's voice out of the silence. An intense listening — and "afterwards," *ahar kakh* — revelation.

This kind of communication between God and the human being has as its purpose *hiba*. Its disadvantages may be obvious — indeterminacy, loneliness, the kind of sterility and palpable absence that *akarut* in its ambiguity poignantly suggests. But the protraction of suspense in time and space is presented as a key to the experience of "love of the command-ment."[50] This quality of love, intimate, familiar, personal, is the strange fruit of a dislocation that threatens Abraham's very sanity. At the core, this is the paradox of Abraham's life from alpha to omega. The crisis of *lekh lekha*, of the Akedah, is a demand for deracination. The words *akira* (barrenness, uprootedness) and *keri'a* (torn-ness, rupture) describe a condition of exile that threatens the very possibility of language. (Con-sider, for instance, Rashi's comment on God's promise of blessing and fruitfulness: this is necessary precisely *because* exile by its nature erodes the sense of self and the connections between self and world.[51]

The expression Rashi uses to describe the menace of groundlessness — *tazuah da'ato alav*, "sending him out of his mind and driving him mad" (22:2) — conveys an overbearing *elation* (literally, being borne out of all structures and limits). That way madness lies, consciousness torn adrift of all the fibers of connection. There is a seductive lure in the call of *lekh lekha*: to cut free of all that one was is to rend the very fabric of consciousness.[52]

And yet *teref natan li-y'reiav* (Psalms 111:5): the gift of rending, *teruf*, of discontinuity, madness, God gives to those who fear Him. This is the hasidic (mis)reading of the text, which translates more literally, "God gives food, daily sustenance [lit., the torn-off portions of meat] to those who fear Him." What the hasidic reading emphasizes is that the man who stands in a certain relation with God (called *yirah*, fear, a condition of balance, limitation) acquires the capacity to find his own sustenance, his inner springs of being, in a modality that isolates him in passionate individuality. But how live a *teruf*, a torn-ness, that is a gift and not a destruction?[53]

The question relates to the innermost quality of Abraham's experience — the "trial in the midst of the trial." What is given is the unmapped space and time, that we call freedom, in which to nurture love. *Hiba* is the organic relation that is developed in spite of, or perhaps only because of the vicissitudes and travails of a world in which God does not reveal His meanings. "We interpret always as transients," writes Frank Kermode in a study of hermeneutics (Hermes, he points out, was the god of *travelers*).[54] The opportunity that is offered by dislocation is of *shehiya* and *tehiya*, of infinite possibilities open to human articulation. In mystery, therefore, the command of God becomes integrated over time into man's fullest creative life.

The peculiar quality of love suggested by *hiba* can be seen, for example, in the statement in B. Berakhot 63b: "The Torah is as beloved (*havivah*) each day to those who learn it as it was on the day it was first given." How do we know this? asks the Talmud. "Because a person reads the *Shema* prayer morning and evening, but if he forgot one evening — it is as though he had never read the *Shema* at all!" In a sense, one missed connection in the web of *hiba* spun from Sinai to "this very day"[55] unravels the whole web. For the very nature of *hiba* is the continuous organic thickening of relationship. The interplay of consciousness with the mitzvah is what creates *hiba*; the uninterrupted murmur of "those who learn" Torah is the cumulative voice of Sinai.[56]

The redemptive possibility of *teruf* lies in the intensity of loss it registers. The word implies a wrenching knowledge of alienation from oneself. In a passage in Midrash Tanhuma,[57] Pharaoh's dreams are compared with Nebuchadnezzar's: — *Va-tipa'em ruho* ("his spirit was agitated") (Genesis 41:8) is compared with *va-titpa'em ruho* (Daniel 2:1) — the more intense reflexive form: "Pharaoh, who knew the dream, but not its interpretation, suffered one *teruf*, one anxiety attack. Nebuchadnezzar, who had forgotten both the dream and its interpretation, suffered a double *teruf* — therefore it is written, *va-titpa'em*."

To be "torn" is to know oneself bereft; on another level, to know oneself diminished. In mourning, one tears one's clothes; but there are certain losses — of parents, of a teacher, of a burnt Scroll of the Law — that represent *kera'in sheheinan mitahin* — gashes that can never be sewn together: these are irreparable losses, that affect the survivor in his very essence. In a poignant narrative in B. Berakhot 42b, Rav's students tear their clothes on his death. A problem immediately arises about the right course of action in a halakhic question (grace after meals). Rav Ida reverses the tear he has already made, in order to tear again: "Rav has left us, and we did not learn how to say the grace after meals from him!" In halakha, *keri'a*, the tearing of clothes, expresses the existential awareness of distance, of not knowing. A source of light is withdrawn: with each throb of that realization comes the increasing appreciation of torn-ness.

## Turmoil and integration

At the core of Abraham's experience is the complex of *akarut, keri'a, tiltul*, and *teruf*. But in the *shehiya*, the *tehiya* that God gives him, he plumbs these experiences to their depths. In the space and time that are his freedom, he contemplates the possible meanings of mystery.

This is the tension at the heart of Abraham's faith, as the midrash portrays him. On the one hand, he is classically praised as one of the fathers of the nation, who had no questioning thoughts about God's ways.[58] The famine that afflicts him immediately when he arrives in Canaan is explained as a test of his unquestioning faith in God's promises: "to test him whether he would have qualms [*hirhurim*] about God's promises" (Rashi, 12:10). But, on the other hand, active *hirhurim*, a term that expresses the imaginative, passionate level of consciousness—perhaps the area of the *id*—is just what Abraham *is* credited with:

"*And it was after these things*" [15:1]: after the *hirhurim*, the troubled thoughts that ensued. Who was troubled? Abraham questioned God, "Master of the universe, You made a covenant with Noah that You would never destroy his children. Then I came along and pleased You better, so that my relation with You overrode his. Perhaps someone else will come along and please You better than me, so that his relation with You overrides mine?" [The reference is to the fact that Abraham had been allowed to kill with impunity descendants of Noah; his fear is that his own descendants may find themselves expendable, if a further process of selection takes place.] God replied, "Among Noah's children there are no righteous people who intercede for others, but among yours there will be."[59]

Abraham brings many responses to bear on his victory over the four Canaanite kings (chap. 14). His vision transcends the immediate gratification of triumph: there are larger questions to trouble him about God's dealings with man. His questionings are not faulted; on the contrary, they lead to an unfolding of meaning in God's response.

Similarly, after the anguish of the Akedah is resolved, there is another "after these things" (22:20), and again the midrash speaks of questioning responses:[60]

> *"And it was after these things"* [22:20]: after the *hirhurim*, the troubled thoughts that ensued. Who was troubled? Abraham questioned God, "If Isaac had died on Mount Moriah, would that not have meant that he died childless? Now that a miracle has been done for him, what shall I do? I shall marry him to one of the daughters of Aner, Eshkol and Mamrei, who are righteous—what do I care for aristocratic connections?" God answered him, "There is no need for you to do that. Isaac's mate is already born—'Milcah too has given birth.'" [22:20]

Again, the *hirhurim* have to do with an unexpected range of responses within Abraham's imagination, an openness to many possible implications in what has just happened to him. Abraham is concerned for eternity, knows himself responsible for providing scaffolding for the future. With that concern uppermost in his mind, he is willing to do what previously had been unthinkable for him—to marry Isaac to a daughter of Aner, Eshkol, and Mamrei. After he has explored the reaches of his apprehensions and commitment, God reveals that He has, in fact, already taken responsibility for the future.

The word *hirhur* in its doubled-root form suggests vagueness, the inchoate dream state that precedes cognition.[61] The *hur* root evokes the state of *herayon*—gestation, conception, in its physiological and its intellectual sense. The *hirhur* is at the opposite pole from the act: a heated, fluid state in which many things are implicit, as opposed to the crystallized realization. "*Hirhurim* of sin are worse than sin itself"—fantasy is more powerful than reality, because it answers more adequately to the infinite demands of the spirit. An anarchic range of consciousness is attributed to Abraham in these classical midrashic sources, although in others he is just as specifically credited with a pure and untraveled faith (in the matter of the famine, and of the land promised but still laboriously purchased as a burial plot).

"There is an angel appointed over *herayon*, over pregnancy."[62] Each state of *hirhurim*, while apparently formless and open-ended, still has its coloration and implicit form. Abraham's *hirhurim* are suffused with the character-istic hues of his concerns: they are unique to him. Conversely, certain sorts of *hirhurim* are not "for him," can never be his.[63] But where he is observed in the world of *hirhur*, he expresses the central paradox of his destiny. Respon-sive to displacement, he probes his condition to its limits; for this purpose, he is given time and space for "play," in Huizinga's sense.[64]

But even here, in the interstice "between place and place" (*me-makom le-makom*), he is animated by the vital quest of his being — " 'You have loved righteousness': he loved God and sought to come closer beneath the wings of His presence."[65] His knowledge of God is not the *result* of an orderly process of inquiry (the Platonic notion of truth that is reflected in Rambam's account: "at age three, he began to explore . . . at forty, he recognized his Creator"), but rather the informing passion of a life in which all forms are to be deconstructed. When he is cut loose in the world, "chaos is come again."[66] In the world of words, of questions asked and questions unasked, Abraham discovers his own being and the *hiba* that is his personal nexus with God.

Midrash Tanḥuma illuminates the paradox with a pun:

> "We have a little sister, whose breasts are not yet formed" [Song of Songs 8:8]. Of whom does the text speak? Of Abraham, when he was thrown by Nimrod into the fiery furnace — he was still "little," for God had not yet done miracles for him. Why is he called "sister"? Because he *sewed the whole world together* in the presence of God! [This is a pun on the words *aḥot* (sister) and *la-aḥot* (to sew); in fact, the sibling concept is integrally related to the paradox of together/separate.] *He was like a person who tears apart and sews together* — therefore he is called "sister" [my italics].[67]

Abraham is called *aḥot*, because he represents the desire to reintegrate (*eḥad* [one], *aḥot* [sister], and *la-aḥot* [to sew] are clearly connected) his own world with God. Paradoxically, however, his radical activity is dual: "tearing and sewing," rending and rendering one. As he comes to understanding and resolution, he uncovers further mysteries, invitations to love.[68]

Perhaps, the midrash even implies in this audacious phrase (rending and rendering one) that the peculiar greatness of Abraham is his response to the hiddenness of God. Despite his distress, he must even "seek for ways of magnifying the breakdown."[69] In this sense, he will "often seem like a man searching at random." But in the current generated between the two poles of "rending and rendering one," there is intensified life.

"I will make of you a great nation" (12:2) — the "small sister" has the potential to grow into a "great nation." For to be great is Abraham's destiny, in the sense of maturity and high evolution — "like a grown-up son who knows how to search in his father's treasuries [his hidden drawers]."[70] The index to Abraham's maturity is the exquisite tension he maintains between the hiddenness, the incommensurate Otherness of God, and the daring activity of his own integrative mind.

# VA-YERA 🌱
## *Language and Silence*

### The demand for sacrifice

Some time afterward, God put Abraham to the test. He said to him,
"Abraham," and he answered, "Here I am." And He said, "Take your
son, your favored one, Isaac, whom you love, and go to the land of
Moriah, and offer him there as burnt offering on one of the heights that
I will point out to you." (22:1–2)

*Aḥar ha-devarim ha'eleh* — "And it was after these things" (or, in the
JPS translation, "Some time afterward"): the subject of this chapter is to
be the culmination of Abraham's life. Here, God demands of Abraham
(*pleads* with him, in Rashi's reading of the word *na* that modulates God's
demand[1]) that he take his beloved son, Isaac (*yeḥidkha*, lit., your only one)
and offer him as a sacrifice. As a burnt offering, Isaac will — technically —
be consumed totally; emotionally, existentially, this will leave Abraham
with nothing to show for his life. "After these things" places the Akedah
test in the sequence of Abraham's life; it suggests, too, that what is at
stake is a judgment on Abraham's whole history.

The Talmud, however, understands the opening clause very specifically:

> "*After these things*": after the words of Satan, as it is written, "The child
> grew up and was weaned, and [Abraham] held a great feast" [21:8].
> Satan said to God, "This old man — You granted him fruit of the womb
> when he was a hundred years old. And yet of all the feasts that he made,
> he did not have a single turtle dove or a young bird to sacrifice to You!"
> God answered him, "He has done nothing that was not for his son —
> and if I were to say to him, 'Sacrifice your son to Me,' he would
> immediately obey." Immediately after that, "God tested Abraham."[2]

Rashi quotes the Talmud (with slight variations), and thus introduces the figure of Satan, who is to be so central in midrashic literature on the narrative. Who is Satan, and how does he function here? It seems that the whole Akedah trial comes about at his instigation: his is the voice (demonic? rational?) that ultimately makes it necessary, in the rhetoric of the midrash, for God to make His demand. ("*Immediately*" — God tested Abraham.)

Compare this version of the Midrash with the one in *Bereshit Rabbah*:

"*After these things*": after the troubled thoughts that ensued. Who was troubled? Abraham was troubled; he thought, "I have rejoiced and I have spread joy everywhere — and yet I have never set aside a bullock or a ram for God." God replied, "In the end you will be told to sacrifice your son and you will not refuse."

(Another view:) The ministering angels said, "This Abraham has rejoiced and spread joy everywhere — and yet he has never set aside a bullock or a ram for God." God replied, "In the end he will be told to sacrifice his son and he will not refuse."

Abraham's inner qualms, on the one hand, and the ministering angels, on the other, accuse Abraham of some defect that Satan summarizes ironically as a kind of poverty: he did not have a single turtle dove. Conspicuous consumption, without sacrifice. What is the relation between the concept of *se'udah*, the banquets that Abraham apparently prepared so lavishly, and the missing sacrificial animal? Is it a kind of hypocrisy that he is being accused of? After all, there are references to altars earlier in Abraham's career.[3] Does the accusing voice insinuate that since Isaac was granted him, he has lived a life of self-indulgence and virtually forgotten God?

In the rhetoric of the midrash in Sanhedrin, Satan dreams up the Akedah; a terrible hypothesis is tested in reality. God is compelled by Satan's logic to defend His beloved, loving Abraham.[4] "*Eelu* — If I were to say to him. . . ." What Abraham knows would be true of himself in an unimaginable ordeal is subject to the attacks of Satan — to the point where confrontation becomes unavoidable. After the crisis is over, God says: "Now I know that you fear God" (22:12). Rashi's comment is: "'From now on, I have a reply for Satan and for other nations who are puzzled by My special love for you. From now on, I can answer back [lit., I have an opening of the mouth], since they see that you do fear God.'"[5]

# Feasting and laughter

God Himself is silenced by Satan's insinuation. Only Abraham can argue his own Satan, his troubled thoughts, to the ground, by the unanswerable force of action. Then Abraham can return to his feasting. What are the implications of the feasting? And what is the subversive force of Satan's sneer?

From the source in Sanhedrin, it would seem that the reference is primarily to the "great banquet" that Abraham made to celebrate Isaac's weaning (21:8). This notion becomes somewhat problematic in view of Satan's phrase, "of all the feasts that he made." This suggests that feasting represents a certain dimension of Abraham's mode of relating to his world; this idea we shall discuss later. What are we to understand about this banquet? Why is specific mention made of it, and of its size?

Rashi's comment focuses attention on the guests at the "great feast": " 'great' because the great personalities of that generation were present — Shem, Ever, and Avimelekh." In this reading, the point of the banquet is to communicate with the representatives of contemporary civilization: a "banquet for the great" (as the version in *Bereshit Rabbah* has it) is an event in which the feasting becomes an occasion for the meeting of worlds. And who are the guests at the banquet? Notably, Avimelekh, king of the Philistines. The irony of the situation is manifest in the midrashic subtext. Avimelekh is, in the view of *leitzanei ha-dor* — the cynics of the time — the obvious biological father of Isaac.[6] Any sophisticated observer can deduce the truth of a situation in which an elderly, sterile couple produce a child shortly after the wife is kidnapped by a lustful king. Yet Avimelekh is high on the guest list. Abraham's way with feasts apparently has to do with feeding those whose thoughts and sensibilities are not only different from his but even threaten him with ridicule.

The atmosphere of laughter that attends the birth of Isaac is essentially ambiguous: "Sarah said, God has brought me laughter; everyone who hears will laugh with me" (21:6). Sarah internalizes the tension set up by laughter as joy at enlarged possibilities, on the one hand, and the laughter that (bitterly? cruelly?) denies any possibility but the quotidian reality. To laugh is to confront the pressures of necessity on one's individual destiny and one's infinite desires. To laugh is to counter Spinoza's first great law of thought: *non ridere, non lugere, neque detestari, sed intellegere* — to laugh, to suffer, to rejoice, to hate, and to weep are to affirm the reality of the self as not simply an undifferentiated part of the world of objects ruled by necessity.[7]

The birth of Isaac (attended by multiple births and healings in the world, according to Rashi) is an outrageous flouting of law and necessity, of common wisdom and stoic, philosophical acceptance. The reaction, the explosion of laughter, may run a long gamut (from mockery to joy, as Ramban puts it),[8] but the very fact of laughter places man firmly, absurdly, at the center of his world.

Abraham and Sarah know of this laughter: they invite it into their home, as they feast with Avimelekh. Like the *se'udah*, the food of the feast, laughter is a mode of communion. Michel Tournier writes of the phenomenon of cryptophasia, the private language of twins, which thrives at the expense of normal speech and of "social intelligence." In the twinless world, the phenomenon is paralleled by that of laughter: "Because when two individuals laugh together — and only then — they come near to the mystery of cryptophasia. At such times they are using a *pseudo-language*, laughter, based on a common ground . . . which, unintelligible in itself, has as its function to narrow the distance between their respective positions which divides them from that common base."[9]

In both pseudo-languages, "the words are incidental, *silence is the essence*" (my emphasis). What is implicit in the dialogue is abnormally large, "so that the explicit always remains *below* the minimum necessary to make it decipherable by outside listeners." This is "a language without diffuseness, radiating nothing, the concentration of everything that was most private and secret in us."[10]

Abraham and Sarah, by inviting the laughter to their table, share in it and modulate it. It is a fully human affirmation of affinity, a nonverbal possibility somewhere "between the wordlessness of animals and the silence of the gods."[11] In the relationship with their peers, it enacts the oral potential that Ramban writes of, in his comment on Sarah's solitary laughter of denial:[12] "'*And Sarah laughed to herself*' [18:12]: For the laughter of joy is from the mouth — 'Our mouths shall be filled with laughter' [Psalms 126:2] — but inward laughter can not be said to be joyful."

The mouth filled with real laughter — like the food of the feast, audible and sensible to others — is an image representing the end of days, the overcoming of separateness and closure. In this world, it remains a mere possibility that constantly destroys itself.

Perhaps Ahasuerus's feast, which opens the book of Esther, can be seen as a grotesque caricature, a surrealistic parody of the meaning of feasts. It is conducted "after the desire of each man" (Esther 1:8) — an oceanic moment of total continuity between subject and world, the me and the not-me, in a social context without restriction or definition. This is the response of the midrash:

> God said to Ahasuerus, . . . It is generally understood in the world that if two men want to marry the same woman she cannot marry both of them. And yet you order your people to behave "after the desire of each man"! Tomorrow, two people will come to you in total confrontation — a Jew and his adversary — will you be able to satisfy both of them? One of them you will promote and the other you will crucify.[13]

In the real world of limitation, two men cannot have one woman: choices are to be made, the demands of the desirous self to be sifted. The problem of *ratzon* (wish, will) subjects human beings to a lifetime of evaluation and — in Freudian terms — to a world of discontents. But *mishteh*, the feast, promises something else: it evokes, along with Nietzsche, "the lightfooted ones" against "the spirit of gravity — through [whom] all things fall. Not by wrath does one will but by laughter. Come, let us kill the spirit of gravity."

The birth of Isaac initiates the period of feasting and laughter, of the bearable lightness of being. It has its precedent, of course, in the feast that Abraham serves the angels who come to announce the imminence of the birth. The passage opens with the cryptic words: "The Lord appeared to him by the terebinths of Mamre" (18:1). Are we to understand that in the midst of a mystical experience (God's "appearance to him"), he notices the three travelers and invites them in so eagerly? On this view, the Sages (and Rashi) base their praise of his hospitality, valuing concern for the guest even above theophanies. But another reading is possible: the theophany *is* the appearance of the angel travelers.[14] This certainly seems a plausible reading of the text: it does, however, turn the screw of paradox much tighter than the other reading.

For this is perhaps the most sensuous description of a meal in the Torah. Abraham's unassuming invitation is belied by the extravagant lengths he goes to, the enthusiasm and energy he displays, in providing a meal for the unequivocally described "three men." The moral point about hospitality is amply made; but details like "choice flour" and "a calf, tender and choice" are read by Rashi, for instance, as directions for a gourmet cookbook (18:6–7). All this gastronomic delight is fed the angels, who then speak the word of God. And the whole event is called a moment of theophany!

For in Abraham's world, feeding is an art, a physical sensual moment, that nurtures the God-in-man. As in Gabriel Axel's film *Babette's Feast*, to feed exquisitely is to bridge the gap between the physical and the spiritual; the feast becomes emblematic of the role of art in transforming the monstrous into the human at its most expansive. In the film, the ascetic Puritan challenge to hedonism is evoked: perhaps the godly folk should eat the delicacies, so as not to offend the cook, but without tasting them.[15] Thus they will achieve heroic spiritual standing. But what happens is something quite different: sensuality is not sidestepped, but mobilized in a movement to a fuller humanity.[16]

Rashi, in focusing on the techniques and delicacies of the feast, as well as on the loving energy of Abraham, seems to be making a similar statement. The fact that these are angels and that (in one reading, at any rate) this encounter represents God's manifesting Himself in Abraham's life, invites the reader to a new understanding of the human and its upper register.[17]

## Abraham's eshel: oral alchemy

The central source for a discussion of Abraham as feast-and-festivity maker ("I have rejoiced and spread joy everywhere") is the passage that immediately precedes the Akedah narrative. In this context, Satan's reproach to Abraham assumes the resonance of an argument against the work of his life: "[Abraham] planted a tamarisk [*eshel*] at Beer Sheva and invoked there the name of the Lord, the everlasting God" (21:33).

The nature of the mysterious *eshel* is discussed in the Talmud:

> R. Yehudah said that this *eshel* was an orchard, while R. Nehemiah said it was a hotel. . . . Resh Lakish said, Do not read the text, "He invoked there the name of the Lord," but read it, "He caused there to be a calling of the name of God" — Abraham caused God's name to ring out in the mouth of every traveler. How was that? After they had eaten and drunk, they would stand up to give him a blessing. He would tell them, "Was it my food you ate? Was it not God's food you ate?" So they

thanked and gave praise and blessing to the One Who spoke and the world came into being.[18]

After the birth of Isaac, it seems, Abraham turns from the construction of altars (12:7–8, 13:4) to that of hotels (or possibly the planting of orchards). A common purpose underlies both ventures — "to invoke the name of the Lord." Only in the *eshel* experience, however, the hotel-orchard modality, does God become the "God of the world," intimately connected with the processes and becomings of the world.

The concept of the orchard (or the hotel with its varieties of comfort and pleasure)[19] is of a place of infinite earthly delight, in which the fantasy and desire of each traveler is satisfied. (*Eshel* is taken by Rashi[20] as an acronym for *Akhilah, Shetiyah, Levayah* — eating, drinking, accompanying on the first leg of the journey — the basic needs of the traveler.) In the *Bereshit Rabbah* version of this midrash, the hotel is described by a play on the letters of *Eshel-Sha'al*: "Ask [*sha'al*] for whatever you desire [*tish'al*] — figs, and grapes, and pomegranates [in the case of an orchard], bread, meat, wine, and eggs [in the case of a hotel]."[21]

This *eshel*, then, is a place where the stranger fulfills limitless desires, the feeding place that is reminiscent of the infant at the breast. Suggested here is the oceanic stage of experience, in which there is no clear boundary between self and not-self. "Just as the breast is tasted by the infant as having a variety of flavors, so the manna."[22] This is Abraham's radical initiative in the world: to nurture himself and others toward a recognition of God. Through the mouth, the opening in the boundary between self and world, nourishment and reassurance enters; and in the mouth Abraham causes the name of God to be uttered — "Abraham caused the name of God to ring out in the mouth of every traveler."

This oral alchemy is Abraham's invention: it takes account, one might say, of the complexities and tensions inherent in the growth to fuller humanity. For if we consider Winnicott's discussion of the development of the infant, the most difficult stage is that between *relating* to an object and *use* of the object. The infant must grow to a recognition of the independent reality of objects (primarily the mother's breast) that he has originally regarded as continuous with his own needs and desires. Once embarked on this painful odyssey of separation from the object, eating becomes an experience fraught with both vulnerability and destructiveness against the object. This is a destructiveness without anger. On the contrary, it is accompanied by joy at the survival of the object. As a result,

"the object is *in fantasy* always being destroyed, [which] . . . makes the
reality of the surviving object felt as such, strengthens the feeling tone,
and contributes to object-constancy. The object can now be used."[23]

In Winnicott's theory, in order to be able to use the object—and,
therefore, to love it, as real and external to the subject's omnipotent
control—both destructiveness and trust must be experienced—trust that
the object will survive one's use of it.[24] Eating is a special case of the
dilemma of use and love; the eater experiences complex emotions toward
the feeder. (Noah feeds the animals in the Ark—and is attacked by the
lion for his trouble!)[25]

In this context, Abraham's answer to his grateful guests is illuminating: "Was it of *mine* [lit., of *me*] that you ate? Was it not of the God of the
world that you ate?" In Winnicott's terms, Abraham is helping his guests
through the anxiety of the transitional phase, to an experience of trust in
an Object who is the inexhaustible source of all life. To eat of Abraham's
substance must generate mixed feelings: to eat of the substance of God is
to be connected with a reality described in another version of the midrash
as "killing and animating, crushing and curing."[26]

Man's omnipotence is gone; the reality of God is beyond human
control, a total power over death and life. But that power is now given for
man's use and the nurturing of his life. In Abraham's alchemy of the feast,
vulnerability and trust, aggression and love find their harmony. The
guests ask: "How shall we bless Him?" (lit., hold onto goodness for
Him?). Abraham answers: "Say, 'Blessed be God who is blessed for ever
and ever! Blessed is He who gives bread and food to all flesh!'" God, in
these words that Abraham literally puts in their mouths after the food, is
the source of all blessing in time and space transcending man's range; He
is also the One who feeds each individual and therefore puts him in
intimate loving contact with that which is Other and incommensurate
with him. These are the words that Abraham teaches; his invention is the
movement from feeding and laughter to first words of separateness and
relatedness.

In the kabbalistic and midrashic literature, Abraham stands as the
paradigm for *ḥesed*, the loving relation with others. In Ketubot 8b, for
instance, we read: "Our brothers act lovingly to one another, and are the
children of those who acted lovingly to one another, who maintain the
covenant of Abraham, our father." Rashi explains "Abraham's covenant"
as referring to the verse we are discussing: "We learn from his *eshel*, his

'orchard-hotel,' that Abraham dealt in loving kindness." This is a rather unexpected piece of deduction: the character of the Jewish people as nurturers is made to spring from this cryptic narrative statement about Abraham. As R. Hutner points out,[27] a more obvious source for such a characterization would be the verse, "I have singled him out, that he may instruct his children and his posterity to keep the way of the Lord by doing what is just and right" (18:19).[28]

Both sources, however, R. Hutner argues, are necessary for a full understanding of Abraham's character of love (*ḥesed*). The latter source stresses love as "the way of God." Rambam illuminates the implications of "keeping the way of God," in a famous passage in *Hilkhot Deot*: "We are commanded to walk in these [median] ways which are good and straight, as it is said: 'You shall walk in His ways' (Deuteronomy 28:9). This is how this commandment is interpreted: 'Just as He is called gracious, so you be gracious; as He is called merciful, so you be merciful.' "[29] To keep "the way of God" means, in Rambam's analysis, to resemble God. Behind all the specifics of compassionate relations with others lies the impulse to relate to God, to place one's feet within His footprints. In this, Abraham acts as paradigm, as father *par excellence*, who teaches his children a passion for God that embraces all his connections with the world.[30]

The "orchard-hotel" initiative, however, represents Abraham in a different dimension. Here, the passion is radically human, the capacity to love others as oneself, which is a reaching out in separateness and empathy, called in Ketubot, "Abraham's covenant." The paradigm of this kind of love that seeks to feed and nurture others simply out of a sense of shared humanity is the cryptic *eshel*, with all the midrashic accretions around the word.

# Reality and play

On this view, Abraham lives on two planes simultaneously, fed from two sources. Radically alone in the world, he desires to approach God by imitating Him; he equally desires to share with others his own human experience of growth and freedom. The feast is his model of appetite braving the hazards of a world of Others and learning to seek its satisfactions in trust and love.

Do these two planes relate to each other? If the feast represents a transitional area between inner psychic reality and external reality,[31] then perhaps its most powerful gift is the "potential space" that Winnicott describes. At the point of emergence (literally, leaving the state of merging-in-with-the-mother) into individuality, the baby repudiates the object as the not-me. This is a dangerous stage, since separation is both necessary and impossible. It is successfully achieved when the separation itself is experienced as a loving gift of enlarged life, as, literally, a play area, that yields limitless new possibilities for being. This area both separates and unites mother and baby. Out of creative playing are generated symbols, a richness "that eventually adds up to a cultural life."[32]

Winnicott's account of this "third area of human living, one neither inside the individual nor outside in the world of shared reality," is enormously fruitful when applied to our texts. Take, for example, this passage from *Tanḥuma*:

> A baby is circumcised at eight days, just as Isaac was circumcised at eight days. There is nothing dearer to a person than his son; and yet he circumcises him. Why? In order to do the will of his Creator. He sees his son gushing blood from his circumcision, and accepts it in joy. Furthermore, he even incurs expense and makes that day a day of rejoicing—which was *not* commanded. That is the meaning of the text in Psalms [71:14]: "As for me, I will hope always, and add to the many praises of You." And furthermore, a person will go and mortgage himself, take out loans, in order to make that day a day of rejoicing. . . . When does a child become precious to his father? When he begins to speak. That is the meaning of the text: "Truly, Ephraim is a dear son to Me, a child that is dandled [*yeled sha'ashuim*]" [Jeremiah 31:20]. What is a child that is dandled? A three- or four-year-old who begins to speak and is playful in the presence of his father.[33]

The midrash begins with the paradigm of Abraham's circumcision of Isaac. Circumcision then becomes a model of human feeling submitting to God's will—"to do the will of his Creator": nothing but this desire to obey God could explain such an obvious violation of paternal feeling. Not only does he obey, however; he unites will and emotion in a new experience of joy. "All joy wills eternity, wills deep, deep eternity" (Nietzsche). He *makes* of the circumcision day a celebration; at great expense (not merely financial?), he makes a feast, a *se'udah shel mitzvah*, and transforms his rudimentary response to that day. The key phrase here, perhaps, is "which was *not* commanded": the father is so passionately concerned to "do the will of his Creator," that, in effect, he begins to improvise.

The paradox is palpable: in order to obey a difficult law, in order to become responsive to a radical demand on his life, the father cannot simply submit. He must find the space between himself and his Creator-Commander, out of which he may generate a kind of godly human play. This is the transforming activity of imagination.

The prooftext focuses the idea: "I will hope always, and add to the many praises of You."[34] Man "hopes" for God not only in crisis, where faith in salvation becomes a necessity. ("There are no atheists in foxholes"?) Faith is a constant, existential awareness of objective reality as only one of many possibilities; both God and man have the power of making and breaking reality. In exercising his imagination, man meets God.

The thematic continuity of the midrash becomes clearer at this point. For what underlies the sharp apparent change of topic, from the circumcision feast to the child's early speech development? Perhaps the theme of the love of father for son? But it is not the baby of the first section who becomes the talkative three-year-old of the second section. Rather, the midrash explores the theme of play — the freedom with words, the puns and jokes of the child beginning to use and love language — as a paradigm for the creative activity of the father circumcising his baby.[35]

The child plundering the resources of language is asserting his separateness, his mastery of the resources of his culture. He is both participant and solitary: in Winnicott's terms, the child is alone only in the presence of someone: "On the seashore of endless worlds, children play": Winnicott quotes Tagore and interprets:[36] babies come up out of the sea of union with the mother and discover the endless worlds of play, of power and danger in the margin that is neither sea nor land. The child in the midrash is most loved, paradoxically, at the point where he asserts separateness. The tension of union and separation, continuity and contiguity,[37] is focused in the two words *mishta'ashea le'aviv* — "he is playful *by himself* in the presence of his father."

The theme of the midrash essentially revolves around the question of *ratzon* (will): the relation between human will (desire, life energy) and God's will (obedience, submission). The passage suggests a third "transitional" area in which man grows in his capacity to *make* the world through language and symbolism. This is the world of the feast, in which there is no need to conquer and suppress one will in order to realize the other.

Maharal carries this notion forward one more stage. In *Netivot Olam*,
in the section on lovingkindness,[38] he quotes from Sotah 14a — a passage
similar to Rambam's discussion, quoted earlier, of the concept of walking
in the way of God. Here, the text is "Follow none but the Lord your God"
[Deuteronomy 13:5]; and the Talmud makes a similar point about imitating the loving acts of God. Maharal, however, inverts the logic of the
traditional equation: it is not the desire to imitate God (come closer to
Him) that generates the loving behavior of *hesed*, but rather it is by
coming to know and express the spontaneous, unforced energy in oneself, that is called *hesed*, that one apprehends the God-like in oneself.

Maharal moves from a theologically centered to an anthropologically
centered universe. In the world of *hesed* (as distinct from that of *mishpat*
[law], in which man acts out of necessity or obedience, and in that sense is
*not* God-like), man is truly in his element; he acts spontaneously and
naturally, and "walks in the ways of God" by acting of his own accord, of
his own free will and unforced consciousness (*me-atzmo me-retzono ume-
da'ato*). What emerges is something close to Berger's "inductive faith": a
"religious process that begins with the facts of human experience." It is
when man knows himself as world-making that he comes closest to the
Father whose creativity asks for the ultimate compliment of imitation.[39]

The playing of freedom and joy, the feast of circumcision, the beginnings of world-creating language, are traced in the passage from Tanhuma back to the birth of Isaac. Word making (*milah* as both circumcision and word) is world making. What God desires of man is discourse
about the world: "How many acrobatics [strategies of indirection] did
God engage in, in order to hear the talk of righteous women!"[40] Here,
the Jerusalem Talmud speaks of the involutions of the scene in which
God sends the angel to announce the birth of Isaac. The whole series of
dialogues and monologues (the angel speaks to Abraham, Sarah laughs
and talks to herself, God speaks to Abraham about Sarah's laughter, and
finally Abraham — or perhaps God? — tells Sarah, "But you did laugh") is
read as a strategy to elicit *siah*, discourse, from Sarah. By multiple
indirection, Sarah is left free to her own spontaneous reactions, in this
case, perhaps, a disappointing reaction. But the Talmud emphasizes the
strenuous importance of such a freedom, even when it involves fear,
skepticism, and prevarication.

In a powerful passage,[41] Rashi writes of the necessity of human discourse, here called prayer, in the creation of the world (2:5):

*"When no shrub of the field was yet on earth and no grasses of the field had yet sprouted, because the Lord God had not yet sent rain upon the earth and there was no man to till the soil":* . . . Before man was created, the vegetation had not emerged, even though God had declared, on the third day of Creation, "Let the earth bring forth grass." The vegetation had stopped growing at the very surface of the earth, and had not emerged until the sixth day. Why? Because God had not sent rain. And why had God not sent rain? "Because there was no man to work the ground" — that is, there was no one who could appreciate the goodness of rain. When man came, and knew that rain is needed by the world, he prayed for it, and it fell, and the trees and grasses grew.

The pun on *siaḥ ha-sadeh* (vegetation/talk about the field) again evokes Winnicott's "transitional space." The grass is both there and not there — "it stood at the very surface of the earth." Man brings it into being by knowing its potentiality and its absence. On the razor edge of trust and need, he plays with the words that make worlds. Out of his own hungers, he finds the language that touches off God's original intent. God holds Himself under restraint ("God had not sent rain") till there exists a subject capable of knowing his separateness from the world, his need and love of the world.

## Language and play

In a famous passage, Abraham negotiates with God about the destiny of Sodom. "Shall I hide from Abraham what I am about to do?" asks God (18:17). In *Bereshit Rabbah*,[42] God's special love for Abraham is expressed thus: "I shall do nothing without his knowledge" — even in a case where other considerations would seem to argue for secrecy. Abraham represents a more mature stage of human development than Adam or Noah: their *da'at*, their knowledge, opinion, was found dispensable on at least one occasion, and they are, respectively, expelled and imprisoned, and so excluded from a significant understanding of their reality. Abraham is never excluded; his consciousness (*da'at*) is valued by God, his reactions courted even where they run, in an obvious sense, counter to the expressed intent of God.

So Abraham pleads for Sodom, "plays" God down from fifty righteous saviors of the city to ten. The core of his plea balances his concern for God with his concern for humanity. "Shall not the Judge of all the

earth deal justly?" (18:25). The midrashic reading transforms this rhetorical cry into a profound either-or statement: "The judge of the whole
earth shall not do justice—if it is a world You want, then strict justice is
impossible. And if it is strict justice You want, then a world is impossible."[43]

To judge the earth is to annihilate it (perhaps a pun on *shofet-shotef*, to
judge/to sweep away). *Mishpat* (justice) is the modality that human beings
can never appropriate as their own. *Ein midat ha-mishpat midat ha-adam*,
as Maharal says: mathematical exactness is not existentially suited to
human life. Inadvertently, or perhaps by the nature of their sensibility
and their language, human beings lie. "We invent for ourselves the major
part of experience," Nietzsche says in *Beyond Good and Evil*. For weal or
for woe, *mishpat*, absolute standards of justice, cannot be realized in this
world as God has created it. To adhere to such standards is to destroy the
world; in order to build the world, *hesed*, the generous perception of
alternative possibilities, is necessary.[44]

In another midrash,[45] the destructive angel of Truth is thrown down to
earth, shattered into a thousand pieces, and can be reassembled only by
the combinations and compositions of human activity. (In an acrostic
formula, *Emet Me-aretz Titzmah*—"Truth springs up from the earth"
[Psalms 85:12]—the initial letters form the word *Emet*, truth. Now truth
is embedded in earth and carries the taste of earth; it has to be decoded
and reintegrated.)

Abraham, on this reading, gives God the benefit of his *da'at*, of his
personal opinion. From where he stands, *hesed* is the only modality in
which a world can survive. For indeed, his whole life has been concerned
with this one theme of potential, transitional space out of which the
creative words can rise. Here, he brings everything he knows back to
God; and God, who will do nothing without Abraham's perspective
being taken into account, enters into a dialogue that must inform His
own intention.

A similar image of "potential space" underlies the description of God
and Wisdom, as father and daughter, in Proverbs 8:30–31 (Soncino
translation):

> Then I was by Him, as a nursling;
> And I was daily all delight,
> Playing always before Him,

Playing in His habitable earth,
And my delights are with the sons of men.

Wisdom speaks here. Created before the world, she describes her own development (vv. 22–29) in the formless void: "When there were no depths, I was brought forth" (v. 24); and her growth in the earliest stages of separation and formation: "when the fountains of the deep showed their might" (v. 28). The passage describes the "play area," the potential space between all-encompassing Father and fully articulated world. This is the area that the kabbalists called the *ḥallal panui*, the empty space evacuated by God, who retrenched His total Presence in order to make it possible for a world to emerge.

The cosmological drama described in Lurianic Kabbalah is understood in psychological terms by writers like R. Nahman of Bratzlav—in terms, indeed, readily translatable into Winnicott's language.[46] For the "vacuum" left by God's loving retreat is tremulous and alive with possibility: *panui* implies "freedom *for*," not "freedom *from*";[47] it suggests an infinite "turning toward" of possible attentions and intentions.

The "nursling" (*amon*), as Wisdom describes its early stages of growth, is an image of total trust and nurturance, containing the paradox of male breast feeding, on the one hand, and a foster-child relationship, on the other. (Moses' image of his relation to the Israelites, "as the nursing father [*omein*] carries the suckling infant" [Numbers 11:12], is a surrealistic masculine projection of the nursing parent.) Rashi, for instance, evokes the associations of the verse in Lamentations (4:5): "children who were reared in [artificially habituated to] purple . . .")

Yet another level of meaning is provided by the association of *amon* ("nursling") with "artistry": the child Wisdom is represented as playing in the transitional area between total union with the nursing Father and the defined identities of the created world. This is the space of the artist, of the child who creates objects expressing his alienation and his connection. And this "play" rejoices the Father; Wisdom speaks out of its own experience, but includes the projected viewpoint of the Father ("Then I was *by Him*, as a nursling"; "playing always *before Him*"; "in *His* habitable earth")—as well as that of created "sons of men."[48]

The interplay between God and man is the area in which Wisdom perpetually moves. This is a dance of ceaseless life ("daily," "always"). The child's play is free of the "anxiety of influence," Harold Bloom's term for the artist's experience of oedipal anxiety—a modality in which predecessors threaten strangulation of new creativity and must be in some sense destroyed, if the new is to survive. Here, the Father is no threat to the son, nor the son to the Father. Instead, the child mysteriously becomes female; in the typology of the Torah, the father-daughter connection is both more fraught with tension than the father-son relation, and less perilous, once its erotic freight is "domesticated."

## Skepticism and joy

In Harold Fisch's phrase, what we find here is not the "anxiety of influence" — the successor-poet feeding on the precursor, but also needing to displace him — but rather the "Joy of Recognition."[49] Fisch writes of theories of literary influence; in terms of Winnicott's notion of the growth to creativity in a more general psychological sense, the Joy of Recognition remains a suggestive phrase.

For example, the opening section of *Midrash Rabbah* quotes our passage from Proverbs, connecting it with the first word of the Torah: *Bereshit*, "In the beginning." ("God made me as the *beginning* of His way" [Proverbs 8:22].) In the midrash, Wisdom is identified with Torah; and the essential activity of Torah is play. "If Your Torah were not my plaything, I would have perished in my affliction" (Psalms 119:92; my translation). The infinite resources yielded by possible combinations of words (the kabbalistic *tzirufin*) in the Torah[50] are not held in check by the presence of the Father. On the contrary, each game leads back to Him and to a knowledge of His delight. For these games create worlds, and are man's intimation of his fearful resemblance to God.

Another association of the word *amon*, "nursling," is given in the opening section of *Midrash Rabbah*. By the use of prooftexts, the midrash sets up a continuum of meanings on the axis of "manifestation-hiddenness." Wisdom is *amun*, in the sense that it is partially revealed, capable of being imparted; but it is also opaque, concealed, inviting the growing child in her separateness to discover/create what no one can tell her. It is this sense of the fecundity of hidden possibilities that "empowers" the child, even as she remains in intimacy with the Father.

The life of Abraham can be viewed as the first biblical engagement with the paradoxes of the potential space. As the incredible is promised him, he laughs; and the age of Isaac ("laughter") begins. This is the age of feasts, of bounty and trust and infinite possibility. But, significantly, to laugh is to make a choice; laughter is two-faced: "here for mockery, there for joy."[51]

Abraham and Sarah represent the dialectics of laughter. When she laughs in response to that which is hidden, yet to be uncovered,[52] the text has her laugh "inwardly" (18:12). Rashi comments: "She looked into her innards and thought, 'Is it possible that these inner organs should carry a child, or that these shriveled breasts should flow with milk?'" She is constrained in her bowels, in a brute and arid factuality. She laughs the hysterical laughter of tension: "*Efshar*—Can it be? How can I find a place for possibility in an inner space that is totally defined? How can I see these reduced particulars as charged, as involved in the uncertain throbbing of life?"

Characteristic of Sarah in its note of grim realism is the midrashic soliloquy put in her mouth, as she awaits rape in Avimelekh's palace: "All that night, Sarah lay on her face and said, 'Master of the Universe, Abraham lives on promises, while I live on faith alone. He is outside the prison, while I am placed inside the prison.'"[53] Sarah's experience is direct, physical, definitive. Matter is intractable and encloses her. God is more effectively hidden in her world; hers, therefore, is a more difficult faith than Abraham's, which is based on promises, transcendent intimations.

The narrative ends with Abraham being reconciled with Avimelekh, and even making the absurdly empathic gesture of praying for him. The midrash responds to this as, effectively, the first prayer-for-the-other.[54] In a poignant phrase, the midrash describes the effect of such a prayer: a knot of resistant reality is loosened by Abraham. The definitions that separate self from other are swept away, a law of nature dissolves, widening possibility. As a result, not Avimelekh alone but Abraham himself finally becomes fertile.

Sarah, however, represents the tension underlying such release. According to Ramban, she is not appeased. The enigmatic speech of Avimelekh to her (20:16) he translates: "With all I could do, you continued resisting, protesting." And she is given credit for a kind of staunch realism. Abraham's generous laughter is heard in contrast with her skeptical laughter.

For Abraham in feasting/festive mode lives dangerously, trustingly in the *ḥallal panui*, in that potential space where all is possible. In the typology of the midrash, he is a mountain—*mafkir lakol*—offering multiple perspectives. His vision is polymorphous; naught is but what is not. "I am dust and ashes," he cries to God (18:27). Rashi comments: "I should already have been dust at the hands of the kings, and ashes at the hands of Nimrod, *were it not [lulei]* for Your mercy which has stood by me." *Lulei* — "Were it not for Your mercy" — this is the characteristic Abraham vision: alternative realities float in space, suspended by the creative will of God. It is a metaphoric vision: "*this* is *that* — I *am* dust and ashes. My existence is held lightly in God's hand."

But by the same token, transforming possibilities that may redeem reality are also present. The work of *ḥesed*, the informing imagination acting on a polymorphous universe, is essential both for God and for man — *hakol tzarikh le-ḥesed* — everything is in need of *ḥesed*. "Is it of my food you have eaten? Nothing is what it seems. The real food growing in my orchard, served in my hotel is not human finite stuff, it is God's substance — infinite, charged with love."

## Metaphor and reality

The ultimate metaphoric statement of Abraham's life, however, is that implied by the midrash with which we began. Satan accuses Abraham: in a life of feasting, did he not have one turtle dove, one young bird for sacrifice? And God answers (or God in Abraham responds, in other versions of the midrash, to his inner doubting): *Ilu . . . If* I were to say to him. . . . An alternative reality is imagined, a horrifying alternative reality in which all Abraham's playing is crystallized into a hard residue. What is the nature of that *ratzon* (wish, will) that has guided him so playfully, so freely, in Maharal's language, to a sense of imitating God? Is it perhaps, after all, mere self-indulgence, self-interest?

"After all these things, God tested Abraham." Cumulatively, through his learning and teaching, an anxiety builds up. Were all these things, this fertile play of consciousness, were they grounded in the authentic desire to be close to God? Or is all this a grotesque Satanic masquerade, in which he is the fool and the victim?

For the main statement of his life has been the *Ilu* statement: I live in the world of feasting and laughter, which imposes no overt constraints; but, really, my life *means* total *korban* (sacrifice), total closeness to God, even if this has never been literally translated into sacrifice. Like the *lulei* statement ("Were it not for Your mercy"), the *Ilu* hypothesis issues from the potential space of conditional realities. It is the ultimate credit note that Abraham has issued on the meaning of his life; now it is called in. A time comes for testing; the hypothesis is unimaginably realized. And in terms of the midrash, Satan's instigation of the test suggests a terrible ambiguity. The need for testing—whose idea is it really? The skepticism that drives Abraham to confirm new depths of himself—is this divine or demonic?

It is within a similar tonal range of self-questioning that the Abraham story is analyzed by the hasidic master, the Ishbitzer, in his book, *Mei Ha-shiloah*. He focuses on the structure of narratives leading up to the Akedah. The final link in the chain of events is the covenant with Avimelech, who tells Abraham: "God is with you in all that you do" (21:22).

Until that point, he had felt distressed about things that were extraneous to his own being (literally, "to his own body"), in case there might result a subversion of God's glory. When, however, Sarah said to him, "Drive out this maidservant and her son," and God supported her by saying, "Whatever Sarah tells you, obey her," then Abraham felt very anxious, since he saw that even in the very seed of his loins there was a force that might subvert God's glory. He was anxious that his deeds were not acceptable to God. But when Avimelekh and Phikhol told him, "God is with you in all that you do"—"all" includes even the marginal products of his life, Ishmael as opposed to Isaac—these too are good . . . then, he was consoled and said, "As a proof that I dug this well" [21:30]—that is, "that I was the first person through whom God's glory was made famous in the world, and who conditioned people to call out in the name of God, God of the world."

And he planted an *eshel* in Beer Sheva, and consoled himself that God was with him. After that, there rose in his mind another anxiety—How could a human being boast about such a thing? And therefore it is said, "And Abraham sojourned in the land of the Philistines many days," on which the midrash comments that days of distress are called "many days" [*Va-yikra Rabba*, Metzora]. Therefore, he had the trial of the Akedah, so that he should begin to evaluate himself and to evaluate all the preceding trials. On this trial depended all the others, and he might have lost all of them, God forbid. . . . But when he saw that it lay in his power to deliver everything to God, then he understood that in everything that he had undergone till now he had done the will of God.[55]

The Ishbitzer here portrays the dialectical tension characterizing Abraham's life. After early episodes, such as the battle to save Lot from the four kings (chap. 14), or Abraham's prayer of intercession for Sodom, he finds himself vulnerable to radical doubts about the ultimate rightness of his generous impulses. The question, "What (who) will come of it?" — good or evil — is never finally resolved, and Abraham experiences all the anguish of indeterminacy in his evaluation of his own acts.

The dialectics of anxiety and consolation are the motif that the Ishbitzer traces; in the case of Sodom, anxiety gives place to reassurance, which spirals into newly intensified anxiety. The secret fear coiled at the base of his tree of life is that he may be responsible for a "subversion of God's glory"; the tragic-ironic possibilities of a destiny undercut by subconscious demons, a destiny acted out in cruel self-deception.

The awareness of forces within himself that may subvert all his conscious intentions comes to a head over the matter of his children. Here, the issue of his own body — Ishmael — is rejected by God. Ishmael is the rapacious hunter, portrayed in the midrash as a highwayman lurking at the crossroads, plundering, demonically connected to others by hunger: "his hand against all, and every hand against him" (16:12).[56] Like Abraham, he creates a new reality, as the world mirrors him back to himself. Ishmael thus represents a parody of Abraham's work in transitional space. But, like all parodies, Ishmael comes from his loins, threatens his life: how can Abraham not be radically suspicious of himself?

He is reassured by Avimelekh's unconsciously gnomic words — "God is with you in all that you do" — which he decodes as an assurance of his essential integrity in all the generous and imaginative acts of his life. Even what seems most questionable in his biography is ultimately in tune with his noblest intentions.

At this point, he formulates his own original contribution to the world: he is the first to engage in the feasting work, the *eshel* of potential space, which teaches men of all kinds to trust and love the God who is not part of them but can be encountered by them. This difficult project he now stamps with the seal of authenticity — only to be assailed once again with a fear of complacency and self-congratulation. In a new shift of perception, Abraham recognizes the inadequacy of such smugness.

In the climactic phase of painful self-examination, the Ishbitzer describes the Akedah as, in fact, inevitable ("*Therefore* he had the trial of the Akedah"). Abraham is compelled at this point to sift through his whole experience and come to some clarity. Existentially, all hangs now on the Akedah, which will prove, crystallize out, the basic truth of all his engagements with the world. What is probed here is the question of being-with-God in all he has done. Now, remorselessly, his search for truth leads him to test the metaphor of his existence: "Is it of my substance you have eaten?"

If the Ishbitzer speaks here of the logic of a life leading inevitably to an Akedah, then perhaps the midrash with which we began can be read in the same way. God answers Satan's aspersions: Abraham's life *is* authentically centered, in spite of its apparent lack of structure. God asserts: "The feasting is *potentially* capable of metamorphosis into *korban* [sacrifice]; in translated form, it *is* a search for closeness to God." And the assertion is *immediately* (*miyad*) followed by "God tested Abraham." Now, Abraham must face his darkest dreams; an act of clarification will decode his whole existence.

## The return to silence

One of the paradoxes of this hermeneutical act is that it invites a return to silence. Abraham's laughter, through which he communed with others, was a "pseudo-language," in which "silence is the essence." Now this essence is explored to its full, almost intolerable, extent. To live in a world in which the essential is experienced implicitly, wordlessly, is to return to the base out of which laughter, feeding, and ultimately speech emerged.

Kierkegaard approaches the paradox of the Akedah, which renders him sleepless, in this way: "Abraham cannot be mediated; in other words, he cannot speak. As soon as I speak, I express the universal, and if I do not do so, no one can understand me."[57] The "teleological suspension of the ethical," in Kierkegaard's phrase, is expressed in the vibration of Abraham's silence. Only after the Akedah, according to Rashi, does Abraham return to the mode of *siḥa*, of language, articulation, personal viewpoint: "Abraham said to Him, 'Let me spread before You my *siḥa*'" (22:12).

In one source for this midrash, Abraham says: "It is revealed and known to You that at the time that You told me, 'Bring him up there as a burnt offering,' I had an answer for You. . . . But I suppressed myself in order to do Your will."[58] "I had an answer for You" — to articulate one's position is normally not only a legitimate defense, but even part of God's education of mankind. Rashi (3:9), for instance, explains God's call to Adam, *Ayeka*— "Where are you?"— as an invitation to response, to dialogue. In confrontation with God, Adam's salvation can only lie in creating his own reality. To foreclose responses is to deny man his limited but essential perspectives. Here, however, Abraham, facing the truth of his life, returns the words to their source; for in potential space there is no simple plotting of positions.

Silence is the ultimate modality of Abraham. In a classic midrash, R. Akiva describes four reactions to suffering: "A king had four sons: one would be silent when beaten; one would kick out; one would entreat forgiveness; and one would ask for more punishment. Abraham was silent when suffering, as it is said, 'Take your son.' He could have said, 'Yesterday, You told me, "In Isaac your seed will be named." ' "[59] "He could have [should have?] responded. . . ." But he says nothing. He leaves the world behind and climbs to cloud-ringed mountains[60] with Isaac, in silence. Now, the emptiness, or the demonic fullness (for Satan accompanies him every step of the way) of that potential space is to be experienced in a muteness that encompasses all words.

R. Nahman of Bratzlav[61] takes this experience as the type of true confrontation with the *hallal panui*, that space from which God has withdrawn. A terrible descent — to the roots of the matter — is involved here. Articulated worlds and words are God's creative expression, but underlying them is the *ma'amar satum* (the blocked word), in which God, it seems, has entirely inhibited His self-expression. Here, nothing is clearly said; and yet all articulate words receive their vitality from this inchoate silence. The only words spoken are, "Where is the sheep?" (22:7). R. Nahman hears in the question the pregnant echoes of all *ayeh* (where?) questions: "Where is the place of His glory?" In this obscurity, man knows God as distant, yielding to no form of words other than the howl of loss and loneliness.

But this very loneliness is the energy that gives life to man: the yearning informs the emptiness as no fulfillment could. "Where is the sheep for the burnt offering?" The burnt offering is traditionally understood as atoning for inner doubts and denials. The redemptive gesture is the *Ayeh* cry, all liquid vowels, emerging inarticulately from silence. It is the cry that atones for loss by expressing loss. So, paradoxically, a return is achieved to that beginning of things, *Bereshit*, before words and structures, the *ma'amar satum*, with which all creativity must firstly engage.[62]

For R. Nahman, this encounter with "potential space," in all its anguish, must precede any original achievement, even in Torah study. Sureness of step involves in its very rhythms a knowledge of vertigo. To speak with the clarity of the poet is to hear in the silence the babble of infinite combinations.

In the end, the "prodigious paradox"[63] of the Akedah focuses on the question of *korban* (sacrifice). Satan insinuates that Abraham's feasting is essentially babble; closeness to God is not Abraham's underlying passion ("He did not have it in him . . . to sacrifice [*le-hakriv*] — to move toward greater involvement with God"). But Abraham's longing for God is manifested most intensely in alienation and obscurity. "And he saw the place *from afar*" (22:4), in a hasidic reading, suggests an essential dimension of the trial.

## The movement toward intimacy

The Talmud teaches that if one travels to a distant synagogue, one receives reward for the journey, even if one might have prayed more conveniently at a nearer synagogue.[64] Maharal questions this: on what principle is this so, since going a distance to fulfill any other commandment (e.g., to reach a Sukkah, where a nearby Sukkah is available) would not bring reward? He answers: "Because God is found in the synagogue, and therefore this is said precisely of traveling to a synagogue, for in this a person is (literally) *drawn after God*."[65]

R. Hutner discusses this cryptic statement.[66] The essential point, he says, is that prayer is existentially different from all other activities. It reflects a situation in which man stands in the presence of God. It is not the words of the prayer that define the situation, for even after he finishes, if he has not physically moved his feet, he "still stands in the presence of the King."[67] Prayer is an act involving body and spirit in relationship with God; it uniquely is called *kirvat Elokim*, a situation of closeness to God. Moreover, Ritva rules that the pilgrim, journeying toward the place of prayer, is already involved in the mitzvah, not merely in its preparatory stages.[68] The concept of traveling toward a place of relationship is then read as part of the mitzvah itself. For traveling, movement toward, is a gesture to diminish distance — and that is the whole point of prayer. So that to travel to a distant synagogue is to express yearning in action. And the situation of man experiencing intimacy with God includes a dynamic process in which desire confronts alienation.

Abraham travels (the word *lekh*, go, is a motif in the narrative; cf. 22:2, 3, 5, 6, 8, 19) far to the place of closeness. *Korban* (sacrifice) and *tefilah* (prayer) are traditionally understood to be based on this common motif of *kirvat Elokim* (closeness to God). The relationship that Abraham seeks is real, but embedded in the *Ayeh* experience of confusion and yearning. In the end, the *korban*, the expression of intimate relationship, is translated into the language of "traveling." The full knowledge of the enigma is turned to redemptive purpose by the sheer force of Abraham's desire.

## The right to feast

Satan's undermining voice acutely associated the feasting with the question of relationship with God: "Of all the feasts that Abraham made, did he not have one turtle dove, one young bird to bring close to You?" The *korban* that is to express Abraham's deepest intentionality must *arise out* of the feast, in order to make sense of (to clarify, in the Ishbitzer's words) his project. It is remarkable, therefore, to read in Tanḥuma an account of Abraham's preparation for the sacrifice:

> Abraham said, "What shall I do? If I reveal it to Sarah, female agitation will certainly overcome her in such an enormous matter. And if I don't reveal it to her now, but only later when Isaac is no longer here, she will kill herself." What did he do? He said to Sarah, "Prepare food and drink for us, and let us eat and rejoice." She asked, "How is today different from other days? What is the nature of this joy?" He answered, "Old people like us, who have had a child in their old age — surely we should eat, drink, and rejoice!" She went and prepared the food. When they were in the middle of the meal, he said to her, "You know, when I was three years old I first knew my Creator, and this boy is already mature and has not been initiated. There is a place, rather far from us, where boys are initiated — let me take him, and initiate him there." She said, "Go in peace."[69]

"Eat, drink, and rejoice — why else were we given a son in our old age?" Abraham re-iterates the meaning of his life, though Satan mocked it. "This old man! You granted him fruit of the womb at a hundred years old — and of all the feasts he made, he did not have one turtle dove . . . !") Now, Abraham is about to justify the intentionality of his feasts.

Unwillingly, Sarah asks the probing question, "What is the nature, the true quality of this rejoicing?" But it is Abraham who has set her up to hear his vindication. "In the middle of the meal," out of the full experience of the feast, Abraham then declares his intent — obliquely, so as to be understood only after the feast.

The climax of the Akedah is the displacement of Isaac by the ram: "He went and took the ram and offered it up as a burnt offering in place of his son" (22:13). Rashi comments on the redundant "in place of his son": Over every part of the ritual that he performed with the ram, he prayed, "May it be Your will that this act should be *as though* [*ke'eelu*] it were done to my son — as though my son were slaughtered, as though his blood were sprinkled, as though he were flayed. . . ."

The rhetorical motif of Abraham's prayer is *ke'eelu* — "Look at it *as though*. . . ." Abraham has earned the right to metaphoric substitution. Now, Abraham can speak again; his prayer rises out of his silence. The ram, created at twilight on the last day of Creation,[70] has been waiting in the wings for the moment at which it *becomes* Abraham's son. (*Taḥat* expresses equi-valence, displacement.)[71] The twilight animal, demonic, creature of potential space, becomes a symbol, vibrant with the meanings that Abraham articulates to all time — to God Himself.

Primary among all blessings, is the blessing of peace. The list of blessings in Leviticus 26 begins with rain, fertility of the soil ("and you shall eat your bread to satisfaction"), and culminates, according to Rashi, in the promise of peace: *And I shall grant peace in the land*: lest you say, "Here is food, here is drink — but if there is no peace, there is nothing" (Rashi, Leviticus 26:6).

One implication of Rashi's comment may be that — in Winnicott's terms — the anxiety and destructiveness arising out of the feeding-experience, in a being who no longer regards the world as an extension of himself, has to be engaged with and mastered. For the infant, "the object is always being destroyed"; it is this that convinces him of its externality. But where the object survives, where the infant can express aggression in ultimate trust, a new balance of connection and independence is set up. Love becomes possible.

Abraham, in his act of "clarification," confronts the hazards of "eating and drinking." Fear and destructiveness are the shadows that he must battle, if he is to achieve a new rigor of love. God is being found, is not simply placed by the subject in the world.[72] If Abraham can live through the reality of his fear of God as totally Other, then his love will become not simply a "bundle of projections" but the love of a real Presence.

This is love as courage, the final praise Abraham receives from God after the trial is over: "Now I know that you fear God, since you have not withheld your son, your favored one [though you were free to do so, might have done so] from Me" (22:12). Abraham, who confronts his fear and his pain, his aloneness and his uncertainty, is a heroic being. Ultimately, he is remembered for his "love of Me" (Isaiah 41:8). "Those who love Him are as the sun when he goes forth in his might" [my translation] (Judges 5:31).[73] The "might" of love is its capacity to confront fears of all kinds, to absorb them in a kind of joy at the survival of lover and beloved.

# ḤAYYEI SARAH 🌺

## Vertigo—The Residue
## of the Akedah

### Sarah's cries

Sarah's lifetime—the span of Sarah's life—came to one hundred and twenty-seven years. Sarah died in Kiryat Arba—now Hebron—in the land of Canaan; and Abraham proceeded to mourn for Sarah and to bewail her. (23:1–2)

Following the climactic moment of Moriah, the Torah turns to the world of procreation and death. There is the chain of continuing births in far-away Haran, with Rebecca's name discreetly introduced to signal a future (22:23); the death of Sarah; and the quest for a wife for Isaac, to continue Abraham's line. Deaths, births, marriages; the Parsha is titled by its opening words, "The life of Sarah"; in a covert sense, Sarah's life is germinal to the whole reading. The problem of her life is manifested just at the moment of her leaving it.

Our starting point is Rashi's comment (23:2), startling in its implications, on the structure of the narrative: "The death of Sarah is narrated directly after the Akedah, the Binding of Isaac, because, as a result of the tidings of the Akedah—that her son had been fated for slaughter, and *had been all-but-slaughtered*—she gave up the ghost [lit., her soul flew away] and died."

Here, Rashi is succinctly summarizing a complex midrashic tradition, which holds at its core a poignant thesis: Sarah is the true victim of the Akedah, her death is its unexplicated, inexplicable cost. Closer attention to Rashi's words, however, heightens the tension even further. For Rashi chooses one among several midrashic possibilities to narrate Sarah's final trauma. It is fascinating to consider the implications of some of these possibilities, and perhaps to arrive at a fuller appreciation of Rashi's choice.

Here, first, is the version found in *Pirkei d'Rabbi Eliezer*:

When Abraham came from Mount Moriah, Samael [Satan] was furious that he had failed to realize his lust to abort Abraham's sacrifice. What did he do? He went off and told Sarah, "Ah Sarah, have you not heard what's been happening in the world?" She replied, "No." He said, "Your old husband has taken the boy Isaac and sacrificed him as a burnt offering, while the boy cried and wailed in his helplessness [lit., for he could not be saved]. Immediately, she began to cry and wail. She cried three sobs, corresponding to the three *Teki'ah* notes of the Shofar, and she wailed (Yelalot) three times, corresponding to the *Yevava*, staccato notes of the Shofar. Then, she gave up the ghost and died. Abraham came and found her dead, as it is said, "And Abraham came [literal translation] to mourn for Sarah and to bewail her."[1]

In this version of the midrash, Satan lies to Sarah. He paints for her the horror and pathos of an old, demented father actually killing a helplessly crying child. Her death from a stroke, or heart attack, might seem naturalistic, evoking no surprise, were it not for the strange detail about her "cries and wails," which are transformed into the throbbing Shofar wails. This surrealistic connection is found in many sources. Essentially, the suggestion is that Isaac's death cries, expressing the unsaveability of the creature in the grip of overwhelming forces, are echoed mimetically by Sarah, also held fast in an irremediable anguish, and that these are reenacted in our ritual to redemptive effect. "The Shofar blasts on the New Year are to transform Sarah's death into atonement, because the *Teru'ah* — the broken Shofar tone — is groaning and wailing."[2]

This enigmatic etiology of the Shofar cry is found in a whole range of midrashic sources. The more obvious notion that the Shofar, the ram's horn, evokes the substitution of the ram for Isaac at the moment of actual sacrifice thus takes on a more tragic and paradoxical cast. Isaac is saved, and the Shofar announces the possibility of redemption, of symbolic substitutions. But Sarah is not saved, and, in the world of her mind, Isaac is not saved, and yet the cries of her — and his — despair are retained in liturgy and ritual, "as an atonement" for her descendants.

How is wailing, the *Yelala* ululation which is the hollow throb of despair, the sound that expresses essential Nothingness,[3] how does this become atonement? For the meaning of this howl, the howl of jackals in a wilderness, is negation. "They did not cry out to Me sincerely, as they lay wailing," Hosea says (7:14). This ululation, *Yelala*, is the opposite of the seeking cry of connection and loss. It echoes inhumanly in the passive anguish of nightmare.

The second midrashic source for Rashi's comment is from Tanḥuma:

> Just as Abraham stretched out his hand to take the knife, a heavenly voice came forth and said to him: "Do not stretch out your hand against the boy." *If it were not for that, he would already have been slaughtered.* At that time, Satan went to Sarah and met her *in the guise of Isaac.* When she saw him, she said, "My son, what has your father done to you?" He answered, "My father took me and led me up hill and down dale, till he took me up to the top of one mountain, built an altar, and laid it out, and arranged the wood, and bound me on top of the altar, and took the knife to slaughter me. If it had not been that God told him, 'Don't stretch out your hand against the boy,' I should already have been slaughtered." Satan did not manage to finish the story when Sarah died [lit., her soul flew away].[4]

In this version, a more subtle anguish, a more terrible irony leads to Sarah's death. For the devastating fact is that Isaac clearly is alive, in Sarah's eyes, as he tells the unbearable saga of his father's murder of him. On the face of it, Sarah dies, simply because of *lo hispik*, because she cannot endure to the end of the story. But before Satan can furnish the redemptive dénouement, he has destroyed, artfully, precisely, Sarah's vision of her husband and of her life's mission. Satan's tale is told as subversion; the ending is almost irrelevant, for Isaac stands before her—a ruined Isaac, who can only elicit horrified questions from her—"What has your father done to you?"

The ironic force of the midrash, then, lies not so much in the *lo hispik*, in the fact that the relief of resolution is delayed (a classic literary strategy, the love letter that arrives fifty years—or one day—late) as in the *eelulei*, the remorseless fatality that is interrupted, almost arbitrarily. Abraham's will to kill Isaac, narrates the midrash, would have known no softening. Effectively, Isaac *would have been dead*, were it not that . . . *eelulei*. . . .

This is part of the truth of the Akedah, and it is this partial truth that Satan "immediately," in the frustration of his larger desire, goes off to exhibit to Sarah. In a voyeuristic trance, Sarah dies of it. Satan's desire is ironically expressed in the previous midrash as the desire to *abort* the sacrifice; in the event, the sacrifice is not literally carried out, but neither is it aborted: in some sense, apparently, it is indeed realized.

The third version of the midrash is the most enigmatic:

> "Abraham did not rejoice in My world and you seek to rejoice?" He had a son at the age of a hundred. And in the end, God said to him, "Take your son. . . ." So Abraham took Isaac, his son, and led him up hill and down dale, and up to the top of one mountain, and he built an altar and arranged the wood, and took the knife to slaughter him. And were it not that the angel called out from heaven, he would already have been slaughtered. Know that it is so, for Isaac then returned to his mother and she said to him, "Where have you been, my son?" He answered, "My father took me and led me up hill and down dale. . . ." She said, "Woe upon the son of the drunken woman! Were it not for the angel, you would already be slaughtered?" He said, "Yes." At that, she screamed six times, corresponding to the six *Teki'ah* notes. She had not finished doing this when she died. As it is written, "Abraham came to mourn for Sarah and to bewail her."[5]

The central thesis of the midrash is the impossibility of full joy in this world. Abraham is the example of a terrible testing, which is resolved in the saving of his son and vindication of his own purity of intent. But this joy is then undercut by Sarah's death. The implied connection between the Akedah and Sarah's death becomes a prooftext for meaninglessness, within the parameters of this life. The midrash continues to speak ultimately even of God's lack of joy in His world: joy belongs to the future, affirms the midrash, not to the troubled middle-distance of temporal reality. "His world" becomes, by definition, an environment hostile to joy.

The paradoxical quality of Sarah's death is brought to a head in this midrash. As in the first midrash (from *Pirkei d'Rabbi Eliezer*), she cries and wails as she dies. But here she dies, not of disinformation, but of a terrible truth. As in the second midrash, her anguish prevails despite — or perhaps because of — Isaac's survival. But here, there is no Satanic figure, even in disguise: *all* is truth — Isaac confronting his mother, her questioning of him — all is an exploration of a truth that the midrash offers to grapple with. "Were it not . . . he would already have been slaughtered." "Know," insists the midrash, "that it is so. . . ."

How terrible is the grace of the *Eelulei* here. *Ḥesed*, God's generosity, illuminates nothing for Sarah; it merely sheds stark light on the endless darkness surrounding it.[6] For Sarah dies of the unbearable lightness of being; the restoration of Isaac in no way palliates the horror of what might well have been. For Sarah, this is not a "test," a three-day trial of faith, culminating in rescue and vindication. She, rather than Abraham, faces the full anguish of the "already slaughtered" one: his survival changes nothing. Her invocation to him holds the full measure of her situation: "Woe to the son of the drunken woman!" The image of her own unhinging, of an ecstasy (literally, a standing outside oneself), in which all stability is undermined, involves mother and son in a miasma of absurdity.

# Vertigo

When Rashi says, therefore, that Sarah dies of the news that her son was all but killed, he is very precisely indicating the full paradox of the midrashic narrative. She dies not simply because she cannot endure to the end of the story: that would constitute a relatively primitive tragic irony. She dies of the truth of *kime'at shelo nishhat*—of that hair's breadth that separates death from life. This is what Sartre calls "contingency," the nothingness that "lies coiled in the very core of being, like a worm."[7]

Maharal explains the concept of Sarah's death from contingency in his own terms: "This is the human reaction of panic, on realizing that *only a small thing* separated one from such a fate."[8] (This is a literal translation of *kime'at shelo nishhat*—"a little thing decided his fate.") The word for panic, *behala*, expresses the notion of vertigo, so central to existentialist philosophy. This is the naked anxiety of "not being able to preserve one's being."[9] Paul Ricoeur speaks of the vertigo of "being already born that reveals to me the non-necessity of being here." "Vertigo comes from the possibility there was of being different, of not having been at all." The potential anguish of the contingency of birth is fully activated only by the "accident which actually makes me die. . . . Only my death will one day fulfill the contingency of my birth and will lay bare the nothingness of this non-necessity of having once been born."[10]

The vertigo of existence in a world of *kime'at shelo nishhat*, a barely and provisionally escaped Nothingness, is expressed by Job: "He it is who stretched out Zaphon over chaos, Who suspended earth over emptiness [*b'li-mah*—lit., without what—devoid of substance, even of questioning]"

(26:7). To be suspended in mid-air is to live in suspense, in a condition of radical and constant doubt of the continuity of one's being.

Such a condition of existential doubt is described in *Deuteronomy* (28:66) as the very nadir of the cursed human condition: "The life you face shall be precarious [lit., suspended in front of you]; you shall be in terror, night and day, with no assurance of survival." In this state, one loses faith in the life thrust, Bergson's *élan vital*. Rashi comments on this suspension of life: "The text speaks of *doubt*. Everywhere, doubt is called the condition of *suspense*, whether one will die today." The knowledge of one's contingency, the vertigo of being, is expressed in the instability, the dizzying symmetry of equivalent possibilities.

On this view, Sarah dies of radical doubt. She suffers an attack of vertigo, and, as the midrash concludes, *lo hispika*, she has not managed to finish her crying and wailing before she dies. It is striking to compare this version with the Tanḥuma version, in which it is Satan who does not manage to furnish her with a happy ending to the story. Here, much more subtly, it is she who is active throughout. No one deceives her, Isaac lives and tells his story, she questions him, she screams six *Teki'ah* notes, and she *dies before she can finish them*. The profundity of her anguish is suggested in every detail. But what does she not finish, what does she not furnish (*sefeka* is power, means, possibility) to herself or to her world, so that her death becomes an interruption, rather than a conclusion? Perhaps it is the very process of *safek*, of doubt, the vertigo of Nothingness, that she has not had the stamina to live through, to its end?

## Isaac's ashes

The problem of Sarah's death is, profoundly, the problem of her life, of *hayyei sarah* — of the contingency of the already born, the all but dead. Her perception of mortal vertigo is displaced onto Isaac's *kime'at shelo nishḥat* experience. In a real sense, as the Sages put it, "His ashes remain piled on the altar,"[11] though he may walk the earth, as large as life. What happened at the Akedah cannot be neutralized, though the sacrifice is not literally consummated. The burden of the "all but" condition is assumed by Sarah, who consummates its meaning in her howls and her death.

The existential status of "Isaac's ashes" — an important theme in the midrash — is explored in an essay by R. Yitzhak Hutner.[12] In some absolute sense, the ashes indicate a negation of life; they represent symbolically the metaphysical pessimism[13] expressed most poignantly by the Sages: "It would have been better [lit., less strenuous] for man never to have been created than to have been created."[14]

The mystery of this negation is felt by many readers: Maharsha,[15] for instance, notes the radical tension it sets up with the primary evaluation of human life — "Behold, it was very good" (Genesis 1:31). The superlative "very" is reserved only for Man. The midrash even points to the anagram of "*adam me'od*": only the human represents the intensified good of creation. The tension between this metaphysical optimism, and the pessimism of the statement in Eruvin is the subject of R. Hutner's essay. He argues that it is precisely out of this tension that *me'od*, the uniquely human intensity, is generated. Only through a fully experienced knowledge of the abyss where "it would have been better for man not to have been created," can a rigorous, even a tragic optimism be achieved.

R. Hutner makes use of the talmudic terms, *hava amina* and *maskana*, to structure his argument. In talmudic discourse, even a hypothesis that is ultimately rejected is examined closely and seriously. In some sense, it remains live, even if it is not the one to be pragmatically adopted. He applies this dialectical principle to the metaphysical question. The dilemma of "To be or not to be" has an ultimately optimistic conclusion; but this can be reached only through an authentic and total involvement in the meaning of negation. There has to be a suspension of belief and affirmation, a kind of philosophical schizophrenia, in which the theoretical optimistic conclusions of faith are ignored, and only the cries and wails of Nothingness are heard.

This dialectical tension prevails in many areas, as R. Hutner indicates.[16] But here, in the existential sphere, it is perhaps most crucial. The groans and wails of the Shofar on Rosh Hashana express the core dimension of human life: "it would have been better for man never to have been created." But in the very heart of this burning recognition arises the affirmative flame of the "*very* good." When the angel negates negation, when he calls out, "Do not raise your hand against the boy" (22:12), Isaac is restored to life. But, at the same time, his ashes remain on the altar; the total surrender of the burnt offering, leaving no residue of hope, no tissue of illusion, is not neutralized.

This core knowledge of paradox — "Without contraries there is no progression" (Blake) — is Isaac's radical experience, bequeathed to his children. "Happy are the people who know the *Teru'ah* [note of the

Shofar]; O Lord, they walk in the light of Your presence" (Psalms 89:16).
To know the brokenness, the hollow resonance of the Shofar, is to
sharpen one's hearing for the affirmations of faith.

## The negation of negation

Yet these are real ashes — the kind out of which nothing can emerge —
quite unlike Abraham's "dust and ashes" (18:27), which contain potential
of fertility; for dust is the *materia* of life. And these cries and howls issue
from the other side of silence, from the "non-silence" (*lo dumiyah*), of
which the Psalmist so bitterly complains: "My God, my God, why have
You abandoned me? . . . My God, I cry by day — You answer not; by
night, and no silence is given me" (Psalms 22:2–3; my translation). André
Neher writes: " 'Nonsilence' is a silence more silent than silence. It is the
fall of silence, into a deeper stratum of nothingness; it is a shaft hollowed
out beneath silence which leads to its most vertiginous depths."[17] The
"opacity" of meta-silence gives rise to terror, the essential *Yirah* of Isaac's
life, with which Sarah, unguarded and unprepared, is fatally assailed.

In a different dimension, Paul Ricoeur writes of negation as the
"privileged language" of the experience of finitude.[18] Want is expressed
negatively as an "I don't have"; the past is "no longer," the future "not
yet," and death "nothingness." This "primal negation" Ricoeur associates with Spinoza's "sadness": "By sadness, I mean a passion by which the
soul passes to a lesser perfection." This leads him to the idea of a "default
of subsistence," which he applies to the experience of "vague vertigo
which flows from the joint meditation on birth and death." To transcend
this primal negation is possible only by a "negation of negation," which
he terms, "denegation." This is the mode of "in spite of," the mode that
differentiates denegation from annihilation. ("I think, I want, *in spite* of
my finitude.")

Ricoeur then proceeds to a brilliant demonstration that "the soul of
refusal, of recrimination, of contestation, and, lastly, of interrogation and
doubt, is fundamentally affirmation." Sartre's *L'Être et le Néant* postu-
lates that nothingness of being is an ontological characteristic of human
life; doubt, interrogation, absence, anguish create the possibility of freedom. The act of "nihilating withdrawal" from the passions, the "suspension" of judgment that frees the thinking "I" from entanglements and
rootedness in the world of nature and the senses — this is the essence of

freedom for Sartre: "the human being putting his past out of play by secreting his own nothingness."[19]

At the heart of Sartre's "nothingness," however, Ricoeur discovers a new affirmation. "I repudiate a past of myself only because I assume another past." What really happens is not a severance of all connections, entanglements: "rather, I am aware of liberating in myself what remained inhibited, refused, impeded. I have only repudiated shackles, denied negations. . . . Hence, by means of negations . . . I have constituted a better continuation of myself."

Ricoeur's model of annihilation and denegation is, I suggest, a useful key to the problematics of the Akedah and Sarah's death. For these take us into that meta-silence of which André Neher writes—into that bitter realm of real ashes. As I want to show, Sarah's life has been profoundly concerned with issues of freedom and disentanglement. And the possibility of transcendence is indeed realized in the narrative—and in midrashic comment on the narrative—in the language of denegation—the negation of negation.

At the resolution of the Akedah, the angel calls out—merely?—"*Do not* raise your hand against the boy, *do not* do anything to him, for now I know that you fear God, since you *have not withheld* your son from Me" (22:12). The double negatives—not to destroy, not to withhold—thus become the basis of blessing and affirmation in the second call of the angel: "Because you have done this—and *have not withheld* your son, I will bestow My blessing upon you" (22:16–17).

Rashi (22:12) quotes the midrash, giving God's answer when Abraham questions Him about His apparent "change of mind" about the sacrifice: " 'I will not violate My covenant, or change what I have uttered' [Psalms, 89:35]. When I told you, 'Take your son,' 'I will not . . . change what I have uttered.' For I did not tell you, 'Slaughter him,' but 'Take him up.' Now you have taken him up—take him down!' "

The annihilation of meaning, inherent in the notion of a god who contradicts himself, is here simply negated. Having acted in a universe of enigma and contradiction—without insisting on resolutions—Abraham is then invited to reconstrue the words of the past. In Ricoeur's terms, he is to "assume another past," to constitute a "better continuation" of God and of himself. The tension between continuity and discontinuity is resolved only ultimately, and only in terms of denegation.

The expression, *kime'at shelo nishḥat* (he was all but slaughtered) also yields the same model of denegation. Survival on such terms is for Sarah contingency and despair, the death of meaning. For her, restoration does nothing to neutralize the terror.

"I did not say to the stock of Jacob, 'Seek Me out in a wasteland [*tohu*]'" (Isaiah 45:19). R. Hutner, in the same essay that we have discussed, analyzes the import of God's denegation. What it implies is that there is a reality called *Tohu*—Nothingness. But the seed of Jacob represents a highly evolved form of consciousness that may transcend this modality. Isaac, on the other hand, lives his life within the parameters of the abyss, and survives for posterity as the realization of this possibility—total nihilation, the burnt offering, the knowledge of "it would have been better for man never to have been created."

This is the *Tohu*, the Nothingness of which Isaiah speaks, and which ultimately he rejects (45:18): "He did not create it [the world] a waste [*tohu*]; but formed it for habitation." The absurdity, the inhuman waste of a world of *Tohu*, ruled by the Greek "moira," the malevolent gods of fate, necessity and silence, is countered by the denegation of *lo tohu*. Rashi's comment spells out the existential force of this denegation; against the meta-silence of *Tohu*—in which human acts are gratuitous, have no effect—God gives the Torah, which is founded in the promise of justice. "Great reward" is the affirmation at the heart of darkness.

## The Torah given in the howling wasteland

At this point, we approach one of the radical forms of the paradox of Nothingness. For, as Moses sings in his last song, the Torah was given in a place of waste, frustration, and death: "He found him in a desert region, in an empty howling waste [*uve-tohu yelel*]" (Deuteronomy 32:10). Rashi comments: "the waste-land where jackals and ostriches howl—*even there*, they were drawn after faith." Here are the *Yelalot*, the voice of waste and absurdity, and here is the denegation, the "in spite of" that Ricoeur describes. The passion to find God, and to be found by Him, leads human beings "even there"—to the delirium, the inspiration that transcends annihilation.

The *Yelalot*, the howlings, are described in the Talmud as the expression of intoxication. ("Wine is called *Yayin*, because it brings *Yelalah*—howling—into the world"[20]—presumably, a reference to the onomatopoetic aspect of the words.) The hollowing out experience of metasilence is the necessary prelude to the words of Torah. Perhaps this is what the midrash indicates in Sarah's cry: "Woe to the son of the drunken woman!"[21]

Sarah achieves the *Yelalot* of the Shofar, but she does not consummate them. "Happy are the people who *know the Teru'ah*; O Lord, they walk in the light of Your presence." To know the broken vibrato of the Shofar is to know "how to seduce the Creator with the *Teru'ah*."[22] For the Shofar represents the consummate paradox of the "very good" creation of Man, apprehended through groans and wails.[23] Involved in a world of negation, all but lost in the wilderness, the human being has the possibility of affirming and transcending.

Satan, who originally desired to abort the Akedah trial, ultimately has all his plans undermined by the Shofar wail.[24] Hoist with his own petard, he is doomed to hear Sarah's wailing brought to its end. For the Shofar evokes the mystical transcendence of Mount Sinai (Exodus 20:15). The Shofar that wails there is described in Targum Jonathan as having the power to revive the dead. For only the wails that issued from the land of ashes can be modulated to signal an ambiguous reality, despair, and redemption.

## Sarah in Abraham's and Isaac's imagination

Sarah *lo hispika* — cannot persist to the end. For her anguish is just this: the perception of the *kime'at shelo*, of disruption, of the "obscure disturbance of [her] whole being."[25] The vertigo that overwhelms her is reflected in midrashic accounts of the anxiety felt for her by Abraham and by Isaac. It is interesting to notice that Sarah's death is a reality in the minds of both, before it happens. The doubt, the dread of their lives is focused on her. As Abraham raises his knife, Isaac begs: "Father, don't tell my mother when she is standing at the edge of a pit or on a roof, lest she throw herself down and die."[26] In a clear vision of Sarah's vertigo and suicide, Isaac speaks out of his own "anima," the Sarah-in-himself, who is a focus of doubt, apprehension, suspense: the modality of *shema*, "lest she. . . ."

Abraham, likewise, fears her suicide when she finds out the truth. He leaves with his son, "early in the morning" — *shema* — "lest Sarah change her mind about letting them go."[27] He, too, is nervously aware of what Sarah represents; she is a part of himself, the part he must evade, if he is to reach Moriah.

The pervasive presence of Sarah in Isaac's imagination is poignantly suggested in this midrash:

Since Satan could achieve nothing with Abraham, he came to Isaac and said, "Son of a miserable woman! He is going to slaughter you!" Isaac replied, "I know." Satan said, "In that case, all your mother's concern about Ishmael will have been for nothing, and your hated rival will inherit in your place. Don't you feel how outrageous this is?" This is like the adage: if poisonous words are not wholly absorbed, they are at least partly absorbed. For "Isaac said to his father, 'Father. . . .'" Why "father," twice? To rouse his pity for him.[28]

What partially undermines Isaac's determination is not the direct voice of self-pity, but the more insidious imagination of Sarah's survival in a world from which he is absent. His pity for his mother, bereft on a personal level, and also deprived of the intentionality of her life, abandoned to an absurd reversal of her hopes, is his access to a sense of his own mortality. How can he make retroactive mockery of her entire perception of the world, in which the conviction of "Isaac-not-Ishmael" is so fierce? Isaac quails before this vision of Sarah, which is the acrid knowledge of his own death:

> By means of the horror-stricken feeling which comes upon me from the silence of those who are absent and who will no longer respond, the death of another pierces me as an injury to our communal existence; death "touches" me; and in so far as I am also another for others and ultimately for myself, I anticipate my future death as my eventual lack of response to all the words of all men.[29]

Through Sarah, death "touches" Isaac, with an anguish which "acquires a sort of intensity that is more spiritual than biological."[30] This *yirah*, the spiritual anguish that has to do with the silence of those who are absent, and the apprehension of that silence, attains a peculiar force in Sarah's situation. For the vertigo, the suicidal potential that Abraham and Isaac sense in her — and in the Sarah part of themselves — always was the hazard implicit in a sensibility that tolerated no equivocation, that was crystal-clear in its perceptions and decisions.

## Sarah's analytical vision

The Sarah who could tell Abraham with such clinical decisiveness: "Cast out that slave woman and her son, for the son of that slave shall not share in the inheritance with my son Isaac" — demonstrates not only inflexible will but an apparently lucid vision of reality that is hidden from the more entangled emotions of Abraham: "The matter distressed Abraham greatly, for it concerned a son of his" (21:10–11). For God confirms her surgical judgment. He tells Abraham not merely to obey Sarah but to accept her vision of things—less confused and multifaceted than his.[31] What she sees is that these two brothers cannot possibly coexist; though they seem to be playing together, there is murder in the wind.

Rashi cites the midrash that presents the game the boys are playing as a kind of William Tell game, with Ishmael shooting arrows at Isaac and then claiming, "But I'm only playing." Ishmael's injured innocence fools Sarah not at all: in the phrase Rashi uses, "They would go out to the field," are caught midrashic harmonics: the field is the world—"Let us prospect our share of the field."[32] There is a mortal struggle under way, here, for a place in the sun; and Ishmael is deadly serious. What Sarah sees is the uncompromising passion of the encounter. Ishmael may be *kimitlahleha* (Rashi, 21:10),[33] he himself may be unconscious of the forces driving him, may really believe in the game. But that does not reduce the necessity Sarah sees to separate the boys before the explosion occurs. For what she sees is Cain and Abel in the field: "Cain said to his brother Abel . . . and when they were in the field, Cain set upon his brother Abel and killed him" (4:8). There, too, there was a strangled attempt at play, at dialogue. But the reality overwhelms them, and murder enters the world.

In a cryptic poetic insight, Midrash Tanḥuma portrays this analytic capacity of Sarah. " 'She looks for wool and flax' [Proverbs 31:13]. This refers to Sarah, who said, 'Cast out that slave-woman and her son.' "[34] Sarah is praised for detecting the incompatible principles that animate Isaac and Ishmael. (According to midrashic tradition, the dubious sacrifice that Cain brings to God is flax.[35] And wool, of course, is associated with Abel's work as shepherd.) In a phrase, the midrash thus suggests the fratricidal potential of an apparently innocent relationship, and places in relief Sarah's acuity in perceiving it.

But this very acuity, the laser beam that disentangles complexity and cuts to the quick, makes Sarah vulnerable when all structures and certainties are undermined. In the vertigo of the *kime'at shelo*, pure thought can no longer help her. Unlike Abraham, whose tendrils of concern involve him with the complex life of those around him, and who is therefore "greatly distressed, for it concerned a son of his," Sarah aspires to an analytical purity that yields her no refuge at the end. "Suicide," says

Kierkegaard, "is the only tolerable existential consequence of pure thought."

On this reading, Sarah dies of her life; or, to put it in Jung's terms, she cannot meet the challenge of later life, which demands reversals, the confrontation with counterpossibilities: "What was true in the morning will at evening have become a lie."[36] The clarity, the habitual gesture of disentangling, which were characteristic of her, can offer her no joy now, when she is suspended in a universe lacking in answerable questions ("Suspended in *bli-ma*" [Job 26:7] — in the Nothingness in which even questions become absurd). In this metasilence, only the howl of negation comes to her lips. *Lo hispika* — she cannot realign herself to complete the howl and discover the difficult "very good," the painful prize of a full humanity.

## Abraham's involvement and conflict

Abraham's history charts a very different course. Entangled in the world, linked by love with all who enter his many doors, he feels himself incapable of the surgical removal of Ishmael that Sarah prescribes. But in this she is right, God says. So he obeys, he submits to her voice. Yet the irony of events leads him later, after Sarah's death, to take Hagar back; according to midrashic tradition, Keturah, whom Abraham marries at the end of his life, is identified with Hagar (25:1–6). In an obvious symbolic reversal, Abraham reaffirms his life's urge to integrate and include. Yet, even in this remarriage, there is a postmortem acknowledgment of Sarah's legacy of discrimination and analysis. He gives presents to the sons of his old age, but he sends them away from Isaac's presence.

Ultimately, he dies in the mode of *bakol* — "And the Lord had blessed Abraham *bakol* [in all things]" (24:1). He is "full of days": in the reading of *Sefat Emet*, this indicates a condition in which nothing is forgotten, nothing censored. Bringing all his days with him, Abraham dies in accord with God's prediction: "You shall go to your fathers in peace" (15:15). According to Rashi, the reference to "your fathers" promises final reconciliation with all that he rejected at the outset of his life. God promises also that Ishmael will be reconciled with Isaac, will acknowledge the preter-natural order of their relationship.[37]

But there is a price to be paid for this idyll, the classical perfection of Abraham's life, from which nothing has to be expunged, and where all complexities find their place. For this idyll does have limits: there is a dark rim edging the sunlight. Abraham must die five years prematurely, in order to preserve the harmony of his vision.[38] Five more years, and he would have seen Esau acting on impulses of his nature that would have disrupted Abraham's peace. To speak of a diminishing of life for the sake of protecting its coherence is to declare the limitation of what Abraham can bear to see.

The point is made vividly in the midrash. The text in Genesis 25:11 reads: "After the death of Abraham, God blessed his son Isaac."

> Not blessings but gifts Abraham gave Isaac. This is like a king who owned an orchard and gave it to a tenant-farmer to tend. Two trees grew there, entangled with one another: one grew vital potions, and the other grew fatal poisons. The farmer said: "If I water the vital tree, the fatal one will be nourished too. But if I don't water the fatal one, how will the vital one live?" He concluded: "I am merely a tenant-farmer, in temporary charge of the orchard. Let me finish my tenure, and then let the owner decide what to do." So said Abraham: "If I bless Isaac now, the sons of Ishmael and of Keturah will be included. And if I don't bless them, how can I bless Isaac?" He concluded: "I am merely flesh and blood—here today and tomorrow in the grave. I have already done what I had to do [Rashi: "in giving birth to them all"]. From this point on, let God do what He wishes in His world." When he died, God revealed himself to Isaac and blessed him.[39]

The mystery at the heart of the midrash radiates from the strange involvement of the trees with one another. Here, Abraham's vision of things, his essential *entanglement* in life, that will not allow him the analytical definitiveness of Sarah, rebounds against its own limitation. To see opposites as viscerally connected with each other, in a complex symbiosis that seems to admit of no separation, is to be overpowered by "thoughts that do often lie too deep for tears." Abraham cannot cut the trees apart; but at this point he cannot simply act on a principle of total inclusiveness. He has given birth to the reality of conflicting principles; only God can preside over the evolving conflict. To be a source of life is to generate tensions that one cannot direct or control. At the point where the essential tension of life grows beyond him, Abraham can only surrender his stewardship.

He was originally blessed, "You shall be a blessing" (12:2). In Rashi's reading, this endowed him with the power to bless at will. But the current of connection fuses at the end of his life. In Rashi's words, "He was afraid to bless" (25:11): he comes to his own form of vital anguish, the modality of Isaac enters his soul, brings them together at the moment when Abraham must hold back blessing from his son.

## Isaac comforted after his mother

If we follow Isaac into the world after Sarah's death, we can detect the veiled structure of a drama that begins with that death and ends with Isaac's marriage and Abraham's remarriage and death, leaving his son unblessed. The whole Parsha (23:1–25:18), a single Torah reading, is titled, "The life of Sarah." The irony of such a naming is only too apparent. For, in reality, the subject of the section is the question of Sarah's life. The statement of the text—the serene, noncommittal numbering of her years—is undermined by the midrashic comment on the cause of her death. Rashi himself reinforces the paradox: on the one hand, all her years were "equal in goodness"; on the other, she dies of "kime'at shelo." The question of Sarah's life is Isaac's legacy: only he can unravel it, though he cannot answer it.

Rashi says, on the intense ending of Isaac's marriage quest—"Isaac brought her into the tent of his mother Sarah, and he took Rebecca as his wife. Isaac loved her, and thus found comfort after his mother's death." (24:67)—"It is human nature that as long as a man's mother is still alive [kayyemet], he is involved (entangled) with her; when she dies, he comforts himself in his wife."

Rashi is pointing a spotlight here on the issue of Isaac's entanglement with his mother's life, her very kiyyum, the problem of her existence. The existential anguish of her last moment, which, in one intuition of kime'at shelo, retroactively confirms the contingency of a life and emerges in a strangled wail—this is what Isaac is involved with. He is caught up in the vertigo of her being. For Isaac, to be comforted is to free himself of this fascination with his mother's pain, and to turn to his own life. Rashi often explains the word, nehama, comfort or regret, as mahshava aheret, "a different thought."[40] The notion is that comfort and regret both imply a shift in paradigms, allowing new questions, new anomalies, to remove one from old preoccupations. In his reading, therefore, Isaac is freed from his preoccupation with his mother's life; he is freed, essentially, for new thoughts, a new way of thinking his existence.

Isaac turns to his wife, to new dialectical struggles, "after" his mother. In his relation with Rebecca, he finds a way of remembering Sarah; of rearticulating the parts of his knowledge of her. The angst of her death is healed in a relation in which Rebecca is both like and unlike his mother. The Oedipal perception that Rashi clearly states ("It is human nature") gains tragic resonance from the death theme.

According to one midrashic source, at least, Sarah has been dead three years, when Isaac marries Rebecca, and what he needs comfort for is not simply the fact of her death:

> Three years Isaac mourned for his mother. Every time he entered her tent, and saw it in darkness [dimmed], he would tear his hair. But when he married Rebecca, and brought her into the tent, the light returned to its place. "And Isaac brought her into the *ohel* [the tent]": *ohel* means "light," as it is said, "Till the moon will no longer shine" [Job 25:5]. He was comforted and [lit.] saw it as though his mother were still in existence. That is why it says: "Isaac was comforted after his mother."[41]

The implicit understanding behind the midrash is that Isaac does, in reality, suffer a kind of death at the Akedah. His mother dies, and with her the light of her tent. In an astonishing fusion of images, the tent of her intimate life becomes the energy that affirms life. Light, claims the midrash, is by definition the meaning of *ohel* (tent). To have left one's tent in darkness is to deny the value of being. The anguish of Isaac's reaction, as he enters the condition of his mother's life, expresses a desperate involvement in the wailing of her end. With Rebecca's coming, the energy of hope returns, because he now can see his mother's life as though she really had her Being. Through the prism of his relation with Rebecca, his mother's existence, her *kiyyum*, becomes vital again.

## The Akedah: the tragic residue

The healing relation with Rebecca, who is and is not Sarah,[42] contains elements that go much beyond the universal Oedipal model. For she comes to resolve a complex tangle of dilemmas. In an obvious sense, as she runs back and forth at the well, eagerly providing for the needs of the servant and the camels, she resembles Abraham welcoming his angel-guests[43] — impatient, energetic, overflowing with love (*ḥesed*). For an Isaac, withdrawn, haunted by the shadows in his mother's tent, she will re-evoke the hopeful involvement of an Abraham, connecting, integrating, generating life. But the need of Abraham's family for Rebecca goes much further than that.

The servant prays for success in his mission, thanks God when success seems imminent. But the motif-word that recurs rather strangely in his prayers is the word, ḥesed (love): "'Act in ḥesed with my master, Abraham'" (24:12). "'Through her, I shall know that You have acted in ḥesed with my master.'" (24:14). "'Blessed be the Lord God of my master, Abraham, who has not abandoned His ḥesed and His truth from my master'" (24:27) (my translation).

The importance of what Rebecca will mean to the family is intimated here. For there is, after all, a tragic residue of the Akedah in Abraham's family. The darkening of Sarah's light is one manifestation. But even in Abraham's case — what can it have meant to him to undergo the test, and then simply, silently, to have Isaac restored to him? It is surely significant that the call on Moriah, to refrain from sacrifice, comes from an "angel of God," not from God Himself. God says not a word to Abraham after the command to sacrifice his son. He restores his son, but Abraham never knows the reason for his experience.

This is the inadequacy of ḥesed to human desire. In this mode of ḥesed, in a world where God is silent, the *status quo* is apparently preserved.[44] Nothing is illuminated by this ḥesed; God's role, His relation to human action, reward, punishment — all the theological mysteries remain intact.[45]

Moreover, the real problem is human recognition of ḥesed as ḥesed. Implicit in the servant's prayers is the need to see a manifest indication of God's ḥesed to Abraham. His main criterion for the rightness of Rebecca's election is that he will sense *in her* the ḥesed that, since the Akedah, has been lacking from his master's experience. He prays to know, by means of her rightness, that ḥesed is being done to his master;[46] not merely that God should be so kind as to make it happen that the girl he speaks to is the right one. The ḥesed he asks for, in other words, is not a means, but an end in itself.

Rebecca represents that essential ḥesed of which *Midrash Rabbah* says: "'*Act in* ḥesed *to my master*': You began something — finish it! Everyone is needy of ḥesed, even Abraham, for whose sake ḥesed charges the world, even he is needy of ḥesed — as it is said, 'Act in ḥesed to my master, Abraham' — You began something — finish it!"[47]

The paradox of *ḥesed* is that it is gratuitous, free of necessity. It is given at God's will, so that even Abraham cannot demand it as a right. But without it, everything fails. The servant speaks of neediness; the knowledge of God's love is the energy that empowers even an Abraham to see coherence in his life. "You began something—finish it!" Implicitly, the servant begs, challenges: Do not withdraw that vital vision from my master—though it is Your right, yet *ḥesed* has a law of its own. To begin a gift commits the giver to a new necessity of giving.

## Abandonment and ingathering

Listening intently to the text, one can detect the tone of renewed hope, the undertow of despair confronted, in the servant's gratitude: "Blessed be the Lord God. . . . who has not abandoned His *ḥesed* from my master" (24:27). *Azav* is the word for both "abandonment" and "binding together," "consolidation."[48] André Neher writes: "Abandonment and ingathering belong together, not because of the compensating healing effect of the passage of time, but through the inner dialectic of their inseparable relationship."[49]

Seeds have been scattered, all seemed fallen apart; but in the disintegration, the servant now recognizes not only the denegation of *lo azav* (He has not abandoned), but the harmonic of affirmation, the promise of a new *emet* to be initiated by Rebecca's entry into Abraham's world. It is as though the metabolic balance of the family is now to be readjusted.

## Pivoting points

The kabbalah characterizes Jacob, born of the new balance, as *emet*—perfect equilibrium, consolidation of extreme modalities, at a point where the center will hold. In reality, and in terms of the contingencies of the narrative, this *emet* is mediated by intense moments of *kime'at shelo*, by the "all but" sense of risk and accident that had proved fatal to Sarah.

There are two such moments. The first is when the servant silently observes Rebecca's lavishly enacted *ḥesed*. On one level, this moment is a full corroboration of God's design, a literal replay of the test-scenario the servant had scripted. Even on this level, however, since Rebecca's words and acts contain anomalies, the immaculate providentiality is subtly shaded, even as it is affirmed.

This is how the Torah describes the servant's reaction: "The man, meanwhile, stood gazing at her, silently wondering whether the Lord had made his errand successful or not" (24:21). The tension of the moment is palpable: the redundant "or not" persuades us of the real anguish of doubt and hope the servant experiences. Silence, tension, waiting for clear knowledge — all the elements are condensed into the unusual word, *mishta'eh*. Rashi lists the gamut of nuances evoked by the word. It enfolds a poetic range of meanings — not simply "surprised," or "waiting," but "transfixed," "devastated," "confused," "dumb," "charged with thoughts."

Clearly, the condition of the servant is not entirely pleasurable. The connotations of desert and silence evoke the vertigo we discussed earlier. This is a moment of suspense, for much hangs on the event. The servant sees Rebecca as Abraham come again. There is a sense of the prodigious possibly about to happen (Rashi: "close to success"). What is at hazard is the living knowledge of *ḥesed* that Abraham had brought to the world: the moment is one of deepest reflection (even the grammatical form expresses this), spanning the poles of abandonment and recollection.[50]

The other moment of suspense occurs when Rebecca and Isaac first meet: "Isaac went out walking [*la-suaḥ*, to meditate] in the field toward evening and, looking up, he saw camels approaching. Raising her eyes, Rebecca saw Isaac. She alighted from the camel and said to the servant, 'Who is that man walking in the field toward us?' And the servant said, 'That is my master.' So she took her veil and covered herself" (24:63–65). Isaac walks in the shadows of the falling night: his meditation is traditionally understood to be the prayer of the evening. For his thoughts since the Akedah and Sarah's death are locked into questions of transition, change, reversal. Rebecca sees him: how does she see him? This apparently is an important question, since *Midrash Rabbah* deals with it, and Rashi quotes: "She saw him majestic, and she was dumbfounded in his presence."[51]

The word used by the midrash, *toheh*, recalls one dimension of that other moment of confusion, doubt, suspense. What Rebecca sees in Isaac is the vital anguish at the heart of his prayers, a remoteness from the sunlit world of *ḥesed* that she inhabits. Too abruptly, perhaps, she receives the shock of his world. Nothing mediates, nothing explains him to her.

"Who is that man," she asks, fascinated, alienated. What dialogue is possible between two who have met in such a way?[52]

A fatal seepage of doubt and dread affects her, so that she can no longer meet him in the full energy of her difference. She veils herself, obscures her light. He takes her and she irradiates the darkness of his mother's tent. She is, and is not, like his mother; through her, his sense of his mother's existence is healed. But the originating moment of their union is choreographed so that full dialogue will be impossible between them.

From this, deceptions, manipulations, maskings, will result—a strange breeding ground for truth! In this new marriage, a new metabolic balance, complex, containing its own seeds of failure and hope, is set up. The result is a condition in which "the twins struggled within her" (25:22). Enmeshed, entangled in her life, truth evolves from conflict and equivocation.

# TOLEDOT 🍎
## *Sincerity and Authenticity*

### Jacob takes Esau's blessings

The dramatic and moral focus of this Parsha is the scene of deception, in which Jacob "takes"[1] from his blind father, Isaac, the blessing intended for his brother, Esau. Both the Torah text and the midrashic tradition have sharp criticism to level against Jacob for this act. Subtly, the narrative voice indicates the ironies of nemesis within Jacob's personal destiny—for instance, in the parallel deception that he has to suffer on his own wedding night. His father-in-law, Laban, replaces his beloved bride, Rachel, with her "hated" sister, Leah, and then ingenuously defends himself with sardonic references to the rights of the firstborn: "It is not the practice in our place to marry off the younger before the elder [lit., the firstborn]" (Genesis 29:26). Outraged, Jacob confronts Leah in the morning. The midrash puts ironic words into her mouth: "He said to her, 'Deceiver, daughter of a deceiver! Did I not call you Rachel and you answered me?!' She replied, 'Is there a master without students? Did your father not call you Esau and you answered him?!' "[2]

Similarly, on the larger scale of national history, the midrash registers the bitter cries of Esau realizing he is supplanted ("he burst into wild and bitter sobbing" [27:34]); these echo in the cries of the Jewish people on the verge of destruction in the time of Haman: "Mordecai went through the city, crying out loudly and bitterly" (Esther 4:1): "Anyone who says that God overlooks misdoing will himself be overlooked. He is merely long-suffering, but ultimately collects His dues. Jacob made Esau break out into a cry just once, and where was he punished for it? In Shushan the capital, as it says, 'And he cried out loudly and bitterly.' "[3]

There is a precise and painful attention paid to Jacob's acts. Nothing is foregone or blurred. The cries of Esau cheated, deprived, resound through

144

history, till they issue in a new ferocious moment of impersonation, when Jacob cries in exact mimicry of the voice of the betrayed Esau.

Morally, then, Jacob's deception is confronted without equivocation or apologetics, both in the narrative itself and in the midrashic tradition. And yet, there is a motif in the midrashic narrative in *Bereshit Rabbah*, which complicates the issue. This is the motif of legal ratification. Three times, the midrash returns to the same imagery, in an attempt to focus the dramatic essence of the "taken" blessing.

The first occasion is at the very moment when Isaac, deeply shaken, realizes he has been deceived: "Isaac was seized with very violent trembling. 'Who was it then,' he demanded, 'that hunted game and brought it to me? And I ate of it all before you came and I blessed him; *indeed, he is blessed*'" (27:33). The strangeness of that coda strikes every reader. Instead of insisting on his unconsciousness at the time of blessing, instead of withdrawing words of blessing extorted from him under false pretenses, Isaac tells his beloved, deprived son, Esau, "indeed, he is blessed."[4] At this point, the midrash comments: "A divorce bill is ratified only when it is signed and sealed. So that you should not say, 'if Jacob had not deceived his father, he would not have acquired the blessings,' the text emphasizes, 'Indeed, he is blessed.'"[5]

After the deception, Isaac himself unexpectedly ratifies the transaction. A dramatic event — the use of certain words called a "blessing" — has transpired. Regardless of moral judgments in the narrative itself or by generations of readers, that dramatic event is here ratified; it is given legal validity in the consciously written "signature" of the agent.

An almost sensuous dimension to this validation is suggested in the commentary of Seforno: "Who brought me venison *to deceive me, and nevertheless* is to be blessed?" Isaac felt, as he blessed Jacob, that the blessing had 'taken' in the one blessed, as is told of R. Hanina, when he used to pray for the sick."

R. Hanina, according to the Babylonian Talmud in Berakhot 34b, could tell if his prayer had been accepted, by its "fluency in his mouth." The capacity to intuit whether a prayer or blessing has "worked" is not, then, a prophetic gift (R. Hanina explicitly denies this) but a sense of *how the words feel in the mouth*. There is a fluency, an organic, almost improvisational flow to the words of a prayer that is "accepted"; a prayer that is rejected (lit., torn apart) lacks this sensed rightness, this flow. On such a reading, Isaac is compelled, in spite of the emotional demands of the

situation, to tell the truth about the transaction that is called "blessing."
His signature ratifies words that, for many reasons, he may have wanted
to gainsay.

The second occasion when the midrash uses the imagery of legal
ratification is when Isaac, in full consciousness, calls Jacob and gives him
the "blessing of Abraham": "And Isaac called Jacob and he blessed
him. . . . 'May Almighty God bless you, make you fertile and numerous,
so that you become an assembly of peoples. May He grant the blessing of
Abraham to you and your offspring, that you may possess the land where
you are sojourning, which God assigned to Abraham'" (28:1, 3–4).
Isaac's "call" signifies the ritual, legal transmission of blessing.[6] The
midrash identifies the essential heritage of the "blessing of Abraham"
with the misappropriated blessings, "taken" by Jacob:

> The blessings were dubious [*mefukpak*, weak, contested, loose, unrav-
> eled] in Jacob's hand. Where were they confirmed [*nitoshashu*, given
> solid foundations] in his hand? Here—"And Isaac called Jacob. . . ."
> Said R. Eliezer, "A divorce bill is ratified only when it is signed and
> sealed. So that you should not say, 'if Jacob had not deceived his father,
> he would not have taken the blessings,' the narrative says, 'And Isaac
> called Jacob and he blessed him.'"[7]

The imagery of ratification is reinforced here by the dual perspective
on the blessings—at first, *weakly* held by Jacob, his grasp enervated—but
then given secure foundations, grasped firmly. What is described is,
apparently, a process of *increasing* reality, as the blessings *become* Jacob's,
and as all questioning of that reality is gradually blocked.

The third stage of the process is the point in the narrative when Jacob
returns after twenty years' absence and confronts his brother for the first
time. Clearly apprehensive of the meeting, he lavishes presents on Esau,
who replies, "My brother, let what is yours remain yours" (33:9). Here,
again, the midrash detects a moment of ratification:

> The blessings were tenuously held in Jacob's hand. When were they
> confirmed? Here—Esau said, "My brother, let what is yours remain
> yours." Said R. Eliezer, "A divorce bill is ratified only when it is signed
> and sealed. So you should not say, 'if Jacob had not deceived his father,
> he would not have taken the blessings,' the narrative says, 'My brother,
> let what is yours remain yours.'"[8]

Here, in a dramatic climax to the midrashic treatment of Jacob's gradual consolidation of his hold on the blessings, Esau himself cedes the reality of what is Jacob's. Rashi marks a similar moment of retroactive acknowledgment, when, on the previous night, Jacob meets the mysterious "man," who wrestles with him until dawn. "Then he said, 'Let me go, for dawn is breaking.' But he answered, 'I will not let you go, unless you bless me' " (32:27). Rashi comments: " 'Acknowledge my right to the blessings that my father gave me.' For Esau questioned his right to them."[9]

Rashi is expressing Jacob's need for a new retroactive understanding of the rightful resentments and angers of the past. When Esau "questions" his right to the blessings, the word used, *me'ar'er*, suggests a legally valid attempt to *undermine* Jacob's claim. In Rashi's reading, the "man," who is midrashically identified with "Esau's guardian angel," " 'blessed him there' — against his will, he acknowledged Jacob's right to the blessings" (32:30).

Rashi is indicating a basic tension between Esau's valid grounds of complaint (Rashi even seems to suggest, by his use of the present tense, that this resentment, and the tension it induces, continues to the present day) and his yielding acknowledgment of Jacob's claim to the blessings. Why, indeed, one must ask, does Esau withdraw from this legal contest? In the midrashic reading, what has changed, what is the process of confirmation, by which the blessings become Jacob's, over a period of time, and are attested to even by those most involved in — and most injured by — the original deception?

## "As a trickster": The problem of voice

At this point, we can look more closely at the narrative itself. When Rebecca presses Jacob to go to his father, in place of Esau, it is striking that nowhere, at first formulation of the plan, does she refer to impersonation or deception. Jacob is simply to bring his father delicacies, "such as he loves . . . in order that he may bless you before he dies" (27:10). The plan follows her account of Isaac's instructions to Esau. Jacob protests: "But my brother Esau is a hairy man and I am smooth-skinned. If my father touches me, I shall appear to him as a trickster and bring upon myself a curse, not a blessing" (27:11–12).

The heart of his protest is the strange phrase, "I shall appear to him *as a trickster.*" Jacob is afraid of *looking like a dissembler* to his father's blind eyes. The question of deception is thus introduced by Jacob as a question of his father's perception of him, rather than as an objective description of Jacob's behavior. The result of this perception will be a curse instead of a blessing. Rebecca counters, "Your curse, my son, be upon me!" and repeats her instructions in condensed form. He fulfills these to the letter: "And he went and he took and he brought" (27:14) and she prepares the food, exactly as she has told him she will: "And his mother prepared a dish such as his father loved." But then follows the description of how she takes Esau's clothes and the skins of the slaughtered kids and uses them to cover Jacob's body, to costume him for his role. Only then, after this act of deception, of which there had been no explicit talk beforehand, does she return to her original scenario, which focuses entirely on the preparation and serving of food to Isaac.

Jacob, it appears, shrinks from the plan, not on objective moral grounds but because his father will perceive—or misperceive—him as a certain kind of person, *ke-metateia*, as a trickster. It is possible that, as Nahum Sarna suggests,[10] in the historical period of the narrative, the "successful application of shrewd opportunism was highly respected." Jacob, therefore, expresses revulsion at the idea that his father might see him as a kind of slick careerist, however unobjectionable such a role might be in contemporary terms.

What is most striking is that Jacob is the first person to bring up the question of deception, which enters as a physical part of the preparations only after he has spoken (27:15–16). Inevitably, if his father touches him, he will be unmasked; he, therefore, is not referring to any disguise of his smoothness when he fears that his father will see him "as a trickster." It is some other act of impersonation, inherent in the original scenario, that he fears will affect his father's vision of him.

To be "like a trickster" has, then, a very specific reference—not to the quasi-burlesque stage business of goatskins and costumes, but to the act of *imitating Esau's voice.* Ramban is troubled by the fact that Jacob never refers specifically to the problem of his voice. The voice is, after all, the central expression of identity, and the sensitivity to voices is a measure of human wisdom. Why, then, is Jacob not apprehensive that his father will simply recognize his voice? Ramban suggests two answers. Either the brothers had very similar voices—which would account for the Sages' interpretation of Isaac's statement, "The voice is the voice of Jacob," as referring to the style and tone of Jacob's speech, rather than to the physical timbre of his voice. Or he changed his voice, to imitate his brother, "for there are people who know how to do that."[11]

If we explore the implications of Ramban's second suggestion, we find, for instance, a statement in the Talmud that clearly understands the "trickster" character as a matter of voice imitation: "Anyone who changes his way of speaking is like one who worships idols — because in one place it is written, 'I shall be like a dissembler [*ke-metateia*] in his eyes,' and in another place, 'They [idols] are delusion, a work of mockery [*ta'atuim*]' " (Jeremiah 10:15).[12]

A startling equation is set up between vocal mimicry, the assumption of inauthentic speech patterns, and idolatry. The premise of the Talmud here is that *metateia*, "dissembler," refers specifically to such a change of voice: Jacob fears that his father will perceive him as manipulating his voice to assume Esau's identity. This the Talmud identifies, without elaboration, with idol worship. One must wonder what was the Sages' sensibility to the voice and its relation to personal identity. Jacob recoils from being perceived as a mimic: a curse is perceived by him as an inevitable consequence of offending against such a radical taboo. What are the implications of assuming the voice of another? Possibly, Rebecca's response — costuming Jacob in animal skins — is a way of partially allaying his anxiety: such a crass imitation of Esau's physical identity will distract his father from concentrating on the question of voice.

## "To thine own self be true"

The concept of *metateia* invites further exploration. The word occurs again in II Chronicles 36:16: "They mocked the messengers of God." The meaning of "mockery," rather than "deception," is important, and is clearly supported by the Targums' translation of the word in our context. Targum Jonathan translates *ki-megahekh* — the same word he uses to translate the description of Lot: "he seemed to his sons-in-law as one who jests" (19:14). Implicitly, what Jacob dreads is not being found out, but being perceived by his father as "one who jests," as fundamentally unserious about his relation to his father and, essentially, to himself. To play with an assumed identity — by changing his voice — is to risk his father's *mis*perception, for he feels himself to be merely *like* a mocker.

Appearance and reality produce multiple distorted inter-reflections; in playing the role of his brother, Jacob risks having his own authentic reality misunderstood; in order to buffer him against such a caricature role, Rebecca must dress him in the gross skins of slaughtered animals.

The most serious issues are at stake. The midrash on Proverbs, for example, asserts: "A scholar who neglects the word of Torah is like one who makes mockery [ki-metateia] of the One who spoke and the world was created."[13] To neglect that which is most essential to one's authentic being—in this case, the responsibility of the scholar to his text—is a criminal act of not taking God seriously. The notion of metateia, therefore, is implicated in the question of gravity, of the "heaviness," the seriousness of being. To jest with this, to play with one's voice, is to disrupt one's access to God-in-the-world. It is to be guilty of a kind of frivolity that dissociates one from others, from continuities and larger purposes. "To thine own self be true," pontificates Polonius, ". . . Thou canst not then be false to any man."[14] To abandon one's individuated selfhood, to trifle with the voices of others, is ultimately to undermine not only the differences, but the connections, between people.

Truth to self is not, however, a simple concept. Rashi introduces his commentary to this Parsha, that deals with role-playing and deception, with an extraordinary—and classic—passage. The Torah text begins: "This is the story of Isaac, son of Abraham. Abraham begot Isaac" (25:19). Rashi accounts for the redundancy:

> Since the text has just said, "Isaac, son of Abraham," does it have to add, "Abraham begot Isaac"? But the mockers of the generation were saying, "Sarah conceived from Avimelekh—she lived with Abraham for many years without conceiving." What did God do? He formed Isaac's facial features like Abraham's, so that everyone testified, "Abraham begot Isaac."

Rashi, drawing on the midrash, focuses the basic problems of paternity and identity. In this one extraordinary case, all the ambiguities—legal and empirical—surrounding the question of paternity are swept aside by the "ocular proof." What can never be conclusively proven—before the age of blood and tissue tests, at any rate—becomes a matter of general consensus: God creates an overwhelming likeness between father and son, whom the mockers so plausibly threaten to dissociate from each other. The knowing laughter of the mockers denies the connection between father and son; to accept this ironic view is to yield to the unbearable lightness of being, to allow appearances to dominate perception.[15]

And yet, God Himself acknowledges the force of the ironic view. In one of Rashi's sources,[16] Isaac's weaning feast is planned to prove to "all the nations of the world" that Sarah is indeed the baby's natural mother: she nurses all the aristocratic infants who are brought to the feast, without nurses, in order to test her. In spite of this, the mockers are not silenced: "Immediately, Isaac's facial features *were transformed*, and resembled Abraham's; everyone cried out, 'Abraham begot Isaac!' "

In this source, God's manipulation of Isaac's appearance is delayed from the fetal stage to his weaning day (at age three). The delay focuses the theme of *change*, of manipulation of the material. Isaac startlingly emerges from this midrashic description as the wearer of a life-long mask. His unequivocal resemblance to Abraham is intended to make a point about connection and continuity. But, in order to make that point, Isaac has to wear Abraham's face, even as he evolves an identity that in every empirical aspect is clearly very different from Abraham's. God makes the change "for the sake of peace."[17] He is prepared to equivocate, whether verbally (by misquoting Sarah's disparaging thoughts about her husband's age, "Now that I am withered, am I to have enjoyment—with my husband so old" [18:22]) or in terms of flesh—by changing Isaac's appearance, "for the sake of peace," for the sake of wholeness, to silence the ironic voices of the fragmenters.

> Great is peace, for the Torah speaks fictions for the sake of peace. . . .
> When the nations of the world said, "Can a hundred-year-old man procreate? She must have conceived from Avimelekh or Pharaoh!," there was suspicion *in Abraham's heart* about this. What did God do? He told the angel in charge of the embryo, "Make him exactly like Abraham, so that everyone will testify that he is Abraham's son.". . . Everyone who saw Abraham said, "Obviously, Abraham begot Isaac."[18]

God prepares visual evidence to counteract the plausible, destructive suspicions of Abraham himself. In the world of appearances, the real nature of things is often thoroughly masked; there is testimony and countertestimony; not even Abraham is exempt from the turbulent processes of interpretation.[19] But here, for once, God intervenes to prevent disintegration and skepticism; in order to do this, however, He has Isaac masquerade in a face whose simple affirmations run counter to the differences that are basic to his being. He lives and explores his truth — his *discontinuity* from his father — while wearing a mask that proclaims continuity and resemblance.

## Isaac: The terror of weightlessness

The question of change, of masking for serious — as opposed to frivolous or disintegrative — purposes, arises with full force in the drama of Jacob's deception of his father. Jacob's dread of seeming "like a dissembler," with its emphasis on a frivolous, disparaging attitude to the fixities and harmonious connections of self and world, is apparently realized when Isaac discovers that he has been deceived. He is "seized with a very violent trembling." Isaac's anxiety is explained by Rashi as a terror at precisely this kind of change in the basic stabilities and relationships of the family structure (27:36):

> Why was Isaac afraid? He said, "Perhaps I have sinned in blessing the younger before the older. I have *changed the order of relationship!*" When Esau cried out, "He has supplanted me twice," Isaac asked, "What did he do to you?" and Esau answered, "He took my birthright." Then Isaac said, "That is what I was anxious about — that I had crossed the straight line of law. Now I realize that I did give my blessing to the firstborn!"

For Isaac, the idea of breaching the given structures is anathema. The "order of relationships," the "straight line of law" — the differences and hierarchies inherent in all structures — are sacred for him. Without them, "chaos is come again." Or, as the midrash puts it, "he saw *gehinnom*, the abyss, open beneath him" (Rashi, 27:33). The idea of disguise provokes profound anxiety about the *weightiness* of things. Nietzsche dreaded the "weightlessness of all things"; perhaps the fascination and fear that the masquerade often arouses registers some profound apprehension about the inauthenticity of all experience. To play the "change" game with skin and voice is to equivocate about that central strength that Rousseau calls the "sentiment of being."[20]

And yet, as we have suggested, it is precisely the voice game, in which identity is most radically compromised, that is basic to Jacob's concept of the masquerade. It is because he is to imitate Esau's voice that he may fall foul of Isaac's terror of weightlessness.

Indeed, the midrash offers a startling reading of Isaac's gnomic assessment of the unseen son standing in front of him: "Jacob drew close to his father Isaac, who felt him and said, 'The voice is the voice of Jacob, yet the hands are the hands of Esau'" (27:22). This is commonly understood as expressing the conflicting evidence presented to Isaac's senses by Jacob's voice, on the one hand, and hairy Esau-like goatskins, on the other. The midrash, however, offers this reading: "The voice is of a wise man, while the hands have been skinning corpses."[21] A super-commentary reads: "The voice is one of indirection and cunning—because Jacob slyly changed his voice to that of Esau."[22]

The "voice of Jacob" is read as the voice of cunning and transformation (the name "Jacob" derives from the root *akov*—crooked, indirect), so that the midrashic reference to a "wise man" is similarly understood as meaning the cunning play with voices. "The hands of Esau" is read as referring to *Jacob's hands* that have completed their task ("Esau" is misread *assoo*—"they have completed") of skinning the animals and covering themselves with the skins.

Such a reading implies that Isaac's sense of the unseen son in front of him is *not* conflicted. Isaac hears Jacob imitating Esau's voice and senses him as wearing a burlesque costume of animal pelts, simulating Esau's skin. That is, on this understanding, the full hybrid role-playing quality of Jacob's project is perceived by Isaac. And yet—astonishingly—"he blessed him" (27:3). And later, as he shakes with anxiety as the fitnesses and fixities of proper relationship gape apart, he confirms the blessing— "And indeed he is blessed" (27:33).

## Impersonation and authenticity

Profound paradoxes of impersonation and authenticity are mobilized in this scene. Lionel Trilling begins his classic study, *Sincerity and Authenticity*, with an anachronistic application of the term "sincerity": "We cannot say of the patriarch Abraham that he was a sincere man. That statement must seem only comical. The sincerity of Achilles or Beowulf cannot be discussed: they neither have nor lack sincerity."[23] A concept suitable to a discussion of Werther or of Marianne Dashwood is, Trilling claims, evidently irrelevant to ancient literary texts. However, to focus on the question of Jacob's sincerity would not, I suggest, be at all comical. It might, indeed, go some way to addressing the same issues that loom large in the midrashic tradition.

Jacob is first introduced as a simple, naif man (*ish tam*—25:27); Rashi comments: "Inexpert at hunting; his words reflect his inner meaning. One who is not sharp at deceiving is called *tam*—naif, sincere." This is the man who fears seeming "like a dissembler"; and who then impersonates his brother, not merely by hanging animal pelts over his flesh, but by the subtle mimicries of voice. As we have seen, according to one reading, at least, Isaac in fact recognizes this as Jacob's special talent. And yet the Talmud in Sanhedrin[24] equates this with idolatry, with a fundamental inauthenticity, an unseriousness about the coherence and continuity of identity. In this act of impersonation, indeed, are focused the powerful tensions that Trilling analyzes in his study of sincerity and authenticity.

By deploying texts from Diderot, Hegel, and Shakespeare, Trilling proposes to us the "dismaying thought that sincerity is undeserving of our respect." The disintegrated, alienated, and distraught consciousness—which Hegel calls "base"—represents a higher mode of freedom than that of the "honest soul," the condition of "nobility," which is committed to accord with the external power of society. To detach oneself from imposed conditions, from the roles assigned by birth and social rank, is to lose one's self, but thereby to gain access to a new authenticity of self.

Trilling uses Hegel's paradoxical analysis of the "honest soul" and the "disintegrated consciousness" as the basis for his study of the historical movement from the admiration of "sincerity" to that of "authenticity."[25] I should like to use this model to suggest a reading of Jacob's entry into the world of "authenticity," the world in which he will look "like a dissembler," and leave behind him his primary sense of himself as *ish tam*, a "sincere," "noble" man. Like Hegel's heroic individual, Jacob must become "base," alienated, a player of many roles, before he can redefine, in his life, the meaning of "nobility." A kind of freedom has to become his, before he can indeed to his "own self be true." He must enter the world of seeming, of enactment, of performance, in which authenticity can be defined only retroactively.[26]

The hazards of such a world are palpable. It is much simpler and safer to remain "sincere"; but Jacob risks entry into the world of ambiguities, equivocations, mimicries. This is, properly, Esau's world, of hunting, tracking, "transformations" of the human-animal margins.[27] Here one becomes whatever one has to become, in order to eat and to feed others. An increasingly complex notion of the "self" becomes Jacob's, as he puts on the costumes, the skin of Esau. The bafflement of the narrative is that, even as he imitates Esau's voice, Isaac recognizes the Jacob-voice of mimicry and, spontaneously, blesses him. Isaac—in whom any obliteration of limits and distinctions rouses profound anxiety—is yet moved both to bless the masquerading Jacob and, later, in full possession of the facts, in a new cognition of reason and order, to confirm that blessing.

## *Isaac's blindness: after-image of the Akedah*

In order to set the enigma of Isaac's blessing in context, it will be helpful, at this point, to explore some dimensions of the "family dynamics" that underlie Jacob's performance and Isaac's response to it. The drama of deception begins with a reference to Isaac's blindness: "When Isaac was old and his eyes were too dim to see" (27:1). Even though the text itself clearly explains the cause of Isaac's blindness, Rashi nevertheless offers three comments:

> "His eyes were too dim to see": Because of the smoke of these daughters-in-law, who were offering incense to idols. Another explanation: When Isaac was bound on the altar and his father wanted to slaughter him, at that moment, the heavens opened up and the ministering angels saw and wept, and their tears came down and fell into his eyes; therefore, his eyes dimmed. Another explanation: so that Jacob should take the blessings.

Rashi's first explanation has the virtue of interpreting Isaac's blindness in its context. The previous verse had spoken of Esau's wives, who were "a source of bitterness to Isaac and Rebecca." The anger and frustration caused by their daughters-in-law, with their alien culture, essentially fogs Isaac's perception. In the Tanḥuma narrative, God brings blindness on Isaac, as a defense mechanism against the frustration of what he has to witness in his household—the absence of the *Sheḥina*, the hollowness of a house without God. On this view, a kind of artificial peace cocoons the sightless Isaac.[28]

The third explanation has a utilitarian thrust; there is a sense of "God's plot"—for the narrative to work, for Jacob to get the blessings,

Isaac *must* be blind. As Rashi's first explanation accounted for the continuity of the narrative preceding Isaac's blindness, so this third explanation accounts for the continuity of the following narrative. Moreover,
from the point of view of Jacob's inner development, one might say that
the process called "Jacob's taking of the blessings" would never have been
launched if Isaac had not been blind and therefore obliged to "know"
Jacob by other means. This is the dimension of the deception scene that
I will explore at a later point.

It is, however, Rashi's second explanation that is most fascinating,
precisely because of its anomalousness. Suddenly, out of context, Rashi
refers to the Akedah — the "almost sacrifice" known as the Binding of
Isaac. Rashi cites the midrash: as Isaac lay on the altar, he looked up, the
angels looked down — their glances met, in the form of blinding tears. Is
there some suggestion of *lèse majesté* here? Does Isaac probe the heavens
with a too-scorching gaze? Is there a decree that his "windows be sealed
up,"[29] to maintain the human boundaries of vision?

What remains opaque, however, is the relevance of the Akedah experience to the present narrative. Possibly, Rashi indicates, by including this
midrashic etiology of blindness, that everything in Isaac's life experience,
his entire "sentiment of being," is shaped by the Akedah. Without the
Akedah, Rashi implies, we understand nothing of Isaac. And this remains
true, despite — or perhaps just because of — the fact that nowhere is the
Akedah moment ever referred to explicitly, *after* the event. Midrashic
readings of the post-Akedah narrative, however, are full of intimated
repercussions and connections, linking it through indirect, subterranean
channels to subsequent events.

If we look at Rashi's source, indeed, a detail emerges that significantly
colors our understanding of the blinding effects of the Akedah:[30]

"Isaac's eyes became dimmed *from seeing*" [literal translation of the
word *me-re'ot*]: from the impact of that vision. For when Abraham
bound his son on the altar, the ministering angels cried, as it is written,
"Hark, the Arielites cry aloud" [Isaiah 33:7]. And tears dropped from
their eyes into his eyes, and were imprinted into his eyes. And when he
became old, his eyes became dimmed, from seeing.

The midrash is finely articulated to respond to the internal tension of
the verse: Isaac's blindness spans the gap between old age and the vision
of the boy bound on the altar. What Isaac experienced in his youth,

helplessly shackled, his eyes alone free to pierce the heavens, is "imprinted" forever on those eyes. The Akedah leaves in him an after-image, a kind of inverted residue, which only in old age assumes its original blinding quality.

What the midrash suggests is that Isaac's blindness is a delayed reaction to the Akedah — "when he became old." Survivor of unbearable trauma, he lives an apparently successful life. He is wealthy and respected, the only one of the patriarchs to be called "great" three times in one verse: "And the man became great, and he became greater until he was very great" (26:13). He is an object of jealousy to the Philistines. His men reopen the old blocked wells of his father's digging and then discover more wells. They acquire "breadth" and "fruitfulness" (26:22). Avimelekh, king of the Philistines, is compelled to make a treaty with him. But after a lifetime of achievement, the deep imprint of the Akedah develops and the whole world falls into darkness.

In recent times, we have become painfully familiar with the notion of a response to trauma that is delayed, repressed, and that emerges in psychosomatic dysfunction. One example is the phenomenon of blindness afflicting women survivors of the Cambodian massacres. A considerable time after the Khmer Rouge horrors, and after they had found refuge in the United States, women began to complain of eyesight problems. No organic disorder was diagnosed, and existing diagnostic categories — such as Freud's hysterical blindness, or Post-Traumatic Stress Disorder — did not entirely fit. What the women had seen, years earlier, had made it necessary to suppress vision, to repress emotional response.

Just such a repression is, I suggest, implicit in the notion of Isaac's delayed blindness. He is a man whose "ashes were as though heaped on the altar,"[31] as the midrash so paradoxically describes the after-effects of the Akedah. After such ashes, what fire? Imprinted deep in Isaac's consciousness is the spectacle, wept by angels, of his own death. In old age, the vision explodes in fatal bloom: his awareness of death fills every moment of life. "Look, now, I am old, and I don't know the day of my death. . . . let me bless you, before I die" (27:2, 4). Death haunts his imagination, the *angst* of one who saw nothing else in an eternal moment of his youth. (Isaac in fact lives sixty years after this "death bed" speech!)

The Midrash Tanḥuma offers a powerful reading of the blindness motif:

You find that one who is blinded is *like the dead*. Said R. Shimeon bar Yohai, God does not generally associate His name with the righteous, in their lifetime, but only after death, as it is said, "As to the holy ones who are in the land" [Psalms 16:3] – When are they holy? When they are buried in the ground ["in the land"]. As long as they are alive, God does not associate His name with them – for He does not believe in them that the Evil Impulse will not still mislead them. Only when they are dead, God associates His name with them. And yet, we find that God associates His name with Isaac, *in his lifetime* – as He says to Jacob, "I am the God of Abraham your father, and the *God of Isaac*" (28:13). There are two understandings of this. The Rabbis say, "He saw Isaac's ashes as though they were heaped on the altar." R. Berakhya says, "Since he was blinded, he was, *as it were, dead* – because he was secluded in his house, and the Evil Impulse ceased troubling him."[32]

To be alive in the world, interacting with others, with the full use of one's senses, is to be volatile, conflicted, exposed to radical transformations. God does not attach His name to those who are still in the process of *becoming*; only after they are "buried in the ground," when their life is a *fait accompli*, does God describe them as belonging to Him. Isaac is the one exception to this rule, but he lives, indeed, a kind of death-in-life, passionless. He has abandoned the vital field, where costumes are worn, and appearances make strident claims on belief. "Off, off, you lendings." If this is holiness, it is a chill, bare recognition of "the thing itself": "Is man no more than this? Consider him well. Thou ow'st the worm no silk, the beast no hide, the sheep no wool, the cat no perfume. . . . Thou art the thing itself; unaccommodated man is no more but such a poor, bare, forked animal as thou art."[33]

## Isaac's family: victims of the Akedah?

There are two symbols for Isaac, the survivor – the ashes of the Akedah, and the constricted lifespan of a blind old man. Hauntingly, the *Bereshit Rabbah* midrash links the two images: the survivor of the Akedah ashes may perform a life of vitality, but the *truth* of the Akedah impress ultimately effaces all the gestures and costumings of the world.

Isaac marries and has two children; but nothing in his life is uncolored by the Akedah experience. Rebecca, whose loving alacrity and energy are reminiscent of Abraham's, meets Isaac in the field, and her whole body falls, she veils herself, before the otherworldliness of an Isaac, rapt in prayer.[34]

A fatal seepage of Isaac's ashen being ultimately changes her: the girl who said, unhesitatingly—in response to her family's demoralizing doubts, "Will you go with this man?"—"I will go" (24:58)[35] becomes the woman who questions, time and time again, the value of her life. Her visceral reaction to her daughters-in-law is a kind of revulsion: "I am disgusted with my life because of the Hittite women. If Jacob marries a Hittite woman . . . what good will life be to me?" (27:46). The "Why life?" question—this is the literal form in the original Hebrew—strikes a new note in the biblical register. She is the philosopher who interrogates life, harshly, skeptically—puts life to the question.

Most striking in this vein, however, is her enigmatic cry, as the infants "struggle" in her womb: "If so, why do I exist?" (25:22). The "Why?" question, here, too, is a bare, rudimentary three-word riddle: *Lama zeh anokhi*—"Why—this—I am?" Rashi amplifies the question: "Why did I desire and pray for pregnancy (if the pain is so great)?" Perhaps Rashi is responding to the *anokhi* ("I am"), as the unitary sense of identity, tormented by the conflict of her pregnant state.

Ramban finds Rashi's amplification not sufficiently grounded in the words of the text. Instead, he emphasizes the central importance of the word *anokhi*: "If this is to be my fate, *why am I in the world?* I wish that I were not, that I would die, or never have had being, as Job said, 'Better . . . had I been as though I never was'" (Job 10:19).

Ramban reads Rebecca's question as a radical challenge to being. Rebecca-as-Job strips the "I am" consciousness of all value. Such a nihilistic protest at the pain and conflict that the self must endure is, for Ramban, the first urge to prayer—"And she went to inquire of the Lord" (25:22). But Maharal, responding to Ramban's reading, expresses some dismay at its existential skepticism. He suggests a modulated translation of *anokhi*: "'Why then am I sitting passively [*batel*], why do I not investigate? It is my task to seek out explanations.'—'And she went to seek God.'"

In Maharal's reading, Rebecca confronts the despair of the self, and discovers that the question of meaning has a dynamic force. Her despair is not to circle hollowly upon itself, but to launch searchings and researchings, inquiries for God. For Ramban, *angst* sends Rebecca into an encounter with God. For Maharal, the questioning itself is a mode of quest.

The self—the sense of "I am"—is threatened by lassitude, by vacancy, by the dearth of given meanings. What is called the *batel* experience—leisured, passive, bored, empty, *unoccupied*, in the dual sense—must be counteracted by an energy generated by absence and longing.

In a family radically shaped by the Akedah experience, Esau can perhaps be seen as the real victim of the sacrifice. In midrashic treatments of the narrative, Esau emerges as the "presenting patient" of the family, to borrow a term from family therapy analyses. In him, an underlying pathology is clinically expressed. For example, in the cooking scene, when he sells his birthright to Jacob for a lentil stew, he disparages the rights and privileges he is relinquishing: "I am going to die, so of what use is my birthright to me?" (25:32). In the Hebrew original, the "Why?" question appears again (lit., Why to me the birthright?). When he is faced with the brute fact of mortality—"I am going to die"—Esau questions the structures, the very language of his culture. This is, in fact, how *Bereshit Rabbah* reads Esau's question—not merely as a figurative expostulation—"I am starved to death; of what use is my birthright?":

> Esau asked Jacob: "What is the stew for?" Jacob answered: "That old man [Abraham] has died." Esau said: "That old man has been struck down by fate!?" He answered: "Yes." Esau then said, "If so, there is no reward, and no resurrection of the dead." The Holy Spirit cried out, " 'Do not cry for the dead and do not lament for them'—this refers to Abraham; 'Weep rather for him who is going' [Jeremiah 22:10]—this refers to Esau."[36]

Abraham, who has died, is not pitiable, in the view of the midrash. Esau, who is "going" toward death, whose mortality obsesses him, is the true object of compassion. The midrash isolates the word, *holekh*—"going"—in Esau's cry: his life is filled with the imminence of death, and all cultural forms and privileges lose substance under that shadow. For Esau, Abraham has been the test case for meaning in absurdity. If he too is subject to the fatality of death, then Esau abandons all belief in an ultimately intelligible reality. In the narrative of the midrash, Esau seems to fall instant prey to existential ennui; but this is clearly the clinching moment of a long process. The question underlying the scene is the question of *anokhi*—"I am": If the self—the sense of "I am"—is going to die, then of what use are all the myths of religion and civilization? Early in his career, Esau has abandoned an essential quest, surrendered an essential energy of being. He begs to "gulp down that red stuff, *for I am tired*" (25:30). Literally, the *anokhi*—the sense of "I am"—is weary.[37]

Esau's *ennui* is prefaced by the innocuous phrase, "And Esau came in from the field" (25:29). The field, however, is Esau's essential place, his heraldic emblem. In the midrashic glossary, it becomes a code word for his situation. The first adult description of him is, "A skillful hunter, a man of the field" (25:27); Rashi comments, "'A man of the field': A vacant man [*batel*], hunting wild animals and birds with his bow." It is striking that while Rashi translates the first part of the description, "A skillful hunter," referring to Esau's Machiavellian manipulation of his father, he reserves the literal description of Esau as hunter for his translation of "man of the field." That is, it seems that he unnecessarily *broadens* the range of meaning of "a skillful hunter" to refer to purely metaphorical "hunting," and then he unnecessarily *narrows* the meaning of "man of the field" to refer specifically to hunting.

The key expression in Rashi's comment, however, is *batel*, "vacant." Esau is a hunter, because he is vacant, empty of meanings, cut loose from the intentional energies of life, conscious of his own vitality only in the act of destroying life.[38] Rashi's source reduces the two-part description of Esau to two words: *sudani tzedani*—a leisured, "unoccupied person, roaming the fields, and a hunter of wild animals and birds."[39] That is, Rashi is offering a basic midrashic reading of the whole description of Esau: the inner code of the man has to do with emptiness and destructiveness. Esau emerges as the "field-sports" man, leisured, purposeless, sensing the pulse of his own life only in the shedding of the blood of others.

On this reading, Esau lives out the family angst at its harshest. The "Why?" question ("Of what use is my birthright?") on his lips expresses deep skepticism about the "uses" of life. ("How weary, stale, flat, and unprofitable / Seem to me all the uses of this world!"[40] It represents the pure philosophical stance, suggested in Plato's "Philosophy is the practice of death." If existence is dominated by the necessity of death, "not even the gods fight against Necessity."[41] Lev Shestov, the Russian-Jewish early existentialist, defines the beginning of philosophy as "only where the kingdom of strict Necessity reveals itself. Our thought, in the final analysis, is only the search for this strict Necessity."[42] That is, Greek thought, filtering down to Western civilization as a whole, is essentially submissive to Necessity. This is the thought of Esau, progenitor and prototype of Greece and Rome, in rabbinic typology.

Shestov characterizes Greek thought as radically "reflective," rather than passionate, its face turned toward death rather than life:

> Philosophy has always meant and wished to mean reflection, *Besinnung*, looking backward. Now it is necessary to add that "looking backward," by its very nature, excludes the possibility and even the thought of struggle. "Looking backward" paralyzes man. He who turns around, who looks backward, must see what already exists, that is to say, the head of Medusa; and he who sees Medusa's head is inevitably petrified.[43]

Esau represents that petrified being of whom Shestov writes. Stony acquiescence is his response to the heaviness, the fatality of existence, to the question that haunts Beethoven's last quartet, "Muss es sein?" (Must it be?). "If so, there is no reward and no resurrection of the dead." He is unable to hope, to struggle, to will, to dream. In him, death has full dominion.

The relation between Isaac and Esau always seems enigmatic. "And Isaac loved Esau, because game was in his mouth, while Rebecca loved Jacob" (25:28). Even if we understand the word *ahav*, love, as merely relative (as, for instance, in the JPS translation, "Isaac *favored* Esau"), the family system clearly falls into two groups. And the nature of Isaac's love for Esau is strangely addressed in that explanatory clause: "because game was in his mouth." A taste for game is the basis of Isaac's preference for the hunting son, the field-sports man.

The Zohar makes the most challenging comment, undercutting our vague assumption that this love is a case of "attraction of opposites," that the blind recluse needs the lusty, outdoors energy of Esau to nourish some inward hunger. On the contrary, the Zohar claims, "Everyone loves his own kind — one who is similar to himself." What Isaac loves in Esau is precisely the hunter, the alienated "disintegrated consciousness" of one for whom all the "noble" privileges and promises of life have dissolved in blood.

Isaac recognizes the fury evoked by animal life: the desire to extirpate what has no proper existence. In his own case, existential helplessness led to withdrawal, to a rigid respect for the priorities and structures of the given world. To Isaac, the spectacle of Esau's despair turned to destructiveness suggests a passion for truth, an intolerance for palliatives, a kind of tortured authenticity. To Isaac, Esau is the analytical mind, obsessed with the unreality of existence. A figure of Byronic melancholy, Esau appeals to his father's heart: this is a son who deeply needs blessing from a father who, despite all external differences, intuits the rhythm of his despair.

The paradoxical similarity of Isaac and Esau is indicated by the notation of "the field." Isaac is first encountered by Rebecca, "meditating in the field toward evening" (24:63). "Meditating" translates the word *la-suaḥ*, for which many translations are offered, ranging from "walking among the shrubbery" (*siḥim*) to "praying"[44] The more mystical understandings of the phrase include in their palette the melancholy coloring of "toward evening," and the midrashic decodings of "the field" as referring to Mount Moriah, the site of the Akedah.

What emerges from such a subtle layering of meaning is a portrait of Isaac imprinted with the deep death-knowledge of his Binding, face turned toward the dying of the light, darkly narrating his story to God. The field in which Isaac walks he transforms into the language of prayer. The field of Esau's darkness, however, is a field of silence; the tension of ambush, the release of bloodshed provides the illusion of a vital heartbeat in emptiness. Isaac's love for Esau is a knowing love that seeks to bless — that is, to animate and populate — that emptiness.

The motif of "walking in fields" that unites Isaac and Esau evokes a passage in Walter Benjamin's essay, "On Some Motifs in Baudelaire." He describes the figure of the *flâneur*, a composite figure drawn from Poe and Baudelaire.[45] In his discussion, the situation of the walker in the field is translated into an account of the *flâneur*, lonely among city crowds. Central to both characters is the *batel* condition. Benjamin describes moving through traffic, or scanning the advertising pages of a newspaper in terms that may lead us to read Rashi's "man of the field" definition with new eyes:

> Moving through this traffic involves the individual in a series of shocks and collisions. At dangerous intersections, nervous impulses flow through him in rapid succession, like the energy from a battery. Baudelaire speaks of a man who plunges into the crowd as into a reservoir of electric energy. Circumscribing the experience of the shock, he calls this man "a *kaleidoscope* equipped with consciousness."

The *flâneur* is compared to the unskilled worker, who is drilled into performing simplified operations. Pedestrians "act as if they had adapted themselves to the machines and could express themselves only automatically. Their behavior is a reaction to shocks."[47]

> The drudgery of the laborer is, in its own way, a counterpart to the drudgery of the gambler. The work of both is equally devoid of substance.[48]

The jolting, disconnected trail of the hunter, the sense of drudgery ("for I am weary"), the work that is "devoid of substance" (*batel*, vacant, void) — most of all, perhaps, the sense of dismissal of the "weighty past" ("Of what use to me is the birthright? . . . And Esau despised the birthright"): all this gives us an Esau who is a prototype victim of the "thousand natural shocks that flesh is heir to."[49] Isaac has retired from the fray: "The Evil Impulse has ceased to trouble him."[50] But Esau staggers from murder to murder (indeed, according to the midrash, from woman to woman),[51] in a search for the consummation that will include and redeem all traumas: "a consummation devoutly to be wished," says Hamlet. "To die — to sleep."[52]

## Jacob and Esau: contrast and symmetry

If we compare the twin brothers, Esau is most clearly visible using his limbs ("the hands are the hands of Esau"; the hunter's legs carry him from shock to shock) to enact his despair in the world; while Jacob is one who "sits in tents," essentially limbless, all mind, as, in the traditional midrashic reading, he studies sacred lore. There is a stark contrast between the two, which the text seems to emphasize at every turn, and which the Sages extend to the future history and cultural profiles of the two peoples who are to descend from them.

But the contrast and symmetry shift considerably, if we look more closely at the text, and at midrashic versions of the narrative. Jacob passively "sits in tents," while his brother vigorously ranges the great outdoors. But what tents are these? The Zohar says enigmatically, "The tents of Abraham and Isaac." There is a suggestion that Jacob is born without a strong *personal* bent of his own. The early years of his maturity are spent in the created worlds of his father and grandfather; he is engaged in a search for God *by indirection*.

There is a smoothness about Jacob, which is not merely a matter of skin texture. "My brother Esau is a hairy man and I am smooth-skinned," says Jacob to his mother (27:11). And the midrash speaks of Esau's disheveled curls in which the stubble from the threshing floor gets tangled.[53] Jacob's smoothness ("baldness") is easily cleaned off by a gesture of the hand over the head. So, teaches the midrash, Jacob may be soiled by sin throughout the year but—unlike Esau—he can find atonement (lit., wiping over) on the Day of Atonement: sins find no essential complexity in him in which to take root. The midrash ends with a comment on its own unparalleled importance: other midrashic parables may be forced or tendentious, but this one expresses an essential truth.

Jacob's smoothness refers to the same quality in him as is suggested by the epithet, "a simple man." He is easily wiped clean: sin finds no deep roosting place in him. The comparison with Esau seems clearly in Jacob's favor: Esau is left with an unruly shag full of stubble.

And yet we cannot but notice that in the first description of the newborn twins, there is no mention made of any such contrast. Esau is vividly, even grotesquely, described: "The first one emerged red, like a hairy mantle all over" (25:25). But of Jacob we know only that "he emerged, holding on to the heel of Esau" (25:26). In other words, we might say that Jacob, unlike Esau, has no strong self-image from birth. He is contrasted with his twin only in not being clearly characterized at all. There is a neutral quality to him; he defines himself as Esau's shadow; he follows in his wake, his perspective filled with his brother's legs.

According to Rashi, Jacob is named by his father alone—"And *he* called him Jacob"—for an opaque, indirect, "follower" quality of his personality; while Esau is named *by all*—"And *they* called him Esau"—for his obvious precocious maturity, as signified by his "mantle" of hair. Nothing is said, in fact, of Jacob's smoothness. Indeed, the midrash strangely emphasizes that the twins are *identical*, in their early years.[54] "'When the boys grew up, Esau became a skillful hunter, a man of the field, while Jacob was a simple man who sat in tents' [25:27]. For thirteen years, they would both go to school and come home from school. At thirteen, one went to the study house, and the other to pagan temples." As Rashi puts it, in their childhood, they were indistinguishable. Only after they achieved maturity did their ways part.

## Jacob constructs his identity

The midrash draws attention to the ways in which Jacob, in particular, chooses to construct his identity. (There is a subtle asymmetry in the verse: "And Esau was a skillful hunter . . . and Jacob a simple man." The lack of a verb in the description of Jacob suggests a less-than-satisfactory identity, hastily assumed for the purposes of differentiation.) If Esau has chosen to be a hunter, a complex "disintegrated spirit," a Byronic sufferer of angst, then Jacob must assume the opposite role, the passive, limbless scholar, absorbed in the worlds of his father and his grandfather. If Esau is a hairy man, then he must be a smooth, sincere man, capable of periodic at-one-ment, unmenaced by ambiguity.

It is only from Jacob's own description that we see an absolute contrast between the twins. To himself, he seems painfully smooth, bald, immature. It is, indeed, not merely as an obvious physical difference between the twins, but as a symbolic measure of perceived difference that Jacob fixes on the hairy-smooth contrast to explain his resistance to his mother's plan. As we have noticed, Rebecca does not, in fact, speak of impersonation. She simply suggests that, whereas Isaac has asked Esau to bring him food, as a preamble to blessing, Jacob should provide food for his father, "as he loves it," and as a preamble to blessing (27:6–10). Rebecca's speech reads almost as a challenge to Jacob to arrive first in Isaac's room, and to earn blessing by the deliciousness of his food.[55] It is Jacob who responds by describing the clearest contrast between himself and Esau. "Esau is hairy," he says, "and I am smooth" (27:11).

One dimension of the contrast is registered in the passage we have quoted from *Bereshit Rabbah*: to be hairy is to become entangled with the world, to find it impossible simply to wipe oneself free of sin. In a real sense, the symbolism of hair suggests impurity, complication, a lodging place for *dirt*, as Mary Douglas defines it: matter out of place.[56] Impurity and danger inhere in this modality. Simple, clear categories — the me and the not-me — are confused. Hair represents the anomalous; it obscures the pattern. As soon as he reaches the age of self-construction, Jacob defines himself as a "simple man" — a word that evokes purity and order.

To be smooth, however, also suggests the lack of a densely evolved sense of self. Surely there is a certain fascination for Jacob in the imagining of his brother. A "hairy man" is a sexually mature man.[57] The midrash even puns on *sa'ir* ("hairy"/"goat-demon") to suggest a demonic, vitalistic quality to the imagined Esau: "a demonic man, as in 'goat-demons shall dance there'" (Isaiah 13:21).[58]

## The will to be tragic:
## Esau's "Dionysiac" temperament

In the course of a famous discussion of the "Dionysian" impulse, as the key to understanding the Greeks, Nietzsche asks rhetorically, "What does that synthesis of god and goat in the Satyr point to? What self-experience, what 'stress,' made the Greek think of the Dionysian reveller and primitive man as a satyr?"[59] The satyr, the goat-god, comes to symbolize the dual desire, the longing for beauty and the longing "*for the ugly*, the good, resolute desire of the Old Hellene for pessimism, for tragic myth, for the picture of all that is terrible, evil, enigmatic, destructive, fatal at the basis of existence." In Nietzsche's view, the Dionysian madness represents a radical paradox: "What if the Greeks, in the very wealth of their youth had the will *to be* tragic and were pessimists? What if it was madness itself . . . which brought the *greatest* blessings upon Hellas?"

Nietzsche's understanding of the Greek tragic temperament may illuminate our reading of Esau, as he is seen by his father and his brother. His pessimism, his fascination with blood and death, can be interpreted as arising "from *joy*, from strength, from exuberant health, from overfullness." Perhaps Jacob sees his twin, ruddy and vigorous as well as possessed with a "longing for the ugly," as a Dionysian type, a complex satyr, dancing a vital, enigmatic dance?

The symbolism of hair, indeed, as it is treated in biblical and midrashic sources, suggests many of the "Dionysian" characteristics. In sheer legal terms, for instance, the appearance of two hairs signifies the onset of sexual maturity.[60] Hair expresses the ambiguous boundary of self and world; in the idiom, for example, "Not a hair of his head shall fall to the ground" (I Samuel 14:45), hair is both part and not part of the body; while the expression, "a wind passed by me, making hair of my flesh bristle" (Job 4:15), suggests that hair is, after all, connected with the nervous system and expresses the inwardness of fear and excitement. Like erectile tissue, hair can stand on end, drawing public attention to private emotion. In an extraordinary midrash, Judah is described as having two hairs that grow out of his chest; when he is angry, they bristle and pierce his clothes.[61] Hair is the interstice between *psyche* and *soma*: Judah's hair expresses his energy, the force of his anger, its penetrating effect on the world.

The Jerusalem Talmud[62] describes Samson's hair as clanging like a bell, with the force of the Holy Spirit moving within him. A voice speaks to Job "from out of the storm [ha-sa'ara]"; this becomes, in provocative midrashic misreading, "from every separate hair [se'ar] of Job's head, God would speak to him." That is, hair represents an ambiguous inner-outer status, originating from within the body, but vehicle of energies that have their source in God. Like lawns of grass, in Calvino's essay, "The Infinite Lawn,"[63] hair exemplifies the particular imbued with the whole, the many, complex resources of vitality of all kinds.

Midrash Tanḥuma gives us yet another provocative case of hair symbolism:

> The story is told of a priest who would inspect skin-infections to diagnose leprosy. He became impoverished and planned to travel abroad to improve his financial situation. He called his wife and told her, "People are accustomed to come to me for diagnosis, so it is hard for me to leave them. Come, I'll teach you how to diagnose. If you see that the root [the "fountain"] of the hair-follicle is dried up, then you will know he is ill — for in every single hair, God has created its own 'fountain' [source of sebumen] to drink from." His wife replied, "If God has provided a source of nourishment for every hair, what about you, who are a human being, with many hairs, and your children depend on you for their livelihood — how much more will God provide resources for you!" So she prevented him from leaving the Holy Land.[64]

With an almost surrealistic focus on the individual hair as vehicle for inward resources that are the gift of God, the midrash presents us with an image of the human being, whose many hairs bristle with a vitality born of a complex hidden nature endowed by God. Such a "hairy" human being becomes a type for the Dionysian energy of which Nietzsche speaks: at one pole, animalic, demonic, the "goat-god," the satyr, and at the other the originator of the tragic vision, longing for beauty and for ugliness, for pleasure and for pain. For such a creature, self-knowledge must, of necessity, be a complex process; self-deception must be a constant hazard.[65] It is not surprising that Jacob opts for smoothness, for simplicity, for sincerity.

# Jacob: from sincerity to authenticity

And yet there comes a time when Jacob clothes his smoothness with goat's hair and goes to his father to be blessed. "And he smelt the fragrance of his clothes and he blessed him" (27:27). "Nothing," comments Rashi, "smells worse than goat's hair; but the fragrance of Eden came in with him." ("'See, the fragrance of my son is like the fragrance of the field that God has blessed.'") Jacob fears that his father will regard him as a dissembler, as one who takes serious matters of his own authenticity lightly, as one who plays with Esau's voice. In answer to his fear, Rebecca dresses him in goatskins, foul-smelling—and Paradisal odors suddenly emanate from him! What notion of selfhood and authenticity can we glean from this midrash?[66]

When Jacob confronts his father in grotesque mimicry of his brother, he significantly reappropriates dimensions of the self that he had "given" to Esau. At the very beginning of their existence, "the boys struggled [*va-yitrotzetzu*] within her" (25:22). The verb seems to derive from the root *rootz*, meaning "to run." Rashi quotes two midrashic readings. On the first reading, each twin tries to escape the womb, when Rebecca passes the place of his own specific predilection—the house of study, or the pagan temple. On the second reading, they struggle (clash) with each other about the inheritance of the two worlds (the temporal world and the spiritual world-to-come).

On the first reading, the "running" of the twins is in opposite directions, driven by congenitally contrary passions. On the second, however, the running expresses conflict: what, asks Maharal, is the basis of the conflict, if each twin desires a different world for himself? Maharal answers by denying the premise: both twins, he asserts, want "the wholeness of existence," physical and spiritual—that is the basis of the conflict. No facile role splitting will resolve this primal struggle. Difference and identity both mark the fetal twins. The intense energy, the global desire of both Jacob and Esau, are equivalent in the womb. This, indeed, is how Ibn Ezra reads the verb: "They raced like streaks of lightning" (Nahum 2:5).

Jacob, like Esau, desires a full-bodied, as well as full-spirited, existence. He has legs for the race and arms for the struggle. But the flashing energy of Ibn Ezra's image is somehow transformed into the image of a Jacob "who sits in tents," who leads a sedentary existence, submerged in the life of study. Perhaps the family memory of Isaac, bound hand and foot, haunts Jacob's life, hangs heavy on his limbs. The very reference to "tents" recalls the powerful description of the studious life, offered by the Sages themselves: "This is the law—a man who dies in the tent . . ." begins the passage in Numbers 19:14 that gives the laws of corpse defilement, which the Talmud deliberately misreads. A man who is truly committed to Torah study, to the "tents of Torah," has to "die" to the pleasures of the world.[67]

In the equally evocative idiom quoted by Rashi (28:9), Jacob will spend fourteen years "buried" in the study house of Shem and Ever. The language of Torah becomes Jacob's trademark; the voice of her son learning that language in all its subtlety is, according to one midrash, what Rebecca most loves.[68] But there is a sacrifice, a "death" involved in the submergence in such a high culture. This is akin to the loss described by Trilling, in *Sincerity and Authenticity*, of "that 'strength' which, Schiller tells us, 'man brought with him from the state of savagery' and which he finds it so difficult to preserve in a highly developed culture. The sentiment of being is the sentiment of being strong." The concern is with "such energy as contrives that the centre shall hold, that the circumference of the self keep unbroken, that the person be an integer, impenetrable, perdurable, and autonomous in being if not in action."[69]

This primitive strength that is diminished by a high culture is the issue on which Jacob's action in "taking" Esau's blessing pivots. Having "given," in his perception and fascinated passivity, the virtues of force, resourcefulness on every level, and complex authenticity to Esau, Jacob is suddenly challenged by his mother to take them back, to recognize the unsuspected ambiguities of his own nature. To bring his father food, "such as he loves," is to commit himself to the totality of his father's "knowing" of him, a knowing that goes beyond words.

Until now, Esau has presented himself to his father in such a way that Isaac has been "nurtured" by him, has received delight from him. That is, Esau has functioned in the world of seeming: he is a good actor, whose force of being arouses passion, the "sentiment of being" in Isaac. Till now, Jacob might have said, like Hamlet, "Seems? . . . I know not seems!"[70] He has engaged in no "action"—in the sense that method actors use the word, to denote the full intent of a particular scene, the desire and struggle that underlie the mere spoken word. Essentially, he has not engaged with either his father or his brother at all.

Now, his mother urges him into his father's room, to replace Esau in the act of "feeding" Isaac. At stake is the question of sincerity and authenticity: Jacob's chosen identity as *tam*, as a simple, sincere man, as against a more complex, "disintegrated" concept of the self. If Jacob is to feed his father, he must engage in an action, expose himself utterly. The risks are radical; Jacob condenses them into that one word, *ki-metateia* — to seem like a frivolous player with identities, sporting with voices. And the measure of the success of his confrontation is the strange aside spoken by Isaac, as the full truth is borne in upon him: "Who was it then that hunted game and brought it me? —*And I ate it all* before you came, and I blessed him. And indeed he is blessed" (27:33). Isaac tasted in Jacob's food worlds of delight that led inevitably to blessing.[71]

In an extraordinary manner, the moment when Jacob confronts his blind father, wearing Esau's skin (goatlike, demonic) and even imitating Esau's voice, becomes a moment when the senses tell spiritual truth. Isaac, who cannot see, and therefore cannot recognize Jacob, uses all his other senses to know him. What happens in the "action" of the encounter is that Jacob as distinct identity, "simple man," withdrawn from the field, disappears from the scene. Up to this point, he has been referred to by name, redundantly; now, Jacob becomes a pronoun. From the moment that Isaac touches his son, through his tasting of his son's food, and the smelling of his clothes (which are of course Esau's clothes), Jacob's name is not mentioned.

## Jacob becomes Esau: the ironic posture

This suggests more than the confusion or doubt in Isaac's mind. It evokes the disappearance of the old self-constructed Jacob, and the birth of a new hybrid being. Isaac perceives this being, through all his functioning senses, and "*does not identify him*, for his hands were hairy, like those of his brother Esau" (27:23). In this condition of totally blurred identity[72] — Isaac not deceived by the hairy hands but recognizing a reality beyond mere naming — Isaac blesses the nameless son, whose voice, touch, taste, smell convince him of his authenticity.

The paradox is, of course, immense. Jacob assumes disguise, he enters the world of seeming, he impersonates Esau, and yet his father, knowing him in a newly intimate mode — suggested by the recurrent word, *va-yigash*, to come close (27:21, 22, 25, 26, 27), composes an image of his nameless son that draws blessing from him. The fact is, moreover, that Jacob speaks an outright lie: in answer to his father's question, "Who are you, my son?" he says, "I am Esau your firstborn" (27:19).

In Hebrew, his self-identification is contained in three words: *anokhi eisav bekhorekha*. Traditional commentaries, clearly embarrassed by what looks like a succinct falsehood, have generally split off the first word *anokhi*—"I am"—from the other two—as though to protect Jacob's integrity from the world of Esau's reality. Rashi, for instance, reads: "*anokhi*—I am the one who is bringing you food; *eisav bekhorekha*—Esau is your firstborn."[73]

There is, however, another possible reading. This rather audaciously takes Jacob's statement as representing a kind of truth, a truth of authenticity, rather than of sincerity. The *Or Ha-ḥaim*, for instance, suggests that since Jacob has bought the birthright from Esau, he has acquired some essential virtue of Esau: "He has *become* Esau, in the birthright dimension."

*Sefat Emet* takes up the idea of impersonation as expressing the desire to expand the range of self. According to a famous rabbinic statement, it is sometimes possible to assume the "part," the "role" of another person in Paradise.[74] Jacob assumes the costume of Esau, takes on what had been Esau's role. This involves Jacob in a new, complex, and dangerous sense of himself. No longer merely simple, "sincere," he now carries all the explosive energies, symbolized by hair, by strong limbs. ("And he went in . . . and he brought . . . the hands are the hands of Esau," which skin animals and assume disguises.) Now, good and evil are intermingled in him; he will be forever involved with the ambiguities of the world of seeming. *Sefat Emet* concludes paradoxically: "Now that he is dressed in Esau's clothes, playing his role, it is written, 'And Isaac smelled his clothes (and blessed him).' And Jacob *spoke truth*, when he said, 'I am Esau your firstborn'—in the sense of inward selfhood and destiny."

Jacob, then, is *really* Esau, as he lays claim to the perceived energies of his twin brother. "Every profound spirit," says Nietzsche, "needs a mask."[75] Emerson, similarly, writes in his journal for 1841, "Many men can write better in a mask than for themselves." Trilling provocatively suggests, "The doctrine of masks proposes the intellectual value of the ironic posture."[76] He points out that the Greek derivation of the word "irony" means "a dissembler"; and defines the concept as "saying one thing when another is meant . . . in order to establish a disconnection between the speaker and interlocutor, or between the speaker and that which is being spoken about, or even between the speaker and himself." Adopting this last phrase, we may say that Jacob achieves, in the conscious irony of "I am Esau your firstborn," the "kind of freedom which we call detachment. If 'existence' is responded to as if it were less than totally in earnest, Spirit is the less bound by it. It can then without sadness accept existence, and without resentment *transact such business with it as is necessary*. . . . The human relation to it need not be fixed and categorical; it can be mercurial and improvisational."[77]

Jacob can, then, be seen as speaking in conscious irony, so as to establish a disconnection, primarily, "between the speaker and himself." This gives him the kind of freedom that is based on detachment, on a salutary sense of *performance* that extends his possibilities of play. He thus enters the world that the Ishbitzer calls the world of *safek*, of doubt, where authenticity can perhaps only be traced retroactively.[78]

"All life," claims Nietzsche, "rests on appearance, art, illusion, optics, necessity of perspective and error."[79] Anathema to such a view, for instance, is Christian dogma, "which is *only* and will be only moral, and which, with its absolute standards, for instance, its truthfulness of God, relegates — that is, disowns, convicts, condemns — art, *all* art, to the realm of *falsehood*."

It is precisely such a perspective, I would suggest, that underlies those midrashic narratives about occasions when God Himself "changes," improvises on the truth, "for the sake of peace."

We looked earlier at the motif of God's changing Isaac's appearance, making him resemble Abraham, in order to convince the mocking world of a hidden truth.[80] This is a case of irony in action: God yields, as it were, to the world of optics, is prepared to "change," to prevaricate with the rigid forms of life, in order to validate improbable continuities. Existence is accepted in the mode of play, which, Schiller says, overcomes "the earnestness of duty and destiny." "Man only plays when he is in the fullest sense of the word a human being, and he is only fully a human being when he plays."[81] This position, Trilling proposes, is not a nihilistic one, but indeed is animated by a real moral earnestness. Within the midrashic tradition, God plays frequently, and with earnest intent; and man is most fully human when he imitates God, in work and at play.

## Crossing the threshold

In a similar vein, Jacob's fear of being misunderstood as *ki-metateia*, as a frivolous player with voices and roles, rises out of the moral earnestness of one who has entered the world of "appearance, art, illusion, optics, necessity of perspective and error." The midrash describes that moment of entry. Rebecca invests Jacob in Esau's clothes and skins, and then accompanies him to the *petaḥ*, the doorway of Isaac's room. There, she says, "Till now, I owed you my support—from now on, your Creator will stand by you."[82] She then puts the food into his hand, and he brings it across the threshold to his father.

The *petaḥ*, the threshold, is that liminal place where status changes, and new realities begin. In halakhic (legal) terms, the *petaḥ* belongs neither to the internal space nor to the external. It is a marginal, ambiguous area with powers and dangers of its own.[83]

The symbolism of the mother accompanying her son to the *petaḥ* evokes the powerful birth parable in the Jerusalem Talmud:[84] " 'The devisings of man's mind are evil from his youth' (Genesis 8:21): Said R. Yudan, ' "From his youth [*mine'urav*]" is spelt defectively. Therefore, read it, 'From the time that he *shakes himself* [punning on the root *na'er*, youth, energetic movement] and comes out into the world.' ' "

Evil begins in man from the moment of birth (and not, as some claim, from the moment of conception): this is the moment of exit, or of entrance into the world, depending on one's perspective. "*At the entrance, sin lies in wait*" [Genesis 4:7], the Talmud[85] quotes God, as he urges Cain to "accept existence and without resentment transact such business with it as is necessary."[86] To be born is to leave the simplicity, the "sincerity," of life-with-mother and to cross a threshold into a world ruled by "appearance, art, illusion, optics, necessity of perspective and error."

Such birth is empowered by the energies of evil; limbs are charged to play the roles of life. Jacob, interestingly, is described in the *Bereshit Rabbah* narrative as crossing that threshold, "compelled, bowed, and weeping."[87] He loses control of his muscles, his heart is as soft as wax, and God has to place two angels on either side of him to support him.[88] He is a novice in the world of the disintegrated consciousness: the passage of birth is palpably traumatic for him.

But by the time he has been touched by his father, he is able to answer Isaac's reiterated question, "Are you really my son Esau?" with the single word, *Ani* — "I am" (27:24). This is the response of authentic being, clear of the strain of role playing. It is this *Ani* of inner freedom that the midrash compares to the *ani* of an angel in a very different narrative. This is the story of the birth of Samson, in the book of Judges. The angel announces the birth of a son (Samson) to Manoah's wife. Rather coarsely, Manoah interrogates the angel when he reappears: "Are you the man who spoke to the woman?" (Judges 12:13). The angel replies, "I am *(Ani).*" And the midrash amplifies: "The angel said, 'You think of me as a man, but I am not a man — I am an angel.' Similarly, when Isaac asked Jacob, 'Are you my son Esau?' he replied, '*Ani* — I am — I am not Esau, but Jacob.' "[89]

The answer, *Ani*, essentially reserves the "sentiment of being" from all public influence. No social or even familial pressure will shape Jacob's sense of his identity. The authentic self disengages from the conceptions of others; the Jacob who can say *Ani* resists any attempt to pluck out the heart of his mystery.

If the entry into Isaac's room represents a kind of moral birth to full personhood, we can identify the climax of the scene as the moment where Isaac recognizes that the hybrid being in his arms carries his own blessedness within himself. Here the paradox of masked authenticity reaches its point of highest tension. Isaac asks his son yet again to "come close," this time not to be touched only, but to be kissed. "And he came close and he kissed him. And he smelled his clothes and he blessed him, saying, 'See, the smell of my son is like the smell of the field that God has blessed. May God give you . . . '(27:27–28). The climax of the encounter is, of course, the blessing; but the blessing emerges seamlessly from the kiss and from Isaac's soliloquy (he is not talking *to* Jacob — "See, the smell of my son") about fragrance and fields already blessed by God.

The word *Re'eh*, with which Isaac begins his speech, means literally, "*Look!* the smell of my son. . . ." The effect of sense-confusion — called by the French symbolist poets *synaesthesia* — yields an impression of mystical transcendence. Limitations of the senses no longer define the knowledge Isaac has of the nameless son in his arms. He sees and smells Jacob's clothes (which include the foul-smelling goatskins), and attains a moment of enlightenment (the JPS translation of *Re'eh* is simply, "*Ah!* the smell of my son"). There is no discontinuity, no jolt, no conscious decision to bless his son. Instead, there is an intimation of a field and of blessedness, the "fragrance of Eden," according to the midrash,[90] so that "his mind becomes calm,"[91] and the words flow spontaneously from a sensuous-spiritual knowledge.

The Zohar[92] carries the notion a step further. The text, "And he said, 'See! the smell of my son' " can be read two ways. The obvious reading is: "Isaac said, 'See! . . .' " But it can also be read: "*God* said, 'See! . . .' " *Meshekh Ḥokhmah* suggests a synthesis: "God spoke out of Isaac's mouth [that is, Isaac was divinely inspired], 'See! There is no longer any need to protect yourself against seeing. You can abandon the defensive strategy of blindness. The one who stands in front of you will irritate no optic nerves.' "

Here, however, the paradox of impersonation and authenticity becomes most challenging. For what Isaac smells in the moment of illumination and inspiration is *not* "Jacob's clothes" but Esau's clothes. That is, it is the deception in its essential expression, the mask, the *irony* with which Jacob now improvises his role, that Isaac apprehends — and apprehends as blessed.

These ambiguous "clothes" become the subject of fascinating midrashic meditation. Goatskins may smell rank, but these clothes are from Eden, the paradisal garb of Adam in the Garden; the "field" is the "field of apples," again a reference to Eden; when Jacob enters Isaac's room, the fragrance of Eden enters with him.[93]

Another line of interpretation suggests that the smell is of the incense which will rise from the Temple on Mount Moriah — a coded reference to Isaac's relation to the "field" ("Isaac called the Temple 'the field' ").[94] A startling connection is suggested between Isaac's Moriah experience (his Binding) and the future offering of incense in that same field, which had become a dream place of despair and mortal *ennui* to his son Esau.

Incense becomes a symbol of what is to redeem that angst of absurdity and weariness that Esau represents. For it is composed of eleven spices — of complex, even esoteric composition — including the spice called galbanum (*ḥelbonah*), which is notoriously foul-smelling. In a classic analogy, the essential rankness in the whole sweet-smelling composition is compared to the essential presence of sinners among the community, particularly on a fast day.[95] The pungency of evil is a necessary ingredient in the social structure of the people, and perhaps also in the personal psychology of the individual. Incense comes to represent the powerful interactions of the Akedah experience, with its dangers and despairs, with life-affirming perspectives. Such perspectives *require* the Akedah dimension, if they are to have force and significance.

## The clothes of impersonation: incense and treachery

As Isaac smells incense from Jacob's clothes, which are the clothes of impersonation, the paradox of the scene reaches its height. As though to emphasize the paradox, the midrash plays on the word for "clothes": " 'And he smelled his clothes' – do not read, 'his clothes [*begadav*],' but 'his traitors [*bogdav*].' "[96] There follows a narrative about the return to the fold of two Jewish traitors, whose passionate repentance becomes a paradigm for the people. Isaac smells the hazards of treachery and evil that are contained within the complexity, the ambiguous perception of the world, that Jacob now bears. No longer simple or sincere, Jacob is forced to be many things, to play many parts. Yet, despite the dangers in this expanded notion of authenticity, Isaac senses a wholeness, a health and strength, that leads him intuitively to blessing.[97]

The Zohar makes the essential comment. Isaac smells the treacherous clothes, the foul goatskins, which the midrashic traditions describe as fragrant with paradise. But how does this alchemy work? How is evil transformed into an essential ingredient of blessing? The text says, "He smelled *his clothes* and he blessed him, saying, 'Look! the smell *of my son* is like the smell of the field that God has blessed.' " And the Zohar comments:[98] Only when Jacob wears the clothes do they smell of Eden – Isaac speaks, significantly, of the "smell *of my son*."

## The sentiment of being

A potential beauty is released from the ambiguities of the "disintegrated consciousness." Jacob searches for his authenticity among all the "lendings" of the theatrical wardrobe. What Isaac senses is the "smell of my son," which transforms the costumes of insincerity.[99] It is ultimately the essence of his son – permeating clothes and skins – that registers as blessing.

The Jacob who leaves his father's presence (lit., his father's face [27:30]) knows himself as he has seen himself mirrored in his father's blind eyes. Like Winnicott's infant, mirrored in his mother's gaze,[100] he is truly born to selfhood, as he "goes out" of the infant stage of growth. To "go out" is to engage in dangerous, necessary separations, to realize one's sentiment of being. In a beautiful passage in *Pirkei d'Rabbi Eliezer*, the midrash describes the inward state of Jacob, at this moment of his life:

> When Jacob left his father's presence, he left adorned like a bridegroom and like a bride in her ornaments. And there descended on him reviving dew from heaven, and his bones were covered with fat; and he, too, became a champion fighter and athlete. That is why it is said: "By the hands of the Mighty One of Jacob—There, the shepherd, the rock of Israel" (Genesis 49:24).[101]

The physical vigor that is described here is first sensed as the "ornaments" of a new status. Jacob is transformed: he "wears" his new, enriched self—even the dew that brings him to new life seems to come down on his skin, from outside himself. (Of course, this is a reference to the words of Isaac's blessing: "May God give you of the dew of heaven and the fat of the earth. . . .")

But ultimately, the description suggests a radiant awareness of new possibilities that springs from deep within the self. The bones that are covered with fat evoke the text in Proverbs 15:30: "Good news puts fat on the bones." The "good news" of the blessings—considered as an existential event, rather than merely as words spoken—gives Jacob a sense of health and power that affects his very bones. In Hebrew, the word for "bones"—*atzamot*—is closely related to the word for "self"—*etzem*. What is nourished—even created anew—in Jacob is the essence of his selfhood. Suddenly, suggests the midrash, Jacob is aware of the complex coherence that holds his bones together. He can articulate his body, with power and control.

What Jacob has gained in his impersonation of Esau is a sense of power in his limbs. He has "mighty hands"; the reference to the shepherd who deals with the stone takes us on to the first stage of Jacob's encounter with the ordeals and promises of Exile. (While Laban's shepherds stand helpless, Jacob effortlessly removes the stone from the well—"like a cork from a jar," says Rashi, "to show you that his strength was great" [29:10].)

"And he, too, became a champion fighter and athlete," continues the midrash. "He, too—like Esau." The impersonation has freed Jacob to a new sense of what Oliver Sacks writes of as "proprioception."[102] Perceptive use of hands and legs is restored. What had been alienated—"given" to Esau—is now reappropriated. With it comes the power to integrate sensations "to the level of perceptions that were related to the world" and to oneself; the power to "to say, 'I perceive, I recognize, I will, I act.' "[103] The experience of "re-realization" often occurs *suddenly*, Sacks notes: "There is, as it were, a critical (functional and ontological) threshold."[104] To be born as a "motor individual," a first impulse of desire for wholeness is necessary. The strength of Jacob's hands is re-realized on the day that he skins the animals and lays them over his own skin.

Sacks poignantly describes the return to proprioception:

> Everything was transformed, absolutely, in that moment, in that leap from a cold fluttering and flashing to the warm stream of music, the stream of action, the stream of life. . . . [It] was essentially and indivisibly a stream, an organic whole, without any separations or seams, but articulate, articulated, articulate with life. An entirely new principle came into effect—what Leibniz called a "new *active* principle of unity"—a unity only present in, and given by, action.[105]

The wholeness of the sentiment of being, of full, integrated articulation, is suggested by the simple description of Jacob walking out into the world: "And Jacob went out of Beer Sheva. . . . And Jacob lifted up his legs and he went . . ." (29:1). Rashi's comment illuminates our theme: "His heart lifted up his legs and he became light on his feet." The active principle of unity harmonizing powerful complexities is the hope that Jacob himself first articulated, when he found it in himself to say, *Ani*—"I am."

The "demon dance" of Esau, which had fascinated Jacob, is now subsumed into the powerful, controlled movements of a different dance. In this way, Isaac's limbs, bound and helpless, are finally released. Jacob leaves his father and, whole in skin and bone, arms and legs articulated by the inner music of the *Ani*—"I am"—he is quickened into life. "Every disease is a musical problem, every cure a musical solution" (Novalis).

The blessings that, according to the midrash,[106] had been tenuously his, are to become consolidated, appropriated by the energy of his own being. This is a process of affirming and confirming, "in his hand." It begins when that hand clothes itself in insincere skins, out of a desire to emerge into greater wholeness.

# VA-YETZE 🍃
## *Dispersions*

*Energy is only Life, and is from the Body. Energy is eternal Delight.*

*— William Blake*

### The imprint of absence

"Jacob left Beer Sheva, and set out for Haran" (28:10).

Jacob embarks on a journey away from his parents — at their bidding — and, in the course of twenty years in Haran, he marries four wives, has twelve children, and amasses a fortune. At this point, he returns with his family and acquisitions to Canaan and, eventually, to his father's house. This is a journey that is pointedly different from his grandfather's originating journey: the *lekh lekha* wandering to the place yet to be shown, the place of promise and destiny. Jacob does not simply "go" (*lekh*); he "leaves" (*va-yetze*). What has been achieved and known for two generations he now relinquishes. And his destination is specific and named: "Jacob had obeyed his father and mother and gone to Padan Aram" (28:7).

Jacob's journey has a clearly delineated beginning and end. But its purpose is ambiguous, as indicated in the subdued irony of that bland clause, "Jacob had obeyed his father and mother." His parents both trigger his journey, but with very different motivations. Rebecca warns him that Esau is out to kill him in revenge for "taking" Isaac's blessing. Using the same compelling admonition as on that previous occasion ("Now, my son, listen to me"), she urges him: "Flee at once [*kum*] to Haran" (27:43). Isaac too summons Jacob and commands him, in a parallel speech: "Up [*kum*] go to Padan Aram" (28:2). In leaving, Jacob obeys both parents. Doubly, perhaps ambivalently motivated, he flees

180

from his vengeful brother and he goes to find a wife abroad, in the Mesopotamian origins of the family. He is moved by forces from both his past and his future.

> Thus we live in a most strange dilemma
> between the distant bow and the too piercing
> arrow.[1]

Neither "fleeing" nor "going," however, is emphasized in the title word, *Va-yetze* ("And he left"). Rashi questions the purpose of this opening clause. He offers a classic midrashic response: "This tells us that the 'leaving' of a righteous person from a place *makes an imprint*. As long as the righteous person is in the city, he is its glory and light and majesty. When he leaves, its glory, light and majesty are evacuated" (28:10).

On one level, this midrash is communicating the perception of absence. There is an imprint, a new awareness of the greatness of a person precisely when his physical presence is removed. Sartre writes in his childhood reminiscences, *Words*, of the occasion on which he first realized the meaning of significant absence. His grandfather

> made a pronouncement which pierced me to the heart: "Someone's lacking here: it's Simonnot.". . . In the centre of a tumultuous circle, I saw a pillar: Monsieur Simonnot himself, absent in flesh and blood. This astonishing absence transfigured him. A great many people connected with the Institute were absent. . . . Only Monsieur Simonnot was *lacking*. It had been enough to mention his name: emptiness had sunk into that crowded hall like a knife. I was amazed that a man had his place fixed. His place: a void hollowed out by universal expectation, an invisible womb from which it seemed one could suddenly be reborn.[2]

The imprint, the full awareness of the indispensable person, is known only after he has removed himself from his place.

Rashi speaks of a void left behind Jacob as he begins his journey. But perhaps the void is *in* Jacob, as well. As he "goes out" of his place, a vacuum separates him from his origins, a kind of necessary detachment.[3] If Jacob is to find a wife, he must separate himself from his parents, body, mind, and heart. "Sometimes," declares the midrash,[4] "one goes toward one's mate, and sometimes one's mate comes toward oneself." In this case, and by contrast with his father, who waited at home for his mate to come toward him, Jacob has to undertake a journey, if he is to marry at all.

This is clearly more than a physical journey: it involves a movement away from the essential place of family and destiny, in order to fulfill not only his father's bidding but perhaps even God's primal statement: "Hence a man leaves his father and mother and clings to his wife, so that they become one flesh" (2:24).

To attach oneself fully to a wife apparently involves an act of abandonment. Only so can Jacob's twenty-year absence be justified. A project has to be completed, which requires a movement away from his parents, a detachment from previous identities and fixities. The purpose of this process is indicated in the enigmatic words—spoken, according to a traditional reading,[5] by God himself—"so that they become one flesh."

Rashi takes this as referring to the child who is the being in whom the separate "flesh" of the parents unites. Rashi here avoids any "romantic" understanding of "one flesh": no full union is possible between a couple other than what is physically created by both of them.

Ramban, on the other hand, rejects Rashi's view as not being specifically *human*: animals, too, produce "one flesh," when they procreate. Here, he claims, is the characteristic of human coupling that marks it off from the matings of the animal world: it is not random and short-lived, but

> since the first human couple were created bone of each other's bone and flesh of each other's flesh, he would cling to her and she would be in his bosom as his own flesh, and he would desire her as his constant companion. As it was with Adam, so with his descendants—the males hold fast to their wives, leave their fathers and mothers, and see their wives as though they were one flesh with them.

In Ramban's reading, to be "one flesh" is the existential ground of marriage: to become one—not simply in a sexual, momentary sense, or in the procreating of children. The couple sets up a new reality, which involves a certain movement away from the givens of heredity and background. The paradigm of Adam and Eve, who of course have no parents to abandon, expresses the totality of the marriage relationship. There is a muted irony in the appeal to such an absolute model, in which betrayals and abandonments, shifts of loyalty, have no place. Future human couples will experience the full problematics of such abandonments, as they attempt to negotiate the paradoxes of separateness and identity.

# The yearning for inner space

In Jacob's case, the issue becomes explicit and central to his whole life. In order to found the "house of Israel," he leaves his parents' house. A unitary innocence is abandoned. He begins his life as a "mild man who stayed in camp" (25:27). In his early years, Jacob is imagined as characteristically inhabiting inner spaces. For fourteen years, narrates the midrash,[6] he is "buried" in the house of Shem and Ever: in the study house, he constructs his internal world of mind and spirit. Then comes a moment of "going out," of birth into the external world; he must leave his parents' home; years later, Laban shrewdly comments, "You were longing for your father's house" (31:30). Through all twenty years of energy and hard work, a profound yearning for the inner space of origin has animated him.

The image of the house is central to Jacob's responses. After his dream at Beth-El, Jacob immediately describes the place as "the house of God" (28:17); and the Talmud notices the importance of the *bayyit*, the house, in his imagination. An important midrashic tradition claims that the site of Jacob's dream is Mount Moriah, the future place of the Holy Temple. This is the center of the universe, the *axis mundi*: all the patriarchs describe it, using the imagery of their deepest experience. Jacob names it Beth-El, the House of God, choosing an image of inwardness and coherence. And God prefers Jacob's image to that of Abraham, who sees a mountain, as the formal image of highest holiness, and to that of Isaac, who sees a field.[7] Therefore, the Talmud affirms, the Holy Temple is called the "house of the God of Jacob" (Isaiah 2:3): it is his lifelong passion for the *bayyit*, for the structure that contains and defines its contents, that will ultimately characterize the religious imagination of his descendants.

But this is no simple nostalgia for home and hearth. In order to achieve the marriage for which he wrenches himself away from parents and promised land, he will have to travel *outwards*, break through many boundaries. Unlike Abraham, his grandfather, he is not traveling, in any simple sense, toward the land of promise. Abraham began his journey in response to God's word. In Jacob's case, God is silent. Without express guidance from God, Jacob has to "go away," to diffuse the focused experience of his father's house, the study house, the land of promise. Unlike Isaac, Jacob will have no servant to bridge the gap between inward and outward, to bring him home a wife.

The very terms in which God blesses him, in the dream at Beth-El, are expansive and even violent in their resonance: "You shall spread out [*u-faratzta*] to the west and to the east, to the north and to the south" (28:14). This, it is true, will lead to blessing for the whole world ("All the families of the earth shall bless themselves by you"). But the word *u-faratzta* ("You shall spread out"), which Rashi reads as an indication of strength, does have explosive, even destructive implications. It often suggests the breaking of structures;[8] indeed the midrash specifically interprets "One who makes a breach [*ha-poretz*] goes before them" (Micah 2:13) as a reference to Jacob, in whose merit God breaks open the Red Sea for his descendants.[9]

This is a strange blessing for one for whom simplicity, harmony, structure, and inwardness are essential elements of his imagination and temperament. God here endows him with a strength that acknowledges no limits, that tears apart and drives through. On a literal level, the blessing is realized in the economic success that Jacob achieves: "*Va-yifrotz ha-ish me'od me'od*" — "So the man burst outwards very, very much, and came to own large flocks, maidservants and menservants, camels and asses" (30:43). The fugitive who crossed the river with a walking stick as his sole property (32:11) has extended his being into the world of possessions. He has "broken through" the opaqueness of things and attached them to himself.

The paradox of Jacob's destiny appears at its clearest, perhaps, in the question of marriage. It is one wife that Isaac and Rebecca have in mind when they send him off to Haran. Jacob's intention in his years of working for Laban is described by the prophet Hosea: "There, Israel served for a wife, for a wife he had to guard sheep" (12:13). The entire focus of Jacob's labor and night vigils is "a wife."[10] Alone among the patriarchs, Jacob is described as loving his wife with a love that transforms time; he loves Rachel at first sight, and he works for seven years, which "seemed to him but a few days because of his love for her" (29:20). There seems to be a natural progression here, from Abraham, with his two wives, to Isaac, who is monogamous but has a servant for matchmaker, and who loves his wife only after marriage, to Jacob, whose love is self-chosen and filled with an energy of intentionality.

When he finishes his seven years of labor for Rachel, he speaks to Laban with a candor that has astonished many readers: "Give me my wife, for my time is fulfilled, that I may cohabit with her" (lit., that I may come into her). In Rachel, Jacob seeks his home, in senses beyond the sexual only. He seeks the unity of which Ramban speaks, when he describes the "one flesh" of human marriage. "A consummation devoutly to be wished," perhaps — but not what God has in store for him. Instead of one wife he gets four. With love comes jealousy and hatred. The plot twists and thickens, in a way that is both blessing and perplexity to Jacob.

## The darkness of exile

In leaving home, Jacob goes out into exile. This is an exile not only from his geographical home but, in some radical sense, from himself. His going out makes an imprint on himself: how is he to know himself in that strange country, that darkness of exile? As he begins his journey, the sun sets (28:11); when he returns, twenty years later, the narrative describes a sunrise (32:32). Both these markers of time, the midrash suggests, are functions of Jacob's personal sense of time.[11] Between these two points, there is darkness, the Dark Night of the Soul.

The most significant event of the Parsha, Jacob's marriage, is diffracted, its single focus shattered, during one dark night. Obviously, a little light on the wedding night would have made Laban's deception impossible. What happens during the night is irreparable, however. All the recognition of the morning cannot alter the reality of what has been transacted between Jacob and Leah. "When morning came, there was Leah!" (29:25). "But during the night, she was not Leah. Rachel had given her the secret code words that Jacob, fearing deception, had given Rachel" (Rashi).

In some real sense, Leah *becomes* Rachel during the night. That is the very nature of the night, of the world of exile. Identities meld into one another, faces and forms swirl in the dark, meeting and splitting off, beckoning and mocking. Where the visual is so untrustworthy, great weight is placed on the voice, on language. And it is primarily in this medium that, according to the midrash, Jacob is most poignantly betrayed.

Describing the preparations for the wedding of Jacob and Rachel, the midrash in *Bereshit Rabbah* emphasizes the oral, voices speaking, hinting at deception, playing with words to reveal or veil the truth:

> All that day, they prepared for the wedding, with song and celebration. Jacob asked, "Why are you doing me so much kindness?" They replied, "You have done us much kindness through your presence

among us," and they praised him and sang, "Ha Lea! Ha Lea!"
[hinting at the deception through the ululations of joy]. In the evening,
they came and put out the lights. He said, "What is this? Why have you
put out the lights, while men and women are mingling with one
another?" They answered, "What do you think— that we are dissolute
as rams?" [Rashi: "We express our modesty by bringing the bride to
the groom *in the dark*."] And all that night, he called her, "Rachel!" and
she answered him. In the morning, "And behold, she was Leah" [lit.].
He said to her, "Deceiver, daughter of a deceiver! Did I not call you
Rachel last night and you answered me?!" She replied, "Is there a
master without students? Did your father not call you Esau and you
answered him?!"[12]

Jacob, it seems, expects voices to tell the truth. He hears neither the
play within the ululation of the wedding guests, nor the tension between
voice and meaning in Leah's responses. The midrash emphasizes the
darkness, not merely as a plot necessity, but as suggesting contrary
symbolisms: to Jacob, darkness means mingling, loss of distinctness and
structure, moral dissoluteness; while Laban's accomplices affirm the
modesty of darkness as a cover for shame.

Jacob's suspicion of darkness is immediately validated: the substitution
of Leah for Rachel is a function of precisely the kind of manipulation of
reality that Jacob most fears. The fully stated clarity of his love is blurred
by the introduction of Leah into his intimate life. From now on, everything will be relative, the echo of the voice of one wife will resound
through the words of the other: "And he came *also* to Rachel, and he loved
*also* Rachel more than Leah" (29:30).

Jacob's love for Rachel is stained by comparison, by *coming after*. His
hate for Leah is palpable to her only after he has married Rachel (29:31–33):
what might have been interpreted as indifference changes color by the
side of the Jacob-Rachel relationship. Eventually, two more wives, Bilhah
and Zilpah, are added to the family. Many children are born: but the
single-minded passion with which Jacob had demanded, "Give me my
wife, that I may come in to her," is diffracted into the jealousies, the side
glances and negotiations of wives vying with each other for favor.

This diffraction, the modality of "more,"[13] increasing complication
and proliferation, breeds in the darkness, in the domain of the oblique,
the illusory, the ambiguous. This is the darkness that begins as Jacob
leaves his parents' house and the land of promise. Instantly, precipitately,

the sun sets. "And Jacob went out . . . and he hit on a place [lit.] and he stayed there overnight, for the sun had set" (28:10–11). The onset of darkness is related in the pluperfect— "And the sun *had* set"— and not as part of the normal order of events ("and the sun set, so Jacob stayed overnight"). Rashi therefore quotes the midrash: "The sun set for him suddenly, earlier than usual, so that he would indeed spend the night there."

## The encounter with darkness: the Evening Prayer

Dramatic, unexpected encounter happens here, in space and in time. "He collided with a certain place"—the word *va-yifga* suggests a dynamic encounter with an object that is traveling toward oneself. The force of the meeting is palpable but mysterious. Traditionally, the "certain place" is identified with Mount Moriah, "where Jacob's father was bound in sacrifice."[14] This is the future place of the Holy Temple, of prayer and sacrifice, of the human attempt to come close to God. It is a place of purity and danger, of great longing and strict distancing. But the *makom*, the "certain place," is equally a metaphoric reference to God Himself, "who is the Place of the universe, while the universe is not His place."[15] Jacob, therefore, makes contact here with God Himself. There is a shock of spiritual recognition, which is hinted at in the classic midrashic translation of *va-yifga*: "he *prayed* . . . Jacob initiated the Evening Prayer. Each of the patriarchs initiated one of the three daily prayers, responding to the three phases of the day: at evening, a person should say, "May it be Thy will, O Lord my God, that You bring me out of darkness into light."[16]

Jacob is, in fact, the first human being to pray in the dark. There is a terror, a "blocking" quality to the night. "He tried to pass through, but the world became entirely like a wall in front of him."[17] Darkness looms suddenly, unexpectedly, barring his passage. But this darkness is deliberately precipitated by God, "so as to speak to Jacob in private—like a king who calls for the lights to be extinguished, as he wishes to speak to his friend in private."

This explanation for the early nightfall—as permitting a certain intimacy of relationship between God and Jacob—is different from the one Rashi refers to: "God made the sun set early, so that he *would spend the night there.*" Rashi's source emphasizes the contrast: God wants darkness, not as cover for intimate dialogue, but simply so that Jacob should *sleep* in that place: "God said, 'This righteous man has come to My lodging house — shall he get off without sleeping the night here?' "[18]

It is Mount Moriah, the place of the Holy Temple, where his father was bound in sacrifice, that Jacob names, with a certain domestic familiarity, the House of God (28:19). It is this local, intimate quality that Jacob brings for the first time to the understanding of God: "Jacob initiated the Evening Prayer." In encountering the darkness, he was the first person to achieve the previously impossible act of *"praying in the dark."* "Obviously," asserts the *Sefat Emet*, "it is not within the power of one who sits in darkness to pray — as in the aphorism, 'One who is bound cannot free himself.' "[19] Leaving all support systems behind him, Jacob moves into the world of the night. Here, nothing is clear, all is shifting, phantasm, illusion. And here, paradoxically, Jacob finds his ground of truth.

This ground of truth is the very meaning of the "certain place" that Jacob suddenly encounters. In the narrative in *Pirkei d'Rabbi Eliezer*, "God met him there. And why is He called The Place? — Because in every place where the righteous are [where the righteous stand: Yalkut], there He is with them, as it is said, 'In every place where I mention My name, I shall come to you and bless you.'" The sacredness of the place, of the encounter with God, is based on the "standing," the stable, vertical being, of the righteous. Wherever the righteous are, in the fullness of selfhood, calling out God's name, they elicit His presence through their prayer.

In this reading, the place of meeting is marked out by human beings: God responds to the intimate but total summons of the righteous. And yet, there is surprise: Jacob prays to God and finds that he has invented a new genre of prayer. For night has fallen. He intended to pray in daylight,[20] in the mode of all human prayer till then, drawing strength from the light of the sun; but God put out the lights and Jacob discovers a new possibility — almost an impossibility, an oxymoron, as the *Sefat Emet* conceives it — called the Evening Prayer.

## The paradox of sleep

There is something essential, if not yet conscious, in Jacob, that prepares him to be the inventor of the Evening Prayer. The place, the prayer,

God's presence — all are contingent on the being of the righteous person. Only the time — the night — falls suddenly in his path, so that he will encounter God in a new way. And here arises the strangeness of God's purpose: the place of night experience is simply called "My lodging house"; all God wants of Jacob is that he *sleep* there, in the most sacred place in the world. "Shall he get off without a night's sleep there?," God asks, as though such sleep is the ultimate religious duty. And so, the Torah tells how "Jacob lay down *in that place*" (28:11). And Rashi sharpens the emphasis: "In that place, he lay down, but during the fourteen years that he lived in the study house of Ever, he never lay down at night, for he was preoccupied with Torah."

For fourteen years, according to this enigmatic midrash, Jacob has turned night into day, relentlessly pursuing the clarities of a scholar's life. The paradox is manifest: the one night of sleep Jacob enjoys is in the holy place. It is followed by twenty more years of sleeplessness, as Jacob himself recounts to Laban: "Scorching heat ravaged me by day and frost by night; and sleep fled from my eyes" (31:40). Alert to sensations, to the differing sensual experience of day and night, Jacob works and watches, from the time he leaves Canaan to the time he returns. In effect, a continuous vigil of sleepless nights over a period of thirty-four years is interrupted by one significant night of sleep, here in the House of God.

Rashi's comment underlines the inner tension of such an experience. When Jacob wakes up, he says, "Surely the Lord is present in this place, and I did not know it" (28:16). Many commentators probe the significance of "I did not know it." Why does Jacob mark out his ignorance of God's presence? How would knowledge have affected his behavior? Seforno, for instance, suggests very plausibly, "If I had known, I would have *prepared myself* for prophecy — and this I did not do." Rashi, however, chooses to follow a midrashic perception: "If I had known, I would not have slept."

On one level, the idea of sleep as a kind of sacrilege in a holy place is quite plausible. The basic text is, "You shall venerate [lit., fear] My sanctuary" (Leviticus 19:30). Belatedly realizing the sacredness of the place, Jacob is filled with penitent awe: "And he was afraid, and he said, How awesome is this place!" The sense of the fearfulness of the place should have prevented him from sleeping here: the sense that Rudolph Otto describes as the numinous awareness of the Other, of that which is incommensurate with humanity. Such a sense finds legal expression in several sources: "One does not behave frivolously in the synagogue . . . and one does not sleep there."[21] "R. Zeira's students asked him, 'How have you deserved such long life?' He answered: 'I did not sleep in the house of study.'"[22] In the Temple, sleep is forbidden; even to *sit* in the courtyard is permitted only to kings of the Davidic dynasty.[23]

The vigilant awe that should be the response to the holy place is dispelled in the posture of sleep. In Rashi's view, Jacob suffers a kind of guilt over this, as he wakes up. But the paradox is clear: if Jacob had not slept, he would not have dreamed of God and angels, would not have received his first message from God, and would not know that this is a holy place. Furthermore, as we have seen, the midrash emphasizes God's wish that Jacob *should sleep here*: God shifts the scenes, alters the lighting, all for the purpose that the "righteous man should sleep there." There is a profound intimation here about the dynamics of sleep, about loss of consciousness and the possible gifts of unconsciousness, about knowing and dreaming.

Sleep is a one-sixtieth part of death, say the Sages.[24] The waking effort is to know, not to miss any detail, to absorb all knowledge into conscious cognitive life. To be awake is the modality of the student who dares not waste a moment. Walter Benjamin writes about Kafka:

> "'But when do you sleep?' asked Karl, looking at the student in surprise. 'Oh, sleep!' said the student. 'I'll get some sleep when I'm finished with my studies.'" This reminds one of the reluctance with which children go to bed; after all, while they are asleep, something might happen that concerns them. . . . While they study, the students are awake, and perhaps their being kept awake is the best thing about these studies. The hunger artist fasts, the doorkeeper is silent, and the students are awake.[25]

The essence of the students' life, the irrational but necessary expression of their artistry, is their wakefulness. One moment's distraction may cause one to miss the single detail that redeems, that construes the whole. Driven by the desire for coherence, how dare one yield to the phantasms of the night? Jacob regrets that during the time he slept, "he was not aware of himself," and therefore was not engaged in the conscious act of developing his relationship with God.[26] So that, despite the inspiration and the promises of his dream, Jacob experiences a paradoxical *fear*, a sense that accompanies any gift of illumination, that one is not large enough, or live enough, to contain this gift.

Though Jacob's sleep, therefore, is the basic condition for God's revelation, it also produces a kind of awe, of estrangement. One extraordinary motif in the midrashic reading of Jacob's dream is the depiction of the angels "going up and down on it [the ladder]" (28:12). In the midrash in *Bereshit Rabbah*, the angels are going up and down *on Jacob*, not on the ladder:

> What can this mean? They are accusing and defending him. They are pushing him, leaping over him, abusing him—as it is said, "You are My servant, Israel in whom I glory" [Isaiah 49:3]—"You are the one whose face is carved out in the worlds above [in the Throne of Glory (*Pirkei d'Rabbi Eliezer*)]." The angels go up and see Jacob's face; they come down and find him sleeping. This is like a king, who would sit in judgment in his council chamber. His people would go up and see him there in his dignity; they would then go down and find him in the corridor, sleeping![27]

Jacob is the focus of the angels' activity. He exists both in the higher worlds—in some ideal, spiritual, and wakeful form—and in the lower worlds—ungracefully, disgracefully asleep. This duality exercises the angels considerably. Their vertical movement—up and down—expresses the contrasts of Jacob's human experience, spiritual and physical. By and large, the angels are antagonistic: they taunt Jacob, who—sleeping—expresses the cloddishness, the static insensibility of the body spread-eagled on the earth, held fast in the grip of gravity.

But God defends Jacob—like a nurse who fans away flies from the sleeping prince.[28] "God was standing beside him" (28:13)—God dispels all the charges of the angels, simply by being there, standing protectively over Jacob, endowing Jacob with the strength of knowing His presence. A certain wordless sense of God redeems the apparent cloddishness of sleep. For it is sleep and the dream-reverie which sleep generates that makes Jacob aware of his sleeping self and the movements of the querulous angels. He dreams their ascent and descent: he himself is the ladder[29] on which, like a music stave, they try to read the mystery of his music. He dreams of them, and of himself, and of God. His sleep, therefore, is far from static:

> Our nocturnal life is an ocean because we float in it. In sleep we never live motionless on the earth. We fall from one sleep into a deeper sleep,

or something in us wants to wake up: then it causes us to rise. We are
forever rising or falling. Sleep has a vertical dynamic. It oscillates
between sleeping more deeply and less deeply.[30]

Jacob oscillates between up and down; but as God stands over him to
protect him, a new synthesis is experienced, a still point in the turning
world. The words describing God's "posture" suggest stability, unconditional attention and support. Rashi comments simply: "to guard him."
There is much fear in Jacob, a live sense of the whole gamut of possibilities in store for him. But God provides reassurance — not by cutting
off the range of oscillation, but by allowing him to experience its full
extent. In a quasi-therapeutic sense, God *contains* Jacob's vertical agitations.

The ladder is placed *toward* the earth; its top reaches *toward* the
heavens (28:12): there are opposing tendencies in man that extend him
endlessly in both directions. But the basis is undoubtedly the earth: the
ladder is *placed*, with full intentionality, in the earthly direction,[31] and
it is from the earth that the angels begin their agitated movement.
The stability that God, standing over Jacob, promises him, is rooted in
the physical image of the sleeper, his body extended horizontally. "The
ground on which you are lying I will assign to you" (28:13). Rashi gives
the image of the sleeping body immense power: "God folded up the
whole land of Israel beneath him, and hinted that it would be easy for his
children to conquer it as the four cubits that are the space of a human
being."[32]

To lie down and sleep can apparently be a mode of large conquest. To
sleep in the place where his father was bound in sacrifice can perhaps be
seen as a gesture of defeat, a refusal to confront the terror of the place.[33]
But God appears to Jacob, as he experiences the full dream-terror, the
oscillation of anger and guilt that the angels project. And Jacob's attention is turned, within the dream, on the power of his own sleeping body,
attached to the earth. All that a man may be is compacted within his
trunk, his head, his limbs. The whole land of Israel is his, if he can fill the
proper shape of humanity, if he can body forth the image of God, on
earth.

## The vertical and the horizontal: God's promise

The paradox of the vertical and the horizontal is here set into dynamic
motion. The ladder on which the angels ascend and descend is an

ironically mechanical prop. For are angels not made to fly? Where are the essential wings? The stepping movement that must, in the dream, connect above with below, the uninspired comparison of the physical and spiritual faces of Jacob, are a travesty of the buoyant impulse without which journeys cannot be undertaken. So, in his dream, Jacob rejects the ladder; and God reveals Himself with a new promise, based on the promises to Abraham and Isaac, but vitally different:

> I am the Lord, the God of your father Abraham and the God of Isaac: the ground on which you are lying I will assign to you and to your offspring. Your descendants shall be as the dust of the earth; you shall spread out to the west and to the east, to the north and to the south. All the families of the earth shall bless themselves by you and your descendants. Remember, I am with you: I will protect you wherever you go and will bring you back to this land. I will not leave you until I have done what I have promised you. (28:13–15)

God promises, firstly, the land—but now, as it relates to Jacob's gravity-held body. His seed "will be as the dust of the earth"—an image as earthly and gross as can be found. But this "low" image produces the "bursting," explosive promise of *u-faratzta* (translated here, "you shall spread out").[34] There is a descent into the concrete reality of the earth, which will produce enormous force and—ultimately—blessing for the whole world. In Abraham's blessing, the perspective had been the empirical wonder of a childless man having many descendants, of a landless alien coming to acquire a whole country clearly dominated by another civilization.[35] Now, however, the wonder of the promise is focused on one body, lying on the ground, and its force for extension and blessing.

The heart of the promise, however, the new note struck in the history of God's speeches to man, is the last verse: "Remember, I am with you: I will protect you wherever you go." Here, on one level, God speaks of ends to be consummated: Jacob will return from exile, all the promises made to his fathers will be fulfilled in him. ("All that I have spoken was *about you*," reads Rashi. "God had never spoken *to* Jacob before this" [28:15]. Jacob is the chosen son, to whom all the promises of destiny referred.) But, essentially, God's message to Jacob goes far beyond this established pattern. "I [*anokhi*] am with you": this suggests an energy that will accompany Jacob constantly through all the vicissitudes of exile. There is a quality of life promised here—a buoyancy Jacob will experience as he walks through the world. By contrast with the angels and their compulsive ascent and descent of the ladder, Jacob will go with an extended *anokhi*, a sense of self that, mysteriously, will *contain* God. This will affect his perspective on the horizontal world, even as he moves outwards upon it.

Rashi places "I am with you" in the context of Jacob's fear. Afraid of both Esau and Laban, of past and future, Jacob is to find essential support in this single phrase. It is not merely that in the end all will be well: it is that a vitality never before known will now be his. Rashi similarly translates God's assurance to Moses, as he responds to God's call with anxious questions ("Who am I that I should go to Pharaoh and free the Israelites from Egypt?"): "I will be with you; that shall be your sign that it was I who sent you" (Exodus 3:11–12). Rashi: "This is in answer to 'Who am I . . . ?' It is My mission, not yours [lit., *It is not yours but mine*] — for I will be with you."

The promise to "be with" Jacob, as with Moses, reveals an electric charge in human life, a new sense of God *involved* in the steps of the journey. Jacob is no longer entirely his own man: he goes on divine business. When, at the end of his life, Jacob goes down to Egypt to rejoin his son, Joseph, God similarly reassures him, "Fear not to go down to Egypt. . . . I Myself will go down with you to Egypt, and I Myself will also bring you back" (46:3–4). The midrash comments: "This teaches that when Israel went down to Egypt, the Divine Presence went down with them; and when they came up from Egypt, it came up with them."[36] The midrash reads the words "with you" as more than a promise of eventual return to the Holy Land, or redemption from Egypt. God will *accompany* Israel in all its troubles, its vicissitudes of Exile and Return, its vertical oscillation of up and down.

Experientially, the promise to "be with you" translates as a mitigation of loneliness for the human being moving downwards and upwards, prey to the contingencies and mutability of destiny. This, in the words of Ramban, is "a great promise: that he will not be in the hands of the angels, but will be the portion of God, and God will be with him always" (28:12). Pulled downwards by the forces of gravity, he will find in himself a strange buoyancy, a dimension that is not entirely his own.

Jacob hears in God's words a concern for the vulnerability of human existence that needs protection at every point — "I shall protect you wherever you go — for I shall not abandon you." In direct response to

God's assurance, Jacob vows next morning: "If God will be with me, if He protects me on this journey that I am making, and gives me bread to eat and clothing to wear . . ." (28:20). God's protective presence is understood by Jacob to refer to the daily needs of existence, food and clothing, the minutiae of human experience.[37] God's care for Jacob is a microscopic matter: out of a sense of God involved in such concerns arises the possibility of wholeness. ("And I shall return in peace" [28:21], Rashi: "In peace [*be-shalom*]" — whole, unfractured by sin).[38]

This concern for wholeness, indeed, is Jacob's central concern, and it is this, essentially, that God addresses in the dream. As Jacob "goes out" into a world of darkness and exile, order and coherence are endangered. To sleep in a holy place is to betray an ideal of heroic stability and consciousness: "If I had known, I should not have slept."

But God wants this sleep. He stage-manages the abrupt darkness so that Jacob will sleep and dream here. At the heart of the dream will be an image of his own sleeping body, with angels querulously attacking the disgrace of his divided self, of the king in his council chamber and asleep in the corridor. And in all the confusion, the oscillation registered by the satirical angels, God will stand firmly by him, proclaiming solidarity, a secret order in the chaos.

Darkness, too, is a way of knowing God. Jacob, who had spent fourteen years turning night into day, studying Torah, preoccupied with order and clarity, suddenly "stood up and turned day into night."[39] In a startling moment, the midrash depicts Jacob as disrupting the God-given order of the world:

> "I realized, too, that whatever God has brought to pass will recur evermore" [Ecclesiastes 3:14]. God's original decree of binary order — upper worlds and lower, sea and dry land, summer and winter, day and night — is changed by the righteous. God decreed that day be eternally day and night eternally night. Jacob stood up and made the day into night, as it is said, "He extinguished the sun" [*kava ha-shemesh*, a play on the words *ki ba ha-shemesh* — "for the sun had set"].

In this version of the narrative, Jacob has the power to cut across the binary system that God has instituted as a model congenial to human thinking. To perceive the world in terms of structural polarities is convenient and, in most cases, productive. But the righteous, men and women of special potency, can shift the boundaries of conventional thinking.

Suddenly, it is Jacob who makes the sun set, who, after years of turning night into day, now turns day into night. In doing this, he opens for himself the treasury of the night: the power of God *with* him in the phantasmagoria of the dark.

The classical, the linear, the predictable and reversible: one might say that these are aspects of Jacob's early life as a "simple man, living in the tents" (my translation) of Torah, in the harmonious interiors of the intellect. What begins with the setting of the sun — and this, according to the midrash we have just cited, on Jacob's own initiative — is a disruption of these classical structures. God speaks of dust, of explosive movements outwards in all four directions, while the angels taunt Jacob with the anomaly of his complex and unpredictable condition. But the turbulence of the night contains an internal structure: "I am with you. . . . I shall not abandon you." There is a structure of dynamic process, which is not known ahead of time. For time bounds ahead of knowledge, as the sun sets and Jacob finds himself praying a new kind of prayer. Chaos, breakdown, disorder contain new possibilities for dynamic structure.

Fusing *the stones: an experiment in integration*

This night of sleep in a holy place, then, becomes an experiment in integration. Before sleeping, with a deliberateness that the midrash takes as experimental, "Jacob took of the stones of that place, he placed them at his head and lay down in that place" (28:11):

> He took twelve stones ["of the stones" suggests more than one stone]. God had decreed that he would raise up twelve tribes. Jacob said: "Abraham did not raise up twelve tribes, nor did Isaac. But if these twelve stones unite with one another, I shall know that I shall raise up twelve tribes." When the stones united with one another ["Jacob woke in the morning and he took *the stone*" (28:18)], he knew that he would raise up twelve tribes.[40]

The fusing of the stones into one is an almost surrealistic image for Jacob's central preoccupation. For stones do not fuse; they stubbornly, stonily preserve their separateness. The enterprise of "raising twelve tribes" seems similarly incapable of producing unity or harmony. This impossible task — of creating structure and meaning in the diverse and the chaotic — is, however, the essentially human act. In a fine, paradoxical sense, the human being—*as* human being—should be able to raise up twelve tribes—simply as the creature formed by the hands of God, and endowed with the unpredictable creativity of God Himself.[41] To raise up twelve tribes is to engage with chaos, with the indeterminate and diverse, and to create harmony, a wholeness out of difference:

> Adam was fit to have twelve tribes rise up from him—as it is written, "This [*zeh*] is the book of the children of Adam" (5:1). *Zeh* has the numerical value of twelve: twelve should be the number of the progeny of Adam. God said, "Adam is the work of My hands—should I not give him twelve tribes?!" But He then said, "When I gave him two sons, one of them rose up and killed his brother. If I had given him twelve sons, how much worse it would have been!" Therefore it is written, "And He said to Adam [*le-Adam*]"—"Not Adam! [*lo-Adam*] I shall not give them to Adam. To whom shall I give them? To Jacob the righteous."[42]

The principle of individuality tends toward anarchy; and the number twelve has mystical implications, a number of maximal diversity. The first siblings introduce murder into the world. God is not willing to expose His human creature to this kind of potentially chaotic creativity, unless He can trust him to read a new order of unity in diversity. Jacob himself sets up the stones *around* his head (not as a pillow *under* his head, according to midrashic readings).[43] He discovers that his head is the focal point, in which unity and coherence can be construed out of chaos.

It is his head which is endangered by the "wild animals."[44] Oliver Sacks writes of the complex, unstable patterns of response exhibited by his post-encephalitic patients, and of the sense of anxiety and helplessness these produced in him. He quotes the chemist Prigogine, facing the "catastrophe" of the breakdown of symmetry and reversibility in physics, classical dynamics, and biological systems, at the end of the nineteenth century: "In some sense, this unlimited predictability is an essential part of the scientific picture of the physical world. We may perhaps even call it the founding myth of classical science. . . . Is this a defeat for the human mind? Is this the end of classical thought?"[45] It is the human mind and its daylight structurings of reality that is endangered; and it is the human mind that sets itself to discern a more complex unity in the apparently random stream of data.

In a poignant variation on the twelve-stones motif, the midrash in *Pirkei d'Rabbi Eliezer*, 35, describes the stones as coming from the altar on which Isaac his father was bound. . . . And they all became one stone, to tell Jacob that they were all destined to become one nation in the land. . . . And in the morning, Jacob sat down to gather the stones together (and replace them in the altar); and he found them all one stone, and he set it up as a pillar. . . . What did God do? He stretched out His right foot [symbolizing eternity] and sank the stone deep into the earth, as one inserts a keystone into an arch. Therefore, it is called *Even Shetiya* — the Foundation Stone of the world.

From the place of utter fear, Jacob takes stones for his experiment. Where his father was almost killed, he asks radical questions about the meaning of the fragments. And a unity is affirmed which is strong enough to support the structure, not only of the Holy Temple, but, through it, of the whole world. Elements of primal terror are rebuilt into a basis for stability: "Did you know, then, that joy is, in reality, a terror whose outcome we don't fear? We go through terror from beginning to end, and that precisely is joy. A terror about which you know more than the beginning. A terror in which you have confidence."[46]

Rilke intuits the unity of joy and fear. Jacob sleeps in the place of his father's fear and wakes to fear. But he also wakes to a new sense of his own strength, his capacity to carry fear to the point of joy. When God blesses him, "*U-faratzta* — You shall spread out," Jacob knows that his destiny involves diffusion, a kind of violent rending of containing structures — but, also, an intimation of growing, irrepressible vigor.[47]

Fear and joy, the sense of cracking apart, of dislocation, and, at the same time, of new power — "I am with you": the paradox of Jacob's feeling is expressed in an evocative suggestion of Ḥatam Sofer. When Jacob "hits the place," there occurs a kind of dislocation; in the words of the midrash, "He saw the Holy Temple in its state of destruction."[48] The structure of sacrifice and sacred meaning created by Abraham and Isaac is uncreated in Jacob's experience of the place. He sees it through the prism of night and exile; the holy place is subtly out of focus, no longer properly aligned with the sacredness of the upper world. As long as the Holy Temple remains truly aligned with its counterpart in heaven, Israel's enemies have no power to enter. Destruction becomes possible when this true positioning of the earthly structure in relation to its spiritual paradigm is lost.[49]

Jacob experiences the moment of catastrophe—the moment of profound dislocation which is called exile. In this moment, God speaks to him of a destiny of diffusion, of apparent formlessness: in the midst of this, Jacob will travel *with* God. As in Coleridge's classic distinction between "mechanical regularity" and "organic form," Jacob is given the power to discover, through the long process called exile, an organic form in his experience. Such form is "innate; it shapes, as it develops, itself from within, and the fulness of its development is one and the same with the perfection of its outward form. Such as the life is, such is the form."[50]

Fullness and form: there is an obvious tension in the concept. Yet the stones come together. And Jacob rises up from the place of his dream with a buoyancy that is subtly expressed in the classic translation of Targum Jonathan, and in Rashi's commentary on Jacob's *motion*, after the dream: "And Jacob lifted up his legs" (29:1, my translation). The Targum adds an adverb, "lightly"; Rashi quotes the midrash, "Since Jacob had been given good news . . . his heart lifted up his legs and he became *light on his feet*."[51] The sense of lightness and freedom gives Jacob a physical sensation, almost a sensation of flying.

## Air and dreams: the imagination of movement

The extraordinary aspect of this midrashic description of Jacob's response to the "good news" of the dream is its physical, dynamic nature. The midrash on which Rashi bases his reading begins with a text from Proverbs: "A calm disposition gives bodily health" (14:30). Where the spirit is at ease, the body becomes light and free, a dreamlike ethereal nature is restored. The body is integrated, moves with an élan, a "really substantiated lightness involving the whole being . . . only the *slightest impulse* is needed to activate the lightness that pervades his whole being. It is easy and very simple: *striking the heel lightly* on the ground gives us the impression of being set free."[52]

In his book, *Air and Dreams*, Gaston Bachelard explores images of flying, in dream or waking reverie. He refers to the "first thesis of Nietzschean Aesthetics": "What is good is light; whatever is divine moves on tender feet."[53]

In an extraordinary way, the midrashic focus on Jacob's feet illustrates Bachelard's thesis. He writes: "Gravity is a very human psychic law. It is a part of us. It is a destiny that we must overcome, and those who have an aerial temperament foresee this victory in reverie."[54] "A human being, in his youth, in his taking off, in his fecundity, wants to rise up from the earth. The leap is a basic form of joy."[55]

Jacob's feet, in midrashic sources, become a symbol for the conflict of lightness and gravity. Lugubriously, the midrash illustrates the theme of the defeat of lightness, youth, and joy: " 'The race is not won by the swift [lit., the light]' [Ecclesiastes 9:11]: This refers to Jacob. Yesterday, 'Jacob lifted up his feet'; today, 'he gathered his feet into the bed' (49:33)."[56] Gravity wins in the end, the retrenching, the concentration. But the midrash invests much dynamic imagination in Jacob's buoyancy, in the integration of body and spirit that is the greatest gift of the dream, and that is expressed as a form of *flight*.

The midrashic tradition conveys the ease, the lightness with which Jacob moves the immovable stone on the well, as he arrives at his destination: " 'You will walk without breaking stride; When you run, you will not stumble' [Proverbs 4:12]. Jacob's steps were not constricted, nor did his strength fail, but like a mighty hero, he rolled off the stone from the mouth of the well."[57] Fatigue does not drag him down, nor does vertigo dizzy him; he covers enormous ground, as though wearing seven-league boots. The classical midrashic assertion that "the ground shrank for Jacob," so that he was suddenly transferred to Haran, is understood in mystical sources as referring to the prodigious high-stepping power of Jacob's walk: his legs become longer and his steps—literally fulfilling the terms of the quotation from Proverbs—become widened.[58] Light and wide-striding, Jacob is, in effect, almost flying: he is a long-distance runner who gains strength and speed by stepping lightly. (In Hugh Hudson's film, *Chariots of Fire*, the Jewish runner, Harold Abrahams, practices a tip-toe run to increase buoyancy and stamina.)

The desire to fly is born of the paradoxical "good news" of Jacob's dream: what was focused but static is to be refracted and dynamic. The movement is to be horizontal—*u-faratzta*, "You shall spread out"—close to the surface of the earth, like its dust, like the sleeping Jacob, embedded in soil and stones. But the imagery of Jacob's feet suggests the paradox of the foot: the basis of stability, and at the same time dynamic, with a complex motion in which the vertical and horizontal interact.

In order to move, one separates the unity of the leg-"pedestal." What drives one to separate, to disperse the coherent strength of the standing position? "At a time of hunger, scatter [*pazzer*] your legs," writes the

Yalkut Shimoni, about the journey into exile of later travelers — Naomi and Elimelech at the beginning of the Book of Ruth.[59] Such scattering is resonant throughout biblical and midrashic texts with nuances of attenuation, fruitlessness, dissipation of energy,[60] poverty,[61] and death.[62] And yet this diffusion is apparently the right response to hunger. One must travel far and wide to seek what one hungers for. A certain static dignity has to be relinquished. Jacob responds to his fate with a long-legged leap, inspired by the knowledge that in his "walking," God is with him: "I shall be with you, wherever you *walk* [lit.]."

He almost flies. Space shrinks in the buoyancy of his motion. But his steps remain earthbound; we hear the heel strike the ground, which "gives power to anyone who rebounds from it."[63]

There is a richness in the earth that gives resilience to Jacob as he goes into exile. His motion, vertical and horizontal at once, has a paradoxical superiority to that of the angels, who can only step up or down the rungs of the ladder at one time. Angels are meant to fly: but in Jacob's dream, they are restricted to the stepping space of the ladder, careful, gradual, perhaps cramped. What Jacob experiences is the power and resilience of his whole being, enriched by the rebound of the earth.

Jacob takes off (*va-yetze*) as he leaves his parents' home. Fear of exile, of that scattering of his energy and will that is the inner meaning of exile (*pezzura* is one of the terms for exile) is transformed through his dream into an acceptance that lends wings to his feet and fecundity to body and mind.

This energy, in itself, is the pure sensation, as the midrash imagines it, of "I shall be with you." It accompanies him in exile, and brings prosperity, not only to himself, but to Laban as well. Using an unusual metaphor, Jacob tells Laban: "God has blessed you *le-ragli* [lit., *through my feet*] because of me" (30:30). Rashi reads: "As a result of my feet coming to you, blessing has come to you." Rambam understands this as a phrase of causation: "because of me."[64] Rashi, too, seems to take the reference to Jacob's feet simply as a synecdoche: "with me came blessing."

But there is a more imaginative thematic understanding of the foot motif in *Pirkei d'Rabbi Eliezer*. Laban's flocks fell to a plague before Jacob's arrival. Jacob nurtures the remaining sheep — "and God blessed them because of my feet": "Do Jacob's feet have the power to increase the fertility of Laban's sheep? From here, the Sages said that sometimes a person's foot brings blessing to a house, while sometimes it brings ruin —

and Jacob's foot brought blessing."[65] Jacob's presence in Laban's house
brings a vitality, a buoyancy, that is the sensed reality of "I am with you."
The sleeping body of Jacob, dreaming in the holy place, becomes instinct
with vigor. For it is, according to the midrash, the very site of God's
presence: wherever the righteous are, there He is.

## Jacob in Padan Aram: fullness and form

The problem of integration, of the coordination of feet, hands, head, and
trunk, still remains with Jacob. Four wives, thirteen children, and enormous wealth present problems in administration, in *husbandry*, in the
fullest sense. But the narrative itself and midrashic and hasidic literature
give us a Jacob who is extended to his ripest contours. To quote Coleridge
again: perfection of form is a process that is organic and innate; "it
shapes, as it develops, itself from within." As the full human being,
seeking life and wholeness, Jacob is portrayed in terms of such process. It
is a history of continual discovery: of error and correction, of "makings
and matchings,"[66] as Jacob struggles for a true perception of the world.

The psychology of visual representation, for example, is indicated by
the use of the simple word *Ve-hine* ("and behold"), which recurs constantly through the Jacob narrative.[67] This gives us a Jacob whose field of
perception is always changing, sharpening its focus. The unpredictable
shocks of present time inform Jacob's world. The word puts the reader
behind Jacob's eyes, experiencing the movement of his perceptions. No
system blunts the startling quality of each encounter in the world of exile.

Jacob's process of integration begins with real fear at the possible
disintegration of the *anokhi*—the self—under the pressures of "poverty,
sickness and malevolent foreigners."[68] When God promises him protection against these erosions of his identity, the words, "And behold I
[*anokhi*] am with you," can be read as an assurance that God's *anokhi*, with
all its resources, is available to Jacob, in his vicissitudes. In his dream, he is
assured of energy and integrity. And when he wakes, he experiences the
buoyancy of his feet and strength of his hands, as he rolls the stone off the
well. His body wakes and discovers its power. "The hands are the hands of
Esau," Isaac said, feeling the Esau-potential in Jacob's arms (27:22). For
Jacob to have strong arms is clearly to mark a new sense of integration:
what he knows, what he sees, he can perform in the world.

And yet, when he sees Rachel, the beloved, for the first time, he weeps. These tears—the first in the Torah narrative—are mysterious. "Then Jacob kissed Rachel, and broke into tears" (29:11). He kisses her, and cries. There is even a similarity between the two verbs, *Va-yishak* and *Va-yevk*: beginning and end of the sentence echo each other. What is the quality of this moment, of these enigmatic tears?

Rashi brings together two views from the midrash:

> "*And broke into tears*": Because he foresaw, through sacred inspiration, that Rachel would not be buried together with him. Also: because he had come with *empty hands*. He said, "Eliezer, my father's servant, had *in his hands* rings and bracelets and delicacies, while I—I have *nothing in my hands*." This happened because Eliphaz, the son of Esau, pursued him, at the command of his father, to kill him. When he caught up with him, he [lit.] *pulled back his hand* from killing him, since he had grown up in Isaac's bosom. He said, "But what shall I do about my father's command?" And Jacob told him, "Take what is *in my hands*—for the poor person is accounted as though dead."

In both readings, Jacob's tears are connected with death. On the one view, he cries *because* of his love for Rachel, and because of their eventual separation: not only death, but even burial will divide them. There is an anguish at the very heart of love—the "invisible worm," of which Blake writes ("O Rose, thou art sick!"). On the second view, he cries because he is "as though dead." His poverty, the emptiness of his hands, declares a loss of autonomy, of the power to do what he wills. Jacob, in effect, cries about the two central concerns of a human life, according to Freud: love and work. As he enters Laban's world, he intuits the profound conflicts that will inform both these concerns.

## *Work: power and authenticity*

On the most basic level, work is a necessity for one who is poor, who has "nothing in his hands." These hands, that have just now freely and proudly demonstrated their strength in rolling the stone off the well, suddenly hang limp. "The poor man is like a dead man," say the Sages. And Maharal explains: The poor man lacks an essential autonomy; he depends on others for his sense of life. There is a "fountain of life" that should flow from the self, unconditioned by the will of others. Without this organic independence, a person is "as though dead."

A humiliating impotence is Jacob's sensation, even as he kisses Rachel, after the triumph of his achievement at the well. Something vital to his full being is eroded by poverty. He must work. Jacob is, indeed, the first worker in the Torah. He is also the first lover. That is, he is the first person to be specifically described as *oved* and *ohev*, engaged in physical labor, and—before marriage—loving a woman.

The incidence of the word *oved*, "work," in this narrative, is very high. Jacob works, primarily, to fill his hands: to acquire a sense of personal power and autonomy. But he works *for* Laban, he must submit to the power of an employer, who tries to prevent that "filling," that autonomy, from ever happening. Ultimately, after all Jacob's work, he says: "Had not the God of my father, the God of Abraham, and the Fear of Isaac, been with me, you would have sent me away *empty-handed*. But God took notice of my plight and the *toil of my hands*" (31:42). It is God who has protected Jacob's hands and their labor: Laban would have sent them away empty as they came. Because God was "with" him (lit., Had not God been *to* me—*mine*), he was able to take full responsibility for any losses incurred by Laban (lit., *from my hand*, you would exact it [31:39]).

The labor of twenty years is an expenditure of energy—first for Laban, and only afterwards for himself (30:30). His hands ultimately build his own empire; but for the first fourteen years, he serves Laban. The word *oved* is used constantly with Laban as object: essentially, Jacob *serves*, he *slaves* for Laban, he is not his own master. The result is paradoxical: through twenty years of labor, Jacob serves his master well; but in doing so, he also discovers his own power. "You know," he says to Laban, "what services I have rendered you" (30:26). And again: "You know how well I have served you" (30:29). And again, to his wives: "You know I have served your father with all my might" (31:6). As Jacob speaks of knowledge in connection with labor, he comes progressively to appropriate for himself the right to his own labor. He knows himself and his own strength; he is intensely aware of "all his might," precisely because he has acquired it through long years of subjugation. His hands have become a conscious expression of his power, of the fountain of life that springs freely within him.

Jacob's success is conveyed in terms of material prosperity: "And the man became very prosperous [*Vayifrotz*]"—a clear fulfillment, on the economic level, of God's promise, "And you shall spread out [*U-fa-*

*ratzta]"* (28:14). Jacob's vitality is expressed in a thickening envelope of property: of things belonging to him, attached to him.

The simple idiom that conveys the idea of property in biblical Hebrew— *Va-yehi lo* (lit., and there was to him)—for the first time in the Torah narrative becomes a central motif. Literally, if inelegantly, translated, the idiom leaves its traces throughout these chapters. "The man became very prosperous, and *there were to him* large flocks, maidservants and menservants, camels and asses" (30:43). Laban's sons claim, "Jacob has taken all *that was our father's*" (31:1). Rachel and Leah affirm: "Truly, all the wealth that God has taken away from our father *is to us and to our children*" (31:16). Laban, in a tantrum, finally reveals his true colors: "The daughters are my daughters, the children are my children, and the flocks are my flocks; all that you see is *to me*" (31:43). Jacob sends messages to his brother, Esau, narrating his success: "and *there were to me* cattle, asses, sheep" (32:6). He also commands his servants to answer Esau, when he asks, "*To whom* are you? And *to whom* are those in front of you?"': "*To your servant*, to Jacob—they are a gift sent to my lord, to Esau" (32:19). And Esau grants Jacob undisputed rights over his own property, with the words, "*There is to me much*—let *what is to you be to you*" (33:9). By contrast, Jacob, who has experienced a night of lonely conflict with a mysterious foe, is able to reply: "*There is to me* everything" (33:11).

Jacob has expanded his personal power, his control over things and people who are in significant relation to him. But, in doing this, he has incurred all the dangers and jealousies attendant on success. He is the first "self-made man" in the Bible—"With my staff alone I crossed this Jordan, and now I have become two camps" (32:11). Solitary and poor, thin as a stick, he began his journey. Dense and complex, his identity is spelled out in wives, children, sheep, cattle, when he returns. But before he confronts Esau, he strips himself: all that belongs to him he places at the other side of the river. In an act of evacuation, he "crosses them over," a displacement, as though to make room for something else. "And Jacob was left alone" (32:24–25). He now has room for his loneliness; gently, he has removed all that he has attached to himself. After such a night, he can say to Esau; "I have everything."

Through his work, then, Jacob acquires, essentially, the energy in his arms and legs. Alone, he can wrestle—arms and legs entwined—with an angel. The hazards of the night, of exile, however, are a factor in this work and this wealth. Perhaps these can be seen most poignantly in Jacob's reference to Laban's changing face: "And Jacob saw that Laban's face was not with him, as it had been in the past" (31:2). Laban's face is "with" Jacob; but later, he repeats to his wives that "Laban's face is not 'to' me, as it was previously" (31:5). Laban's face is part of Jacob's world; he carries its impress, its changing looks around with him. It is part of the "envelope" of his life. Laban's smiles and frowns affect Jacob, even as he affirms that the stability of "the God of my father has been with me."

For to work *for* someone is to make oneself vulnerable, dependent on approval for one's fundamental sense of self. It is this dependence on the face of another that Jacob has to confront in his "service" of Laban. Literally, he has "left his father's face" (27:30): that, too, had its terrors for him ("I shall be in his eyes as a trickster" [27:12]), but nevertheless it expressed the noble expectations of his home. Now, it is to the changing moods of a Laban that he must accommodate.

This relation to Laban's face represents a profound challenge to Jacob's integrity. The Talmud in Berakhot 6b speaks of the debilitating effect of dependence on others: "When a person is needy of people, his face changes like a *kroom*, as it is said, 'One who humiliates himself before people is like a *kroom*' [Psalms 12:9]. What is a *kroom*? There is a bird in the seaboard cities whose name is *kroom*. When the sun rises, it turns many colors." Like the *kroom* bird, one who is too much affected by others' faces finds his own face turning all colors, blushing and paling in response to their changing expressions.

R. Nahman of Bratzlav discusses this passage.[69] For him, what is at issue here is personal authenticity. Someone who is "needy of others" — financially, or in terms of self-esteem — will find it very difficult to pray with the community. He will be excruciatingly aware of the gaze of others, which will induce a fatal self-consciousness in him. His prayers will then become affected, marked with theatrical expressions, in order to please and impress others. His face will lose its natural coloring: chameleonlike, he will respond to the imagined expectations of others.

With great subtlety, R. Nahman describes the effects of emotional dependence: the false complexity that replaces the simple expression of the integrated self. At its truest, that is what the human face represents — a forceful integration of the authentic self that can confront other selves, other faces, without fear or favor.

This is the challenge that Jacob faces, in his relation to Laban. He must acquire strong hands, but not at the expense of his face. R. Nahman quotes: "Grant truth to Jacob" [Micah 7:20]; and "Such is the circle of those who turn to Him, Jacob, who seek Your presence" (Psalms 24:6). He reads: those who seek God's face seek the Jacob face in themselves — the authentic human face of one who struggles for truth. And he finishes his discussion with a reading of Psalms 146:2: "I shall praise God with my life." When one is needy of others' approval, one does not live from the sources of one's own life. Such a person's life is not life, say the Sages[70] — not authentic life. Only one who has freed himself of such needs can truly pray to God: "I shall praise God with *my* life."

Jacob's authentic life is constantly threatened by his relation to Laban. The truth of his own face must survive the necessary masks of an alienated existence. This is one of the radical tensions of exile, of work *for another*. If Jacob's face survives, his truth will be the stronger, perhaps. But this reality of work is the reality of a post-Eden world. When Adam was originally placed in the Garden, his brief was to "work it and to tend it" (2:15). The two verbs (*avad* and *shamar*) are identical to those systematically used of Jacob, as he works by day and "watches" by night. The idyllic situation of the Garden made an organic nurturing and self-nurturing activity of work. But the reality of Jacob's life in exile — doubly alienated from paradisal simplicity — is one of conflict, threatened integrity, jealousies, and resentments.

## Love: union and separation

Similarly, in relation to that other main human concern — love — the paradise model only seems to throw the reality of Jacob's life into higher relief. For Eve was made of Adam's rib; and Adam said, "This time, bone of my bone" (2:23). *Only this time* is the full organic unity of man and wife to be achieved. They are, literally, of the same body: Adam recognizes a part of himself restored to him — transformed, visible, but intimately his. Other love stories will contain memories, intimations perhaps of this primal unity. But separate identities and viewpoints will make for a tension that will complicate the desired union.[71]

Jacob is, in a sense, the first lover in the Torah narrative. By this, I mean that he aspires to an ideal, all-consuming love. Isaac is also of course described as loving his wife (24:67), but this is a love of marriage, of comfort after bereavement. Jacob, on the other hand, loves Rachel from the moment he sees her. "And when Jacob saw Rachel . . . Jacob went up and rolled the stone off the mouth of the well" (29:10). Jacob's feat with the stone on the well is clearly inspired by the sight of Rachel: his kiss and his tears express an intensity that is not explained in the text. Rashi, as we have seen, speaks of a love that foresees its own ultimate frustration. Jacob desires eternal union with Rachel, and in the very moment when desire is born, he knows that he will be separated from her, by death and burial.

It is a strange passion that brings Jacob to tears. Who would think of the grave at the moment of live encounter? Jacob lives in that moment the full paradox of union and separation that will characterize his whole relation to Rachel. She will be his, but not as he imagined. There will be "also" Leah, and Bilhah, and Zilpah. He will love her, but his love will generate jealousy and hatred in his household, now and in generations to come. And, ultimately, they will be buried apart.

The knowledge that full unity cannot be achieved is like a sword between them. It is in this sense that Jacob is the first lover in the Torah — in the European, romantic sense, in which a central component of passion is unattainability.[72] From the tales of courtly love, knightly adventures engaged in for the sake of the beloved, a notion of self-validation through love has emerged. Prominent in such tales is the theme of the impossible, even illicit, love, whose fire burns stronger for the taboo. Both themes — work for the sake of love, and frustration as a catalyst of passion — inform the story of Jacob and Rachel.

The connection between work and love is made lucidly in the famous description of Jacob's courtship: "So Jacob served seven years for Rachel and they seemed to him but a few days because of his love for her" (29:20). Jacob has already demonstrated the energy that the sight of Rachel has released in him, when he rolled the stone off the well. In a sense, the whole of Jacob's experience in the darkness of exile is an inquiry into the relation of desire, frustration, and action. When Jacob "works for Rachel," the verb *avad* is used without the usual suffix or object that denotes his employee status with Laban — "I have served you." Here, instead, "working *for* Rachel" [*be-Raḥel*] expresses the energy source of his work, its purpose and motivation. The *be-* prefix conveys a sense almost of the saturation of the work with the idea of Rachel. Because the work is inspired by desire, time goes fast. In a state of high vitality, he drives toward the accomplishment of his desire; his arms become stronger, and the society he has adopted becomes wealthier.

As when the sun set early at the beginning of his journey, and as when the ground shrank under his leaping feet, after his dream, so during this period of his life Jacob experiences the "shrinking" of time, in relation to human buoyancy and will. There is a strength that is connected with desire—a taut-limbed sense, sleepless, highly articulated: "The hunger artist fasts, the doorkeeper is silent, and the students are awake"—and Jacob works and watches for Rachel. Perhaps, in the same way as Benjamin suggests that the students' being kept awake is the best thing about their studies, Jacob's working and watching is the best thing about his love.

Even on the level of animal husbandry, a point is made in the narrative about this connection of strength and desire. Jacob's strategy for increasing his wealth is described thus: "Moreover, when the sturdier animals were mating, Jacob would place the rods in the troughs, in full view of the animals, so that they mated by the rods" (30:41). The word translated here, "sturdier," *mekusharot*, is derived by Ramban from the word, *kesher*, meaning "bond, relationship." The males, writes Ramban, were "bound by desire" to the females: the young born of such matings are called the "bound ones." Ramban also cites a view that the sturdier animals have a taut-limbed vigor, which is related to good health and strong desire.

The compulsion of desire—"His own life is *bound up* with his" (44:30) is the later description of Jacob's love for Benjamin—gives a clearly erotic focus to Jacob's working courtship of Rachel. At the end of seven years, he says to Laban, with almost brutal directness: "Give me my wife . . . so that I may come in to her" (29:21). He wants, in the fullest sense, to come home. And he is cheated by Laban: Leah replaces Rachel under the wedding canopy. On the surface, the deception is not tragic: after the elapse of seven days, he marries Rachel; the work and the desire come to their fulfillment. But in reality, a wholeness has been fractured.

# Rachel: barrenness and prayer

Jacob is now married to two women: a storm of emotion—hatred, jealousy—replaces the calm harbor of fulfillment. And a profound frustration underlies the relationships between Jacob and his two wives. Leah loves Jacob—names her children as a record of her changing relation to her husband; Jacob loves Rachel; while Rachel's main passion is for children. Essentially, all the protagonists most want what they cannot have. In this sense, the compulsion of desire continues to drive them, even after the apparent resolution of marriage.

The only recorded dialogue between Jacob and Rachel can perhaps be read in the light of such an understanding of the dynamics of desire and frustration. Jacob is strangely angry with Rachel, when she begs for his help in "giving her children": "And Rachel said to Jacob, 'Give me children, or I shall die.' Jacob was incensed at Rachel, and said, 'Can I take the place of God, who has denied you fruit of the womb?'" (30:1–2).

Rachel cries for children, "or I shall die." Literally, the Hebrew translates as "or *I am dead*." Rashi, quoting the midrash, writes: "One who has no children is accounted as dead."[73] Seforno quotes from Isaiah 56:3: "I am a withered tree." Both commentators understand Rachel not to be having a feminine tantrum—threatening her husband with dire consequences, if he does not "give" her children.[74] Rather, she is simply describing a dull meaninglessness, a loss of sap in her life. And Jacob's anger becomes comprehensible. It is painful for him to hear his wife— whom he loves for herself, not as a means for procreation[75]—declare so plainly that her primary passion is not for him.

Rashi reads his apparently callous reply: "You say that I should do as my father did—pray for you. But I am not like my father: he had no children, while I do have children. *It is you He has denied, not me*."

In Rashi's reading, the callousness of Jacob's answer seems, if anything, exacerbated. Jacob seems to proclaim his satisfaction, his lack of involvement in Rachel's pain. But perhaps Jacob speaks out of the anger of a man whose love meets with poor response. On one level, he is simply saying that his life would be amply fed by his relationship with her: her deprivations are different from his and must inform her own personal relationship with God.

In this scene, as in the scene where Jacob weeps on meeting Rachel, Rashi emphasizes the midrashic statements about life conditions that are "accounted as deathly." Poverty and childlessness: in an emotional sense, these are the two *life-threatening* conditions. In a Torah portion that deals with the question of energy, Rashi reads the paradoxes of desire and frustration. Poverty drives Jacob to work and prosperity in an alienated world; childlessness drives Rachel to authentic prayer and fertility: "Now God remembered Rachel; God heeded her and opened her womb" (30:22).[76]

## *Leah: the dynamic imagination*

Leah, by contrast, is patently unloved by Jacob—and, *therefore*, given children: "The Lord saw that Leah was unloved and he opened her womb" (29:31). The balance of frustration and desire is translated into an "unromantic" fertility. Leah names her children for her wistful, ever-hopeful pain: "The Lord has seen my affliction. . . . Now my husband will love me. . . . The Lord heard that I was unloved. . . . This time my husband will become attached to me. . . ." (29:32–34).

Her relationship with Jacob is, essentially, an act of will; for, in some enigmatic sense, it was never meant to be. Even before Jacob arrives on the scene, midrashic tradition asserts she was destined to marry Esau: familial and social consensus had allocated her to her elder cousin. Her anguished protest at her fate is expressed in her "weak eyes"—reddened from weeping:

> "*Leah had weak eyes*" [29:17]: This is to her credit. She would hear people talking at the crossroads: "Rebecca has two sons, and Laban has two daughters—the elder daughter will marry the elder son, the younger daughter the younger son." She sat at the crossroads, asking: "The elder son—what kind of person is he?" "A bad person, a robber." "And the younger son—what kind of person is he?" "A mild man, who sits in the tents of Torah." And she cried till her eyelashes fell off.[77]

"*Everyone said*, the elder daughter will marry the elder son" (Rashi): there is a destined quality, a kind of fitness about the matches projected between the two sets of cousins. In some sense, Leah really belongs to Esau. Another version of the midrash in fact reads, "Leah was fit to marry none but Esau."[78] In this version, she cries in protest: " 'Rachel and I both came out of one womb—and Rachel is going to marry the righteous Jacob, while I marry the wicked Esau!' And she wept, till her eyes became weak."

In effect, Leah defies her fate. She refuses to accept the "fit" marriage. Sitting at the "crossroads," where destinies fork, she interrogates her fate, demands to know the implications and consequences of what "must be." Her tears generate her many children. For a formidable energy builds up in her, in her deprivation; she takes Rachel's place under the marriage canopy; and in the darkness, in which forms and structures become fluid, in which transformations, fantastic combinations, and splittings become possible, Leah *becomes* Rachel.[79]

"When morning came, there [*ve-hine*—behold!] was Leah!" (29:25).
Rashi comments: But at night she was not Leah. The effect of *ve-hine* is to
convey a real jolt of perception. Jacob had experienced her during the
night as Rachel: "But I called you 'Rachel,' and you answered me!"[80]
Leah had found in herself the potential to *be Rachel*. And when, in this
devastatingly ironic midrash, she replies: "But did your father not call you
'Esau,' and you answered him!" she re-evokes in Jacob the power of his
old desire to *be other*, to reappropriate the qualities projected on the rival
brother.

Essentially, Leah tells Jacob that there are other possibilities of relationship than that of idyllic, total love. There is the dynamic imagination,
through which Jacob becomes Esau, Leah becomes Rachel.[81] There is
the world of the night, in which shadow selves, maskings, word plays
baffle and fascinate the dreamer. Both Jacob and Leah play their fuller
selves: they are both audacious actors in the *poretz* mode. *U-faratzta*—
"You shall spread out" God commanded/promised Jacob in his dream.
*Va-yifrotz*—And the man did indeed burst through the boundaries of a
simple prescribed identity. He extended his register in all directions.
Leah simply invites him to recognize her as a fellow spirit in the world of
the night.

The marriage of Leah and Jacob, therefore, represents one type of
possible marriage, the type that is characterized by children, by the
multiple consequences of a complex self-knowledge. This is Rashi's
concept of "one flesh": the child, the fruit of two people struggling to
understand who they may be, singly and together. Even in his anger, even
in the "hate" that the narrative ascribes to him, Jacob looks at his
children and says, "The mother of these—can I divorce her?"[82] The
children represent possible "makings and matchings" of self and other:
possible integrations of parts of himself that Leah has mirrored back to
him. There is no divorcing the source of such intimations.

## Jacob's house: fractured perspectives

Jacob and Leah are buried together. The irony is manifest. The struggling, complex couple, with their many children, remain forever together
in the Cave of Makhpelah, the Cave of Couples; while Rachel, the only
true wife of intention and desire, is buried separately, on the road to
Bethlehem.

Sadly, Jacob remembers, at the end of his life: "I, when I was returning from Padan, Rachel died, to my sorrow, while I was journeying in the land of Canaan, when still some distance short of Ephrath; and I buried her there on the road to Ephrath" (48:7). A relationship that began with tears of foreboding at the ultimate separation of himself and Rachel ends as he explains to Joseph, the son of that marriage, why this separation was necessary.

Rashi penetrates the unspoken layers of dialogue:

> "*I buried her there*": I did not even take her to Bethlehem, bring her into the Holy Land, proper. I know you resent this. But know that it was at the command of God that I buried her there, so that she might be a help to her children. When Nebuchadnezzar will send them into exile, and they pass her grave, "there, on the road," Rachel will come out of her grave and cry and ask for mercy for them — as it is said, "A cry is heard in Ramah — wailing, bitter weeping — Rachel weeping for her children. She refuses to be comforted for her children, who are gone. Thus said the Lord: Restrain your voice from weeping, your eyes from shedding tears; for there is a reward for your labor — declares the Lord: they shall return from the enemy's land. And there is hope for your future — declares the Lord: your children shall return to their country" [Jeremiah 31:14–16].

Jacob explains to Joseph why Rachel — with whom he desired nothing more than to be "one flesh," in Ramban's understanding of the concept: total and eternal union, without conflict or variation — had to be buried "there, on the road," in an alienated wayside grave on the boundary of the Holy Land. At that border place, her eternal yearning for her children will generate redemptive force. Her tears will win a response from God: her children will not disappear into the night. Through the sheer power of her yearning for her children, "who are not" (lit., who are gone), and practiced by much longing for children, who were not, Rachel will bring them back into real, coherent being.

Maharal adds a poignant note. Why, he asks, does Rachel weep more that the other mothers of the exiled children of Israel? He quotes a midrash, in which Rachel protests to God:

> "What have my children done, that You have brought such punishment upon them? If it is because they worship idols — which are called *tzarah* — a rival wife — then consider my case. I loved my husband,

Jacob, and he worked seven years for me, and, in the end, my father
gave him my sister as a wife, and I suppressed my love for my husband,
and gave my sister the code words. I am flesh and blood, while You are a
compassionate King — how much more should you have pity on them!"
And God acknowledges the truth of her words: "There is reward for
your labor."[83]

Maharal understands this midrash as Rachel's most personal, most
philosophical reading of reality. The world is not a coherent, integrated
world. Such unity as would be symbolized by Jacob's marriage to Rachel
is an ultimate, messianic vision. Jacob must marry two wives, because his
"house" must represent a truth about existence in this world, the truth of
fractured perspectives. Rachel accepts this truth, though it defaces the
purity of her love, with love. Such an acceptance puts her on the high
moral ground: can God not similarly accept with love an Israel who sins
because of that inherent defect, that lack of clear coherence, with which
God Himself has fashioned the world? Rachel sees the separation in her
married life, the frustration of total unity, as an indication of the nature of
things. She alone, therefore, has the power to ask God for mercy.

In this reading, Maharal cuts to the heart of Jacob's tragic experience.
Everything in his life is shaped by the threat of a breakdown of desired
form. The integrated harmony of his vision is diffracted into pieces with
jagged edges. Reality reveals itself to him in the sharp, successive, provisional images of *ve-hine* . . . *ve-hine* . . . ("Behold . . . behold . . ."); of
*gam* . . . *gam* . . . ("also . . . also . . ."). Perception changes reality from
moment to moment.

This is, Maharal says, a world of *perud* — of disjunction: Jacob and
Rachel live that *perud* bravely, with imagination, with awareness that
through the disjunctions, through the catastrophic shards, *anokhi imkha* — "I am with you." There is an inner architecture, which only the
desirous imagination can fathom. Through the imagery of physical
buoyancy and strength, of flight, sleeplessness, and unfulfilled desire,
Jacob traces the outlines of a human profile — of head, trunk, arms, legs,
and face — the person in the image of God, alive "with his own life."

# Translating pain into strength

Exile, dislocation, and disjunction are not, it seems, absolute states. They
hold at their heart the seed of unity, coherence, and continuity. For — as

Galileo asserted of the physical planet—"Nevertheless—in spite of everything—it moves": there is a constant process of change, a shifting of the patterns, which, paradoxically, tends to order. Rachel, buried in "no place," on the wayside, in the volatile, ever-changing world of her exiled children, has the power to generate their reintegration and return.

Rachel dies in childbirth. In one sense, this is a most poignant example of fragmentation and absurdity: to be cut off at the very beginning of creativity, just as new life breaks into the world. And, in fact, she calls her baby, Ben-oni, "the son of my sorrow." "But his father called him, Ben-yamin—the son of my strength" (35:18).[84] On the face of it, the child is named twice, to record the anguish of his dying mother, and the virile triumph of his father.

But Ramban suggests a different reading. He notes that all the children of Jacob were named *by their mothers*. Jacob does not rename the child; he *translates* the word, *oni*, to mean, "goodness and strength." Responding to an enigmatic expression in *Bereshit Rabbah*[85]—"the child's father named him Ben-yamin, *in the Holy Tongue*"—Ramban writes: "Jacob translated Rachel's language into goodness."

Jacob is the translator, the one who senses the ambiguous, changing meanings of language. The word *oni* in Hebrew means both pain and strength. It is the very nature of holiness to translate pain into strength—even to intuit the strength within the pain, the coherence within chaos.

It is for this purpose, perhaps, that Jacob goes abroad: in order to become a translator, to speak the Holy Tongue, his mother tongue, with a new awareness of its complexity. For though he has learned the language of his exile—the apparently unequivocal language of pain and alienation—he brings this knowledge to a fullness of experience, in which it reveals its "holiness," to a point at which terror fuses with joy, sorrow with strength. A skilled translator, he can play with meanings, faithful both to Rachel's pain and to the integrative energy at the heart of that pain.

# VA-YISHLAḤ 🦋
## The Quest for Wholeness

S*afe return: God's promise and Jacob's commitment*

Jacob returns to the Holy Land, after twenty years' absence. Return proves to be a complex experience of confrontations, deaths, and disasters. His first act as he reenters the Holy Land is to send messengers to his estranged brother, Esau, parleying for peace and bearing gifts of reconciliation. Fearful for his life, he prays to God—the first quoted prayer in the Torah—and prepares for war. And during the night before meeting Esau with his four hundred men, Jacob encounters a mysterious "man," with whom he wrestles all night, till the sun rises and he limps toward his brother.

No sooner has he placated his brother than his daughter, Dinah, is raped by Shekhem, a local prince, and the whole town of Shekhem is massacred by his vengeful sons Simeon and Levi. Then, Rebecca's nurse, Deborah—whose presence in Jacob's camp has not previously been mentioned—dies, and the mourning is marked by the naming of the oak tree under which she is buried, *Allon Bakhut*, "the oak of weeping" (35:8).[1] This is followed by the death of Rachel in childbirth, and by the enigmatic brief narrative, in which Reuben "lay with Bilhah, his father's concubine. And Israel found out" (35:22).

This brief survey of the tribulations afflicting Jacob on his return to the Holy Land casts a shadow over God's promise to Jacob, as he left the land twenty years earlier. In his dream at Beth El, Jacob had heard God say, "I will bring you back to this land" (28:15). And, on waking, he had vowed his response to the promise: "If God remains with me, if He protects me . . . and if I return safe [*be-shalom*] to my father's house—the Lord shall be my God. And this stone, which I have set up as a pillar, shall be God's abode" (28:20–22). In his vow, Jacob had added *be-shalom*— "safe, in peace"—to the words of God's promise: his concept of return

216

involves an idea of wholeness. Rashi, in fact, reads *be-shalom* as "intact, uncontaminated by sin. May I not learn from Laban's ways." Jacob understood God's promise—read it back to Him—as culminating not merely in a physically safe return to his country, but in a spiritually unaffected return to his father's house. He desires a wholeness and a closing of the circle, as he imagines the end of his exile, and his reabsorption into his father's house.

There may even be more than a nuance of commitment to Jacob's hope for the future; possibly, his call for integrity throughout his exile is part of his vow, and not—as usually read—part of the conditions he lays down before he will fulfill his vow.[2] On such a reading, Jacob takes a certain responsibility for returning whole, "unspoiled," from his wanderings, and, equally, for closing the circle of his travels by returning to his father's house. He does not merely desire such a return, but sets himself in full intentionality on a course of preserving a certain original integrity.

How far does reality consummate God's promise and Jacob's intention? As far as integrity is concerned, the text seems to vouch for Jacob that he does indeed return intact from his travels: "And Jacob arrived safe [*shalem*, lit., whole] in the city of Shekhem" (33:18). Rashi here expands the notion of wholeness to multiple areas of human concern: "Whole in his body, as he was cured of his limp; whole in his financial resources, as he lost nothing by his munificent gift to Esau; whole in his Torah, as he forgot nothing of his learning in Laban's house."

In an acute midrashic play on words, Rashi places Jacob's hidden concern with integrity in almost surrealistic focus. Jacob sends a message to Esau, in which he speaks of his "sojourn" (*garti*) with Laban: *garti* expresses a way of seeing his time in Laban's house as provisional, temporary.[3] Rashi quotes a classic midrash: "*Garti* has the same numerical value as *taryag*—the 613 commandments: 'I sojourned with Laban, but I kept all 613 commandments, and did not learn from Laban's ways.'" In other words, he encodes in his message to his brother what he feels to be his real strength—the fact that his identity has remained unaffected by all his vicissitudes.

If, however, we examine more closely the midrash quoted by Rashi, in which wholeness—physical, financial, and intellectual—is unpacked from the word *shalem* (33:18), an implicit tension is exposed at each level of the description. Physical health is a matter of having been injured—the

limp with which Jacob emerges from his night of wrestling with the man-
angel — and of having been cured of his injury. Financial health follows on
a moment when Jacob is compelled to sign away a large chunk of his
property to Esau; in spite of this, claims the midrash, his holdings suffer
no loss. Intellectually, too, the claim is that Jacob loses none of his
learning in the course of twenty years in Laban's house. From all three
descriptions, a tension of loss and gain becomes manifest. To be whole,
apparently, means to have been in great danger and to have been saved.
Jacob's integrity has been significantly assailed on many levels, but losses
have been recouped, injuries healed, the erosion of memory successfully
fought.

Rashi continues with a parable: "like a man who says to his friend: X
emerged from between the lions' teeth and arrived home intact. So here,
'And he arrived intact . . . from Padan Aram': from Laban and Esau, who
both attacked him on his journey." There is an anarchic pleasure in
telling of the voracious danger and of the immaculate escape. But these
are the pleasures of myth and fairy tale; the narrative form is emphasized
in Rashi's framing device, where what sounds like a tall tale is being told.
In a more realistic context, the image of lions' teeth generates a tension in
which wholeness becomes a dynamic rather than a static idea. What is the
history of such wholeness? To mix the metaphor — how did the anti-
bodies work, how were they developed, as Jacob's organism encountered
the infections of the world of Laban and Esau?

The question of "wholeness," in fact, is central and problematic in
Jacob's concept of himself and his destiny. First described as a "simple
man" (25:27), he desires — even vows his commitment to — a more complex process of health, in the Anglo-Saxon meaning of the word ("wholeness"). This is a problem in equilibrium, in the managing of contrary
forms, in the husbanding of divergent energies. In Rashi's reading (32:5),
Jacob seems to pride himself on a certain impervious quality, a holding
fast to his own course, unstirred by alien winds. In other words, he seems
to see himself as successfully returned, exactly in the terms he had used
twenty years before to commit himself to a paradoxical stability in
vicissitude. This stern imperviousness is a different thing, however, from
the "wholeness" that the narrative voice, as read by Rashi, attributes to
him. Here, the midrash gives us the troubled dynamic of loss and gain,
sickness and health, oblivion and awareness.

# The *return to Isaac's house: ambiguous nostalgia*

As for the second "hidden" promise, implicit in Jacob's vow ("I shall return whole *to my father's house*"), here, too, Jacob's desire, even his commitment, to a certain act of closure is fulfilled in an unforeseen, troubled manner. On the one hand, Jacob clearly yearns for his father's house: he unilaterally introduces it into his reading of God's promise; and Laban, with shrewd insight, analyzes Jacob's underlying passion during the years of his exile: "you were longing for your father's house" (31:30). This is a chronic nostalgia, not simply for home, but for the home of his *father*. That, at least, is how Laban sees Jacob's motivation in leaving him so stealthily.

But here, the issue of nostalgia becomes ambiguous. For the startling truth is that Jacob never spontaneously mentions his father again, after his vow at Beth El. On the two occasions when he speaks of return — to Laban (30:25) and to his wives (31:13) — his desire to see his father simply does not figure among his reasons for ending his exile. And even when he refers to the God of his fathers, who has preserved him from Laban's rapacity, he speaks ambiguously and enigmatically of "the God of my father, the God of Abraham and the Fear of Isaac" (31:42). From its position in the sentence, "my father" can be understood as referring to Abraham, while Isaac is not even credited with a relationship to God, other than the oblique reference to fear.[4] Highly guarded in speaking of his father, Jacob in fact returns to him only toward the end of the Parsha: "And Jacob came to his father Isaac at Mamre" (35:27). His return to source is followed by a summation of Isaac's life — clearly constitutes its consummation — and by Isaac's death. It is as though Isaac waited to die until Jacob finally arrives back home; a sense is subtly conveyed of long delay, of a return deferred, perhaps even avoided.

The subtext of Jacob's vow, then, presents us with a problem of deferral, as well as a problem of wholeness. The midrash gives us a clue of the time that elapses before Jacob actually returns home. After he has made peace with Esau — perhaps an unavoidable preliminary to returning home — "Jacob journeyed on to Succoth, and built a house for himself and made stalls for his cattle" (33:17). Rashi quotes the Talmud: "He stayed there eighteen months — a summer [Succoth, stalls], a winter [a house], and a summer [stalls]."[5] From there, he moves on to Shekhem, where his daughter is raped and his sons massacre the townspeople. After

that, he moves on to Beth El, where he fulfills the main thrust of his
vow — to set up a stone pillar in the place of his original dream and to offer
a libation to God. There follow the deaths of Deborah and Rachel;
Reuben lies with Bilhah, in a new camping site, Migdal Ha-Eder, where
Jacob "settles"; and, finally, Jacob returns to his father.

At least eighteen months, therefore, and probably a considerably
longer period, elapses before Jacob closes the circle and returns to his
point of origin. How is one to understand this delay, this absence of Isaac
from Jacob's consciousness, from the morning after his dream until he
finally arrives home, only to bury him?

## The problem of delay

The problem of delay can be approached obliquely, if we explore the
implications of the one surprising criticism leveled against Jacob in the
midrashic narratives. The Rabbis, in general, breathe no word of disap-
proval for any of Jacob's apparently more dubious acts: his acquisition of
the birthright, his "taking" of the blessing, his financial negotiations with
Laban. The harshest criticism — and the suggestion that he was terribly
punished — is leveled against Jacob's delay in fulfilling the overt thrust of
his vow at Beth El. God finally has to tell him, with some exasperation:
"Arise, go to Beth El and remain there; and build an altar there to God
who appeared to you when you were fleeing from your brother Esau"
(35:1). On this, Rashi comments, condensing the Midrash Tanḥuma
narrative: "Because you delayed on your journey, you were punished by
this, your daughter's fate."

The extraordinary midrashic claim is that Jacob is delinquent in
delaying his return to Beth El, where he had vowed that the stone pillar
he had erected would "become a house of God." What are the repercussions of this vow? And why is delay in fulfilling it considered so gravely as
to be punishable by the agony of his daughter?[6]

Even while he is still in Padan Aram, God has to remind him of his vow:
"I am the God of Beth El, where you anointed a pillar and where you
made a vow to Me. Now, arise and leave this land and return to your
native land" (31:13). Rashi reads this as implicit reproach: "'*Where you
made a vow to Me*': — and you must [lit.] pay it, since you said, 'It will
become a house of God' — that you would offer sacrifices there." This
reference to Jacob's vow does not appear in the original account in which

God tells Jacob to return home (31:3). It is Jacob, in fact, who fills in this detail—he must pay off what he has promised—when he explains to his wives why he must return. The narrative thus suggests, most subtly, the workings of Jacob's subconscious mind, the guilt that he feels at a profound ambivalence he senses in himself.

Specifically, however, to "pay off" a vow has a precise meaning, which Rashi here indicates. At root, a vow is a *vow to sacrifice*.[7] When one is in trouble, one promises to give of oneself, of one's real resources, to God, if He will act to save one's life. The animal sacrificed, the money allocated to the Holy Temple, is a metaphoric, even a metonymic, displacement for the life of a person. "When you make a vow to the Lord your God, do not put off fulfilling it, for the Lord your God will require it of you, and you will have incurred guilt" (Deuteronomy 23:22). The statutory period of "delay" is declared to be a cycle of three pilgrim festivals.[8] Once this period has passed, a person finds himself guilty of delay (*ihur*) in "paying" his obligations of sacrifice, be they animal or money equivalents.

Even before he returns to the Holy Land, therefore, Jacob is aware of a reluctance to "pay the sacrifice." Technically, he must transform the place of the dream into a house of God, by sacrifice. Symbolically, something unwhole in himself remains unresolved, according to Rashi, until God finally and explicitly urges him to "arise, go to Beth El."

Rashi's source, in Midrash Tanhuma, is vividly evocative of the troubled condition of "delay":[9]

There are three conditions where a person's ledger is examined: if one goes on a journey alone, if one sits in a house that is in danger of collapse, and if one vows and does not pay [lit., make whole] one's vow. . . . How do we know about the problem of vowing and not paying? Because it is written, "When you make a vow to the Lord your God, do not put off fulfilling it" [Deuteronomy 23:22]; and "It is a snare for a man to pledge a sacred gift rashly, and to give thought to (examine) his vows only after they have been made" [Proverbs 20:25]. If one delays paying one's vow, one's ledger is examined, and the angels assume a prosecutorial stance, and speak of his sins. . . . Come and see: when Jacob went to Aram Naharayim, what is written? "And Jacob made a vow. . . ." He went and became wealthy, and returned and settled down, and did not pay his vow. So God brought Esau against him, bent on killing him, and he took all that huge gift from him—200 goats, etc.—yet Jacob did not pay attention. He brought the angel against him; he wrestled with him but did not kill him, as it is said:

"Jacob was left alone. And a man wrestled with him until the break of dawn" — that was Sammael, Esau's guardian angel, who wanted to kill him, as it is said, "He saw that he could not prevail against him." But Jacob was crippled. And when he still did not pay attention, the trouble with Dinah came upon him: "And Dinah went out." When he still did not pay attention, the trouble with Rachel came upon him: "And Rachel died and was buried." Then God said, "How long will this righteous man take punishment and not pay attention to the sin for which he is suffering? I must inform him now: 'Arise, go to Beth El.' — These troubles have come upon you only because you delayed fulfilling your vow. If you do not want any more trouble — arise and go to Beth El, and make an altar there, in the very place where you vowed to Me. In time of distress, you made a vow, and in time of ease, you let it slip from your mind?!"

When Jacob made his vow, he prayed to be preserved from the three cardinal sins: idolatry, immorality, and bloodshed. Because he delayed fulfilling his vow, he became guilty of all three: idolatry — " 'Rid yourselves of the alien gods in your midst' " (35:2); immorality — the story of Dinah; and bloodshed — "They [Simeon and Levi] killed every male [in the city of Shekhem]" (34:25). This teaches you that delaying the fulfillment of a vow is a graver offense than all three cardinal sins!

"It is better not to vow at all than to vow and not fulfill" (Ecclesiastes 5:4). R. Meir said: It is better than both alternatives [vowing and not fulfilling one's vow, or even vowing and fulfilling one's vow] not to vow at all. A person should simply bring his lamb to the Temple Courtyard and slaughter it. R. Yehuda said: It is better than both alternatives [vowing and not fulfilling one's vow, or not vowing at all] to vow and fulfill one's vow, as it is said, "Make vows and pay them to the Lord your God" (Psalms 76:12). One then receives reward, both for the vow and for the fulfillment.

The main statement of the midrash is, of course, that the making of a vow creates a sacred, dangerous reality. To delay fulfilling a vow is not so much a moral issue as it is a question of disturbing an essential balance. Like going on a journey, unaccompanied, or sitting in a house that is about to collapse, the unfulfilled vow suggests a state of disequilibrium: the whole structure may collapse around one's ears, the forces of chaos are free to attack, one has exposed oneself to the baneful stare of the accusing angels.

While solitary journeys and dilapidated houses are obviously dangerous, however, the peculiar peril of the unfulfilled vow needs some clarification. It is as though one has enjoyed a special kind of oral pleasure, as in the quotation from Proverbs: one has eaten of the sacred, of the animals set aside for ritual purposes. To vow is to break a rational limitation, a clear boundary between hand and mouth, as another midrash puts it: "Let your hand [the fulfillment of your vow] be close to your mouth. The Sages said: Let your hand be *in front* of your mouth — that is, hold the object to be vowed, ready in your hand, *before* uttering vows."[10] If the mouth is not underwritten, as it were, by the hand, if words correspond to nothing, then one finds that one has created a reality-that-is-not-reality.

Language has the power to create such marginal — sacred and dangerous — realities. In making a vow, one constructs an image of an intended future, and thereby opens a Pandora's box of conflicts and resistances, of hitherto hidden fears and fantasies: the ledger of one's inner being, in the imagery of the midrash, is exposed to searching angelic gaze. The unbalanced books are audited, and one may find, even if only in subconscious form, the three cardinal sins traced within. The gap between hand and mouth is a perilous space; by bringing trouble after trouble upon him, God tries to make Jacob aware of the need to close the gap. But Jacob does not pay attention: he is insensitive to the implications of catastrophe, to the single message encoded in the many blows that rain down on him.

The midrash insists that the root of all Jacob's vicissitudes on his return to the Holy Land is the problem of delay, that dangerous space of *unawareness* that separates the vow from its fulfillment. In the end, God gives up on symbolic codes of reminder and — baldly, literally — tells Jacob to close the gap between symbolic language and realization: "Arise, go to Beth El." For the vow claims to transcend, to transgress the limits of space and time. It pretends to a stake *now* in a portion of reality that is not, empirically, *now.* This is the great joy of utterance before the fact: it puts into words what must be deferred, and translates the exigencies of action into the freedom of symbolic language.

> At times. . . . I would let myself daydream; I would discover, in a state of anguish, ghastly possibilities, a monstrous universe that was only the underside of my omnipotence; I would say to myself: anything can happen! and that meant: I can imagine anything. Tremulously, always on the point of tearing up the page, I would relate supernatural

atrocities. If my mother happened to read over my shoulder, she would
utter a cry of glory and alarm: "What an imagination!"[11]

## Glory and alarm

Glory and alarm: the power of imagination and of language arouses
ambivalent responses. In the midrashic argument, the alarmed response
is that of R. Meir, who declares: better not to vow at all. For there is always
risk in utterance, in the work of the mouth. Better simply to act: language
is unnecessary and potentially dangerous. Its danger is formulated in the
reproach God directs at Jacob: "When you were in distress, you made a
vow—now you are at ease, you let it slip from your mind." What could
make one utter what is not there, if one were not in such distress as impels
one to a vow, rather than die? One offers one's real substance in words,
substituting for the life that is under duress. But this offer of words is
intrinsically an irresponsible, perilous substitute. It is a gesture of sacrifice without the blood, without the real cost. In the best of cases, even
where the gap is eventually closed, one should not do it, says R. Meir: the
alarming power of words is too great.

R. Yehuda, on the other hand, insists on the glory of avowals. The
highest possibility is that of vowing and fulfilling one's vow, achieving a
kind of equilibrium that will contain the originating anguish that led to
words in the first place. Such words are informed by the pressure of
reality. Just to take the animal and slaughter it is a brief, inglorious act: to
vow the sacrifice, to lay claim to a territory in time not yet one's own, is to
be most fully human.

In the vow, imagination and will press for words to embody a radical
sense of power. "Every intention is an attention, and attention is I-can,"
writes Merleau-Ponty.[12] In making a vow ("Man is the only creature who
can make promises" [Nietzsche]),[13] one experiences one's identity, one's
ability to see and construct a future. But consciously to intend an act—an
act of closure, in particular—and then to feel oneself incapable of making
good on that intention, is to be plunged into a radical despair, in which all
the books are opened to the accusing stare of the vengeful angels.

This, I suggest, is the implication of the midrash about Jacob's condition at the time of his return to the Holy Land. Returning is a harrowing
experience: vows have to be made good, what was begun in words has to
be completed, made whole (*shalem*—to pay, fulfill, make whole). If Jacob

had fulfilled his vow, according to R. Yehuda, he would have received reward both for the vow and for the fulfillment. He would have been the first human being[14] to engage in this most alarming, glorious act of interfusing words and acts, so that each informs the other. Jacob, however, does not make good on his vow; mysteriously, in a way that is never made explicit in the text, he avoids such a closing of the circle.

The notion of delay in fulfilling a vow is profoundly equivocal. Jacob does not, after all, refuse to fulfill his vow: he simply delays, hangs back (*aḥer*, the word for "delay," is rooted in the idea of "behind, at the back"). This is a passive, not active, denial. But, effectively, repression is the gravest form of refusal (graver than the three cardinal sins), since it will not engage with—avow or disavow—the vow. Through all the symbolic bombardments of fate, he remains unaware, not reading the signs of his condition. In the imagery of the midrash, the books are open and fatally unbalanced: he alone fails to decipher the traces of his own debt.

The problem that is called "delay" is most clearly inscribed in the issue of the vow: God finally sets aside the challenges and risks of symbolic disclosure and *tells* Jacob to return to Beth El and bring his sacrifices. This issue is then apparently resolved, immediately preceding the death of Deborah and Jacob's renaming (35:7). The main thrust of the vow is fulfilled, language is made whole in action, as Jacob builds an altar and offers sacrifices in the very place of his vow.

This, however, is only the visible tip of the iceberg. The fulfillment of the vow with animal sacrifices can be seen as the "objective correlative" (T. S. Eliot's term) for a much larger and more pervasive problem. Rashi hints at a more diffuse issue of delay: " '*While Jacob stayed in that land*' (35:22): during the period before he came to Hebron, to Isaac, all these things happened to him."

## Dinah's tragedy: Jacob's responsibility

The issue is not simply one of delay in the technical fulfillment of a vow (as in the *Tanḥuma* passage), but of what Rashi himself, in a subtle recasting of the words, calls a "delay *on the journey*" (35:1).[15] The implication, spelled out in Mizraḥi's supercommentary on Rashi (35:22), is that Jacob's delay is *in returning to his father*. It was because of this delay that "all these things happened to him." There is an intuition here of reluctance, of hanging back. And it is this reservation, this *arrière-pensée*, that will claim much of our attention from this point.

For what, indeed, holds Jacob back? Among the criticisms that the Sages level at Jacob, perhaps the most unexpected is his responsibility for the rape of Dinah. This, specifically, according to Rashi (35:1), happened because of "delay on the journey." But Rashi himself quotes midrashic sources to suggest an apparently different etiology for that disaster: " '*His eleven children*' (32:22): And where was Dinah? He placed her in a box and locked it, so that Esau should not lay eyes on her. For this, Jacob was punished, for withholding her from his brother — perhaps she would have redeemed him? — and she fell into the hands of Shekhem."

Mizrahi strikingly diagnoses Jacob's refusal to let Esau see and marry Dinah as the root of the tragedy that leads to Dinah's rape. There is something in Jacob that expresses itself in putting Dinah in a box. Because of this — presumably because he is afraid to confront Esau with Dinah visible — Jacob has to delay in Succoth for eighteen months and incurs the terrible punishment of the Shekhem catastrophe. On such a reading, there is a radical connection between Jacob's refusal to let Esau see Dinah and his "delay on the journey": Dinah's tragedy is a consequence of both, the final point in a narrative chain that goes back to Jacob's failure in love for his brother, Esau:[16] "He said: This wicked man has presumptuous eyes — let him not look at her and take her from me. . . . God said to him: 'A friend owes loyalty to one who fails' (Job 6:14) — You have withheld love from your brother."[17]

Beneath a plausible surface — Jacob protects his only daughter from Esau's lust — the midrash detects a kind of avarice: "he will take her from me." Augustine's insight about incest comes to mind: it is forbidden because it represents the sin of avarice[18] — love is being hoarded, kept "locked up," in the family. Precisely here, within Jacob's apparently reasonable fear for his daughter, the Sages decipher a failure in *ḥesed*, in that imaginative risk-taking that leads one to vow and to make good on vows.

The connection between Dinah's fate and Jacob's attitude to the future is again imaginatively sketched in the following midrash:

> R. Yehuda bar Simon said: "Do not boast of tomorrow" [Proverbs 27:1] — yet you said, "Tomorrow, let my honesty testify for me" [Genesis 30:33]. Tomorrow, your daughter will go out and be tormented by

Shekhem. R. Ḥanina said: "A friend owes loyalty to one who fails" [Job 6:14]—you have withheld love from your brother.[19]

Two views of the root cause of Dinah's tragedy are juxtaposed here: R. Ḥanina speaks of the failure in love, which we touched on in the previous midrash, while R. Yehuda points to a speech of Jacob's in quite a different context. Guaranteeing his own future probity in fulfilling the terms of their salary agreement, Jacob speaks of the morrow with great confidence. R. Yehuda finds this confidence about the future objectionable. He mobilizes the verse from Proverbs: "Do not boast of tomorrow," to suggest that Jacob is guilty of a kind of hubris about his righteousness "tomorrow." The verse continues, "for you do not know what the day will bring" (lit., what the day will give birth to). In this reading, Jacob is found radically responsible for Dinah's fate: he speaks of the future with an arrogance that is inappropriate to the real mystery, the discontinuity of history, as seen by one fully participating in its contingencies. The birth image conveys this sense of the unknowable: Jacob charges at the future with a bravado not of confidence, but of fear. What happens to Dinah is a terrible reminder of the hollowness of such bravado.

This criticism of Jacob may seem excessively rigorous. But taken in conjunction with R. Ḥanina's view—about a failure in ḥesed, in imaginative love—and with a third, enigmatic criticism, a profile begins to emerge, a subtle tracing of what the Sages see as Jacob's main problem— the problem we have indicated as deferral, delay, hanging back.

The third criticism occurs strangely after Jacob is reconciled with Esau and after his stay in Succoth. He arrives at Shekhem, buys a plot of land, and constructs an altar: "And he called Him, El, God of Israel" (33:20). The rape of Dinah follows immediately. The Hebrew text is highly ambiguous: it is not clear who called whom (or what). Rashi, for instance, offers two explanations: Jacob commemorates his new relationship to God in that place by the name he gives the altar; and God names Jacob, El, indicating strength.[20] Most extraordinary, however, is the reading in *Bereshit Rabbah*:

> *"And he called him, God"*: Jacob said, "You are the God of the upper worlds, and I am god of the lower worlds." Even the cantor in the synagogue does not arrogate authority to himself [cannot assume the privilege of reading the Torah unless he has first been summoned]— and you would arrogate authority [*serara*] to yourself! Tomorrow, your

daughter will go out and be tormented — as it is written, "Now Dinah went out."[21]

In a provocative, deliberate misreading of the text, the midrash has Jacob call *himself*, "El, God of Israel," arrogating to himself divine powers "in the lower worlds." Again, some form of hubris seems to be involved, a tragic miscalculation of the range of his own control over the lower worlds. Jacob has a certain consciousness of his ability to create worlds, to impose order and meaning on his experience. But this self-consciousness is faulted by the Sages: there are limits to control.

Indeed, the problem of authority [*serara*] is raised implicitly in the very name that the angel has given to Jacob: "Your name shall no longer be Jacob but Israel" (32:29). Rashi explains the name change:

> "No longer shall it be said that the blessings came to you through insinuation and trickery, but by *authority* [*serara-yisra-el*] and openly [lit., with a revealed face]. God will reveal Himself to you at Beth El, and He will change your name, and there He will bless you. And I will be there and confirm them for you." Hence, it is written: "And he [Jacob] strove [*sara*] with an angel and prevailed — the other had to weep and implore him" [Hosea 12:5]. What did the angel implore him? "At Beth El, God will meet us and there He will speak with us. Wait for me [let me go], until He speaks with us there." But Jacob did not agree and, against his will, the angel confirmed the blessings to him — "And he blessed him *there*" [32:30].

Jacob insists on assuming his changed name immediately. The angel acknowledges that "you have striven [*sarita* — exerted power, authority] with God and with men," but begs that Jacob's new modality of control be properly defined by God at Beth El. Jacob will not wait. One modern reading[22] has, in fact, seen in this premature assumption of the name, Israel, the fault that the midrash decries: "Jacob called himself Israel" before he had any authority to do so (35:10).

What Jacob reveals in this enigmatic episode is a profound fascination with the idea of authority. Subtly, the midrash suggests that such a power to structure his reality is both genuinely his, proven by the encounter with the angel, and yet somehow beyond him, desired by him with too much passion. The question of timing is central: Jacob will not let the angel go and wait for God's confirmation of his new sense of power. It is as though an old skin is being sloughed off, a sense of uncongenial identity is rejected, with an impatience that provokes criticism: "you arrogate authority to yourself."

## Jacob on power: fascination and fear

Jacob's concern for *serara*, for control over his experience, invites further exploration. When he first sends messengers to placate Esau, he uses the expression, "I have sojourned [*garti*] with Laban" (32:5). Rashi offers two readings. In one, as we have seen, Jacob proclaims his spiritual integrity—untouched by Laban's culture, he has kept all 613 commandments. In the other, however, he assumes a low profile, presumably in order to pacify Esau: "I have not become powerful [*sar*—a prince] or important, but have simply been a stranger [*ger*]. It is not worth your while to hate me for father's blessings, since he blessed me, 'Be master [*g'vir*] over your brothers' [27:29], and you see that has not been fulfilled in me."

Jacob placates Esau by insisting that one of the main issues of Isaac's blessing has not, in fact, been realized in him: he has no power, he is marginal to all societies. In Rashi's reading, his intention seems clearly tactical—to defuse Esau's hatred. But perhaps there is another dimension to his disclaimer. Perhaps Jacob protests too much, with the excessive humility of one fascinated by the concept of authority. Fascinated and afraid—for to be weak means to be killed, while to be strong means to kill.

In such simple terms, the midrash focuses the dilemma of power, as it analyzes the description of Jacob's feelings before meeting Esau: "*'He was greatly frightened and anxious'* (32:8): He was afraid of being killed. And he was anxious at the idea of killing. 'If he prevails [*yitgaber*] over me, he will kill me, while if I prevail over him, I will kill him.' "[23]

Beyond deflecting Esau's jealousy, Jacob's disclaimer is a meditation on powers not yet realized. The full blessing of *serara* and *gevura* is not yet his. The question of his own survival seems poised against Esau's survival: will the struggle for power take the form—the primal, essential form—of fratricide?

Sharpened by the issue of survival, then, Jacob's concern about control dominates this period of his life. Prematurely calling himself Israel, even naming himself "god of the lower worlds," assuming mastery of the future, keeping Dinah in a box so that Esau does not set eyes on her and force a change in Jacob's structuring of his integrity—all these are facets of a single will: to master, comprehend, and control his experience. This is a concern for form, for the coherence of the parts and the integrity of the whole. If Jacob is to achieve such authority over his life, his camp, his future, he must box up Dinah, he must "withhold love" from Esau. For "love spoils the straight line";[24] it breaks through pre-imposed patterns, it opens gaps in secure defenses. Jacob must be able to guarantee his future righteousness, and he must call himself, unequivocally, Israel.

## Jacob's wisdom: lastness and lateness

The central image that expresses Jacob's dilemma at this period of his life—the dilemma of mastery—is of Jacob *behind*. He sends ahead herds of livestock, as propitiatory gifts, and instructs his servants: "And you shall say, 'He himself is behind us. . . . Your servant Jacob is behind us.'" (32:19, 21). Arranging his encounter with Esau, he structures his camp with great deliberation: the secondary wives with their children in front, "Leah and her children behind [*aharonim*] and Rachel and Joseph last [*aharonim*]" (33:2). The emphasis on "lastness" leads Rashi to quote the well-known aphorism: *aharon aharon haviv*—"the further back [the later], the more loved."

Spatially, there is a principle of lastness, corresponding to the temporal principle of lateness, of delay, that the midrash defined as the key to Jacob's history at this time of return. The same Hebrew root, *aher*, covers both spatial and temporal "deferment." Jacob has, in fact, choreographed both his personal camp of wives and children and his propitiatory gifts ("He told his servants, 'keep a distance between droves'" [32:17]). He has organized the gifts for effect, instructing each of his servants, walking behind each of the flocks (32:20), exactly what to say to Esau. From his position at the rear, he has planned ahead of time what Esau will ask, and what the servants will reply: "Why did he not send Esau all the flocks mixed together? In order to astonish him at the immensity and range of the gift. And why did he not send them all at once [the flocks immediately following one another]? In order to satisfy the eye of that wicked man."[25]

Subtly, Jacob plans the presumed effect of his gift. For maximum impact, he allows the suspense of a space between flocks, playing with Esau's constant surprise, as he assumes that the procession of animals has ended—only to find it begin again.

Characteristically, then, Jacob *leads from behind*: he is the thinker, the one who projects in images and words, the director behind the scenes. This is, properly speaking, the position of the hunter, tracking his prey from the rear. Jacob comes into the world behind: "After that (*aḥarei khen*), his brother emerged, holding on to the heel of Esau; so they named him Jacob" (25:26). Esau cries out, deprived of his blessing, "He has outwitted [*va-ya'akveni*] me twice" (27:36)—playing on Jacob's behind-the-scenes name. (*Akev* is the heel, the back of the foot.) Esau sees him as the snake, who comes up from behind and attacks the heel.[26]

But the ambiguous quality of such lateness is marked by Rashi and the Targum, in their translations of Esau's cry: "He has been too *clever* [*ve-ḥakmani*] for me." It is the essential meaning of *ḥokhma*, wisdom—not to rush in where angels fear to tread, but to imagine and manipulate realities from the sidelines. The sophistication of one who lies in wait, who bides his time, who plans his strategies from the rear, is Jacob's character and destiny. He is the ultimate man—born second, his destiny deferred. This is the classic midrashic reading of his position at birth, a historical vision of the eventual triumph of Jerusalem over Rome.[27]

Such a celebration of lateness in history has its roots in the promise to Abraham, in the Covenant of the Pieces. It will be *after* all the suffering and slavery in Egypt, God tells Abraham, that "in the end [*aḥarei khen*], they shall go free with great wealth" (15:14). He who laughs last laughs best. It is Jacob who will see the end of the story, the whole meaning of history.

There is, however, a darker aspect to lateness. Jacob—about to become Israel—lives the full ambiguity of being behind. In the midrash, his tragic flaw was defined as being related to lateness: "You delayed on the journey." There is a tendency in Jacob that can be called sophistication, subtlety, imagination, but that exposes him to less flattering epithets:

> Rabbi and R. Yossi ben R. Yehuda were walking along, when they saw a Roman police officer coming toward them. Rabbi said: He will ask you three questions—"Who are you? What is your profession? And where are you going?" "Who are you?"—"Jews." "What is your profession?"—"Businessmen." "And where are you going?"—"To allocate wheat for the granaries at Dibnia." Rabbi presented himself to the police officer to see what he would ask him, while R. Yossi waited beside him to catch any further questions—so that there should be no discrepancy in their answers. R. Yossi then asked Rabbi: Where

did you learn to prepare the answer before the question? And Rabbi replied: From Jacob our father—"So you shall say . . . behold, he is behind us."[28]

The Roman militia are experienced as embodying all the sinister aspects of Esau, with "game in his mouth" (25:28)—which, as reported by Rashi, is midrashically understood as "trying to trap the unwary with sophistical questions." The situation of the two sages, menaced by hostile authority, generates a prototypical response: Rabbi rehearses the answer before the question. Compelled by experience of the hunter, the prey develops its own evasion strategies: the prey, in fact, becomes hunter, subtly tracking the enemy, "knowing from behind." Their paradigm is Jacob, characteristically "behind," late, wary, conscious of all possibilities. The sages and their paradigm assume a purely reactionary role: they will not take the initiative, they merely prepare their responses to the initiatives of others.

This, of course, is an eminently reasonable stance in a situation where all the power is with the enemy. But it is not so much the political as the psychological aspect of the midrash that commands our attention. The sages, faced with brute power, firmly ground that power in the arena of language. Who wins in that arena wins the game. The obliquities of language, the rhetorical power attributed by the sages to Esau, are met by a truthful, but thoroughly rehearsed use of language on the part of Jacob. Always cautious, alive to the possible implications of a narrative, to the fatal consequences of discrepancies between texts, the sages hone and harmonize their story—as Jacob writes the script for the dialogues of his servants and Esau, choreographs the eloquent movements of the herds of livestock.

What is at issue is indicated in the expletive effect of Jacob's name, as Esau so derisively and bitterly utters it: "Was he then named Jacob that he might outwit me these two times?" (27:36). It is not a question of deception, of lying to his brother: the sages tell the truth under interrogation. What maddens Esau is Jacob's reluctance to confront, his distrust of the face of the other. He will wait offstage, preparing his lines until they are word-perfect. He will parley for peace, but he will not trust the immediacy of a relationship with his brother, however sincere his kisses may seem to be.[29]

Spontaneity, therefore, is not Jacob's strong suit. Time must elapse, meanings must be allowed to emerge, before one hazards a reaction.

What is to be must be as fully preconceived in the mind as possible.[30] This is, of course, a kind of control, a way of mastering a perilous reality. Oblique, subtle, Jacob plans ahead, previsioning Esau's responses, choreographing sheep and goats, so that they send messages of endless stimulation, induce in his brother spasms of an almost erotic excitement. His own camp he structures with an equal deliberation: what is most loved is behind, what is behind is most beloved. Love flourishes where the deferred, the symbolic meanings are most in play, in the spaces, the fissures, where imagination traces out infinite possibilities.[31]

## Becoming Israel: confrontation and mastery

The ultimate — and absurd — recourse of such a dynamic of reservation and deferral is the image of Dinah in a box. Jacob has "withheld love" from his brother; he has lost hope and trust in a reality of confrontation and change. The paradoxical hazard of too sophisticated, too "delaying" a consciousness is a kind of impotence. To be obsessed with controlling the issues in a complex world is to risk losing all dynamic contact with that world.

But the Jacob of our Parsha is Jacob-about-to-become-Israel. From his first message to Esau, he is concerned with the fact that he has not yet consummated his father's blessing: "Be master over your brothers" (27:29): "I have not become powerful or important" (Rashi, 32:5). On a conscious level, Jacob is deflecting his brother's jealousy and hatred, but, unconsciously, he is exercised by the problem of *serara*, of mastery. What is the meaning of authority, how does one control the contingencies, the absurdities of experience, how does one, in effect, *author* one's own life? Up to now, Jacob acknowledges, "I have been on the margins of Laban's world, a sojourner, a stranger; I have been in the *ahor*, in the rear, the late position." Anticipating events — the story of the striped and speckled sheep is a paradigm here — orchestrating responses of animals and people — Jacob has capitalized on his intelligence and foresight. In his dialogues with Laban and with his wives, he has deployed all his verbal resources to outwit his enemies. But now, the modality of "behindness" begins to irk him, for it has not led to the fulfillment of his father's blessing. In order to be a *sar*, a person of power and authority, something else is needed — a capacity to confront, a passionate will that exposes one to loss and injury.

In a magnificently ironic moment, the narrative sets Jacob's "behindness" in perspective, by comparing it with—of all things—Shekhem's
passion for Dinah. Dinah's brothers demand that Shekhem and all the
males in his town circumcise themselves, as part of the marriage agreement. "And the youth lost no time [*lo iḥer*] in doing the thing, for he
wanted Jacob's daughter" (34:19). Shekhem, the villain-rapist, is presented in an unexpectedly sympathetic light: he wants, he desires, he
loves.[32] Exposing himself to circumcision, he risks his manhood; he does
not "hang back," "lose time," delay. On this axis, Jacob and Shekhem
emerge as polar opposites: subtle, aware of suspended meanings, Jacob
lacks something in passion.

It is in this context that his confrontation with the man-angel becomes
most significant. The mysterious "man" seems to come upon him unawares. Before he knows, before he can put himself on guard, he is
embraced and held in the loving-hostile grip of the wrestler. Rashi's
reading of the word, *va-ye'avek* ["wrestled"] is illuminating: he emphasizes nuances of twining, knotting round one another, being tied together—"for this is the way of two people who strain to push each other
down to the ground—they embrace and struggle [*ḥovko ve-ovko*] with each
other" (32:24). This is clearly a passionate experience, involving the
closest confrontation (literally face-to-face)[33] of the whole body.

We described Jacob as taken unawares by the strange "man." But
perhaps, in some enigmatic sense, Jacob is the aggressor, who has waited,
"alone," for the man, whose struggle is expressed in the passive form—as
though it is Jacob who engages with him, or who has conjured the man's
spirit out of the lonely air. Who is this man? The classic midrashic answer
is that he is Esau's guardian angel, literally his *sar*—his authority, the
principle of his authenticity. (The Greek ancestry of the word resonates
with violence. *Authenteo*: to have full power over; also, to commit a
murder. *Authentes*: a master, a doer; also, a perpetrator, a murderer, even a
self-murderer, a suicide.)[34]

Another midrashic tradition, however, suggests a more ambiguous
identification: " 'I shall not let you go till you tell me your name.' And he
called his name Israel—like his own (the angel's) name, for his name was
Israel."[35]

In this reading, the angel has come for no hostile purpose but "to save
and rescue him." This angel is called Israel, perhaps because that is the
purpose of his mission, to show Jacob, in a therapeutic encounter, how to

become Israel. Since angels are named for their mission, this may be the reason for the angel's response to Jacob's question ("What is your name?") — "Why do you ask my name?" Jacob already knows in himself the purpose of the angel's coming, for, essentially, he is facing himself, the desired-feared necessity of a new name. He has summoned the angel to save him from the condition of being Jacob.

The struggle between Jacob and the Israel principle has no unequivocal outcome. Two approaches to power, to authority, even to authenticity, are mobilized here. There is a dialectical confrontation, in which, as the Netziv puts it, "both of them prevailed."[36] Jacob emerges with a thigh injury. Even if we take into account the midrashic reading that the rising "sun brought him healing" (Rashi, 32:31), the Netziv suggests that this healing cured only the immediate pain and made it all the clearer to Jacob that he would, in fact, limp all his life: "he realized that the angel, too, had prevailed over him to some extent."

Evenly matched, Jacob wants to prevail, to absorb into himself the power of his partner. He wants to become Israel, by mastering the angel. The wrestling match is an occasion for clarification, for discovery of the parameters of personal power.[37] At a certain point in the match, the angel sees that he cannot prevail over Jacob and injures his thigh. He then begs for release: " 'Let me go, for dawn is breaking.' But he answered, 'I will not let you go, unless you bless me' " (32:26).

Another midrash deciphers a connection between the injury and Jacob's refusal to release the angel: "He said, 'You have injured me and hurt me — I shall not let you go.' "[38] Jacob is given a certain moral advantage by his injury. Against all the arguments of the angel ("It is time for me to sing God's praises — if I miss today, I will never be allowed to sing again — I was not sent to bless you — if I obey you, I will be expelled from my place in Heaven"), against all rational and mystical objections, Jacob insists on holding the angel, and gaining the blessing — *because* he has been injured. His Jacob-identity suffers a pang of inner knowledge. This identity is not sufficient: the angel who has the face of Israel must yield up his secret of "more life."[39] The pain Jacob suffers empowers him to defy convention and claim a larger range of authenticity.

Ultimately, of course, Jacob and Israel both remain his names. The dialectical confrontation between his two personae is never entirely resolved. This is true throughout the biblical and prophetic writings, where the passionate power of confrontation and the sophisticated "knowing from behind" both remain essential aspects of the man and the nation, undergoing mutations and reworkings throughout history.[40] Certainly, before God confirms the angel's blessing, Jacob's unequivocal assumption of the name Israel is unjustified. It betrays Jacob's ongoing conflict, the dilemma of double identity, and his desire for unambiguous resolutions.

## Jacob-Israel: a "crippling sense of belatedness"

Jacob-Israel is indeed an uneasy combination. Jacob desires both knowledge and power, both subtlety and potency. If the sages criticize him for failing in love for Esau, for a premature arrogation of authority, or for an overconfidence about what the morrow will yield, essentially their criticisms can all be focused on the basic issue of *ibur*: "You have delayed on the journey." To be behind or in front, to be late or early, deferring or confronting: it is along this axis of possibilities that Jacob must plot his course.

When he meets Esau, after his night encounter with his Israel-self, "he himself went on ahead" (33:3). He is held in close embrace by his brother: *Va-y'habkehu* clearly evokes the love-hate ambiguities of the wrestler's grip—*va-ye'avek*. There is a tension that is both erotic and agonistic, since each brother wants of the other what he lacks, and each fears to lose his place on the earth. As Jacob's family move forward to meet Esau, it retains its highly formalized structure, the dearest last. But Jacob himself embraces and is embraced. He offers Esau his "blessing" (33:11), by which he means, according to Rashi, his gift, his salute to Esau, in the moment of true encounter: he greets the godliness in Esau's face (33:10) and, implicitly, he wishes him, too, more life. This is a moment of equilibrium, in which Esau is genuinely moved by Jacob's courage and generosity.

Such a courage is composed of multiple levels of readiness, say the sages—readiness for war, for peace, for prayer. His enlarged sense of his own power leads Jacob, paradoxically, to an equivalent awareness of his brother's power; underlying both is the equalizing knowledge of man's condition in the presence of God. Emerson's definition of courage seems relevant here: "Courage consists in the conviction that they with whom you contend are no more than you. If we believed in the existence of strict *individuals*, natures, that is, not radically identical but unknown, immeasurable, we should never dare to fight."[41] A certain mystique of the individual, "unknown, immeasurable," has to be shed if Jacob is to confront Esau as "no more" than himself, as "radically identical" with himself.

Harold Bloom deploys this passage from Emerson, as part of his argument about the problem of power in the growth of poetic genius. Emerson manifests "acute apprehension of the sorrows of poetic influence. . . . If the new poet succumbs to a vision of the precursor as the Sublime, 'unknown, immeasurable,' then the great contention with the dead father will be lost. . . . Emerson, shrewdest of all visionaries, early perceived the accurate enemy in the path of aspiring youth: 'Genius is always sufficiently the enemy of genius by overinfluence.' "

At root, the question of "overinfluence," the Oedipal problem in the area of psychological and spiritual development, lies at the base of all Jacob's "delays." Jacob suffers, literally and figuratively, from a "crippling sense of belatedness," in Bloom's rhetoric. In the simplest sense, he is the *last* of the patriarchs; the essential, dramatic directions have been plotted by his father and grandfather. If we adopt the kabbalistic formula of *ḥesed* (love) and *gevura* (strength), Abraham has traced out the course of love, daring, expansiveness, and imagination, while Isaac has lived the inward life, shadowed by fear, by constriction, by a knowledge of what it is to be bound on an altar. This, too, yields its wisdom, generates a subtlety, a fine-tuned awareness of structures and differences. What is left for Jacob to do?

The answer offered in classic midrashic sources is that, in some sense, Jacob is to be the ideal "true" synthesis of the polar characteristics of Abraham and Isaac. But, in real terms, the problem of a Jacob is not capable of simple solutions. R. Hutner offers a colloquial Yiddish epigram: Abraham was the *geworrener*—the one who became; Isaac was the *geborrener*—the one who was born into it; while Jacob was the *farfallener*—the one who no longer had any choice. Thesis, antithesis, and synthesis: the role of the third generation is clearly the most complex, precisely because in an obvious sense everything has already been done.

Bloom's argument, worked out in *The Anxiety of Influence*, *A Map of Misreading*, and *The Breaking of the Vessels*, is that to be born later is, for the poet, for the creative person, a "crippling" experience. One cannot avoid saying what has already been said: one suffers from the Oedipal dilemma of having been preceded: "A poet . . . is not so much a man speaking to men as a man rebelling against being spoken to by a dead man (the precursor) outrageously more alive than himself. A poet dare not regard himself as being *late*, yet cannot accept a substitute for the first vision he reflectively judges to have been his precursor's also."[42]

This is Jacob's dilemma. At the core, what "cripples" him is his sense of his father's crippling. Isaac, in the branding moment of his life, was bound hand and foot; and Jacob, in spite of all his movements of hand and feet, in spite of the freedom and energy he expresses in love and work during the years away from his father's house, remains profoundly absorbed by his father's trauma.

This, I suggest, is the conflict indicated by his translation of God's promise in the dream at Beth El: where God had said, "I shall bring you back to this land," Jacob declares, "if I come back *in wholeness to my father's house.*" Thereafter, as we have noticed, Jacob avoids any mention of his father, apart from one enigmatic reference to "the God of my father, the God of Abraham," and to "the Fear of Isaac" (31:42). It seems as though, in order to hew out a possible identity for himself, he flinches from confronting the image of his father, the fear that is his father's genius: "Genius is always sufficiently the enemy of genius by over-influence." And he most poignantly expresses this "overinfluence" by delaying his return home, to his "father's house."

## The necessary synthesis

It is this delay, with its refusal to confront, to take account of the past, by acknowledgment or by repudiation, that is diagnosed as the tragic flaw of this period of his life. Hanging back, reserving his options, reluctant to return, Jacob refuses to negotiate the necessary synthesis between his father and his grandfather, between subtlety and passion. He is radically afraid to speak of his father's God as anything other than fear,[43] afraid to engage with that fear and move toward love.

Harold Bloom articulates the general human dilemma:

> If we are human, then we depend upon a Scene of Instruction, which is necessarily also a scene of authority and of priority. If you will not have one instructor or another, then precisely by rejecting all instructors, you will condemn yourself to the earliest Scene of Instruction that imposed itself upon you. The clearest analogue is necessarily Oedipal; reject your parents vehemently enough, and you will become a belated

version of them, but compound with their reality, and you may partly free yourself.[44]

Jacob, afraid of fear, is fixed in fear ("Jacob was greatly frightened and anxious" [32:8]); he is a "belated version" of Isaac, just because he rejects, he defers the encounter with what Isaac represents. To compound with his father's reality would be to achieve his own freedom — what Ramban calls his own *ḥelek*, his unique synthesis of the worlds of his precursors.[45]

For Bloom, this involves first a willingness to be instructed by the experience of one's father, and, ultimately — as in the case of the "strong poet" — a capacity to "misread," to engage in vital, original reinterpretations, which necessarily involve falsifications, of the work of one's precursors. The "willful re-interpretation of all reality" (de Man) must involve such "misreading," because "every strong reading insists that the meaning it finds is exclusive and accurate."[46]

Jacob's career, according to Ramban, who draws on kabbalistic sources, is a quest for equilibrium, for *emet*, truth on the psychological as well as the cognitive plane. Jacob seeks his true self, in R. D. Laing's use of the term. He wants to "read strongly" the texts his precursors have bequeathed to him; paradoxically, though, such a reading must be both faithful and "false," he must both submit to instruction and rebel against his late condition, if he is to avoid being a mere replica, helplessly branded, of his precursor.

This he achieves, Ramban claims, at the end of his life, when he goes down to Egypt to rejoin his lost son, Joseph: "So Jacob set out with all that was his, and he came to Beer Sheva, where he offered sacrifices to the God of his father Isaac. God called to him in a vision by night" (46:1–2). Why, asks Ramban, is his father Isaac so clearly specified as the paradigm of relationship with God, at this time of his life? Rashi had quoted the general principle that "one owes respect to one's father more than to one's grandfather." Ramban comments that it might have been more courteous simply to write of "the God of his fathers," without giving preference to one or the other, as Jacob in fact does later, for the first time (48:15),[47] or else to avoid any mention of his family. The point is, however, that Jacob, as he reaches a maturity of his own "strong" identity, relates fully to both his precursors, and *especially* to his father Isaac. For it is the Fear of Isaac (31:42, 53), Isaac's modality of worship, his reading of reality, that has haunted Jacob throughout his life.

The nodal experience is, Ramban asserts, the "Akedah day," the existential dread that he lived on that day he was bound in sacrifice to God. As Jacob begins his journey down to Egypt, he has agonized premonitions of the exile and slavery of his children; he offers sacrifices — specifically, peace offerings (*zevaḥim* or *shelamim*) — to the God of his father Isaac, who is known in dread and blind anguish. He engages fully with that dread, and prays that it may be moderated in him, that he may find a new vital equilibrium.

Jacob is the first person to offer such peace offerings, expressing his longing for peace, for wholeness. But in order to realize that desire, he must begin with the difficult, the overwhelming experience, of his immediate precursor, his father. He must, in Bloom's terms, compound with Isaac's reality; only then can he seek to balance the fear, the sense of mystery and complexity, in which the human is dwarfed, with the opposing sense of *ḥesed*, of love, connection, spontaneous expansion and encounter with all that exists. This search for equilibrium, for a sense of his "own quick'ning power,"[48] Ramban calls the search for "truth." It is consummated through sacrifice, through "peace offerings," which generate a new revelation of God, in a "vision by night" — a revelation of modified dread, irradiated by hope and promise.

## The struggle for stability

On this reading, Jacob's life is a struggle to synthesize, to "misread" strongly, the lives of his precursors. He knows the "crippling sense of belatedness," of coming *after* the originators. He is shadowed by the stringent agony of his father, while he wants to realize the possibility of love, of compassion, of imaginative connection.[49] But only through a certain sacrifice, suggested in the need to "make good" on vows (*le-shalem*, "pay off," "make whole"), can he engage with and transcend the crippling psychology of belatedness.

This is the core irony. In order to overcome the debilitating anxiety of his belatedness, Jacob must expose himself to fear, to face-to-face encounter with what he most dreads. He must confront the nameless horror of the man who grips him, binds him arm and leg, if he is to acquire the partial freedom of a limping hero, who has learned his new name — and, incidentally, the mirror identity of the face of his dread. He comes to know his courage and his vulnerability, simultaneously. The sun that rises "for him" may, indeed, as the midrash claims, bring him healing; but still he limps, even as the sun shines for him. He has gained and lost, a paradigm experience that sets the tone for his whole life, and for the lives of his descendants.

What he has gained, primarily, is courage: the "conviction that they with whom you contend are no more than you." He contends, essentially, with himself, with his dread, his sense of evil,[50] his need to control and structure a cogent world, safe from the mystery of his father's binding. Seeking wholeness, he struggles for a new sense of the good, that will endure through all evil.

"I am too small," he cries to God, before engaging with Esau, "for all the kindnesses [*ḥasadim*] and all the truth [*emet*]" (32:11). Strangely, the Targum translates *emet* as *tavevon* ("goodness"). Ramban suggests that the kindnesses may refer to all the episodes of rescue, the acts of grace, by which God mysteriously intervenes in Jacob's life; while the word *emet* refers to the *enduring* goodness of his life, the stable consciousness that does not change with time and vicissitude. "I am too small," says Jacob, with modesty and, perhaps, with realism. His whole life will be a struggle to grow, to achieve the stability, the wholeness for which he yearns.

"You said," he reminds God in his prayer, " 'I will deal with you in great goodness' " (32:13). God, in fact, did not say this: He never spoke of goodness in relation to Jacob, who twice speaks of God's "goodness," in the course of a short prayer (32:10, 13). Jacob "misreads" God's promise: he interprets in the way most vital to him the words, "I shall be with you,"[51] since what he most desires is that enduring consciousness of the goodness of God that permeates and integrates a life.

The *Sefat Emet* makes the point elegantly: "I will deal *with* you (*imkha*) in great goodness" suggests that God promises Jacob that his sense of his own life will share in the experience of God's goodness.[52] God will not merely be good *to* Jacob: He will make Jacob accomplice in the benign self-creation of Israel.

A strong goodness—a paradoxical, "whole" condition in which passion and subtlety, safety and love are interfused: Jacob-Israel plays many variations on this basic theme to the end of his life. *Emet*—truth—in this sense is not overnight work: to encounter an angel is not to be healed for ever. Jacob's instinct to delay, to defer encounter, to lie in wait and be wise, is to be tempered by much experience of solitude and encounter.

But this dialectical mode of learning has the very texture of human freedom: "You hedge me before and behind; You lay Your hand upon me" (Psalms 139:5).[53] God's hand laid on man in creation set him apart from all other creatures, according to Rashi (1:27); they were made "by His word," determined, made precisely according to His will, while man was formed out of the symbolic freedom of the unmediated creative process.[54] Rashi quotes this verse from Psalms, in his commentary on the creation of man, to sharpen the contrast between the human and the nonhuman, between freedom and determinism.

The first part of the verse, equally, I suggest, evokes the peculiar process by which human beings are created. *Aḥor* and *kedem* ("Behind and before"): between delay, belatedness, anxiety, and structure, on the one hand, and spontaneity, courage, and passionate encounter, on the other, the human being is besieged, challenged, pressed by God's hand. The image conveys all the tension of a condition both constrained and — strangely — free.[55] Invisibly to the naked eye, Jacob dances in place, the human dance in which he assumes the multiple postures between fore and aft, passion and deliberation, love and fear.

# VA-YESHEV 🍎
## Re-membering
## the Dismembered

The *quest for peace*

> Now Jacob was settled in the land where his father had sojourned, the land of Canaan. (37:1)

The narrative of Jacob's later life, after his return to Canaan, is ironically captioned by this opening verse. From the earliest midrashic commentaries, microscopic attention has been paid to the apparently innocuous opening — and titular — word of the Parsha — *va-yeshev*. On the surface a neutral account of Jacob's "settling down" in the Holy Land, after twenty years' exile in Padan Aram, the verse, the verb, has classically been read as resonant with forebodings, with a sense that Jacob has fatally misread the structure, the plot, the moral motifs of his own life: " '*Jacob was settled*': Jacob sought to settle in peace — there leapt upon him the agitation of Joseph. The righteous seek to settle in peace — God says, 'Is it not enough for the righteous, what is prepared for them in the world to come, that they seek to settle in peace in this world?' "[1]

There is a poignant undertow to the word *va-yeshev*, as Rashi reads it. Quite reasonably, in the way that all righteous people do — the statement about the desire for peace is unqualified (without "if" or "when") — Jacob would like to settle his life, to find some measure of tranquillity after all his troubles. One might even say that it is characteristic of righteous people to yearn for such a "settling," a clarification of the turbulences and anguish of life. But God rebuffs this yearning, in a tone of strange sarcasm: "Is it not enough?" In God's rhetoric, the righteous are made to seem importunate, almost greedy, their desire for peace in this world wrongheaded, in view of the treasure awaiting them in another world.

243

Neither Rashi nor his source midrash speaks of "peace," as the nature of "what is prepared" in the world-to-come; so that one cannot read this as simply a matter of actuarial computation — as though a certain measure of peace were allocated to the righteous, who may not overdraw on their this-worldly allowance. God simply asks an ironic, enigmatic question about the desire of the righteous, and implicitly answers by the savage "leap upon him" of "the agitation [*rogez*] of Joseph." What is the meaning of God's question, of His implicit reproach to the righteous, and, specifically, to Jacob?

We may perhaps find some clue to understanding in a phrase in the source midrash: "When the righteous settle in peace — and seek to settle in peace — in this world, Satan comes to accuse them."[2] Subtly, the midrash indicates a possible imbalance in the attitude of the righteous. Given a time of tranquillity, they discover in themselves a passion for tranquillity — they *seek* to settle in peace — which arouses the anger of Satan. (Compare Rashi's version, where it is God, judicious and unanswerable, who criticizes the universal desire of righteous people for peace.) In the original midrash, the righteous make themselves vulnerable to Satan's attack, they release a certain force of evil in the world, by their overweening desire to settle, to discern, *in this world*, the innate structure of meaning in their lives.

If we respond to this nuance in the midrash, we understand that it is not wrong to "settle in peace," but to seek, with too great a need, such a "settling." The quest for peace is problematic: Rashi telescopes the text of the midrash, assuming that the emphasis on "seeking" is abundantly evident. What he changes is the speaker of reproach — it is not Satan, but God, who asks the ironic question; it is not so much evil as misjudgment that is at issue in Rashi's reading.

Taking the emphasis on "quest for peace" into account, Jacob's "settling" becomes not a fact, but an attitude, a mode in which he seeks to appropriate his life. In the most obvious sense, he would like to "settle down" in the Holy Land, after his years in exile and danger. He would like to read the narrative of his own life as entering a period of fulfillment, of closure, after the difficult conflicts and confrontations of his youth.

## Reading history: the desire for aesthetic composure

Possibly, too, he would like to read the history of his family as having arrived at its consummation. Perhaps the promise to Abraham, "between the pieces" (15:13–16), a promise heavy with exile, slavery and suffering but culminating in eventual redemption, is to be realized in this latter period of his life?

> "*And Jacob was settled*": Jacob speculated, "God said to Abraham that his children would be 'sojourners'—I have been a 'sojourner' for twenty years in the house of Laban, 'enslaved' to the care of his sheep." And when he saw that Esau had gone to live in another city, he said, "With this, the 400 years' slavery is fulfilled," and his mind was settled. But God said, "My thoughts are deeper than yours, as it said, 'For My thoughts are not your thoughts'" [Isaiah 55:8], and immediately brought upon him the plot [*alilah*] of Joseph's story. When did He bring this plot upon him? When he thought there would be no slavery in Egypt and his mind became settled—"Now Jacob was settled."[3]

Jacob tries to interpret history in the light of God's promise. God had spoken of sojourning, alienation in "a land not theirs"—Jacob had indeed been exiled to a land not his. Precisely as God had specified in His covenant, He had been enslaved (the word *la 'avod* [to work] is a *leitwort* of the narrative of his relation to Laban) and afflicted (31:42). And the four hundred years clearly does not represent a fixed sum of years in Egypt, even in the normal reckoning of the fulfillment of the Covenant: God "calculated the end" of slavery; in accord with His desire to make it bearable, He began the calculation with the birth of Isaac (Rashi, 15:13), who all his life is characterized as a "sojourner."

The family history of alienation in a "land not theirs" is, therefore, not confined to the Egyptian episode. Even in Canaan, Isaac was a "stranger," unable to appropriate the land. In the view of this midrash, then, Jacob's speculation is quite plausible: if God can reduce the 400-year exile to 210, allowing for the broadest definition of exile to cover the 400-year stipulation, then He can reduce it still further, so that the rootlessness of the patriarchs will be read retroactively as having fulfilled the terms of covenantal suffering. Jacob's clue is the fact that Esau has left the Holy Land, to find his own separate destiny: this seems to indicate the end of the vicissitudes of the Covenant. Now, "Jacob's mind was settled": things seemed to fall into proper perspective, a kind of clarity and coherence invested the narrative of family history, as he set himself to read it. God, however, reads the plot differently. However plausible Jacob's reading may seem, however satisfying aesthetically and cognitively, he has to face the shock of participation in a very different "plot." The story of Joseph is that shock that rouses Jacob from his aesthetic composure.

If Jacob craves a certain gratification that is hinted at in the word *va-yeshev*, yet the moral criticism implicit in Rashi's reading—"It is not enough for the righteous"—remains enigmatic. After all, the desire for cogency—for *yishuv ha-da'at*, as the midrash calls it—is normally praised in rabbinic literature: "The older they grow, the more clear-minded they grow."[4] *Yishuv ha-da'at* is opposed to *tiruf ha-da'at*—literally, to be of torn mind—to be confused, bewildered, not fully conscious. This is a question of order as against disorder, clarity as against confusion.

More pointedly, it is a question of composition, of composure. To be able to connect the parts of an experience, of a text into a cogent whole, is the task of the writer, the artist, the critic; it is properly, Rashi says (Psalms 16:7), in quite a different context, the task of the reader of sacred texts: "'*My conscience* [lit., kidneys] *admonish me at night.*' The sages applied this to Abraham, who learned Torah from his own experience (from his inward parts), before it was revealed at Sinai. So we too should [lit.] settle [*yashev*] the texts in order."

Rashi comments here on his own lifework; his primary concern in reading Torah is the discovery of order, which, as in Abraham's pre-Sinai experience, is never *given* entirely. It has to emerge out of one's own kidneys, in the bizarre image of the midrash:[5] one has to undergo the torments of wakeful darkness to "create" Torah, to find, in the intimate encounter between reader and text, a new composition of the elements. The satisfaction, the composure that results from such a "settling" is not merely innocent but, even Rashi seems to assert, an ideal condition of being: "so we too should settle. . . ."

In view of this, Jacob's attempt to resolve, to "read" the text of God's covenant in the light of his own life seems impeccable. And yet, as we have seen, God does not merely override Jacob's reading (as in the above midrash), but—much more radically—He mocks such an attempt, wherever it occurs, as vulgar misreading, a lack of aesthetic tact.

The opening verse seems to contrast Jacob's desire to "settle," to interpret his life and God's word, with the "sojournings" of his father, Isaac. The provisional, God-directed quality of his father's life has been replaced by a new enterprise in Jacob's life—the enterprise that the kabbalists called *emet*—truth. Jacob wants to read the family texts strongly, to synthesize the contrasting elements of his father's and his grandfather's worlds. In a word, Jacob wants to compose a whole world of his own: "He sought to settle in peace" indicates a cognitive and aesthetic ambition to see history resolved, sojournings over, in this world. What "leaps upon him" is the wild animal that tears Joseph apart—*tarof toraf Yosef*. Instead of *yishuv ha-da'at*, clarity, composure, coherence, there is *tiruf ha-da'at*, confusion, bewilderment, loss of consciousness.

## The Joseph story: turbulence and cruelty

It is in this sense that the opening, titular word of the Parsha—*va-yeshev*—puts into play a concept, a human desire, that is immediately—and literally—savaged. The chapter that tells of Joseph's being sold into slavery by his brothers, chapter 37, begins with *va-yeshev* and ends with *tarof toraf*. Jacob has attempted a reading that proves to be woefully wrong. From a human perspective, there seems to be an irreducible disorder in things. No elegant composure can veil the organic disease of this world. And the full tension of composure and discomposure, of *yishuv* and *tiruf*, is felt most acutely by the righteous, by those whose sense of beauty, whose desire for harmony, exposes them to the shock of reality.

The point is made in Rashi's first comment on the Parsha. He contrasts the account of Esau's *toledot*—his children and descendants—with that of Jacob's *toledot*. (The two accounts are consecutive—the previous Parsha ended with Esau's genealogy, culminating in many generations of kings, "before there ever was a king in Israel" [36:31].)

> "And Jacob was settled": After narrating the settlings of Esau and his children, in a brief manner—because they were not distinguished or important enough to explain how they settled down and the order of their wars, how they dispossessed the Hurrites—the Torah explains the settlings of Jacob and his children, in a full way, all the changes in their fortunes, since they were significant before God to relate them at length. So you find also with the ten generations from Adam to Noah—"So and so begat so and so," but when it comes to Noah, the text deals with him at length. So, too, with the ten generations from Noah to Abraham—they are covered briefly and only Abraham is described at length.

The main difference between the two accounts of settlings and offspring is a matter of length. Esau's children produce children in no more time than it takes to read the words on the page; Esau himself "settles in the hill country of Seir" (36:8), with equal, uncomplicated promptitude. The narrator is simply not interested enough to give us the complexities of a story of settlings and childbearings. When it comes to Jacob and his *toledot*, his *yishuvim*, however, the story is told in all its complication, in all the terrible, heart-stopping details. The turnings of the wheel of fortune, the wrenching reversals of the plot, which — retroactively — can be seen to create a chain of causality, all this is given in full, circumstantial detail in Jacob's case.

The difference between the two narratives, however, is clearly more than a matter of length. The real issue is one of importance. Esau's family is not, literally, worth thinking about (*hashuvim*), their lives resolve themselves predictably and simply; there are no secret areas (*sefunim*), no crevices out of which God can speak. They settle down in their own country; they bear children; they even produce kings — exemplars of national coherence — many generations before Jacob's children are ready to do so.

Jacob's children are individual, unique, unclassifiable. The story of their "settling" is a long and tortuous process:

> "*These are the* toledot *of Jacob*" (37:2): These are the stories of the children of Jacob — these are their settlings and their vicissitudes — till they arrived at the reality of settlement. The first cause was, "Joseph was seventeen years old . . .": as a consequence of that, they went through many turns of fate until they went down to Egypt. (Rashi, 37:2)

Rashi here offers an answer to the problem of the word *toledot*. He insists that it refers to Jacob's children[6] (even though only Joseph is listed), but that *eileh* — "these" — refers back to the key word *va-yeshev*: it signifies the zig-zag processes, by which Jacob's children finally arrived at the point called *yishuv* — full settlement. This concept of process exerts explosive pressure on the surface meaning of the word *va-yeshev*. In Esau's case, it is indeed true to say, simply and flatly, that he "settled down." In Jacob's case, Rashi implies, a discomposed, unsettled movement of lives, relationships, and locations begins here.

This turbulence — Rashi's word *gilgul*, for example, refers to a field full of hills and depressions — ultimately leads to resolution, to a resettling in the land of Canaan. But this will be many years later, more than 250 years later, after much suffering, much turbulence in the story line. Interpretation in the midst of history will not be easy; and in a sense, the whole

Torah is narrated in the midst of the turbulent process of history. Arrival at the Promised Land, the full settlement of which Rashi speaks, is always in the future, promised, imagined, but, within the framework of the biblical narrative proper, never consummated.

Jacob's settling is a long story; it is also a story of contingency and cruelty that tears apart the elegant closure that Jacob speculated he could read in his own lifetime. But for this very reason, paradoxically, Jacob and his children are called *sefunim va-ḥashuvim*. They are substantial, complicated, with secret potentialities, which take time to explore.

## Jacob and Esau: the choice of alienation

Rashi conveys a further sense of the contrasting destinies of Jacob and Esau, in his comment on Esau's choice of territory (36:6–7):

> "Esau went to another land [lit., to a land] because of his brother Jacob. For their possessions were too many for them to dwell together." Because of his brother Jacob, because of the writ of obligation of the decree, "for a stranger will be your seed" [15:13], which was placed on the seed of Isaac. Esau said, "Let me go away from here, I have no part either in the gift, for this land was given to him, or in paying the obligation."

Esau leaves for "a land": the strange indefinite article indicates that his main urge is to remove himself from Canaan and Jacob, to find a place to settle, wherever it may be. He rejects any share in the Covenant between the Pieces; he will have neither the gift of the land nor the suffering preceding it. The Covenant is, interestingly, represented as a writ of obligation: it represents something to be *paid*, to be worked through, its elements dismantled, torn open, uncovered (*lifro'a* has all these nuances of meaning). Through time, through the 400-year period specified by God, a process of analysis and testing is to take place; only after that process has been lived through can the Land be possessed. Esau wants no part of the process of piecemeal self-realization and ultimate gift. He chooses instead the instant gratification: "So Esau settled in the hill-country of Seir — Esau being Edom" (36:8).

Another midrash fleshes out Esau's choice:

> Esau said to Jacob, Let us divide all that father has left us into two parts, and I shall choose my share, for I am the elder. What did Jacob do? He

divided the property: all that his father had left, as one part, and the Land of Israel, as the other part. What did Esau do? He went to consult Ishmael, in the desert, as it is said, "So Esau went to Ishmael" [28:9]. Ishmael said to Esau, The Emorites and the Canaanites are now in possession of the land, and Jacob trusts that he will inherit the land! Take all that your father left you, and Jacob will be left with nothing! So Esau took all that his father left him, and the Land of Israel and the Cave of Makhpelah he gave to Jacob, and they wrote an eternally valid contract between them. And Esau took his wives and all his property, as it is said, "He went to another land because of his brother Jacob" [36:6]. As a reward for removing all his things from Jacob's land, he received a hundred states, from Seir to Magdiel.[7]

Esau takes the issue of inheritance under advisement. In worldly terms, his decision is shrewd: he takes all that the world can immediately offer him and leaves Jacob nothing to take hold of, no *eretz aḥuzah*, such as Esau's descendants, spread over a hundred states, with kings and princes to lead them, are granted.

"These are the chiefs of Edom . . . by their settlements in the land which they hold" (36:43). So reads the verse that precedes "Now Jacob was settled." Seeing his brother's destiny, the tangible power and coherence of his world, Jacob seeks the same security in the land where his father had accepted a provisional, wandering existence.[8] But the writ has not yet been paid off. Jacob has chosen the Land, and with it he has chosen a distinctly unsettled existence:

"*So Jacob was settled*": Esau's princes settled in the land of "their holding"—that is, in the land they took hold of, as an everlasting possession. But Jacob lived as a sojourner, like his father, in a land not theirs but Canaan's. This means that they chose to live as sojourners in the chosen land, and that "Strangers shall your seed be in a land not theirs" was fulfilled in them, and not in Esau, for Jacob alone represents the seed of calling.[9]

Ramban's reading of the word *va-yeshev* fades it into the associations of "his father's sojournings": his father's essential modality is continued into Jacob's life, and, Ramban emphasizes, constitutes an existential choice of a profoundly paradoxical nature. The Land is chosen by God; but it is also chosen by Isaac and Jacob. They choose to sojourn in it, although it is "not theirs." Here, Ramban executes an astonishing sleight-of-hand: God had warned Abraham of a 400-years' exile in a "land not theirs," clearly — or, at least, with the clarity of hindsight — referring to the Israelite slavery in Egypt. But Ramban adopts the coinage of alienation for the patriarchs' experience of the Holy Land: it is Canaan that is the "land not theirs," the land in which they are strangers.

Technically, of course, this is no novel idea, since it forms the basis for the classic understanding that the 400-years' exile began with the birth of Isaac (Rashi 15:13). But Ramban's comment goes far beyond the technical. Isaac and Jacob make a choice of a certain kind of existence — squatters in a land not possessed by them. And they are contrasted in this with Esau — who takes fast hold of his land, and who, in that very act, disqualifies himself from the "seed of calling." The paradox is manifest: Ramban, unlike Rashi, emphasizes the free choice of a rootless existence in the Holy Land, and not the search for peace or stability. What identifies the seed of destiny is the capacity to choose a troubled, unsettled life, with nothing in one's hand.

The contrasting destinies of Esau and Jacob, therefore, are plotted on a graph of "settledness." *Va-yeshev* marks the divergence of the two lines, the choice of immediate realization and appropriation, on the one hand, or the ambiguous endowment of suffering and ultimate gift, on the other. This is Ramban's understanding of Jacob's *va-yeshev*: he "settles for" the long way, the way of a complex, "significant" race, whose potential energies are to be discovered through a history of extreme experience. By accepting responsibility for the "writ of obligation," Jacob chooses the process rather than the fact of "settling": the many turns of the wheel, the unlikely causalities, the unpromising beginnings.

The midrashic notion of a contract under which Jacob and Esau assume separate destinies is referred to again, at a significant moment in Jewish history. Before entering the Promised Land, after forty years' wandering in the wilderness, the people send messengers to the king of Edom, descendants of Esau: "Thus says your brother Israel: You know all the hardships that have befallen us; that our ancestors went down to Egypt, that we dwelt in Egypt a long time, and that the Egyptians dealt harshly with us and our ancestors. . . . Allow us, then, to cross your country" (Numbers 20:14–15, 17). Rashi quotes the midrash:

> *"Your brother Israel"*: Why did Moses mention brotherhood here? Moses told him, We are brothers, children of Abraham, who was told, "A sojourner shall be your offspring." That writ was laid on both of us to pay off.

*"You know all the hardships"*: for this reason, your father separated from our father, "and he went to another land, because of his brother Jacob" — because of the writ of obligation that was laid on them, and that he left Jacob to carry.

*"The Egyptians dealt harshly with us"*: we suffered many troubles.

*"Allow us, then, to cross your country"*: you have no grounds for appeal about our inheritance of the Land of Israel, since you did not pay off the writ of obligation.

Rashi conveys a sense of the burden of destiny: Esau reneged on his share in this complex destiny, and has therefore no legitimate claim to its promise, while Jacob has been left to bear its full weight. Free choice is not the emphasis here; unlike Ramban, Rashi depicts an almost involuntary endurance of a divine decree. The midrashic narrative gives us an Esau who sidesteps this destiny, leaving Jacob to endure all its painful implications.

It seems, therefore, that there are two different emphases in the midrashic tradition, which are expressed in the two commentaries of Rashi and Ramban. In one reading — that of Rashi and *Bereshit Rabbah*[10] — a writ of obligation, the Covenant of the Pieces, with its drama of frustration and gift, is imposed on Abraham's family. Jacob is compelled to pay the full amount, since his brother has opted out of the family's responsibilities. In the other reading — that of Ramban and *Pirkei d'Rabbi Eliezer* — there is a *voluntary* assumption by Jacob of the experience of the Land of Israel, which, by its very nature, involves unsettledness, a life lived not by the grip of the hand, but by the words of the promise.

## Inexorable causality

It is this latter view, with its strange notion of freedom, that teases us out of thought. For the idea that Jacob *chooses* the modality of indirection, of volatile vicissitude, is contradicted by a central motif in the midrashic readings of the Joseph narrative. Rashi, for instance, speaks of a concatenation of events, an inexorable causality: "The first cause was, 'Joseph was seventeen years old.' As a result of this, they had to turn around and go down to Egypt" (37:2). The apparent disaster, the misdirection, of the family's emigration to Egypt, is precipitated by a "first cause" (the term ironically plays on the Aristotelian notion of the Prime Mover, the great "cause of causes," that sets all the spheres in motion): the fact of Joseph's youth, his father's special love for him, his brothers' jealousy and hatred.

In the family narrative, what sets the wheels turning is the fact that Joseph was seventeen, a *na'ar*, a youth, immature in his management of relationships. (The Baal Ha-Turim notes that *na'ar* and *shoteh* [fool] have the same numerical value!) The word implies much more than biological age (that, as Mizrahi points out, is already given): Joseph behaves with the narcissism of youth, with a dangerous unawareness of the inner worlds of others.

Later, the butler will tell Pharaoh of the dream interpreter in prison, describing him as a *na'ar ivri*, a Jewish lad; on which Rashi comments: "This is a disparaging term, meaning, fool, unfit for greatness" (41:12). Joseph has greatness thrust upon him, before the day is out—which seems to indicate that his *na'ar* nature has matured considerably, as a result of his adventures. And yet, apparently, there is a *na'ar* quality that accompanies him throughout his vicissitudes, and that, in his early life, explosively combines with his cleverness and closeness to his father. ("Son of his old age," as quoted by Rashi [37:3], is read midrashically to refer to his wisdom, his direct tutorial relationship with his father's intellectual tradition, his clonelike resemblance to his father.) He is a child prodigy, prematurely knowledgeable, devastatingly unaware.

Joseph's growing wisdom is indicated by an apparently minor detail: he becomes sensitive to people's faces, to their changing expressions. When the butler and the baker meet him on the day after their dreams, he asks them, "Why do you appear downcast today?" (40:7). Instead of launching into a direct account of their dreams, the text records this trivial question, to make a point about sensitivity: "for this is the way of the wise person, to ask his companion, why his face looks different today from other days."[11] Joseph's progress in sensitivity to the human face, which hides and reveals invisible worlds, is a token of the deepening of his wisdom.

But it is his clever folly, his narcissism, which precipitates the narrative crisis. First causes, trivial, oblique data—youth, precocity, unawareness—lead to exile and slavery. Rashi emphasizes the inexorable chain of events. Behind him stands a powerful midrashic tradition that emphasizes the fatality of human life, and God's manipulation of human passions and follies.

It is in view of this tradition that Ramban's insistence that Jacob *chose* the life of alienation, or the motif in *Pirkei d'Rabbi Eliezer* of a deliberately worded contract in which Jacob assumes the burdens of the Covenant of the Pieces, seems enigmatic. The element of free choice seems tenuous in this narrative, particularly in the perspective of midrashic readings.

## God's plot

Perhaps the most powerful midrash in this fatalistic vein, for example — the midrash that poses the most provocative challenge to the concept of human freedom — is this passage in *Tanḥuma*, 4:

> "*And Joseph was brought down to Egypt*" [39:1]: This is an example of "Come and see the works of God, who is held in awe by men for His acts" [Psalms 66:5]. Even the awesome [lit., terrible] things that You bring upon us, You bring through a plot [*alilah*, translated here as "acts"]. Come and see: when God created the world, from the first day, He created the Angel of Death — "with darkness over the surface of the deep" [1:2] — that is the Angel of Death, who darkens the faces of human beings. And Adam was created on the sixth day and a pretext [*alilah* — lit., plot] was found to blame him for bringing death to the world, as it is said, "As soon as you eat of it, you shall die" [2:17]. This is like a man who wants to divorce his wife, and, before going home, writes a bill of divorce. He enters his house with the divorce in his hand, and seeks a pretext [*alilah*] to give it to her. He asks her for a cup of beverage, and she pours it for him. As he takes the cup from her, he says, "Here is your divorce." She says, "What have I done wrong?" He says, "Leave my house, for you have poured me a lukewarm drink!" She says, "But you knew that I would pour you a lukewarm drink, for you had already written the divorce bill and brought it in your hand!" In the same way, Adam said to God, "Master of the Universe, before You created Your world, two thousand years ago, the Torah was as a confidant with You . . . and in the Torah, it is written, 'This is the ritual: When a person dies in a tent . . .' [Numbers 19:14]. If You had not already planned death for Your creatures, would You have written this in the Torah? But You came to me with a pretext to make me responsible for death — 'terrible to man are Your plots.' ". . .

God wanted to fulfill the decree of "Know well that your offspring shall be strangers in a land not theirs" (15:13), so He brought about the plot of all this narrative, so that Jacob should love Joseph, and his brothers should hate him, and sell him to the Ishmaelites, who would bring him down to Egypt. Do not read, "Joseph was brought down to Egypt," but "Joseph brought his father and brothers down to Egypt.". . . This is like a cow whose owners want to place a yoke on her neck. She refuses the yoke, so what do they do? They take her calf away from her, and pull him to the field they want ploughed. The calf bellows for his mother, who hears and involuntarily follows her son. In the same way, God sought to fulfill the decree of the Covenant, so He engineered the plot of this whole narrative, and the family went down to Egypt and paid off the writ—"Terrible to man are Your plots."

The striking characteristic of the midrash is its conscious bitterness about God's relationship to human autonomy. Centering on the concept of *alilah*, "plot," the midrash evokes complex responses. For the word works on multiple levels of meaning: the plot of a story, a malicious stratagem to entrap the victim—as well as simply the causality through which one plans the future. The latter, neutral meaning is overshadowed by a sinister quality on the other two levels. (This meaning-complex works in both Hebrew and English: *alilah* and "plot" both suggest manipulation, as the Author moves his material, characters, feelings, and events, to His own will.)

The midrash presents human beings as participants in a drama of God's devising. Though ultimately not malicious, God's intents are inexorable, and human beings are for the most part unconscious actors in His plot. How is the Author to get His characters down to Egypt? He achieves His plot-purposes, through a realistic technique of apparent freedoms—freedom to love, to hate, to kill, to sell into slavery. This apparent life-likeness granted to the characters is, however, only a tribute to the skill of the Author. In reality, all is decided ahead of time. Human life is instrumental—like the cow, whose maternal passion is manipulated to bring her just where her master wants her, human beings feel and act—and may never themselves realize to what purposes they have been used.

"It is possible to be in a plot and not understand it," writes Thomas Mann of the "God-story."[12] More than possible, one might add: it is of the very nature of life inside an *alilah*, inside a plot, that one does not understand its whole structure. The wife who is handed the divorce is acute enough to observe that her husband must have determined beforehand to give her the divorce. But this homely parable sets up the basic tension of the midrash: the husband has not in any way deceived or compelled his wife into failure. He simply set the scene for her to do what she presumably tends to do—he knows that she usually prepares luke-warm drinks! His knowledge of her habitual responses opens up a plot-possibility that enables him to give her the divorce, without being unfaithful to the demands of realism. The analogy with the plotting of a good dramatist, however, does not make his behavior any the less sinister.

This, it seems, is the essential point of the midrash. God is the omniscient, skillful Narrator, whose plot rests, apparently without arti-fice, on the plausible motivations of His characters. And yet, there is a peculiar and subtle horror in such a perspective. For God not only fulfills His own intentions through the agency of human beings; He also makes them feel, through His plot-stratagems, fully responsible.

There comes a moment when the unconsciousness of the character is superseded by knowledge: the woman understands what her husband had intended, Adam resorts to complex exegesis of texts, to convey his sense that he is both responsible for death, and a mere instrument executing God's prior determination to bring death to the world. And Joseph, at the very end of the narrative (45:5, 8; 50:19–20), speaks ambiguously of God's thoughts and human thoughts, of responsibility and fatality.

But this moment of anagnorisis, of retroactive knowledge, in the first two cases, at any rate, is full of disenchantment, as the reality of the experience is undermined in the light of the revealed plot. It is interesting that in both cases, written texts reveal the script of the plot—the divorce bill serves as evidence of prior intention, while the Torah text, preceding all life and contingency, tells of God's original invention of death. Human beings suddenly perceive their lives as less real than the written texts that they have been manipulated to enact. Even when Joseph offers his brothers his observations about God's thoughts, His turning of evil to good, as consolation, as an alleviation of their torturing guilt, the notion of being actors in an *alilah* is not without its chilling aspect.

The question of the freedom and responsibility available to those involved in an *alilah* is evoked in a classic midrashic hyperbole: "Jacob, our father, should have gone down to Egypt in chains and iron collar, but God said, 'He is my first-born son—shall I bring him down in shame? . . . I shall draw his son down before him, and he will go down after him, unawares, and he will bring God's presence down with him to Egypt.' "[13]

Here, the cow-calf parable is explicitly applied to Jacob and Joseph. Jacob in chains—the image evokes horror and humiliation. Prometheus, chained to the rock, his liver endlessly torn by vultures, provides one analogy—helpless, unjustly tormented. But since the biblical Author has ends in view, other than simple retribution for hubris, He chooses a less brutal, a less direct way of bringing Jacob down to Egypt.

In the terms of the midrash, dignity is related to privacy: Jacob will go down to Egypt obeying his own personal motivations, not publicly humiliated by Pharaoh's blatant power. But exactly how dignified is this descent, in fact? In what sense is it better to go down as a result of a plot that has evoked so much pain and loss—involving betrayals, quasi-fratricide, and incarcerations in pit and prison—than simply to "go down in chains"?

The question seems to relate to the basic contrast between the short and long way of telling a story. The short, summary way of achieving the novelist's ends is to apply whatever fictional artifice may be necessary to move one's characters about. The hand of the author rests heavy on his work, in such a case. *Deus ex machina* becomes not merely a technique for mechanically resolving the ending of the story, but a continual resource at every juncture of the plot. When God comes to deal with significant, complex people, on the other hand, their substantiality demands a different approach. God's plot is not set aside, but is molded to the shape of their personalities, of their uniqueness. The sheer length and privacy of Jacob's sufferings, the complication of the devices used to move him to Egypt, is a tribute to the massiveness of his personhood.

The problem of authentic, autonomous life and the concept of "God's plot" is basic to midrashic understandings of the Joseph story. To seek to "settle in peace" is, on one level, to seek an ordering of experience, a personal construction of one's own reality, that should be both coherent and realistic. It is, in effect, to articulate the narrative of one's own life. This is, in an aesthetic, or even an epistemological sense, Jacob's desire; but, sparing no sarcasm, God thwarts his desire. For God has His counternarrative; and it is in the space between the two narratives that Jacob stands, a Job-like figure, suffering losses on many levels.

## Jacob as Job: consummated anxiety

"When suddenly a scourge brings death, He mocks as the innocent fail" [Job 9:23]: Antoninus asked Rav, What is the meaning of this? Rav answered, This is like a king who decreed that one of his people receive a hundred blows of the whip, and be given a hundred dinars—the same amount of dinars as blows: if he accepted the blows, he would get the dinars, but if he could not bear the pain, or died in the middle, he would receive nothing, and seem ludicrous for enduring the blows for nothing—"He mocks as the innocent fail." When the righteous settle in peace, and seek to settle in peace in this world, Satan comes and accuses them. He says, Is it not enough what is prepared for them in the world-to-come, but they seek to settle in peace in this world? Know that it is so; because Jacob sought to settle in peace in this world, and Satan leapt upon him with the agitation of Joseph. "Now Jacob was settled"; but "I had no repose, no quiet"—no repose from Esau, no quiet from Laban, "no rest" from Dinah, "and agitation came" [Job 3:26]—there came upon him the agitation of Joseph.[14]

The human condition is imagined as a kind of endurance test, on a win-all, lose-all basis. Job cries out against universal fate: "It is all one; therefore I say, He destroys the blameless and the guilty" (9:22). There seems to be no moral discrimination: if the righteous seem to live longer than the wicked (8:21–22), then their lives are a protracted torment, which may turn out to have been suffered in vain. It may be preferable, indeed, to die suddenly, like the wicked, than to suffer the whips and scorpions of outrageous fortune, like Job in all his innocence.

The ending of the midrash provides us with the key to the connection between Job and Jacob: "I had no repose, no quiet, no rest, and agitation came" (Job 3:26). Jacob ventriloquizes Job's cry of long suffering, which expresses an essential motif of his own life. The context of Job's protest about restlessness is significant: it comes at the end of a chapter of radical despair, chapter 3, where Job's sense of malaise, of feeling *mal dans sa peau*, is traced back to the very moment of his conception: "Perish the day on which I was born, and the night it was announced" (3:3). He wishes darkness and oblivion had fallen on the world before he was born: "Why did I not die at birth, expire as I came forth from the womb? Why were there knees to receive me, or breasts for me to suck? For now I would be lying in repose, asleep and at rest" (3:11–12). Wishing for death, Job imagines peace: "There the wicked cease from troubling [*rogez*, "agitation"]; there rest those whose strength is spent" (3:17). All of life becomes a tormented gasping for release; even the mother's breasts and knees become sinister decoys to a world of suffering.

Job finishes this, perhaps his most radically nihilistic chapter, with a strange coda—the words that the midrash puts into Jacob's mouth: "For what I feared has overtaken me; What I dreaded has come upon me.

I had no repose, no quiet, no rest, And trouble [*rogez*, "agitation"] came" (3:25–26). It seems that the peculiar form of suffering of which Job complains, the reason that he wishes never to have been born, is anxiety, dread—in Heidegger's term, angst. All his life he has been wracked by premonitions, even in times of apparent prosperity.[15] His worst apprehensions are realized in the *rogez*, the trouble that finally comes upon him.

It is this nightmare condition of consummated anxiety that the midrash applies to Jacob, as it makes him cry Job's cry. It is as though all Jacob's constant sufferings—with Laban, Esau, Dinah—have engendered in him a radical disease, as he senses the catastrophe potential in every moment. The *rogez* of Joseph—the trouble that leaps upon him at that time in his life when he had hoped to find some peace, is a savage affirmation of all his life's intimations of vertigo. The peace that Job associates with death is precisely the peace that Jacob desires: a release from the deep troubling of his spirit that time and again sweeps over him.

## *The problem of Being*

The extraordinary perspective of the midrash yields a view of this disease as essential to human experience. The wicked may gain quick release from angst; the righteous, however, are asked to suffer it to the end, if they are to gain any reward at all. To seek peace prematurely is to beg off from reality. Job speaks elsewhere of the "peace" of the wicked, who die in immaculate tranquillity (21:23); that very peace is an index to a profound disqualification for the human project. "It would have been better [more comfortable, more restful] for man never to have been created," say the Sages, in a rare moment of apparent nihilism.[16] But through Job's perspective, in this chapter, this is a realistic nihilism, for comfort, ease, are signally lacking in the life of a human being, an *adam*. Or—to reverse the terms—it is characteristic of a human being to find life uncomfortable, filled with angst and unease.

"Man is the only being to whom Being is a problem," says Heidegger. The midrash applies this notion to a theology of which Jacob-Job becomes the paradigm. A fundamental vertigo afflicts him, a sense of being a stranger in the world. When he tries to "settle in peace," he looses the vengeful furies of the Joseph story—not because his is a moral offense, but because it constitutes a wrong understanding of the human condition.

Such an artificial peace, a simulation of death in life, can be expressed in terms of the storytelling model. Jacob seeks to order his experience, to construct his world, in such a way that the texts of God's promise knit with his reality, each giving solid being to the other. Such a desire, as we have seen, may even represent the duty of a human being to seek out the meaningful structure of text and world.[17] And yet this commendable passion for order becomes, in the metaphoric texture of Jacob's narrative, a temptation, from which he is savagely barred. Just as he thinks he has arrived at a cogent version of his own narrative, "trouble comes."

# Rogez: *the narrative disturbed*

*Rogez*, translated here as "trouble" or "agitation," means, of course, something akin to "anger" — a strange nuance to evoke in speaking of Jacob's loss — subjectively, his bereavement — of Joseph. But this is a word specifically used by Joseph in a context where it seems equally enigmatic. When he sends the brothers home to their father, after he has revealed his true identity, he instructs them: "Do not be quarrelsome [*tirgezu*] on the way" (45:24). Rashi comments: "The plain meaning of the text is that since they were ashamed [of their crime against Joseph], he was anxious lest they quarrel on the journey about who had been responsible for selling him, by slandering him and causing the others to hate him." From Rashi's reading, one might understand *rogez* as that irritability of conscience that leads to the attempt to shift responsibility. *Rogez* is thus a peculiarly human, indeed moral response to the discomfort of shame — a radical agitation, a disturbance of the narrative one tells oneself. Such irritability leads to investigating "first causes," almost insignificant knots in the texture of human relationships.

The brothers experience this undercutting of their own narrative, when Joseph, as Egyptian viceroy, accuses them of spying, and demands that they bring their youngest brother in proof of their story. The illogic of such a demand engenders in them the vertigo of an alternative narrative. Suddenly, they see the narrative connections of their lives as very differently articulated: "They said to one another, 'Alas [*aval*— lit., but], we are being punished on account of our brother, because we looked on at his anguish, yet paid no heed as he pleaded with us. That is why this distress has come upon us" (45:21).

The strangely used word *aval*—"but"—suggests the vertigo of plot transformation. The brothers become dizzyingly aware of another narrative than the one they have been telling themselves all along. The uncanny, even savage irrationality of Joseph's charge has forced them out of the "peace" of their narrative constructions, so that another, perhaps truer story can emerge.[18] Perhaps the unifying motif of the story is, after all, as the brothers begin to perceive, *tzara*—grief, trouble. Only now, feeling the pinch of anguish and outrage as their plot, in the largest sense, collapses, can they "replay" the scene of Joseph's anguish and hear his cries.

Similarly, the *rogez* of Joseph's disappearance comes to Jacob as an agitating realization of many premonitions: it reminds him conclusively of the nonsense of his narrative, of his attempts at constructing a coherent reality. Instead of *yishuv ha-da'at*, instead of that sanity of the admirable projects of consciousness, shaping, plotting experience, there is, finally and fatally, *teruf ha-da'at*, the insanity in which the center will not hold, and things fall apart.

The extremity of Jacob's condition is indicated in the classic midrashic comment: "The Presence of God abandons him." Effectively, he is left with his narrative torn, but with no alternative narrative to replace it. A coherent narrative gave him a sense of life; without it, notes Rashi (37:35), he cries that he is doomed to the inferno of fragmentation: " '*I shall go down mourning to She'ol*': This is *Gehinnom*—the inferno—for this sign was given me by God, that if none of my sons died in my lifetime, I was assured that I would not see *Gehinnom*."

A wholeness has been fractured, as Jacob is bereft of the plot of his life. When he cries out at the sight of the torn coat: *tarof toraf yosef*—"Joseph is torn in pieces"—the midrash describes a startling verbal connection: " 'Why do you say, O Jacob, Why declare, O Israel, My way is hid from the Lord' [Isaiah 40:27]. So said Jacob: 'Till now, while I guarded Laban's sheep, no wild animal ever attacked them—and now they have set upon the son of my old age!' "[19]

Jacob recalls his protest to Laban at the end of his twenty years of faithful service: "That which was torn by beasts [*trefa*] I never brought to you; I myself made good the loss; you exacted it of me, whether snatched by day or snatched by night" (31:39). In all that time, he claims, there was no case of a sheep torn by lion or bear (see Rashi). With savage irony, Jacob notes the violent "rhymings" of fate: Laban's sheep were kept intact from tearing, and his beloved son is torn apart by wild animals! "My way is hid from the Lord!" He expresses the loss of all meaningful narrative; he cannot even conceive of a map of his life course, even from God's perspective, that should make his experience intelligible.

The irony in this midrash is, in fact, taken a significant stage further, in another provocative reading: Jacob's scrupulous guarding of the sheep from *trefa*, from being torn by wild animals, is seen as an offense against the balance of things: " 'I myself made good the loss' [lit., I would sin against the lion]. For God had decreed that the lion should tear and eat of Laban's sheep. 'Snatched by day' — 'I was called a thief by day and by night.' "[20]

In protecting the sheep against the depredations of the wild animals, Jacob made a kind of ecological error. Depending on one's perspective, one can consider this as a virtue or a vice: Laban's property is kept intact, by his heroic efforts, but the lion is cheated of his legitimate prey. The word *teref* — "torn" — is, in fact, the word for "food," "daily needs," in relation to wild animals and, by metaphoric extension, even in relation to human beings.[21] There is a passionate, absolute quality to the needs that Jacob frustrates with all the determination he can command. By day or by night, in freezing cold or burning heat, he sets himself against *trefa*, against that savaging of integrity that God, it seems, has made the law of the lion's nature. The midrash offers a moment of shocked recognition, as Jacob, who has invested all his energy in sanity, consciousness, wholeness, reels under the backlash effect of *teruf*.

There is a terrible symmetry in the plot that is reminiscent of *The Bacchae*. In Euripides' tragedy, King Pentheus defies and attempts to suppress the "bacchic forces," the orgiastic, drunken, anarchic energies, only to be torn in pieces by the ecstatic, dionysiac women, among them his own mother. Subtly, the midrash suggests a similar motif: Jacob's passion for wholeness denies the rights of the lion. With the poignant incommensurateness of tragedy, Jacob's whole world is torn apart, so that no peace, no coherent narrative seems possible.

"My way is hidden from the Lord" — both Jacob and Job express a radical sense of absurdity, through this image of the "hidden way." Here, indeed, is the focus of the Jacob-Job analogy. The midrash, as we have just seen, puts Isaiah's words into Jacob's mouth, as his profound response to the motif of "tornness" in his life. And Job, in chapter 3, which we have read as his central text on angst, on the basic restlessness, disease, of man in the world, cries at the climax of his lament, "Why does He give life . . . to the man whose way is hidden, whom God has hedged about?" (3:19–22). This text, too, is put into Jacob's mouth (or at least the final verse of the chapter—"I had no repose") in the midrash we considered earlier. And here, Jacob-Job's "mal-aise" is clearly defined as a sense of not-being-seen by God. "My way is hidden," conveys the experience of a life lived through time but not held in any kind of steady perspective.

And yet, as the midrashic play on the *trefa* motif suggests, pure contingency is not the real problem of the Joseph story. What the characters have to contend with, rather, is a sense of *alilah*, of a plot that transcends and, essentially, ignores the realities of human experience. For to be in an *alilah* means to be caught in the purposes of another, whether for benign or malignant ends. To be *alul* is to have one's being totally accounted for, used for its plot value, to be incapable of surprising.[22] There is something undignified in such a condition: a significant human freedom—to tell the tale of one's own life—seems to be overridden.

## Joseph and his brothers: bewilderments of interpretation

The sense of not being able to understand their own story also constitutes the radical anxiety that Joseph inflicts on his brothers. His technique is a series of enigmatic questions whose drift is opaque to his victims. To be interrogated in such a way that one cannot construe the significance of the interrogator's "plot" is to experience the authentic terror of one caught in an *alilah*. Even the benign questions of, for example, a doctor may induce this special terror; for the doctor has a "narrative" in mind, a possible diagnosis, in the light of which he examines for symptoms. This narrative is "about" the patient, but he cannot decipher its meaning.

In Kafka's *The Trial*, for instance, K. suffers from this anxiety, as he tries unsuccessfully to decipher the plot, the case that he has to answer. There are multiple possibilities, which constantly interpose between K. and any single solution. As in any interpretation of a text, "The scriptures are unalterable and the comments often enough merely express the commentator's bewilderment."[23] When K. and the priest debate interpretation of the story of the doorkeeper before the Law, K. finally experiences fatigue, a sense that he is not qualified for the task of interpretation:

> He was too tired to survey all the conclusions arising from the story, and the trains of thought into which it was leading him were unfamiliar, dealing with impalpabilities better suited to a theme for discussion among Court officials than for him. The simple story had lost its clear outline, he wanted to put it out of his mind.[24]

Joseph's brothers suffer a similar vertigo, as they lose control of their own "simple story," under Joseph's questioning. Finally, Judah, as their spokesman, expresses their radical outrage: "My lord asked his servants, 'Have you a father or another brother?'" (45:19). Judah begins his own narrative of the enigmatic relations between the ruler and his brothers: "You asked . . . we said . . . you said . . . we said . . . you said. . . ." On the surface, Judah is simply focusing the narrative on the issue of Benjamin, whose loss will send his father "in evil to the grave," and on his own responsibility for his brother. But Rashi quotes the midrash to pivot Judah's speech on the issue of Joseph's interrogation, which Judah presents as a kind of terror-tactics: "My lord asked . . . : from the beginning, you came upon us with a plot [alilah]. Why did you have to ask all those questions? Were we seeking your daughter in marriage, or were you seeking our sister in marriage? But nevertheless, 'we said to my master . . .' — we hid nothing from you."

In this midrashic account, Judah protests against the libel, the malicious narrative in which the ruler has tried to involve them. But even when it is not malicious, the experience of being in an alilah is painful and humiliating, for it undermines the central importance of intention in human life. The midrash calls on the intentionality of matchmaking as a sardonic example of personal purposes that justify submitting to interrogation. Judah protests not against the questioning as such but against the unnerving sense of being mere figures in the cryptic narrative ends of a "plotter." His words may sound conciliatory, but, in Rashi's reading, they breathe angry reproach.[25]

For Rashi, this aspect of Joseph's treatment of his brothers seems to be radically significant. He evokes the problem of the alilah on another occasion, earlier in the story; but on this occasion, it is God whom the brothers sense as "plotting" their narrative. They find the money they have paid for corn returned inside their sacks — "Their hearts sank; and, trembling, they turned to one another, saying, 'What is this that God has done to us?' " (42:28). Rashi comments: " '*What is this that God has done to us?*' — to bring us to this *alilah*, for the money was returned only in order to torment us."

The word *alilah* is used twice here, the second time in the verbal form (here translated "to torment"). It implies the humiliation, the sporting with the victim, by reducing his subject status — in effect, by removing his capacity to narrate his own experience.[26] Clearly, the brothers fear that false charges will be brought against them: they will be victims of a libel. But Maharal describes their basic *ḥarada* — "trembling" — the anxiety with which they respond to the returned money, as the unnerving effect of *any* sudden change in one's perception of reality.[27] The integrity of one's world, one's capacity of describe one's own story, is undermined by unclassifiable, cryptic events.

Suddenly, the brothers feel that — like the prisoner in Kafka's story, *In the Penal Colony* — they are being written on, rather than writing their own narrative. And, like the wretched prisoner, who will be "written to death," they squirm with the effort to read what is written. Unlike Kafka's victim, however, the brothers have no mirror-mechanism in which to read their sentence. They strive to recategorize their perceptions, to find new meanings that will accommodate the invasion of the uncanny into their lives. But the main verb of the sentence describing their response is *va-yeḥerdu* — which the Targum translates *u-tevahu* — they were perplexed, disoriented. The word indicates a shudder, almost of disgust, at a reality suddenly become unreadable.

This is the authentic *alilah* experience, as Isaac, for example, knew it, when Esau stood in front of him, crying betrayal: "Isaac was seized with very violent trembling [*Va-yeḥerad . . . ḥarada gedola*]" (27:33). Rashi quotes the Targum, which again translates *u-tevahu*: "an expression of wonder and horror. The midrash reads, 'He saw Gehinnom — the inferno — open beneath him.' "

This vertigo of the ground cut away from beneath one's feet is precisely what the brothers experience — a glimpse of the inferno. For, as they themselves say, it is not only the ruler, but God, who has precipitated them beyond their safe mappings of their own reality. The secure perspectives they have cultivated fall apart, as they sense multiple possible "plots" hedging them round. Interrogated by the ruler, trapped in the details of their answers, they become aware of the many possible connections, the many synapses in the "blooming, buzzing chaos" of their new experience.

What Joseph has engendered in them is, in effect, not paranoia, but the condition of radical doubt, in which many possible constructions of reality seem equally valid. This is no simple act of revenge, but an invitation to them to live through that fragmentation of a given reality that has been his own experience. A primal coherence has been shredded in his life. Before he can be at one with his brothers, it seems, it is essential that they too know that fragmentation of the *alilah* awareness.

## The brothers' crime: Joseph stripped and flayed

The question that arises at this point is of the actual nature of the brothers' crime. In the account of the sale of Joseph, there is confusion, even explicit contradiction: Judah suggests they sell him to the Ishmael-ites, but the Midianites then come and pull him out of the pit; they sell him to the Ishmaelites for twenty pieces of silver, and take him down to Egypt. There follows a mysterious statement that the *Midianites* sell him to Potiphar. There are many attempts among the commentators to resolve the problems of the text; but one effect of the confusion seems to be to alleviate the brothers' responsibility for the sale — as if to say, not only do they not kill Joseph, they do not even, it seems, personally sell him.[28] Whatever their intention, God's plot overrides theirs, and their responsibility for Joseph's fate seems attenuated.

Such a blurring effect on the actual crime of the brothers, however, is neutralized by the savage statement that they themselves obliquely make about their act. In thrusting Joseph's coat, torn and bloodied, at Jacob, and in saying, "Please recognize it; is it your son's tunic or not?" — they in fact feed him the words with which he interprets its meaning: "He recognized it, and said, 'My son's tunic! A savage beast devoured him! Joseph is torn in pieces!'" (37:32–33). *Tarof toraf Yosef* — "Joseph is torn apart": the words, I suggest, express the brothers' deep intent. The poignancy of the moment lies not in deception, but in the accurate, if unconscious, decoding of the symbolism of the coat. What the brothers had wanted to do to Joseph — indeed, what they had done to him — is truly articulated by their father.

In a sense, the coat is Joseph. His brothers strip it from him as they fall on him, and before they cast him into the pit. Only later, after Judah has prevailed and Joseph is sold to the traders, do they take the coat, dip it in the blood of the slaughtered kid, and send it in evidence to their father. That is, the coat as deception is only an afterthought; originally, in a primary intuitive act, before any calculating intent has intervened, they strip Joseph of his coat—of that *ketonet ha-passim* that, as Rashi comments, his father had given him "in excess" of his brothers. They remove that which is additional, unique about Joseph. Indeed, the word for "excess" — *hosafa* — is another form of the root of Joseph's name: they tear from him that superlative, individual quality that they most envy.

The concept of "stripping" occurs here for the first time in the biblical text. It is at root a violent idea, with connotations of flaying skins of animals. In biblical language, it is characteristically used of the preparation of an animal as burnt offering: it is flayed (*hafshata*), dissected (*nituah*), and totally burnt.[29] Essentially, the desire of the brothers is the absolute destruction of Joseph — of that "excessive" quality in Joseph that is both grace and irritant. The ritual of the burnt offering reenacts, sublimates a basic savage human instinct—to strip, to dismember, to "tear apart living structures," as Erich Fromm defines the "necrophilous" instinct.

Fromm uses the term "necrophilous" to "denote a character, rather than as a perverse act in the traditional sense." He adopts the term from the Spanish philosopher Miguel de Unamuno (from a speech delivered in response to the nationalistic motto, "Viva la Muerte!" [Long live death!]), and includes in his description, "the exclusive interest in all that is purely mechanical."[30] In "flaying" Joseph of the "excessive," vital coat of many colors, the brothers express an intense, almost unbearable necrophilia: what they are doing to him is, in a radical sense, just what Jacob later articulates, as he "reads" the coat: *tarof toraf Yosef*—the Joseph, "additional" quality of him is flayed, dismembered, so that it need constitute no threat to them ever again.

For to tear apart living structure is to assert control, to reduce volatile vital forces to mechanical parts. On a subconscious level, the brothers' impulse to *hafshata* and *nituah* is also an impulse to "abstraction" and "analysis" — which, indeed, are the modern Hebrew meanings of the words. In order to analyze a subject, one must, in a sense, kill it. Fromm discusses the connection between necrophilia and the worship of technique (for instance, "music lovers for whom listening to music is only the pretext for experimenting with the technical qualities of their record players. . . . Listening to music has been transformed for them into studying the product of high technical performance."[31]

He relates his terms "necrophilia" and "biophilia" to Freud's concept of the death instinct and the life instinct (Eros):

> It is the effort of Eros to combine organic substance into ever larger unities, whereas the death instinct tries to separate and to disintegrate living structure. . . . The biophilous person prefers to construct rather than to retain. He wants to be more rather than to have more. He is capable of wondering, and he prefers to see something new rather than to find confirmation of the old. He loves the adventure of living more than he does certainty. He sees the whole rather than only the parts, structures rather than summations.[32]

Adopting this model, I suggest that Joseph's brothers committed on Joseph a fully necrophilous act. A fundamental hatred and fear of life is projected in the torn and bloodied coat that Jacob so responsively diagnoses. Like the burnt offering, Joseph is to be consumed utterly: dismembered, so that nothing, essentially, remains of him. "The boy is gone," says Reuben (37:30): *einenu*—"he is not."

With extraordinary intuition and knowledge of biblical and midrashic sources, Thoman Mann conveys just such an image of the brothers' crime:

> They fell upon him as the pack of hungry wolves falls upon the prey; their blood-blinded lust knew no pause or consideration, it was as though they would tear him into fourteen pieces at least. Rending, tearing apart, tearing off—upon that they were bent, to their very marrow. "Down, down, down!" they panted with one voice; it was the *ketonet* they meant, the picture-robe, the veil. It must come off, and that was not so easy. . . .

Joseph's reaction is that of a man rent apart by the hail-storm of brutality:

> . . . cutting into very little pieces his trust, his whole notion of the world. . . . To him, the most horrible and incredible thing of all was what happened to the *ketonet*. That was worse, crueler, even, than all this howling horror about him. Desperately he tried to protect the garment and keep the remnants and ruins of it still upon him. Several

times he cried out: "My coat! My coat!" and even after he stood naked, still begged them like a girl to spare it.[33]

## The coat: Joseph dismembered

The symbolism of Joseph's coat is complicated by the goat's blood in which it is dipped. The characteristic of goat's blood, Rashi says, is that it is similar to human blood (*damo domeh le-dam adam* [37:31] — the word-play is highly suggestive, reflecting a basic identity of the human and the animal, at the level of blood). This is more than a tactical comment on the shrewdness of the substitution. It is a comment on the substitution itself; to all intents and purposes, the brothers have shed Joseph's blood; wild animals have, in effect, dismembered him.

The brothers' involvement in the *teruf* — the dissection — of Joseph is the central theme of the narrative. "They saw him from afar, and before he came close to them they conspired to kill him. They said to one another, 'Here comes that dreamer!'" (37:18–19). The midrash comments on the brothers' "distanced" vision of Joseph: "Come, let us set the dogs on him!"[34] They would like to kill him by remote control, as it were: if pressing a button would wipe him out, that would fulfill their desire at this point. This oblique form of murder is suggested by the word *va-yitnaklu*, with its nuances of craftiness, of detached cunning. According to Seforno, they construct an image of Joseph as plotting against them: they see themselves as endangered by him and try to arrange a "clean," uninvolved murder.

Only after this plan has failed do they speak of killing him and throwing him into a pit,

> and we can say a savage beast devoured him. . . . But when Reuben heard it, he tried to save him from their hands. He said, "Let us not take his life." And Reuben went on, "Shed no blood! Cast him into that pit out in the wilderness, but do not touch him with your own hands" — intending to save him from their hands and restore him to his father. (37:20–22)

Reuben is obsessed by the imagery of hands. Three times, the text avows his intent — to prevent the horror of hands tearing apart the living body. "Shed no blood," he pleads, more concerned about the direct "hands-on" involvement in blood than about Joseph's fate. But the brothers, while formally accepting his plea, lay their hands on Joseph, "strip" him, "take" him, and "throw" him into the pit (37:23–24) – all verbs emphasizing the contact of hands with body. What had begun as an elegant murder plot, to be executed at an aesthetic distance, is played out in horrifying immediacy: with their own hands, they strip and dismember him, ironically realizing the images of their cover story ("we can say a savage beast devoured him").

Then, surprisingly, Judah speaks up, and deplores their act: "What do we gain by killing our brother and covering up his blood?" (37:26). Joseph is by now in the pit, so that any direct responsibility for his death seems to be shuffled off. Moreover, there is no literal "blood" shed at all at this stage. Rashi deals with Judah's reference to blood, by saying simply, "Covering up his blood – hiding his death." But a primal horror of blood dominates Judah's speech, and is joined to the imagery of hands: "Come, let us sell him to the Ishmaelites, but let our hands not be upon him. After all, he is our brother, our own flesh" (37:27).

The physical sensation of hands shedding blood haunts Judah, who persuades his brothers to sell Joseph by his rhetoric of fratricide as quasi-suicide ("our brother, our own flesh"). But the paradoxical aspect of this speech is precisely the fact that the brothers have not, in any physical sense, killed Joseph – there is no blood on their hands. And yet, after Joseph is definitively removed from the scene – "The boy is gone" – after all ugliness and terror is expunged, the brothers, as of one accord (without rhetoric, or special appeals), slaughter a kid, and dip the coat in its blood – and Jacob "reads" the coat as Joseph, torn by wild animals. And when, years later, they stand in front of the Egyptian ruler, the memory of that day returns to them, in a new narrative-connection with the anguish of the "plot" in which they are trapped: "They said to one another, 'Alas, we are being punished on account of our brother, because we looked on at his anguish. . . .' Then Reuben spoke up and said to them, 'Did I not tell you, "Do no wrong to the boy"? But you paid no heed. Now comes the reckoning for his blood'" (42:21–22).

Reuben expresses the intuitive feeling of all the brothers that "now comes the reckoning for his blood." Blood, however, has not been shed; they themselves, in the depth of their contrition, accuse themselves of no more than callousness, insensitivity. They "saw" Joseph's anguish, but did not "listen" to him: that is why anguish has come to them. In this context, to see and to listen are very different modes of response. The brothers see Joseph's begging face, coldly, in detachment, but they absorb neither what he is saying, nor what Reuben says in defense of him.

In memory, it seems, the original interaction among the brothers takes on a new coloring: instead of Reuben successfully saving his brothers from bloodshed, we are given a scene of violence and callousness, with Reuben unsuccessfully pleading, "Do no wrong to the boy." The brothers' act is remembered, after all, as an act of blood, though their failure is twice described as, simply, "not listening."

Rashi compounds the difficulty of Reuben's reference to blood, by interpreting the word *gam* — lit., *also* his blood is required — as including Jacob's blood. Clearly, Rashi takes "blood" as a metaphor for "anguish," the pain caused by the fear of death. (David speaks of blood, in a similar mode, when he cries, "Oh, let my blood not fall to the ground, away from the presence of the Lord!")[35] Ramban, too, speaks of Joseph's blood in a metaphorical sense: "It will be accounted to you, as though you had shed his blood." Blood is identified here with cruelty, with the indifference with which the brothers refused to "listen" on that terrible day.

In this sense, they are physically incriminated for the anguish they have caused, not only to Joseph but to Jacob as well. Their involvement with blood, according to Rashbam, thus carries on a chain of violence going back to the massacre of Shechem: Jacob ironically sends Joseph to the place of his dismemberment, to Shechem, out of anxiety for his sons in that place of violence (37:13). Their constant references to blood indicate a primal instinct — the necrophilous instinct — that they themselves unconsciously recognize, when they kill the goat and dip Joseph's coat in its blood. This becomes a symbolic utterance of their guilt, of the radical meaning of their act.

## The original sin?

The brothers' crime remains throughout Jewish history as a kind of ineradicable original sin, with proliferating effects. Because of it, ten sages are martyred at the time of the Roman persecution.[36] Rambam refers to this original sin of our forefathers; in constant self-reminder of this evil, we sacrifice a goat for all communal sin-offerings; the goat that was substituted for Joseph remains a symbol of hatred and violence in the consciousness of the whole people.[37]

A Yemenite manuscript, contained in the Sassoon collection, focuses on this goat:

> The goat had no horns and it said to the brothers, "You are killing two lives"—this teaches that it was a female and pregnant. [*Se'ir izzim* indicates *two* goats.] When they came to slaughter it, it cried out in a voice that reached the heavens, so that the angels came down to see, "Joseph lives and I die! Who will tell Jacob?" One of the winds went and told Jacob what the goat said. But in the end, "His heart went numb, for he did not believe them" (45:26). So the goat cried out, "Earth, do not cover up my blood!" And till now, the goat's blood is damp on the earth, until the Messiah comes, as it is written, "I will smelt them as one smelts silver" [Zekhariah, 13:9]—the silver for which they sold Joseph, as it is said, "They sold Joseph for twenty pieces of silver." (37:28)

This enigmatic midrash treats the sale of Joseph and slaughter of the goat as the paradigm for all violence from the beginning of human existence to messianic times. Resonances from Cain's murder ("You shall be more cursed than the ground, which opened its mouth to receive your brother's blood from your hand" [4:11]), from Job's sufferings ("Earth, do not cover my blood" [Job 16:18]) make this midrash a lament for the pain and injustice of human existence. The goat's insistence on her pregnancy, on being heard, on her blood's eternal staining of the earth is an appeal for consciousness of this anguish, for utterance of its ineradicable effects. Against oblivion (the earth's sin in Cain's murder of Abel), against incredulity (Jacob's failure to absorb the wind's report), the midrash poignantly addresses the reality of evil.

For this blood—though metaphorically displaced from human blood—comes to represent the human responsibility for suffering—the "necrophilous" instinct, wherever it is found. Rashi defines it as including Jacob's anguish as well; one midrashic source deciphers this mortal anguish in Jacob's cry, "I will go down mourning to my son in Sheol" (37:35)—the brothers have "shed their father's blood," in causing him to set his sights on death.[38] And a medieval source conceptualizes the meaning of such responsibility: "Know and understand that one who murders or does evil to another is punished not only for that specific victim but for all who sorrow for him, as it is said, 'Now comes the reckoning for his blood'" (42:22).[39]

If the emotional repercussions of an act are traced back to the agent, then bloodshed, dismemberment, the "necrophilous" acts for which the brothers remain responsible, are not simply a matter of *intention*, but constitute the very stuff of the story. They not only *intend* to strip, dissect Joseph: they in fact do so. Far beyond their intent, in fact, is the anguish of *teruf*, of dismemberment, that they cause in the world. "The blood of the old man," as the midrash has Reuben refer to Jacob, is shed. Something essential in him dies; and comes alive again, only when Joseph is restored ("the spirit of their father Jacob revived" [45:27]).

## Joseph in Egypt: re-membering the self

It is Joseph, of course, who is both the intended and the real victim of dismemberment. "His notion of the world," as Mann puts it, "is cut into very little pieces." A certain trust in the correspondence between external and internal, between face and heart, is torn with the precious coat. Mann imagines Joseph as desperately trying to hold the "remnants and ruins" of the coat upon him, as begging the brothers to spare it, even when he is stripped of it. For it is his excellence, his "additional" quality—the main victim of his dismemberment.

The story of Joseph in Egypt is a history of his continued, desperate attempts to re-member himself, to reintegrate the broken pieces of his identity. He names his elder, Egyptian-born son, Manasseh—"for God has made me forget completely my hardship and my parental home" (41:51). He remembers only the pain of his father's home, the last vision, perhaps, of his brothers' animal faces, tearing him apart—and he is grateful for oblivion. His son's name continually evokes the paradox of his dismemberment: he has forgotten, but he knows, he experiences his oblivion. His is a repression, in the process of becoming conscious.

Earlier, his desire to repress had prevailed over his conscious efforts to remember:

*"And his master saw that the Lord was with him"* [39:3]: But in the end, he forgot, as it is written, "for God has made me forget completely my hardship and parental home." He would come in whispering, and go out whispering. Potiphar would tell him to pour him boiling water, and the water would boil as he poured—or tepid water, and it poured at the right temperature. Potiphar said, "What! Joseph, are you bringing

straw to Ofraim?". . . How long did this last? Till "his master saw that
the Lord was with him."[40]

In the early days of his captivity in Potiphar's house, Joseph goes about
repeating (whispering) the Torah he learned in his father's house. This is
his strenuous attempt to "re-member" his identity and culture, to keep
"God with him." Since small domestic miracles constantly happen to
him (such as the instantly boiling water), Potiphar assumes that he is
muttering spells—hence, his aphorism about bringing witchcraft to
Egypt. Eventually, it seems, Potiphar does recognize the heroic subjectivity of Joseph, as he strives to remember God, Torah, and himself. But
in the end, the midrash begins—as though this end to heroic memorizing
were inevitable—Joseph forgot.

The problems of remembering and forgetting inform the whole narrative. The butler, in spite of Joseph's pleas, does not remember to
mention him to Pharaoh: he "did not remember Joseph; he forgot him"
(40:23). But this failure signals a moment when he does, in fact, remember certain aspects of Joseph, in a context where such reconstructions have become essential to Pharaoh, and, indeed, to the whole
country. His memory is fragmentary, but reassembles a Joseph who is
both nonthreatening and a talented interpreter. (Rashi emphasizes the
"clever fool" motif in his reading of "a Hebrew youth, a servant" [41:12].)

Similarly, Joseph has disappeared down a pit, into the deathly oblivion, of which the Talmud says, "If one fell into a pit full of snakes and
scorpions, we bear witness [that he is dead and we allow his wife to
remarry, for he surely died there.]"[41] He is lost to memory, his own as well
as his family's conscious memory. Thomas Mann describes his dismemberment as "cutting into very little pieces his trust, his whole notion of
the world." A wholeness, an intuitive ordering of experience, is disrupted
forever. Now Joseph must learn to study the faces of others, to piece
together evidence of their inner worlds and of where he stands in the
context of those worlds. He must become sensitive to changing surfaces
and find ways of constructing a world of his own in the kaleidoscope of
exile. Joseph's conscious memory of himself fails, as he works to survive in
pit, prison, and palace.

When his brothers appear before him to buy food in the famine,
"Joseph remembers his dreams" (42:9)—not their cruelty, but the dreams
that had been the catalyst of jealousy and hatred so many years before.

What begins for Joseph at this point is a process that Walter Benjamin calls "involuntary recollection":

> The important thing for the remembering author [Proust] is not what he experienced, but the weaving of his memory, the Penelope work of recollection. Or should one call it, rather, a Penelope work of forgetting? Is not the involuntary recollection, Proust's *mémoire involontaire*, much closer to forgetting than what is usually called memory? And is not this work of spontaneous recollection, in which remembrance is the woof and forgetting the warp, a counterpart to Penelope's work rather than its likeness? For here the day unravels what the night has woven.[42]

The weaving work of forgetting, that Benjamin so strikingly describes in this passage, is the experience of Joseph, as he "involuntarily" reassembles fragments of his repressed past.[43] He involves his brothers, in his reconstruction of the past, imprisoning Simeon as he was imprisoned, insisting on Benjamin's being "brought down" to Egypt, as he was brought down. He weeps three times in the course of a protracted charade, in which the past returns to him in terror and pity. And as he experiences the new reweavings from the loom of forgetting, he subjects his brothers, too, to the radical anxiety of loss and recollection. Like him, they find themselves disintegrated, whirling in the "blooming, buzzing chaos" of a reality whose plot is hidden from them.

In the most literal sense, Joseph's accusation that they are spies constitutes an *alilah*, a narrative of causalities, linking the fragments of their experience in a plausible but insane scenario. Moreover, a spy proposes to assemble a narrative, to weave empirical observations into a version of the unknown. *Le-ragel*, "to spy," implies "footwork" — the restless assembly of evidence for a thesis. Throughout the dialogue, Joseph insists on his "reading" of their purpose — they are *meraglim*, "spies"; he finally agrees to test their claim that they are *kenim*, "honest," by having them bring Benjamin in evidence of the truth of their family history (42:19–20).

The relation of their family narrative to their claims of innocence is unclear: if they are sons of the same man, with a younger brother still in Canaan, does this disqualify them as spies? But the word *kenim*, "honest," supplies an essential clue: the brothers protest that they are "solid citizens," well grounded in family and society, the circumstances of their lives conventionally ordered — not *meraglim* — foot-loose adventurers, making their fortune by constructing narratives about foreign worlds.[44] Joseph proposes to test the organic certainties of their world and, in effect, to engender in them the tornness, the disorientations of his own experience. Only so, can they be induced to re-member the repressed cruelty of the past, to construct, as spies on the unthinkable, a new sense of family unity.[45]

For this to happen, Joseph and his brothers must reinterpret the fragments, must survive the perils of the plot by attempting their own version of narrative. The intrusion of the uncanny into their lives forces them to reconstitute themselves. The climax of the process is reached when Judah tells Joseph a story of pain, empathy, and responsibility, as he explains why Benjamin cannot be held prisoner in punishment for the stolen goblet; at this point, Joseph can no longer control his "plot," which collapses at Judah's masterful narrative. But the beginning of the process is an encounter with the uncanny, with strangeness: *Va-yit-naker* — "He made himself strange to them" (42:7). They do not recognize him;[46] Joseph reinforces the strangeness by his arbitrary behavior, by the return of the money and of the goblet. Out of this uncanniness and the anxiety it generates comes re-cognition: before identities are revealed, narratives must be rearticulated.

## Judah re-collects the fragments

It is Jacob who narrates a final dreamlike — and largely unconscious — version of the story, and, particularly, of Judah's role in it. Before his death, Jacob blesses Judah (in Rashi's narrative, there is a painful, almost comic moment when, after hearing his elder brothers castigated, Judah tries to evade his father's attention): "Judah is a lion's whelp; from prey, my son, have you risen up" (49:9). Rashi reads the word *teref*, "prey," as a coded reference to the *teref*, the "tearing," that had pulled Joseph's life" apart:

> "*From prey*": my suspicions of you, when Joseph was torn to pieces: *tarof toraf Yosef*. The "wild beast" was Judah, who is compared to a lion.

> ". . . *my son, have you risen up*": You have removed yourself [from the tearing of Joseph] when you said, "What do we gain by killing our brother?"

In an extraordinary midrashic misreading, "my son" is no longer the vocative form, addressed to Judah, who as lion rises up from his prey, but refers to Joseph: Judah has managed to *transcend* the act called the "tearing of Joseph."

He has done this by his characteristic response of *hoda'a*, "acknowl-edgment." The midrash puns on his name: "You acknowledged your responsibility [*hodeita*] in the affair of Tamar—so your brothers will acknowledge you [*yodukha*] as king."[47]

The play on Judah's name (Yehuda—*hoda'a*) is, in effect, a translation of the word used of Judah's moment of recognition in the Tamar narra-tive—"Judah recognized [*va-yaker*] the pledges, and said, 'She is more in the right than I'" (38:26). What Judah recognizes is not simply his pledge to Tamar—the seal and cord and staff that symbolize his author-ity. He recognizes, in effect, himself. In response to Tamar's weighted invitation, "Please recognize [*haker na*]," he rises above the dismember-ings of experience. From the loom of forgetting fall his own words to Jacob, as he presented him with Joseph's torn coat: "Please recognize [*haker na*] . . ." (37:32).[48] Then, Jacob had been asked to acknowledge tornness; now, Judah is asked to reassemble that tornness. In the words of the midrash, Tamar pleads with him, "Please, recognize your Creator, and do not hide your eyes from me."

## From philosophy to poetry

The irony is poignant: Jacob, like Joseph, has had his blood shed, has been dismembered by the act of his sons. God has departed from him, he has suffered the dislocated perplexity of dulled consciousness for twenty-two years. But in the end, he recognizes Judah as "king" of his sons—because of his power of re-cognition, in relation to Tamar, and in relation to Joseph. It is Judah who is able to reconstitute the fragments of a repressed past into a narrative of pity and responsibility; the shards cut by callousness are recollected in acts of awareness that Tamar simply calls "recognizing God."

"Jacob sought to settle in peace. . . ." The simplicity of the narrative Jacob would have liked to tell is shattered by acts of *teruf*, such as he has always set himself against. God speaks to him in a strange tongue: "Is it not enough for the righteous, what is prepared for them in the world to come, that they seek to settle in peace in this world?" There is, it seems, a painful law that obtains in this world—particularly painful for the righteous who would like to retain memory intact, to be loyal to all of life as it was experienced. This law has to do with the "Penelope work of forgetting," with restlessness and brokenness and anxiety, and with the work to be done on the "few fringes of the tapestry of lived life, as loomed for us by forgetting."[49]

Jacob's cognitive and spiritual dilemma is traced by the Ishbitzer, the nineteenth-century hasidic writer of *Mei Ha-Shiloaḥ*:

> "*Jacob was settled in the land of Canaan, in the land of his father's sojournings*": in the land of *megurei aviv*—his father's *fear*; and in the land of Canaan, of *humility* [*kana*]—and he sought to dwell in peace. This peace obtains when a person behaves in such a way as to keep far from all doubt, and guards himself from any evil act. That is the modality of peace. But in response to Jacob's desire for such peace, God told him that as long as a human being lives a bodily existence, it is impossible to behave with extreme wariness and fear and humility. For God wants human acts, and in this world human beings must act *in love, in ways that are not completely clarified*. For this reason, it is said only of the future human condition: "And Jacob shall again [*shav*] have calm and quiet with none to trouble him" (Jeremiah 30:10)—*shav* means "tranquil," as in "He gives my soul tranquillity" (Psalms 23:3).[50]

In this reading, Jacob's desire for a stable, coherent reading of his own experience, based on cognitive certainty and moral scrupulousness (which the Ishbitzer calls "fear" and "humility," respectively), is countered by God's insistence on the tragic nature of existence in this world. Only in the future will the yearning for *ve-shav Ya'akov*, for intellectual and aesthetic integration, be fully satisfied. In this world, what is most needed is not fear, which deprives man of initiative beneath the sleepless eyes of God,[51] but love—the capacity to act in a world where absolute clarity is not obtainable.

In his characteristically dialectical mode, the Ishbitzer suggests an eternal oscillation between extremes of fear and love, certainty and courage, in the face of perplexity. A worldview based on fear and humility, in his paradoxical terms, risks human atrophy; for such fear and humility grant all power to God. Only a vision in which the plot is unclear, in which anomalies bewilder serene faith and integrities are torn apart, can open the possibility of human action. Cognitively, action means the capacity to reintegrate the fragments of experience into new wholes: in re-membering, to create something unprecedented, a personal language of self-description.

The Ishbitzer gives us a Jacob who is Everyman, perplexed by contingency, searching for philosophical and spiritual calm. In a sense, God turns Jacob's quest away from philosophy, from the search for certainties, to the world of poetry. Poetic language is the loving act of the human being, who seeks to redescribe his reality, in the midst of, and against, *teruf*. Richard Rorty, for instance, writes of Freud, that he "sees every . . . life as an attempt to clothe itself in its own metaphors." He quotes Lionel Trilling on Freud: "[He] showed us that poetry is indigenous to the very constitution of the mind; he saw the mind as being, in the greater part of its tendency, exactly a poetry-making faculty."[52]

Using this model, one might say that Jacob is precipitated into the world of poetry, from the moment that the *va-yeshev* mode falls apart. His immediate response to anguish is in formal verse: *haya ra'a akhalathu / tarof toraf Yosef* — "a savage beast devoured him, Joseph is torn in pieces." Robert Alter has pointed to the semantic parallelism that scans with three beats in each hemistich: "Poetry is heightened speech, and the shift to formal verse suggests an element of self-dramatization in the way Jacob picks up the hint of his son's supposed death and declaims it metrically before his familial audience."[53]

Alter writes of self-dramatization, of the extravagance of Jacob's mourning, indicating a kind of posturing response to the bloodied coat. I would suggest, however, that the formal, heightened quality of Jacob's speech, the many different expressions of grief, convey a Jacob who has been thrust out into the maelstrom of contingency, of the bitter dismemberments of a world of *hafshata* and *nituah*, of flayings and dissections, abstractions and analysis. The *va-yeshev* project abruptly fails, and Jacob responds intuitively with the redundancies of poetry. In gesture and language, he describes the death that has befallen him. *Tarof toraf Yosef* gathers resonance as the central metaphor for intimate disconnections, until he finally addresses Judah, in his death-bed poem: *Alita mi-teref beni* — "You have risen above *teruf* by acts of self-creation." ("You have recognized your Creator!")

When Jacob is precipitated beyond the certainties of philosophy, he is compelled — by despair, by fear of extinction — to the project of poetic self-description. In terms of the Covenant between the Pieces, as read by

Rashi and the midrash, the "writ of obligation" now devolves entirely upon him, since Esau has opted out of a destiny of alienation, slavery and suffering. He must pay the debt of the "sojourner" in this world, must endure the fragmentation of self and undertake the project of constant redescription (the "*writ* of obligation") that the Ishbitzer calls the project of love. In Rashi's view, this is the destiny of Jacob, of the righteous, in general: they are given no choice—the writ must be paid.

Ramban, however, writes of a free choice. As we saw, in his text is implicit the alternative midrashic perspective[54] of a contract, drawn up by Jacob himself, in which a life of contingency in the Holy Land is set against the tenacious clarities of settling in the land of possession. Jacob chooses to live as a stranger, in the Chosen Land, and thus to realize the meaning in his own life of the Covenant: "Your offspring shall be strangers in a land not theirs" (15:13). There is a decision here, a readiness for the "long story" of contingency, vicissitude, fragmentation, and reintegration. Implicitly, the family chosen to experience on its own flesh the historical condition of protracted alienation lends its free consent to its difficult enterprise.

## Serah's song: poetry and prayer

From dismemberment comes re-membering: for Jacob, Joseph is reconstituted first through words—"And they told him, 'Joseph is alive'" (45:26). He responds with incredulity, with heart failure ("His heart went numb, for he did not believe them"). Only after he sees the wagons, the physical evidence of Joseph's bounty,[55] does his spirit come back to life. That incredulity, that failure of the heartbeat, is the natural response to language, to yet another possible description of reality. "It is passing strange," say the brothers in Mann's version of the narrative, "that we shall have to talk him out of something we once talked him into by means of the bloodstained garment, so that he clings to it now."[56] Having precipitated Jacob, through language and symbol, into the world of poetry, shall they now draw him, through language and symbol, back into the world of philosophy, of certain, clear truth? "How Shall We Tell Him?" is Mann's chapter heading.

A poignant midrashic tradition has it that Jacob is told of Joseph's survival and identity, not by the brothers themselves, but by a young girl, Serah, the daughter of Asher. Mann makes wonderful use of the tradition, having Serah, the poet-musician, sing the words of revelation to Jacob. She herself has no access to certainty: the brothers say, "Believe it or not, just sing it and then we will come and prove it. But it would be better if you believed it, for you would sing the better."[57]

Through her song, she induces in Jacob a yearning response, as she plays "teasingly and riddlingly" on her strings. For art has the effect of performance—Jacob "even clapped his hands benevolently, just like the audience at a play." But this is its seduction and danger, he chides her: "Sense and senses lie close together, and song rhymes all too easily with wrong."[58]

Against his resolution, however, he is moved by the beauty of her description. When the brothers arrive with carts and asses and the prosaic voice of truth, he is "half-absent," his "gaze was bewildered." Serah's poetry and music have engendered a fantasy of loss and restoration that he partly deplores, partly fears. The brothers speak judiciously at first, of "some truth in her harping," and finally of "The truth! . . . She sang the truth!"[59]

In Mann's version, a poetry that is both beautiful and true "now for once is here achieved." Serah's strategy is to have Jacob "think it / Beautiful awhile but yet not true, / Lest the cup if suddenly you drink it / Fling you on your back and lay you low."[60] The effect of music, of rhyme is to induce a dreamlike state, where ideas penetrate, though conscious reason repudiates them. This gives Jacob breathing space, as it were, to adjust gradually to the truth of the poem.

The essential elements of Mann's narrative derive from the *Midrash Ha-Gadol* and *Pirkei d'Rabbi Eliezer*:

[The brothers said:] If we tell him right away, "Joseph is alive!" perhaps he will have a stroke [lit., his soul will fly away]. What did they do? They said to Serah, daughter of Asher, "Tell our father Jacob that Joseph is alive, and he is in Egypt." What did she do? She waited till he was standing in prayer, and then said in a tone of wonder, "Joseph is in Egypt / There have been born on his knees / Menasseh and Ephraim" [three rhyming lines: *Yosef be-mitzrayim / Yuldu lo al birkayim / Menasheh ve-Ephrayim*]. His heart failed, while he was standing in prayer. When he finished his prayer, he saw the wagons: immediately the spirit of Jacob came back to life.[61]

Mann has clearly mobilized this and the *Pirkei d'Rabbi Eliezer* midrash (which speaks of Serah's playing on an instrument) in his own narrative.

The semihypnotic effect of rhyme becomes the basis in Mann's account for Jacob's discussion of the "falseness" of art.

One important detail of the midrash, however, is ignored in Mann's version; it is this detail that must inform our reading of the midrash and, indeed, of the problems of fragmentation and integration in the narrative. For Jacob is "standing in prayer" when Serah sings to him. This is the enigmatic but focal detail, on which our attention is centered. "What did Serah do?" indicates a forthcoming act of initiative: she does not simply obey her uncles' command, but adds elements of her own to her "performance." She "waits" until Jacob is standing in prayer, and she includes in her rhyming song more than the content dictated by her uncles: the birth of Joseph's two sons. She sings "in a tone of wonder," and Jacob's heart fails, while he is standing in prayer. There is apparently no problem in continuing his prayer in a state of "heart failure." He concludes his prayer, sees the wagons, and returns to life.

The act of prayer is the most expressive act of man situated in the modality of "doubt," unclarity, and contingency, of which the Ishbitzer writes. Serah bides her time until Jacob assumes his familiar stance: not "sitting" at peace, ensconced in the spiritual certainties of his desire, but standing in the characteristic posture of prayer, alert, attentive to all intimations from within and without. Le-hitpalel, "to pray," is, literally, to "think about oneself": it is to attempt yet another redescription of the self, in the presence of God. In a situation of unclarity, such as obtains in this world, any human act requires great courage, a motive force to appropriate and transform experience into the making of a world. Prayer is the quintessential act of this kind; and Serah deliberately sings her rhyming song to fuse with Jacob's prayer.

The "wonder" with which she sings does not crash through the web of Jacob's thoughts: it intertwines with them, tentative, almost questioning. Her song does not include philosophical discussions about truth and beauty, and therefore it does not generate them in Jacob. It does not reflect on the nature of poetry: it is a poem, affirming relationship between fragmentary, rhyming statements. (What has "Egypt" to do with "knees," or either with "Ephraim"?) Past, present, and future are contained in three simple lines, as she offers Jacob a possible narrative, a re-membering of his life.

And Jacob is indeed almost overwhelmed, as the song gently filters through his consciousness. But still he stands in prayer, working to metabolize Serah's poem into his own poem, even as the dangers of *teruf*, of total loss of consciousness, reach their highest pitch. The news of Joseph's survival does not, as in Mann's version, return Jacob to "The Truth," from the shadowy teasings and riddlings of music. Rather, it confirms the tentative, "wondering" nature of reality in this world. It may be the sight of the prosaic wagons that restores Jacob to life, but "love of life" — "biophilia" — is restored at the moment that Jacob describes himself yet again, under the influence of music. The "quickening art," as Kant called music, brings life to Jacob, even as he faints from excess of desire.

Serah has not done as the brothers asked — introduced him gradually to the new reality, so that his life is not endangered. She has sung the words of unbearable desire to the music of longing and recollection. And she has invited Jacob to re-member a world in which despair and hope, discontinuity and continuity, are interlaced in the poetry of his prayers.

# MI-KETZ 🐏

## *The Absence of the Imagination*

J*oseph names his sons*

Joseph is released from his Egyptian jail, as the result of an interpretation: he has released Pharaoh from the perplexity of his double dream, by translating the imagery of fat and lean cows, of healthy and blasted ears of

284

corn, into terms of famine and plenty. He is appointed viceroy of Egypt, after he has advised Pharaoh—going beyond his brief as a mere interpreter, a diagnostician of dreams—to appoint a "man of discernment and wisdom" (41:33) to supervise the collection of corn during the years of plenty, against the rigors of the forthcoming famine years. Pharaoh responds to Joseph's suggestion on cue: "There is none so discerning and wise as you" (41:39). He bestows symbols of power upon Joseph, changes his name, and marries him into the aristocracy. Joseph immediately sets about his essential task of gathering food against the famine: "Joseph collected produce in very large quantity, like the sands of the sea, until he ceased to measure it, for it could not be measured" (41:49).

It is in this context of spectacular success as provider of food, of life, to a whole nation, that we read of the birth of Joseph's two sons, "before the years of famine came. Joseph named the first-born Manasseh, meaning, 'God has made me forget completely my hardship and my parental home.' And the second he named Ephraim, meaning, 'God has made me fertile in the land of my affliction'" (41:51–52). The narrative then resumes telling of the end of the years of plenty and the beginning of the famine; and of the apparently—and bizarrely—instant starvation that overtakes the population, so that they have to appeal to Pharaoh—and, at his behest, to Joseph—for food.

Interrupting the flow of this narrative is the description of the birth and naming of Joseph's sons, "before the years of famine came." The timing here is enigmatic: Rashi, quoting the Talmud,[1] suggests that the clause specifying when the children were born—"before the famine came"—is to make the point that procreation—even marital relations—is forbidden in time of famine. This seems to reinforce a view of Joseph's situation of ease, success, and normal human functioning, during these first years of plenty. In the names he gives his sons, he tenders an account of his life-drama, as he perceives it at this moment of its course, when his own fertility mirrors the general prosperity.

Indeed, nowhere does Joseph reveal as nakedly as in these names his own feeling about the strange vicissitudes of his life. Nowhere does he comment so openly on its bitterness and its sweetness as in these namings that encode his sense of God's dealings with him. Before the central drama of his relations with his brothers gains momentum—before the famine that will bring them to Egypt—we are given important access to Joseph's thoughts about his own life.

*M*anasseh: *oblivion and survival*

Both names are fraught with paradox. Manasseh is named for forgetfulness. Joseph seems to celebrate the oblivion, not only of his suffering, but
of "all my father's house" (lit.), that God has granted him. The midrashic
tradition indicates that he is referring specifically to his spiritual heritage
(his "Torah learning"): he names his first-born son for the alienation that
he experiences from his native culture, from "the best that has been
thought and known," as Matthew Arnold defines the nature of culture, in
general.[2] It is difficult not to read this naming as celebratory: what
gratitude is Joseph expressing at this moment of his experience?

One suggestion, offered by *Ha'amek Davar* (41:51), is that Joseph is
acknowledging the mercy in oblivion: he is grateful not to be haunted by
memory. The dangers of obsession with the past are very real for Joseph;
they have the power to cripple him in the essential task he has undertaken.
Not only the evils of the past but its loves, its beauty, and its sweetness —
all have become perilous to one whose business is sheer survival. Joseph's
task, quite simply, is to ensure — in the phrase that is used more than once
to express the overriding value of survival — "that we may live and not
die" (43:8; 47:19). Nostalgia, yearning for the "sweetness and light"[3] of
his own culture, might hamper him in his single-minded role as life-
sustainer for many nations.

It is in these terms that Joseph ultimately accounts for God's plot in
sending him down to Egypt, with all the suffering that entailed: he has
been sent, he tells his brothers, *le-miḥya* — for the sake of life (45:5).
Anesthetized to the disabling prods of memory, Joseph acknowledges his
own necessary alienation. The word *nashani*, indeed — "He has made me
forget" — the root of Manasseh's name, is translated by Rashi to mean,
"to spring out of place" (as in 32:31, where Jacob's sinew shrinks and is
dislocated).[4] Implicitly, the word suggests dislocation, the discontinuity
of a leap into a new place, a new mode of being.[5] There is a clenching, a
shrinking, a contraction. The rupture of experience that sets Joseph at a
radical distance from his previous life has the virtue of allowing him to
concentrate totally on the imperative of his new condition.

There is, of course, a brutal quality to situations in which sheer
survival overrides all other considerations. Spiritual and cultural values
tend to be assimilated to primary, physical needs. This, according to
Ramban, is the meaning of the strange imagery in Pharaoh's dream: the
fat cows are swallowed by the lean cows, "but when they had consumed

them, one could not tell that they had consumed them, for they looked just as bad as before" (41:21).

From this surrealistic image, Joseph understands that he should tell Pharaoh to collect all the available resources of the good years, for all that can be accumulated will ensure only sheer survival. No vestige of plenty, or beauty, will be perceptible in the rigor of the bad years; there will be no sign of the huge investment of the resources of prosperity. All will be consumed, assimilated to the needs of mere survival. This, Ramban asserts, is the meaning of the image of weird "disappearance" in Pharaoh's dream: the lean cows do not even bulge, achieve no look of health or prosperity, as they consume the fat cows. Joseph, therefore, is not offering gratuitous advice in telling Pharaoh to hoard all the corn in the years of plenty: he is simply "reading" the dream imagery, releasing its message.

"The best that has been thought and known" is suddenly, abruptly, "unknown," under the pressure of a single imperative. The very prospect of hunger and death can erode all values. In this way, *Ha'amek Davar* reads Joseph's words to Pharaoh, "No trace of the abundance will be left in the land *because of the famine thereafter*" (41:31). Even in the good years, there is no enjoyment of plenty, under the shadow of impending hunger. Cultural values that normally thrive in prosperity are eroded by the anticipation of brutal times ahead. "Thus conscience does make cowards of us all," says Hamlet, meditating on the disabling effect of consciousness.[6] The imagining of famine makes it impossible to live well, even in the good years. Seforno, indeed, quotes the aphorism of the sages in this context: "One who has bread in his basket [that is, one whose future life is assured] is quite different from one who has no bread in his basket."[7] In a reality framed by famine, food does not satisfy. The impending rift undermines one's basic hold on life.

This grim perspective on ultimate priorities is reinforced by the narrative at several points. Most obviously, the Egyptian people are ready to yield everything—property, land, even personal liberty—for the sake of food (47:19). But, more subtly and, therefore, more devastatingly, it is Jacob himself who comes to exemplify the power of necessity, the subversive effect of the survival imperative on all other values.

Jacob, faced by the command of the mysterious Egyptian viceroy to send his youngest son, Benjamin, down to Egypt, at first responds with all the force of his being: "My son must not go down with you!" (42:38).

(This becomes a formula for unequivocal rejection of an idea, as the midrash relates: "R. Tarfon would use these words to disparage an untenable statement.")[8] But Judah is not impressed by his father's recalcitrance, his passionate refusal to endanger the only surviving son of Rachel. In a radical sense, indeed, Benjamin is *his* only surviving son, as Judah recognizes: "Your servant my father said to us, 'As you know, my wife bore me two sons'" (44:27). The heart of the matter, as Jacob articulates it in time of stress, is that he had only one wife, only two sons. Yet confronting his father's absolute refusal to relinquish Benjamin, Judah pragmatically predicts, in the words of the midrash, "Just wait till the bread is gone from the house!" (Rashi, 43:2).

And, indeed, when the provisions are exhausted, Jacob's principled passion crumbles in the face of the bare cupboard and Judah's succinct argument: "Let us live and not die" (43:8). Sure death faces the family if Benjamin is not sent to Egypt, notes Rashi, while disaster to Benjamin, of which Jacob has such complex foreboding, is only a possibility. Rationally, the prospect of certain death must argue louder than possible loss, even of that which is most valuable, which makes life worth living. So Jacob, in the *persona* of *paterfamilias*, with a due sense of posterity and destiny ("their father Israel" [43:11]) yields to necessity.

It is this confrontation between certainty and possibility that Joseph traces in naming Manasseh. A certain mercy of oblivion has allowed Joseph to turn his back on the world of loves and values and possibilities, to turn his face unequivocally toward the single necessity of the moment. But by naming his son for that oblivion, he expresses his ambivalence.[9] There is regret in the ironic celebration of forgetfulness, in the imagining of dislocation. Possibly, there is even hope, a bracketing of present reality in the flow of time. The question of physical and cultural survival, with their implicit tensions, engages Joseph to the depths of his being. He names Manasseh for that tension.

# Ephraim: *life-giving and life-preserving*

Ephraim, his second son, is also named out of Joseph's passionate concern with survival: "God has made me fertile in the land of my affliction." The paradoxical thrust is palpable: fruitfulness and affliction are inseparable in Joseph's life. The irony of this association is compounded by the fact that fruitfulness is seen, in the midrashic tradition, as an essential characteristic of Joseph (Rashi, 49:22), while Egypt is described in the Covenant between the Pieces as the place where Abraham's descendants will be "afflicted" (15:13). Joseph, therefore, names his son for the ironic fulfillment of God's promise. The terror of great darkness (15:12), in which God had informed Abraham of the fate of his children, comes to rest on Joseph, with an unexpected twist of sweetness. It is, apparently, possible to be fruitful, to create life, even in that place, that no-place ("a land not theirs" [15:13]) of affliction.

Joseph is involved on many levels with the question of life-giving—he is the Feeder, the Sustainer of life for many nations. Essentially, Ramban suggests, his wisdom consists of the capacity to preserve corn against rotting (41:33). His is basically a technical expertise: he knows what additives to mix with the produce to preserve it against lice, worms, and other destructive insects.

This is the central problem in preserving life: the corruption that rises spontaneously from the very heart of life. (The belief in the spontaneous generation of insects was traditionally held till recent times.) How to stop things rotting is, for Joseph, a much more vital problem than that of fertility itself. He knows, Rashi comments, a technical secret of preservation: he puts a little of the soil in which the produce grew into the storehouse, and the corn will not rot (41:48). There is a relation, chemical or mystical, between life and the soil out of which it grows. Joseph's intuition about this (which Ramban simply calls *ḥokhmah*—"wisdom"), indicates a general sensitivity to the relations between life and land, to the need of the fruit for its place of origin, if it is not to rot and die.

In naming Ephraim, therefore, Joseph meditates on the real problems of life-giving, the hazard of corruption, the tendency of life to breed death. Desiring fruit for himself, Joseph is aware of a more complex version of Kafka's description of his own condition: "Without forebears, without marriage, without heirs, with a fierce longing for forebears, marriage, and heirs."[10] Joseph has all three. But all are problematic for him; in all, fierce longing is mixed with other feelings.

His forebears are illustrious and forbidding in their effect on his freedom. The midrash has him reject the advances of Potiphar's wife with the words, "God is in the habit of choosing among the loved ones of my father's house for burnt offerings."[11] He cannot act as he might desire, because of his responsibility as child of his forebears. He carries with him a predilection, an availability to God, almost a genetic passion, that is liable to flare up at any moment. His marriage to an Egyptian and his children by her are similarly fraught with ambivalent feelings. As he names his children, he meditates on the problems of true "heirship"; he fiercely longs, not only to procreate — to be fruitful — but to negotiate the deathly perils of life, the tendency to corruption in an alien soil.

The irony of Ephraim's name is compounded by the invariable description of Egypt as a *fertile* country: Sodom, for example, is described as well watered, "like the garden of the Lord, like the land of Egypt" (13:10). The main problem of the famine, the midrash suggests, is not lack of produce, or even neglect in collecting the produce during the good years. It is simply, as Rashi (41:55) has the Egyptians complain to Pharaoh, that "we collected a great deal, but it rotted."

There is a frighteningly *immediate* character to this rotting: suddenly, at the very onset of the seven famine years, "there was famine in all the lands." "The seven years of abundance that the land of Egypt enjoyed came to an end, and the seven years of famine set in" (41:53–54): playing on the words *va-tikhlena* ("they came to an end") and *va-teḥilena* ("they began"), the midrash speaks of a terrifying transformation, from joy to sickness — "In the time it took them to sit down at table, there was no bread to be found."[12] Such an instant famine is explained by the notion that all the corn immediately rotted, at the end of the seven good years.

The terror of corruption, the anxiety that Paul Tillich describes, "of not being able to preserve one's own being,"[13] is Joseph's deep concern. He has been fruitful; but his fierce longing is to have heirs, in the fullest sense. Again, the tension between physical and cultural survival is central; replete with forebears, marriage, and heirs, Joseph must meditate on the hazards affecting his continued being. At the moment of childbearing, Joseph is fixed on the paradoxes of rupture and preservation, of staying alive, giving life, and keeping alive, of forgetting and remembering.

## The pit of oblivion

For the essential fact of his life is that he is a man who was thrown into a pit, into one of many pits, into more than one pit. The experience of the pit is the informing image of his life.

Both the pit into which his brothers throw him and the prison in which Potiphar incarcerates him are called *bor*. The word usually connotes a cistern, used to hold water. For this reason, the text makes a special point about the *bor* into which Joseph is thrown by his brothers: "The pit was empty; there was no water in it" (37:24). Unusually, this *bor* has no water in it. But the text then proceeds to use the same word of Joseph's prison: he calls it a *bor*, in his outraged description of his undeserved fate: "For in truth, I was kidnapped from the land of the Hebrews; nor have I done anything here that they should have put me in the dungeon (*bor*)" (40:15).

Fate has dealt enigmatically with him: his mysterious kidnapping from his homeland is paralleled by his equally unjustified incarceration in Egypt. Clearly, the essential characteristic of a *bor* in this context—in Joseph's imagination—has nothing to do with water. It is, in Rashi's definition, simply a concave space (41:14), a hole, in which Joseph unexpectedly finds himself, and from which it is impossible to climb out.

This is indeed something of a world apart from the world. In this space, normal logic and law do not seem to function; it is an absurd, hollow space in which one can cry out and not be heard (42:21), and in which one feels cut off from past and future. In *A Tale of Two Cities*, Dickens describes the experience of being imprisoned in the Bastille as that of being "Buried Alive." The full terror of the *bor* is precisely that of disappearing, without explanation, down a hole, to be forgotten by the world.

This implication of the *bor* is detected by the Talmud, within the text of the Torah: "They cast him into the pit" (37:24). "Wherever the word "cast" [*hashlakha*] is used, it means to a depth of at least twenty cubits":[14] that is, to a depth that, in halakhic terms, is *beyond eyeview*. Joseph, therefore, becomes invisible when he is thrown into the *bor*, into both *borot*—pit and prison. In the fullest sense, he is forgotten by the world.

The specific case of forgetting that the text narrates is that of the butler, whom Joseph begged, "But remember me when all is well with you again, and do me the kindness of bringing me to Pharaoh's mind, so as to free me from this place" (40:14). Nevertheless, he "did not remember Joseph; he forgot him" (40:23).

To be remembered would mean release from live burial. But once fallen into the pit, Joseph enters a kind of black hole, unimaginable to those outside. This is a private inferno, in which he cannot imagine himself into any real relation with his past. When he narrates his history to the butler, he speaks in the passive, or impersonal form: "I was kidnapped . . . they put me in the dungeon" (40:15). There is, indeed, an impersonal quality to his brothers' silent fury, as they strip him and hurl him into the pit. In memory, Joseph cannot relate that moment to what came before. It seems uncaused, a rupture in the fabric of things. He can only see it as equivalent to his blamelessness when he is caught up in the vengeful fire of Potiphar's jilted wife. The fibers connecting him with the world of reason and continuity are cauterized.

To be thrown into a pit is, effectively, to be declared dead in the mind of others. The Talmud states that the presumption of death is so strong that the victim's wife may remarry. An overpowering conviction consigns the *bor*-victim to death.

Joseph's brothers, in fact, originally plan to kill Joseph first, and then to "throw him into one of the pits" (37:20). Reuben pleads that they keep their hands clean of blood—of direct contact with blood—and that they throw him directly into a pit. Although the text vouches for Reuben that he intends to save Joseph by this strategy, as far as the brothers are concerned, throwing him into a pit is equivalent to killing him. More precisely, it is a way of making him disappear without trace, so that *any* story can be fabricated to account for his absence ("we can say, 'A savage beast devoured him'" [37:20]). Out of the hollow into which Joseph disappears emerges a narrative, a fiction. On the basis of circumstantial evidence—the coat realistically daubed with blood—a full-blown theory of dismemberment and death will become current in the world.

## "Joseph is not"

The presumption of death is applied in the talmudic case we have just quoted, when the pit was "full of snakes and scorpions." This detail is just the circumstance given in Rashi's famous comment on Joseph's pit: "*'The pit was empty; there was no water in it'* [37:24]. If it was empty, is it not obvious that there was no water in it? There was no water, but there were snakes and scorpions." Emptiness, in this case, means emptiness of water. The pit is, in fact, full—of snakes and scorpions. This is, essentially, a description of emptiness: to be in emptiness, to be assigned to a hole, discontinuous with past and future, gone from the minds of others, is to be assailed by all the horrors with which emptiness is pregnant.

Joseph has been projected into such an emptiness. In the next chapter, Tamar uses all her cunning and courage to fill her internal emptiness—literally—with child. The Jerusalem Talmud has her pray in fear and desire: "Master of the Universe, let me not go empty from this house!"[15]

Internal emptiness is the specific site of fulfillment, in the biological lives of women. Tamar speaks of a desire, at once physical and metaphysical, to be filled by the seed of the house of Jacob. She recognizes the terror of "going out empty," and will risk the fire to fill herself. Her sense of the hollow space at her core gives her passion and guile to choose her own destiny.

Joseph, however, is enveloped in a world of nothingness that threatens his life with its own spawn, its "snakes and scorpions." In the extraordinary expression, repeatedly used in this narrative, Joseph "is not." When Reuben returns to the pit, hoping to save him, "Behold! — Joseph is not [*ein*] in the pit. And he tore his clothes" (37:29). Reuben is affected by a sense of Joseph's "not-being": there is an absence, a horror of "not-Joseph" in the pit, that leads him to tear his clothes in desperate mourning. He cries to his brothers: "The boy is gone [*einenu!* — lit., is not!]! Now, what am I to do?" (37:30).

The word *ein* ("is not") conveys the sudden disappearance, the reverberation of absence. Reuben plays poignantly with the word, with its hollow resonance — *einenu va-ani ana ani* — ("he is not — and I, whither am I"). Identity, direction, being itself — all are put to question by this mysterious disappearance. Faced with the empty space of the pit, Reuben knows that he too is inescapably consigned to a world of hollowness. "Where shall I flee from father's sorrow?" he asks, in Rashi's reading.

Reuben's *einenu* expresses the mystery of disappearance. The brothers speak of Joseph as *einenu*, when they explain their family situation to Joseph, in his role of Egyptian viceroy: "The youngest is now with our father, and one is no more [*einenu*]" (42:13). The brothers know what has happened to Joseph until the point when they sold him to the passing traders (Midianite or Ishmaelite). One might say that they are being evasive, not wishing, for obvious reasons, to tell the truth about Joseph's disappearance, but also unwilling to lie and speak of his death. *Einenu*, in that case, would be a usefully ambiguous word to describe "lostness."

What gives added poignancy and an uncanny force to the word, however, is the brothers' real ignorance of Joseph's fate. According to an important midrashic tradition, indeed, one reason for their journey into Egypt is to seek their lost brother. When they stand in front of Joseph, therefore, they evoke his palpable loss, the effect on them of his not-being.

The irony goes beyond the obvious dramatic irony of ignorance that Joseph himself is their interrogator. It lies in the magnetic force that Joseph's "not-being" has exerted on them: "For the sake of the one who is not, we have scattered throughout the city to seek him." This is Rashi's reading of the relation between the whole family—"We your servants were twelve brothers, sons of a certain man"—and the one lost son. Joseph's "lostness" has sent his brothers in all directions, entering Egypt by ten different gates, according to Rashi (42:12). Emptiness, not-being, loss, demonstrate their power to move, to break up unities, and make the fragments volatile.

## Losing and finding

The brothers again use the word *einenu*, when they repeat the dialogue to their father. And Jacob tellingly accuses them: "You have bereaved me! Joseph is no more [*einenu*] and Simeon is no more, and now you would take away Benjamin!" (42:36). Jacob's startling talk of his sons' responsibility for bereaving him of Joseph and Simeon, and the fact that he perceives their fates as symmetrical—both are "no more" [*einenu*]—leads Rashi to comment: "Anyone whose sons are lost is called 'bereaved.'"

Perhaps similarly to the relation in English between the words "bereaved," and "bereft," there is a play of concepts covered by the words *shakul* ("bereaved/bereft"), *avud* ("lost"), and *einenu* ("he is not"). Each term can mean, unequivocally, "dead"—as in "bereaved." But each can also mean an absence, a distance, shimmering with perplexities and possibilities.

Rashi justifies the use of the word *shakul* (usually signifying bereavement of one's children) in a case where the child is simply *avud*—"lost." The range of this latter word can be sensed in its usage in biblical and prophetic texts. When the Israelite would bring his first fruits to the Temple, for example, he would make a declaration, tracing his personal history back to the time of Jacob: "An Aramean destroyed [*oved*] my father" (Deuteronomy 26:5). This is read as a reference to Laban, who represents the experience of exile for Jacob.[16] *Oved*, therefore, can mean to destroy by destructuring one's relation to one's proper place.

To be lost, in this sense, is to lose that ease in which outer and inner worlds meet: "There is no sense of ease like the ease we felt in those scenes where we were born, where objects became dear to us before we had known the labor of choice, and where the outer world seemed only an extension of our personality."[17] And to lose someone, a child, is to be left with the husk, the outer world, with a vacuum at its core—*einenu*.

When this concept of loss occurs in biblical and prophetic texts, it often generates a disturbing awareness of ambiguity. Is death, final destruction, the meaning? Or, on the contrary, is it "loss," "displacement," which carries with it the companion notion of recovery, return?

When Esther says stoically, "If I am to perish [*avadti*], I shall perish!" (Esther 4:16), she means, clearly, that she is prepared to risk martyrdom in her effort to save her people. Or when the sailors on Jonah's ship pray, "Do not let us perish on account of this man's life" (Jonah 1:14); or when the king of Nineveh urges prayer, "so that we do not perish" (3:14); or when God describes the gourd as having "appeared overnight and perished overnight" (4:10)—clearly, they all speak of the dread and mystery of death.

On the other hand, when Isaiah says: "On that day, a great ram's horn shall be sounded; and the strayed (*ha-ovdim*) who are in the land of Assyria and the expelled who are in the land of Egypt shall come and worship the Lord on the holy mount, in Jerusalem" (27:13); or when Ezekiel accuses the false shepherds: "You have not brought back the strayed, or looked for the lost. . . . I will look for the lost, and I will bring back the strayed" (34:4, 16)—they are describing loss, exile, as a situation that demands restoration; the false shepherds have reneged on their duty, if they do not seek the lost sheep.

In these texts, it is of the very nature and meaning of the lost being, the *aveda*, that it is to be sought. If the Psalmist compares himself to a "lost [*oved*] sheep," there follows naturally an appeal to the shepherd to seek him out: "I have strayed like a lost sheep; search for Your servant, for I have not forgotten Your commandments" (Psalms 119:176). This appeal is based on the claim that the lost one has not entirely lost all connection with home. The Psalmist still "remembers" God's commandments: they are not "lost" to him, as Ibn Ezra puts it. Here, the danger of being lost is focused in the problem of forgetting. And the real drama, the dialectical tension of "lostness," lies in the consciousness of the lost one, in the vestiges of memory that appeal for reintegration.

In these texts, the meanings of *avad* seem clearly distributed. But how is one to read "*Va-avadtem* [You shall perish / be lost] soon from the good land that the Lord is assigning to you" (Deuteronomy 11:17)? The

Sifrei reads it as referring to exile.[18] But a similar text—"*Va-avadtem* among the nations" (Leviticus 26:38)—becomes the subject of real controversy among the Sages. R. Akiva takes it as meaning absolute destruction: "It refers to the Ten Tribes who were exiled for ever";[19] "the ten tribes were exiled from their place to distant lands and are not destined to return."[20] Others say, "*Ovdan* means simply exile";[21] "the ten tribes *are* destined to return. . . . Just as the day darkens and lightens, so the ten tribes who have gone into darkness are destined to emerge into light."[22]

Here, two views of time—linear and cyclical—oppose one another. If *va-avadtem* means final destruction, this is congruous with a view of time as irreversible—"One never crosses the same river twice" (Heraclitus). If, however, it means exile, diffusion, loss, this is congruous with a cyclical view of time and a dialectical view of history: the darkness is a phase in a returning cycle; the exile moves both away from home and toward it.

But the question of reading remains unresolved: the concept of "loss" invites radically different responses, on every level of gravity. There is a perspective from which even the most trivial loss (of household objects, the memory of a name, a number) can induce the panic reaction of final, irrevocable disappearance. And there is a different perspective from which even the death of a loved child is a temporary, subjective "loss," which contains the seeds of recovery. In a sense, such losses generate the energy for great "findings."

The Talmud, for instance, speaks in these terms of the search for a wife: "It is the way of a man to go around searching for a wife—like a person who has suffered a loss."[23] Presumably, the loss of Adam's rib is the primary myth here, but the notion of loss makes the finding a matter of restoring an imagined part of the self. Knowing one's incompleteness, narrating the history of an absence, generates the desire to find, to fill the emptiness.

The same dynamic of losing and finding informs the famous midrash that tells of the moment of birth as a moment of forgetting.[24] The embryo in the womb knew the whole Torah and forgets it as it emerges into the world. Implicitly, the whole of life is a process of recovery, of restoring the loss, of filling the vacancy.

This is the "peculiar possibility of the negative," as Henri Bergson puts it. "Every human action has its starting point in a dissatisfaction, and thereby in a feeling of absence."[25] Kenneth Burke writes:

[Bergson] jolted me into realizing that there are no negatives in nature, where everything simply is what it is. To look for negatives in nature would be as absurd as though you were to go out hunting for the square root of minus-one. The negative is a function peculiar to symbol systems, quite as the square root of minus-one is an implication of a certain mathematical symbol system. . . . One of the negative's prime uses . . . involves its role with regard to unfulfilled expectations. If I am expecting a certain situation and a different situation occurs, I can say that the expected situation did *not* occur. But as far as the actual state of affairs is concerned, some situation positively prevails, and that's that.[26]

The "actual state of affairs" can be flatly described. The "expected state of affairs" can generate infinite negative descriptions, expressing disappointment, surprise, disillusion, hope. Here, language comes into its own; as Burke rather mischievously puts it, "Language and the negative 'invented' man."

Unfulfilled expectations represent one aspect of the experience of loss. Human life, according to the Talmud in Tractate Niddah, is founded on this experience and on the profound sense of the negative it engenders. However, it is essential to the process of recovery that the loser own his own loss, that he become conscious of an absence.

When, for example, Moses speaks of the people coming to him "to seek God," this can be understood as a psychotherapeutic encounter in which the leader helps his followers to "recognize what they have lost."[27] There is no finding without that sense of loss. The leader-teacher helps the seeker to identify the hollowness, the absence, that will move him to a passion of quest. A primal "forgetting" (the neo-Platonic notion of anamnesis) leads to a process of approximate reconstructions, of "makings and matchings,"[28] to which the teacher-tzaddik can hold up therapeutic mirrors—but only, as R. Nahman says, if the seeker is genuinely the loser, if there is no inauthenticity in the search.[29] Such a genuine awareness of loss is the only basis for hope of recovery.

There emerges a notion of the intimately imaginative nature of loss. To speak of what is not may be an academic linguistic exercise, unless the loss is passionately appropriated as one's own. It is only a "mind of winter" that perceives "the nothing that is not there and the nothing that is."[30]

Only such a mind, a snowman's mind, could attend to the frozen trees without adding to them some increment of language, of humanity, even if that increment is misery . . . There is no "inert savoir"; to speak as if there were is already to speak as if. Metaphor begins to remodel the plain sense as soon as we begin to think about it. If Stevens is right in saying that the words of the world are the life of the world, then metaphor runs in the world's blood.[31]

## Limited perspectives: despair and hope

"The child is not," "the one is not," "Joseph is not," say Joseph's brothers and father. What Jacob means may cover a range of possibilities. At both ends of the range, he speaks explicitly of these possibilities: Joseph is dead (42:38); or, merely, minimally, "One has gone from me, and I said: Alas! he was torn by a beast! And I have not seen him since" (44:28). Jacob recognizes that positive identification of the corpse is simply the work of human language, a remodeling of that nothingness: "I said: Alas! he was torn . . ." The only fact is a negative one: "I have not seen him till now."

Jacob will speak of Joseph as dead, when it suits his rhetorical purpose—that is, when he is passionately opposing his sons' intention of taking Benjamin. But when Judah makes his great speech before the Egyptian viceroy, he delineates a Jacob who refuses the easy pleasures of rhetoric, who speaks simply, movingly of his real experience, his real loss: "The one has gone from me . . . and I have not seen him till now." He says all that a human being can realistically say about loss: to be bereaved is to be bereft, the one who has gone can no longer be seen. To be *einenu* is to enter a blind spot; "we have suffered a loss," the brothers say to the viceroy, in the midrashic narrative.[32] As a result of this loss, they disperse throughout the city, in search of Joseph. They are prepared to change their original position, to break ranks, so as to "catch sight" perhaps of their elusive brother, to bring him into view.

*Einenu*, then, is a word that describes mystery, the limits of human perception. As Jacob uses it, it resounds with a profound cognitive skepticism. This is reflected in the translation of Targum Jonathan: "and we do not know what has happened to him" (42:13). Apparently unequivocal—what could be more absolute than its declaration of not-being—*einenu* is strangely redolent with possibility. It is a frankly subjective owning of loss.

It can, however, reach a pitch of yearning that kills the loser: "When he sees that the boy is not [*einenu*] with us, he will die" (44:30). Judah imagines his father seeing Benjamin's absence: "that the boy *is not*." For Benjamin, like Joseph, has a tendency to disappear, to become *einenu*. In his speech in Joseph's unrecognized presence, Judah three times refers to the impossibility both of going down to Egypt for corn and of returning to Canaan, if Benjamin *einenu itanu*—"is not with me / us" (44:26, 30, 34). In Benjamin's case, however, the significant word *itanu* ("with us") is added each time to the word *einenu*. It is no longer a matter of sheer disappearance. Judah acknowledges personal responsibility—on behalf of his brothers—for Benjamin's continued being. On a profound level, Judah must make a place for Benjamin, *with* himself, so that if he is lost, his "not-being," his lostness, is to be thoroughly owned by Judah and his brothers.

*Einenu* has, then, an ambiguous thrust, in the direction of absolute negation, on the one hand, and of a subjective skepticism, on the other. The word both cuts off imagination or speculation and encourages them. Before Joseph, there was a man called Enoch, who "was not": "He walked with God, and he was not [*einenu*], because God took him" (5:24). Rashi explains the force of *einenu*: "He was a righteous man, but easily seduced to return to evil ways. So God hastened to remove him from the world, and killed him before his time. That is why the text describes his death in such an unusual way: 'and he was not in the world'—to live out his full life."

Rashi quotes the midrash to give us a sense of the rupture, the unfulfilled expectation, evoked by *einenu*. Suddenly, there is an absence. But "he is not in the world" suggests, by its qualification, that there is an elsewhere, where Enoch is. The midrash claims this verse as a proof against heretics, who would like to set Enoch up as an immortal, that he did indeed die.[33] But, as the commentaries to the midrash point out, there is a kabbalistic tradition that Enoch did not, in fact, die. Without entering into the substance of this claim, one can notice the ambiguity with which the word *einenu* resonates. It does and does not mean death. All one can realistically speak of is the surprise, the shock, the speculations, the hope, that "not-being" evokes.

This complex response to *einenu* is depicted in the midrashic understanding of Jacob's mourning for Joseph: "'*And he refused to be comforted*': One does not accept comfort for someone who is still alive, even though one thinks he is dead; for it is in reference to the dead that a decree has been issued that he be forgotten from the heart, and not in reference to the living" (Rashi, 37:35).

Jacob, on some subconscious level, *knows* that Joseph is alive; while, consciously, he thinks him dead. That is why he cannot accept comfort for him. The point is obviously paradoxical: normally, one might imagine that a mourner who refuses to be comforted is overinvolved in the despair of death. The midrash shifts the reader's perspective: the willingness to be comforted becomes a mode of despair at the finality of death—it is a "decree" that allows the dead to recede from the heart of the living, a kind of treachery to the loyalty of memory. Conversely, the refusal to be comforted is a refusal to yield up the dead, to turn one's mind to other thoughts.[34]

Jacob has every evidence for his reasonable view ("one thinks"—*savar*) that Joseph is dead. Not only the stained coat but a veritable conspiracy of silence, in which the midrash imagines God Himself to be involved, ensures that the truth is not revealed to him. Nevertheless, a "glimmer of inspiration" makes it impossible for him to accept the despair of his own rational mind:

> *"A savage beast devoured him"*: The Holy Spirit glimmered in him, showing him that Joseph would be attacked by Potiphar's wife [the "savage beast"!]. Why did God not reveal the truth to him? Because the brothers had placed a ban and a curse on anyone who would reveal this truth, and they had included God in their ban! Isaac knew that Joseph was alive, but he said, "How shall I reveal it, if God Himself does not want to reveal it?" (Rashi, 37:33)

Rashi delicately balances the question of perception and truth. The truth is that Joseph is alive; but Jacob does not know this on any conscious level[35]—indeed, God does not *want* him to know it, in Isaac's words. Instead, he inhabits a field of perception, in which he "plausibly thinks"—*savar*—that Joseph is dead, while experiencing "glimmers" of intuition—rationally, quite irreconcilable with his conscious opinion—about Potiphar's wife, and while finding it impossible to "give up" on Joseph.

There is, indeed, an active force to the verb, *va-yima'en*, "he refused." Something in Jacob stubbornly bars him from oblivion: he *will* remember Joseph, keep him alive-in-absence in his mind. Jacob is conscious of his limited perspective, as a human being. He is aware that he has a "blind spot," and allows for it; Joseph has disappeared, but Jacob knows that the plausible interpretation of the bloody coat is just that—an interpretation—a *sevara*, in the language of talmudic logic. The totality of the blank—not even a corpse to fill it—and the totality of the conspiracy of silence around him evoke glimmerings of intuition. If Joseph "is not" here, in Jacob's field of perception, perhaps he is elsewhere? If he is lost, perhaps he is to be sought, to be imagined as continuing, not ended?

In quoting this midrash about comfort and oblivion, Rashi is, I suggest, making a rare and audacious statement about the workings of the conscious mind. Like an aura beyond consciousness, there is an awareness of truth—Joseph is, in reality, not dead. Jacob has a certain access to this truth, though Rashi insists that God does not want it revealed to him. In the tension between the two kinds of knowledge—rational, perspectival knowledge and the awareness of the limitations of perspective—the *einenu* sense grows: a profound skepticism, finally summarized in Judah's report of his father's view: "The one has gone from me. . . . And I have not seen him since" (44:28).

## Shever / Sever: *the dialectical vision*

A kind of twilight zone between despair and hope is evoked by the expressions of loss, of not-being, in the narrative. Radically ambiguous, *einenu* closes and opens avenues of speculation. Just this dialectical tension is the subject of a central midrash on the narrative:

> "Jacob saw that there were food rations [*shever*] to be had in Egypt" (42:1): "Happy is he . . . whose hope [*sever*] is in the Lord his God" (Psalms 146:5). "Whatever He tears down cannot be rebuilt" (Job 12:14). When God destroyed the plan of the tribes, it was not rebuilt. "Whomever He imprisons cannot be set free"—these are the ten tribes, who traveled to and from Egypt, and did not know that Joseph was alive. But to Jacob it was revealed that Joseph was alive, as it is said, "Jacob saw that there was *shever* in Egypt." "There was *shever* [brokenness]"—that is the famine; "there was *sever* [hope]"—that is the plenty. "There was *shever* [brokenness]"—"Joseph was taken down to Egypt" (39:1); "there was *sever* [hope]"—"Joseph became the ruler" (42:6). "There was *shever* [brokenness]—"They shall enslave and afflict them" (15:13); "there was *sever* [hope]"—"in the end they shall go free with great wealth" (15:14).[36]

On this reading, Jacob "sees" much more than the fact that corn rations are to be had in Egypt. ("Heard" would be a more appropriate verb to describe the arrival of such news in Canaan, as Jacob himself describes it in the next verse: "I hear that there are rations"). What he sees distinguishes him from his ten sons, who have no sense that Joseph is alive. Extraordinarily, the midrash affirms: "to Jacob it was revealed that Joseph was alive."

The revelation takes the form of a vision of *shever*—a Janus-headed concept, suggesting both brokenness and hope. The midrash gives three examples of Jacob's bifocal vision: the famine and the plenty; Joseph's kidnapping and his rise to power; God's promise of suffering and slavery in Egypt, on the one hand, and of triumphant redemption, on the other.

The relation of *shever* to *sever*, of brokenness to hope, is not, however, merely sequential. Jacob does not merely see an end to suffering and a new phase of prosperity. Indeed, the historical order of the plenty and the famine does not allow of such an optimistic reading: the midrash in fact reverses the order to adjust it to the conceptual scheme of brokenness and hope. What Jacob sees is a dialectical vision of *shever / sever*. When things fall apart, the opportunity for *sever* arises. Before such a crisis, in a condition of wholeness and security, hope is irrelevant. After it, some plausible reconstruction of the shards becomes essential.

This is *sever*; the word for hope (the midrash quotes the verse from Psalms, "Happy is he . . . whose hope [*sever*] is in the Lord his God") is intimately related to the idea of shattering, of crisis. It is also related to the notion of "thought," of "plausible opinion." *Sevara*, as we have noticed, is a plausible interpretation. It is the conventional talmudic expression for thinking: for speculation, ingenuity in constructing a pleasing hypothesis. Thinking is an act of trust; there are no guarantees that one is right in one's interpretation. *Savoor* is often used, in fact, to describe a mistaken opinion (as we have just seen, Jacob *savar* that Joseph was dead). To think, then, is to respond with a kind of courage to the evidence, the surfaces of reality. To hope, likewise, is to dare to trust the more cheerful facets of a shattered condition.

What Jacob sees, then, is the necessary relation between disaster and hope. He sees the condition of the *bor*, of emptiness, disappearance, loss, as generating hopeful hypotheses. The fundamental polarity of disaster and hope is thus expressed in the single word *shever*, as the midrash refracts it. The two concepts are related by an inner dialectic; they are simultaneous.

This, the midrash affirms, is what is "revealed" to Jacob. He must act on the basis of hope, of a vision of life-in-death. He may turn out to be mistaken; but that is the nature of the *shever* world, into which Joseph has disappeared. "Not to have is the beginning of desire."[37]

## Rachel and her children: the battle against non-being

Jacob sees *einenu* as that condition of elusiveness, of not-being-there, that is characterized by Joseph and Benjamin, the sons of Rachel. It is a kind of genetic endowment; for Rachel, too, was a mistress of the *einenu* mode. "Give me children," she cried to Jacob, in her extremity, "or else I die!" (30:1). Literally, the text says: "and if *ayin* ["nothing"], I die!" Some commentators read this as the suicidal threat of a pampered wife.[38] But we can read it simply as Rachel confronting *ayin*, nothingness. If she has no children to fill her emptiness, Rachel cries, she is dead. This is no threat: it is an intimate existential description. "One who has no children is accounted as dead," Rashi comments. There is a psychological and emotional wasteland consciousness, to which Rachel is singularly sensitive.

Jacob responds with a strange anger to her plea. And *Akedat Yitzḥak* offers a striking reading of the scene, setting Jacob up as philosophical opponent to Rachel's despair. The background is the two names that were given to Eve, to signify her two roles: Eve [*Ḥava*—"life-giver"] signifies her sexual, procreative function, while *isha*—"woman"—signifies her intellectual, spiritual role, parallel to that of man. The first role is instrumental, which subordinates her to the procreation of life; the second is autonomous. A woman who cannot bear children still has what the commentator calls her greatest purpose in living—her moral and spiritual role, equivalent to a man's.

It is for this reason that Jacob is angry with Rachel: she has invested all her life energy in the procreative role, has surrendered to *ayin*, once that role seems denied to her. "Let not the eunuch say, 'I am a withered tree.' "[39] The pathos of Rachel's cry is understood but rejected. Poignant as is the sense of life denied in childlessness, the prophet Isaiah maintains that a vital identity—even a kind of immortality—is awarded to those people, men or women, eunuch or foreigner, who fulfill their destiny as moral and spiritual beings.

On this view, Jacob is angered by Rachel's despairing acceptance of *ayin*. She sees herself—mistakenly, according to *Akedat Yitzḥak*—as having only one avenue of escape from nothingness. But this is, nevertheless, Rachel speaking her truth. It is, indeed, the only speech that Rachel makes in the whole narrative, aside from her naming of Joseph.

In all her beauty, Rachel is the one who is not there. During their wedding night, Jacob "knew" that Rachel was there, but in the morning, "Behold! she was Leah!" (29:25). "All night," he accuses Leah, "I called you 'Rachel!' and you answered!"[40] For Jacob, Rachel always represents an absence, as beauty perhaps always arouses the desire for what cannot be possessed.

And, suddenly, *ba-derekh*, on the journey back to the Holy Land, she dies in childbirth. Rashi reads Rachel's death "on the way," as setting up a dangerous precedent, creating in her family a kind of genetic sensitivity to the *derekh*, to the road between places, that is no place. In the light of this he understands Jacob's reluctance to let Benjamin travel to Egypt with his brothers. The whole family is aware of the hazard: if Benjamin "leaves his father, he will die" (44:22). Rashi comments: "If he leaves his father, we are anxious that he will die on the *derekh* [journey], since his mother died on the *derekh*." From the beginning, Jacob is most protective of Benjamin, apparently because of the family history of *asson* — the blow of fate on the journey between places. There is almost an *expectation* that the children of Rachel will disappear into nothingness, into the modality of *einenu*.[41]

The central text for a study of Rachel and *einenu*, however, is the famous poignant description in Jeremiah 31:15–17:

> Thus said the Lord: A cry is heard in Ramah — wailing, bitter weeping — Rachel weeping for her children. She refuses to be comforted for her children, who are gone [*einenu*]. Thus said the Lord: Restrain your voice from weeping, your eyes from shedding tears; for there is a reward for your labor — declares the Lord: They shall return from the enemy's land. And there is hope for your future — declares the Lord: your children shall return to their country.

Like Jacob, Rachel refuses comfort. It is as though she has been reconciled to his view of things, to the dialectical view of crisis. She refuses the comfort that means despair, *because* her children are *einenu* — they have gone out of her line of sight. Radak explains the word: "The ten tribes have not yet returned, since their exile [unlike the tribes of Judah and Benjamin], and their place is unknown." Rachel, always sensitive to *ayin*, registers the disappearance of her children[42] from her field of perception: therefore, she will not give up on them. They are lost: therefore, they will be found. They are dispersed and placeless: therefore, they will be gathered together. This is the burden of her tears; this is the "labor" of hope, enacted in her weeping.

The dialectic of *shever* and *sever*, of rupture and reintegration, is evoked in the place of Rachel's burial. On his deathbed, Jacob explains the reason for burying her *ba-derekh*, on the way, "no place": "As for me, when I was returning from Padan, Rachel died, to my sorrow, while I was journeying in the land of Canaan, when still some distance short of Ephrath; and I buried her there on the road to Ephrath" (48:7).

Rashi comments on Jacob's emphatic references to her burial "there on the road":

> *"And I buried her there"*: I did not even bring her into Bethlehem, to bring her into Israel proper. I know you [Joseph] resent this — but know that it was by the word of God that I buried her there, so that she should be a help to her children: when Nebuzzaradan sends them into exile and they pass by *on the road there*, Rachel will come out over her grave and weep and beg mercy for them, as it is said, "A voice is heard in Ramah" [Jeremiah 31:15] — and God will reply, "There is a reward for your labor, says the Lord, and your children shall return to their country."

Rachel is buried between fixed places of human concourse, in a no-man's land, which is the metaphysical space her children will traverse on their way into exile.[43] She meets them, as it were, at the border, in that exposed place, where they move off into not-being; she weeps their *einenu* into provisional absence.

In mystical sources, Rachel becomes a code word for *Kenesset Yisrael*, the principle of cohesion in a dispersed people. As her children scatter, are broken up, the magnetic force of Rachel's desire, of her battle against *ayin*, manifests itself, and generates the dialectical movement of "return to their borders." Rachel becomes a word for imagination and desire, for the essential unity of a diffused Israel.[44]

## Joseph and his brothers: the recognition of absence

Like his mother Rachel, Joseph is *einenu*, and learns to use the energy of his disappearance to reconstitute his dispersed identity. For Joseph is

lost—both to his family and to himself. There is a need to recognize that
lostness, to gauge the space he has placed between himself and his
memories. And so he names his sons for discontinuity and survival. He
defines the real dilemma of "Let us live and not die," which is the
problem of both giving life and preserving life, of growing corn and
preserving it against corruption, of forgetting and remembering. And
when his brothers appear before him in the Egyptian court, he enacts the
*einenu* which is his family's account of him, as a means of realizing more
clearly the contours of his own absence.

"When Joseph saw his brothers, he recognized them; but he acted like
a stranger toward them and spoke harshly to them" (42:7). Joseph sets
himself to act a role of total alienation. Rashi reads *va-yitnaker*: "He acted
to them like a non-Jew, in his way of speaking—his language was harsh."
He tests his actual alienation, his lostness, by taking it almost to a point
of caricature. Conscious of the perils of assimilation, of forgetting his native culture, he acts—more, he *speaks*—in a style and tone barbaric to a
Jewish ear.

His purpose is hinted in the fact that the root of *va-yitnaker* ("he acted
like a stranger") is the same as that of *va-yakirem* ("he recognized them.")
The root—*nakar*—means "to perceive by making strange"—that is, to
know by breaking up the smooth continuities of things and focusing on
the singularity of the object. In order finally to be known by his brothers
in a way that will heal the rifts of the past, Joseph makes himself strange to
the point of uncanniness. His accusations that they are spies constitute
bizarre probes of their responses, while his inquisitorial *persona* is so
incomprehensible that his brothers are freed, in a sense, from any
attempt to communicate with him.

He is an enigmatic sovereign presence, his true face unseen,[45] set at a
distance from them by the presence of an interpreter. In this way, he can,
for the first time, hear them, as they remember their deafness to Joseph's
cries from the pit:

> They said to one another, "Alas, we are being punished on account of
> our brother, because we looked on at his anguish, yet *would not listen* as
> he pleaded with us." Then Reuben spoke up and said to them, "Did I
> not tell you, 'Do no wrong to the boy'? But you *would not listen*." They
> did not know that Joseph understood [lit., *was listening*], for there was
> an interpreter between him and them. (42:21–23)

This has not, apparently, been a listening family. In a quasi-therapeutic situation, Joseph understands (this secondary meaning of *shama* ["to hear"] is the primary meaning in this context) and accepts[46] his brothers' appalled memory of their refusal to understand and accept him. Acceptance means allowing the other—strange, singular as he is—into one's heart: the brothers speak not of active cruelty—murder, the sale of Joseph—but of a negation, a blankness, where acceptance should have been.

As Joseph hears his brothers recognize what *was not* in the past, an overwhelming emotion wells up in him: "He turned away from them and wept. But he came back to them and spoke to them; and he took Simeon from among them and had him bound before their eyes" (42:24). He has to turn away from them to hide his outburst of tears.

## Joseph's tears: retrieving absence

This is the first of three occasions on which Joseph weeps, in the course of his masquerade with his brothers. In fact, Joseph sheds most of the tears in Genesis; before him, Jacob and Esau wept, on meeting again after so much hatred and fear (33:4). From them Joseph learns to weep— the irrational collapse of tears, the genuine, unassimilated force of that flow.[47]

Each time he weeps, something opens up in him, an unplanned response, which is at first a mere parenthesis, as he turns away and then turns back to his tyrannical role. In the course of that "parenthesis," he knows himself lost and remembered by his brothers. As they speak of what was not in the past, a new relationship is suggested, woven of regret, empathy, loss. Listening to them, Joseph begins to be; his real life takes on imagined luster in their words, in their contrition.

He weeps again, when Benjamin appears in front of him. Again, spontaneously, anarchically, tears force him away from his brothers: even more emphatically, the narrative stresses this withdrawal: "Joseph hurried out, for he was overcome with feeling toward his brother and was on the verge of tears; he went into a room and wept there. Then he washed his face, reappeared, and—now in control of himself—gave the order, 'Serve the meal'" (43:30–31). The effect is of a kind of slow-motion lingering on the experience of weeping—before, during, and after. This is time out of time, after which Joseph returns to the routines of his host role ("Serve the meal"). Again, a profound, repressed consciousness breaks through with his tears.

Here, Rashi quotes the midrash to provide a subtext to Joseph's weeping:

> *"He was overcome with feeling"*: Joseph asked Benjamin, "Do you have a full brother [from your mother]?" He answered, "I had a brother, but I don't know where he is." Joseph asked him, "Do you have children?" And he answered, "I have ten children." Joseph asked, "What are their names?" Benjamin answered, "Bela, Bekher, etc." Joseph then asked, "What do these names mean?" And Benjamin replied, "They are all for my brother and the troubles that have befallen him: Bela—because he was swallowed up among the nations; Bekher—because he was first born to my mother; . . . Hupim—because he did not see my wedding, nor did I see his; Ard—because he went down among the pagans." (43:30).

In this midrashic narrative, Joseph's compassion is stirred, not simply by nostalgia and love for his true brother Benjamin, but because his own existence is suddenly fleshed out in absence. Through all the years of *einenu*, out of the line of Benjamin's sight, he has continued to be an object of imagination and regret for his brother. The naming of Benjamin's sons responds to the enigma that had inspired the naming of his own sons; indeed, it is clearly he who takes the initiative in eliciting information from Benjamin about the *meaning* of his sons' names—as though he seeks precisely the mirroring consolation that Benjamin gives him. For—absent, forgotten, swallowed up—Joseph has lived on in Benjamin's mind, as a continuous presence, manifested in the names of his sons: an elder brother, pleasant, his father's prime student, marrying in some unknown place, captive, alienated.

It is this fusion of absence and presence, of alienation and empathy, this understanding of Joseph's "lostness" to himself that Benjamin has recorded, through the years of separation. In naming his children, he has registered irremediable loss: for words, names are, in George Steiner's phrase, an indication of "real absence": "That which endows the word *rose*, that arbitrary assemblage of two vowels and two consonants, with its sole legitimacy and life force is, states Mallarmé, *'l'absence de toute rose.'*. . . The truth of the word is the absence of the world."[48] And yet, as Steiner himself argues, words, names, constitute a "counterworld"; they are a gesture of human creativity, defiant of the blankness of reality. Joseph's tears are the sign of a wild hope in brokenness.

Nevertheless, he "controls himself." There is a plot afoot to reveal his brothers' response to Benjamin under duress. Repressed memories of their cruelty to him rise to the surface, as their responsibility to Rachel's other son, Benjamin, is tested. Will they abandon him, as they abandoned Joseph in the past? This question — of abandonment, of alienation, rather than of active cruelty — is the essence of Joseph's plot, in its final stage. When Judah offers himself in place of Benjamin, simply because it is unbearable to him to witness his father's anguish, if he should return without him (44:34), Joseph again bursts out in weeping.

This time, however, he cannot restrain himself:

> Joseph could no longer control himself before all his attendants, and he cried out, "Have everyone withdraw from me!" So there was no one else about when Joseph made himself known to his brothers. His sobs were so loud that the Egyptians could hear, and so the news reached Pharaoh's palace. Joseph said to his brothers, "I am Joseph. Is my father still alive?" (45:1–3)

As on previous occasions of weeping, Joseph has time, before his tears overwhelm him, to make preparations. But this time, he "could no longer control himself," he cannot hold himself to his scheme. The implication is that his plot collapses prematurely. If he could, he would have turned the screw yet again. In empirical terms, his experiment is incomplete.

Before he breaks down, instead of withdrawing, this time he sends away all onlookers. And the passion of his tears is almost orgiastic. A whole verse is given to the description of his weeping, as it echoes through the palace. There is an intensified sense of the mystery and anarchy of tears. One can only imagine the terror and strangeness of those moments, for the courtiers beyond the doors, certainly for the foreigners left alone in his presence. Only after that long hiatus of sheer release does Joseph speaks to his brothers.

His weeping is an eruption of the pain of his loss, intensified to a point that compels him to give up the masquerade. It is prompted by Judah's repeated evocation of his *einenu*, and of its effect on his family. In a convoluted narrative — as in a hall of mirrors — Judah speaks of his father, who quotes himself: " 'And I said, Alas, he was torn by a beast!' " (44:28). He remembers the rememberings of his father, and he imagines his future response, if "he sees that the boy is not with us" (44:31). That is, Judah experiences his father's experience of *ayin*; and he cannot bear it. ("Let me not see . . . when he sees that the boy is *ayin*.") At this point, Joseph, overwhelmed by the reality of his own absence, weeps for the third time and reveals himself.

By "making himself strange," by using an interpreter, by "disappearing" for his brothers, Joseph has gained access to his lost self. His brothers, equally, have recovered a vital sense of pain at their loss. But when he reveals himself, saying simply — inarticulately — "I am Joseph. Is my father still alive?" they are dumbfounded: "They could not answer him, so dumbfounded were they on account of him" (45:3). Their single most powerful emotion is of shame, says Rashi. But then, they never could speak to him, respond to his greeting ("They could not speak a friendly word to him" [37:4]).

## The therapeutic narrative

If Joseph cannot find the right words at this point, then all is lost; the story has returned full circle to alienation, bafflement, conflict. But Joseph has found himself, a process of confirmation[49] has come to a head. And he succeeds in finding the nexus between their different realities: going beyond "I am Joseph," he talks of his connection to them — "I am *your brother* Joseph" (45:4) — and narrates their joint story:

> Then Joseph said to his brothers, "Come forward to me." And when they came forward, he said, "I am your brother Joseph, he whom you sold into Egypt. Now, do not be distressed or reproach yourselves because you sold me hither; it was to save life that God sent me ahead of you. . . . God has sent me ahead of you to ensure your survival on earth, and to save your lives in an extraordinary deliverance. So, it was not you who sent me here, but God; and He has made me a father to Pharaoh, lord of all his household, and ruler over the whole land of Egypt." (45:4, 5, 7, 8)

Joseph finds himself in relation to his brothers: his story is balanced on the axis of "I . . . you . . ." and "You . . . me. . . ." It is an honest, but discriminating account of what they did and did not do to him, of the limits of their responsibility for his disappearance: "You sold me hither" (45:5); but "it was not you who sent me here" (45:8). The nexus between their realities is God, who has choreographed their relationships, their absences and losses, in order to "save life." He is the One who "sent" Joseph to Egypt. The word is used three times, to express God's purposeful perception. From the human perspective, Joseph was *einenu*, he had ceased to be in the line of sight. From God's perspective, he had been just where he was meant to be, swallowed up, giving and saving life.

This is Joseph's therapeutic narrative, full of expressions of relationship, unblinking of the basic facts of the distance between "you" and "me," but allowing God to take up the slack of that distance. Out of the brokenness has come a rethinking of the past, a redeeming of the past, a hope for wholeness in the house of Jacob.

Joseph's tears, like Rachel's, confirm the value of the *einenu*. "Is not value this lack, this hole, which I hollow out before me and which I fill by acts . . . ?"[50] Such tears, as a response to the *bor*, are perhaps those of which the Psalmist sings: "Though he goes along weeping, carrying the seed bag, he shall come back with songs of joy, carrying his sheaves" (Psalms 126:6). André Neher writes of these tears:

> What is to weep? To weep is to sow. What is to laugh? To laugh is to reap. Look at this man weeping as he goes. Why is he weeping? Because he is bearing in his arms the burden of the grain he is about to sow. And now, see him coming back in joy. Why is he laughing? Because he bears in his arms the sheaves of the harvest. Laughter is the tangible harvest, plenitude. Tears are sowing; they are effort, risk, the seed exposed to drought and to rot, the ear of corn threatened by hail and by storms. Laughter is words, tears are silence. . . . It is not the harvest that is important; what is important is the sowing, the risk, the tears. Hope is not in laughter and plenitude. Hope is in tears, in the risk and in its silence.[51]

## The pit: hollowness and birth

This sense of hope in tears informs the midrashic narrative at important points. There are biblical characters who are singularly sensitive to the *ayin*, to the hollowness of the pit. Sarah, for instance, who is the subject of Isaiah's prophetic vision: "Listen to me, you who pursue justice, you who seek the Lord: Look to the rock you were hewn from, to the quarry [*makevet*] you were dug from. Look back to Abraham your father and to Sarah who brought you forth" (Isaiah 51:1–2).

In Rashi's reading, the *makevet* is not a quarry, not a hole, but the hammer that hollowed out the hole. This is Sarah: not a biological cavity, generating a people, but a woman whose painful vision "decompressed" the plenitude of things,[52] who gave birth to a nation by "inventing" and confronting emptiness and vertigo. ("Sarah, *who brought you forth*" — *teholelkhem* — refers both to birth and to the hollowness from which the birth emerges.) All creation emerges from such emptiness. Sarah dies of it, endowing her children with the will to fill hollowness.[53]

Adam was first, however. At the beginning of the second account of the Creation process, the narrative tells of the world before man: "When the Lord God made earth and heaven — when no shrub of the field was yet on earth and no grasses of the field had yet sprouted, because the Lord God had not sent rain upon the earth and there was no man to till the soil" (2:5). Rashi comments:

> There was no vegetation on the earth when creation was completed on the sixth day, before man was created. Even though God had commanded, "Let the earth sprout vegetation," on the third day, it had not emerged, but remained just at the rim of the soil, until the sixth day. Why? Because God had not sent rain. Why not? Because "there was no man" [*adam ayin*] to till the soil, and so there was no one to realize the goodness of the rains. But when man arrived and realized that they are a necessity for the world, he prayed for them, and they fell, and the trees and vegetation grew.

Vegetation cannot grow, life cannot flourish, unless there is a human being who can recognize their absence, his need. Such a man can pray, can express his sense of *ayin*, his hope and desire. One might mistranslate *adam ayin* as "Man is *ayin*"; man is the source of that consciousness of *ayin* that leads to all value.

In considering the relations of *shever* and *sever*, brokenness and hope, as a theme with many manifestations in midrashic thought, we return to Joseph as the Master-*Mashbir*, the one who in the very flesh — in no merely metaphoric sense — descended into a pit. The midrash recognizes the seminal importance of that experience. At the end of the narrative, when Joseph returns to Canaan to bury his father, he passes the pit, where the story began: "He went and looked into that pit."[54] "His brothers saw that Joseph went to make a blessing over that pit where they had thrown him. He made a blessing over it, as one should do over any place where a miracle happened to one: 'Blessed be God who did a miracle for me in this place.' "[55]

Joseph stares into the pit and blesses God (literally called *ha-makom*—"the Place"), who miraculously transformed this nonplace into a source of life. "How many wonders has God done for me, in saving me from this pit!"[56] The midrash seems to suggest that the pit and Joseph's salvation from it is not an isolated incident but the matter of his whole life. "I am rebegot / Of Absence, Darknesse, Death, things which are not."[57] He first came to know himself in this pit; his rebegetting has been a history of many wonders, as he appropriated and interpreted its emptiness.

# VA-YIGGASH ✿
## The Pit and the Rope

The *stolen goblet: four sentences*

Perhaps the most dramatic break between Parshiot of the Torah is the one that precedes Judah's great speech to Joseph, pleading for Benjamin's liberty. The tension that fuses the scene is strangely broken before the words *va-yiggash eilav yehudah* — "Then Judah went up to him and said, 'Please, my lord . . .'" (44:18). For the narrative is clearly one seamless unit — the discovery of Joseph's goblet "planted" in Benjamin's sack, the brothers returned to the palace in astonished silence, Joseph's reproach, and Judah's response, which directly precipitates Joseph's revelation of his true identity. And yet in uncanny counterpoint to that seamlessness, that thrust of dramatic intention toward the dénouement of the plot, a different structure imposes itself, with an ending and a new beginning, in the very midst of the dialogue between Joseph and Judah.

A closer look at this structure will lead us to focus on an apparently simple question: what, according to the different voices in the drama, is to happen to the brothers, if the goblet is indeed found with them?[1] The terms of punishment change several times, and in suggestive ways, in the course of a few lines.

At first, when the brothers are accused by Joseph's servant, they answer in innocent outrage: "Whichever of your servants it is found with shall die; the rest of us, moreover, shall become slaves to my lord" (44:9). They have no knowledge of any such theft, and can speak with utter innocence of the goblet's being found in anyone's possession, and of the death penalty for the guilty one. Implicitly, however, they distance themselves as a group from such a hypothetical — though at this point inconceivable — offense: if there were to be such a finding, then they assert their difference from the criminal — they will be slaves, while he will die.

The servant replies, "Although what you are proposing is right, only the one with whom it is found shall be my slave; but the rest of you shall go free" (44:10). He changes the terms of their punishment, while strangely asserting that he agrees with their offer. Essentially, he is addressing their sense of distance, of noninvolvement with the crime: he agrees that only the guilty shall be punished, though he reduces the severity of the punishment from the death penalty to slavery, and dismisses their rhetorical offer to remain as slaves, despite their innocence.

When the goblet is discovered in Benjamin's sack, all the brothers tear their clothes, in sign of mourning, and return in silence to the palace. There, Judah responds to Joseph's reproach with its mysterious emphasis on a kind of clairvoyance: "Do you not know that a man like me practices divination?" (44:15). "What can we say to my lord? How can we plead, how can we prove our innocence? God has uncovered the crime of your servants. Here we are, then, slaves of my lord, the rest of us as much as he in whose possession the goblet was found" (44:16).

Judah's speechlessness is poignant but enigmatic: his primary response is a gesture of confession, of guilt, that allows of no defense. "What can we say?" seems, on the face of it, a defeated response. He cannot justify himself, God has indeed "found" the sin of all of them: the "finding" of the goblet is an objective correlative for another kind of coming to roost, another kind of horrifying reality suddenly impressed on the vagueness, the malleability of memory. In very concrete imagery, Rashi quotes the midrash to convey this sense of the sudden pressure of reality: "The creditor has found an occasion to exact payment for his bill of debt."

The debt, the paper on which it is recorded—these can remain abstractions, legal fictions, until the moment when the debtor exacts payment: in place of paper and ink, he demands hard coin, the very image for a reality that cannot be gainsaid. So what is there to say in the face of such a demand for payment? Words fail Judah: he speaks of it three times, before launching into his great speech. Ironically, the inarticulate shudder of an inescapable guilt generates the speech that will transform the whole context of that guilt.

First, however, there is another transaction between Judah and Joseph about the exact terms of payment. In his inchoate despair, Judah offers himself and all his brothers as slaves to Joseph. This seems inexplicable: he *extends* the punishment that the servant had declared, including all the brothers in Benjamin's fate, without, at this stage, any benefit to Benjamin. Joseph replies in righteous horror, "Far be it from me to act thus! Only he in whose possession the goblet was found shall be my slave; the rest of you go back in peace to your father" (44:17).

Joseph repeats, in effect, his servant's just sentence; he accepts that the brothers are not accomplices in the crime and that only the guilty should be punished; the innocent brothers should return "in peace" to their father. The force of Joseph's reply ("Far be it from me!") expresses his image of himself as a rational, just ruler: in a civilized society, this is obviously the right sentence. It reflects the thrust of Abraham's argument with God over Sodom, for example: "Will you sweep away the innocent along with the guilty?. . . . *Far be it from You!* Shall not the Judge of all the earth deal justly?" (18:23, 25). The very nub of justice, human or divine, is this distinction between innocent and guilty.

Yet Joseph's rightness throws into relief Judah's strange offer of slavery for all, with its implication of shared guilt. In a paroxysm of recognition, Judah mutely acknowledges that other guilt, the bloodshed, the flaying, displaced onto a goat.[2] He is in no debating mood: all distinctions are blurred between the technical, apparent guilt of Benjamin and the profound residue of a crime committed by the brothers a generation before.

But when Joseph has declared his just sentence, the narrative of the Parsha comes to an end. It is as though a certain course of logic has been brought to its legitimate conclusion. Judah has refused the opportunity to plead for a lighter sentence for Benjamin: in the despair of guilt, he has simply thrown in his lot with Benjamin. This apparent madness is rebuked by Joseph's sanity, his rational discrimination. A balance is struck, and the Parsha ends with characters and reader contemplating that balance. Even the expression "Go back *in peace*" lends a sense of closure to Joseph's sentence.

"Then Judah went up to him." The effect is of an almost gratuitous movement on the part of Judah, of an equally gratuitous burst of eloquence from the man who has just proclaimed his wordlessness.[3] Judah launches into one of the longest speeches in the Torah. What he asks for, in essence, is that he be accepted in place of Benjamin; he alone will stay as a slave, while all his brothers go free. He entirely ignores the fact that he has just offered the whole family as slaves, in spite of their proclaimed innocence. Responding to Joseph's essential distinction between guilty and innocent, he moves from a position in which the innocent will be punished along with the guilty to one in which only the innocent will be punished, while the guilty one goes free.

On the face of it, this is an unconscionable position: Judah makes no attempt to plead Benjamin's innocence, nor does he adduce new data to change Joseph's judgment of the situation. He simply retells the story of the brothers' relations with the enigmatic Egyptian viceroy, retells it with great pathos, particularly in dealing with their unseen father, whose pain in losing one son of Rachel will now be compounded by losing the other. It is purely on this basis—of the pathos of the bereaved father—that Judah pleads for an exchange of victims: he will stand in for the precious Benjamin. The aim of his speech, therefore, is to influence the viceroy—who has shown himself to be arbitrary and unpredictable in his mood swings—by means of rhetoric, by emotional word-painting, to change a just verdict into one inspired by compassion for a Jacob who becomes a purely literary figure—the creature of Judah's words, the almost classical type of bereaved fatherhood.

Many commentators have noted that Judah effectively brings no new data in his long speech. What justifies this long recounting of the narrative is what Ramban calls the plea for grace, the attempt to arouse compassion by words describing suffering: the brothers, their father, Judah himself—all are victims of fate, circumstance, the imperatives of survival. The need for food, Joseph's stern questionings, Judah's pledge to his father to bring Benjamin back alive—all have conspired to place the family in an impossible situation. What Judah asks is that Joseph tinker with the scales of justice, so that the intimate equilibrium of the family may not be totally disrupted.

The purely emotional nature of Judah's speech, with its—in judicial terms—outrageous plea, leads directly to Joseph's unmasking. This speech presents the last of four different sentences for the theft of the goblet: the death penalty for the guilty, combined with slavery for the innocent brothers; the rational sentence of slavery for the guilty one, with freedom for the innocent; slavery for all the brothers; and an exchange of guilty and innocent victims. The point of these transactions seems rather elusive.

We can notice, however, that Benjamin is at the crux of the problem. Before the brothers know that he is the butt of the investigation, they affirm the judicial distance between the fate of the guilty one and the innocence of the rest. Once Benjamin has been incriminated, however, Judah, representing his brothers, refuses to accept any distinction between Benjamin's fate and theirs—even if this means, absurdly, that they will all stay together as slaves. Joseph and his servant propose a rational sentence, based on the essential distinction between guilty and innocent. But Judah—after the silent contemplation of the journey back to the palace—pleads for a blurring of this distinction: Benjamin must return *with* his brothers, the guilty with the innocent, while Judah, representative of the innocent, remains in Benjamin's place.

The involvement of Benjamin with his brothers is thus the main force at work in these transactions. And the break in the narrative before Judah's great speech draws attention to the outrageous, the irrational nature of Judah's plea. It is as though Joseph's judiciousness has given him courage for the leap into a quite different field of discourse.

## Judah's speech: plea or menace?

*Va-yiggash eilav yehuda*—"Then Judah went up to him": traditional commentaries, midrashic narratives, and hasidic meditations have all paid extraordinary attention to the drama of this confrontation between Judah and Joseph. Particularly in midrashic readings, Judah's "coming close" to Joseph resonates with a challenge, a tension that continues throughout history, until messianic times. The two brothers become quasi-allegorical figures, representing opposing principles. Without entering into the substance of this kind of reading, it will be illuminating to explore the enlarged dimensions of this confrontation, as the midrash reads it.

In a classic analysis, for example, the word *va-yiggash* is refracted into three possible modalities of intimacy (lit., he drew close): war, appeasement, and prayer.[4] Appeasement and prayer seem quite compatible with the context of a Judah trying to stir compassion in the breast of the inscrutable viceroy, or with a reading that has Judah ever-conscious of God as the ultimate arbiter of the family's fate.

The motif of belligerence, however, seems difficult to assimilate to a conventional reading of the text. And yet, in a whole range of midrashim, Judah's speech is not simply a plea for mercy: it becomes an angry, reproachful, even menacing attack on Joseph. The very thought of separating Benjamin from his brothers—Joseph's judicious sentence,

with its prospect of *shalom*, "peace," for the other brothers — sends Judah
into a paroxysm of rage:

> When Judah's anger swelled, two hairs would go out of his heart and
> tear through his garments. And when he wanted his anger to swell, he
> would fill his belt with brass pellets, take some of them and grind them
> between his teeth — and his anger would swell. When Joseph saw
> Judah's power (for of him it is said: "The king's wrath is a messenger of
> death, but a wise man can appease it" [Proverbs 16:14] — the "king's
> wrath" refers to Judah, while the "wise man" refers to Joseph, as it said,
> "There is none so discerning and wise as you" [Genesis 41:39]) — when
> Joseph saw Judah's anger swelling, he said, "Now Egypt will perish."
> This is like two athletes who were held in a tense struggle — when one
> was about to be defeated, he said, "Now he will defeat me, and I shall be
> shamed in front of everyone." What did he do? He kissed his rival's
> hand, and the stronger athlete's anger abated. So when Joseph felt
> Judah's anger, he was afraid lest he be shamed in front of the Egyptians:
> immediately, he said to his brothers, "I am Joseph your brother," and
> they could not answer him.[5]

This unexpected reading of the confrontation between Judah and
Joseph is paralleled by many others. In all, the encounter is marked by
anger, royal power, and menace on the side of Judah, and by a strategic
retreat on the part of Joseph. In some of these readings, the animal
typology of Judah as a lion, and Joseph as an ox (from Jacob's deathbed
blessings) is deployed.[6] In others, the opposition between Judah's power
and Joseph's wisdom is elaborated. But the basic notion of a belligerent
encounter, with Judah as the aggressor, does seem highly unexpected. A
realistic dramatic sense of the situation would seem to cast Judah in the
role of eloquent pleader, playing on the chords of empathy and sentiment, flattering Joseph's omnipotence and moral conscience, beseeching
him to move beyond justice, even beyond the generous justice of exon-
erating the innocent brothers of any share in the crime.

This mode of eloquence, which the midrash calls *lashon rakah*, "the
soft tongue," does not, however, according to a wide range of midrashic
sources, and according to Rashi's reading, characterize Judah's tone.
Instead, these sources attribute to him *lashon kashah*,[7] "the harsh tongue."
Like Joseph himself (42:7), he speaks harshly, challenging the ruler with
all his personal power, attacking him for his past dealings with the
brothers — even threatening to assassinate him and his royal master, or, in

other sources, to run amok in the city, massacring the population. For example, here is Rashi's commentary on one phrase of Judah's speech:

"for you are the equal of Pharaoh": "You are as important in my eyes as the king." This is the plain meaning. The midrashic reading: "You will in the end be afflicted with leprosy, as Pharaoh was, when he kept Sarah, my great-grandmother, for one night in his palace." Or— another reading—"Just as Pharaoh decrees and does not fulfill his decree, promises and does not perform, so do you. Is this what you meant when you promised to keep your eye on Benjamin?" Or— another reading—"You are just like Pharaoh—if you provoke me, I shall kill both you and your master."

In this passage, Rashi understands the obviously conciliatory tone of Judah's rhetoric as the plain meaning of the text, with the menacing, reproachful notes detected by the midrash as undertones. Ramban elaborates on this idea, which possibly originates in the midrashic comment that Judah spoke "both softly and harshly":[8] he emphasizes the covert nature of Judah's attack on the ruler, and particularly on the "plot" that Joseph had woven to entangle them from the beginning (the gratuitous questions about their family background, the charge of spying, the demand to bring Benjamin as evidence of the truth of their story). In Ramban's view, there is anger hidden in Judah's words, though he dare not express it unambiguously.

In the midrashic sources, however, the anger is isolated and becomes dominant. In the extraordinary surrealistic imagery of the *Tanḥuma* passage, hairs protrude erect from his chest and pierce his clothes. Or— with a telling precision—when he *wants* to swell with anger, he chews on brass pellets to feed his rage. This is a Judah who intentionally becomes the very personification of an anger that is identified in the midrash with kingly power. There is an appropriateness to this anger; through his capacity to feel and to express feeling, Judah defeats Joseph in the contest that, with a kind of formality—it is a game, a sport—is being fought by the two of them.

Joseph concedes defeat to Judah. In the midrash, he reveals himself to his brothers, not because he is overcome by emotion, but because he has to put an end to the contest before he is embarrassingly trounced by Judah's power. By revealing himself, he limits the damage Judah is able to do to him—his brothers are "unable to answer him": he has achieved a paradoxical equipoise of power in surrender.

This reading of the confrontation sits uncomfortably on the text, on conventional understandings of the narrative. What is the quality of Judah's anger? A moment before, he proclaimed his guilt and speechlessness, overwhelmed by memories of the past. He was ready to accept slavery for all eleven brothers. And now—arguing for an obfuscation of justice, the innocent replacing the guilty—he suddenly seethes with deliberate, self-generated anger, which breaks up Joseph's game, and proves Judah's rights to royal status in the family?

This change of mood, corresponding to the break in the narrative, is precipitated, I suggest, by Joseph's use of the word *shalom*: "the rest of you go back *in peace* to your father" (44:17). *Shalom*, peace, wholeness—the notion strikes Judah's ear as exquisitely wrong in this context.

For Jacob's family had been raised to the ideal of *shalom*, of wholeness. The objective correlative of that ideal was the birth of twelve children; the number twelve (as, for instance, in the twelve signs of the zodiac) is commonly treated in midrashic sources as suggesting cosmic completeness. The loss of Joseph was a fatal fracture of that symbolic wholeness.[9] Ironically, he was lost on a mission to "see the *shalom*, the peace of your brothers and of the sheep" (37:14). Jacob sent him to investigate the apparent idyll of household integrity; while engaged on this research project ("See . . . and bring me back word"), he disappeared. Jacob's wholeness is shattered; thereafter, Simeon disappears (he "is not" [42:36]); and now Joseph wants to remove Benjamin too.

From the reader's perspective, there is an outrageous quality to Joseph's bland direction to his brothers to "go back in peace"; all three disturbances of the family's wholeness can, in a sense, be laid to his door. He is personally responsible for the progressive fragmentation of the family, because of his tendency to "see . . . and bring back word." As the household detective, he "brought evil report to their father" (37:2). Rashi comments: "Every evil that he would see in his brothers he would tell his father." From the beginning, there was a kind of seeing in Joseph that broke the peace, that probed beyond the surfaces, and that led to the disintegration of the family.

Clearly, the irony of Joseph's use of the word *shalom* is more manifest to the reader than to the participants in the drama. Even from the brothers' viewpoint, however, there is a tension in the scene where Joseph greets his brothers, when they bring Benjamin down to Egypt: he insistently inquires after their *shalom*—and especially after their father's *shalom*: "He greeted them [*le-shalom*], and he said, 'How [*ha-shalom*] is your aged father of whom you spoke? Is he still in good health [lit., still alive]?' They replied, 'It is well [*shalom*] with your servant our father; he is still in good health.' And they bowed and made obeisance" (43:27–28).

This dialogue, its formal courtesy indicated by the obeisance, covers dangerous depths. Both Joseph and his brothers know of the pressures that assail Jacob's *shalom*. Joseph focuses the question onto the minimal matter of survival: "Is he still alive?" And the brothers answer, confirming that he is still alive, but skimming over the incommunicable problems evoked by the mention of *shalom*, in connection with their father.

This encounter, however, takes place at a moment when the brothers are hopeful of restoring both Simeon and Benjamin to Jacob. But when Joseph speaks of their returning *le-shalom* — at the very moment when he condemns Benjamin to slavery — something snaps in Judah. "They said to Joseph: 'What *shalom* can there be, when it is all darkened [or poured away]?' "[10] Judah savagely picks up on Joseph's word *shalom*; the whole of his speech can be read as a demand to restore the disintegrated wholeness of Jacob's house.

## Joseph and Judah: the pit and the rope

Such a belligerent reading of Judah's speech still remains difficult. The dynamic of his speech becomes enigmatic: what is the nature of this transaction that leads to Joseph's revealing his identity? If it is not pathos only that informs Judah's words, what is the force, the "kingly" power he brings to bear on Joseph that pressures him to a tactical retreat?

> *"Then Judah went up to him"*: "The designs in a man's mind are deep waters, but a man of understanding can draw them out" [Proverbs 20:5]. "The designs in a man's mind are deep waters" refers to Joseph. But as much as Joseph was wise, Judah came and defeated him, as it is said, "Then Judah went up to him." What does this resemble? A deep pit into which no one could climb down. Then a clever person came and brought a long rope that reached down to the water so he could draw from it. So was Joseph deep, and Judah came to draw from him.[11]

According to this midrash, the relation between Joseph and Judah is based on the notion that Joseph represents an absolute, inaccessible quality that only Judah knows how to reach and to negotiate. Only he can draw up the deep water with his rope: this is his "conquest" of Joseph. Joseph, in his wisdom, has an inscrutable quality; Judah has the pragmatic ability to make that wisdom work in the world. In William James's terms, Judah knows how to test the "cash value" of Joseph's hiddenness and power. James writes: "The truth of an idea is not a stagnant property inherent in it. Truth *happens* to an idea. It *becomes* true, is *made* true by events. Its verity *is* in fact an event, a process: the process namely of its verifying itself, its veri-*fication*. Its validity is the process of its valid-*ation*."[12] Judah, I suggest, encounters Joseph in a similar mode of process against essence: he is the rope that draws the deep (stagnant?) water into the sunlit, changing world.

This is signified by the word *va-yiggash*.[13] Judah comes close to Joseph's pulse of secret life and forces it into expression. In doing so, Judah claims a certain power of kingship — a pragmatic power to communicate, to influence, to shape the public articulations of private desire and perception. Joseph, on the other hand, expresses a pure principle of kingship: holding his own counsel, owing explanation to no one, responsible to no one, secret, provident.

In this view, Judah's anger is part of the armory of the leader who knows how to make things happen in the world. Judah knows about change, about sin and repentance, about contingency and a pain that alters perception. In another version of the *Tanḥuma* midrash, he knows how to "tie rope to rope, cord to cord, twine to twine,"[14] in order to reach down into Joseph's pit. He is a master of instrumentality, of expression. The image of the rope evokes distance and connection: Judah acknowledges the opaqueness, the differences among human beings, but he engineers techniques to draw what is most private into the public area — "until he penetrated to his heart."

At first, he is silent; he in fact proclaims his necessary silence ("What can we say?"). But then he takes hold of the rope and he speaks, at great length and to radical effect. Indeed, in several midrashic sources, Joseph challenges him: Who has appointed him spokesman (*dabran*, or *patit*) of his brothers, since he is not the eldest? To speak is, implicitly, to lead, to tie rope to rope, and bring hidden things to the surface. What gives Judah the energy to undertake, even usurp this role? This is his answer:

> "In spite of the fact that there are brothers older than me, they stand outside the relationship, while I [lit.] feel my bowels cramping [twisting] like a rope." Joseph asked him, "How?" And Judah replied,

"Because I am surety for him." Joseph said, "If it is a question of silver or gold, I shall give you the amount." And Judah said, "It is not a matter of silver or gold. For this is what I told Father: 'I shall be banished in this world and in the world to come.'"[15]

Judah speaks, assumes the responsibility to achieve something beyond guilty silence, because he must. A visceral involvement with Benjamin, painful (the word *ḥevel* means both "rope" and "suffering," particularly, "labor pains"), undeniable, binds him to all eternity. When he proclaimed himself surety for Benjamin to his father, "I was tied in a strong knot to be banished in both worlds" (Rashi, 44:32).[16]

The recurrence of the rope image is fascinating. The twisting and folding of the fibers of the rope expresses the complicated, painful involvements by which a Judah gains his power of leadership, his capacity to probe depths and retrieve what was hidden for public use. His pragmatism, his empirical approach to reality, come to a head in the question of "surety," in his strange commitment to Jacob for Benjamin's safe return.

## "The one who must pay"

Jacob had refused to let Benjamin go to Egypt: an absolute refusal ("My son shall not go with you" [42:38]), which even Reuben's melodramatic offer—to kill his own two sons, if Benjamin failed to return—cannot affect. But Judah waits "till the bread is consumed from the house," as the midrash puts it. At the right moment, he speaks—at length and to good effect. He evokes the magical "seeing of the king's face," which means life: without Benjamin, there will be no further audiences with the food provider in Egypt.[17] For the sake of life, he appeals to Jacob: "I myself will be surety for him [*e'ervenu*]; you may hold me responsible:[18] if I do not bring him back to you and set him before you, I shall stand guilty before you forever" (43:9). Unlike Reuben, Judah himself offers to stand in for Benjamin, to bear the total responsibility for him. Benjamin will be "with" him personally; Judah will be legally liable to pay, personally, intimately, and eternally, if Benjamin should fail to return.

The legal imagery of "standing surety" (*arev*) traces the precise parameters of Judah's commitment to Jacob. In economic situations, the guarantor commits his own resources to cover the debt of others. To promise to return goods given to oneself is simply to commit oneself to pay back a loan. The concept of "surety," however, is much more far-reaching, even, one might say, fundamentally absurd. For the guarantor assumes responsibility that properly belongs to others, to the real debtor, and covers for situations where chance, pure contingency, may cause disaster.

This concept of "surety" finds its first narrative paradigm in Judah's offer to Jacob.[19] He does not merely take Benjamin and promise to return him: that would be equivalent to a debtor's promise to return a loan. Rather, he *personally* assumes total responsibility for a communal obligation. Jacob says, in plural form, "Take your brother" (43:13), while Judah emphasizes the first-person singular form in his commitment: "*I* shall stand surety . . . from *my* hand you may seek him."

Surety thus involves an obscuring of boundaries, particularly of the most basic boundary that separates individuals. It is based, in a sense, on a legal fiction. It proclaims a confusion (*arov* means "to mix") of identities that can come to roost in sheer economic terms: the debtor fails to pay, and the guarantor finds himself solely responsible, a grotesque economic surrogacy giving reality to the fiction. For the basic definition of the "guarantor" is that "he is the one who must pay."[20]

Judah, similarly, is the one who must pay, through whom the "cash value" of words is to be most rigorously validated. He stands personally responsible for Benjamin, though all the brothers take him down to Egypt. When the goblet is found in Benjamin's sack, the midrash relates: "Each of the other brothers turned his face aside. And who stood against Joseph? The guarantor—'Then Judah went up to him.'" Implied in the guarantor position is an ability to "stand against," to resist: to summon up resources of anger, irony, and menace in protection of that with which one is identified. For the "guarantor," the barriers of personhood are down: he becomes real, as the rope of pain and involvement twists in his bowels.

## Judah's growth to moral vision

A poignant suggestion about Judah's growth to his full stature is made in *Tanḥuma*, 9. Immediately after Jacob cries for the loss of his son Joseph, Judah "goes down" to Timna, marries, has three children, and is bereaved of two of them, in circumstances that seem to incriminate his daughter-in-law, Tamar. It is this theme of the death of children that the midrash takes up: "'And his father wept for him' [37:35]. God said to

Judah, 'You have had no children until now, and you do not know the pain of children. You have tortured your father, and misled him to say, "Joseph was torn by a beast!" As you live, you shall marry a woman and bury your children, and you shall know the pain of children.'"

The midrash continues to tell of Judah's personal responsibility for Joseph's sale, and of his resulting loss of status among his brothers ("Then Judah went down"). Only when he stands surety for Benjamin, and Joseph reveals himself, is he reinstated as leader of the family. Then, Jacob's suspicions of his role in Joseph's murder are allayed, and Jacob chooses him to represent the family, "sending him ahead" to blaze the trail to Egypt (46:28).

This midrash connects Judah's moral growth with his experience of the "pain of children." His experience of bereavement, the wrenching in the bowels at his own losses, teaches him empathy—belatedly—with Jacob, in his loss. The "pain of children" is, moreover, a hauntingly general expression, seeming to indicate something of the notion that children are hostages of fortune. A peculiar vulnerability is experienced only through parenthood; a pristine arrogance is punctured when one has children, to whom anything can happen. The full contingency of the human condition is known when one's children are touched by fate. Judah becomes human when his children are born; the midrash mentions his children's deaths as the extreme example of the fatality to which he is laid open.

With the carelessness of the childless, Judah has tormented his father. *Tiganta*—the word used to express torment—has basic meanings of an instrument of torture and execution, unimaginable physical agony. The midrash focuses on this anguish and on Judah's responsibility for it. His growth to responsibility and leadership is calibrated on a gauge of pain and empathy. Initiated into the fellowship of pain, Judah becomes capable of investing the whole force of his personhood into preventing its recurrence.

Judah stands surety for Benjamin: just as previously, in the context of his children's deaths, he had left with Tamar—twice-widowed of his two sons—a pledge (*eravon*), in lieu of payment for sleeping with her. The pledge that Judah had left was his seal, his cord, and staff: the emblems of his leadership. Symbolically, Tamar demands his *self* in pledge. She produces these emblematic expressions of his responsibility, just as, pregnant with his children, she is about to be burnt for profligacy: "I am with child by the man to whom these belong. . . . Please recognize these: whose seal and cord and staff are these?" (38:25).

When she says, "Recognize these," she appeals for a kind of vision, a way of seeing her and their connection that is tantamount to spiritual recognition: "Recognize your Creator, and do not hide your eyes from me," she says in the midrashic narrative.[21] For Judah had not been visually proficient, earlier in the story: "When Judah saw her, he took her for a harlot; for she had covered her face" (38:15).

The same midrash explains the logic of his blindness. It was not that the veil convinced him that she was a prostitute; rather, because she had constantly veiled herself in her father-in-law's house, he had never really seen her face, and was, therefore, easily duped. The fact that he did not recognize her, therefore, was rooted in their past relationship. He had never really seen her. On the one hand, this is praised as a proper modesty between father-in-law and daughter-in-law;[22] but on the other, it is held up as an example of dangerous and even immoral blindness.[23] The latter midrash implies that Judah should have insisted on seeing the face of Tamar. She, however, "*saw* that Shelah was grown up, yet she had not been given to him as wife" (38:14). Her sense of purpose had informed a strong, empirical vision of her reality; and had led her to unconventional but necessary action.

Now, Judah responds to her plea for moral vision: for a complex sense of connection and responsibility: "Judah recognized them, and said, 'She is more in the right than I'" (38:26). Judah's public confession is praised in the same midrash as "sanctifying God's Name in public." It is the *public* nature of his acknowledgment that distinguishes him from Joseph, who "sanctified God's Name in private" (in his sexual encounter with Potiphar's wife).

These are two different kinds of heroism. Joseph emphatically rejects his master's wife, so that—if she had not revealed the affair—nothing need ever have been known of it; for this he is rewarded with one letter of God's Name.[24] Judah, however, sins, both in withholding his youngest son from Tamar and in sleeping with her, and when the results of his act have become visible, a public fact, he justifies her behavior and publicly confesses; for this, the midrash notes, his name is read as including the whole of God's Name (*Yehuda* includes the four letters of the Tetragrammaton).

The difference between Judah and Joseph, which the Talmud, in Sotah, indicates here, relates to publicity, to acts consummated, confessed, and repented. Judah acts in full consistency with his nature, registering in his speech and behavior the changes in his inwardness. He is a person invested in the process of "becoming": the root meaning of God's Name, as God explains it to Moses: "I shall be what I shall be" (Exodus 3:14).

Vulnerable, dynamic, responsive with all his being, Judah becomes the paradigm of responsibility and leadership. When Tamar appeals to him, "Please recognize these," another appeal for recognition resonates in the words. Judah, now schooled in pain and loss, hears within her voice his own voice, saying to his father, "Please recognize it; is it your son's tunic or not?" (37:32). The midrash notices the irony of this spot in time, the double exposure effect of the same words, spoken in two different contexts: "With the word *haker* [recognize], he brought news to his father; with the word *haker*, he had news brought to him." His own callousness revives in his memory and generates a full acknowledgment, an act of vision that registers his own "becoming," the processes by which he learns to see better.

Robert Alter discusses the version of the midrash that appears in *Bereshit Rabbah* 84:19: "You said to your father, *Haker na*; as you live, Tamar will say to you, *Haker na.*" Alter objects to the direct moral rebuke that God administers to Judah in this version of the midrash. His objection is primarily to the suggestion that Judah is conscious of the connections between the two situations. The dramatic irony is palpable to the audience, but should not be to the protagonist:

> The preservation of Judah's ignorance here is important, for the final turn of his painful moral education must be withheld for the quandary in which he will find himself later when he encounters Joseph as viceroy of Egypt without realizing his brother's identity. The Midrash, on the other hand, concentrating on the present moment in the text and on underscoring a moral point, must make things more explicit than the biblical writer intended.[25]

To this, one might respond that the two different versions (*Bereshit Rabbah* and Sotah) present two options of interpretation: the passage in Sotah advises the reader of the irony of the echo, while the *Bereshit*

*Rabbah* passage suggests that God speaks directly to Judah, eroding his ignorance, even at this early stage of his moral career.

Even if one focuses on the latter reading, however, the midrash, it seems, is contributing to precisely what Alter claims is the innovative effect of the biblical narrative: the "indeterminacy of meaning . . . [which is] conceived as a *process*, requiring continual revision." When God draws Judah's attention to the echoing appeal for recognition, this echo is not "spelled out with a thematically unambiguous closure." In midrashic rhetoric, God's rebuke is an evolving idea in Judah's mind; he is free to ignore it, to ponder it, to act on it in multiple ways.

The echoing *haker na* urges him to ever-clearer vision of his reality, and of his own standing within that reality. But his "moral education," as Alter puts it, surely begins here, in this episode of recognition based on painful experience. His own deception of his father lies at the base of that whole education.

"As wisdom grows, vexation grows" (Ecclesiastes 1:18). R. Nahman comments: the greater the sensibility, the greater the pain.[26] There is no acquiring knowledge, or understanding, without a sense of the enlarged dimensions of the world. This sense R. Nahman calls *yirah* — fear; and from this kind of fear comes pain. From this point of view, Judah lives in an ever-enlarging world: his consciousness grows, and with it the pain that is his human response to the tug of the rope.

From Tamar, he learns the meaning of the word *arev* — pledge, guarantee: the total symbolic replacement of one for the other. This is always, in a sense, an outrageous notion. It requires an act of imagination, a way of seeing, to validate the legal fiction. Judah might have denied that poetic surrogate force of the pledges, as he earlier manipulated the surrogate force of Joseph's coat. *Haker na*, in its pleading form, acknowledges Judah's freedom to accept or reject the symbolic displacement of the objects Tamar holds out to him. She will not force his hand.

Similarly, when Judah comes to confront Joseph, he is free to acknowledge or ignore that bizarre confusion of separate identities that he has evoked in his commitment to his father: *anokhi e'ervenu*, "I shall stand surety for him." Justice is with Joseph, as he discriminates between guilty and innocent. As a first response, recognizing a primal guilt, the "innocent" brothers tear their clothes together with the "guilty" one. Then, Judah takes command: "Then Judah and his brothers came into Joseph's house . . ." (44:14).

## Judah redescribes himself: direct optics as ethics

The moment is fraught with significance: the brothers, always considered as a plural, communal entity, are suddenly represented by an individual, a personal voice. Joseph continues to address them as a group ("He said to *them*"); but Judah alone answers, bewailing the inadequacy of words, speaking of God who has brought the sediment of an old sin to the surface, and offering all the brothers as slaves. Judah puts into words, in a first formulation, his sense that Benjamin cannot be separated from his brothers. Joseph rejects this unjust sentence, and Judah launches into his speech.

Poignant, belligerent, or prayerful—or all simultaneously—Judah's speech makes one basic statement. Attaching "rope to rope," phrase to phrase, he recounts the narrative that is already known to us.[27] In speaking of the past, however, and in imagining the future, Judah is doing something new. *Sefat Emet* expresses the point in a play on the words: *va-yiggash eilav*—"Then Judah went up to *himself*, to his own essence."[28]

This is a speech of self-analysis, of redescription. In it, Judah discovers a new vocabulary to say something that had never been said before. What he says, quite simply, is this: "I have seen my father's anguish at the loss of Joseph—I have heard him describe an absence ["I have not seen him since"]. My eyes have learned to cross his line of sight, to see that absence too.[29] And if I should have to see another such absence, I should not be able to bear the sight."

Essentially, Judah has transformed the story into his own story. Ultimately, it is not his father's anguish, or the family's trouble, that he is describing: it is his own pain of involvement and empathy. Before Joseph's eyes, he constructs the anger and pathos of his own consciousness. The climax of his speech is his last sentence, which provokes Joseph's collapse: "For how can I go back to my father unless the boy is with me? Let me not see the woe that would overtake my father" (44:34). He has redescribed himself in a new vocabulary of intimate relationship: a vocabulary that suggests what it is like to *see* the other seeing, and not to be able to bear seeing what he sees.

Emmanuel Levinas writes: "The Torah is given in the Light of a face. The epiphany of another person is *ipso facto* my responsibility toward him: seeing the other is already an obligation toward him. *A direct optics— without the mediation of any idea—can only be accomplished as ethics.*"[30] The "direct optics" in Judah's speech leads him to understand the painful twisting of the rope wherever it exists: in the empathy between Jacob and Joseph — "His life is bound up with his"; between Judah and Jacob; ultimately, between Joseph and Judah.

Judah speaks the simple language of personal feeling, contingent, without recourse to theoretical or moral propositions. It is not because it is wrong, on a metaphysical level, to leave Benjamin in slavery, that Judah makes his plea: it is because from his private and idiosyncratic perspective, it is impossible for Judah to see his father seeing "that the boy is not" (44:30).

Judah redescribes the whole narrative, beginning with Joseph's strange questions, the plot in which he entangled his brothers.

All he wanted was to get out from under finite powers by making their finitude evident. He did not want to befriend power nor to be in a position to empower others, but simply to free himself from the descriptions of himself offered by the people he had met. He wanted not to be merely the person these other people thought they knew him to be, not to be frozen in the frame of a photograph shot from another person's perspective. He dreaded being, in Sartre's phrase, turned into a thing by the eye of the other. . . . His method of freeing himself from those people — of becoming autonomous — was to redescribe the people who had described him.[31]

This passage is taken from Richard Rorty's analysis of Proust as "ironist liberal," in which he argues that the ironist is the rebel against "final vocabularies," the received notions of propositional truths. Proust

had written a book, and thus created a self — the author of that book — which these people could not have predicted or even envisaged. He had become as much of an authority on the people whom he knew as his younger self had feared they might be an authority on him. This feat enabled him to relinquish the very idea of authority, and with it the idea that there is a privileged perspective from which he, or anyone else, is to be described.[32]

Judah, too, rejects privileged perspectives in his speech. Even the name of God — with which Judah is so totally identified, by his capacity for public confession[33] — does not figure in this act of self-creation. His one reference to God, as having "uncovered the crime of your servants"

(44:16), had used the Name *Elohim* and had led to silence and acquiescence in guilt and indiscriminate punishment.

Now, he is after different game: the unit of persuasion is "a vocabulary rather than a proposition"; his method is "redescription rather than inference."[34] Using his anger and his pathos, he invests old words with new meanings, so that by the end of a narrative in which no detail is new he has constructed a radical criticism of Joseph and all he stands for. "Nothing," writes Rorty, "can serve as a criticism of a person save another person . . . for persons . . . are, for us, incarnated vocabularies."[35]

In this sense, Judah's speech can be read as a personal litany,[36] a chain of words and images that have peculiar resonance for himself. In a project of self-creation, he lists the events, the experiences that have meshed together to created the unique world of his selfhood. His inspired articulation of contingency, of the particulars of his own life, represents a recognition of God, without reference to the authoritative perspective of a privileged vocabulary.

A classic midrash narrates that the angel of transcendental truth advised God against creating man. God threw it down to earth; it shattered, and must now grow out of the earth in splintered, contingent shards — "Truth springs up from the earth" (Psalms 85:12).[37] The personal litany of a human being is such a project of producing personal truth "from the earth." And Judah's greatness lies precisely in this capacity to redescribe himself, rooted in earth, aspiring to a personal vocabulary, in which the splintered letters of God's Name can be detected.[38]

## Judah inspires Joseph: the personal litany

The power of such a personal litany is paradoxical. Precisely because Judah presents himself in his contingency, in the intimate vocabulary that weaves his uniqueness, he moves Joseph to remove his mask. Speaking with all the force of his private experience, Judah evokes the lost wholeness of the family, and stirs Joseph to his own attempt at self-redescription.

Essentially, what Joseph does in response to Judah's speech is — not reveal himself — but create himself in words. First, he says, "I am Joseph. Is my father still alive?" His anxious question about his father is logically redundant — he had asked them the same question when they arrived in Egypt shortly before (43:27). Moreover, when his brothers "could not answer him, so dumbfounded were they on account of him" (45:3), he repeats and amplifies his self-description: "I am your brother Joseph, whom you sold into Egypt" (45:4) — but he does not repeat his question about his father, in the course of the long speech that follows. In fact, although he refers to his father several times in the course of his speech, he does not express any further anxiety about his survival.

This spontaneous question: "Is my father still alive?" should, however, be understood as Joseph's first, poignantly incoherent attempt to find a vocabulary in which to describe himself. Judah's confession of personal truth inspires him to a similar spontaneity; and he uncovers the two hidden preoccupations of his masquerade: his identity, and his concern that the masquerade, compounding with his original disappearance, has made his father's life impossible.

## The *narrative against shame*

Here, one of the central questions about Joseph's behavior arises. Ramban asks it, as do many other commentators: how could Joseph not communicate with his father, at least during the years of his success and power? Some powerful restraint bars him from relieving his beloved father of his anguish. The question is, of course, exacerbated by the protracted torment to which he subjects his whole family — his charge that his brothers are spies, the money hidden in their sacks, the "planted" goblet. These make an enigma of the whole narrative.

*Or Ha-ḥayyim* offers a simple, but totally convincing answer:[39] Joseph is paralyzed by the prospect of his brothers' shame, if he reveals himself to his father. This is a genetic sensitivity: his mother, Rachel, according to a classic midrash, had been so horrified at the idea that her sister, Leah, masquerading as Rachel, would be shamed on her wedding night, that she gave her the secret signs that Jacob had given her, to prevent just such a deception (Rashi, 29:25) To prevent his brothers' shame, Joseph has, like his mother, kept silent, while his heart yearned to express itself.[40]

When his brothers actually appear before him for the first time, passivity and silence are neither possible nor necessary. From this point on, Joseph engages in an active project of discovery, the aim of which is to produce evidence that will allow his brothers to endure his "resurrection" without shame.

We shall return to this project of Joseph; here, we can simply notice the irony that, in spite of Joseph's prophylactic strategy, the brothers are "dumbfounded" when he first reveals himself. It is shame, says Rashi (45:1, 4, 15), that silences them. One effect of this shame, as Joseph had feared, is violence and anger: in several midrashic sources, Joseph's life is in danger, at the moment he identifies himself, so tormented are his brothers by the disgrace of their situation.[41]

For while shame, in classical theological thought, is often considered as forerunner to a positive rearticulation of one's life,[42] it is also a volatile, potentially dangerous response. The lowering of the brothers' moral profile threatens to have self-fulfilling effects; it may drive them to despair, to silence — even to murder the source of their shame. It is for this reason that Joseph, seeing that his first attempt at self-description is generating just that response that he had most feared, engages in a much fuller, more elaborate attempt to create himself, to discover a vocabulary that his brothers will be able to appropriate for themselves in their future narratives of their history.

He begins, surprisingly, by squarely attacking their sore point: "I am your brother Joseph, whom you sold into Egypt" (45:4). His reference to the unmentionable fact of the sale is, however, made in a context of brotherhood. On one level, he is simply identifying himself in the only way that is totally convincing: this secret of the sale is the most potent proof of his identity. But he defuses some of the tension of this memory, by describing himself — in spite of everything — as "your brother."

He then tells them: "Now, do not be distressed or reproach yourselves because you sold me hither." He lets them know that he understands their ambivalent response to his reappearance: they are heartbroken at what they did to him, so many years before, and they are frustrated at their own humiliation. They are genuinely saddened by their cruelty of the past; at the same time, they are resentful at the way they have been hoist with their own petard. Unwilling to bow to the adolescent Joseph, they sold him into slavery; now they find themselves bowing to him, in entire subjugation.[43]

Joseph's strategy is essentially to reveal to his brothers a Joseph empathic with their inner conflicts. The main thrust of his speech serves to show them his loving interpretation of his own history: the sale was for the sake of life, his cruel experience was, in fact, a mission to save his family from starvation in the famine years. God's plot is the only level of the narrative that matters to him, he tells them. And ultimately, the purpose of his speech is to provide them with a narrative to tell their father, to defuse the shame of their situation. The core of his speech is: "Now, hurry back to my father and say to him: Thus says your son Joseph . . ." (45:9)—a message to his father that will proclaim Joseph's personal credo, his vocabulary of self-creation.

This is the central point: Joseph's speech of reassurance is full of references to God—unlike Judah's speech. It seems replete with theological propositions. But in fact Joseph is not making sententious, theoretical statements; he is talking about his personal perspective on his own life, and he is doing so in order to provide his brothers with the only stratagem that will help them to scotch their own shame. He gives them a story to tell their father, to ground the electric furies of their own humiliation. Formally, his message to his father includes only assurances of economic security in Egypt. Implicitly, however, Joseph's whole speech is intended to convey to Jacob—as well as to his sons—that Joseph has discovered a vocabulary in which to articulate his life.

There is no hatred in his heart: this is the implicit message of his speech, according to Rashi (45:12). His status and wealth are the direct result of their guilty act. This is not merely a fact; it forms the basis of Joseph's most personal life litany.

The point is made succinctly by *Sefat Emet*, who comments on Joseph's opening statement: "I am your brother Joseph, he whom [*asher*] you sold." For him, Joseph is neither simply identifying himself, nor pouring salt on their wound. Instead, he cites the midrash on a parallel statement, where God speaks to Moses of the Tablets of Stone, "which [*asher*] you broke" (Exodus 34:1): "Congratulations [*yishar koḥakha*] that you broke them!"[44] In the long view, the dynamic by which the second set of Tablets is created is to be more useful to the Jewish people—psychologically and spiritually—than the instant gift of the first Tablets. Cataclysms are often retrospectively seen as fortunate, the gains outweighing the losses. In the same way, *Sefat Emet* suggests,[45] Joseph views his life since he was sold: he comforts his brothers with words only he can utter, testifying to an inner conviction that his fall into the pit was a fortunate moment in their shared history.

Joseph succeeds in allaying the anguish of the moment: "only then were his brothers able to talk to him" (45:15). But the shame and fear never disappear entirely. At the very end of the narrative, after Jacob's death, they surface again, as Joseph's brothers appeal to him for their lives, in such terms as to reduce him, yet again, to tears (50:15–18). A residue of that shame poisons their relationship to the end.

## Joseph's project abandoned

In a sense, then, Joseph was premature in ending his masquerade: "Joseph could no longer control himself" (45:1). Self-control (*hit'apek*) is a concept that has been deployed before, to describe a previous paroxysm of Joseph's tears (43:31). It is an unusual word; Rashbam suggests that it describes a mode that had been Joseph's consistently until this point, when he "could no longer" maintain it. The word implies "strength":[46] Joseph had previously succeeded, despite his yearning and his tears, in holding himself in strength; now, he "cannot" keep himself firm in his resolve.

A graphic sense of his emotional conflict is given in Rashi's etymology of *nikhmeru*, the word that describes his yearning towards his brother Benjamin: "'*He was overcome*' [43:30]: *nikhmeru* means 'was heated.'. . . In the Bible [Lamentations 5:10]: 'Our skin as by an oven was heated'—it was heated and shrank into many wrinkles because of the pangs of hunger; such is the nature of every skin when it is heated, it wrinkles and shrivels." This vivid description of the shriveling effect of emotion is then balanced by the statement, *va-yitapak*—"but he made himself firm, strong in resolve."

There is an idea at work in Joseph, that he holds on to, through all the erosive effects of compassion. After Judah's speech, he "cannot" maintain his strength. Implicitly, his resolve collapses. A project tenaciously pursued since the brothers appeared in the Egyptian court is discarded. Joseph, the all-powerful ruler [*mekhalkel*—the provider, which can be read punningly to yield the sense of complete control of resources, *hakol yakhol*] finds himself suddenly, like his brothers, in the helpless condition of *lo yakhol*—incapacity.

From the beginning, the brothers are described in terms of such an incapacity: "they *could not* speak a friendly word to him" (37:4). Tangled in Joseph's plot, their characteristic response is one of helpless bewilderment (42:28). Forces incomprehensible to them lie in ambush to deceive and trap them (43:18). But it is in Judah's speech to Joseph that the motif of *lo yakhol*, of a kind of trapped impotence, fully emerges.

Judah recalls how the ruler had demanded that they bring Benjamin to Egypt, "that I may set eyes on him. We said to my lord, 'The boy *cannot* leave his father; if he were to leave him, his father would die' " (44:22). They had returned home, and Jacob had demanded that they return to Egypt for more food: "We answered, 'We *cannot* go down; only if our youngest brother is with us can we go down, for we may not show our faces to the man unless our youngest brother is with us' " (44:26).

Judah conveys a powerful sense of their "double-bind" situation: without Benjamin, they cannot buy food, but to take him is equally impossible — their father will inevitably die. Hemmed in by legal and psychological impossibilities, the brothers know the full pressure of their existential situation. They had been "unable to speak in peace to Joseph" — compelled by purely inward forces. Like the Egyptians who "could not" eat together with the Hebrews ("for it was an abomination to the Egyptians" [43:32]), the brothers are subject to the human condition, in which cultural or psychological barriers limit possibility.[47] When Joseph reveals himself, their hypothetical freedom of response is similarly cramped by the paralysis of shame: they "could not answer him, so dumbfounded were they" (45:3).

In a startling moment of collapse, Joseph rejoins the human race. He surrenders his project, shriveled, reduced to human size. A sinister grandiosity had informed that project; now, compassion, the benign infection of Judah's words, compels him to relinquish his secret idea.

## Joseph's experiment: the demand for "ocular proof"

The nature of that idea he had indicated when, in their first interview, he had told his brothers: "By this you shall be put to the test. . . . that your words may be put to the test . . . you must bring me your youngest brother, that your words may be verified and that you may not die" (42:15, 16, 20).

Joseph's vocabulary had been based on the notion of *proof*: by bringing Benjamin back with them, they will bring evidence of the truth of their story. Clearly — and puzzlingly — Benjamin is being used as evidence of their authenticity. Rashi's comment is: "Your words will be verified and established [set firmly in reality]" (42:20). The issue thus seems to be Joseph's suspicion of language: words can lie, any description of reality can be uttered, without any necessary basis in fact.

This skepticism of Joseph about the existence of "final vocabularies" (Rorty's expression) leads him to demand indubitable "ocular proof." He uses the language of empirical research to make his demand for clear knowledge, in the form of the visible person of Benjamin. What he wants to know is not simply that there is a younger brother at home: his whole experiment aims to elicit visual information about who his brothers are now — *ha-emet itkhem* — "Is there truth in you? Have you found a solidity of being, a loyalty that will not allow you to repeat the crime of the past?"

The experiment is not for his information only. It is, as we have suggested, a strategy for dealing with the problem of shame, potentially so dangerous to the survival of the family. It is for his father's sake that he wants to know, to make empirically obvious, of what stuff his brothers are now made. It is, most of all, for their information, that he probes and presses them.

This is the experiment that collapses, that shrivels in the face of Judah's personal, passionate litany. At this point, however, the purpose of Joseph's experiment is not our main interest. It is the very notion of an experimental approach in human affairs that we shall explore: Joseph's mode of resolving the anguish and silence of his life.

"A wise man has eyes in his head" (Ecclesiastes 2:14): Joseph is the prototype of the *hakham*, of the wise man. He is first described as the "child of Jacob's old age" (37:3); the Targum translates the Hebrew expression (*ben zikunim*) as *bar hakima*, the wise son, precocious, intellectually developed. The wise person makes use of his eyes: he understands the implications of events. He is vigilant, aware of consequences, provident, canny. He can read what is unintelligible to others. For these qualities, Pharaoh chooses Joseph as viceroy, "for there is none so discerning and wise as you" (41:39).

But there is a sinister side to this optical awareness. What angered the brothers in their youth was precisely this sage understanding of the underside of their lives. He "brought bad reports of them to their father" (37:2); Rashi comments: "Any evil that he saw in them he would report." Joseph does not slander his brothers;[48] he reports what he sees, but what he sees is evil, weakness. His is a critical sensibility; his eye does not merely collate information, but is active in structuring a sinister vision.

The type of the intellectual — abstracting, analyzing, testing — Joseph is described by Thomas Mann as "always knowing far too well what was being played."[49] The reality-appearance problem — the fundamental problem in Western philosophy—continually concerns him. He willingly engages in play acting, but only in order to elicit the truth from the other actors, who are less enlightened than he. He seeks clear, indubitable knowledge, an unblurred version of the "blooming, buzzing chaos," that he is precipitated into, when his brothers throw him into the pit. The confusion, the bewilderment, the helplessness of the pit is with him always; but it translates into a desire to achieve the highest possible definition in his perception of reality.

A congenital tendency is confirmed by experience. The visual awareness that is so strong in him is the linchpin in Jacob's final assessment of him: "Joseph is a fruitful bough, a fruitful bough *alei ayin*" (49:22). These last words—as indeed many words of Jacob's blessing—have been translated in very different ways. *Ayin*, however, does most commonly mean "eye"; and Rashi's first translation emphasizes the visual grace of Joseph—the beauty that strikes the eye of others (including the Egyptian girls who are referred to in the second part of the verse). Rashi's final reading closes in on a midrash that explains the verse in context of the whole narrative:

> When Esau came to greet Jacob, the mothers went first, in front of their children, to bow down to him. But regarding Rachel it is written: "Joseph came near and Rachel and they bowed down" [33:7]. Joseph said, "This wicked man has haughty eyes—perhaps he will cast his eyes on my mother?" So he went out in front of her and enlarged his stature so as to cover her. That is why his father blessed him, saying *ben porat*—"You have made yourself large, Joseph, over the eyes of Esau. Therefore, you have earned greatness."

In this passage, Joseph is praised by his father for recognizing the arrogant power of the eye, and for attempting to limit it. The dialectical thrust of the midrash emphasizes both Joseph's empathy with Esau, in his visual arrogance, with its components of eroticism and power, and his greatness in taming that arrogance. Because of his beauty, Joseph is the object of visual admiration and rapacity; but he is see-er, as well as seen, manipulating the field of vision available to others, arriving at his own conclusions about their perspectives.

This encounter with Esau becomes emblematic of Joseph's visual transactions throughout his life. He is driven to master reality, to appropriate it through his eyes. Clear knowledge is his aim. Judah concisely summarizes Joseph's expressions of his empirical quest ("You shall be put to the test . . . your words shall be verified"), when he reports to his father: "The man who is lord of the land said to us, 'By this I shall *know* that you are honest men' " (42:33).

From Judah, too, we hear a key expression of Joseph's purpose in bringing Benjamin down to Egypt: "that I may *set eyes* on him" (44:21). Implications of surveillance emerge from this image — protective surveillance, perhaps — which leads Judah to retort, in the midrashic narrative: "Is this what you meant by *setting eyes* on him? Is this concerned attention? Or is it blindness, neglect (a pun on *simat ayin* and *samyut ayin*)?" [50]

Through this key expression, Joseph articulates his primary need: for a clear, visual perception of reality, evidence unequivocal of the truth behind words. But, as Michel Foucault has demonstrated in *Discipline and Punish*, the connections between surveillance, power, and scientific experiment are awkwardly close. As Joseph watches, his brothers will be manipulated into the proper situations for discovery and knowledge. Judah's pun raises questions about the relation between Joseph's "apparatus of observation, recording and training," [51] and a kind of moral obtuseness. In Judah's experience, seeing has come to mean something different, more involved, vulnerable, volatile.

# Knowledge and power

Joseph's image of himself as the all-knowing subject, examining the world under his microscope, comes to almost parodic expression in his reproach to his brothers for the presumed theft of the goblet: "Do you not know that a man like me practices divination?" (44:15). His reproach is based on a field of shared assumptions: everyone knows, surely, that "a man like me" would know things not accessible to the ordinary person.

Rashi conveys this nuance in his reading: "Do you not know that an *important* person like me knows how to practice divination and to *know through knowledge, and rationality, and understanding*, that you have stolen the goblet?" [italics mine]. Joseph is speaking of "power knowledge" — the fact that "power produces knowledge . . . that power and knowledge directly imply one another; that there is no power relation without the correlative constitution of a field of knowledge, nor any knowledge that does not presuppose and constitute at the same time power relations." [52]

Rashi's translation of *naḥash* (divination) deemphasizes the magical or clairvoyant notion of Joseph's knowledge. After all, the goblet is supposed to be his source of clairvoyance (44:5), and this was not in his possession at this time of his knowledge. Instead, the whole apparatus of intellectual activities is in his power; it constitutes his eyes, with which he pries open the secrets of the world.

This is his *ḥokhmah*, his wisdom, in the sense of an almost technical skill in the using of the objects. Rashi's source may be Targum Onkelos, who translates *naḥash* with *badak*—the capacity to examine, scrutinize, research the truth. This is especially interesting, since Onkelos always offers a "magical" translation of *naḥash*, where this is clearly appropriate;[53] here, however, in connection with Joseph's powers, he feels free to translate the word to mean "inquire, investigate, experience."[54]

In spite of this "intellectual" translation, however, something of the "magical" connotations of the word remain, and invest Joseph with a mystique, a prestige, that sets a distance between their limited perceptions ("Do you not know . . . ?") and his superior knowledge. This is a manifestation of the power-knowledge mechanism that underlies his relationship with them, from the time of their appearance in the Egyptian court. Even his accusation that they are spies implies that they are guilty of transgressing the power-knowledge system: trying to gain illicit knowledge, to "see the nakedness of the land." His accusation, in all its absurdity, reinforces in them a sense of their own limited perception; there is so much that he knows, that they do not know.

The brothers express a kind of astounded appreciation of his *ḥokhmah*, his wisdom, in the *Bereshit Rabbah* narrative, when they tell their father, "Even the wood of our cradles he revealed to us!"[55] This extraordinary midrash seems to emphasize Joseph's clairvoyant talents: he could describe to his brothers what kind of wood their cradles were made of. The idea is based on the brothers' words in the text: "The man kept asking about us and our family" (43:7). *Moladtenu*, the word for "family," is translated by Maharal as "our rearing as infants."

On this reading, Joseph reveals to them the details of their early infancy, symbolized in the midrash by the "wood of our cradles." But this revelation is not, after all, a matter of simple clairvoyancy: "the man kept *asking* us" suggests that by dint of asking many questions, Joseph elicited information from the brothers.

In effect, Joseph engages in a kind of psychoanalysis of his brothers: he asks questions that lead them to a knowledge beyond any they could have achieved alone. This is Joseph as inspired therapist, uncovering (the literal meaning of *gilah* — "he revealed") buried truths: the wood of their cradles symbolizing the repressed memories of the earliest time in the "family romance."

There is, to the brothers' sense, something uncanny about such a power to elicit knowledge. Rightly, they assume that he saw what was unseen to them; the dynamic of his questions generated their own understanding: "'*and we answered him accordingly*' [43:7]: in accordance with his questions" (Rashi). The therapeutic experience reinforces their sense of his superiority. "How were we to know that he would say?" expresses the submission of the patient to the manipulation of the therapist. This process of "transference" experienced by the brothers is summarized by the word *va-yitmehu* (43:33) — "they were in a state of wonder," of dependency tinged with fear of the uncanny. "They wondered at his *hokhmah*,"[56] at his power to see things, not by clairvoyancy, but through an intellectual discipline transcending their own.

## Joseph yields to Judah: two ways of knowing

Joseph as master knower, with his eyes in his head to examine and organize the apparent formlessness of the world, uses the vocabulary of investigation. His aim is clarity, evidence: what he sees he will believe. The basis of this experimental approach is the fact that people are not transparent: one cannot master them at a glance, or verify that their words correspond to reality. Therefore, Joseph's strategy is to set them to act in ways that will test the credibility of their words.

This strategy is conceived as a response to the real problem of *emunah*, of verification, of knowing when and what to believe ("that your words may be verified" — *ve-ye'amnu* [42:20]). Even Jacob, after all, did not believe his sons, when they told him that Joseph was alive and ruler in Egypt: *lo he'emin* — he could not grant credence, he could not say *amen* with his whole being.[57]

To "believe," then, is to say "yea"; the word *amen*, if its letters are shuffled, becomes *ma'en*, to refuse, to say, "Nay" — "He refused to be comforted" (37:35). These are the binary positions of human response to language: at some subconscious level, Jacob could not accept his sons' story of death and mangling (Rashi, 37:35); but, after twenty-two years, he could not quite accept their second story of resurrection.

The trouble with *emunah* — "yea-saying" — is that one is dealing with words. Treacherous, opaque, words can distort, mislead. So Joseph demands clear, visual evidence "that your words may be verified." Then, Judah stands before him and redescribes himself, creates himself as empathic seer of his father's seeing, as painfully involved in love and responsibility; and Joseph's empirical resolve shrivels up. Joseph yields to the puckerings, the wrinklings of compassion. He yields, essentially, to the power of Judah. Judah, living the life of constant redescription, revision, overwhelms Joseph, the searcher for clarity, absolute truth.

Judah's descendant, David, confronts the genetic dilemma of *beḥina*, of empirical testing and its inadequacy as a way to knowledge of human beings. He presents himself to God, in one of his Psalms, as an object of testing, of training: "Probe me [*beḥaneni*], O Lord, and try me, test my heart and mind" (26:2). In a classic passage, the Talmud shows David's realization that no human being should invite such an "investigation" of himself; immediately after inviting God to "probe" him, he sins with Batsheva.[58]

This is, apparently, a statement about human fallibility. It also, however, expresses the radical "wrongness" of the language of *beḥina*, of empirical research as a way of knowing human beings. David comes to recognize the central role of what *Sefat Emet* simply calls "the help of heaven" in his life.[59] The project of knowing oneself or other human beings is so complex and entangled that an empirical rationality, a search for "a final vocabulary," will not do:

> Why, look you now, how unworthy a thing you make of me! you would play upon me, you would seem to know my stops, you would pluck out the heart of my mystery, you would sound me from my lowest note to the top of my compass — and there is much music, excellent voice, in this little organ, yet cannot you make it speak.[60]

Judah, confronting Joseph with all the limitations and the power of language, is an implicit argument against Joseph's modality of *beḥina*, of rigorous investigation. Joseph is criticized in midrashic sources, as the ox who "goes forth and all the animals flee from him; he kicks this one, and gores that one. Then comes the lion, and he cannot stand before him."[61] Joseph is depicted as wreaking havoc among his brothers, in the willfulness of his resolve to know. Confronted with Judah, and with Judah's anger at being the object of knowledge, Joseph is compelled to let the whole therapeutic project collapse: "he could no longer control himself" — armor himself against the force of his brother's words, his self-creation. Joseph can no longer hold his stance of intellectual immunity. The habit of "control," of a self-contained, observatory power, that had informed all his actions till now, shrivels in the heat of a different way of seeing.[62]

A rigidity dissolves as he reveals, uncovers, a Joseph never before seen.[63] He speaks many words, achieving the purpose — not of knowledge — but of giving his brothers and his father a narrative — questionable, not entirely credible — a redescription of the meaning of their lives. His radical desire at this point is to have them able to speak to him — "Only then were his brothers able to talk to him" (45:15) — to overcome the paralysis, the dangerous shame of those who know themselves observed.

## Plausible constructions of reality

The problem of knowledge remains. Even if the brothers believe that he really is the long-vanished Joseph (and the midrash suggests that, despite all his eloquence, Joseph has to show them his circumcision before they will credit his words),[64] how will they convince their father? All they have is words: no photographs for the hungry eye to devour. In the event, Jacob does not believe their words.

Joseph addresses the problem quite deliberately: "You can see for yourselves, and my brother Benjamin for himself, that it is indeed I who am speaking to you" (45:12). The sentence is strange; on the surface, it seems to mean either too little or too much ("You can see that I am speaking to you"; or "You can see that it is I, your brother Joseph, who am speaking to you"). Joseph seems to offer visual evidence of his identity — lit., your eyes see that my mouth is speaking to you.

Rashi comments: "'Your eyes see' my glory; and that I am your brother, for I am circumcised like you; moreover, that 'my mouth is speaking to you' in the Holy Tongue." According to Rashi, there are two proofs here of Joseph's identity: his circumcision (visual) and his speaking Hebrew (aural). Ramban objects to the latter evidence. He claims that Hebrew is the general language in Canaan, and that many educated Egyptians would speak it. Joseph, therefore, is not offering his use of Hebrew as evidence of his identity: he is simply drawing attention to his authority ("my mouth") and power to fulfill his promises of economic well-being for his family.

Rashi's other proof of identity—Joseph's circumcision—is similarly open to objection. For circumcision is not an exclusive property of Jacob's family: all the Ishmaelites were circumcised, as well as the children of Ketura, Abraham's second wife—and even the Egyptians, according to some midrashic sources. What kind of evidence, then, does Joseph offer his brothers and his father?

Maharal offers an ingenious solution. Each piece of evidence alone—circumcision, or Hebrew speech—is not conclusive. But both together in the same person makes coincidence unlikely: a Canaanite who is circumcised like an Ishmaelite, or an Ishmaelite who speaks Hebrew like a Canaanite.

The truth is, of course, that this conjunction of mental sets would not stand as conclusive identifying evidence in any court. But Joseph recognizes it as good enough evidence. In offering it to his brothers, he implicitly abandons his compulsive need for certainty: he is born into the world of plausible constructions, with which one works until they are proven false.

This is an adult world, where conjectures and hypotheses lead one to beliefs, whose main character, as Karl Popper defines it, is that they are falsifiable. Both circumcision (*milah*) and the Hebrew language (*lashon*) evoke associations with the nature of language itself, as a structure of perception, with which human beings explore their reality. These are not "final vocabularies"; perception is a constructive process, using whatever models are available to build a perceptual world.

Jerome Bruner cites a fascinating experiment with infants. He took a rubber pacifier and linked it up to a projecting system on a screen above the baby's head. The baby could bring blurred pictures into focus by sucking on his pacifier; he soon learned to step up his sucking rate in order to bring the picture into focus. He would then stop and look at it. When the picture drifted out of focus, he would turn away, suck until the picture was back in focus, and look at it again. He could also master the opposite, counter-intuitive situation; in this case, sucking drove the clear picture out of focus. He would look at the clear picture for as long as possible without sucking and then "have an exuberant burst of sucking," while looking away.[65]

The infants in Bruner's experiment can learn to construct their visual world, so that clarity is achieved. The blurred picture is not acceptable; even the pleasure of sucking gives place to the need for a sharp visual definition.

This need has informed Joseph's transactions with his world, until his confrontation with Judah. Now, he has recourse to a less crystalline, conclusive type of perception: he offers his brothers and his father data of the eye and of the ear, neither incontrovertible. Together, they form a plausible construction of reality. Perhaps, after all, the need for absolute clarity is a property of infants?

This cognitive shift in Joseph, as Judah "defeats" him, allows him to send his father evidence of a kind that, in the event, his father cannot believe. For Jacob, too, is a highly visual person, whose suffering for twenty-two years is summed up in the statement, "I have not seen him since" (44:28). Jacob's eye works differently, however. "But when they recounted all that Joseph had said to them, and when he saw the wagons that Joseph had sent to transport him, the spirit of their father Jacob revived" (45:27). He hears and he sees: he hears the full narrative that Joseph has conveyed through his brothers, and he sees the *agalot*—the wagons—that, according to a powerful midrash, act as a coded reminder of the last Torah passage he had studied with Joseph before his disappearance.[66] Only then, his eyes and ears informing each other, memory becoming usable at last, does his spirit revive.

Jacob sees with the eyes of one seeking a narrative: remembering his complicity in study with Joseph, and knowing it remembered by him, his one desire is to "see him before I die." A certain force of longing to see, to understand something essential about his life, revives in him: "The Holy Presence that had departed from him, dwelt over him again" (Rashi, 45:27).

And indeed, in this sense, he "sees" Joseph: "And Joseph was seen by him. . . . Then Israel said to Joseph, 'Now I can die, since I have seen that you are still alive'" (46:29–30).[67] A residual doubt is resolved in Jacob only when he sees Joseph's face. The anxiety that would not let him die in peace is the anxiety at a narrative that had turned into babble. Now, the picture clears: he sees life in Joseph's face, the kind of spiritual vitality of which the Sages say, "The righteous are called the *living*."[68]

This is the kind of vision of which Jacob has been deprived for twenty-two years. One might say that as soon as Joseph yields his single-minded pursuit of the "ocular proof," Jacob regains the imaginative, re-visionary use of his eyes.

## Jacob: knowing blindness

There are two strange codas to this theme of surrendered vision and regained vision. In the first, God tells Jacob, as he halts at the Egyptian border, suddenly afraid, to "go down": "Fear not to go down to Egypt, for I will make you there into a great nation. I myself will go down with you to Egypt, and I myself will bring you back; and Joseph's hand shall close your eyes" (46:3–4). Some commentators think that this last sentence describes the presence of the closest mourner, the beloved Joseph, at Jacob's deathbed; Jacob is promised that Joseph will close his eyes, in the devout act of the surviving son.

But a different reading is suggested by *Meshekh Ḥokhmah*. Joseph's hand on Jacob's eyes is directly related to the anguish Jacob feels about "going down" to Egypt. Jacob sees no sense in being compelled to go into exile, an exile he intuits will be longer than the time for a visit to his son. What is the purpose of a journey away from his proper place?

God tells him that the mystery of Joseph's fate — his descent and rise to power — should serve as a paradigm for movements downwards and upwards, in general. It should act as a "hand on the eyes," preventing his restless intelligence from probing the ultimate meanings of phenomena that seem empirically absurd. Joseph's rise to power serves purposes, some of which become evident with the passage of time; others remain opaque to human perception.

Joseph's experience, then, is the paradigm of the limitations of vision, in the sense of rational understanding. The irony is that he, whose dominant desire had been to see clearly and indubitably, is now primed to teach his father a kind of blindness, in the face of historical contingency.

This reading of God's words may not be precisely comforting; rather it reaffirms a tragic sense of the unintelligibility of life, to human eyes. But — and this is the second coda — Jacob has his own ways of seeing, even in blindness. On his deathbed, he asks to bless his grandsons:

Then Israel saw Joseph's sons and asked, "Who are these?" And Joseph said to his father, "They are my sons, whom God has given me here."

"Bring them up to me," he said, "that I may bless them." Now, Israel's eyes were dim with age; he could not see. So [Joseph] brought them close to him, and he kissed them and embraced them. And Israel said to Joseph, "I never expected to see you again, and here God has let me see your children as well." Joseph then removed them from his knees, and bowed low with his face to the ground. Joseph took the two of them, Ephraim with his right hand — to Israel's left — and Manasseh with his left hand — to Israel's right — and brought them close to him. But Israel stretched out his right hand and laid it on Ephraim's head — thus crossing his hands — although Manasseh was the first-born. . . . When Joseph saw that his father was placing his right hand on Ephraim's head, he thought it wrong [lit., it was evil in his eyes]; so he took hold of his father's hand to move it from Ephraim's head to Manasseh's. "Not so, Father," Joseph said to his father, "for the other is the firstborn; place your right hand on his head." But his father objected, saying, "I know, my son, I know. . . ." (48:8–14; 17–19).

The whole scene is focused on the theme of vision. Jacob sees Joseph's sons and, enigmatically, does not recognize them. Rashi comments that inspiration, the creative seeing that is Jacob's restored treasure, abandons him, because evil kings will descend from these two grandsons. An alienation settles on him, and Joseph hastens to assure him that they are the offspring of a true marriage. Inspiration returns; but, the text continues, Jacob is physically blind. Yet, as he kisses and embraces the two, he speaks of the wonder of vision: "God has let me see your children."

Joseph then sets his sons in proper order by Jacob's right and left hands; but Jacob, acting apparently on the disability the text has just mentioned, crosses [sikel] his hands, and blesses them with the wrong hand. Joseph sees this and "it was evil in his eyes." He tries to change his father's hands. But Jacob refuses — va-yima'en: once again, as in his refusal to be comforted after Joseph's presumed death, Jacob says "Nay" to the words of others, to the version of reality offered him by his son. This time, however, his "Nay" is expressed with consummate confidence: "I know, my son, I know."

The drama of this confrontation between Jacob and Joseph has many dimensions. In it, the whole story of blindness and perception from Isaac's blessing onward is encapsulated. Now, Jacob is the blind one, knowing in his sightlessness. The would-be deceiver of the past knows that his father was never deceived. With the confidence of that knowledge, filled with the same kind of perception as gave him that original blessing at his father's hands, Jacob can speak not only of knowledge ("I know"), but of seeing ("God has let me see your children"). This is a vision informed by love and imagination; clouded by evil; restored by a sense of possibilities.

He sees something in the boys that leads him to cross his hands. The word *sikel* (translated here, "he crossed") is translated simply and powerfully by Rashi and the Targum: "he guided his hands with understanding and wisdom [*sekhel*]. He was aware that Manasseh was the firstborn, and nevertheless he did not place his right hand on him" (48:14). On this reading, Jacob, in the very act of crossing his hands, is moved by a total cognitive understanding of reality. His eyes are physically dimmed, but his mind and other senses are preternaturally alert; just because he knows Manasseh is the firstborn, he assumes that Joseph has placed him at his right hand, and *therefore* he crosses his hands.[69]

A subtly different reading is given by Seforno: "*Sikel*: he knew and understood through the touch of his hand, without seeing." Jacob's hands are credited with wisdom; like Isaac, in his blindness, Jacob uses his other senses, his body, as avenues of knowledge.

The difference between the two readings is perhaps a matter of emphasis: Rashi maintains that Jacob is fully conscious of what he is doing in changing his hands, while Seforno writes of an intuitive body-knowledge. Wherever the source of Jacob's awareness, however, the outcome is clear, in his serenely repeated answer to Joseph's protest: "I know, my son, I know." Jacob is fully at peace with his closed eyes and his full understanding.

He goes on to speak specifically of the relative greatness of the two boys and of their descendants. He seems to offer reassurance to Joseph, in his firm assessments of younger and older, great and small. He allays Joseph's anxiety about delusion—does his father not realize who is the elder grandson? or does he think Joseph has misarranged his sons, using his own right hand to place the firstborn? does he underestimate Joseph's own foresight, or spatial intelligence?

"I know, my son, I know" answers many specific, unspoken anxieties; but its resonance seems to transcend such specifics. It has a vatic quality, seeming to imply, in its repetition, a knowledge beyond the empirical. It contains and grounds Joseph's most radical anxieties, about favoritism, displacements of firstborn children, and the violence that can unleash. And it evokes Jacob's own most radical experience of firstborns displaced, of deception and error in the context of blessing. An intimate and ultimate sense of order radiates from these words, a patriarchal confidence that includes and transcends his own father's affirmation: "And indeed blessed he shall be!" (27:33).

## Joseph and Judah: the conflict of vocabularies

Joseph, however, remains in the world of the sons, after his father has received his inspired vision and blessing. When the fathers have receded into metaphysical certainty, each standing firmly by his own form of knowledge, the sons are left to struggle with the dilemmas, the irritations of vision. "When Joseph saw . . . it was evil in his eyes" (48:17). Joseph's irritable confidence in the truth of his perceptions – "Not so, Father" – is countered by the calm conviction of his dying father. There is a moment of archetypal confrontation, between the world of the fathers and the world of the sons. From this point of view, Joseph never graduates to the status of "father," of patriarch. He is the first of the sons; he has not the gift of inspiration, but must struggle with his own experience of vision, to the end believing in the evidence of his eyes.

This is to say that Joseph remains Joseph, seeking for what is certain. "*Lo ken*," he says to his father, "It is not so." The same emphasis on the absolutely proved, on a solid, well-based *rightness*, had informed his challenge to his brothers; he had picked up on their word, as they protested their innocence of his charge of spying: "No, my lord! . . . we are honest men [*kenim*]; your servants have never been spies!" (42:10–11). "If you are honest men [*kenim*] . . . you must bring me your youngest brother" (42:19–20).

To be honest, in this sense, is opposed to being a spy, a *meragel*, a vagabond, cut loose from social and cognitive proprieties. A *meragel* is defined by his visual ambition: he aims to "see the nakedness of the land" (42:9). It is in response to this specific charge, of an unseemly, disordered kind of looking at what should not be exposed to the gaze, that the brothers protest that they are *kenim* – "honest." Respectable, solidly defined in their visual projects, the brothers give Joseph what is essentially his word – *ken*. And what it expresses in terms of the desire for clear, authentic knowledge remains with him even after the central experiment of his life has been abandoned, even after his father has serenely countered his empiricism with vision of a different order.

Between Joseph and Judah remains, then, an unbridgeable space. For an instant, Judah overwhelmed Joseph with his full, generous use of language to redescribe himself; with his personal, imaginative vision and re-vision of his reality. But the union of the two modalities—the Joseph quest for a "final vocabulary," for metaphysical certainty in the relations between human beings and reality, and the Judah "ironist" sense of the contingency of all vocabularies, a sense that only increases his responsibility to create a personal vocabulary—is a union of "approachings," of *va-yiggash*, in appeasement, prayer, and belligerency. Like the two trees that are brought close to one another, in Ezekiel's prophecy (37:15– 20),[70]—the tree of Joseph and the tree of Judah—they will become one only in some ultimate, messianic time, and in the hand of God. In this world, the tension between the two remains, a source sometimes of frustration, sometimes of fruitful confrontation.

# VA-YEḤI 🍃
## The Beginning of Desire

*Jacob's deathbed: weakness and power*

> Thus Israel settled in the country of Egypt, in the region of Goshen; they acquired holdings in it, and were fertile and increased greatly. Jacob lived seventeen years in the land of Egypt, so that the span of Jacob's life came to one hundred and forty-seven years. (47:27–28)

Jacob's final period is described as a time of *yeshiva* and of *ḥayyim*, of settling down and of living. It is Israel, the man, the family, the nation in germinal form, that finds a niche (*va-ye'aḥazu*, lit., they were held by it) in Egypt, this land of essential foreignness. There, paradoxically, they flourish, realizing all the blessings of fertility. But it is Jacob, the mortal man, who is described at the opening of the Parsha as "living" in the land of Egypt, an apparent redundancy that releases unexpected resonances.

For if the English word "lived" is ambiguous, its meanings divide, in Hebrew, into the two connotations of "settled, resided" and "was alive." *Va-yeḥi*, therefore, carries a peculiarly questioning ring, as if to impress a meaning of unexpected, almost incongruous vitality. After those many years of suspended vitality in the darkness of Joseph's absence, Jacob's life is rediscovered and sustained in the land of Egypt. This is the opening statement of the Parsha, its virtual redundancy belied by the force of the word *va-yeḥi*, "he lived."

This seventeen-year period of grace culminates in the main subject matter of the Parsha: Jacob becomes conscious of approaching death, and communicates his final wishes to his children. In speaking to define a reality that he is about to leave, Jacob is unique among the patriarchs. His is, in fact, the only deathbed scene in Genesis, indeed in the whole Torah.

Abraham's death, for instance, is simply narrated after a summary of his years (25:7–8). As the midrash notices, he conspicuously fails to bless

352

his children: the power of blessing that God had given him[1] is surrendered, as he senses the complexity encoded within Isaac's being. With Jacob and Esau as grandchildren, Abraham is simply afraid, in the language of the midrash, to endorse Isaac by blessing him.[2] Isaac's death is narrated as following on Jacob's return from Padan Aram (35:28–29). His "deathbed" blessing to Jacob, masquerading as Esau, occurred twenty-two years earlier. ("And he said, 'I am old now, and I do not know how soon I may die. . . . So that I may give you my innermost blessing before I die'" [27:2, 4].) Consciousness of mortality is a feature of Isaac's "inscape," but his time of real death arrives without rehearsal and without declaration of will or blessing.

Jacob is the only patriarch who speaks his will, in full awareness of his own end. A striking midrashic tradition tells of a new human experience—sickness or weakness presaging death.[3] Previously, man had died on a sneeze. Now, Jacob consciously asks for sickness, for a time in which to prepare, to transact essential death business with his children:[4] "Jacob instituted the sickness that tends toward death."[5]

The midrashim on this theme cluster around the narrative preamble to Jacob's blessings: "Joseph was told, 'Your father is ill'" (48:1). The first use in the Torah of the word *ḥoleh* (ill), together with the word *hineh* (behold), with its implications of fresh perception,[6] form the underpinning for a new mode of consciousness. Jacob is aware of his own impending death and wants to set his affairs—in the largest sense—in order. An unprecedented sense of responsibility to life informs Jacob's expression, on his deathbed, of his "living will."

His first concern is with his own burial. In language of entreaty ("Do me this favor"), he asks to be buried in Canaan, not in Egypt. Implicit in his speech are the power relations between an old dying man and his ruler son, who has "power in his hand to execute his will" (Rashi, 47:29). There is a pathos in Jacob's insistence on an oath from Joseph, and in his bowing to his son at the end of the interview. Worldly wise, the midrash comments, "The fox in his time, bow down to him" (Rashi, 47:31). Among the losses of old age is the loss of power. Jacob's primary need has to do with his own body and its accommodation after death; but with only words at his disposal, he will use every verbal convention, making Joseph swear acquiescence, to realize his will.

A provocative midrash, quoted by Rashi (50:6), traces the effects of this oath on reality. Because of it, Pharaoh is compelled to allow Jacob's burial in Canaan:

*"According as he made you swear"*: "Were it not for the oath, I should not
have permitted you to go." But Pharaoh was afraid to say, "Transgress
the oath," lest Joseph say, "If so, I shall transgress the oath I swore to
you, that I would not tell about the Holy Language I know in addition
to the seventy languages you know, but which [i.e., Hebrew] you do not
know."

At stake is the strength and weakness of language, its power and
vulnerability. An oath is easily broken, but with it collapses the whole
delicate tissue of transactions and commitments on which society stands.
And ultimately, not to be master of all the languages, especially of the
"seventy-first" language, the *ur* language, is to be exposed in a shameful
nakedness, a powerlessness, that even a Pharaoh cannot endure. By
making his royal son swear to bury him in Canaan, Jacob evokes the
equivocal authority of words to shape reality.

When Joseph comes a second time to his father in his illness, "Israel
strengthened himself, and sat upon the bed" (48:2); he makes conscious
efforts to greet his princely son with the respect due to his station — even
though, on this occasion, it is Jacob who is about to bestow a gift of
unexpected blessing on Joseph.[7]

The midrash isolates the motif of brutal and conscious mortality, the
sense of the dying that they are absent from the drama of life, while still
in life:

*"The time approached for Israel to die"* [47:29]. It is written: "No man has
authority over the lifebreath — to hold back the lifebreath; there is no
authority over the day of death" [Ecclesiastes 8:8]. When Jacob in-
clined toward death, he began to lower himself before Joseph and said,
"If I have found favor in your eyes. . . ." When was this? When he drew
close to death, as it is said, "The time approached for Israel to die."[8]

There is a strained note of humiliation in Jacob's voice, as this midrash
reads his speech to his son.

Dialectically opposed to this, however, is the sense of spiritual power
that clearly emanates from him, as he allocates blessings and destinies to
his children and grandchildren. They wait breathlessly, silently, on his
words. Even Joseph's one protest at the apparent error — as Jacob crosses
his hands over his grandsons' heads (48:14) — is informed by the urgency
of his desire to waste no drop of the precious substance that Jacob is
dispensing. The patriarch is at the center of a force field called "bless-

ing": the position of his hands, the words he articulates, create a reality that his children regard with great awe, even with trepidation.

Jacob's apparent weakness—generic to the situation of the dying—is belied, therefore, by a power that rests in words spoken by the dying. The mythic fascination of deathbeds here—uniquely in the Torah—becomes central. Here, it is not saintly behavior in the face of death, nor meditations at the margin, that mark Jacob's last minutes. Instead, his essential act is indicated, as he concludes, "When Jacob finished his instructions [*le-tzavot*—commanding, charging] to his sons" (49:33). He sits up in bed and "charges" his children. This was the purpose of his self-induced "illness"—the opportunity to charge, to make some vital contact with the life he is leaving, to speak words that will help his children to live.[9]

## Blocked consciousness: the presence of God departs

The problem is one of survival. A deathly darkness falls over Jacob, as he confronts his family and their future. Egypt is quintessential exile: the first exile, the paradigm exile. The whole family, in search of bread, has "gone down" into Egypt—an idiom not merely geographical, indicating a movement southward, but existential in resonance. Downward is deathward. If, to Hamlet, Denmark is a prison, then to Jacob, Egypt is a grave that threatens to swallow all his family's aspiration for a distinct destiny.[10] His last speech is, therefore, "fraught with background," in Erich Auerbach's famous phrase:[11] in a reality of exile and diffusion, how is the identity of this family to be preserved?

This identity, that began to be forged in a heroic abandonment of all known paradigms, in an exquisite training of vision to sights never before seen, now threatens to end in a peculiar blindness, a failure of the senses and the sensibilities.

This is the strange burden of Rashi's opening comment on the Parsha. Responding to the graphic layout of the Torah text at the point of juncture between Parshat Va-yiggash and Parshat Va-yehi, Rashi asks, "Why is this Parsha *setuma* [blocked, closed]?" (47:28).

By this, he means that there is no space at all, marking the Parsha break. This is, in fact, the only instance where not even a minimum nine spaces separate the new Parsha from the previous one. (An "open" Parsha would leave space to the end of the line and begin on the next line. This is, therefore, in the words of Rashi's source, the "most closed of all Parshiot in the Torah.")[12]

Rashi's question has all the air of a technical query, but his answer is far from merely technical: "For when Jacob our father died, the eyes and hearts of Israel were closed because of the affliction of the bondage with which the Egyptians began to afflict them. Another explanation: Jacob desired to reveal the end to his sons, but it was closed [*nistam*] from him."

He gives two answers to his question, both puns on the concept of the "blocking" of the text, the loss of intervening space. In the first, the "blocking" mimes a kind of stupidity that clouds the eyes and hearts of Jacob's children, as soon as he dies. This is a historical-psychological observation: slavery brings with it, even in its incipient stages,[13] a condition in which the victims are diminished in their basic ability to read and understand their own reality.

The closing of the eyes and heart evokes a midrashic expression used of the Greeks: "they *darkened the eyes* of Israel."[14] Light or darkness in the eyes is a metaphor for understanding, intellectual or spiritual. Similarly, Isaiah decries a nation, whose "eyes are besmeared, and they see not; their minds, and they cannot think" (44:18). The parallelism indicates the connection between eyes and heart/mind, seeing and understanding. Idioms of "light in the eyes" are common in the Talmud: "the elders illuminate the eyes of Israel"; Mordecai was named "ben Yair," because he "illuminated the eyes of Israel";[15] and in the liturgy, "illuminate our eyes in Your Torah, open our hearts in Your commandments."[16]

The closing of intellectual apertures on Jacob's death becomes, on one reading in the Zohar, independent of the question of slavery.[17] R. Yaakov makes no mention of slavery, simply connecting Jacob's death with the blocking of understanding. A heavy mystery lies over so unexplained a statement. There seems to be a fatality at work, less rational than specific factors of slavery and physical suffering. In itself, Jacob's death brings in its wake a failure to read reality as though it constituted an intelligible text.

The problem with this first of Rashi's answers to the blocked Parsha question is that at the beginning of the Parsha, Jacob is alive; the whole Parsha, in fact, as we have noticed, is named for his "aliveness" — *va-yeḥi*. And for most of the Parsha, he remains alive, conscious of approaching death, trying to assure life to his children. What relevance, then, does the sealed Parsha break have to his situation? Its symbolism would possibly be more evocative if the blocking happened in the next Parsha break, after Jacob's death.

Rashi's second answer comes as a partial response; it moves into Jacob's own consciousness. It is he who is blocked in his desire to "reveal the end." The tragic experience of blocking is now his; intimately, he knows, in the last hours of his life, that condition which will, after his death, be the fate of his survivors.

"Jacob wanted to reveal the end." This is the moment when Jacob calls his children around his deathbed and proclaims his intent to speak to them of the "last things": "And Jacob called his sons and said, 'Come together that I may tell you what is to befall you at the end of days. Assemble and hearken, O sons of Jacob; Hearken to Israel your father'" (49:1–2).

What follows is a description of each son, with no eschatological reference. It is this discontinuity between Jacob's preamble and the content of his final speech that generates the midrashic narrative. Rashi here quotes the midrash again: "He sought to reveal the end, and the Presence of God departed from him, and he began to say other things."

The whole deathbed speech is, it seems, a diversion from Jacob's original intent. It bears at best an oblique relation to the final meanings that Jacob would have wished to communicate to his children. The "other things" that he finds himself telling his children are quite different from the "final things" he had projected — "what is to befall you at the end of days."

By this expression, Jacob refers to scenarios unfolded in later prophetic books, of ultimate redemption, of return from exile, of messianic harmony and coherence.[18] Jacob is the first to refer to this historic, or perhaps metahistoric, theme, to the "sense of an ending,"[19] that shall make intelligible all the complexities and contingencies of experience. But the midrash narrates a drama of vision and frustrated speech: "the Presence of God departed from him"; "it was blocked from him." Is he prevented from seeing that vision of "the end," or from speaking it? Is it the eyes or the mouth that strain against their seal?[20] What is it to have the Presence of God depart from one, on one's deathbed?

*Sefat Emet* makes a powerful suggestion:[21] to "reveal the end" is simply to communicate the *idea* of ultimate harmony. It is not a matter of graphic descriptions of the manner and the timing of redemption. It is to convince Jacob's children, on the verge of exile and diffusion, about to lose all sense of autonomy, of the intelligibility of their destiny, that their experience really does have a *ketz*, an implicit order, a movement toward meaning.

A certain vitality of vision is given to Jacob—and then blocked off from him. For if Jacob had succeeded in conveying to his children a strong, unequivocal vision of "the end," the experience of exile would have been entirely robbed of its necessary sting. That experience knows of no easy resolution. Jacob's children will have to live its absurdity and its pain, its apparently fruitless yearnings, without intoxicating visions of harmony to sustain them. What resolutions, what orderings they achieve, they will have to achieve in the immediacy, the vulnerability, the confusion of their own lives.

On such a view, Jacob has a vision that in its very luminousness prevents him from speaking it. This notion is conveyed in the midrash in *Bereshit Rabbah*:

> This is like the king's friend, who was about to depart the world, and his children were gathered round his bed. He said to them, "Come, I shall reveal to you the secrets of the king." He raised his eyes and saw the king. Then he told them, "Beware of the glory of the king." So Jacob our father raised his eyes and saw the Presence of God standing over him. He told them, "Beware of the glory of God." (98:3)

In place of the "secrets" that the king's friend would have revealed (liberating, resolving the imprisoned meanings of their condition), he can only—overwhelmed by the king's presence—stammer his silence and acquiescence. The paradox is poignant: the end is "blocked," "covered" by too dazzling a vision. The departure of the Shekhina becomes the looming Presence (*al gabav*) that opens his eyes to their widest extent (*talah einav*) and seals his mouth.

One implication of the paradox, however, is that his children do, from his very silence, receive an oblique sense of the king's presence. This is not an immediate, "usable" experience, as revealed secrets are "usable." But, obliquely, the "other things" that Jacob says to his children do convey a deflected vision. "Everything that Jacob wanted to reveal," says the Zohar, "he did indeed reveal, in a manner that was both hidden and revealed."[22] Cryptically, in a mode of indirection, Jacob communicates a vision of blinding, even perilous order: "Beware of the glory of the king."

# Jacob's bed: the question of coherence

A radically different understanding of the "departure of the Shekhina" is given in the Talmud:[23]

> *"And Jacob called his sons and said, 'Come together that I may tell you what is to befall you. . . . Reuben, you are my first-born. . . .'"* Jacob wanted to reveal the end of days to his sons and the Shekhina departed from him. He said, "Is there perhaps — God forbid — a blemish in my bed? Like Abraham, from whom Ishmael emerged, and like my father Isaac, from whom Esau emerged?" His sons said to him, "Hear, Israel, the Lord our God, the Lord is one." They said, "Just as there is nothing in your heart but oneness, so there is nothing in our hearts but oneness." Then, Jacob exclaimed, "Blessed be the name of His kingdom's glory for ever!"

Here, the sensed "absence of God" generates anxiety in Jacob: "is there perhaps a blemish in my bed?" The notion of the "blemish in the bed" refers to the genetic pattern established by his father and grandfather, by which one out of two children, products of the bed, is "waste matter" in the destiny of the family — excrescence, "matter out of place," in Mary Douglas's famous definition of impurity.[24]

Jacob — so much more prolific than they, with an expansive vitality expressed in thirteen children — is concerned with the question of coherence. His terror is precisely a terror of the wasted, the excess, the unusable. The ultimate compliment that is paid him in midrashic rhetoric — "His bed was whole, complete" — comes to symbolize a life fully used, energies fully metabolized, its parts tending toward integral meaning. But the compliment carries with it an undertow of anxiety: on his deathbed, Jacob is still unsure about the project of his life. Shakespeare's bitter line on a sexuality felt to have issued forth in meaninglessness — "Th' expense of spirit in a waste of shame"[25] — expresses perhaps some of Jacob's dread. This is a moment in which the readability of his life is in question; it is called a moment in which the Shekhina departs.

The poignancy of the moment is underscored by his sons' response. They cannot prove to their father that they all belong to the family destiny. All they can do is speak back to him — counterpointing his address, "Hear, O sons of Jacob" — with their own claim to the creation of meaning in language: *Shema Yisrael* — "Listen, father, for we, too, must speak . . . with all our diversity, our extreme differences and conflicts, we too are concerned with the question of coherence." In a moment of vindication, Jacob says aloud, in the mode accessible only in rare times of unitary vision: "Blessed be the name of His kingdom's glory for ever!" The striking character of the midrash lies in its dialectical tension. It is the father's anxious sense of *pesul*, of anarchy, of meaninglessness, that generates an affirmation of equivalent concern from the children. That, in turn, leads the father into an articulation of blessing and integration. The absence of the Shekhina, that is, evokes a new sense of presence; the dread of chaos a new sense of order.

Jacob "blocked," suddenly unable to see or speak, becomes a premonitory figure, telling of the opaqueness, the confusions of exile. Before the startled eyes of his children, he enacts a drama of disintegration and oblique reintegration, that speaks volumes about their own destiny.

# The absence of God: the poetic blank

The pathos of this drama is illumined by the fact that, as the midrash reads Jacob's life, it is no new phenomenon. For long periods, he has suffered the "absence of the Shekhina." The twenty years in Padan Aram, in the course of which he amassed wives, children, servants, cattle, sheep, gold, and silver, are years in which "the Presence of God does not rest on him."[26] In some radical sense that has to do with the effect of Laban's society, God is not "with him." Then, again, during the twenty-two years of Joseph's disappearance, "the Shekhina departed from him"; his life force is drained and wells up again only on the news of Joseph's survival: "the spirit of Jacob revived."[27]

These long periods of God's absence are, then, a leitmotif in Jacob's life. Rambam offers a clinical psychological diagnosis:

> Because of Jacob's sorrow and anxiety, during all the days of his mourning for Joseph, the holy spirit departed from him, until he was brought tidings that Joseph was alive: then, "the spirit of Jacob revived" — which the Targum translates, "The spirit of prophecy rested upon their father Jacob." The Sages make the point in this way: "Prophecy does not come to rest in the midst of lethargy, or of melancholy . . . but only in the midst of joy."[28]

Jacob's condition becomes a paradigm for that joyless condition in which prophetic vision cannot flourish. Writing as a clinician, Rambam diagnoses the absence of God as a function of depression ("lethargy and melancholy"). In this condition, it is impossible to attain full human stature; the prophet, in Rambam's view, is the fully developed human being.

Jacob survives long periods of this "absence of God," to win seventeen years of grace, of "life" in Egypt. And then, like the flickering of a candle, at the moment when he most needs prophetic inspiration, it fails him. Twice in these last hours — once with all his children around his bed, and once before, as he is about to give special blessing to Joseph's two children, Ephraim and Manasseh — the midrash recounts this failure. In Rambam's reading, this is no arbitrary movement of God, present and then absent, but a movement within the intimacies of Jacob's spirit. There, something flickers and goes out.

This recurrent experience of a kind of extinction is, I suggest, related to the trope that Harold Bloom describes in *The Breaking of the Vessels* — the trope of the blank.[29] This may be taken as a model for the specific poetic crisis that Jacob endures in his last hours. The blank is a figure that Bloom traces through poets from Milton to Wallace Stevens. Obviously derived from the French, "blanc," "white," it is also — paradoxically — related to the word "black": both black and blank have the same root, *bhel*, "to shine or flash." To be assailed by the blank is to be assailed by emptiness or density, unintelligible, like an unreadable page:

> It is difficult to read. The page is dark.
> Yet he knows what it is that he expects.
>
> The page is blank or a frame without a glass
> Or a glass that is empty when he looks.
>
> — *Wallace Stevens,*
> *Phosphor Reading by His Own Light*

The tradition of the blank that Bloom uses as an example of transumptive literary criticism — "instances of the interpretive and revisionary power of a poetry perpetually battling its own belatedness" — goes back to Milton's *Paradise Lost*:

> Thus with the year
> Seasons return; but not to me returns
> Day, or the sweet approach of even or morn,
> Or sight of vernal bloom, or summer's rose,
> Or flocks, or herds, or human face divine;
> But cloud instead, and ever-during dark
> Surrounds me, from the cheerful ways of men
> Cut off, and for the book of knowledge fair
> Presented with a universal blank
> Of Nature's works to me expunged and razed,
> And wisdom at one entrance quite shut out.
>
> *(Book 3, 40–50)*

The sense of being "cut off," "shut out," from wisdom, from an intelligible vision of things is the pain of a "universal blank." Milton's physical blindness provides the trope that Coleridge then takes up:

> O Lady! in this wan and heartless mood,
> To other thoughts by yonder throstle wooed,
> All this long eve, so balmy and serene
> Have I been gazing on the western sky,
> And its peculiar tint of yellow green:
> And still I gaze—and with how blank an eye!
>
> *(Dejection: An Ode)*

> I see them all, so excellently fair,
> I see, not feel, how beautiful they are!
>
> *(The Ancient Mariner)*

and Wordsworth, describing the "void of decreation:"

> Blank misgivings of a Creature
> Moving about in worlds not realized
>
> *(Intimations of Immortality)*

or, in *Tintern Abbey*, bemoaning his "blind man's eye," and Emerson:

The problem of restoring to the world original and eternal beauty is solved by the redemption of the soul. The ruin or the blank that we see when we look at nature is in our own eye. . . .

and the harsh despair of Wallace Stevens:

> Shall a man go barefoot
> Blinking and blank?
>
> *(The American Sublime)*

The blank is in the eye of the beholder, but no mere chiding will transform the unmeaning colorlessness/blackness of things. This is the poetic crisis, as Bloom isolates it: "the mere horror of blank naught-at-all" (Coleridge, *Limbo*). It is this trope, I suggest, that will help us translate the "departure of God" in the midrashic narrative of Jacob's last hours. The anxiety of the "blemish in the bed" reduces Jacob's life to "blank naught-at-all," a parody life, deprived of that "shaping spirit of Imagination" (*Dejection*), that envisages and speaks meaning.

When Jacob comes to bless his children, he calls them to "gather round," to "come together" (*he'asfu, hikavtzu*). There is a tension in dealing with their disparateness: he would weld them into a core unity that will make prophecy possible. But the poetic crisis overwhelms him: the sheer blackness, the diverse detail and difference of his children congests his vision. There is no space for structurings, not even the minimum nine letters' space that allows Parshiot to mean. So that when he does begin to speak to his massed children, it is without the clear vision of blessedness that should inform a blessing.

> This passage is not prefaced by the word "blessing," since he did not yet have clearly in focus what he would say to them. Moses, however, began immediately with the words, "And this is the blessing." The word "this" [*ve-zot*] indicates that everything was clearly focused for him, at the moment he began to speak. In Jacob's speech, on the other hand, the word "this" is not used, till after all the blessings have been uttered. Only then, after everything had acquired clear focus for him, did his blessings seem manifestly to come from God — but not earlier.[30]

The Ishbitzer, a nineteenth-century hasidic commentator, here describes Jacob's confusion as a function of repressed resentment and suspicion: he is angry with his sons, who put him through the torment of the Joseph story. This anger is reflected in harsh words to the first three sons, Reuben, Simeon, and Levi, who are traditionally understood to have played the most active roles in the deception of Jacob. Only gradually, in the course of utterance, he finds himself able to "see" his subject, through the blur, the blank of his disenchantment. By the time he has finished, the "poetic crisis" is long over, signaled by the use of the word "this": "All these were the tribes of Israel, twelve in number, and *this* [*ve-zot*] is what their father said to them, blessing them each according to his own blessing he blessed them" (49:28).

*The poetic crisis resolved*

Ample reference to blessing is the harvest of his poem, though it was not its seed. And what had begun as *eileh* — as a diffuse mass, a blurred indistinctness — becomes "this" — a firm object of perception. The prolific issue of his bed becomes coherent: he blesses each son separately, but, as Rashi notices, he blesses *them* all with the blessings of all. A kind of benign seepage of color replaces the original dry blankness. Even the sons he most resents from the Joseph episode are suffused by the newly organic conception he now has of his family:

> "Every part of you is fair, my darling" [Song of Songs 4:7]: this speaks of the tribes. And if you object, "When Jacob blessed the tribes, he criticized Reuben, Simeon, and Levi, so how can you say, 'Every part of you is fair'?"... Nevertheless, he did go back and bless them, as it is written, "All these were the tribes of Israel, twelve in number." What is the meaning of "And this is what their father said to them, blessing them"? Said R. Elazar, "He made them [lit.] nurse from one another."[31]

The fluid, vital quality of his children affects Jacob's vision, so that what had seemed diffuse and dry now comes together in fluent blessedness. This happens in the course of his poem — inspiration arrives belatedly, unexpectedly, with imagery of liquids, and of animals.

The associations of fluidity are rich in sensuousness and in their paradoxical philosophical implications. The fluids that interfuse the poem begin with the negative connotations of water. This is the simile for Reuben: "Unstable as water, you shall excel no longer" (49:4). Hasty, rash, volatile, Reuben cannot dominate his family, cannot be the force that will bind them into a significant structure. The water image suggests that he has no self-possession.

But water is then replaced by wine and milk, when Jacob comes to speak of Judah:

> He tethers his ass to a vine,
> His ass's foal to a choice vine;
> He washes his garment in wine,
> His robe in blood of grapes.
> His eyes are dark from wine;
> His teeth are white from milk.
>
> *(49:11–12)*

These are sensuous images of eyes and teeth colored by the abundance of fermenting wine and nurturing milk. Finally, Joseph is also described in water images ("A wild ass by a spring" [49:22]) and blessed with "the blessings of the deep that couches below" (49:25) — the symbol of female sexuality and fertility, moistness, and receptivity. Water, connoting impulse, sexuality, release, is now not a negative image, but a figure for erotic and procreative force.

Fluidity comes to express motion, energy, and fertile receptivity. It is as though Jacob, in the course of speaking, revises his view of the passionate and the sensual — the currents in his family that had caused pain and disruption in the past, and that — as the Ishbitzer suggests — generate a poetic crisis in Jacob, as he comes to bless his children. Searching for clear focus, he discovers a new way of seeing fluidity: ultimately, these passionate connections among his children are the stuff of life itself. In the form of anger and jealousy, they destroy, but when the midrash describes Jacob's ultimate blessing of his sons, it is to transform them into the mode of "nursing from one another" (*Pesikta Rabbati*). They nurture one another: the suckling image is a startlingly direct expression of a vital, even a subconscious drawing on one another's being.

This revision of Jacob's use of fluid imagery is profoundly connected to the question of integration that so troubles him. The sense that God has departed from him, the vision of things as falling apart, is, on a tactile level, an experience of *dryness*: of discrete parts, without possibility of attachment or relation.

Ezekiel's vision of the dry bones, for example, is essentially a vision of despair of this kind; from the outset, it is the dryness of the bones that is emphasized. "He led me all around them; there were very many of them spread over the valley, and they were very dry" (37:2). These two features—many and dry—convey a landscape of total fragmentation, as though the entire world had fallen apart into its basic constituents, never again to be reconstructed.

Dryness is precisely what makes renewed life impossible; here, nothing flows, nothing streams. God's question to Ezekiel is almost humiliatingly rhetorical: "Can these bones live again?" And the prophet's response is nothing more than a silent acquiescence: "I replied, 'O Lord God, only You know'" (37:3). When God translates the vision into contemporary terms, He refers to the dry bones as a mode of consciousness equivalent to total despair: "And He said to me, 'O mortal, these bones are the whole House of Israel. They say, "Our bones are dried up, our hope is gone; we are doomed"'" (37:11). The bones suggest not merely death but a desiccation of some vital stuff, for lack of which the bones lie in stark objective isolation. In this dry condition, there can be no hope;

> We had come to the end of the imagination,
> Inanimate in an inert savoir.
>
> —*Wallace Stevens,*
> *"The Plain Sense of Things"*

Imagination, ways of constructing parts into new wholes, intimate joinings and fruitions—these are the meaning of God's final promise. After all the bodies have been reconstructed, bones reassembled, sinews, flesh, skin, after breath is restored—"You shall know that I am the Lord" (37:6). The final stage of a knowledge that is not merely an "inert savoir," not an expression of a "mind of winter,"[32] is what makes hope possible. Beyond the humiliating blankness of "Lord God, only You know," it is a mode of dynamic, desirous connection with a world of infinite possibilities.

This is God's promise; but in the vision of the reconstructed bones, the promise is not realized. The first stage of resurrection is the wind, the spirit entering the bodies—"and they came to life and stood up on their feet, a vast multitude [*ḥayil gadol me'od me'od*]" (37:10). The imagery is of vast numbers—*me'od me'od*, very very many, as compared with the strewn bones that were merely *rabbot me'od*, very many (37:2). But there is no description of transformed consciousness, of motion. The host of reconstructed bodies stands with a fearsome rudimentary force, uninspired, almost robotlike. The despair of the House of Israel is not, therefore, assuaged.

Only when God speaks, sending a direct message to the people, does the word *yediah*, knowledge, recur. Twice, God says, "And you shall know that I am the Lord"; suffusing all the miraculous mechanics of reconstituted bodies, lungs filled with air, restoration to the Holy Land, is the ultimate gift of consciousness, connecting language and reality, narrating a story of transformation (37:13–14).

Within Ezekiel's vision, the possibility of full redemption from the "dry bones" condition remains a matter of hope: "You *shall* know that I am the Lord." Indeed, such an experience of passionate transformation is the radical desire of prophets and poets: a fluidity of becoming that represents the very pulse of life:

> *Will* transformation. Oh be inspired for the flame
> in which a Thing disappears and bursts into something else;
> the spirit of re-creation which masters this earthly form
> loves most the pivoting point where you are no longer yourself.
>
> What tightens into survival is already inert;
> how safe is it really in its inconspicuous gray?
> From far off a far greater hardness warns what is hard,
> and the absent hammer is lifted high!
>
> He who pours himself out like a stream is acknowledged at last by
>     Knowledge;
> and she leads him enchanted through the harmonious country
> that finishes often with starting, and with ending begins.[33]

Even Plato—who in his early dialogues had set the claims to genuine understanding of the philosopher, with his self-possessed good sense, far above those of the poet—came, in *Phaedrus*, to reassess his earlier position. Martha Nussbaum discusses this movement, from an ideal of self-possession (*sophrosune*) to a reappreciation of the virtues of *mania*, erotic appetite and passionate inspiration. In *Phaedrus*, Plato uses imagery of streaming, melting warmth, the flood of passion, the release of imprisoned waters, the growth of the soul's wings, which captures the "feeling of being in a state of *mania*. . . . The very madness criticized [previously by Plato] can be an important, even a necessary part of moral and philosophical development."[34]

This movement from self-possession to a more complex, inspired, and receptive vision of things is, I would suggest, relevant to the process that brings Jacob from a discrete, "mind of winter" view of his children to one that allows him to see them as flowing, feeding ("nursing") one another, growing, passionate, and capable of transformations.

The imagery of water, wine, and milk expresses this movement, as does the persistent animal imagery. Judah is a lion, Issachar a donkey, Dan a serpent, Naftali a hind, Joseph an ox, Benjamin a wolf. Most obviously, these metaphors exude vitality: the very word for animal is *ḥaya*, its root meaning "life," as, indeed, does the Latin root of the English word, "animal." The life force that Jacob senses in his sons is a capacity—the basic animal capacity—to procreate further life. Jacob's vision of his family as animals conveys a primal creative energy.

Rashi quotes from the Talmud,[35] referring to this animal imagery to explain the claim of the midwives, as they justify their failure to kill Israelite male babies (Exodus 1:19): " '*The Hebrew women are not like the Egyptian women: they are vigorous [ḥayot]*': They are compared to animals of the field, which need no midwives. And where are they compared to animals?—'a young lion,' 'a preying wolf.' "

The basic definition of an animal, a *ḥaya*, is that it can deal unaided with the life-business of procreation. Jacob sees in his children a similar vital competence to realize in the world what is potential within them, to tend to sustaining and increasing life.

As animal visions of this kind succeed one another, Jacob's conviction of blessing, of a significant creativity in his family, becomes more focused; until, at the end, he is able to vindicate the integrity of his own bed, in the word *ve-zot*—"this." It is a lucid focus gained, paradoxically, through the medium of the "other things," the "other words," that he has had to speak, in the "blank cold" of his poetic crisis. These words of a deflected purpose, the products of a failure, a forgetting, a blurring of focus, lead him by indirection, by the organic flow of their imagery, their contingency, to a blessing inconceivable at first.

## Jacob blesses his Egyptian grandsons: "They are mine"

The poetic crisis, the experience of the "blank," is, then, the model for our understanding of the theme of "blocking," of the "absence of God," that is so pervasive in midrashic readings of Jacob's deathbed words. A similar midrashic narrative attaches to that earlier scene where Jacob gives a special blessing to Joseph's children, Manasseh and Ephraim. Here, however, the tension of the sudden "blank" is more extreme and, on the face of it, inexplicable.

In slow motion, the Torah tells of Joseph bringing his two sons to his father, of Jacob struggling to sit up to greet and bless his beloved son. If there is any doubt as to the purpose of Joseph's visit, Rashi spells it out: he brings his sons "so that Jacob may bless them before his death" (48:1). Within the narrative gap, the silence about Joseph's purpose, the midrash detects an undertow of anxiety: " 'My sons were born in Egypt—will Jacob bless them nevertheless?' Therefore, when he went to his father, he took his two sons with him."[36] In another midrash, Osnat, his wife, urges Joseph to take their children to their grandfather, because "I have heard that if one receives a blessing from a righteous person, it is like receiving it from the Shekhina."[37] What emerges from these midrashic narratives is the anxiety of diffusion: the sons born in exile, the question of the coherence of the family, the need for a reaffirmation of the "presence of God."

Jacob begins his speech by referring to the past, to God's blessing of him at Luz (Beth-El) (48:3–4). This mode of beginning a blessing is a way of asserting stability: Jacob is not doing anything rash or unfounded when he declares, as he does in the next verse (48:5), that he is adopting his grandchildren as his own children.[38] He is simply decoding the enigmatic phrase in God's blessing: "I will make you fertile and numerous, making of you a *community of peoples.*"

This last phrase, as Rashi points out, refers to the expression that God had actually used: "A nation, yea a community of nations, shall descend from you" (35:11). Decoding precisely, therefore, Jacob understands that the "nation" meant Benjamin, the one son still unborn on Jacob's return to Canaan. But the "community of nations" constitutes a mystery unsolved till this day of Jacob's death; for Jacob had no more children, and at least two more seem to be promised in this phrase. Therefore, he concludes, this must refer to a "splitting" of one of his tribes—a doubling of rights and blessings for one of his sons; this gift he now bestows on Joseph: "Now, your two sons, who were born to you in the land of Egypt before I came you in Egypt, shall be mine; Ephraim and Manasseh shall be mine no less than Reuben and Simeon" (48:5).

"Now" conveys Jacob's intention to interpret God's promise as applying to his two grandsons. There is a sense of embarking on a new project:
in adopting Ephraim and Manasseh, he includes both Egyptian-born
children—the first fruits of exile and fragmentation, of an "otherness"
that might indeed invite questions about the "integrity of his bed"—
within the "envelope" of his own identity.

These are the children of separation and forgetting (Manasseh is so
named because "God has made me forget completely my hardship and
my parental home," and Ephraim because "God has made me fertile in
the land of my affliction" [41:51–52]). Jacob re-members them into the
structure of promise and blessing on the most intimate level.

For his core statement is *li hem . . . yiheyu li*—"they shall be mine"
(lit., to me). The dative form for possession is, as we have seen,[39] the
characteristic stamp of Jacob's being in the world. He, alone among the
patriarchs, is described everywhere as acquiring property—cattle, sheep,
servants, but also wives and children—a thickening envelope of things
and people belonging to him, attached to him—indicated by the simple
idiom *va-yehi lo*—"they were to him." This "envelope" is an index to his
vitality, his control over an ever more complicated reality. It is a fulfillment of God's promise: "You shall spread out [*u-faratzta*] to the west and
to the east, to the north and to the south" (28:14). "So the man grew
exceedingly prosperous [*va-yifrotz . . . me'od me'od*—lit., spread out very,
very much] and came to own [*va-yehi lo*—lit., there were to him] large
flocks, maidservants and menservants, camels and asses" (30:43).

## "*W*ho are these?"—the poetic crisis

By the work of his hands, he has realized his own power, economically,
sexually. And now, again using his hands to contain and to bless, he speaks
the same idiom with almost primitive passion: *li hem*—"they are mine."
What had seemed to spin off into the alien deathworld of Egypt—foreign
grandchildren, born in oblivion—he adopts as integral parts of his own
wholeness.

What follows is all the more enigmatic. There is, first, a strange
reference, apparently unconnected to this adoption project, to the death
of Rachel: "I . . . when I was returning from Padan, Rachel died, to my
sorrow [lit., upon me], while I was journeying in the land of Canaan,

when still some distance short of Ephrath; and I buried her there on the road to Ephrath (now Bethlehem)" (48:7).

That haunting, intrusive first person—"I . . . died upon me" betrays a profound trace of feeling, an involvement with the radical question of his own life. It is poised against the *lekha yiheyu*—"they shall be yours" of the previous verse: Joseph's later children will be his own—but "as for me. . . . she died on, for me. . . ." What is the suppressed narrative that links these verses ("they are *mine*. . . . as for *me*. . . . she died for, on me. . . .")? About to bless his grandchildren as his own children, Jacob is apparently caught up in a ground swell of emotion that is ultimately—and in no crudely narcissistic sense—about himself.

Stranger yet is the following passage: "Noticing Joseph's sons, Israel asked, 'Who are these?'" On the face of it, this must be one of the most startling moments in the entire Torah. Jacob has just been declaring his intent to adopt these children; he turns, sees them, and clearly does not recognize them. What is the reader to imagine? That he is not familiar with them, that they have grown beyond recognition, since their last visit, that they are dressed in Egyptian fashion (as one midrash in fact suggests), that he is blind (but this, if it is the crucial factor, should be narrated here, and not two verses later [v. 10]—instead, the text insists, "Israel *saw* the children of Joseph")?[40]

Midrash Tanḥuma heightens the tension of the question: "Did he really not recognize them? But surely they sat in his presence every day and occupied themselves with Torah? And now he says, 'Who are these?'—after they attended him for the seventeen years he was in Egypt, he did not recognize them?" Then it offers a radical answer: "He saw Jeroboam ben Nevat and Ahab ben Omri—idolators, who would descend from Ephraim; and the holy spirit departed from him."[41]

According to this midrash, Jacob looks at his grandchildren and sees evil and alienation engendered by them: kings of misrule and worshipers of strange gods. His gaze instantly turns blank: "Who are these?" expresses a rupture, a dryness, an "inert savoir." In this condition, he can clearly not bless them. A certain kind of vision is essential to blessing as it is to poetry.[42] What he sees throws him into silence.

Rashi subtly alters his Tanḥuma source: "He sought to bless them but the Divine Presence departed from him, because Jeroboam and Ahab were destined to issue from Ephraim and Jehu and his sons from Manasseh." In his version, Jacob simply experiences the blank, without seeing visions of evil kings. He intends to bless, and knows that God has departed. His question, "Who are these?," refers directly to Ephraim and Manasseh (and not to the future kings): it expresses his horrified alienation in the indubitable experience of the moment. What can be the nature of these children, if such a blank cold suddenly possesses him? The explanation about the evil kings is offered to the reader but plays no part in Jacob's consciousness. For him, there is only the unmediated, undeniable fact of the blank.

Joseph's reply is then read strongly by Rashi: " '*And Joseph said to his father, "They are my sons, whom God has given me here*" ' [*ba-zeh*]: *bazeh* indicates that Joseph showed him his document of betrothal and his marriage contract, and Joseph supplicated for mercy about this. Then, the holy spirit rested upon him" (48:9). Joseph allays Jacob's anxiety about "Who are these?" — about the meaningless proliferation of his life — with the word *ba-zeh* — "with *this*": he points to the marriage document that testifies to his own intentionality, even in the midst of exile and oblivion. *Zeh* is the word that expresses focus, clarity, integrity of vision. For lack of it, Jacob has been lost in the "waste and welter" of the unintelligible *eileh* — "Who are *these*?" — just as, later, he will be unable to preface his blessings to his whole family with *ve-zot ha-berakha*.

Joseph assuages Jacob's anxiety, so that, eventually, Jacob is able to bless Ephraim and Manasseh. But when, precisely, does inspiration return? When is the "universal blank" transformed into a readable "book of knowledge"? Rashi gives one answer: immediately after he has been shown Joseph's *ketuba*, his marriage document, Jacob's power to read the world in the mode of blessing returns: "Bring them up to me, that I may bless them" (48:9). The crisis, essentially, is over.

There are, however, other, more tortured readings. In *Bereshit Rabbati*, for instance, the crisis continues unresolved through the description of Jacob's blindness, his embraces of his children, till the point where Joseph withdraws in anguish at his father's anguish and prostrates himself: "And Israel said to Joseph, 'I never expected to see you again, and here God has let me see your children as well.' Joseph then removed them from his knees, and bowed low with face to the ground" (48:11–12).

In a deliberate misreading, the midrash gives us this prostration, not as a bow of gratitude to his father for forthcoming blessing, but as a final desperate — and lonely — entreaty to God to transform Jacob's vision:

"[When you disappeared,] I did not debate in my mind [*lo pilalti*—lit., I did not *think*, engage in all the resources of thought about you],[43] 'Is he alive or dead?' But I cut off my thinking/hoping [*sivri* has the double meaning of rational thought and openness to possibilities] from my Creator about you. And I said: 'My way is hidden from the Lord' [Isaiah 40:27]."

When Jacob saw that the Holy Spirit had departed from him, he began speaking to Joseph: "I think it is because I cut off from God my thinking/hoping about you that now God does not answer me with inspiration about your children. . . . I have nothing to plead [lit., no opening of the mouth] to appeal for His mercy. You go out and appeal for mercy, that the Holy Spirit may rest upon me, to bless your children." Immediately, Joseph took his children out from between his knees, and when he saw his father's distress, he took them and fell on his face before God. . . . And immediately, the word of God leapt [lit.] upon Jacob.[44]

In this radical midrash, Jacob assembles the fragments of his own life. He holds himself culpable of despair: he has closed a certain inner debate, in which hope might have held open the dialectical possibilities of his situation. Such hope had carried too high a price. There was a paradoxical ease in reducing the complexity of the debate to a single thin strand of despair, in interrupting the exhausting process of thought, the finality of the blank. Jacob quotes a prooftext from Isaiah: "My way is hidden from the Lord."[45] Essentially, his feeling was that his way was hidden from *himself*: it is precisely the experience of the blank, of the too-dense, too-empty human condition, that baffles him into silence.

Now, again, such a paralyzing silence grips him; but by now, he is ready to hold himself accountable for despair. Because he cut short a certain vital inner discourse at that time, he now has no "opening of the mouth"; a genius for hopeful interpretations has dried at the root. Only Joseph can save the situation. Separating himself from his father's despair, he regains by the passion of his own vision a time of grace for his father.

What the midrash conveys so wonderfully is a sense of the infrastructure of Jacob's spiritual life. Daringly, it evokes a Jacob who thinks himself accountable for his own blankness in the face of a tormenting complexity. The deep traces of old feeling about expansiveness and harmony, contingency and transcendent purpose, underlie this penultimate moment of poetic crisis. But why—at this least appropriate of moments—does the sensation of the "universal blank" overwhelm him? Why—just after so bravely asserting that his Egyptian grandchildren, in all their apparent otherness, "are mine," are integrated into his vision of his life—does the center not hold, why do things fall apart?

## The memory of Rachel: unity and fragmentation

Jacob's mysterious reference to Rachel's death and burial comes between Jacob's intention to adopt Ephraim and Manasseh and the moment of poetic crisis. Here, I would suggest, is the bridge, the thought that discomposes Jacob to the point of paralysis.

Enigmatically, he pivots the sentence on himself: "As for me. . . . She died on, for me. . . ." Is this a certain guilt speaking, as Jacob remembers how he cursed the unknown thief of the Teraphim (31:32)?[46] Or how he delayed fulfilling his vow to return to Beth El, to return to his father, and assume the authority, the originality of his own being?[47] Or is he explaining that Rachel's death was, on the level of erotic feeling, a desiccation of his own faculty for vital feeling (*meita alai*—"her death was my death")?[48] But why does he focus on the place of Rachel's burial—"there, on the way to Ephrath"?

Rashi quotes a midrash that implicitly resolves all the enigmas:

> *"And I buried her there"*: and I did not carry her even to Bethlehem to bring her into the Land. And I know that you have a complaint in your heart against me. But know that it was by the word of God that I buried her there, so that she might be of help to her children: when Nebuzaradan sends them into exile, they will pass by there, and Rachel will come out of her grave and weep and entreat God for mercy for them, as it is said, "A voice is heard in Ramah—wailing, bitter weeping—Rachel weeping for her children. She refuses to be comforted for her children, who are gone. Thus said the Lord: Restrain your voice from weeping, your eyes from shedding tears; for there is reward for your labor, says the Lord" (Jeremiah 31:15–16).

In this poignant passage, Jacob feels guilt—projected as Joseph's resentment[49]—at burying Rachel so unceremoniously. But this burial was designed by God, so that in a time of need, centuries later, Rachel would be strategically placed so as to intercede for her exiled children.

A closer reading of Rashi leaves us uneasy, however, even on the most factual level. In what sense is it true to say that Jacob did not carry her body "into the Land"? Was she buried abroad? Clearly, the text describes her place of burial ("near Ephrath, which is Bethlehem"), and Rashi himself makes the point that Benjamin was the only one of Jacob's children to be born *within* the borders of the Land (35:18). Rachel's death and burial followed immediately. To "carry her into the Land" may, therefore, simply indicate a failure to bury her in recognizably holy land — which, in the time of the Patriarchs, may have meant land legally purchased by them for burial plots. This suggestion[50] reinforces the sense that Jacob might have acted to create a real place, consciously consecrated, to bury his loved wife, rather than simply bury her in a "no place" (*ba-derekh* suggests the transitional space between place and place).

It is this "liminality" that Ramban emphasizes, as he scrutinizes the text for a basis for Rashi's midrashic narrative. That basis he finds in the word *ba-derekh*, repeated, signifying a strategic placing on the route her children would take on *their* way out to exile. She is buried at the interstice between holy land and exile. This is not a proper burial at all, as Rashi's midrashic source makes clear:[51] the problem is not that she was buried apart from Jacob, but that such an unceremonious burial leaves her exposed, unplaced — and therefore responsive to her children's pain at their point of dispersal.

Jacob recalls the pain, guilt, and strange promise associated with Rachel's burial, at the very moment when he is reintegrating the lost fragments of his life — the two grandchildren of Rachel, born of beauty, jealousy, hatred, and exile.

But there is a further dimension to what is stirred in him, as he recalls Rachel's tears for her children. Maharal, in his super-commentary to Rashi,[52] discusses the peculiar prestige of Rachel's tears. What, he asks, is Rachel's power of intercession? Why does God instruct Jacob to bury her so that it is *her* tears that will restore her children from exile? Why does she cry more than the other mothers of Jacob's children? He refers to *Eikhah Rabbah*:[53]

> Rachel says to God, "What have my children done, that You have brought such punishment upon them? If it is because of their idolatry [called *tzara*, a rival wife] — I loved my husband, Jacob, and he worked for me for seven years, and in the end my father gave my sister to him in marriage. And I constrained my love for my husband and handed over

to my sister the identifying signs. . . . I am flesh and blood, while You
are the compassionate King—how much more merciful should You be
to them!" And God answers, "There is a reward for your labor."

Rachel's entreaties win God's ear as no other intercession succeeds in
doing (Abraham, Isaac, and Jacob try in vain). Maharal understands her
to be speaking of theological issues—monotheism and idolatry, sin and
forgiveness—in terms of her most intimate experience. This is the core of
Maharal's discussion. The story of Jacob and Rachel's love for each other
becomes a paradigm for metaphysical reality:

> Rachel knew that there is a rightness in Jacob's marrying two wives, for
> this world, which is a world of division and separation, does not lend
> itself to total unity. If Jacob had had only the one wife of his desire, the
> family and the nation would have been unified, the basic split of the
> people into two kingdoms (Judah from Leah, and Ephraim from
> Rachel)—a split that will endure till messianic times—would have been
> avoided. But because Rachel saw that such a split is congruous with the
> nature of this world, she suppressed her love and jealousy. She, there-
> fore, is uniquely qualified to plead that God similarly forgive Israel for a
> sin—idolatry, the "rival wife"—that is a direct outcome of the frag-
> mented reality of this world. She is most personally tutored in the pain
> of incompleteness; God listens to the weeping that teaches Him about
> the world He has created.

Maharal's assumption is that the personal dramas of the patriarchs and
matriarchs are always indicative of metaphysical reality. Here, he touches
on the classic philosophical problem of the One and the Many, and
proposes a tragic acceptance of this world as one of multiple, conflicting
versions of truth. Without a single indubitable focus, human beings
naturally tend to "other gods," to "rival wives." This, Rachel argues, is in
the very nature of this world, as God made it, and as she has experienced
it, in her most intimate knowledge of "otherness." This is not a world of
perfect love, of pure forms, but rather one of diffracted, partial relationships, of kaleidoscopic, shifting appearances. Rachel, passionately in love
with her husband, nevertheless achieves a kind of acquiescence, even a
muted optimism, in her acceptance of the "rival wife."

For Rachel, in Maharal's reading, is poised at the fulcrum of unity and
fragmentation. She personifies total passion—Jacob works for her and
only for her; she is the primary and ultimate symbol of integration, the

dream mother of the Jewish people. It is she, therefore, who suffers the diffusion and exile of her children, accepting the tragic "rightness" of such displacements, yet expressing, in that very acquiescence, the most poignant appeal to the creator of such a world. "If I could tolerate incompleteness, fragmentation of my desire, why cannot You?" And God, moved by the human being reinventing the world in the shape of her own experience, promises reward for her "labor" — hope for ultimate integrations.

The point is a fine one. Rachel reflects back to God the split reality of a human being. Exposed, buried in no place (*ba-derekh*), in the liminal space in which exile begins, she acts as a potent magnet: the very force of her yearning will draw her children back toward coherence. In all their diffusion, they will live with an undertow of desire for oneness. It is this desire, the eternal yearning that Rachel, buried at the border, will restlessly articulate.

Her "labor," her significant act that earns reward, is simply her tears. God bids her restrain them, but she never will — until "the end," the time beyond history and its shatterings, when "those who sowed in tears shall reap in joy" (Psalms 126:5). Till then, she "refuses to be comforted"; a terrible, disconsolate passion possesses her. Like Jacob mourning for his lost son Joseph ("He refused to be comforted" [37:35]), she cannot accept comfort, for that would mean final despair; the lost fragments would never cohere again.[54]

Her fierce tears are a response to her children's fate — "who are gone." *Ki einenu* — they are not, they have "gone from her sight." She longs for them, strains to see them, and sees only their absence. But like Jacob, whom Judah painfully records as saying of Joseph, "He is gone from me. . . . and I have not seen him since" (44:28), Rachel draws paradoxical, stubborn hope from this ambiguous notion of *einenu*. She will not be comforted, she refuses the simplifications of despair, because her children's absence is situated in the refracted, limited perspectives of this world. The word *einenu* itself contains skeptical reservations:[55] human perception is partial, subject to constant change in a world of "division and separation."

Rachel's sense of what "is not" engenders imaginings beyond the visible: these are the "labor" of her tears.

> For there is a reward for your labor — declares the Lord:
> They shall return from the enemy's land.

And there is hope for your future — declares the Lord:
Your children shall return to their country.

God rewards her with "hope" alone; for the passage is circular in its
implications, it comes to no final apotheosis. God may tell her to hold
back her tears; but it is just her refusal to do this, to "be comforted," that
constitutes the work of faith in this world.

In Maharal's reading, therefore, heroic complexity, a kind of tragic
optimism, radiates from the figure of Rachel, buried "by the way." It is
this painful radiance, I suggest, that overwhelms Jacob's memory, just at
the moment when he is about to synthesize the exiled fragments of his
world. The thought of Rachel becomes a mirror, reflecting, same and yet
inverted, some of his own deepest dilemmas. For, if she could tolerate the
diffractions of her experience, Jacob, it seems, cannot. Rachel can hold a
position at the margin between reality and appearances, on the border
between meaning and meaninglessness. For Jacob, the tension underlying such a position is sometimes unbearable. At the very moment of
reintegration, it precipitates him into the blank.

## Between meaning and mystery

Robert Alter writes of "the most characteristic moments of biblical
narrative": "The world is seen as offering all sorts of access to human
understanding, but there is also no absolute fit between the nature of
reality and the human mind. The biblical tale is fashioned in ways that
repeatedly remind us of that ontological discrepancy."[56]

This ontological discrepancy is one meaning of exile. Rachel's sense of
the fragmentary occlusions, limited perspectives, and blind spots of this
world is an extension of the core symbolism of exile. On his deathbed,
Jacob lives the repeated shocks to coherence that his children will experience over thousands of years. In most intimate form, he suffers the
blanking of meaning, the poetic crisis, that threatens to seal off language,
as well as vision.

In this peculiar suffering, he serves as paradigm to his children, in
their looming worlds of exile. As Ramban notices, in his opening comment to the Parsha, Jacob dying in Egypt is an emblematic figure,
premonitory of those exiles, that will endure much longer than expected:
"And our exile has extended immensely over us, its end is not known, as

the ends of previous exiles were, and we are in it like the dead who say, 'Our bones dried up, we are cut off' (Ezekiel 37:11)."[57]

Unlike Rachel, however, Jacob's work is not to be the work of tears, but of words. He must find "other words" to accommodate the plain sense of things to human need. The disenchantments, the dry incoherencies of exile are to be the very subject of his poem. "Not to have is the beginning of desire."[58] Between meaning and meaninglessness, he must find the energy to create a world; for "the words of the world are life of the world."[59]

The prophet Amos articulates this idea succinctly: *dirshuni vi-ḥeyu* — "Seek Me and live" (5:4). Out of the human response to God's absence, to the unintelligible and the fragmented, life is generated. *Dirshuni*, moreover, means the process of inquiry, interpretation, re-membering, that creates meaning. *Derisha, midrash*, is the work of continuing translations in the face of mystery.

A story by Italo Calvino will help us realize the abstraction. In "Serpents and Skulls," Mr. Palomar is visiting the ruins of Tula, ancient capital of the Toltecs.

A Mexican friend accompanies him, an impassioned and eloquent expert on pre-Columbian civilizations, who tells him beautiful legends about Quetzalcoatl. . . . In Mexican archeology every statue, every object, every detail of a bas-relief stands for something that stands for something else that stands, in turn, for yet another something. . . . Mr. Palomar's Mexican friend pauses at each stone, transforms it into a cosmic tale, an allegory, a moral reflection.

A group of schoolchildren moves among the ruins: stocky boys with the features of the Indios, descendants perhaps of the builders of these temples, wearing a plain white uniform, like Boy Scouts, with blue neckerchiefs. The boys are led by a teacher not much taller than they are and only a little more adult, with the same round, dark, impassive face. They climb the top steps of the pyramid, stop beneath the columns, the teacher tells what civilization they belong to, what century, what stone they are carved from, then concludes, "We don't know what they mean," and the group follows him down the steps. At each step, each figure carved in a relief or on a column, the teacher supplies some facts and then invariably adds, "We don't know what it means."

. . . Though Mr. Palomar continues to follow the explanation of his friend acting as guide, he always ends up crossing the path of the schoolboys and overhearing the teacher's words. He is fascinated by his friend's wealth of mythological references: the play of interpretation, allegorical readings, have always seemed to him a supreme exercise of the mind. But he feels attracted also by the opposite attitude of the schoolteacher: what had at first seemed only a brisk lack of interest is being revealed to him as a scholarly and pedagogical position, a methodological choice by this serious and conscientious young man, a rule from which he will not swerve. . . . The refusal to comprehend more than what the stones show us is perhaps the only way to evince respect for their secret; trying to guess is a presumption, a betrayal of that true, lost meaning.

. . . The boys go by. The teacher says, "This is the wall of the serpents. Each serpent has a skull in its mouth. We don't know what they mean."

Mr. Palomar's friend cannot contain himself: "Yes, we do! It's the continuity of life and death; the serpents are life, the skulls are death. Life is life because it bears death with it, and death is death because there is no life without death. . . ."

The boys listen, mouths agape, black eyes dazed. Mr. Palomar thinks that every translation requires another translation and so on. . . . And yet he knows he could never suppress in himself the need to translate, to move from one language to another, from concrete figures to abstract words, to weave and reweave a network of analogies. Not to interpret is impossible, as refraining from thinking is impossible. Once the school group has disappeared around a corner, the stubborn voice of the little teacher resumes: "*No es verdad*, it is not true, what that *señor* said. We don't know what they mean."[60]

"Not to interpret is impossible, as refraining from thinking is impossible." And yet, the imperviousness, the closedness of the fragments demands a "respect for their secret," for their "true lost meaning." Exquisitely poised between this respect for what is hidden, the forbidding blank, and the need to translate, to understand—though provisionally—that very enigma, Mr. Palomar communicates a radical and all-but-paralyzing paradox.

Precisely where primary, privileged enlightenments have failed, the need to translate, to seek meaning through the "other words" of human discourse, remains the endless project of human life. As in the Mexican friend's interpretation of the serpents and the skulls, "death is death because there is no life without death": what is hidden, what has been repressed, generates an ever-new "gaiety of language."[61]

Mourning the loss of the "brightness and the gleam," Wordsworth comes in the end to give thanks precisely for

> those obstinate questionings
> Of sense and outward things,
> Fallings from us, vanishings;
> Blank misgivings of a Creature
> Moving about in worlds not realized.

*(Intimations of Immortality)*

The worlds of exile are "not realized," blank, unintelligible, for Jacob, as they will be for his children. But, insists Amos, in the face of devastation and exile, *dirshuni vi-ḥeyu*: "Seek Me, inquire for Me, interrogate Me, weave networks of meaning about My hidden face." And Jacob, containing within himself the infinite tension of life in such worlds not realized, must utter words that will merge mystery and meaning, and teach his children to speak themselves toward blessing.

# Notes

## INTRODUCTION

1. Gerald Bruns, *Inventions: Writing, Textuality, and Understanding in Literary History* (Yale University Press: 1982), 1–2.
2. George Steiner, *Real Presences* (University of Chicago Press: 1989), 139.
3. Steiner, 139.
4. Franz Kafka, *Parables and Paradoxes* (Schocken: 1975), 31.
5. Nadezhda Mandelstam, *Hope against Hope* (Atheneum: 1970), 70–71.

## BERESHIT

1. Lev Shestov, *Athens and Jerusalem* (Simon and Schuster: 1968), 75.
2. Michael Fishbane, *Text and Texture* (Schocken: 1979), 8.
3. *Bereshit Rabbah* 5:3. Other sources are quoted in the commentary of Rabbenu Bahya on Leviticus 2:13. R. Hutner bases a discussion of the problematics of human free choice on this midrash (*Pahad Yitzhak*, Rosh Hashanah 13:1).
4. Rosh Hashanah 31a: "The Psalm assigned to the second day of the week is Psalm 48, beginning, 'The Lord is great and much acclaimed,' because on the second day He divided up His works and reigned over them."
5. J. Berakhot 1:5.
6. E.g., *Va-yikra Rabbah* 14:9.
7. E.g., *Bereshit Rabbah* 20:17: "The woman in childbirth vacillates about the costs of her sexual role; she therefore is obligated to bring a 'fluttering' sacrifice [birds]"!
8. Aristotle, *Metaphysics*, 1015a, 32.
9. Kenneth Burke, "The First Three Chapters of Genesis: Principles of Governance Stated Narratively," in *Genesis: Modern Critical Interpretations*, ed. Harold Bloom (Chelsea House: 1986), 17.
10. See Ramban and Radak on 1:28.
11. Gaston Bachelard, *The Poetics of Space* (Beacon Press: 1969), 173.

12. See 9:1–2, 6–7: "God blessed Noah and his sons, and said to them, 'Be fertile and increase, and fill the earth. The fear and dread of you shall be upon all the beasts of the earth and upon all the birds of the sky—everything with which the earth is astir [*tirmoss*]—and upon all the fish of the sea; they are given into your hand. . . . Whoever sheds the blood of man, by man shall his blood be shed; For in His image, did God make man. Be fertile, then, and increase; abound [*shirtzu*] on the earth and increase on it.'" The Rabbis (see Rashi, 9:6) define this as both a blessing and a commandment—the imperative of "après le déluge." Even the word *sheretz*, with its specifically reptilian quality, is now incorporated into the imperative of human fertility. But here, too, the proliferation motif is set beside the motif of man's godlikeness.

13. Elias Canetti, *Crowds and Power* (Penguin: 1973), 109.

14. Ibid., 126.

15. Ibid., 128–29.

16. Bachelard, *The Poetics of Space*, 173.

17. *Bereshit Rabbah*, 26:16; B. Sotah 34b.

18. Ibn Ezra explains the name *Nephilim* as a reference to the dejection (the "fallen heart") experienced by those who are dumbfounded at their stature.

19. Stanley Cavell, *Conditions Handsome and Unhandsome* (University of Chicago Press: 1990), 47.

20. William Shakespeare, *Hamlet*, III, i, 121–29.

21. *Tanḥuma*, Noah, 18.

22. Quoted in Elias Canetti, *Kafka's Other Trial* (Penguin: 1982), 68.

23. B. Ḥulin 60a.

24. Gur Arye, 1:16.

25. B. Baba Batra 74b. See also Gur Arye on 1:21.

26. See, too, 5:1–2.

27. B. Ketubot 8a. See also B. Berakhot 61a and B. Eruvin 18b.

28. B. Ḥagiga 16a.

29. *Bereshit Rabbah*, 99:12.

30. *Devarim Rabbah* 2:22.

31. B. Sanhedrin 37a.

32. W. B. Yeats, "Sailing to Byzantium."

33. Mircea Eliade, *The Sacred and the Profane*, trans. Willard R. Trusk (Harvest: 1959), 20.

34. B. Berakhot 61a.

35. Franz Kafka, *Parables and Paradoxes* (Schocken: 1975), 31.

36. *Pirkei d'Rabbi Eliezer*, chap. 11

37. See *Pirkei d'Rabbi Eliezer*, 11, note 38 (Radal).

38. Aristotle, *Metaphysics*, 1015a, 32.

39. *New Yorker*, 17 December 1990, 48.

40. Erich Neumann, *Art and the Creative Unconscious* (Princeton University Press: 1973), 193.

41. Rainer Maria Rilke, *The Sonnets to Orpheus*, trans. Stephen Mitchell (Touchstone: 1986), 95.

42. B. Sanhedrin 38b.

43. B. Eruvin 100b.

44. The word *etzev* occurs again in this early part of the biblical narrative, when Adam is punished: "Cursed be the ground because of you; by toil [*be-itzavon*] shall you eat of it" (3:17). Rashi's comment stresses the unpredictable, willful nature of the earth's response to man's curse. Man will be compelled by necessity to accept the "thorns and thistles" that the earth will offer him, after he has invested his best resources in it. This doom is reflected again later, when Noah is born, and there is new hope for "relief from our work and for the toil [*itz'von*] of our hands, out of the very soil which the Lord placed under a curse" (5:29). There, again, Rashi reiterates his theme of *itzavon* as the frustration of the worker who sows wheat and reaps thorns and thistles. There, *itzavon* is clearly associated with the "hands-on" involvement and risks that are confronted by creativity.

45. Emmanuel Levinas, *Nine Talmudic Readings*, trans. Annette Aronowicz (Indiana University Press: 1990), 14.

46. *Pirkei d'Rabbi Eliezer*, 11. There is a number of different versions of the timetable of the sixth day—see, for instance, B. Sanhedrin 38b.

47. B. Sanhedrin 38b.

48. Canetti, *Crowds and Power*, 451.

49. B. Megilla 31a.

50. J. Nazir 7:2.

51. *Ba-midbar Rabbah* 11.

52. *Bereshit Rabbah* 19:16.

53. Ibid., 21:9.

54. *Shemot Rabbah* 32:1.

55. Shakespeare, *Hamlet*, III, iii, 36.

56. *Perush HaGra*, Jonah, 1:3.

57. Yeats, "The Second Coming."

58. See *Bereshit Rabbah* 9:5: "In R. Meir's text of the Torah, they found it written: 'Behold it was very good'—behold, death was good."

59. *Midrash Ha-Gadol*, 3:23.

60. *Tanḥuma*, Massei, 11.

61. *Midrash Ha-Gadol*, 3:24.

62. René Descartes, *Second Meditation*.

63. Mircea Eliade, *Myth and Reality* (Harper & Row: 1963), 43–44.

64. See *Bereshit Rabbah* 17:5 for an account of man's "wisdom" in naming not only the animals but himself and God too.

65. The pivotal role of language is stressed by Rashi. God asks, redundantly, "Where are you?" only in order that Adam's version of his experience should not be inhibited by fear. God's desire is to "enter into words with him." Adam's response is inadequate to the occasion.

66. See the complex image of the cradle, in which man sleeps before Creation (*Bereshit Rabbah* 2:3). The earth-nurse watches the cradle with apprehension (*toha u-boha*); the sleeping infant is contained, at peace, in this primary reality. But a secondary reality is already implicit: the sleeping child will awake to his full powers and destroy both himself and the world.

67. Another version of Rashi: On the sixth of Sivan, when Israel received the Torah, all the works of beginning were strengthened, and it was as if the world was created then.

68. B. Shabbat 88a.

69. *Pesikta Rabbati*, 21 (100a).

70. *Va-yikra Rabbah* 36:4. I have slightly changed the play on words here, to make it accessible in English.

71. Jerome Bruner, *Actual Minds, Possible Worlds* (Harvard University Press: 1986), 95.

72. Ibid., 97.

73. Ibid., 102–3. Bruner here cites the famous "map," popularized by the physiologist Lord Adrian in his *The Basis of Sensation*, "depicting the monkey with each part of the body enlarged to correspond to its density of sensory innervation—its lips and tongue in this caricature grossly larger than its trunk and torso."

74. *Bereshit Rabbah* 3:9.

75. B. Shabbat 88a.

76. Levinas, *Nine Talmudic Readings*, 45.

77. Ibid., 42.

78. Mircea Eliade, *The Myth of the Eternal Return* (Harper and Row: 1969), 92.

79. Ibid., 34.

80. Bachelard, *Poetics of Space*, 198.

81. *Shemot Rabbah* 29:9.

82. The angels are of course the paradigms of "standing" beings. Their substantiality is not physical, but rather a matter of specific, unambiguous identity and role.

83. B. Gittin 43a.

84. See *Pahad Yitzhak*, Rosh Hashanah, 7:10.

85. Neumann, *Art and the Creative Unconscious*, 162–63, 196.

86. Shestov quotes Spinoza as representative of the "Athenian" conception of a reality entirely constrained by Necessity: *non ridere, non lugere, neque*

*detestari, sed intellegere*—"not to laugh, not lament, not to curse, but to understand" (*Athens and Jerusalem*, 195).

87. Richard Rorty, *Contingency, Irony, and Solidarity* (Cambridge University Press: 1989), 96.

88. The skeptic asks: "Does God see the *nolad*—that which is born . . . ?" R. Yehoshua answers: "*Nolad?* Was there born to you a son?" His retort brings the "philosopher" down to earth, to the existential knowledge of fathers of mortal children. It is here, and not in the sublime certainties of metaphysical knowledge, that human understanding of God begins.

89. *Bereshit Rabbah* 27:4.

90. The source for the ending is *Bereshit Rabbah* 8:9.

91. *Bereshit* is the construct form of the noun. So, "In the beginning of the creation of heaven and earth. . . ."

92. Rilke, *Sonnets to Orpheus*, second part, 12.

## NOAḤ

1. There is a midrash that connects Noah's birth with Adam's death, and the end of the curse ("Cursed be the ground because of you . . . until you return to the ground" [3:17, 19]). (*P'sikta d'Rabbi Eliezer*, in *Torah Shelemah* 5:81).

2. Martin Buber, "The Tree of Knowledge," in *On the Bible* (Schocken: 1982), 17.

3. Joseph is also described as "righteous," in Amos 2:6, and he, too, is described as feeding and sustaining his world.

4. See Ramban on 6:9.

5. See 6:5, 12–13, 17; 7:4.

6. *Bereshit Rabbah* 29:4

7. Compare *Torah Shelemah* 6:37 on the wordplay of *gopher* (the wood of the ark) and *gophrit* (sulfurous fire).

8. *Tanḥuma*, Re'eh, 3.

9. See Rashi on Genesis 6:4: one third of the world was flooded in the time of Enosh.

10. See Rashi on 6:13.

11. See Ramban on 7:18: "The waters swelled. . . ."

12. Rashi's main source is *Bereshit Rabbah* 26:5.

13. *Bereshit Rabbah* 32:8.

14. See, for example, *Tanḥuma*, Ba-midbar, 26.

15. The reference to the Tower of Babel generation is missing from the first edition of Rashi. There are, however, midrashic sources that suggest that at least some of the builders of the Tower were also destroyed. See *Bereshit*

*Rabbah* 38:16. This midrash plays on the words *va-yafetz* and *va-yatzef*—"God *scattered* the builders" becomes "God *swept them away.*"

16. *Tanḥuma*, Tissa, 17.

17. *Tanḥuma*, Va-yera, 8.

18. *Tanḥuma Yashan*, Va-yera 10.

19. *Bereshit Rabbah* 52:8.

20. *Va-yikra Rabbah* 20:2.

21. *Bereshit Rabbah* 28:2.

22. *Tanḥuma*, Noah, 11.

23. See, for example, *Sefat Emet* 5662, p.40.

24. *Sifrei*, Ha'azinu, 7.

25. Leviticus 20:17: "If a man marries his sister, the daughter of either his father or his mother, so that he sees her nakedness and she sees his nakedness, it is a disgrace (*ḥesed hu*)." Rashi notes that in Aramaic *ḥisuda* is the term for "disgrace" — which leaves us with the paradox of *ḥesed* as root for two contrary ideas, "grace" and "disgrace." Ramban clearly finds this distasteful and asserts (claiming the support of the Sages) that *ḥesed* posits the right, generous mode of relationship that the sinner is transgressing: instead of disinterested concern to marry off his sister, he demonstrates selfish lust. However, the radical possibilities in a paradoxical conception of *ḥesed* remain intriguing.

26. *Bereshit Rabbah* 26:5.

27. See Mary Douglas, *Purity and Danger* (Penguin: 1966), 145, on the dangers inherent in margins.

28. See Bachelard, *Poetics of Space*, 224: "How concrete everything becomes in the world of the spirit when an object, a mere door, can give images of hesitation, temptation, desire, security, welcome and respect. If one were to give an account of all the doors one has closed and opened, of all the doors one would like to re-open, one would have to tell the story of one's entire life."

29. *Bereshit Rabbah* 38:6.

30. Rorty, *Contingency, Irony, and Solidarity*, 177–78.

31. Ibid., 165.

32. Ibid., 163.

33. Ibid., 158.

34. Ibid., 160.

35. Bachelard, *Poetics of Space*, 222.

36. See Rashi, 6:11. Targum Onkelos translates *ḥamas* (which Rashi, in the wake of the midrash, translates as *gezel*, "robbery") with the word *ḥatufin*, "snatching," "rapaciousness."

37. See *Bereshit Rabbah* 27:3 for an analogy between the uses of the word *rabbah* in both narratives and the fates of both worlds.

38. Nahum M. Sarna, *Understanding Genesis* (Schocken: 1970), 52.

39. Rambam, *Mishneh Torah, Hilkhot Melakhim* 9:14.

40. The requirement of *dinim* — of instituting the structures of legality in society — is one of the Seven Noachide Commandments.

41. See *Bereshit Rabbah* 70:12.

42. B. Sanhedrin 108b. See also *Meshekh Hokhmah* on 8:19.

43. Gordon S. Haight, *George Eliot: A Biography* (Clarendon Press: 1968), 464.

44. *Tanhuma*, Noah, 7.

45. See his commentary to Job 24:20.

46. *Bereshit Rabbah* 29:4.

47. André Neher, *The Exile of the Word* (Jewish Publication Society: 1981), 101.

48. *Tanhuma*, Noah, 5. See also Rashi, 6:14.

49. Sexually, too, he refuses to articulate his being: he has children late in life (at 500 [5:32]) "because of the sin of his generation, which he saw. Only when God told him to build the ark, he married and had children, a hundred years before the Flood" (*Ba-midbar Rabbah* 14:12).

50. *Bereshit Rabbah* 30:9.

51. Ibid., 31:19.

52. Emmanuel Levinas, *Totality and Infinity* (Duquesne University Press: 1969), 110–15.

53. Ibid., 116.

54. "The righteous man knows the needs of his beast" has traditionally been understood to refer to this relation to *one's own needs*, and their wise management.

55. *Tanhuma*, Noah, 9.

56. See Ramban 6:19

57. *Bereshit Rabbah* 32:4.

58. Ibid., 32:8.

59. *Ma'aseh Ha-shem* 68:1. See also Targum Onkelos.

60. Bachelard, *Poetics of Space*, 224

61. See *Tanhuma*, Noah, 11, and our earlier discussion of this midrash. This reading is based on the fact that Noah and his sons are listed *separately* from their wives, in the original instructions to enter the ark (6:18; 7:7; 7:13), but *in pairs* when they are told to leave the ark (8:16) — and, in the same breath, God tells them of the fertility-imperative implicit in "coming out." Noah, however, leaves in sexually *segregated* groups (8:18).

62. *Pirkei d'Rabbi Eliezer*, chap. 23.

63. Shakespeare, *Hamlet*, II, ii, 257.

64. *Pirkei d'Rabbi Eliezer*, chap. 23.

65. *Baal Ha-Turim* suggests that Og is a decoding of the words "Only Noah," since they have the same numerical value (*gematriya*). This would imply an intimate – perhaps dialectical – relation between the Noah who is enclosed in the ark and the obsessional force of the giant king.

66. Bachelard, *Poetics of Space*, 222–23.

67. See Rashi, 8:13, and B. Rosh Hashanah 12b.

68. *Bereshit Rabbah* 18:1.

69. Ibid., 18:3.

70. John Keats, "On First Looking into Chapman's *Homer*."

71. *Bereshit Rabbah*, 34:8

72. *Pirkei d'Rabbi Eliezer*, chap. 23.

73. "You have *brought us into* a net" (v.11); "We have *come into* fire and water" (v.12); "You have *brought us out* to the fresh air" (v.12). Ibn Ezra reads *revaya* as air, neither desiccating like fire, nor obliterating like water. Fire and water are both dimensions of the Flood in midrashic literature.

74. See Radal on *Pirkei d'Rabbi Eliezer* chap. 23.

75. See *Tanhuma*, Tavo, 1.

76. Compare 6:5.

77. *Rabbenu Bahya* 8:21.

78. *Bereshit Rabbah* 34:10.

79. *Kohelet Rabbah* 9:22.

80. George Eliot, *Middlemarch* (Penguin English Library: 1965), 243.

81. Quoted from *Torah Shelemah* 9:119.

82. D. W. Winnicott, *Playing and Reality* (Penguin: 1971), 12–13.

## LEKH LEKHA

1. Henri Bergson, "The Idea of Nothing," in *Creative Evolution*, trans. Arthur Mitchell (Modern Library: 1944), 323.

2. *Bereshit Rabbah* 38:21.

3. It is interesting to notice, however, that the first *ein* in the Torah (2:5) speaks of the absence of Man himself. ("When the Lord God made earth and heaven – when no shrub of the field was yet on earth and no grasses of the field had yet sprouted, because the Lord God had not sent rain upon the earth and there was *no man – adam ayin –* to till the soil. . . .") Without human consciousness of need and desire, without the experience of the "peculiar possibility of the negative," there can be no prayer, indeed no reality that is humanly appropriated. See Rashi's comment on this passage.

4. Ramban, 12:1.

5. Cf. ibid., 20:13.

6. Cf. Rashi's comment on *me-artzkha* (12:1) – "'*Go forth . . . from your*

*land*': Move even further away from there"—his native land he has already left with his father: the point now is to move on, away, with no specified destination.

7. *Tanḥuma*, Lekh Lekha, 3.

8. *Y'lamdenu*, quoted in *Torah Shelemah* 12:107.

9. See Rashi on this verse: "'*Therefore shall a man leave*': The Holy Spirit makes this declaration, forbidding incest to all mankind." The incestuous bond is primary not only chronologically, in the history of the child's development, but culturally and spiritually. A primal unity must be ruptured in order that generation take place—the removal of the rib from Adam's body becomes in Rashi's comment the paradigm for alienation-become-fruition.

10. *Bereshit Rabbah* 53:6.

11. Ibid., 39:16. The imagery of coinage suggests the capacity to "mint" and reproduce, to beget in one's own image. Abraham and Sarah come to represent a transformative mode that captures the human imagination.

12. Cf. the commentary of *Etz Yosef*: "Their two situations that are reversed by the lovingkindness of God."

13. *Tanḥuma*, Lekh Lekha, 3.

14. Rambam, *Mishneh Torah*, Hilkhot Teshuva 2:4.

15. B. Rosh Hashanah 16b.

16. My wordplay on *kri'ah* and *akirah*, with their identical but inverted root letters, is not, I hope, entirely perverse. The state of alienation/barrenness (*akirah*) is one of ground torn away (*kri'ah*)—filaments of connection with past and future rent apart. Discontinuity is the essential experience Abraham comes to represent.

17. *Midrash Ha-Gadol* 12:1.

18. Cf. Rashi: "'*Lekh lekha*': Go from your land—for your good, for your benefit" (12:1).

19. See the comment of the Netziv on "And Abram went *as* God had told him" (12:4)—"Abram went *instantly*, in response to God's word."

20. William James, *The Varieties of Religious Experience* (Fontana: 1960), 201.

21. Rambam, *Mishneh Torah*, Hilkhot Avodah Zarah 1:3.

22. Thomas S. Kuhn, *The Structure of Scientific Revolutions* (University of Chicago Press: 1962), 55.

23. Ibid., 62.

24. Ibid., 63.

25. Ibid., 64.

26. Ibid., 65.

27. But see ibid., 208: his theses should be of wide applicability, "for they are borrowed from other fields." Kuhn claims originality mainly in *applying* them to the sciences.

28. Ibid., 64, note.
29. Ibid., 150
30. *Midrash Ha-Gadol*, Genesis 12:1.
31. Cf. Erasmus, *In Praise of Folly.*
32. Kuhn, *Structure of Scientific Revolutions*, 37
33. See, e.g., Isaiah 22:17 and *Va-yikra Rabbah* 5:5.
34. *Bereshit Rabbah* 39:2.
35. Ibid., 39:1.
36. Rorty, *Contingency, Irony, and Solidarity*, 30.
37. Peter Berger, *A Rumor of Angels* (Anchor: 1970).
38. See, e.g., *Sefat Emet* 5648.
39. JPS translates *ohavi*, "my friend." See also B. Sotah 32b.
40. Rambam, *Mishneh Torah*, Hilkhot Teshuva 10:3.
41. Cf. 1 Samuel 26:21 and Proverbs 5:19.
42. In his comment on Proverbs 5:19, he cites an Arabic source for the translation, "preoccupation"; and then adds the rabbinic reading, which emphasizes "distraction."
43. Cf. Deuteronomy 28:34: "until you are driven mad by what your eyes behold." And the comment of *Ha'amek Davar*: the madness comes not from physical suffering but from the disruption of normal causal relationships.
44. W. B. Yeats, *Easter, 1916.*
45. Conversely, language always conspires to close off as it discloses meaning: "There is also another sense in which we can never quite close our fists over meaning, which arises from the fact that language is a temporal process. When I read a sentence, the meaning of it is always somehow suspended, something deferred or still to come" (Terry Eagleton, *Literary Theory* [University of Minnesota Press: 1983], 128). Deferral, writes George Steiner (*Real Presences* [University of Chicago Press: 1989], 122) is "that postponement of settled signification, that keeping in flickering motion which adjourns the illusion, the sterile fixity of meaning."
Note that Rashi has changed the text of his source in *Bereshit Rabbah*, which speaks of a reward for each *step*, an image obviously more appropriate, as Abraham sets out on a journey, each step of which is shrouded in doubt. Perhaps Rashi is thinking primarily of his supporting prooftexts, where delayed language is an appropriate expression of indeterminacy. The third example Rashi gives ("on one of the mountains") is his own addition to the quotations in *Bereshit Rabbah*: for him, evidently, this theme is central to the Abraham idea, and it is crucial to consider the three quotations as an organic structure.
46. E.g., *Sifrei Deuteronomy*, 326: "When God punishes Israel, He, as it were, regrets it." J. Nedarim, 9, 41b: "Is not regret of a vow like a novel [unforeseen] circumstance?" *Shemot Rabbah*, 43:11: in Moses' prayer of

intercession, "Turn back from Your burning anger and think better of the evil decreed against Your people" (Exodus 32:12), the word for "think better" (*hinnahem*) is translated, "Let *tehiya* exist for You."

47. Cf. B. Shavuot 17a: "When he did not *stand still*, he walked constantly." B. Berakhot 5a: "The pious *spend an hour in silent contemplation* before prayer." B. Berakhot 32b: "They would *contemplate* an hour, pray an hour, and again *contemplate* an hour."

Compare George Steiner's discussion of Derrida's "famous neologism, *la différence*, [which] is crucial to the deconstructionist and post-structuralist counter-theology of absence." Particularly in the sense of "deferral" – "that postponement of settled signification, that keeping in flickering motion which adjourns the illusion, the sterile fixity of definition" (*Real Presences*, p 122).

48. Cf. B. Yevamot 36b: "A human birth that *survived* thirty days is not considered an abortion."

49. The expression is borrowed from John Keats, "On First Looking into Chapman's *Homer*." Compare B. Hulin 75b: "Reish Lakish *gazed at him* (when R. Yohanan gave his opinion) and was silent."

50. Note that the double cry, "Abraham! Abraham!" as God's angel reveals himself after the Akedah (22:11) is described by Rashi as "an expression of love [*hiba*]." Here, God reciprocates Abraham's love, *after* the suspension in space and time is resolved.

51. Cf. R. D. Laing's clinical description of *akarut* as peril and opportunity:

> Something happens that is incompatible with [this] pivotal identity, perhaps hidden, that determines his whole system of meaning. A linch-pin is removed that had been holding a whole world together, The whole meaning of reality crumbles. It *"takes the ground from under his feet"* [my italics]. Participation in the world, such terms as "contact with" and "sense of reality" are empty sounds. A desperate crisis indeed. Either one re-structures one's whole "real" view of others and the world and redefines one's "real" self; or one annuls the chasm between what is the case and what one *knows* to be the case, by taking one's stand on what one *knows*. There is nothing more real and indubitable than pure phantasy; nothing more obvious; nothing less necessary and more easy to prove. (*Self and Others* [Penguin: 1961], 93)

52. The repeated second-person singular possessive suffix in the *lekh lekha* summons – "Go forth from *your* land, *your* birthplace, *your* father's house" brings an almost hypnotic focus to bear on self. This suggests a fascination in abandonment.

53. Compare the use Rashi makes of the words *teruf* and *meshugga* in his account of the drowning of the Egyptians. Their self-infatuation gives them a fatal buoyancy that will not allow them the mercy of a quick death.

54. Frank Kermode, *The Genesis of Secrecy* (Harvard University Press: 1979), 145.

55. The text discussed in the Talmud is "Today you have become the people of the Lord" (Deuteronomy 27:9). "Today" suggests a "double exposure" effect: the day of Moses' speaking, or indeed the day of the reader's reading, becomes elided with the day of the Giving of the Torah on Sinai.

56. Cf. the comment of *Ha'amek Davar* on Exodus 19:19.

57. *Tanḥuma*, Miketz, 2.

58. See Rashi on Exodus 6:9, citing B. Sanhedrin 111a.

59. *Bereshit Rabbah*, 44:6.

60. Ibid., 57:2. Cf. Rashi on 22:20. The midrash is apparently playing on the similarity between *aḥar ha-devarim ha-eleh* ("after these things") and *hirhurim*.

61. Cf. Isaiah 59:13.

62. B. Niddah 16b.

63. It is interesting to notice the "timing" of Abraham's *hirhurim*, in the midrashic sources—e.g. *Bereshit Rabbah* 56:12: "Abraham *began* to wonder: All these events are bewildering—yesterday You told me, 'In Isaac, seed shall be named for you'; then You said, 'Please take your son'; and now You tell me, 'Do not stretch out your hand against the boy'—I am full of wonder!" It is only after a certain crisis of commitment is past that he opens himself to the complex contradictions (literally, the *counterdictions*—mutually exclusive speech acts) of his situation: characteristically, *after* these things. Compare also the version of this midrash in J. Ta'anit 2:4: "Master of the universe, it is fully revealed to You that *at the time* that You told me to offer up my son, *I had what to answer You.*" The timing of Abraham's musings on contradiction is of the essence here. "I had a response" indicates the thought that is immediately submerged in the movement of love for God. Only when he has acted out that commitment do the full implications of contradiction surge up in his mind. This is the time for meaning-making.

64. J. Huizinga, *Homo Ludens* (Routledge and Kegan Paul: 1949), 13. Huizinga defines play as "a free activity standing quite consciously outside 'ordinary' life as being 'not serious,' but at the same time absorbing the player intensely and utterly. It is an activity connected with no material interest, and no profit can be gained by it. It proceeds within its own proper boundaries of time and space according to fixed rules and in an orderly manner."

65. *Midrash Ha-Gadol*, Genesis 12:1

66. Chaos, the formless emptiness of the uncreated world, is described in Genesis as *tohu va-vohu*: the cosmological dimension of a full emptiness out

of which everything is engendered holds both horror and fascination for
human beings, whose essential need is for structure. (See Rashi's comment
on these words, Genesis 1:2.) *Tehiya* is *tohu* on the existential plane.

67. *Tanḥuma*, Lekh Lekha, 2.

68. In *Paḥad Yitzḥak* (Pesaḥ, 17:5), Rav Yitzhak Hutner explores the
theme of the necessity of the question. Often, he suggests, the answer is in
greater need of a good question than the question is in need of an answer.
Only when imperfection, need, tension are authentically experienced, (the
"anomaly" of which Kuhn writes) does man progress toward wholeness.
Resolution without tension is a joyless triumph. In these terms, Rav Hutner
discusses the indeterminacy of Abraham's journey: knowledge comes to him
"as the answer to a real question, not as an arbitrary answer" — as response to
an existence fabricated out of questions. "When God caused me to wander
away from my father's house" (Genesis 20:13) — "God led me to know Him
precisely through the experiences of felt not-knowing."

69. Kuhn, *Structure of Scientific Revolutions*, 87.

70. *Sefat Emet* 5648.


## VA-YERA

1. *"Take please"*: Na is an expression of request. God said to Abraham,
"Please stand firm for Me in this test, so that people should not say, The first
tests had no substance to them."

2. B. Sanhedrin 89b.

3. See Genesis 12:7–8 and 13:4.

4. Isaiah 41:8.

5. Rashi's comment is based on *Tanḥuma*, Shelaḥ, 14. It is interesting to
notice that in the original midrash, the prooftext is, "Go, eat your bread in
gladness . . . for your action was long ago approved by God" (Ecclesiastes
9:7). Abraham is vindicated and the effect is — bathetically? — that he can
return to his *se'udah*, to the feasting that generated the doubts that made the
test necessary in the first place.

6. See Rashi, 25:19.

7. See the discussion of this in Shestov, *Athens and Jerusalem*, 57–71.

8. See Ramban, 17:1.

9. Michel Tournier, *Gemini* (Minerva: 1989), 131.

10. Ibid., 33–4.

11. Ibid., 134.

12. Ramban, 18:15.

13. *Esther Rabbah* 2:14.

14. See Ramban's discussion of this verse and of Rambam's reading.

15. Cf. the discussion in *Bereshit Rabbah* 48:16, as to whether the angels really ate, or only appeared to eat.

16. Cf. Ruth 3:7: "Boaz ate and drank, and in a cheerful mood went to lie down"; and the comment in *Ruth Rabbah*: " '*in a cheerful mood' (lit., his heart was good)* — he made a blessing over his food. Or, he ate a variety of sweets that train the tongue for Torah." The implication is that Boaz is fully nurtured by the world, and can make use of reality: by an act of alchemy, food is metabolized to creative play in Torah. (See *Likutei Moharan* 1, 19:7.)

17. Cf. Harvey Cox, in *Feast of Fools* (Harper and Row: 1969), writes of the prodigality and fantasy, the "calculated excess" implied in feasting and living it *up*, dressing *up*. Cf. Abraham's teaching to Sarah: "This is no time for austerity [modesty] — uncover your breasts and nurse all the princes of the world!" (*Bereshit Rabbah* 53:13).

18. B. Sotah 10b. Cf. Rashi on this verse.

19. See Rashi on this verse: "hotel, a place where the stranger is lodged, and *where there are all kinds of fruits*."

20. Rashi, B. Ketubot 8b.

21. *Bereshit Rabbah* 54:8.

22. B. Yoma 75a.

23. D. W. Winnicott, *Playing and Reality* (Basic Books: 1971), 93.

24. It is interesting to notice that the word for feast that is used in B. Sanhedrin 89b — *se'udah* — is rooted in the invitation that Abraham extends to the angels — "*Sa'adu libkhem*" — "you may refresh yourselves" — lit., support your heart (18:5). This is the primary concept of eating; as Rashi points out, the expression "heart support" is used throughout Scriptures for "food." What Abraham is offering is an experience in which dependency is overcome and the hazards of growth and separation are mediated.

25. See Rashi on 7:23.

26. *Tanhuma*, Lekh Lekha, 12.

27. R. Hutner, *Pahad Yitzhak*, Pesah, 18:5.

28. Cf. B. Yevamot 79a, where this source is chosen as the prooftext for characterizing the kindness of the Jews.

29. Rambam, *Hilkhot Deot* 1:6

30. Cf. Hutner, *Pahad Yitzhak*, Shavuot, 15:14.

31. Compare Winnicott's account of play in *Playing and Reality*, 96.

32. Ibid., 110

33. *Tanhuma*, Tetzaveh, 1.

34. See the commentary of Malbim on this verse (Psalms 71:14).

35. The pun on *milah* ("circumcision," "word") is a commonplace in hasidic writings.

36. Winnicott, *Playing and Reality*, 95.

37. Ibid., 101.

38. Maharal, *Netivot Olam* (Yahadut, Bnei Brak: 1980), 148.

39. The Zohar expresses this in its comment on Isaiah 51:16: " 'I have said to Zion, You are My people.' Do not read *ammi* [my people], but *immi* [with me]: Just as I create heaven and earth by My word, *so do you*." (See *Likutei Moharan*, 64:4.)

40. J. Sotah 7:1.

41. Based on B. Hulin 60b.

42. *Bereshit Rabbah*, 49:5.

43. Ibid., 49:20.

44. See Maharal, *Netivot Olam*, 164, where he discusses the statement that "Jerusalem was destroyed only because its inhabitants stood on the letter of the law" (B. Baba Metzia 30b).

45. *Bereshit Rabbah* 8:5.

46. I owe this insight—the analogy between the *hallal panui* and the "potential space"—to R. Daniel Epstein.

47. Cf. Matthew Arnold, *Culture and Anarchy*.

48. Rashi suggests (on v.31) that the historical reference here is to the two thousand years before Abraham's time: the fully human phase of "sons of men" begins with Abraham, whose work it is to grow "sons of men" out of the culture of a merely potential universe.

49. "The Hermeneutic Quest in *Robinson Crusoe*," in *Midrash and Literature*, ed. Geoffrey H. Hartman and Sanford Budick (Yale University Press: 1986), 232.

50. See Ramban, Introduction to the Torah.

51. See Ramban, 17:17.

52. This is Rashi's translation of the angel's response: "Is anything too wonderful [Rashi: "covered, blocked off"] for God?" (18:14). Belief in God means that there is a reality transcending division, law, impossibility.

53. *Bereshit Rabbah* 52:14.

54. Ibid.

55. Ishbitzer Rebbe, *Mei Ha-shiloah*, Va-yera, 11.

56. See Rashi and *Tanhuma*, Shemot, 1. Ishmael is an inversion of Abraham, in relation to feeding and the question of separateness and relationship.

57. Søren Kierkegaard, *Fear and Trembling*, ed. and trans. Howard V. Hong and Edna H. Hong (Princeton University Press: 1983), 60.

58. J. Ta'anit 2:4.

59. *Semahot*, chap. 8.

60. See Rashi on 22:4: "And he saw the place from afar"—the place [the rabbinical mode of describing God] is marked by a cloud.

61. R. Nahman, *Likutei Moharan*, 11:12

62. R. Nahman quotes the Zohar's reading of *Bereshit*: unscrambling the letters to form the words *Bara tayish* ("He created a ram"), the Zohar produces the redemptive lamb of alienation and yearning.

63. Kierkegaard, *Fear and Trembling*, 53.

64. B. Sotah 22a.

65. Maharal, *Netivot Olam, Netiv Ha-avodah*, chap. 5.

66. R. Hutner, *Paḥad Yitzḥak*, Rosh Hashanah, 5:3–4.

67. B. Berakhot, 29b; *Mishnah Berurah* 122:5.

68. B. Sukkah 25a.

69. *Tanḥuma*, Va-yera, 22.

70. Pirkei Avot 5:6.

71. Cf. Rashi on 22:16: "May God see *the ashes of Isaac* gathered eternally upon the altar." In this formulation, there is not even the fig leaf of the *ke'eelu* ("as though") to cover the fact of substitution. Abraham has created a world.

72. Winnicott, *Playing and Reality*, 94.

73. See Albo, *Sefer Ha-Ikarim*, 3, 314.

## ḤAYYEI SARAH

1. *Pirkei d'Rabbi Eliezer*, chap. 32.

2. *Midrash Aggadah*, quoted in *Torah Shelemah*, Bereshit, chap. 23, n. 17.

3. See, for instance, the repeated cries of King Lear at the height of his tragedy: "Howl, howl, howl, howl!" (V, iii, 259). "Never, never, never, never, never!" (V, iii, 310). The theme of nothingness is central to this play.

4. *Tanḥuma*, Va-yera, 23.

5. *Va-yikra Rabbah* 20:2.

6. Cf. Jonah 4:2: "For I know that You are a compassionate and gracious God." Jonah fears the mutability of a world ruled by *ḥesed*, by apparently arbitrary acts of love. What solid knowledge of good and evil can be gained in such a world? His fear, according to Rashi, is of being "a liar in their eyes." How can truth be known, if God masks His power, restrains His dramatic interventions, and simply allows life to continue?

7. Jean-Paul Sartre, *L'Être et le néant* (Paris: 1948), 57.

8. Gur Arye on Genesis 23:2.

9. Paul Tillich, *The Courage to Be* (Yale University Press: 1952), 39.

10. Paul Ricoeur, *History and Truth* (Northwestern University Press: 1965), 290.

11. See Rashi 22:14.

12. R. Hutner, *Paḥad Yitzḥak*, Sukkot, 19.

13. Miguel de Unamuno defines the foundation of metaphysical pessimism: "Our desire is to make ourselves eternal, to *persist*, and whatever con-

spires to this end we call good, and evil is whatever tends to lessen and annihilate our consciousness" (*The Tragic Sense of Life* [Princeton University Press: 1972], 269).

14. B. Eruvin 13b.

15. "Everyone feels anxiety on reading this mysterious statement" (Maharsha on B. Makkoth 23b).

16. E.g., the question of evil and free will. The God-fearing person detests evil and desires its end, yet he values and requires it for the energetic life of his spirit. In Jung's imagery, confrontation with evil provides the gradient, which allows his energy to express itself in the world.

17. Neher, *Exile of the Word*, 68.

18. Ricoeur, *History and Truth*, 317–22.

19. Sartre, *L'Être et le néant*, 66.

20. B. Yoma 76b.

21. *Va-yikra Rabbah* 20:2.

22. *Yalkut Tehillim* 89:16.

23. R. Hutner, *Paḥad Yitzḥak*, Rosh Hashanah, 7:11

24. "All the claims of Satan are strangled by the Shofar" — See *Torah Shelemah*, chap. 23, n. 17.

25. Ricoeur, *History and Truth*, 318.

26. *Tanḥuma*, Va-yera, 23.

27. *Tanḥuma*, 21.

28. *Bereshit Rabbah* 56:5

29. Ricoeur, *History and Truth*, 289.

30. Ibid., 290.

31. See Rashi, 21:12.

32. *Bereshit Rabbah* 53:15.

33. This strange word occurs in Proverbs 26:18 and implies unintentional violence.

34. *Tanḥuma*, Ḥayyei Sarah, 4.

35. See Rashi, 4:3.

36. Carl Jung, *Modern Man in Search of a Soul* (Routledge and Kegan Paul), 125.

37. See Rashi; also Rashi and Seforno, 25:8–9.

38. See Rashi, 25:30.

39. *Bereshit Rabbah* 61:5.

40. See 6:6 with Rashi's comment on "God repented that He had made man."

41. *Midrash Ha-Gadol* 24:67.

42. See Rashi, 24:67: " '*to the tent—Sarah, his mother*': lit, he brought her to the tent, and she became Sarah, his mother—that is, she became like Sarah, his mother. For as long as Sarah was alive, there was a lamp lit from

Sabbath eve to Sabbath eve, and there was blessing in the dough, and a cloud attached to the tent. When she died, they ceased; and when Rebecca came, they returned."

43. Compare verbs of *hastening* in both narratives.

44. This is the root of Jonah's anger at God's *ḥesed* to Nineveh. The effect of such *ḥesed* is mere unintelligibility. The world continues as though there were no justice, no judge. To Jonah, this is an outrage against *emet*, the Truth, that is so conspicuously missing from his list of divine attributes (4:2). Without Truth, *ḥesed* seems to him a deplorable, even self-destructive foible of God.

45. Cf. *Mishneh Torah*, Hilkhot Teshuva, chap. 7, in which Rambam traces the complexities of sin, penitence, reward, and punishment. Rambam reiterates constantly that the transcendent truth is in no way derivable from experience. On the contrary, "Do not say. . . . ," "Let the penitent not imagine that. . . . ," "A person should always see himself as though. . . ."

46. See Rashi, 24:14.

47. *Bereshit Rabbah* 60:2.

48. See, for instance, the injunction, "*Azov ta'azov imo* — You shall indeed come to the aid of your enemy, whose donkey has collapsed under its burden" (Exodus 23:5). The ambiguities and rhetorical questions involved in this text are the subject of much rabbinic commentary. For an unequivocal example of *azav* as "reinforcement," see Nehemiah 3:8.

49. Neher, *Exile of the Word*, 285–86.

50. This is not a moment of joy; for doubt and suspense make awkward bedfellows with joy. The legacy of Sarah's death is her last cry. According to the *Midrash Ha-Gadol* (23:2), Kiryat Arba, the place of her death ("the city of four"), is called so because of her four death cries — expressing sadness on hearing her son's fate; wailing for her son; the bitterness of her death; and mourning for the fact that there is no perfect joy. These carefully differentiated modes culminate in the "reversibility of joy," as the Midrash *Or Afela* has it. Realization of the volatile nature of experience and consciousness is not easily neutralized.

51. *Bereshit Rabbah* 60:14.

52. See the commentary of *Ha'amek Davar* on this meeting.

## TOLEDOT

1. It is striking that even the cheated Esau in the heat of his bitterness has no stronger recrimination than "and now he has taken my blessing" (27:36).

2. *Bereshit Rabbah* 70:17.

3. Ibid., 67:4.

4. Ramban focuses on the unexpectedness of Isaac's reply. He mobilizes this to intensify the outrage of Isaac's question, which now covers the *involuntary* nature of the blessing: he trembles all the more violently for knowing that the blessing is a reality, *in spite* of his intention and present feeling.

5. *Bereshit Rabbah* 67:3.

6. Compare "And Jacob called his sons" (49:1), which introduces his deathbed blessings.

7. *Bereshit Rabbah* 67:10.

8. Ibid., 78:14.

9. Rashi is reponding here to the past tense form of *berakhtani*. He translates literally, "till you admit my *having been blessed*, in the past."

10. Sarna, *Understanding Genesis*, 188.

11. Ramban, 27:12

12. B. Sanhedrin 92a.

13. *Midrash Mishlei* 10:17.

14. Shakespeare, *Hamlet*, I, iii, 78–80.

15. See R. Hutner, *Paḥad Yitzḥak*, Sukkot 21:8.

16. B. Baba Metzia 87a.

17. Ibid.

18. *Tanḥuma*, Toledot, 1.

19. The striking feature of this version of the midrash is that Abraham cannot come to his own just assessment of the facts, even *after* God has changed Isaac's appearance. It is because of the consensus of opinion of others, who can see both father and son, that Abraham's suspicions are allayed. The visual factor, the criterion of perspective and opinion, remains central, even after the miracle.

20. Lionel Trilling discusses this concept, and its relation to the "sentiments of art," in *Sincerity and Authenticity* (Harvard University Press: 1971), chap. 3.

21. *Bereshit Rabbah* 65:16.

22. *Matnot Kehunah*, Genesis 27:22.

23. Trilling, *Sincerity and Authenticity*, 2.

24. B. Sanhedrin 92a.

25. See Trilling, *Sincerity and Authenticity*, chap. 2.

26. See *Mei Ha-Shiloaḥ*, 10: "And indeed, whenever a person exposes himself to ambiguities, in his religious life — if he succeeds in dealing authentically with these ambiguities, then he is greater than a person who kept himself clear of ambiguities."

27. See Canetti, *Crowds and Power*, 126–32.

28. *Tanḥuma*, Toledot, 8.

29. *Bereshit Rabbah* 65:5.

30. Ibid.

31. See, for instance, *Tanḥuma*, Va-yera, 23 and Toledot, 7.

32. *Tanḥuma*, Toledot, 7.

33. Shakespeare, *King Lear*, III, iv, 105–11.

34. Genesis 24:64–65. See the interpretation of the *Ha'amek Davar*, who discusses this meeting as the pivotal moment of the relationship of Isaac and Rebecca.

35. Note the vocabulary of "going," which marks Rebecca as kin to Abraham, whose motif-word is, of course, the verb "to go" — *lekh lekha* (12:1, 22:2).

36. *Bereshit Rabbah* 63:16.

37. Rashi quotes the midrash (ibid.) describing Esau as "tired of murder": Esau takes life, to express his disappointment and despair of life.

38. Even the ordinary words for "wild animals and birds," *ḥayot ve-ofot*, used by Rashi, suggest life and movement, while Esau lies in ambush, focusing his energies on the point of his arrow.

39. *Bereshit Rabbah* 63:15.

40. Shakespeare, *Hamlet*, I, ii, 133–34.

41. Plato, *Protagoras*, 345D.

42. Shestov, *Athens and Jerusalem*, 89.

43. Ibid., 90.

44. See Ibn Ezra, Rashbam, and *Bereshit Rabbah* on 60:14.

45. Walter Benjamin, "On Some Motifs in Baudelaire," in *Illuminations* (Collins/Fontana Books: 1973), 174ff.

46. Ibid., 177.

47. Ibid., 178.

48. Ibid., 179.

49. Shakespeare, *Hamlet*, III, i, 62.

50. *Tanḥuma*, Toledot, 7.

51. *Bereshit Rabbah* 63:16. The midrash refers specifically to betrothed women.

52. Shakespeare, *Hamlet*, III, i, 63.

53. *Bereshit Rabbah* 65:14.

54. Ibid.

55. Since Rebecca will prepare the food, it is her skill that will arouse love and blessing (a libidinal energy that is now poignantly focused on food, but that, in some form, is essential to the act of blessing, see Ramban, Bahya). Jacob's role is minimal, but does involve the use of his hands and legs: "Go . . . take . . . bring. . . ."

56. Mary Douglas, *Purity and Danger* (Penguin: 1970), chap. 2.

57. Targum Jonathan, in fact, translates *sa'ir* as "a mature man."

58. *Bereshit Rabbah* 65:10.

59. Friedrich Nietzsche, *The Birth of Tragedy*, in Geoffrey Clive, ed. *The Philosophy of Nietzsche* (Mentor: 1965), 145.

60. J. Sotah 1:16.

61. *Tanḥuma*, Va-yiggash, 3

62. J. Sotah 1:8.

63. Italo Calvino, *Mr. Palomar* (Picador: 1986), 26–29.

64. *Tanḥuma*, Tazria, 6.

65. See *Mei Ha-Shiloaḥ*, Toledot, 10a for a discussion of Jacob and Esau in relation to the question of simplicity and ambiguity.

66. *Bereshit Rabbah* 65:22.

67. B. Berakhot 63b.

68. *Bereshit Rabbah* 63:15.

69. Trilling, *Sincerity and Authenticity*, 99. The expression, "the sentiment of being," comes from Rousseau's *Second Discourse*, where he compares the savage who "lives within himself" with the sociable man who "knows how to live only in the opinion of others, and it is, so to speak, from their judgment alone that he draws the sentiment of his own being" (quoted in Trilling, 62).

70. Shakespeare, *Hamlet*, I, ii, 76.

71. Rashi comments on "I ate of it all": "All delicacies that I sought to taste, I tasted in his food." Isaac experiences the triumph of the desiring imagination, fusing the sensual with the spiritual — a similar notion to the classic midrashic descriptions of the taste of the manna, and the experience of receiving the Torah at Mount Sinai.

72. Compare Abarbanel's reading of *lo hikiro*. Unlike most commentators, he translates, "he did not identify him," rather than "he did not recognize him."

73. In the *Bereshit Rabbah* source, Jacob describes his *anokhi* differently: "*I am destined* to receive the Ten Commandments" — a word-play on the opening statement of the Ten Commandments: "*I am* the Lord your God." In this reading, Jacob's identity will find full standing only in the *anokhi* encounter of Sinai, where man will achieve an unprecedented strength to "stand" in the presence of God. [See essay on "Bereshit," especially pp. 20–36.] See also the comment of Ibn Ezra on Jacob's "disinformation:" he rejects all attempts to split the sentence and argues that the sentence must be tolerated as it stands.

74. *Sefat Emet*, 5647.

75. B. Yoma 39a.

76. Trilling, *Sincerity and Authenticity*, 119.

77. Ibid., 120

78. *Mei Ha-Shiloaḥ* 10a.

79. Clive, *Philosophy of Nietzsche*, 147.

80. B. Baba Metzia 87a.

81. Trilling, *Sincerity and Authenticity*, 121.

82. *Bereshit Rabbah*, 63:14.

83. See Douglas, *Purity and Danger*, where she discusses pollution and purity, in terms of the interstitial in social structure.

84. B. Yevamot 3:5.

85. B. Sanhedrin 91b.

86. Trilling, *Sincerity and Authenticity*, 21.

87. *Bereshit Rabbah* 65:11.

88. Ibid., 65:15.

89. *Bemidbar Rabbah* 10:6.

90. *Bereshit Rabbah* 65:22.

91. *Tanḥuma*, 11.

92. Zohar 242:2.

93. See Rashi, who condenses complex midrashic traditions.

94. B. Pesaḥim 88a. *Meshekh Ḥokhmah* explains the focus on incense (see *Targum Jonathan* and *Tanḥuma Yashan* 22): incense is that aspect of Temple ritual that is *exclusive* to the Temple — it may not be offered in any other place. Incense, therefore, becomes a metonymy for the field-Temple idea.

95. B. Kritot 6b.

96. *Bereshit Rabbah* 65:18.

97. See *Or Gedalia*, Toledot, 2, 3, for a reading of this text that has substantially informed my own reading.

98. Zohar 142:2.

99. The clause, "that God has blessed," is in itself ambiguous: it could refer to the field, on the one hand, and to "my son," on the other. "The smell of my son . . . whom God has blessed—is like the smell of the field," is a workable reading of the text. See the commentary of Mizrahi on the verse.

100. See Winnicott, *Playing and Reality*.

101. *Pirkei d'Rabbi Eliezer*, 32.

102. This is a common theme in Sacks's books—e.g., *A Leg to Stand On* (Picador: 1986) and *The Man Who Mistook His Wife for a Hat* (Picador: 1986).

103. Sacks, *Hat*, 58.

104. Ibid., 61.

105. Ibid., 111.

106. *Bereshit Rabbah* 67:10.

## VA-YETZE

1. Rainer Maria Rilke, "Groves," *Vergers*, 52, 56

2. Jean-Paul Sartre, *Words* (Penguin Books: 1967), 58.

3. See Kli Yakar's commentary on 28:10.

4. *Bereshit Rabbah* 68:3.

5. See Rashi, 2:24.

6. See Rashi, 28:9.

7. B. Pesaḥim 88a.

8. See Exodus 19:22: "The priests, also, who come near the Lord, must stay pure, lest the Lord break out [*yifrotz*] against them." See Rashi: " '*Break out*': Kill them and make a breach in their ranks."

9. *Bereshit Rabbah* 69:3. In line with this, the psalmist asks, "What alarmed you, O sea, that you fled . . . ? Tremble, O earth . . . at the presence of *the God of Jacob*" (Psalms 114:5–6).

10. The grammatical form, "to work for a wife [*be-isha*]" (lit., to work *in*), suggests the suffusion of the labor with the image of the beloved.

11. See Rashi, 28:11: "for the sun had set": The sun set early, so that he would spend the night in the place later called Beth-El. Rashi 32:31: "The sun rose upon him": The sun rose for him, bringing healing on its wings (after the wrestling match with the mysterious man, who names him Israel).

12. *Bereshit Rabbah* 70:17.

13. The word *gam*, "also," is a motif word in the Parsha, expressing the thickening "envelope" of Jacob's identity in the world.

14. *Pirkei d'Rabbi Eliezer*, 35.

15. *Bereshit Rabbah* 68:10.

16. Ibid., 68:11.

17. Ibid., 68:12.

18. B. Sanhedrin 95b.

19. *Sefat Emet*, Va-yetze, 5636.

20. See Gur Arye, 28:11.

21. Tosefta, Megilla, 82:11.

22. B. Ta'anit 20b.

23. B. Tamid 25a, 27a. See *Rashi Ha-shalem*, note 31, for further discussion.

24. B. Berakhot 57b.

25. Walter Benjamin, *Illuminations*, 136.

26. *Sefat Emet*, 5632.

27. *Bereshit Rabbah* 68:18.

28. Ibid., 69:1.

29. See *Sefat Emet*, 128.

30. Gaston Bachelard, *Air and Dreams* (Dallas Institute Publications: 1988), 56. In a footnote, Bachelard quotes Gerard de Nerval: "On that particular night I had a wonderful dream. . . . I was in a tower, so deep on the earth side and so high on the sky side that my whole existence seemed to be spent going up and down" (*Aurelia*, ed. Corti [Paris: 1927], 154).

31. See *Sefat Emet*, 5639.

32. Rashi's source is B. Ḥulin 91b.

33. Compare Jonah's sleep in the hold of the ship — a paradigm of regression and denial, the final stage in a series of "descents."

34. See Seforno, 28:14.

35. See Rashi, 12:6.

36. *Mekhilta*, Be-shallaḥ, Massekhta d'Shira, 3.

37. See Rashi, 28:20.

38. See Seforno, who analyzes God's promises — and Jacob's vow — as focusing on three areas: protection from sickness, poverty, and the dangers presented by foreigners. In all three cases, the central point is that they disturb mental equilibrium and distract from a fully human focus.

39. *Kohelet Rabbah* 3:17.

40. *Bereshit Rabbah* 68:13.

41. See the first chapter of this volume.

42. *Kohelet Rabbah* 3:14.

43. See *Ha-ketav Veha-kabala*, 28:11.

44. See Rashi, 28:11.

45. Oliver Sacks, *Awakenings* (Harper Perennial: 1990), 353–54.

46. Rainer Maria Rilke, *Selected Works I: Prose*, trans. G. Craig Houston (New Directions: 1967), 24.

47. This is the translation of the word *u-faratzta* in Targum Jonathan and in Rashi: "You shall become strong." Jacob's economic prosperity — the proliferation of "body" (30:43) — is paralleled by Laban's equally unexpected prosperity: "For the little you had before I came has grown to much" (30:30). The verb *paratz* is used to describe the process of "little" becoming "much" — the unpredictable proliferation of possibilities.

48. *Bereshit Rabbah* 69:7.

49. The prooftext of the midrash is "The Lord has . . . disdained His Sanctuary" (Lamentations 2:7). The midrash and the discussion of Ḥatam Sofer is quoted in *Or Gedalia*, 93.

50. S. T. Coleridge, *Lectures*, in *Shakespeare Criticism, 1623–1840*, selected by D. Nichol Smith (Oxford University Press: 1916), 231–32.

51. *Bereshit Rabbah* 70:8.

52. Bachelard, *Air and Dreams*, 28.

53. Ibid., 33.

54. Ibid., 56.

55. Ibid., 63.

56. *Kohelet Rabbah* 9:11.

57. *Pirkei d'Rabbi Eliezer*, 36.

58. See Radal's commentary on *Pirkei d'Rabbi Eliezer*, 36. He quotes R. Chaim Vital as source for this idea.

59. Yalkut Ruth, 598.

60. A famous example is Haman's disparaging description of the Jewish people—"a people scattered and dispersed" (Esther 3:8). In the midrashic reading in B. Megilla 13b, his argument turns on the profitlessness of this people.

61. See Psalms 112:9.

62. See Psalms 141:7.

63. Bachelard, *Air and Dreams*, 62.

64. Rambam, *Guide for the Perplexed* 1:28.

65. *Pirkei d'Rabbi Eliezer*, 35.

66. The term is from Ernest Gombrich, who uses it to describe the learning process of artists, as they move from a conventional to a realistic representation of objects. See his *Art and Illusion* (Princeton University Press: 1961).

67. See, for example, 28:12, 13, 15; 29:2, 25; 31:2. Several verses contain the word *ve-hine* two or even three times.

68. See B. Eruvin 41b. See also Seforno, 28:20–21.

69. *Likkutei Moharan*, 66:3.

70. B. Betza 32b.

71. See *Ha'amek Davar*, 2:20, 24.

72. See Denis de Rougemont, *Passion and Society* (Faber and Faber: 1956).

73. *Bereshit Rabbah* 71:6.

74. Ramban reads the dialogue in just this vein. In spite of his love, Jacob is compelled to reprove her, to shock her back to herself, and to a sense of her religious autonomy—her own power to pray to God for children.

75. See Seforno, 29:9.

76. See Ramban, 30:2.

77. B. Baba Batra 123a.

78. *Tanhuma*, 4.

79. The narrative stresses the evening/morning polarity (29:23, 25). See Ramban on the contrasting modes of evening (when forms intermingle) and morning ("when one can critically discriminate between them"): 1:5.

80. *Bereshit Rabbah* 70:17.

81. See *Sefat Emet*, 5647.

82. *Bereshit Rabba* 71:2.

83. *Eikha Rabbati*, Petihta, 24.

84. Ramban relates *yamin*—the right hand—to the motif of strength: a classic kabbalistic symbolic move.

85. *Bereshit Rabbah* 82:9.

## VA-YISHLAH

1. Midrashic tradition associates this death with the death of Rebecca herself—a covert way of referring to a death too painful to describe. (*Allon* is "other" in Greek: "another weeping" encodes a reference to an undescribed death.) See Rashi and Ramban, 35:8.

2. Compare the disagreement between Rashi and Ramban on whether the following clause— "the Lord shall be my God" — belongs to the condition or the promise part of the vow.

3. Compare the terms of Rebecca's directions to him: "Stay [*ve-yashavta*] with him" (27:44). "He stayed with him a month's time" (29:14). In retrospect, what had at the time been experienced as a real settling and cooperation dwindles into an episode, radically unimportant. There may, of course, be a tactical element in Jacob's presentation of himself to his brother as unchanged.

4. See Rashi: Jacob is afraid to repeat God's words, crediting Isaac with a relationship to God, even while he is still alive and his "godliness" is still in question.

5. B. Megillah 17a.

6. The moral question about Dinah's responsibility for her own fate does not arise in these midrashic treatments. To all intents and purposes, Dinah becomes a dream figure in Jacob's consciousness—as, indeed, do all the characters in his narrative—as the midrash traces the patterns, shadowy and often repressed, of his experience.

7. See *Pirkei d'Rabbi Eliezer*, 35: "Jacob fell on his face on the ground, in front of the Stone of Foundation, and prayed to God: Master of all worlds, if you bring me back to this place in wholeness, I will sacrifice before You offerings of thanks and burnt offerings—as it is said, 'And Jacob made a vow.'" Targum Jonathan also indicates that the core meaning of a vow is sacrifice.

8. B. Rosh Hashanah 90b.

9. *Tanhuma*, Va-yishlah, 8.

10. *Bereshit Rabbah* 81:2.

11. Sartre, *Words*, 94.

12. Rollo May, *Love and Will* (Dell: 1969), 230.

13. Ibid., 241.

14. Before this, only God has made promises; and—as Rashi comments in a classic passage (Exodus 6:3–8)—His promises have made human beings peculiarly aware of the "dangerous" quality of words unfulfilled.

15. See *Rashi Ha-Shalem* on 35:1, for a list of sources using either of these formulations.

16. Maharal describes the connection differently: Jacob's tragic flaw, expressed covertly when he withholds Dinah from Esau, becomes visible, cries out to high heaven, after he has delayed on his return home. His delay acts as a catalyst: the ledgers fall open for rigorous inspection (Gur Arye, 32:22).

17. *Bereshit Rabbah* 76:9.

18. Saint Augustine, *The City of God* (Hafner Library: 1948), 78–81.

19. *Bereshit Rabbah* 80:3.

20. B. Megillah 18a.

21. *Bereshit Rabbah* 79:10.

22. *Ha'amek Davar* 33:20.

23. *Bereshit Rabbah* 76:2.

24. Ibid., 55:8.

25. Ibid., 76:8.

26. Compare Genesis 3:15: "you shall strike at their heel." See Rashi.

27. *Bereshit Rabbah* 63:13.

28. Ibid., 76:7.

29. This issue of sincerity, when Esau embraces Jacob, acquires a strange significance among the commentators, evidently for historical reasons. See Rashi, 33:4; Sifrei, Be-ha'alotkha, 69.

30. In a striking passage, Terry Eagleton puts the point in post-structuralist terms:

> Since the meaning of a sign is a matter of what the sign is *not*, its meaning is always in some sense absent from it too. Meaning, if you like, is scattered or dispersed along the whole chain of signifiers: it cannot be easily nailed down, it is never fully present in any one sign alone, but is rather a kind of constant flickering of presence and absence together. . . . There is also another sense in which we can never quite close our fists over meaning, which arises from the fact that language is a temporal process. When I read a sentence, the meaning of it is always somehow suspended, something deferred or still to come. . . . There is always more meaning where that came from. (*Literary Theory* [University of Minnesota Press: 1983], 128)

This idea of the constant modification of meaning in a text is a characteristic "Jacob approach" to reading: "There is always more meaning where that came from."

31. See p. 89–93 for a discussion of this theme, in connection with the Binding of Isaac. God *delays* giving information to the righteous—in order to generate *love* for the commandment. Mystery, the unspoken edge of words, is the source of interpretation and self-knowledge.

32. There is an extraordinary midrash (*Bereshit Rabbah* 80:6) that focuses on three words signifying Shekhem's love (*davek, hashek, hafetz*) as the paradigms for the relation between God and Israel. Savage and lawless as Shekhem's act is, the feelings become a kind of pure ore, something raw and undistilled, which provides a glossary, as it were, for the texts of spiritual passion.

33. "I have seen a divine being face to face" (32:31) suggests naked confrontation with a powerful force in human guise.

34. See Trilling, *Sincerity and Authenticity*, 131–32, where he describes the violence in modernist art as necessary "to startle . . . to retrieve the human spirit from its acquiescence in non-being."

35. *Pirkei d'Rabbi Eliezer*, 37.

36. *Ha'amek Davar* 32:32.

37. See Ramban, who traces a fascinating etymological chain, through the Targum: wrestling comes to evoke seduction, strategy, and clarification.

38. *Bereshit Rabbah* 78:3.

39. Harold Bloom uses this expression to translate the word *berakha* ("blessing"): an apt translation, since the word everywhere suggests "moreness," increase, as *kelala* ("curse") suggests diminution. See Ibn Ezra, 49:7.

40. See *Ha'amek Davar* 35:10.

41. Quoted in Harold Bloom, *A Map of Misreading* (Oxford University Press: 1975), 163.

42. Ibid., 19.

43. See Ramban, 31:42. The "Fear of Isaac" is explicitly traced to the Akedah experience.

44. Bloom, *Map of Misreading*, 38.

45. Ramban, 46:1.

46. Bloom, *Map of Misreading*, 69–70.

47. In his prayer before meeting Esau's army, Jacob does speak of "God of my father Abraham, and God of my father Isaac" but, as Rashi implies, he is effectively *quoting* God's previous promise to him, in the dream at Beth El. He himself is "afraid" (Rashi, 31:42) to speak of his father and his relation to God in any terms other than that of "fear" in his father's lifetime.

48. John Milton, *Paradise Lost*, quoted in Bloom, *Map of Misreading*, 63.

49. See *Meshekh Hokhmah* 35:1: " 'Arise, go to Beth El and remain there; and build an altar there to the God [El] who appeared to you.' There he built an altar . . . for it was there that God [Elohim] had revealed Himself to him" (35:1, 7). The name El refers to the God of love, while the name Elohim refers to the God of Justice, or Dread. Jacob acquires the personal, active vision of El, on the basis of a revelation of Elohim, in which he is not active (God imposes the knowledge of dread on man, while man works actively to see God as the God of love). In terms of our reading, Jacob's *passive* relation

to Elohim is a function of his overinfluence by his father and his father's vision of reality.

50. At crucial points of his life, Jacob refers to his sense of *ra*, of evil besetting his consciousness. See 44:29, 34; 47:9; 48:16.

51. See Ramban, 32:13: "All these references to *tov* ["goodness"] are derived from God's promise – 'I shall be with you.'"

52. *Sefat Emet*, 5649.

53. This verse figures importantly in midrashic and hasidic reflections on this Parsha: see, e.g., *Sefat Emet* 5652, 5653.

54. See the first chapter of the present volume for a discussion of this idea.

55. The verse is quoted several times in the Talmud, as proof that "Adam was created with two faces," facing front and back (e.g., B. Eruvin 18b; see Rashi). Sexual differentiation results from the splitting apart of this original androgynous being.

## VA-YESHEV

1. Rashi, 37:1.

2. *Bereshit Rabbah* 84:1.

3. *Yalkut Talmud Torah*; manuscript in Sassoon Collection in London. Quoted in *Torah Shelemah* 37:1.

4. *Kinnim* 3:6.

5. *Bereshit Rabbah* 61:1.

6. Compare Ibn Ezra on the same verse. He translates *toledot* as "events."

7. *Pirkei d'Rabbi Eliezer*, 38.

8. See 26:3, "Stay a stranger in this land," and *Midrash Ha-Gadol* on this verse: "This teaches you that when the righteous settle in this world it is a mere sojourning to them" and on 26:6 – Isaac accepts God's command, somewhat against his own view of things, and stays in Canaan, in time of famine. This self-subjugation to God is signified by the idea of "sojourning."

9. Ramban, 37:1. " 'It is through Isaac that offspring shall be continued [called] for you' [21:12]: *through* Isaac, but not all of Isaac's offspring" (B. Nedarim 31a).

10. *Bereshit Rabbah* 82:13.

11. *Lekah Tov* 40:7.

12. Mann, *Joseph and His Brothers*,

13. *Bereshit Rabbah* 86:1.

14. *Bereshit Rabbah* 84:1.

15. See Rashi on 3:24. He refers back to 1:5: Job's burnt offerings in time of prosperity marked a constant premonition of evil.

16. B. Eruvin 13b.

17. See Rashi, *Psalms*, 16:7.

18. See Rashi, quoting the Targum: *"Aval*— 'in truth.' " Hirsch gives a similar reading of *aval.*

19. *Sekhel Tov* 37:33.

20. *Bereshit Rabbah* 74:7.

21. See Psalms 111:5 and Proverbs 30:8.

22. In chapter 3, Job speaks of *olalim*— babies — as a figure of rudimentary being, the product of pure causality, "all dirt and laughter," as Rashi wonderfully puts it (3:16). They represent most clearly the humiliating human fate of "being already born" (see Ricoeur, *History and Truth*, 290).

23. Franz Kafka, *The Trial* (Penguin: 1953), 240.

24. Ibid., 243.

25. The anger is explicit in the source of the midrash (*Tanhuma*, 5). Judah lists Joseph's "plots," and concludes, "I swear . . . that if I pull my sword out of its sheath, I shall fill the whole of Egypt with corpses." Ramban softens the unequivocal anger of the midrashic reading — which does not seem to emerge clearly from the biblical text — and suggests that Judah's accusation against the ruler is only implicit, "hinted in his words."

26. See Elaine Scarry, *The Body in Pain* (Oxford University Press: 1987), for a study of *mute* pain as the aim of the torturer, who hopes to deprive his victim of language and of a connection with human institutions. This is what Scarry calls the "unmaking of the world."

27. Gur Arye, 42:28.

28. See Rashbam, 37:28, who suggests that while the brothers were waiting to sell him to the Ishmaelites, Midianite traders passed by and drew Joseph out, without the brothers' knowledge.

29. See Leviticus 1:6.

30. Erich Fromm, *The Anatomy of Human Destructiveness* (Fawcett Crest: 1973), 369.

31. Ibid., 381

32. Ibid., 406

33. Mann, *Joseph and His Brothers*, 373–74.

34. *Bereshit Rabbah* 84:13. The emphasis on Joseph's distance from them and the use of the word *ha-lazeh* (see *Ha'amek Davar*) both suggest a lack of passionate involvement, which perhaps constitutes a defense strategy.

35. See *Ha-ketav Ve-ha-kabala* 42:22.

36. See the piyyut, *"Eileh ezkera,"* on the Ten Martyrs, in the Musaf prayer for the Day of Atonement.

37. Rambam, *The Guide for the Perplexed*, 3:46.

38. *Midrash Ha-Gadol* 42:22.

39. *Sefer Ḥasidim*, 131.

40. *Bereshit Rabbah* 86:6.

41. B. Yevamot 121a.

42. Walter Benjamin, "The Image of Proust," in *Illuminations*, 204.

43. See Regina Schwartz, "Joseph's Bones and the Resurrection of the Text: Remembering in the Bible," in *The Book and the Text: The Bible and Literary Theory*, ed. Regina M. Schwartz (Basil Blackwell: 1990), 40-59, for a discussion of the Freudian motifs in the Joseph narrative.

44. See *Ha'amek Davar* 42:11.

45. See Schwartz, "Joseph's Bones," 50, for a perceptive reading of the "nakedness of the land," as "the sight of something that should remain hidden, something that is illicit to see. Only Joseph's recent effort to repress his past can make sense of this response, for the very presence of the brothers violates what Joseph is trying to hide from himself: his memory of their abuse."

46. The root *nakar* is common to both the verb "to recognize" and the verb "to make oneself strange."

47. *Bereshit Rabbah* 99:9.

48. B. Sotah 10b.

49. Benjamin, "Image of Proust," 204

50. *Mei Ha-Shiloah*, 1, Va-yeshev, 14.

51. This definition of "fear," as the human response to divine providence, is the Ishbitzer's, earlier in the passage.

52. Rorty, *Contingency, Irony, and Solidarity*, 36.

53. Robert Alter, *The Art of Biblical Narrative* (Basic Books: 1981), 4.

54. *Pirkei d'Rabbi Eliezer*, 38.

55. Rashi (45:27) cites a midrash associating the wagons (*agalot*) with the work of memory: Joseph sends word reminding his father of the last Torah issue they had studied together, before his kidnapping—the laws of *egla arufa*, the heifer whose neck is broken, in token of the self-exoneration of society when a corpse is found, unaccounted for. The heifer becomes a powerful poetic metaphor, recollecting motifs from the past—brokenness, murder, the extent of responsibility, the shared culture of father and son. On this reading, Jacob comes to life under the impact of a potent poetic image and of the demands of interpretation that it makes on him.

56. Mann, *Joseph and His Brothers*, 1124.

57. Ibid., 1127–28.

58. Ibid., 1133.

59. Ibid., 1136.

60. Ibid., 1130.

61. *Midrash Ha-Gadol* 45:26.

## MI-KETZ

1. B. Ta'anit 11a.
2. Matthew Arnold, *Culture and Anarchy*, ed. J. Dover Wilson (Cambridge University Press: 1963), 70.
3. Ibid., chapter 1.
4. Rashi translates *nasha* in his commentary to 32:31, and quotes our verse (41:51) as a prooftext.
5. *Kefitza* ("leap"), the word Rashi uses to translate *nasha*, usually means a jump with both feet (as opposed to *rikud* ["dance"] and *dilug* ["skip"], for instance). This conveys a sense of total, unmitigated dislocation, relocation.
6. Shakespeare, *Hamlet*, III, i, 83.
7. Seforno, 41:21. The source is B. Yoma 74b.
8. *Bereshit Rabbah* 91:12.
9. Thomas Mann writes of Joseph's "polite flourish," his "tact," in pretending to have forgotten his past: he "had not forgotten at all but had always in his mind what he said he had forgotten" (*Joseph and His Brothers*, 1012).
10. Franz Kafka, *Diaries* (Schocken: 1949), 2:207.
11. *Bereshit Rabbah* 87:5.
12. *Bereshit Rabbah* 90:6.
13. Paul Tillich, *The Courage to Be* (Yale University Press: 1952), 38.
14. See *Torah Temimah* on 37:24.
15. J. Sotah 1:4.
16. See Sifrei: "Jacob went down to Aram in order to be lost [exiled from his place], and Laban the Aramean is held responsible for making him disappear."
17. George Eliot, *The Mill on the Floss* (Collier: 1962), 177.
18. *"From* the land" lends itself to this reading, rather than to the simple meaning, "You shall be destroyed from [?] the land."
19. *Torat Kohanim* on Leviticus 26:38.
20. B. Sanhedrin 110b.
21. *Torat Kohanim* on Leviticus 26:38.
22. B. Sanhedrin 110b.
23. B. Kiddushin 2b.
24. B. Niddah 30b.
25. Henri Bergson, "The Idea of Nothing," in *Creative Evolution*, 323.
26. Kenneth Burke, *Language as Symbolic Action* (University of California Press: 1966), 9–10.
27. Ramban, Exodus 18:15.
28. This is Ernest Gombrich's term for the alternating sequence of constructions and modifications by which "the artist gradually eliminates the

discrepancies between what is seen and what is drawn." See Jonathan Miller, *States of Mind* (Pantheon: 1983), 214.

29. *Likkutei Moharan*, 188.

30. Wallace Stevens, "The Snow Man," in *Poems* (Vintage Books: 1959), 23.

31. Frank Kermode, "The Plain Sense of Things," in *Midrash and Literature*, 180, 192.

32. *Tanhuma*, Mi-ketz, 8.

33. *Bereshit Rabbah* 25:1.

34. Rashi translates the concept of "comfort" (*nehama*) in several places, as "having other thoughts" — for example, on Genesis 6:6. Thus, both "comfort" and "regret" are covered by this single concept of a change in cognitive gestalt.

35. There are midrashic sources that claim that Jacob does not believe his sons' story. See *Rashi Ha-Shalem* on 37, note 80. But Rashi clearly reads Jacob as believing that Joseph is dead.

36. *Bereshit Rabbah* 91:1.

37. Wallace Stevens, "Notes towards a Supreme Fiction."

38. Ramban takes this view of the dynamic between Jacob and Rachel.

39. Isaiah 56:3. See Seforno, who also quotes this verse to explain Rachel's sense of herself as "dead."

40. *Bereshit Rabbah* 70:17.

41. See 42:4, 38. See also B. Hulin 95b and J. Shabbat 6:5, where the chain of disappearances is implicitly traced back to Rachel's death "on the way." See *Torah Temimah* on 42:36.

42. In this reading, it is interesting that Rachel is considered the genuine mother of all twelve tribes. In intention and desire, all Jacob's work for Laban was for her. She is the wife and the mother who is "not there" in reality, but who persists in imagination.

43. See Ramban, who translates "on the road there" in temporal, rather than spatial terms: Rachel is buried at the point of contact with the future passage of her children.

44. See Gur Arye, 48:7. See also the translation in Targum Jonathan of Jeremiah 31:15: "*Kenesset yisrael* is called Rachel."

45. Rashi comments on the masking effect of a beard (42:8).

46. See the translation of *shama* (21:22) in Targum Onkelos.

47. Samson Raphael Hirsch comments on the relation between *bakha* ("to weep") and *baka, pakah* ("to burst out"). Rashi quotes a midrashic discussion about the genuineness of Esau's kiss. But tears are self-evidently genuine and need no discussion.

48. George Steiner, *Real Presences* (University of Chicago Press: 1989), 96.

49. "The basis of man's life with man is twofold, and it is one — the wish of every man to be confirmed as what he is, even as what he can become, by men; and the innate capacity in man to confirm his fellow-men in this way." R. D. Laing quotes this passage from Martin Buber as epigraph to his discussion of "Confirmation and Disconfirmation," in *Self and Others* (Penguin: 1968), 98. He begins his discussion by emphasizing the partial, complex nature of human confirmation: in Buber's words, it "is always 'to some extent or other.'"

50. Paul Ricoeur, *History and Truth*, 322.

51. Neher, *Exile of the Word*, 236.

52. Ricoeur, *History and Truth*, 322.

53. See the chapter on *Hayyei Sarah* in this volume.

54. *Bereshit Rabbah* 100:8.

55. *Tanhuma*, Va-yehi, 17.

56. *Mishnat Rabbi Eliezer*, 87, 94, 130a.

57. John Donne, "A Nocturnall upon S. Lucies Day."

## VA-YIGGASH

1. See Ramban, 44:10, for a discussion of the implications of these changing formulations of punishment.

2. See the chapter on *Va-yeshev* in this volume.

3. The irony of using this rhetorical gesture ("What can we say?") as preface to a flood of words is picked up in the introductory passage to the *Selihot* (the penitential prayers), which quotes Judah's inarticulate cry, before launching into the many-worded prayers of the Days of Atonement.

4. *Bereshit Rabbah* 93:4.

5. *Tanhuma*, 3.

6. This image is found in the passage immediately preceding the quotation from *Tanhuma*.

7. See Rashi, 44:18: "*'Do not be angry with your servant'* — from here, you learn that he spoke harshly to him."

8. *Tanhuma*, 5.

9. See Rashi, 37:35: "*'I shall go down as a mourner to She'ol'*: The midrashic reading is 'to the inferno. . . . This sign was given me by God: if no one of my sons dies in my lifetime, I am assured that I shall not see the inferno.'"

10. *Bereshit Rabbah* 92:9.

11. *Tanhuma Yashan*, 2.

12. See "Pragmatism's Conception of Truth," in William James, *Essays in Pragmatism* (Hafner: 1968), 160–61.

13. See *Midrash Ha-Gadol* 44:18: *"Va-yiggash* means 'to examine.'"

14. *Bereshit Rabbah* 93:3.

15. Ibid., 93:8.

16. The midrashic tradition narrates that, in spite of Judah's fulfillment of his guarantee to his father, he is in fact doomed to an eternity of restless alienation: "All forty years that the Israelites were in the wilderness, Judah's bones were rolling around in his coffin, because of the excommunication that he accepted upon himself, as it is said, 'And I shall be a sinner to my father all the days'" (44:32). (See Rashi, Deuteronomy 33:7.) He is ultimately released from his fate; but the striking notion here is the absolute, unconditional nature of his assumption of a fate of alienation. It is as though so complete a commitment to the pain of others brands one apart from those others.

17. Judah puts the words, "You shall not see my face" into Joseph's mouth — twice, in fact (43:3, 5) — although in the original version of Joseph's decree, these words do not occur. This is Judah's pragmatic translation of the meaning of Joseph's more "academic" statement: "Let your words be verified, so that you do not die" (42:20).

18. Lit., *from my hand you may seek him.* The play on hand imagery goes back to the scene by the pit, where the direct "hands-on" involvement in murder had led both Reuben and Judah to suggest less direct methods of disposing of Joseph. Now, Judah recognizes an immediate physical responsibility, as a necessary feature of full moral agency.

19. See *Torah Shelemah* 43:13. In a passage in B. Baba Batra 173b, the sages disagree over whether Judah's offer can be considered conceptually as *arevut* — "standing surety." The long footnote discusses the implications of this disagreement.

20. *Tanḥuma*, 1.

21. B. Sotah 10b.

22. Ibid.

23. *Bereshit Rabbah* 85:9.

24. Joseph is referred to as Je*h*oseph, including the letter *heh* from God's name, in Psalms 81:6.

25. Robert Alter, *The Art of Biblical Narrative*, 11–12.

26. *Likkutei Moharan* 2:77.

27. See, however, Joel bin Nun's provocative suggestion that Jacob's reported speech, "Alas, he was torn by a beast!" (44:28), does constitute news for Joseph, who has assumed that Jacob's failure to search for him in Egypt stems from neglect, or undue influence by the other brothers. In this reading, Joseph's whole understanding of his father's attitude is changed by Judah's speech; he now knows of the brothers' deception, and can no longer refrain from revealing his identity (*Megadim*, 1, 20).

28. *Sefat Emet*, 5637.

29. See Jerome Bruner, *Actual Minds, Possible Worlds* (Harvard University Press: 1986). In his chapter on "the transactional self," he cites a study in which he found that "by their first birthday children are already adept at following another's line of regard to search for an object that is engaging their partner's attention" (60). Apparent egocentrism, he suggests, is really a failure to grasp the structure of events (68). Using this model, one might say that Judah's capacity to take Jacob's perspective depends on his growing understanding of the human situation.

30. Levinas, *Nine Talmudic Readings*, 47; italics mine.

31. Rorty, *Contingency, Irony, and Solidarity*, 102.

32. Ibid., 102–3.

33. B. Sotah 10b.

34. Rorty, *Contingency, Irony, and Solidarity*, 78.

35. Ibid., 80.

36. The expression is Rorty's, who uses it to describe Proust's success and to discriminate between the successes and failures in the work of Nietzsche and Heidegger.

37. *Bereshit Rabbah* 8:5. The idea is reflected in the initial letters of the quotation from Psalms: *Emet Me-eretz Titzmaḥ*. These constitute the word *Emet*: truth is woven from the separated letters, grounded in earth and becoming.

38. See *Sefat Emet*, 5637.

39. *Or Ha-Ḥayyim* 45:26.

40. *Or Ha-Ḥayyim* quotes the sages' classic dictum about the taboo of causing shame: "A person should rather throw himself into a fiery furnace than shame his friend" (lit., cause his face to go pale).

41. See *Bereshit Rabbah* 93:9.

42. See, for instance, Rambam, *Hilkhot Teshuva* 1:1, which includes shame as one aspect of regret for past actions.

43. See *Or Ha-Ḥayyim* 45:4.

44. B. Menaḥot 99b.

45. *Sefat Emet*, 5643.

46. See Targum Onkelos, Rashi, and Ramban.

47. Traditional readings of *lo yakhol* in many biblical contexts similarly emphasize the force of an idea to "incapacitate," and, in effect, to mold the moral personality. See, for instance, Deuteronomy 31:2, with Rashi's commentary.

48. Ramban distinguishes between two expressions for evil report (*meivi* and *motzi*), on the basis of the truth or falsehood of the report.

49. Mann, *Joseph and His Brothers*, 1207.

50. *Bereshit Rabbah* 93:5.

51. Michel Foucault, *The Foucault Reader*, ed. Paul Rabinow (Penguin: 1984), 191.

52. Ibid., 175.

53. See Leviticus 19:26; Deuteronomy 18:10.

54. See Genesis 30:27. For a full discussion of the issue, see *Rashi Ha-Shalem*, 44, note 10.

55. *Bereshit Rabbah* 91:13.

56. From *Yalkut Midrash Teiman*, a manuscript quoted in *Torah Shelemah* 43:86.

57. "But wherefore could not I pronounce 'Amen'?" (Shakespeare, *Macbeth*, II, ii, 32).

58. B. Sanhedrin 107a.

59. *Sefat Emet*, 5648.

60. Shakespeare, *Hamlet*, III, ii, 366–72.

61. *Tanḥuma Yashan*, 3.

62. See Rashbam 45:1.

63. See *Sefat Emet*, 5644.

64. *Bereshit Rabbah* 93:8.

65. Jonathan Miller, *States of Mind* (Pantheon: 1983), 40–41.

66. *Bereshit Rabbah* 94:3. The passage studied was the law of the broken-necked heifer (*eglah larufa*), which deals with the problem of an unidentified corpse and society's responsibility for the murder. The coded message works on several levels at once, therefore: the theme of death and responsibility is obviously appropriate, while the intimacy of the learning experience is evoked as the surest proof of identity. Seeing the *agalot* is a trigger for a complex response, in which aural, linguistic memory, and associations are central.

67. Both Rashi and Ramban resolve the ambiguity of the pronouns in this verse in this way; though Rashi consistently reads Joseph as the subject of the whole sentence, while Ramban changes the subject of "he kissed," and "he fell on his neck" to Jacob ("Who cries more, father for son, or son for father?").

68. See *Or Ha-Ḥayyim* 46:30.

69. See *Or Ha-Ḥayyim* 48:14.

70. This forms the beginning of the Haftara—the additional reading—for the week.

## VA-YEḤI

1. See Rashi, 12:2, on the words, "And you shall be a blessing."

2. See Rashi, 25:11.

3. See B. Baba Metzia 87a.

4. See *Yalkut Shimoni*, Lekh Lekha, 77; *Pirkei d'Rabbi Eliezer*, 52.

5. *Midrash Ha-Gadol* 48:1.

6. See Rashbam, 29:25.

7. From here, according to Rashi (48:2), we learn the principle of respectful behavior toward kings, even non-Jewish kings. *Siftei Ḥakhamim* emphasizes the paradox of this principle, in a situation where Joseph is, as it were, "needy" of his father's blessing.

8. *Bereshit Rabbah* 96:3.

9. The most obvious reading would limit this "charge" to his burial instructions (49:29–33). But midrashic readings broaden the scope of the "charge" to cover the largest disposition of Jacob's spiritual estate. See *Torah Shelemah*, 49, note 403.

10. In his first anguish at the loss of Joseph, Jacob says: "I will go down mourning to my son in She'ol [the grave, the underworld]" (37:35). This is realized when he in fact "goes down" to Egypt to see his son again after twenty-two years.

11. Erich Auerbach, *Mimesis: The Representation of Reality in Western Literature*, trans. Willard R. Trask (Princeton University Press: 1953), 12.

12. *Bereshit Rabbah* 96:1. The "closedness" of the text would represent the seamless nature of the narrative: there is, of course, no narrative break between verses 27 and 28. But the very meaning of the word Parsha has to do with "separation," with spacing the text, as an aid toward interpreting it, toward perceiving its structures, explicit and implicit. Sometimes, the break seems forced; here, it is both forced and neutralized by "blocking."

13. The traditional understanding is that enslavement properly speaking began only after the entire generation of Jacob's children had died.

14. *Bereshit Rabbah* 2:5.

15. Rashi, B. Ta'anit 24b; B. Megilla 22b.

16. This entreaty comes at the end of the *amidah*, the main prayer, suggesting the move from the prayer mode to the intellectual mode of Torah study, in which one needs "light of the eyes and of the heart/mind." See B. Berakhot 16a.

17. *Zohar*, 1, 209b, quoted in *Torah Shelemah*, 47 [50].

18. See Isaiah 2:2; Ezekiel 38:16; Hosea 3:5; Micah 4:1; Daniel 10:14.

19. See Frank Kermode, *The Sense of an Ending* (Oxford University Press: 1967), a study of apocalyptic movements in history and of "endings" in literature.

20. Moses' famous cry that he is "of uncircumcised lips" is translated by Rashi to mean "blocked, impassible, sealed." The imagery of the foreskin can be used to suggest an excess that prevents proper functioning, of the ears (Jeremiah 6:10), the mind (Jeremiah 9:25), or even of fruit trees, banned

from harvesting for the first three years (Leviticus 19:23). This notion of *atum*, of the impediment that weighs down and closes off, is related to our theme of *setima*, the "block."

21. *Sefat Emet*, Va-yeḥi, 5635.
22. Zohar 234b.
23. B. Pesaḥim 56a.
24. Douglas, *Purity and Danger* (Penguin: 1966).
25. Shakespeare, Sonnet 129.
26. See Rashi, 31:3: "*'Return to the land of your fathers'*—and there I shall be with you. But as long as you are associated with the impure one, it is impossible to rest my Presence upon you."
27. See Rashi, 45:27.
28. *Shemona Perakim*, 7.
29. Harold Bloom, *The Breaking of the Vessels* (University of Chicago Press: 1982), espec. 75–85.
30. *Mei Ha-Shiloaḥ*, 17b.
31. *Pesikta Rabbati*, 7.
32. Wallace Stevens, *The Snow Man*.
33. Rilke, *The Sonnets to Orpheus*, 95.
34. Martha Nussbaum, *The Fragility of Goodness* (Cambridge University Press: 1967), 215.
35. B. Sotah 11b.
36. *Pesikta Rabbati* 83:10.
37. *Midrash Ha-Gadol* 48:1.
38. See *Ha'amek Davar* 48:2. Israel "strengthens himself," in the realization that his transaction with Joseph is indicated in God's blessing at Luz— his singling out of Joseph is rooted in God's words.
39. See the chapter on *Va-yetze* in this volume.
40. See Seforno, who suggests that what he sees is a blurred double presence that he cannot identify.
41. *Tanḥuma*, Va-yeḥi 6.
42. See Seforno, who relates the need for vision to the capacity for blessing, in the context of Moses' death.
43. Several commentators—e.g., Mizraḥi—read *pilalti* as a reference to a rigorous thought process that would hold open positive possibilities. Jacob accuses himself of a precipitate despair, a closing of the issue without further internal debate. See also Targum Onkelos, who translates *la sivarit*.
44. *Bereshit Rabbati*, 227–28.
45. This text is often quoted in midrashic narratives, as a key to Jacob's later life. See, e.g., *Midrash Sekhel Tov*, quoted in *Torah Shelemah*, 87 [189]; *Bereshit Rabbah*, 94:4.
46. See *Or Ha-Ḥayyim*, 48:8

47. See the chapter on *Va-yishlaḥ* in this volume, and especially *Tanḥuma*, Va-yishlaḥ, 8.

48. See Seforno, 48:8.

49. In most midrashic sources, it is Jacob, and not Joseph, who raises the question of Rachel's burial. See, however, Targum Jonathan.

50. Ḥatam Sofer, *Torat Moshe*, 47:1.

51. See *Pesikta Rabbati*, 3.

52. Gur Arye, 48:7.

53. *Petiḥta*, 24.

54. See Rashi, 37:35. Jacob's refusal is a subconscious intuition of Joseph's survival.

55. See Rashi, 5:24: "*'Enoch walked with God; then he was no more [einenu] for God took him'*: God removed him from the world before his time — therefore the unusual expression about his death: he was not in the world to fulfill his years." *Einenu* implies the removal from one world to some other beyond man's perspective.

56. Robert Alter, *The World of Biblical Literature* (Basic Books: 1992), 22.

57. Ramban, 47:28.

58. Wallace Stevens, "Notes towards a Supreme Fiction."

59. Frank Kermode, "A Plain Sense of Things," in *Midrash and Literature* (Yale University Press: 1986), 180.

60. Calvino, *Mr. Palomar*, 86–89.

61. Stevens, "L'Ésthetique du Mal."

# Glossary

ABRABANEL, DON ISAAC (1437–1508): Spanish Bible commentator, philosopher and statesman.

AGGADAH: literally "telling," referring to the ethical imaginative and homiletic portions of talmudic literature, as opposed to the halakhic, the legal-ritual part.

AKEDAH: the Binding of Isaac, signifying Abraham's readiness to sacrifice his son at God's command.

AKEDAT YITZHAK: philosophic commentary to the Torah by Isaac Arama (1420–94), Spanish Talmudist and exegete of Expulsion Period.

AVOT D'RABBI NATAN: tannaitic amplification on tractate Avot, by R. Natan, an older contemporary of R. Judah Ha-Nasi.

BAHYA: Spanish fourteenth-century commentator on the Torah.

B.C.E./C.E.: abbreviations for "Before the Common Era" and "Common Era," traditional Jewish designations for B.C. and A.D.

DA'AT: knowledge, opinion.

EMET: truth. In mystical sources, psychological and spiritual attribute of Jacob.

EMUNAH: faith.

GUR ARYE: supercommentary to Rashi of Judah Loew ben Bezalel, known as Maharal of Prague (1525–1609).

HA'AMEK DAVAR: commentary on the Torah of Naftali Zvi Yehuda Berlin, known as the Netziv (1817–93).

HAFTARA: selection from the Prophets read in the synagogue after the Torah reading on Sabbaths and festivals.

HA-GRA: Eliahu ben Shlomo, the Gaon of Vilna (1720–97), greatest of talmudic authorities of recent centuries.

HA-KETAV VE-HA-KABBALAH: commentary on the Torah of Jacob Zvi Mecklenburg (1785–1865).

422

HALAKHAH: literally "going," "the way one should go." Law as it is formulated by rabbinic tradition.

ḤASIDISM: religious movement founded by Israel ben Eliezer, known as the Ba'al Shem Tov, in the eighteenth century.

ḤAYYIM: life.

ḤESED: love, kindness.

HIRSCH, SAMSON RAPHAEL (1808–88): German rabbinical leader and commentator on the Torah.

ḤOKHMAH: wisdom.

IBN EZRA, ABRAHAM (1080–1164): Spanish Bible commentator, poet, and grammarian.

ISHBITZER: R. Mordecai Yosef Leiner (d. 1854), author of *Mei Ha-Shiloaḥ*, a collection of his writings on the Parshiot of the Torah. Controversial in many of his theological positions, particularly in his skepticism about the existence of human freedom.

KABBALAH: Hebrew term for medieval Jewish mysticism.

K'LI YAKAR: homiletic commentary on the Torah of Ephraim Solomon ben Ḥayyim of Luntshitz (1550–1619).

KORBAN: sacrifice.

LIKKUTEI MOHARAN: see Nahman of Bratzlav.

MAHARAL: Judah Loew ben Beẓalel (1525–1609), author of philosophical, legal, and exegetical works; see Gur Arye.

MAHARSHA: Shemuel Eliezer ben Yehuda Halevi Edels (1555–1631), author of foremost commentary to Talmud after Rashi and the Tosafists.

MALBIM: initials of Meir Yehuda Leibush ben Yeḥiel Mikhal (1809–1880), Russian rabbi chiefly noted for his commentary on the Torah.

MASHAL: parable.

MEI HA-SHILOAḤ: see Ishbitzer.

MEKHILTA: tannaitic midrash on Exodus, both halakhic and aggadic.

MESHEKH ḤOKHMAH: commentary on the Torah of Meir Simḥa Ha-Kohen of Dvinsk (1843–1926), Talmudist and rabbinic leader.

MIDRASH: from the root meaning "to seek out" or "to inquire": a term in rabbinic literature for the interpretive study of the Bible. The word is also used in two related senses: first, to refer to the results of that interpretive activity, the specific interpretations produced through midrashic exegesis; and, second, to describe the literary compilations in which the original interpretations, many of them first delivered and transmitted orally, were eventually collected.

MIDRASH HA-GADOL: collection of midrashim on the Bible compiled from ancient tannaitic sources by David ben Amram Adani, a Yemenite scholar in the thirteenth century.

MIDRASH RABBAH: collection of ten midrashim, from various periods, on the five books of the Pentateuch and on the Five Scrolls (Ruth, Esther, Lamentations, Ecclesiastes, and Song of Songs).

MILAH: circumcision.

MISHPAT: law, justice.

MITZVAH: "commandment" — divine mandate in Jewish law.

MIZRAHI, ELIAHU (1440–1525): author of supercommentary to Rashi on the Torah.

NAHMAN OF BRATZLAV (1772–1811): author of *Likkutei Moharan*, a collection of theological teachings, in which he expounded a paradoxical concept of faith, the centrality of the tzaddik, and the importance of doubt and self-criticism, as well as of melody and dance, in the life of the spiritually aspiring.

NEHAMAH: comfort.

NISAN: first month of the Jewish calendar.

OR HA-HAYYIM: commentary on the Torah of Hayyim ibn Attar (1696–1743), Moroccan Kabbalist, Talmudist, and leader of Moroccan-Jewish resettlement in Israel.

PAHAD YITZHAK: collected discourses of R. Yitzhak Hutner (b. 1907), representing a synthesis of talmudic conciseness, hasidic mysticism, and ethical sensitivity.

PARSHA: weekly Torah reading.

PESHAT: the plain meaning or contextual sense among the different levels of interpretation.

PESIKTA RABBATI: collection of midrashim for the festivals and special Sabbaths. According to Zunz, the work was "certainly not composed before the second half of the ninth century."

PETIHTA: literally, "opening." A midrashic proem beginning each section of classical collections of midrash.

PIRKEI D'RABBI ELIEZER: a description of the workings of God in creation and in the oldest history of Israel. The book was probably written in Palestine, some time about the beginning of the ninth century.

RADAK: initials of Rabbi David Kimhi (1157–1236), author of commentary on the Torah.

RAMBAM: initials of Rabbi Moshe ben Maimon, or Maimonides, (1135–1204), author of a master code of Jewish law, *Mishneh Torah*, a philosophical handbook to Judaism, *Guide of the Perplexed*, and a compendium of the 613 commandments, Sefer Ha-Mitzvot.

RAMBAN: initials of Rabbi Moshe ben Nahman, or Nahmanides (1194–1270), Spanish biblical and talmudic commentator.

RASHBAM: initials of Rabbi Shemuel ben Meir (1080–1158), member of Tosafist school, grandson of Rashi, renowned for his *peshat* – plain sense – commentary on the Torah.

RASHI: initials of Rabbi Shelomo Yitzhaki, foremost commentator on the Torah (1040–1105). Lived in Troyes, France.

RATZON: will.

SAFEK: doubt.

SE'UDAH: feast.

SEFAT EMET: collected writings of Judah Aryeh Leib Alter (1847–1905), Polish Jewish leader and head of Hasidim of Gur. Characterized by wide scholarship, profundity of ideas, and clarity of exposition. Reflects the influence of Maharal.

SEFORNO, OVADIAH BEN YA'AKOV (1475–1550): Italian Talmudist, physician, and commentator on the Torah.

SHEKHINA: from the Hebrew for "dwell," it indicates the divine presence in the natural world.

SHOFAR: ram's horn used ritually in days of awe, especially on Rosh Hashanah, the New Year.

SIFREI: tannaitic midrashim on the books of Numbers and Deuteronomy, containing both halakhah and aggadah.

SIFTEI HAKHAMIM: the most important of Rashi's supercommentaries, usually printed alongside Rashi. The author is Shabtai ben Yosef (1641–1718), usually known as Meshorrer Bass.

TALMUD: code of Jewish law, lore, philosophy, and ethics, compiled between 200 and 500 C.E. in both Palestine and Babylon. Here, the two codices are referred to by J. and B.

TANAKH: the Holy Scriptures, comprising Torah (the Pentateuch), Prophets, and Writings.

TANHUMA: homiletic midrash on the Pentateuch known in a number of collections.

TANNAIM: mishnaic teachers, 20–200 C.E.

TARGUM: Hebrew for "translation." Any of the Aramaic translations of the Torah done in the last centuries B.C.E. and the early centuries C.E. Often exegetical in nature.

TEFILAH: prayer.

TESHUVAH: repentance.

TISHREI: the seventh month of the Jewish calendar, sometimes reckoned as the first month, since it begins with Rosh Hashanah, the New Year.

TOLEDOT: generations, offspring.

TORAH: Hebrew for "instruction." Designates the Five Books of Moses: Genesis, Exodus, Leviticus, Numbers, and Deuteronomy.

TORAH SHELEMAH: compendium of early rabbinic commentary on the Torah, by Rabbi Menaḥem Kasher, begun in 1926.

TORAH TEMIMAH: commentary on the Torah of Rabbi Barukh Ha-Levi Epstein, Russian Talmudist (1860–1942), in which he appended to the written text his own selection of the main dicta of Oral Tradition selected from talmudic literature, with his commentary explaining their relevance.

TZADDIK: righteous person, saint.

YALKUT SHIMONI: a midrashic thesaurus on the whole of the Bible compiled from more than fifty works. Probably composed in the first half of the thirteenth century.

YIRAH: fear. In mystical sources, psychological and spiritual attribute of Isaac.

ZOHAR: the Book of Splendor, the most important text of Jewish mysticism, purportedly written by R. Shimeon bar Yoḥai, but in fact composed in Spain in the thirteenth century.

# Bibliography

## LIST OF TEXTS CITED

### BIBLICAL

*Tanakh — The Holy Scriptures: The New JPS Translation according to the Traditional Hebrew Text* (1988)

### RABBINIC

Avot d'Rabbi Natan
Babylonian Talmud
Bereshit Rabbati
Eikhah Rabbati
Mekhilta
Midrash Ha-Gadol
Midrash Rabbah
Midrash Tanhuma
Palestinian Talmud
Pesikta Rabbati
Pirkei d'Rabbi Eliezer
Rashi Ha-Shalem
Sifrei
Targum Jonathan
Targum Onkelos
Torah Shelemah
Yalkut Shimoni

### MEDIEVAL AND LATER

Abrabanel*
Akedat Yitzhak*
Albo, *The Thirteen Principles of Faith*
Ba'al Ha-Turim*

* *Commentary on the Torah*

Bahya*
Ibn Ezra*
Likkutei Moharan
Maharal, Commentary on Rashi on the Torah (Gur Arye), Netivot Olam
Mei Ha-Shiloah
Mizrahi, Commentary on Rashi on the Torah
Or Ha-Hayyim*
Radak*
Rambam, Guide for the Perplexed, Mishneh Torah
Ramban*
Rashbam*
Rashi*
Sefat Emet
Seforno*
Siftei Hakhamim, Commentary on Rashi on the Torah

MODERN

Ha'amek Davar*
Ha-Ketav ve-Ha-Kabbalah*
Malbim*
Meshekh Hokhmah*
Or Gedaliah
Pahad Yitzhak
Samson Raphael Hirsch*
Torah Temimah*

## BIBLIOGRAPHY OF WORKS IN ENGLISH

This bibliography is only of works referred to in the text. It does not represent a comprehensive reading list on biblical or midrashic topics.

Alter, Robert: The Art of Biblical Narrative (Basic Books: 1981)
Arnold, Matthew: Culture and Anarchy (Cambridge University Press: 1963)
Auerbach, Erich: Mimesis: The Representation of Reality in Western Literature (Princeton University Press: 1953)
Bachelard, Gaston: Air and Dreams (Dallas Institute: 1988)
———: The Poetics of Space (Beacon Press: 1969).
Benjamin, Walter: Illuminations (Collins/Fontana: 1973)
Bergson, Henri: Creative Evolution (Modern Library: 1944)

* Commentary on the Torah

Bloom, Harold: *A Map of Misreading* (Oxford University Press: 1975)

——: *The Breaking of the Vessels* (University of Chicago Press: 1982)

Bruner, Jerome: *Actual Minds, Possible Worlds* (Harvard University Press: 1986)

Bruns, Gerald L.: *Inventions—Writing, Textuality, and Understanding in Literary History* (Yale University Press: 1982)

Buber, Martin: *On the Bible* (Schocken: 1982)

Burke, Kenneth: "The First Three Chapters of Genesis: Principles of Governance Stated Narratively," in *Genesis: Modern Critical Interpretations*, ed. Harold Bloom (Chelsea House: 1986)

Calvino, Italo: *Mr. Palomar* (Picador: 1986)

Canetti, Elias: *Crowds and Power* (Penguin: 1973)

——: *Kafka's Other Trial* (Penguin: 1982)

Cavell, Stanley: *Conditions Handsome and Unhandsome* (Open Court: 1990)

Coleridge, Samuel Taylor: *Lectures*, in *Shakespearean Criticism, 1623–1840*, ed. D. Nichol Smith (Oxford University Press: 1916)

Cox, Harvey: *Feast of Fools* (Harper and Row: 1969)

Douglas, Mary: *Purity and Danger* (Penguin: 1966)

Eagleton, Terry: *Literary Theory* (University of Minnesota Press: 1983)

Eliade, Mircea: *Myth and Reality* (Harper and Row: 1963)

——: *The Myth of the Eternal Return* (Harper and Row: 1959)

——: *The Sacred and the Profane* (Harvest: 1959)

Eliot, George: *Middlemarch* (Penguin: 1965)

Fisch, Harold: "The Hermeneutic Quest in *Robinson Crusoe*," in *Midrash and Literature*, ed. Geoffrey H. Hartman and Sanford Budick (Yale University Press: 1986)

Fishbane, Michael: *Text and Texture* (Schocken: 1979)

Foucault, Michel: *The Foucault Reader*, ed. Paul Rabinow (Penguin: 1984)

Fromm, Erich: *The Anatomy of Human Destructiveness* (Fawcett Crest: 1973)

Haight, Gordon S.: *George Eliot: A Biography* (Oxford University Press: 1968)

Huizinga, J.: *Homo Ludens* (Routledge and Kegan Paul: 1949)

James, William: *The Varieties of Religious Experience* (Fontana: 1960)

——: *Essays in Pragmatism* (Hafner: 1968)

Jung, Carl: *Modern Man in Search of a Soul* (Routledge and Kegan Paul: 1976)

Kafka, Franz: *Diaries* (Schocken: 1949)

——: *Parables and Paradoxes* (Schocken: 1975)

——: *The Trial* (Penguin: 1953)

Kermode, Frank: *The Sense of an Ending* (Oxford University Press: 1967)

——: *The Genesis of Secrecy* (Harvard University Press: 1979)

——: "The Plain Sense of Things," in *Midrash and Literature*, ed. Geoffrey H. Hartman and Sanford Budick (Yale University Press: 1986)

Kierkegaard, Søren: *Fear and Trembling* (Princeton University Press: 1983)

Kuhn, Thomas S.: *The Structure of Scientific Revolutions* (University of Chicago Press: 1962)

Laing, R. D.: *Self and Others* (Penguin: 1961)

Levinas, Emmanuel: *Nine Talmudic Readings* (Indiana University Press: 1990)

———: *Totality and Infinity* (Duquesne University Press: 1969)

Mann, Thomas: *Joseph and His Brothers* (Knopf: 1948)

Miller, Jonathan: *States of Mind* (Pantheon: 1983)

Neher, André: *The Exile of the Word* (Jewish Publication Society: 1981)

Neumann, Eric: *Art and the Creative Unconscious* (Princeton University Press: 1973)

Nietzsche, Friedrich: *The Birth of Tragedy*, in *The Philosophy of Nietzsche*, ed. Geoffrey Clive (Mentor: 1965)

Nussbaum, Martha: *The Fragility of Goodness* (Cambridge University Press: 1967)

Ricoeur, Paul: *History and Truth* (Northwestern University Press: 1965)

Rilke, Rainer Maria: *Selected Works 1: Prose* (New Directions: 1967)

———: *The Sonnets to Orpheus* (Touchstone: 1986)

Rorty, Richard: *Contingency, Irony, and Solidarity* (Cambridge University Press: 1989)

Rougemont, Denis de: *Passion and Society* (Faber and Faber: 1956)

Sacks, Oliver: *A Leg to Stand On* (Picador: 1986)

———: *Awakenings* (Harper Perennial: 1990)

———: *The Man Who Mistook His Wife for a Hat* (Picador: 1986)

Sarna, Nahum M.: *Understanding Genesis* (Schocken: 1970)

Sartre, Jean-Paul: *Words* (Penguin: 1967)

———: *L'Etre et le néant* (Paris: 1948)

Scarry, Elaine: *The Body in Pain* (Oxford University Press: 1987)

Schwartz, Regina, ed., *The Book and the Text: The Bible and Literary Theory* (Basil Blackwell: 1990)

Shakespeare, William: *Works*

Shestov, Lev: *Athens and Jerusalem* (Simon and Schuster: 1968)

Steiner, George: *Real Presences* (University of Chicago Press: 1989)

Stevens, Wallace: *Poems* (Vintage: 1959)

Tillich, Paul: *The Courage to Be* (Yale University Press: 1952)

Tournier, Michel: *Gemini* (Minerva: 1989)

Trilling, Lionel: *Sincerity and Authenticity* (Harvard University Press: 1971)

Unamuno, Miguel de: *The Tragic Sense of Life* (Princeton University Press: 1972)

Winnicott, D. W.: *Playing and Reality* (Basic Books: 1971)

# Index of Sources

# General Index